I0006170

A HISTORY

OF THE

SEPOY WAR IN INDIA.

1857—1858.

BY

JOHN WILLIAM KAYE, F.R.S.,

AUTHOR OF THE "HISTORY OF THE WAR IN AFGHANISTAN."

VOL. I.

SEVENTH EDITION.

LONDON:

W. H. ALLEN & CO., 13, WATERLOO PLACE.

1875.

I SHOULD HAVE DEDICATED

THESE VOLUMES

TO

LORD CANNING,

HAD HE LIVED;

I NOW INSCRIBE THEM REVERENTIALLY

TO HIS MEMORY.

CONTENTS OF VOL. I

CHAPTER IV.

PROGRESS OF ENGLISHISM.

————————

BOOK II.—THE SEPOY ARMY: ITS RISE, PROGRESS, AND DECLINE.

CHAPTER I.

EARLY HISTORY OF THE NATIVE ARMY.

CHAPTER II.

DETERIORATING INFLUENCES.

CHAPTER III.

THE SINDH MUTINIES.

CHAPTER IV.

THE PUNJAB MUTINIES.

CHAPTER V.

DISCIPLINE OF THE BENGAL ARMY.

BOOK III.—THE OUTBREAK OF THE MUTINY.

CHAPTER I.

LORD CANNING AND HIS COUNCIL.

CHAPTER II.

THE OUDE ADMINISTRATION AND THE PERSIAN WAR.

PREFACE.

IT was not without much hesitation that I undertook to write this narrative of the events, which have
imparted so painful a celebrity to the years 1857-58,
and left behind them such terrible remembrances.
Publicly and privately I had been frequently urged
to do so, before I could consent to take upon myself
a responsibility, which could not sit lightly on any
one capable of appreciating the magnitude of the
events themselves and of the many grave questions
which they suggested. If, indeed, it had not been
that, in course of time, I found, either actually in
my hands or within my reach, materials of history
such as it was at least improbable that any other
writer could obtain, I should not have ventured upon
so difficult a task. But having many important
collections of papers in my possession, and having
received promises of further assistance from surviving actors in the scenes to be described, I felt that,
though many might write a better history of the
Sepoy War, no one could write a more truthful one.

So, relying on these external advantages to compensate all inherent deficiencies, I commenced what I knew must be a labour of years, but what I felt would be also a labour of love. My materials were too ample to be otherwise than most sparingly displayed. The prodigal citation of authorities has its advantages; but it encumbers the text, it impedes the narrative, and swells to inordinate dimensions the record of historical events. On a former occasion, when I laid before the public an account of a series of important transactions, mainly derived from original documents, public and private, I quoted those documents freely both in the text and in the notes. As I was at that time wholly unknown to the public, it was necessary that I should cite chapter and verse to obtain credence for my statements. There was no ostensible reason why I should have known more about those transactions than any other writer (for it was merely the accident of private friendships and associations that placed such profuse materials in my possession), and it seemed to be imperative upon me therefore to produce my credentials. But, believing that this necessity no longer exists, I have in the present work abstained from adducing my authorities, for the mere purpose of substantiating my statements. I have quoted the voluminous correspondence in my possession only where there is some dramatic force and propriety in the words cited, or when they appear calculated, without impeding the narrative, to give colour and vitality to the story.

And here I may observe that, as on former occasions, the historical materials which I have moulded into this narrative are rather of a private than of a public character. I have made but little use

of recorded official documents. I do not mean
that access to such documents has not been extremely serviceable to me; but that it has rather
afforded the means of verifying or correcting statements received from other sources than it has supplied me with original materials. So far as respects
the accumulation of facts, this History would have
differed but slightly from what it is, if I had never
passed the door of a public office; and, generally,
the same may be said of the opinions which I
have expressed. Those opinions, whether sound or
unsound, are entirely my own personal opinions—
opinions in many instances formed long ago, and
confirmed by later events and more mature consideration. No one but myself is responsible for them;
no one else is in any way identified with them. In
the wide range of inquiry embraced by the consideration of the manifold causes of the great convulsion of
1857, almost every grave question of Indian government and administration presses forward, with more
or less importunity, for notice. Where, on many
points, opinions widely differ, and the policy, which
is the practical expression of them, takes various
shapes, it is a necessity that the writer of cotemporary history, in the exercise of independent thought,
should find himself dissenting from the doctrines and
disapproving the actions of some authorities, living
and dead, who are worthy of all admiration·and respect. It is fortunate, when, as in the present instance, this difference of opinion involves no diminution of esteem, and the historian can discern worthy
motives, and benevolent designs, and generous strivings after good, in those whose ways he may think
erroneous and whose course of action he may deem
unwise.

Indeed, the errors of which I have freely spoken were, for the most part, strivings after good. It was in the over-eager pursuit of Humanity and Civilisation that Indian statesmen of the new school were betrayed into the excesses which have been so grievously visited upon the nation. The story of the Indian Rebellion of 1857 is, perhaps, the most signal illustration of our great national character ever yet recorded in the annals of our country. It was the vehement self-assertion of the Englishman that produced this conflagration; it was the same vehement self-assertion that enabled him, by God's blessing, to trample it out. It was a noble egotism, mighty alike in doing and in suffering, and it showed itself grandly capable of steadfastly confronting the dangers which it had brought down upon itself. If I have any predominant theory it is this: Because we were too English the great crisis arose; but it was only because we were English that, when it arose, it did not utterly overwhelm us.

It is my endeavour, also, to show how much both of the dangers which threatened British dominion in the East, and of the success with which they were encountered, is assignable to the individual characters of a few eminent men. With this object I have sought to bring the reader face to face with the principal actors in the events of the Sepoy War, and to take a personal interest in them. If it be true that the best history is that which most nearly resembles a bundle of biographies, it is especially true when said with reference to Indian history; for nowhere do the characters of individual Englishmen impress themselves with a more vital reality upon the annals of the country in which they live; nowhere are there such great opportunities of independent action; nowhere

are developed such capacities for evil or for good, as
in our great Anglo-Indian Empire. If, then, in such
a work as this, the biographical element were not
prominently represented—if the individualities of
such men as Dalhousie and Canning, as Henry and
John Lawrence, as James Outram, as John Nicholson, and Herbert Edwardes, were not duly illustrated, there would be not only a cold and colourless,
but also an unfaithful, picture of the origin and progress of the War. But it is to be remarked that, in
proportion as the individuality of the English leaders
is distinct and strongly marked, that of the chiefs of
the insurrectionary movement is faint and undecided.
In the fact of this contrast we see the whole history
of the success which, by God's providence, crowned
the efforts of our countrymen. If the individual
energies of the leaders of the revolt had been com-
mensurate with the power of the masses, we might
have failed to extinguish such a conflagration. But
the whole tendency of the English system had been
to crush out those energies; so again, I say, we found
in the very circumstances which had excited the
rebellion the very elements of our success in sup-
pressing it. Over the Indian Dead Level which that
system had created, the English heroes marched triumphantly to victory.

In conclusion, I have only to express my obligations to those who have enabled me to write this
History by supplying me with the materials of which
it is composed. To the executors of the late Lord
Canning, who placed in my hands the private and
demi-official correspondence of the deceased statesman, extending over the whole term of his Indian
administration, I am especially indebted. To Sir
John Lawrence and Sir Herbert Edwardes, who have

furnished me with the most valuable materials for
my narrative of the rising in the Punjab and the
measures taken in that province for the re-capture of
Delhi ; to the family of the late Colonel Baird Smith,
for many interesting papers illustrative of the operations of the great siege ; to Sir James Outram, who
gave me before his death his correspondence relating
to the brilliant operations in Oude ; to Sir Robert
Hamilton, for much valuable matter in elucidation of
the history of the Central Indian Campaign ; and to
Mr. E. A. Reade, whose comprehensive knowledge
of the progress of events in the North-Western Provinces has been of material service to me, my warmest
acknowledgments are due.   But to no one am I
more indebted than to Sir Charles Wood, Secretary
of State for India, who has permitted me to consult the official records of his Department—a privilege which has enabled me to make much better use
of the more private materials in my possession.   No
one, however, can know better or feel more strongly
than myself, that much matter of interest contained
in the multitudinous papers before me is unrepre-
sented in my narrative.   But such omissions are the
necessities of a history so full of incident as this.   If
I had yielded to the temptation to use my illustrative
materials more freely, I should have expanded this
work beyond all acceptable limits.

London, October, 1864.

. . . For to think that an handful of people can, with the greatest courage and policy in the world, embrace too large extent of dominion, it may hold for a time, but it will fail suddenly.—*Bacon.*

. . . As for mercenary forces (which is the help in this case), all examples show that, whatsoever estate, or prince, doth rest upon them, he may spread his feathers for a time, but he will mew them soon after.—*Bacon.*

If there be fuel prepared, it is hard to tell whence the spark shall come that shall set it on fire. The matter of seditions is of two kinds, much poverty and much discontentment. It is certain, so many overthrown estates, so many votes for troubles. . . . The causes and motives for sedition are, innovations in religion, taxes, alteration of laws and customs, breaking of privileges, general oppression, advancement of unworthy persons, strangers, dearths, disbanded soldiers, factions grown desperate; and whatsoever in offending people joineth and knitteth them in a common cause.—*Bacon.*

HISTORY OF THE SEPOY WAR.

—•—

BOOK I.—INTRODUCTORY.

[1846—1856.]

—•—

CHAPTER I.

THE ADMINISTRATION OF LORD DALHOUSIE—HIS FAREWELL MINUTE—
RETROSPECT OF THE FIRST SIKH WAR—THE MILITARY OCCUPATION OF
THE PUNJAB—THE COUNCIL OF REGENCY—THE SECOND SIKH WAR—
THE ANNEXATION OF THE PUNJAB—ITS ADMINISTRATION UNDER THE
LAWRENCES—THE CONQUEST OF PEGU.

BROKEN in bodily health, but not enfeebled in spirit,
by eight years of anxious toil, beneath an Indian
sun, Lord Dalhousie laid down the reins of government and returned to his native country to die. Since
the reign of Lord Wellesley, so great in written history,
so momentous in practical results, there had been
no such administration as that of Lord Dalhousie;
there had been no period in the annals of the Anglo-
Indian Empire surcharged with such great political
events, none which nearly approached it in the rapidity
of its administrative progress. Peace and War had
yielded their fruits with equal profusion.

On the eve of resigning his high trust to the hands
of another, Lord Dalhousie drew up an elaborate state-

B

1856.   paper reviewing the eventful years of his government. He had reason to rejoice in the retrospect; for he had acted in accordance with the faith that was within him, honestly and earnestly working out his cherished principles, and there was a bright flush of success over all the apparent result. Peace and prosperity smiled upon the empire. That empire he had vastly extended, and by its extension he believed that he had consolidated our rule and imparted additional security to our tenure of the country.

Of these great successes some account should be given at the outset of such a narrative as this; for it is only by understanding and appreciating them that we can rightly estimate the subsequent crisis. It was in the Punjab and in Oude that many of the most important incidents of that crisis occurred. Lord Dalhousie found them Foreign States; he left them British Provinces.

1845-46.   Lord Hardinge conquered the Sikhs; but he spared
First occupa- the Punjab. Moderate in victory as resolute in war,
tion of the
Punjab.   he left the empire of Runjeet Singh, shorn only of its outlying provinces, to be governed by his successors, and strove to protect the boy-prince against the law-lessness of his own soldiers. But it was felt that this forbearance was only an experimental forbearance; and the proclamation which announced the restora-tion of the Punjab to the Maharajah Duleep Singh sounded also a note of warning to the great military autocracy which had well-nigh overthrown the State. "If this opportunity," said the victor, "of rescuing the Sikh nation from military anarchy and misrule be neglected, and hostile opposition to the British army be renewed, the Government of India will make such

other arrangements for the future government of the
Punjab as the interests and security of the British
power may render just and expedient." Thus was the
doubt expressed; thus were the consequences foreshadowed. It did not seem likely that the experiment would succeed; but it was not less right to
make it. It left the future destiny of the empire,
under Providence, for the Sikhs themselves to determine. It taught them how to preserve their national
independence, and left them to work out the problem
with their own hands.

But Hardinge did more than this. He did not
interfere with the internal administration, but he established a powerful military protectorate in the Punjab.
He left the Durbar to govern the country after its
own fashion; but he protected the Government against
the lawless domination of its soldiery. The Sikh army
was overawed by the presence of the British battalions;
and if the hour had produced the man—if there had
been any wisdom, any love of country, in the councils
of the nation—the Sikh Empire might have survived
the great peril of the British military protectorate.
But there was no one worthy to rule; no one able to
govern. The mother of the young Maharajah was
nominally the Regent. There have been great queens
in the East as in the West—women who have done
for their people what men have been incapable of
doing. But the mother of Duleep Singh was not one
of these. To say that she loved herself better than
her country is to use in courtesy the mildest words,
which do not actually violate truth. She was, indeed,
an evil presence in the nation. It rested with her to
choose a minister, and the choice which she made was
another great suicidal blow struck at the life of the
Sikh Empire. It may have been difficult in this

emergency to select the right man, for, in truth, there were not many wise men from whom a selection could be made. The Queen-Mother cut through the difficulty by selecting her paramour.

Lal Singh was unpopular with the Durbar; unpopular with the people; and he failed. He might have been an able and an honest man, and yet have been found wanting in such a conjuncture. But he was probably the worst man in the Punjab on whom the duty of reconstructing a strong Sikh Government could have devolved. To do him justice, there were great difficulties in his way. He had to replenish an exhausted treasury by a course of unpopular retrenchments. Troops were to be disbanded and Jagheers resumed. Lal Singh was not the man to do this, as one bowing to a painful necessity, and sacrificing himself to the exigencies of the State. Even in a country where political virtue was but little understood, a course of duty consistently pursued for the benefit of the nation might have ensured for him some sort of respect. But whilst he was impoverishing others, he was enriching himself. It was not the public treasury, but the private purse that he sought to replenish, and better men were despoiled to satisfy the greed of his hungry relatives and friends. Vicious among the vicious, he lived but for the indulgence of his own appetites, and ruled but for his own aggrandisement. The favourite of the Queen, he was the oppressor of the People. And though he tried to dazzle his British guests by rare displays of courtesy towards them, and made himself immensely popular among all ranks of the Army of Occupation by his incessant efforts to gratify them, he could not hide the one great patent fact, that a strong Sikh Government

could never be established under the wuzeerat of Lal
Singh.

But the British were not responsible for the failure.
The Regent chose him; and, bound by treaty not to
exercise any interference in the internal administration of the Lahore State, the British Government had
only passively to ratify the choice. But it was a state
of things burdened with evils of the most obtrusive
kind. We were upholding an unprincipled ruler and
an unprincipled minister at the point of our British
bayonets, and thus aiding them to commit iniquities
which, without such external support, they would
not have long been suffered to perpetrate. The compact, however, was but for the current year; and
even for that brief period there seemed but little probability of Lal Singh tiding over the difficulties and
dangers which beset his position.

Very soon his treachery undid him. False to his
own country, he was false also to the British Government. The province of Cashmere, which was one of
the outlying dependencies taken by the British in payment of the war-charges, had been made over to Gholab
Singh, chief of the great Jummoo family, who had
paid a million of money for the cession. But the
transfer had been resisted by the local governor, who
had ruled the province under the Sikh Rajahs, and
covertly Lal Singh had encouraged the resistance.
The nominal offender was brought to public trial, but
it was felt that the real criminal was Lal Singh, and
that upon the issue of the inquiry depended the fate
of the minister. It was soon apparent that he was a
traitor, and that the other, though for intelligible
reasons of his own, reluctant to render an account of
his stewardship, was little more than a tool in his

hands. The disgrace of the minister was the immediate result of the investigation. He left the Durbar tent a prisoner under a guard, an hour before his own body-guard, of Sikh soldiers; and the great seal of the Maharajah was placed in the hands of the British Resident. So fell Lal Singh; and so fell also the first experiment to reconstruct a strong Sikh Government on a basis of national independence.

Another experiment was then to be tried. There was not a native of the country to whose hands the destinies of the empire could be safely entrusted. If the power of the English conqueror were demanded to overawe the turbulent military element, English wisdom and English integrity were no less needed, in that conjuncture, to quicken and to purify the corrupt councils of the State. Sikh statesmanship, protected against the armed violence of the Prætorian bands, which had overthrown so many ministries, had been fairly tried, and had been found miserably wanting. A purely native Government was not to be hazarded again. Averse as Hardinge had been, and still was, to sanction British interference in the internal administration of the Punjab, there was that in the complications before him which compelled him to overcome his reluctance. The choice, indeed, lay between a half measure, which might succeed, though truly there was small hope of success, and the total abandonment of the country to its own vices, which would have been speedily followed, in self-defence, by our direct assumption of the Government on our own account. Importuned by the Sikh Durbar, in the name of the Maharajah, Hardinge tried the former course. The next effort, therefore, to save the Sikh Empire from self-destruction, embraced the idea of a native Government, presided over by a British statesman. A Council of Regency was instituted, to be composed of Sikh chiefs, under the superintendence and control of the Resident ; or, in other words, the British Resident became the virtual ruler of the country. 1844.

And this time the choice, or rather the accident, of the man was as propitious; as before it had been untoward and perverse. The English officer possessed well-nigh all the qualities which the Sikh Sirdar so deplorably lacked. A captain of the Bengal Artillery, holding the higher rank of colonel by brevet for good service, Henry Lawrence had graduated in Punjabee diplomacy under George Clerk, and had accompanied to Caubul the Sikh Contingent, attached to Pollock's retributory force, combating its dubious fidelity, and controlling its predatory excesses on the way. After the return of the expedition to the British provinces, he had been appointed to represent our interests in Nepaul; and there—for there was a lull in the sanguinary intrigues of that semi-barbarous Court—immersed in his books, and turning to good literary purpose his hours of leisure, he received at Catamandoo intelligence of the Sikh invasion, and of the death of George Broadfoot, and was summoned to take the place of that lamented officer as the agent of the Governor-General on the frontier. In the negotiations which followed the conquest of the Khalsa army, he had taken the leading part, and, on the restoration of peace, had been appointed to the office of British Resident, or Minister, at Lahore, under the first experiment of a pure Sikh Government hedged in by British troops. 1842.

If the character of the man thus placed at the head of affairs could have secured the success of this great compromise, it would have been successful far beyond the expectations of its projectors. For no man ever undertook a high and important trust with a more solemn sense of his responsibility, or ever, with more singleness of purpose and more steadfast sincerity of heart, set himself to work, with God's blessing, to turn a great opportunity to great account for the benefit of his fellows. In Henry Lawrence a pure transparent nature, a simple manliness and truthfulness of character, were combined with high intellectual powers, and personal energies which nothing earthly could subdue. I may say it here, once for all, at the very outset of my story, that nowhere does this natural simplicity and truthfulness of character so often as in India survive a long career of public service. In that country public men are happily not exposed to the pernicious influences which in England shrivel them so fast into party leaders and parliamentary chiefs. With perfect singleness of aim and pure sincerity of purpose, they go, with level eyes, straight at the public good, never looking up in fear at the suspended sword of a parliamentary majority, and never turned aside by that fear into devious paths of trickery and finesse. It may be that ever since the days of Clive and Omichund an unsavoury odour has pervaded the reputation of Oriental diplomacy; but the fact is, that our greatest successes have been achieved by men incapable of deceit, and by means which have invited scrutiny. When we have opposed craft to craft, and have sought to out-juggle our opponents, the end has been commonly disastrous. It is only by consummate honesty and transparent truthfulness that the Talleyrands of the East have been beaten by such mere children in the world's ways as Mountstuart Elphinstone, Charles Metcalfe, James Outram, and Henry Lawrence.

Henry Lawrence, indeed, was wholly without guile.
He had great shrewdness and sagacity of character,
and he could read and understand motives, to which
his own breast was a stranger, for he had studied well
the Oriental character. But he was singularly open
and unreserved in all his dealings, and would rather
have given his antagonist an advantage than have
condescended to any small arts and petty trickeries
to secure success. All men, indeed, trusted him; for
they knew that there was nothing selfish or sordid
about him; that the one desire of his heart was to
benefit the people of the country in which it had
pleased God to cast his lot. But he never suffered
this plea of beneficence to prevail against his sense of
justice. He was eminently, indeed, a just man, and
altogether incapable of that casuistry which gives
a gloss of humanity to self-seeking, and robs people
for their own good. He did not look upon the misgovernment of a native State as a valid reason for the
absorption of its revenues, but thought that British
power might be exercised for the protection of the
oppressed, and British wisdom for the instruction and
reformation of their oppressors, without adding a few
more thousand square miles to the area of our British
possessions, and a few more millions of people to the
great muster-roll of British subjects in the East.

Above the middle height, of a spare, gaunt frame,
and a worn face bearing upon it the traces of mental
toil and bodily suffering, he impressed you, at first
sight, rather with a sense of masculine energy and
resolution than of any milder and more endearing
qualities. But when you came to know him, you saw
at once that beneath that rugged exterior there was a
heart gentle as a woman's, and you recognised in his
words and in his manner the kindliness of nature

1846.

which won the affection of all who came within its reach, and by its large and liberal manifestations made his name a very household word with thousands, who had never felt the pressure of his hand or stood in his living presence. But, with all this, though that name was in men's mouths and spoken in many languages, no unknown subaltern had a more lowly mind or a more unassuming deportment.

Such was the man who now 'found himself the virtual sovereign of the empire of Runjeet Singh. The new protectorate, established at the end of 1846, gave to Henry Lawrence "unlimited authority," "to direct and control every department of the State." He was to be assisted in this great work by an efficient establishment of subordinates, but it was no part of the design to confer upon them the executive management of affairs. The old officers of the Sikh Government were left to carry on the administration, guided and directed by their British allies. Under such a system corruption and oppression could no longer run riot over the face of the land. It was a protectorate for the many, not for the few; and for a while it seemed that all classes were pleased with the arrangement. Outwardly, indeed, it did not seem that feelings of resentment against the British Government were cherished by any persons but the Queen-Mother and her degraded paramour.

1847.

And so, in the spring of 1847, the political horizon was almost unclouded. The Council of Regency, under the control of Henry Lawrence, seemed to be carrying on the government with a sincere desire to secure a successful result. Tranquillity had been restored; confidence and order were fast returning. The Sikh soldiery appeared to be contented with their lot, and to be gradually acquiring habits of discipline and obedience, under a system which rendered them dependent on the British officers for whatever most promoted their interests and contributed to their comforts. But it did not escape the sagacious mind of the Resident, that serene as was the aspect of affairs, and promising as were the indications of continued repose, there were, beneath all this surface-calm, dangerous elements at work, waiting only for time and circumstance to call them into full activity. The memory of frequent defeat was still too fresh in the minds of the humbled Khalsa to suffer them to indulge in visions of at once re-acquiring their lost supremacy. But as time passed and the impression waxed fainter and fainter, it was well-nigh certain that the old hopes would revive, and that outbursts of desperate Asiatic zeal might be looked for in quarters where such paroxysms had long seemed to be necessary to the very existence of a lawless and tumultuous class. It is a trick of our self-love—of our national vanity—to make us too often delude ourselves with the belief that British supremacy must be welcome wheresoever it obtrudes itself. But Henry Lawrence did not deceive himself in this wise. He frankly admitted that, however benevolent our motives, and however conciliatory our demeanour, a British army could not garrison Lahore, and a British functionary supersede the Sikh Durbar, without exciting bitter discontents and perilous resentments. He saw around him, struggling for existence, so many high officers of the old Sikh armies, so many favourites of the old line of Wuzeers now cast adrift upon the world, without resources and without hope under the existing system, that when he remembered their lawless

1847.   habits, their headstrong folly, their desperate suicidal zeal, he could but wonder at the perfect peace which then pervaded the land.

But whatsoever might be taking shape in the future, the present was a season of prosperity—a time of promise—and the best uses were made by the British functionaries of the continued calm. Interference in the civil administration of the country was exercised only when it could be turned to the very apparent advantage of the people. British authority and British integrity were then employed in the settlement of long-unsettled districts, and in the development of the resources of long-neglected tracts of country. The subordinate officers thus employed under the Resident were few, but they were men of no common ability and energy of character—soldiers such as Edwardes, Nicholson, Reynell Taylor, Lake, Lumsden, Becher, George Lawrence, and James Abbott; civilians such as Vans Agnew and Arthur Cocks—men, for the most part, whose deeds will find ample record in these pages. They had unbounded confidence in their chief, and their chief had equal confidence in them. Acting, with but few exceptions, for the majority were soldiers, in a mixed civil and military character, they associated with all classes of the community; and alike by their courage and their integrity they sustained the high character of the nation they represented. One common spirit of humanity seemed to animate the Governor-General, the Resident, and his Assistants. A well-aimed blow was struck at infanticide, at Suttee, and at the odious traffic in female slaves. In the agricultural districts, a system of enforced labour, which had pressed heavily on the ryots, was soon also in course of abolition. The weak were everywhere protected against the strong. An

entire revision of the judicial and revenue systems of
the country—if systems they can be called, where
system there was none—was attempted, and with
good success. New customs rules were prepared, by
which the people were greatly gainers. Every legitimate means of increasing the revenue, and of controlling unnecessary expenditure, were resorted to, and
large savings were effected at no loss of efficiency in
any department of the State. The cultivators were encouraged to sink wells, to irrigate their lands, and
otherwise to increase the productiveness of the soil,
alike to their own advantage and the profit of the
State. And whilst everything was thus being done
to advance the general prosperity of the people, and
to ensure the popularity of British occupation among
the industrial classes, the Army was propitiated by the
introduction of new and improved systems of pay
and pension, and taught to believe that what they
had lost in opportunities of plunder, and in irregular
largesses, had been more than made up to them by
certainty and punctuality of payment, and the interest
taken by the British officers in the general welfare of
their class.

As the year advanced, these favourable appearances
rather improved than deteriorated. In June, the
Resident reported that a large majority of the disbanded soldiers had returned to the plough or to
trade, and that the advantages of British influence to
the cultivating classes were every day becoming more
apparent. But still Lawrence clearly discerned the
fact that although the spirit of insurrection was at
rest in the Punjab, it was not yet dead. There were
sparks flying about here and there, which, alighting
on combustible materials, might speedily excite a
blaze. "If every Sirdar and Sikh in the Punjab," he

1847.   wrote, with the candour and good sense which are so
conspicuous in all his communications, "were to avow
himself satisfied with the humbled position of his
country, it would be the extreme of infatuation to
believe him, or to doubt for a moment that among
the crowd who are loudest in our praise there are
many who cannot forgive our victory, or even our
forbearance, and who chafe at their own loss of power
in exact proportion as they submit to ours." People
were not wanting even then, in our camp, to talk with
ominous head-shakings of the " Caubul Catastrophe,"
and to predict all sorts of massacres and misfortunes.
But there was no parallel to be drawn between the
two cases, for an overweening sense of security had
not taken possession of the British functionaries at
Lahore. They had not brought themselves to believe
that the country was "settled," or that British occupation was "popular" among the chiefs and people of
the Punjab. With God's blessing they were doing
their best to deserve success, but they knew well that
they might some day see the ruin of their hopes, the
failure of their experiments, and they were prepared,
in the midst of prosperity, at any hour to confront
disaster.

Even then, fair as was the prospect before us, there
was one great blot upon the landscape; for whilst the
restless nature of the Queen-Mother was solacing itself
with dark intrigues, there was a continual source of
disquietude to disturb the mind of the Resident with
apprehensions of probable outbreaks and seditions.
She hated the British with a deadly hatred. They
had deprived her of power. They had torn her lover
from her arms. They were training her son to become a puppet in their hands. To foment hostility
against them, wheresoever there seemed to be any

hope of successful revolt, and to devise a plot for the murder of the Resident, were among the cherished objects by which she sought to gratify her malice. But she could not thus labour in secret. Her schemes were detected, and it was determined to remove her from Lahore. The place of banishment was Sheiko-poor, in a quiet part of the country, and in the midst of a Mussulman population. When the decision was communicated to her by her brother, she received it with apparent indifference. She was not one to give her enemies an advantage by confessing her wounds and bewailing her lot. She uttered no cry of pain, but said that she was ready for anything, and at once prepared for the journey.

The autumn passed quietly away. But an important change was impending. Lord Hardinge was about to lay down the reins of government, and Colonel Lawrence to leave the Punjab for a time. The health of the latter had long been failing. He had tried in August and September the effect of the bracing hill air of Simlah. It had revived him for a while, but his medical attendants urged him to resort to the only remedy which could arrest the progress of disease; and so, with extreme reluctance, he consented to quit his post, and to accompany Lord Hardinge to England. He went; and Sir Frederick Currie, a public servant of approved talent and integrity, who, in the capacity of Political Secretary, had accompanied the Governor-General to the banks of the Sutlej, and who had been subsequently created a baronet and appointed a member of the Supreme Council of India, was nominated to act as Resident in his place.

Meeting the stream of European revolution as they journeyed homewards, Hardinge and Lawrence came

1848. overland to England in the early spring of 1848. Brief space is allowed to me for comment; but before I cease to write Lord Hardinge's name in connexion with Sikh politics and history, I must give expression, if only in a single sentence, to the admiration with which I regard his entire policy towards the Punjab. It was worthy of a Christian warrior: it was worthy of a Christian statesman.   It is in no wise to be judged by results, still less by accidents not assignable to errors inherent in the original design.   What Hardinge did, he did because it was right to do it. His forbearance under provocation, his moderation in the hour of victory foreshadowed the humanity of his subsequent measures.   It was his one desire to render British connexion with the Punjab a blessing to the Sikhs, without destroying their national independence. The spirit of Christian philanthropy moved at his bidding over the whole face of the country—not the mere image of a specious benevolence disguising the designs of our ambition and the impulses of our greed, but an honest, hearty desire to do good without gain, to save an Empire, to reform a people, and to leave behind us the marks of a hand at once gentle and powerful—gentle to cherish and powerful only to sustain.

Conquest of the Punjab.   The portfolio of the Indian Government now passed into the hands of Lord Dalhousie, a young statesman of high promise, who, in the divisions of party politics at home, had been ranged among the followers of Sir Robert Peel, and professed the newly-developed liberalism of that great parliamentary chief.   Held in esteem as a man of moderate views, of considerable administrative ability, and more than common assi-

duity in the public service, his brief career as an
English statesman seemed to afford good hope that, in
the great descriptive roll of Indian Viceroys, his name
would be recorded as that of a ruler distinguished
rather for the utility than for the brilliancy of his administration.   And so, doubtless, it seemed to himself. What India most wanted at that time was Peace.
Left to her repose, even without external aid, she
might soon have recovered from the effects of a succession of wasting wars.   But, cherished and fostered
by an unambitious and enlightened ruler, there was
good prospect of a future of unexampled prosperity—
of great material and moral advancement—of that
oft-promised, ever realisable, but still unrealised
blessing, the "development of the resources of the
country." The country wanted Railroads, and the
people Education, and there was good hope that Dalhousie would give them both.

When he looked beyond the frontier he saw that
everything was quiet. The new year had dawned
auspiciously on the Punjab. The attention of the
British functionaries, ever earnest and active in well-
doing—for the disciples of Henry Lawrence had
caught much of the zealous humanity of their master
—was mainly directed to the settlement of the Land
Revenue and the improvement of the judicial system
of the country. They had begun codifying in good
earnest, and laws, civil and criminal, grew apace
under their hands. In a state of things so satisfactory
as this there was little to call for special remark, and
the Governor-General, in his letters to the Home
Government, contented himself with the simple observation, that he "forwarded papers relating to the
Punjab." But early in May intelligence had reached
Calcutta which impelled him to indite a more stirring

1848.   epistle.   The Punjab was on the eve of another crisis.

In September, 1844, Sawun Mull, the able and energetic Governor* of Mooltan, was shot to death by an assassin.   He was succeeded by his son Moolraj, who also had earned for himself the reputation of a chief with just and enlightened views of government, and considerable administrative ability.   But he had also a reputation very dangerous in that country: he was reputed to be very rich.   Sawun Mull was believed to have amassed immense treasures in Mooltan; and on the instalment of his son in the government, the Lahore Durbar demanded from him a succession-duty† of a million of money.   The exorbitant claim was not complied with; but a compromise was effected, by which Moolraj became bound to pay to Lahore less than a fifth of the required amount.   And this sum would have been paid, but for the convulsions which soon began to rend the country, and the disasters which befel the Durbar.

On the re-establishment of the Sikh Government the claim was renewed.   It was intimated to the Dewan that if the stipulated eighteen lakhs, with certain amounts due for arrears, were paid into the Lahore Treasury, he would be allowed to continue in charge of Mooltan; but that if he demurred, troops would be sent to coerce him.   He refused payment of the money, and troops were accordingly sent against him.   Thus threatened, he besought the British Government to interfere in his favour, and consented to adjust the matter through the arbitration of the Resident.   The result was, that he went to Lahore in the

* I have used the word most intelligible to ordinary English readers, but it does not fitly represent the office held by the "Dewan," who was financial manager or revenue-farmer of the district, with the control of the internal administration.

† Nuzzurana.

autumn of 1846; promised to pay by instalments the
money claimed; and was mulcted in a portion of the
territories from which he had drawn his revenue. The
remainder was farmed out to him for a term of three
years. With this arrangement he appeared to be
satisfied. He was anxious to obtain the guarantee of
the British Government; but his request was refused,
and he returned to Mooltan without it.

For the space of more than a year, Moolraj remained in peaceful occupation of the country which
had been leased out to him. There was no attempt,
on the part of the British functionaries, to interfere
with the affairs of Mooltan. That territory was especially exempted from the operation of the revenue
settlement, which had taken effect elsewhere, and of
the new customs regulations which had been established in other parts of the Punjab. But the compact which had been entered into with the Lahore
Durbar did not sit easily upon him. He thought, or
affected to think, that its terms were too rigorous;
and accordingly, about the close of 1847, he repaired
to the capital to seek some remission of them. He
soon began intriguing with the Durbar for the reduction of the stipulated rents; and not coming to any
satisfactory arrangement, intimated his wish to resign
a charge which he had found so little profitable. He
was told that his resignation, when formally tendered,
would be accepted; but was recommended to reflect
upon the subject before finally coming to a determination, which could not be subsequently revoked.
Moolraj quitted Lahore; and sent in first a somewhat
vague, and afterwards a more distinct, resignation of
his office; and the Durbar at once appointed a successor. Sirdar Kan Singh, who was described as "a
brave soldier and intelligent man," was nominated to

1848.

the Governorship of Mooltan, on a fixed annual salary. At the same time, Mr. Vans Agnew, a civil servant of the Company, and Lieutenant Anderson, of the Bombay army, were despatched to Mooltan with the new Governor, and an escort of five hundred men, to receive charge of the place. On their arrival before the city there were no symptoms of any hostile intentions on the part of its occupants. Moolraj himself waited on the British officers on the 18th of April, and was peremptorily called upon to give in his accounts. Disconcerted and annoyed, he quitted their presence, but next morning he met them with a calm aspect, and conducted them through the fort. Two companies of Goorkhas and some horsemen of the escort were placed in possession of one of the fort-gates. The crisis was now at hand. Moolraj formally gave over charge of the fort; and as the party retired through the gate, the British officers were suddenly attacked and severely wounded. Moolraj, who was riding with them at the time, offered no assistance, but, setting spurs to his horse, galloped off in the direction of his garden-house, whilst the wounded officers were carried to their own camp by Kan Singh and a party of the Goorkhas.

In the course of the following day all the Mooltanee troops were in a state of open insurrection. Moolraj himself, who may not have been guilty in the first instance of an act of premeditated treachery, and who subsequently pleaded that he was coerced by his troops, sent excuses to Vans Agnew, who, with the generous confidence of youth, acquitted him of all participation in the outrage. But he was soon heart and soul in the work; and his emissaries plied their trade of corruption with unerring effect. Before nightfall, the commandant of the escort, with all his

men, went over to the enemy. The building in which
the wounded officers lay was surrounded. A motley
crew of ruffians—soldiers and citizens—men of all
classes, young and old, moved by one common impulse, one great thirst of blood, came yelling and
shouting around the abode of the doomed Feringhees.
In they rushed, with a savage cry, and surrounded
their victims. The wounded officers lay armed on
their beds, and helpless, hopeless as they were, put
on the bold front of intrepid Englishmen, and were
heroes to the last. Having shaken hands, and bade
each other a last farewell, they turned upon their
assailants as best they could; but overpowered by
numbers, they fell, declaring in the prophetic language of death, that thousands of their countrymen
would come to avenge them. The slaughter thoroughly accomplished, the two bodies were dragged
out of the mosque, and barbarously mutilated by the
murderers, with every indignity that malice could
devise.

Irretrievably committed in the eyes both of our countrymen and his own, Moolraj now saw that there was
no going back; he had entered, whether designedly
or not, on a course which admitted of no pause, and
left no time for reflection. All the dormant energies
of his nature were now called into full activity. He
took command of the insurgents—identified himself
with their cause—bestowed largesses upon the men
who had been most active in the assault upon the
British officers, retained all who would take service
with him, laid in stores, collected money, and addressed letters to other chiefs urging them to resistance. He had never been looked upon by others—
never regarded himself—as a man to become the leader
of a great national movement; but now circumstances

had done for him what he would never willingly have
shaped out for himself; so he bowed to fate, and became a hero.

Thus was the second Sikh War commenced. Outwardly, it was but the revolt of a local government—
the rebellion of an officer of the Sikh State against
the sovereign power of the land. But, rightly considered, it was of far deeper significance. Whether
Moolraj had been incited to resistance by the promptings of a spirit far more bitter in its resentments, and
more active in its malignity than his own, is not very
apparent. But it is certain that when he raised the
standard of rebellion at Mooltan, he did but anticipate a movement for which the whole country was
ripe. Already had ominous reports of ill-concealed
disaffection come in from some of the outlying dis-.
tricts, and though the mortifying fact was very reluctantly believed, it is certain that the state of things
which Henry Lawrence had predicted was already a
present reality, and that the Sikhs, chafing under the
irritating interference of the European stranger, were
about to make a common effort to expel him. A finer
body of officers than those employed under the British
Resident in the Punjab seldom laboured for the good
of a people. That they worked, earnestly and assiduously, animated by the purest spirit of Christian
benevolence, is not to be doubted. But it was not
in the nature of things that even if the thing done
had been palatable to the Sikhs, they would have
reconciled themselves to the doers of it. Habituated
to rule in all parts of the world, and to interfere in
the affairs of people of all colours and creeds; Englishmen are slow to familiarise themselves with the
idea of the too probable unpopularity of their interference They think that if they mean well they
must secure confidence. They do not consider that

our beneficent ways may not be more in accordance with the national taste than our round hats and stiff neckcloths; and that even if they were, alien interference must in itself be utterly distasteful to them. It is not to be doubted, I say, that the young Englishmen first employed in the Punjab laboured earnestly for the good of the people; but their very presence was a sore in the flesh of the nation, and if they had been endowed with superhuman wisdom and angelic benevolence, it would have made no difference in the sum total of popular discontent.

But it is probable that some mistakes were committed—the inevitable growth of benevolent ignorance and energetic inexperience—at the outset of our career as Punjabee administrators. The interference appears to have been greater than was contemplated in the original design of the Second Protectorate. At that time the God Terminus was held by many of our administrators in especial veneration. The Theodolite, the Reconnoitring Compass, and the Measuring Chain were the great emblems of British rule. And now these mysterious instruments began to make their appearance in the Punjab. We were taking sights and measuring angles on the outskirts of civilisation; and neither the chiefs nor the people could readily persuade themselves that we were doing all this for their good; there was an appearance in it of ulterior design. And, as I have hinted, the agents employed were sometimes wholly inexperienced in business of this kind. "My present *rôle*," wrote a young ensign[*] of two years' standing in the service, whose later exploits will be recorded in these pages, "is to survey a part

---

[*] W. R. Hodson ("Hodson of Hodson's Horse"), January, 1848. This young officer narrowly escaped the fate of Anderson at Mooltan, for he had been selected in the first instance to accompany Vans Agnew.

of the country lying along the left bank of the Ravee and below the hills, and I am daily and all day at work with compasses and chain, pen and pencil, following streams, diving into valleys, burrowing into hills, to complete my work. I need hardly remark, that having never attempted anything of the kind, it is bothering at first. I should not be surprised any day to be told to build a ship, compose a code of laws, or hold assizes. In fact, 'tis the way in India; every one has to teach himself his work, and to do it at the same time." Training of this kind has made the finest race of officers that the world has ever seen. But the novitiate of these men may have teemed with blunders fatal to the people among whom they were sent, in all the self-confidence of youth, to learn their diversities of work. As they advance in years, and every year know better how difficult a thing it is to administer the affairs of a foreign people, such public servants often shudder to think of the errors committed, of the wrong done, when they served their apprenticeship in government without a master, and taught themselves at the expense of thousands. The most experienced administrators in the present case might have failed from the want of a right understanding of the temper of the people. But it was the necessity of our position that some who were set over the officers of the Sikh Government knew little of the people and little of administration. They were able, indefatigable, and conscientious. They erred only because they saw too much and did too much, and had not come to understand the wise policy of shutting their eyes and leaving alone.

And so, although the rebellion of Moolraj was at first only a local outbreak, and the British authorities were well disposed to regard it as a movement against the Sikh Government, not as an outrage especially directed against ourselves, that fiction could not be long maintained—for every day it became more and more apparent that the whole country was ripe for another war with the intruding Feringhee. The Durbar officers did not hesitate to express their conviction that to send Sikh troops to act against Moolraj would only be to swell the number of his adherents. To have despatched with them a small English force would have been to risk its safety and precipitate the conflict. An overwhelming display of force, on the part of the British Government, might have crushed the rebellion at Mooltan and retarded the general rising of the country. But the season was far advanced; the responsibility was a great one. The Commander-in-Chief of the British army in India was not far distant. Currie, therefore, though his own judgment inclined to the commencement of immediate hostilities, rightly referred the momentous question to the military chief. Lord Gough was against immediate action; and the head of the Indian Government unreservedly endorsed the decision.

The remnant of the old Khalsa army eagerly watched the result, and were not slow to attribute our inactivity, at such a moment, to hesitation—to fear—to paralysis. I am not writing a military history of the Second Sikh War, and the question now suggested is one which I am not called upon to discuss. But I think that promptitude of action is often of more importance than completeness of preparation, and that to show ourselves confident of success is in most cases to attain it. The British power in India cannot afford to be quiescent under insult and outrage. Delay is held to be a sign of weakness. It encourages enmity and confirms vacillation. It is a disaster in

itself—more serious, often, than any that can arise
from insufficient preparation, and that great bugbear
the inclemency of the season.   On the other hand,
it is not to be forgotten that to despise our enemies is
a common national mistake, and that sometimes it
has been a fatal one.   We have brought calamities
on ourselves by our rashness as we have by our
indecision.   The History of India teems with examples of both results; the most profitable lesson to
be learnt from which is, that, however wise we may
be after the event, criticism in such a case ought to
be diffident and forbearing.

But whilst the Commander-in-Chief, in the cool
mountain air of Simlah, was deciding on the impossibility of commencing military operations, a young
lieutenant of the Bengal army, who had been engaged
in the Revenue settlement of the country about Bunnoo, was marching down upon Mooltan with a small
body of troops, to render assistance to his brother-
officers in their perilous position, and to support the
authority of the Lahore Durbar.   A letter from
Vans Agnew, dictated by the wounded man, had providentially fallen into his hands.   He saw at once the
emergency of the case; he never hesitated; but abandoning all other considerations, improvised the best
force that could be got together, and, with fifteen
hundred men and two pieces of artillery, marched
forth in all the eager confidence of youth, hoping
that it might be his privilege to rescue his countrymen from the danger that beset them.

The name of this young officer was Herbert Edwardes.   A native of Frodley, in Shropshire, the son
of a country clergyman, educated at King's College,
London, he had entered the Company's service as a
cadet of infantry, at an age somewhat more advanced

than that which sees the initiation into military life of the majority of young officers. But at an age much earlier than that which commonly places them in possession of the most superficial knowledge of the history and politics of the East, young Edwardes had acquired a stock of information, and a capacity for judging rightly of passing events, which would have done no discredit to a veteran soldier and diplomatist. He had served but a few years, when his name became familiar to English readers throughout the Presidency to which he belonged, as one of the ablest anonymous writers in the country. His literary talents, like his military qualities, were of a bold, earnest, impulsive character. Whatever he did, he did rapidly and well. He was precisely the kind of man to attract the attention and retain the favour of such an officer as Henry Lawrence, who, with the same quiet love of literature, combined a keen appreciation of that energy and fire of character which shrink from no responsibility, and are ever seeking to find an outlet in dashing exploits. In one of the earliest and most striking scenes of the Punjabee drama, Edwardes had acted a distinguished part. When the insurrection broke out in Cashmere, he was despatched to Jummoo, to awaken Gholab Singh to a sense of his duty in that conjuncture; and there are few more memorable and impressive incidents in Sikh history than that which exhibited a handful of British officers controlling the movements of large bodies of foreign troops,—the very men, and under the very leaders, who, so short a time before, had contested with us on the banks of the Sutlej the sovereignty of Hindostan.

On the reconstruction of the Sikh Government, after the deposition of Lal Singh, Herbert Edwardes

1848. was one of the officers selected to superintend the internal administration of the country ; and he had just completed the Revenue settlement of Bunnoo, when the startling intelligence of the Mooltanee outbreak reached his camp. He marched at once to succour his brother-officers; crossed the Indus, and took possession of Leia, the chief city in the Sindh Saugor Doab. But tidings by this time had reached him of the melancholy fate of Agnew and Anderson, and there was then no profit in the immediate movement on Mooltan to compensate for its certain danger. But the demonstration still had its uses. It was something that there was a force in the field with a British officer at the head of it to assert the cause of order and authority in the name of the Maharajah of the Punjab. Such a force might, for a time at least, hold rebellion in check in that part of the country. But Edwardes dreamt of higher service than this. To the south of Mooltan, some fifty miles, lies Bahwulpore, in the chief of which place we believed that we had a staunch ally. In the name of the British Government, Edwardes called upon him to move an auxiliary force upon Mooltan; and he had little doubt that, after forming a junction with these troops, he could capture the rebel stronghold. The confidence of the young soldier, stimulated by a victory which he gained over a large body of rebels on the great anniversary of Waterloo, saw no obstacle to this enterprise which could not be overcome if the Resident would only send him a few heavy guns and mortars, and Major Napier, of the Engineers, to direct the operations of the siege. He knew the worth of such a man in such a conjuncture, and every year that has since passed has made him prouder of the youthful forecast which he then evinced.

The Bahwulpore troops were sent, the junction was formed, and the forces marched down upon Mooltan. Placing himself at the head of a considerable body of men, the rebel chief went out to give them battle, but was beaten by Edwardes, aided by Van Cortlandt, a European officer in Sikh employ, who has since done good service to the British Government, and Edward Lake, a gallant young officer of Bengal Engineers, directing the Bahwulpore column, who has abundantly fulfilled, on the same theatre of action, the high promise of his youth. But much as irregular levies, so led, might do in the open field, they were powerless against the walls of Mooltan. Again, therefore, Edwardes urged upon the Resident the expediency of strengthening his hands, especially in respect of the ordnance branches of the service. Only send a siege train, some Sappers and Miners, with Robert Napier to direct the siege, and—this time, for the difficulties of the work had assumed larger proportions in his eyes—a few regular regiments, under a young brigadier, and we shall "close," he said, "Moolraj's accounts in a fortnight, and obviate the necessity of assembling fifty thousand men in October."

In the early part of July this requisition was received at Lahore. The interval which had elapsed, since the disastrous tidings of the rebellion of Moolraj had reached the Residency, had not been an uneventful one at the capital. Early in May, discovery was made of an attempt to corrupt the fidelity of our British Sepoys. The first intimation of the plot was received from some troopers of the 7th Irregular Cavalry, who communicated the circumstance to their commanding officer. The principal conspirators were one Kan Singh, an unemployed general of the Sikh army, and Gunga Ram, the confidential Vakeel of the

1848.   Maharanee. These men, and two others, were seized,
tried, and convicted. The two chief conspirators
were publicly hanged, and their less guilty associates
transported. That they were instruments of the
Maharanee was sufficiently proved. The conspirators
acknowledged that she was the prime instigator of the
treacherous attempt, and her letters were found in
their possession. With this knowledge, it could no
longer be a question with the Resident as to what
course it behoved him to adopt. The mother of the
Maharajah and the widow of Runjeet Singh could no
longer be suffered to dwell among the Sikhs. She had
already been removed from Lahore to Sheikopoor.
It now became necessary to remove her from the
Punjab. Accordingly, certain accredited agents of
the Lahore Durbar, accompanied by two British
officers, Captain Lumsden and Lieutenant Hodson,
were despatched to Sheikopoor, with a mandate
under the seal of the Maharajah, directing her removal from that place. Without offering any resistance, or expressing any dissatisfaction, she placed herself under the charge of the deputation; and, when
it became clear to her that she was on her way to the
British frontier, she desired—not improbably with
that blended irony and bravado which she so well
knew how to employ—that her thanks might be conveyed to the Resident for removing her to the Company's dominions, out of the reach of the enemies
who would destroy her. With a considerable retinue
of female attendants, she was conveyed to Ferozepore,
and eventually to Benares, where she was placed under
the charge of Major George Macgregor, an Artillery
officer of high personal character and great diplomatic
experience, who had well sustained in the Punjab the
brilliant reputation which he had earned at Jellalabad

Such was the apparent growth visible at the British Residency, recognised in our State-papers, of those three months in the Punjab. But in the hands of a Sikh historian these incidents would form but a small part of the national annals, for all over the country the great chiefs were actively maturing the plan of their emancipation, calling upon all true Sikhs, in the name of the great Founder of their Faith, to exterminate the Christian usurpers, and even those nearest to the throne were among the arch-promoters of the movement. The daughter of Chuttur Singh and the sister of Shere Singh was the betrothed wife of the Maharajah; but these Sirdars, though anxious to veil their designs until the whole country was ripe for a simultaneous rising, were intriguing and plotting for our overthrow. The former was in the Hazareh, where his fidelity had been for some time suspected by James Abbott—another officer of the Bengal Artillery, friend and comrade of Henry Lawrence, who had been settling that part of the country—one of those men whose lot in life it is never to be believed, never to be appreciated, never to be rewarded; of the true salt of the earth, but of an unrecognised savour; chivalrous, heroic, but somehow or other never thoroughly emerging from the shade. He was not one to estimate highly the force of the maxim that "speech is silver, silence is gold;" and his suspicions are said not to have been acceptable at Lahore. But though it may be good to suspect, it is doubtless good, also, not to appear to suspect. And if Currie, in that conjuncture, had betrayed a want of confidence in the Sikh Sirdars, he would have precipitated the collision which it was sound policy to retard. So, whatever may have been his genuine convictions, he

1848.   still appeared to trust the chiefs of the Regency; and
Shere Singh, with a strong body of Sikh troops, was
sent down to Mooltan.   It was wise to maintain, as
long as possible, the semblance of the authority of
the Sikh Durbar—wise to keep up the show of sup-
pressing a rebellion by the hand of the native Government. To send down that undeveloped traitor to
the great centre of revolt may have been a hazardous
experiment, but it was hazardous also to keep him
where he was; and the master-passion of the Sikh
soldiery for plunder might have kept his battalions
nominally on the side of authority, until they had
glutted themselves with the spoils of Mooltan, and preparations had, meanwhile, been made in the British
provinces for the commencement of military operations
on a scale befitting the occasion. But the repeated re-
quisitions of Edwardes for British aid at last wrought
upon the Resident, and Currie determined to send a
force to Mooltan, with a siege-train for the reduction
of the fortress.   In General Samson Whish, of the
Artillery, under whose command the force was despatched, there was not literally what Edwardes had
asked for—" a young brigadier"—but there was a
general officer of unwonted youthfulness of aspect
and activity of body, who could sit a horse well,
could ride any distance at a stretch, and was generally esteemed to be one of the best artillery officers
in the service.   This forward movement was not
countenanced in high places.   The Commander-in-
Chief shook his head.   The Governor-General shook
his head.   But the Resident had ordered it, and it
could not be countermanded, without encouraging a
belief that there was a want of unanimity in British
councils.

So the besieging force marched upon Mooltan, and

arrived before the city in high health and excellent spirits. On the 5th of September, in the name of the Maharajah and Queen Victoria, the British General summoned the garrison to surrender. No answer was returned to the summons, and the siege commenced. But on the 14th, when our guns were within breaching distance of the walls of the town, Whish, to his bitter mortification, was compelled to abandon the siege. The Sikh force under Shere Singh had gone over to the enemy.

This event had long been matter of anxious speculation in the British camp, and now took no one by surprise. It was known that the hearts of the soldiery were with Moolraj; but there was something of a more doubtful character in the conduct of the Rajah himself, who had on more than one occasion testified his zeal and loyalty by voluntary acts of service in our cause. In his own camp, the Khalsa troops said contemptuously, that he was a Mussulman. With Edwardes he was outwardly on the best possible terms; spoke freely of the conduct of his father, Chuttur Singh; declared that he washed his hands of all the old man's rebellious projects; and candidly avowed his mistrust of the Sikh troops. But in all this he was playing a part. He had written to his brother to say that he intended to go over to the enemy on that very 14th of September, and he kept his word to the letter. On the morning of that day, the whole Durbar force sought entrance into the city. Doubtful of the real nature of the movement, Moolraj at first refused them admittance; but soon satisfied of their intentions, he opened his gates; the long dreaded and fatal junction was effected; and the British General was under the mortifying necessity of raising the siege of Mooltan.

The whole truth was now visible before the world. It was impossible any longer to maintain the fiction of a local rebellion, to pretend that the Lahore Government, assisted by British troops, was endeavouring to coerce a refractory subject. The very heads of that Government were in open hostility to the British, raising the standard of nationality in the name of the Maharajah. It was obvious that the war now about to be waged, was between the British and the Sikhs. Some hope was at one time to be drawn from the fact of long-standing feuds among the different Sikh families. Then there was the not unreasonable conviction that the Mahomedan population of the Punjab might easily be kept in a state of enmity with the Sikhs. But these assurances soon melted away. Hostile families and hostile religions were content to unite for the nonce against the Feringhees; and the Commander-in-Chief, as the cold weather approached, was gratified by finding that there had been no premature birth of victory—that the work was yet to be done — and that an army of twenty thousand men, under his personal command, was required to take the field.

And from that time Mooltan ceased to be the focus of rebellion and the head-quarters of the war. In the Hazareh country Chuttur Singh had thrown off all vestments of disguise, and plunged boldly into the troubled waters that lay before him. The thoughts of Shere Singh soon began to turn towards that quarter—indeed, such had been his desire from the first—and before the second week of October had passed away, he had marched out of Mooltan to join his father. The whole country was now rising against us. Having used the name of the Maharajah, the Sikh leaders were eager to possess themselves of

the person of the boy-King, and but for the vigilance
of the Resident they would have achieved an object
which would have added a new element of strength
to the national cause.   Duleep Singh remained in our
hands virtually a prisoner at Lahore.

All this time the Governor-General was at Calcutta, watching from a distance the progress of
events, and betraying no eagerness to seize a favourable opportunity for the conquest of the Punjab.   Indeed, it has been imputed to him, as a grave political
error, that he did not at an earlier period make due
preparation for the inevitable war.   But, it would seem
that in the summer of 1848, his desire was to recognise as long as possible only internal rebellion in the
Sikh country — to see, not the rising of a nation
against a foreign intruder, but the revolt of a few un-
loyal chiefs against their own lawful sovereign.   But
with the first breath of the cool season there came a
truer conception of the crisis, and Lord Dalhousie prepared himself for the conflict.   " I have wished for
peace," he said, at a public entertainment, early in
October ; " I have longed for it ; I have striven for
it   But if the enemies of India determine to have
war, war they shall have, and on my word they shall
have it with a vengeance."   A few days afterwards
he turned his back upon Calcutta, and set his face
towards the north-west.   All the energies of his
mind were then given to the prosecution of the war.

The British army destined for the re-conquest of
the Punjab assembled at Ferozepore, and crossed the
Sutlej in different detachments.   On the 13th of
November the head-quarters reached Lahore.   At
that time it could hardly be said that British influence extended a rood beyond the Residency walls.
In all parts of the country the Sikhs had risen against

D 2

1848.   the great reproach of the English Occupation.   In
many outlying places, on the confines of civilisation, our English officers were holding out, in the
face of every conceivable difficulty and danger, with
constancy and resolution most chivalrous, most
heroic, hoping only to maintain, by their own personal gallantry, the character of the nation they represented.   There was, indeed, nothing more to be
done.   We had ceased to be regarded as allies.   So
eager and so general was the desire to expel the
intruding Feringhee, that the followers of Govind
sank for a time all feelings of national and religious
animosity against their Afghan neighbours, and invoked Mahomedan aid from the regions beyond the
passes of the Khyber.   .

On the 21st of November, Lord Gough joined the
army on the left bank of the Sutlej.   A veteran commander, who within the space of a few years had
fought more battles in different parts of the world
than were crowded into the lives of most living warriors—a general whose uniform good fortune had
glossed over his want of forecast and science, and
whose repeated successes had silenced criticism—he
was now about to engage in military operations greater
than those of his antecedent campaigns, with, perhaps,
even less knowledge of the country and less consideration of the probable contingencies of the war.   But all
men had confidence in him.   India had been won by
a series of military mistakes that would have disgraced an ensign before the examination period, and,
perhaps, would not have been won at all if we had
infused into our operations more of the pedantry of
military science.   He was a soldier, and all who fought
under him honoured his grey hairs, and loved him
for his manly bearing, his fine frank character, and

even for the impetuosity which so often entangled his legions in difficulties, and enhanced the cost of the victories he gained.

The arrival of the Commander-in-Chief was the signal for the immediate commencement of hostilities. The force then under his personal command consisted of upwards of twenty thousand men, with nearly a hundred pieces of artillery, and Gough was in no temper for delay. On the day after his arrival in camp was fought the battle of Ramnuggur, the first of those disastrous successes which have given so gloomy a character to the campaign. The enemy had a strong masked battery on the other side of the river, and very cleverly contrived to draw the British troops into an ambuscade. The operations of the Commander-in-Chief, commenced with the object of driving a party of the rebels, who were on his side of the Chenab, across the river, had the effect of bringing his cavalry and artillery within reach of these concealed guns; and twenty-eight pieces of ordnance opened upon our advancing columns. The cavalry were ordered to move forward to the attack as soon as an opportunity presented itself. They found an opportunity, and charged a large body of the enemy, the Sikh batteries pouring in their deadly showers all the while. Many fell under the fire of the guns, many under the sabre-cuts of the Sikh swordsmen, many under the withering fire of a body of matchlockmen, who, taking advantage of the nature of the ground, harassed our horsemen sorely. Nothing was gained by our "victory;" but we lost many brave and some good soldiers; and our troops returned to camp weary and dispirited, asking what end they had accomplished, and sighing over the cost.

Some days afterwards a force under General Thackwell was sent out to cross the river, but being scantily supplied with information, and grievously hampered by instructions, it succeeded only in losing a few men and killing several of the enemy. No great object was gained, but great opportunities were sacrificed. The Commander-in-Chief pompously declared that "it had pleased Almighty God to vouchsafe to the British arms the most successful issue to the extensive combinations rendered necessary for the purpose of effecting the passage of the Chenab, the defeat and dispersion of the Sikh force under the insurgent Rajah Shere Singh and the numerous Sikh Sirdars who had the temerity to set at defiance the British power." These "events, so fraught with importance," were to "tend to most momentous results." The results were, that the field of battle was shifted from the banks of the Chenab to the banks of the Jhelum. The enemy, who might have been taken in rear, and whose batteries might have been seized, if Thackwell had been free to carry out the most obvious tactics, escaped with all their guns; and on the 13th of January bore bloody witness to the little they had suffered, by fighting one of the greatest and most sanguinary battles in the whole chronicle of Indian warfare.

By this time Henry Lawrence had returned to the Punjab. The news of the outbreak at Mooltan had reached him in England, whilst still in broken health, and had raised within him an incontrollable desire, at any hazard, to return to his post. He had won his spurs, and he was eager to prove that he was worthy of them, even at the risk of life itself. It has been said that he ought not to have quitted the Punjab, and that if he had been at Lahore in the spring of 1848, the war would not then have been precipitated by the rebellion of Moolraj, for "any one but a civilian would have foreseen that to send Vans Agnew and Anderson down to Mooltan at the time and in the manner selected was almost sure to produce an ebullition of feeling and violence." But if Lawrence had not gone to England at that time, he would, in all human probability, have died; and though he might not have sent the same men to Mooltan, he would have sent a mission there for the same purpose. " I meant to have sent Arthur Cocks," was his remark to the present writer, when the disastrous news reached us in London. He saw at once that the Mooltanee revolt was but the prelude to a great national outbreak, and though his friends trembled for his safety and counselled delay, his strong sense of duty to the State overruled all personal considerations, and so he carried back his shattered frame and his inexhaustible energies to the scene of the coming conflict. Leaving London at the end of October, he reached Bombay early in December, and pushing up the Indus with characteristic rapidity of movement, joined the camp of General Whish, before the walls of Mooltan, two days after the great festival of Christmas.

On the second day of the new year, Whish, reinforced from Bombay, carried the city of Mooltan. Long and obstinate had been the resistance of the besieged; and now that our storming columns entered the breach, the garrison still, at the bayonet's point, showed the stuff of which they were made. Frightful had been the carnage during the siege. Heaps of mangled bodies about the battered town bore ghastly witness to the terrible effects of the British ordnance. But many yet stood to be shot down or bayoneted in the streets; and the work of the besieging force was

1848.

Calcutta Review.

1849.

yet far from its close. Moolraj was in the citadel with some thousands of his best fighting-men; and the fort guns were plied as vigorously as before the capture of the town. The strength of this formidable fortress seemed to laugh our breaching batteries to scorn. Mining operations were, therefore, commenced; but carried on, as they were, beneath a constant discharge from our mortars, it seemed little likely that the enemy would wait to test the skill of the engineers. The terrible shelling to which the fortress was exposed dismayed the pent-up garrison. By the 21st of January they were reduced to the last extremity. Moolraj vainly endeavoured to rally his followers. Their spirit was broken. There was nothing left for them but to make a desperate sally and cut their way through the besiegers, or to surrender at once. The nobler alternative was rejected. Asking only for his own life and the honour of his women, Moolraj tendered on that day his submission to the British General. Whish refused to guarantee the first, but promised to protect the women; and on the following morning the garrison marched out of Mooltan, and Dewan Moolraj threw himself upon the mercy of the British Government.

Meanwhile, Henry Lawrence, having witnessed the fall of the city of Mooltan, hastened upwards to Ferozepore, conveyed to Lord Dalhousie the first welcome tidings of that event, took counsel with the Governor-General, made himself master of the great man's views, then hurried on to Lahore, communicated with the Resident, and on the same evening pushed on to the camp of the Commander-in-Chief, which he reached on the night of the 10th of January. He was there in no recognised official position, for Currie's tenure of office did not expire until the beginning of the ensuing month; but he was ready for any kind of service, and he placed himself at Lord Gough's disposal, as an honorary aide-de-camp, or any other subordinate officer, in the fine army which was now stretching out before him.

Three days after Lawrence's arrival in camp the battle of Chillianwallah was fought. The time had arrived when a far less impetuous general than Gough might have deemed it incumbent on him to force the Sikh army into a general action. It is true that the final reduction of the fortress of Mooltan would have liberated a large portion of Whish's column, and greatly have added to the strength of the British army on the banks of the Jhelum. But the Sikh Sirdars, on this very account, were eager to begin the battle, and would not have suffered us to wait for our reinforcements. Gough already had a noble force under him, equal to any service. It was panting for action. There had been a lull of more than a month's duration, and all through India there was a feeling of impatience at the protracted delay. Gough, therefore, prepared for action. Ascertaining the nature of the country occupied by the Sikh army, and the position of their troops, he planned his attack upon sound tactical principles, and fully instructed his generals in the several parts which they were called upon to play. On the afternoon of the 13th everything was ready, and the battle was to have been commenced early on the following morning. But, unwilling to give the British General the long hours of the morrow's light, from daybreak to sunset, that he wanted, to fight his battle according to approved principles of modern warfare, the Sikh leaders, when the day was far spent, determined, if possible, to aggravate him into an immediate encounter. They

knew their man.   So they advanced a few guns, and
sent some round-shot booming in the direction of the
British camp.   The bait took.   The warm Hibernian
temperament of the British leader could not brook the
insult.   He moved up his heavy guns, responded with
some chance shots at the invisible enemy, and then,
there being little of the day left for his operations,
gave the command for his line to advance.

The story of what followed has been often told, and
it is not so gratifying a page of history that I need
care to repeat it.   Night closed upon the fearful
carnage of that terrible engagement, and both armies
claimed the victory.   What it cost us is written in
the Gazette.   Never was an official bulletin received
in England with a wilder outcry of pain and passion.
The past services, the intrepid personal courage, the
open honest character, the many noble qualities of
the veteran Commander were forgotten in that burst
of popular indignation, and hundreds of English
families turned from the angry past to the fearful
future, and trembled as they thought that the crowning action with that formidable enemy had yet to be
fought by a General so rash, so headstrong, and so
incompetent.

In the high places of Government there was universal discomposure, and the greatest military authority in the country shook his head with an
ominous gesture of reproach.   Then arose a wild
cry for Napier.   The conqueror of the Beloochees was
sent out in hot·haste to India to repair the mischief
that had been done by Gough, and to finish off the
war with the Sikhs in a proper workmanlike manner.
But the hottest haste could not wholly annihilate time
and space, and though this sudden supersession of the
brave old chief, who had fought so many battles and

won so many victories, might shame his grey hairs, it could not bring the war to a more rapid or a more honourable close. The carnage of Chillianwallah shook for a time the confidence of the army in their chief, but it did not shake the courage of our fighting-men, or destroy their inherent capacity for conquest. It was a lesson, too, that must have scored itself into the very heart of the British chief, and made him a sadder man and a wiser commander. The errors of the 13th of January were to be atoned for by a victory which any leader might contemplate with pride, and any nation with gratitude. Scarcely had his appointed successor turned his back upon England when Gough fought another great battle, which neither Napier, nor Wellington himself, who talked of going in his place, could have surpassed in vigour of execution or completeness of effect.

Anxiously was intelligence of the surrender of Moolraj looked for in the camp of the Commander-in-Chief. Since that disastrous action at Chillian-wallah, Gough had been entrenching his position, and waiting reinforcements from Mooltan. The surrender of that fortress set free some twelve thousand men, and Whish, with unlooked-for rapidity, marched to the banks of the Jhelum to swell the ranks of the grand army. A great crisis was now approaching. Thrice had the British and Sikh forces met each other on the banks of those classical rivers which had seen the triumphs of the Macedonian—thrice had they met each other only to leave the issue of the contest yet undecided. A great battle was now about to be fought—one differing from all that had yet been fought since the Sikhs first crossed the Sutlej, for a strange but not unlooked-for spectacle was about to present itself—Sikhs and Afghans, those old heredi-

1849.   tary enemies, fighting side by side against a common
foe.   The Sikh Sirdars, I have said, had been intriguing to secure the assistance of the Ameer of
Cabool.   For some time there appeared little likelihood that old Dost Mahomed, whose experience
ought to have brought wisdom with it, would lend
himself to a cause which, in spite of temporary successes, was so sure to prove hopeless in the end.   But
neither years, nor experience, nor adversity had
taught him to profit by the lessons he had learned.
The desire of repossessing himself of Peshawur was
the madness of a life.   The bait was thrown out to
him, and he could not resist it.   He came through
the Khybur with an Afghan force, marched upon the
Indus, and threatened Attock, which fell at his approach; despatched one of his sons to the camp of
Shere Singh, and sent a body of Douranee troops to
fight against his old Feringhee enemy, who for years
had been the arbiter of his fate.   How deplorable an
act of senile fatuity it was, the events of the 21st of
February must have deeply impressed upon his mind.
On that day was fought an action—was gained a
victory, in the emphatic words of the Governor-
General, " memorable alike from the greatness of the
occasion, and from the brilliant and decisive issue of
the encounter.   For the first time, Sikh and Afghan
were banded together against the British power.   It
was an occasion which demanded the putting forth of
all the means at our disposal, and so conspicuous a
manifestation of the superiority of our arms as should
appal each enemy, and dissolve at once their compact
by fatal proof of its futility.   The completeness of the
victory which has been won equals the highest hopes
entertained."   And there was no official exaggeration
in this; none of the vain boasting of the interested

despatch-writer. At Goojrat, to which place the
enemy had unexpectedly moved their camp, Lord
Gough fought a great battle as a great battle ought
to be fought, coolly and deliberately, by a British
Commander. Every arm of his fine force was brought
effectively into play; each in its proper place, each
supporting and assisting the others, and each covering
itself with glory. From the early dawn of that clear
bright morning the cannonade commenced. Never
had the Bengal Artillery made a nobler display;
never had it been worked with more terrible effect.
Resolute and well handled as was the Sikh army, it
could not stand up against the steady fire of our guns.
By noon the enemy were retreating in terrible disorder, "their position carried, their guns, ammunition, camp equipage, and baggage captured, their
flying masses driven before their victorious pursuers,
from mid-day receiving most severe punishment in
their flight." And all this was accomplished with
but little loss of life on the side of the victorious
army. It pleased the Almighty that the bloody
lessons of the Chenab and the Jhelum should not
be thrown away.

A division under Sir Walter Gilbert, an officer of
great personal activity, unequalled in the saddle, was
ordered to follow up the success of Goojrat, and to
drive the Afghans from the Punjab. And well did he
justify the choice of his chief. By a series of rapid
marches, scarcely excelled by any recorded in history,
he convinced the enemy of the hopelessness of all
further resistance. The Barukzye force fled before
our advancing columns, and secured the passage of
the Khybur before British influence could avail to
close it against the fugitives. By the Sikhs themselves the game had clearly been played out. The

Khalsa was now quite broken. There was nothing left for Shere Singh and his associates but to trust themselves to the clemency of the British Government. On the 5th of March, the Rajah sent the British prisoners safely into Gilbert's camp. On the 8th, he appeared in person to make arrangements for the surrender of his followers; and on the 14th, the remnant of the Sikh army, some sixteen thousand men, including thirteen Sirdars of note, laid down their arms at the feet of the British General.

The military chief had now done his work, and it was time for the appearance of the Civil Governor on the scene. Lord Dalhousie was on the spot prepared for immediate action. Already was his portfolio weighty with a proclamation which was to determine the fate of the empire of Runjeet Singh. I do not suppose that a moment's doubt ever obscured the clear, unsullied surface of the Governor-General's resolution. It was a case which suggested no misgivings and prompted no hesitation. The Sikhs had staked everything on the issue of the war, and they had lost it in fair fight. They had repaid by acts of treachery and violence the forbearance and moderation of the British Government. We had tried to spare them; but they would not be spared. First one course, then another, had been adopted in the hope that eventually a strong native Government might be established, able to control its own subjects, and willing to live on terms of friendly alliance with its neighbours. Our policy had from the first been wholly unaggressive. There was no taint of avarice or ambition in it. But it had not been appreciated; it had not been successful. The whole system had collapsed. And now that again a British ruler was called upon to solve the great problem of the Future of the

Punjab, he felt that there was no longer any middle course open to him; that there was but one measure applicable to the crisis that had arisen; and that measure was the annexation of the country to the territories of the British Empire. So a Proclamation was issued announcing that the kingdom founded by Runjeet Singh had passed under British rule: and the wisdom and righteousness of the edict few men are disposed to question.

The last Sikh Durbar was held at Lahore. The fiat of the British conqueror was read aloud, in the presence of the young Maharajah, to the remnant of the chiefs who had not committed themselves by open rebellion; and a paper of Terms was then produced by which the British Government bound themselves to pay the annual sum of forty or fifty thousand pounds to the boy-Prince and his family,* so long as he should remain faithful to his new master and abide by his sovereign will. It was a happy change for Duleep Singh, born as he was for the Sikh shambles; for in his new state he had abundant wealth, perfect safety, freedom from all care, and the insurpassable blessing of a saving faith. Becoming, in his twelfth year, the ward of the Governor-General, he was placed under the immediate tutelage of an Assistant-Surgeon of the Bengal Army,† who was so fit a man for the office, so worthy of the confidence reposed in him, that the little Sikh Prince, under his wise ministrations, developed into a Christian gentleman, an English courtier, and a Scotch laird. And it may be recorded here, before I pass on to the history of British rule in the Punjab, that the mother

---

* This is not the loose diction of doubt. The agreement was, that the British Government should pay not less than four, or more than five, lakhs of rupees.

† Afterwards Sir John Login.

1549. of Duleep Singh, the widow of old Runjeet, that restless, turbulent Chund Kowr, whose intrigues did so much to precipitate the fall of the Sikh Empire, after a series of strange romantic vicissitudes, prematurely old, well-nigh blind, broken and subdued in spirit, found a resting-place at last under the roof of her son, in a quiet corner of an English castle, and died in a London suburb.

1863.

1849.
Administration of the
Punjab.

The Proclamation which turned the Punjab into a British province was not the only weighty State-paper in the portfolio of the Governor-General. Whilst Gough had been preparing to strike the last crushing blow at the military power of the Khalsa, Dalhousie, with Henry Elliot at his elbow, never doubting the issue, was mapping out the scheme of administration under which it seemed good to him to govern the country which was about to pass under our rule. The crowning victory of Goojrat found everything devised and prepared to the minutest detail. The men were ready; the measures were defined. There was no hurry, therefore—no confusion. Every one fell into his appointed place, and knew what he had to do. And never had any Governor better reason to place unbounded confidence in the men whom he employed; never was any Governor more worthily served.

The country which had thus fallen by right of conquest into our hands embraced an area of fifty thousand square miles, and contained a population of four millions of inhabitants. These inhabitants were Hindoos, Mahomedans, and Sikhs. The last were a new people—a sect of reformed Hindoos, of a purer faith than the followers of the Brahminical superstitions. It was a Sikh Government that we had supplanted; and mainly a Sikh army that we had conquered; but it must not be supposed that Punjabee is synonimous with Sikh, that the country was peopled from one end to the other with the followers of Nanuk and Govind, or that they were the ancient dwellers on the banks of those five legendary rivers. The cities of the Punjab were Mahomedan cities; cities founded, perhaps, ere Mahomed arose, enlarged and beautified by the followers of the Ghuznivite. The monuments were mainly Mahomedan monuments, with traces here and there of Grecian occupation and Bactrian rule. Before Delhi had risen into the imperial city of the Moguls, Lahore had been the home of Indian kings. But the rise of the Sikh power was cotemporaneous with our own, and the apostles of the new Reformation had not numbered among their converts more than a section of the people. And as was the population, so was the country itself, of a varied character. Tracts of rich cultivated lands, the corn-field and the rose-garden, alternated with the scorched plain and the sandy desert. Here, as far as the eye could reach, a dreary level of jungle and brushwood; there, a magnificent panorama, bounded by the blue ranges and the snowy peaks of the Himalayah. And ever the great rivers as they flowed suggested to the cultured mind of the English scholar thoughts of that grand old traditionary age, when Porus fought, and Alexander conquered, and Megasthenes wrote, and the home-sick Argive, on the banks of those fabulous streams, sighed for the pleasant country he had left, and rebelled against his leader and his fate. It was a country full of interest and full of opportunity; and it grew at once into the pet province of the

E

British Viceroy, the youngest and the most hopeful of all.

That a country so situated, so circumstanced, and so peopled, should not be brought under the system of administration prevailing in our long-settled provinces was a mere matter of course. But Dalhousie had no disposition to rush into the opposite extreme of a purely military government. He had at no time of his career any class prejudices, and he did not see why soldiers and civilians should not work harmoniously together in the administrative agency of the province. He had faith in both; each in his appointed place; for there was rough soldiers' work to be done, and much also that needed the calm judgment and the tutored eye of the experienced civilian. So he called in the aid of a mixed Staff of civil and military officers, and at the head of this he placed a Board of Administration, presided over by Henry Lawrence.*

The Board was to consist of three members, with secretaries to do the pen-work of the administration, and to scatter its instructions among the subordinate functionaries of the province. It was not a controlling authority which a man of Dalhousie's stamp was likely to affect; scarcely, indeed, could he be supposed to tolerate it. But he could not set aside the great claims of Henry Lawrence, nor, indeed, could he safely dispense with his services in such a conjuncture; yet he was unwilling to trust to that honest, pure-minded, soldier-statesman the sole direction of affairs. The fact is that, with a refinement of the justice and moderation which were such conspicuous features of Henry's character, he dissented from the

---

* Sir Frederick Currie had by this time resumed his seat in the Supreme Council of India.

policy of annexation. He thought that another effort 1849. might have been made to save the Sikh Empire from destruction. Out of this difficulty arose the project of the Board. It was natural that Dalhousie should have desired to associate with one thus minded some other statesman whose views were more in harmony with his own. A Board of two is, under no circumstances, a practicable institution; so a Triumvirate was established. But sentence of death was written down against it from the very hour of its birth.

The second seat at the Board was given to the President's brother, John Lawrence. An officer of the Company's Civil Service, he had achieved a high reputation as an administrator; as one of those hardworking, energetic, conscientious servants of the State, who live ever with the harness on their back, to whom labour is at once a duty and a delight, who do everything in a large unstinting way, the Ironsides of the Public Service. He had taken, in the earlier stages of his career, an active part in the Revenue Settlement of the North-Western Provinces, and had subsequently been appointed Magistrate of the great imperial city of Delhi, with its crowded, turbulent population, and its constant under-current of hostile intrigue. In this post, winning the confidence of men of all classes and all creeds, Lord Hardinge found him when, in 1845, he journeyed upwards to join the army of the Sutlej. There was an openness, a frankness about him that pleased the old soldier, and a large-hearted zeal and courage which proclaimed him a man to be employed in a post of more than common difficulty, beyond the circle of ordinary routine. So, after the campaign on the Sutlej, when the Jullindur Doab was taken in part payment of the charges of the war, John Lawrence was appointed to superintend the administration of

1849. that tract of country; and on more than one occasion, during the enforced absence of Henry from Lahore, in the first two years of the British Protectorate, he had occupied his brother's seat at the capital, and done his work with unvaried success. That there were great characteristic differences between the two Lawrences will be clearly indicated as I proceed; but in unsullied honesty and intrepid manliness, they were the counterparts of each other. Both were equally without a stain.

The third member of the Lahore Board of Administration was Mr. Charles Grenville Mansel, also a covenanted civilian, who had earned a high reputation as one of the ablest financiers in India, and who supplied much of the knowledge and experience which his colleagues most lacked. His honesty was of as fine a temper as theirs, but he was a man rather of thought than of action, and wanted the constitutional robustness of his associates in office. Perhaps his very peculiarities, rendering him, as it were, the complement of the other two, especially marked him out as the third of that remarkable triumvirate. Regarded as a whole, with reference to the time and circumstances of its creation, the Board could not have been better constituted. It did honour to the sagacity of Lord Dalhousie, and fully justified the choice of agents he had made.

The system was one of divided labour and common responsibility. On Henry Lawrence devolved what was technically called the "political" work of the Government. The disarming of the country, the negotiations with the chiefs, the organisation of the new Punjabee regiments, the arrangements for the education of the young Maharajah, who had now become the ward of the British Government, were among

the immediate duties to which he personally devoted
himself; the chief care of John Lawrence was the
civil administration, especially the settlement of the
Land Revenue; whilst Mansel superintended the
general judicial management of the province; each,
however, aiding the others with his advice, and having
a potential voice in the general Council. Under these
chief officers were a number of subordinate administrators of different ranks, drawn partly from the civil
and partly from the military service of the Company.
The province was divided into seven divisions, and to
each of these divisions a Commissioner was appointed.
Under each of these Commissioners were certain
Deputy-Commissioners, varying in number according
to the amount of business to be done; whilst under
them again were Assistant-Commissioners and Extra
Assistants, drawn from the uncovenanted servants of
Government—Europeans, Indo-Britons, or natives of
pure descent.

The officers selected for the principal posts under
the Lahore Board of Administration were the very
flower of the Indian services. Dalhousie had thrown
his whole heart into the work which lay before him.
Resolved that it should not be marred by the in-
efficiency of his agents, he looked about him for men
of mark and likelihood, men in the vigour of their
years, men of good performance for the higher posts,
and sturdy, eager-spirited youths of good promise for
the lower. It mattered not to him whether the good
stuff were draped in civil black or military red. Far
above all petty prejudices of that kind, the Governor-
General swept up his men with an eye only to the
work that was in them, and sent them forth to do his
bidding. Some had already graduated in Punjabee
administration under the Protectorate; others crossed

1849. the Sutlej for the first time with honours taken under Thomason and his predecessors in the North-West Provinces. And among them were such men as George Edmonstone, Donald Macleod, and Robert Montgomery from the one service; Frederick Mackeson and George Macgregor from the other; such men, besides those already named,* as Richard Temple, Edward Thornton, Neville Chamberlain, George Barnes, Lewin Bowring, Philip Goldney, and Charles Saunders; soldiers and civilians working side by side, without a feeling of class jealousy, in the great work of reconstructing the administration of the Punjab and carrying out the executive details; whilst at the head of the department of Public Works was Robert Napier, in whom the soldier and the man of science met together to make one of the finest Engineer officers in the world.

They found much to do, but little to undo. The Government of Runjeet Singh had been of a rude, simple, elementary character; out of all rule; informal; unconstitutional; unprincipled; one great despotism and a number of petty despotisms; according to our English notions, reeking with the most "frightful injustice." But somehow or other it had answered the purpose. The injustice was intelligible injustice, for it was simply that of the strong will and the strong hand crushed down in turn by one still stronger. Petty governors, revenue-farmers, or kardars might oppress the people and defraud the State, but they knew that, sooner or later, a day of reckoning would come when their accounts would be audited by the process of compulsory disgorgement,

---

* *Ante*, p. 12. I have here named only those distinguished during the earlier period of our Punjabee career. Others there were, appointed at a later period, equally entitled to honourable mention.

or in some parts of the country settled in the noose of 1849. the proconsular gibbet. No niceties of conscience and no intricacies of law opposed an obstacle to these summary adjustments. During the existence of that great fiction the Council of Regency, we had begun to systematise and to complicate affairs; and as we had found—at least, as far as we understood the matter— a clear field for our experiments, we now, on assuming undisguisedly the administration of the country, had a certain basis of our own to operate upon, and little or nothing to clear away.

The system of administration now introduced into the Punjab, formal and precise as it may have been when compared with the rude simplicity of the old Sikh Government, was loose and irregular in comparison with the strict procedure of the Regulation Provinces. The administrators, whether soldiers or civilians, were limited to the discharge of no particular departmental functions. They were judges, revenue-collectors, thief-catchers, diplomatists, conservancy officers, and sometimes recruiting serjeants and chaplains, all in one. Men trained in such a school as this, and under such masters as the Lawrences, became equal to any fortune, and in no conjuncture, however critical, were ever likely to fail. There was hardly one among them who did not throw his whole heart into his work; who ever thought of ease, or leisure, or any personal enjoyment beyond that which comes from an honest sense of duty done. They lived among the people of the country, their tents open to all the points of the compass;* and

* Sir John Malcolm used to say that the only way to govern the people of a newly-acquired country was by means of *char durwaseh kolah*, or four doors open. That the Punjabee officials well understood this, here is a pleasant illustrative proof, from a paper written by one of them : —" For eight months in the year the tent is the proper home of him who loves his duties and his people. Thus he comes to know and be known of

1849.   won by their personal bearing the confidence and the
admiration of all who came within their reach.

And so, far sooner than even sanguine men ventured to predict, the Punjab began to settle down
under its new rulers. Even the old Khalsa fighting-
men accepted their position, and with a manly resignation looking cheerfully at the inevitable, confessed
that they had been beaten in fair fight, and submitted
themselves to the English conqueror. Some were
enlisted into the new Punjabee Irregular Regiments,
which were raised for the internal defence of the province. Others betook themselves, with the pensions
or gratuities which were bestowed upon them, to their
fields, and merged themselves into the agricultural
population. There was no fear of any resurrection
of the old national cause. For whilst the people were
forced to surrender all their weapons of war—their
guns, their muskets, their bayonets, their sabres, their
spears—the whole province was bristling with British
arms. An immense military force was maintained in
the Punjab. It was a happy circumstance that, as
the Indus had now become our boundary and the
country of the Sikhs our frontier province, it was
necessary for purposes of external defence, after the
apparent settling down of our newly-acquired territories, still to keep our regular troops, European and
native, at a strength more than sufficient to render
utterly harmless all the turbulent elements of Punjabee society. Had the British army been withdrawn

them; thus personal influence and
local knowledge give him a power
not to be won by bribes or upheld
by bayonets. The notables of the
neighbourhood meet their friend and
ruler on his morning march; grey-
beards throng round his unguarded
door with presents of the best fruits
of the land, or a little sugar, spices,
and almonds, according to the fashion
of their country, and are never so
happy as when allowed to seat themselves on the carpet and talk over
old times and new events—the promise of the harvest and the last
orders of the rulers."—*Calcutta Review,* vol. xxxiii.

from the Punjab, as at a later period it was from Oude, it is hard to say what might not have resulted from our confidence and incaution.

On the acquisition of a new country and the extinction of an old dynasty, it has commonly happened that the chief sufferers by the revolution have been found among the aristocracy of the land. The great masses of the people have been considerately, indeed generously treated, but the upper classes have been commonly prostrated by the annexing hand, and have never recovered from the blow. This may be partly attributed to what is so often described as the "inevitable tendency" of such a change from a bad to a good government. It has been assumed that the men whom we have found in the enjoyment of all the privileges of wealth and social position, have risen to this eminence by spoliation and fraud, and maintained it by cruelty and oppression. And it is true that the antecedents of many of them would not bear a very jealous scrutiny. Now, so far as the substitution of a strong and pure for a weak and corrupt government must necessarily have checked the prosperous career of those who were living on illicit gains and tyrannous exactions, it was, doubtless, the inevitable tendency of the change to injure, if not to ruin them, as the leaf must perish when the stem dies. But it must be admitted that for some years past the idea of a native aristocracy had been an abomination in the eyes of English statesmen in India; that we had desired to see nothing between the Sircar, or Government, and the great masses of the people; and that, however little we might have designed it, we had done some great wrongs to men, whose misfortune, rather than whose fault, it was that they were the growth of a corrupt system. There was at the bottom of this a strong desire for the welfare of the people—an eager and a generous longing to protect the weak against the tyranny of the strong; but benevolence, like ambition, sometimes overleaps itself, and falls prostrate on the other side, and out of our very love of justice come sometimes unjust deeds.

To the great chiefs of the Punjab the annexation of the country to the British Empire was a source of sore disquietude.* Mercy to the vanquished in the hour of victory was not one of the weaknesses they had been accustomed to contemplate. They had played for a great stake, and they had lost. They had brought their losses on themselves. They had invited by their own acts the conflict which had ruined them. In no one instance had our policy been aggressive. We had not coveted the possession of the Punjab. We had not invited either the first or the second great conflict between the British and the Sikh armies. A brave nation fighting for its independence is one of the noblest spectacles of humanity; and the leaders of such a movement have just claim to sympathy and respect. But these men had risen against us whilst they pretended to be our friends. They had soiled their patriotism by treachery, and forfeited their honour by falsehood and deceit. Still, to a man of large mind and catholic spirit like Henry Lawrence, it could not seem right to judge these Sirdars as he would the

---

* This was admitted in the first Punjab Report, the following passage of which may be advantageously quoted :—" A great revolution cannot happen without injuring some classes. When a State falls, its nobility and its supporters must to some extent suffer with it ; a dominant sect and party once moved by political ambition and religious enthusiasm, cannot return to the ordinary level of society and the common occupations of life without feeling some discontent and some enmity against their powerful but humane conquerors. But it is probable that the mass of the people will advance in material prosperity and in moral elevation under the influence of British rule."

flower of European chivalry. So he dealt gently
with their offences; and when he came to consider
their position under the new Government, he respected their fallen fortunes, and laid a lighter hand
upon their tenures than higher authority was altogether willing to sanction. That a large portion of
the revenue would be alienated by grants to military
chiefs and to priestly sinecurists was certain; not
less certain did it appear that the money might be
better bestowed. Still, it might be politic, even in
a financial aspect, to tolerate for a time abuses of
this kind, as not the most expensive means of reconciling the influential classes to our rule. Thus
argued Henry Lawrence. So these privileged classes
received from him, in many instances, though not all
that he wished to give, more perhaps than they had
dared to expect. Existing incumbents were generally
respected; and the privileges enjoyed by one generation were to be only partially resumed in the next.

Thus, by a well-apportioned mixture of vigour and
clemency, the submission, if not the acquiescence, of
the more dangerous classes was secured; and our
administrators were left, undisturbed by the fear of
internal revolt, to prosecute their ameliorative measures. It would be beyond the scope of such a narrative as this to write in detail of the operations
which were carried out, under the Lahore Board, at
once to render British rule a·blessing to the people,
and the possession of the Punjab an element of
strength and security to the British Empire. These
great victories of peace are reserved for others to
record. That the measures were excellent, that the
men were even better than the measures, that the
administration of the Punjab was a great fact, at
which Englishmen pointed with pride and on which

foreigners dwelt with commendation, is freely admitted, even by those who are not wont to see much that is good in the achievements of the British Government in India. Under the fostering care of the Governor-General, who traversed the country from one end to the other, and saw everything with his own eyes, the " Punjab system" became the fashion, and men came to speak and to write of it as though it were a great experiment in government originated by Lord Dalhousie. But it was not a new system. It had been tried long years before, with marked success, and was still in force in other parts of India, though it had never been carried out on so large a scale, or in so fine a country, or been the darling of a viceroy. The only novelty in the construction of the administration was the Lahore Board, and that was abandoned as a failure.

I do not say that it *was* a failure; but it was so regarded by Lord Dalhousie, who, in 1853, remorselessly signed its death-warrant. A delicate operation, indeed, was the breaking up of the Punjabee Cabinet and the erection of an autocracy in its place. It was the will of the Governor-General that the chief direction of affairs should be consigned to the hands, not of many, but of one. And when the rumour of this resolution went abroad, there was scarcely a house, or a bungalow, or a single-poled tent occupied by an English officer, in which the future of the Punjab— the question of the Lawrences—was not eagerly discussed. Was Henry or was John Lawrence to remain supreme director of affairs? So much was to be said in favour of the great qualities of each brother, that it was difficult to arrive at any anticipatory solution of the question. But it was in the

character of the Governor-General himself that the
key to the difficulty should have been sought. Lord
Hardinge would have chosen Henry Lawrence. Lord
Dalhousie chose John. No surprise is now expressed
that it was so ; for, in these days, the character and
policy of Dalhousie are read by the broad light of
history. No regret is now felt that it was so ; for,
when the great hurricane of which I am about to
write swept over India, each of those two great
brothers was, by God's providence, found in his
right place. But there were many at the time who
grieved that the name of Henry Lawrence, who
had been for so many years associated with all their
thoughts of British influence in the Sikh country, and
who had paved the way to all our after successes,
was to be expunged from the list of Punjabee administrators. It was said that he sympathised overmuch
with the fallen state of Sikhdom, and sacrificed the
revenue to an idea ; that he was too eager to provide
for those who suffered by our usurpation ; whilst Dalhousie, deeming that the balance-sheet would be regarded as the great test and touchstone of success, was
eager to make the Punjab pay. John Lawrence, it
was said, better understood the art of raising a revenue.
He was willing, in his good brotherly heart, to withdraw from the scene in favour of Henry ; but the Governor-General needed his services. So he was appointed Chief-Commissioner of the Punjab, and a
new theatre was found for the exercise of Henry
Lawrence's more chivalrous benevolence among the
ancient states of Rajpootana.

Outwardly, authoritatively, and not untruthfully,
the explanation was, that the work of the soldier-statesman was done, that the transition-period in which

1853.

1853.   Henry Lawrence's services were so especially needed
had passed; that the business of internal administration was principally such as comes within the range
of the civil officer's duties; and that a civilian with
large experience, especially in revenue matters, was
needed to direct all the numerous details of the Executive Government. Dalhousie never liked the Board.
It was not a description of administrative agency
likely to find favour in his eyes; and it is not impossible that he placed, with some reluctance, at the
head of it a man who had not approved the original
policy of annexation.   But he could not have read
Henry Lawrence's character so badly as to believe
for a moment that, on that account, the policy once
accomplished, he could have been less eager for its
success, or less zealous in working it out.   There was
the indication, however, of a fundamental difference of
opinion, which as time advanced became more and
more apparent, for Henry's generous treatment of his
fallen enemies came from that very source of enlarged
sympathy which rendered the policy of annexation distasteful to him.   It was natural, therefore, that the
Governor-General, who had resolved to rid himself
of the Board on the first fitting opportunity, should
have selected as the agent of his pet policy, the
administrator of his pet province, the civilian who
concurred with, rather than the soldier who dissented from, his views.   The fitting opportunity
came at last, for there was a redistribution of some
of the higher political offices;* and Dalhousie then

* The Hyderabad Residency was
about to be vacated. It was an
office that had been held by Sir
Charles Metcalfe and other eminent
men. I believe that Henry Lawrence suggested (for the days of the
Board had been for some time numbered) that either he or his brother
should be sent to Hyderabad. Lord
Dalhousie, however, sent General
Low to the Court of the Nizam, and
gave Henry Lawrence the scarcely
less honourable appointment of Governor-General's agent in Rajpootana.

swept away the obnoxious institution, and placed the
administration of the Punjab in the hands of a single
man.

Henry Lawrence bowed to the decision, but was not
reconciled to it. He betook himself to his new duties
a sadder and a wiser man. He did not slacken in
good service to the State; but he never again had the
same zest for his work. Believing that he had been
unfairly and ungratefully treated, he had no longer
his old confidence in his master, and as the Dalhousie
policy developed itself, under the ripening influence
of time, he saw more clearly that he was not one to
find favour in the eyes of the Governor-General.
Much that he had before but dimly seen and partly
understood now became fully revealed to him in the
clear light of day. Once, and once only, there was
any official conflict; but Henry Lawrence saw much
that whilst he deplored he could not avert, and he
sighed to think that his principles were out of date
and his politics out of fashion.

In the mean while, John Lawrence reigned in the
Punjab. The capacity for administration, which he
had evinced as a Member of the Board, had now free
scope for exercise, and was soon fully developed. His
name became great throughout the land, and he deserved the praise that was lavished upon him. Right
or wrong he did all in accordance with the faith
that was in him. He was a fitting agent of Dalhousie's
policy, only because he believed in that policy. And
happily the greater part of his work lay along the
straight road of undebatable beneficence. How he
worked, day after day, early and late, and how all
men worked under him, is a history now well known.
He was emphatically a man without a weakness.
Strong himself, bone and muscle, head and heart, of

1853. adamantine strength, that would neither bend nor break, he expected others to be equally strong. They sighed, perhaps they inwardly protested, but they knew that the work he exacted from them he gave, in his own person, unstintingly to the State; and they could not regard as a hard task-master one who tasked himself hardest of all. From moral infirmities of all kinds he appeared to be equally free. He did not even seem to be ambitious. Men said that he had no sentiment, no romance. We so often judge our neighbours wrongly in this, that I hesitate to adopt the opinion; but there was an intense reality about him such as I have never seen equalled. He seemed to be continually toiling onwards, upwards, as if life were not meant for repose, with the grand princely motto, "*I serve*," inscribed in characters of light on his forehead. He served God as unceasingly as he served the State; and set before all his countrymen in the Punjab the true pattern of a Christian gentleman. ⋅

And it was not thrown away. The Christian character of British administration in the Punjab has ever been one of its most distinguishing features. It is not merely that great humanising measures were pushed forward with an alacrity most honourable to a Christian nation—that the moral elevation of the people was continually in the thoughts of our administrators; but that in their own personal characters they sought to illustrate the religion which they professed. Wherever two or three were gathered together, the voice of praise and prayer went up from the white man's tent. It had been so during the Protectorate, when, in the wildest regions and in the most stirring times, men like the Lawrences, Reynell Taylor, and Herbert Edwardes, never forgot the

Christian Sabbath.* And now that peace and order 1853.
reigned over the country, Christianity asserted itself
more demonstratively, and Christian churches rose at
our bidding. There was little or none, too, of that
great scandal which had made our names a hissing
and a reproach in Afghanistan. Our English officers,
for the most part, lived pure lives in that heathen
land; and private immorality under the administration of John Lawrence grew into a grave public
offence.

And so the Punjab administration flourished under Conquest of
the Chief-Commissioner and his assistants;† and the Pegu.
active mind of Lord Dalhousie was enabled to direct
itself to new objects. Already, far down on the
south-eastern boundary of our empire—at the point
farthest removed of all from the great country whose
destinies we have been considering—the seeds of war
had been sown broad-cast. Ever since 1826, when
the first contest with Ava had been brought to a close
by the surrender to the English of certain tracts of
country in which no Englishman could live, our relations with the Burmese had been on an unsatisfactory
footing. In truth, they were altogether a very unsatisfactory people; arrogant and pretentious, blind
to reason, and by no means anxious to manifest their
appreciation of the nice courtesies of diplomatic in-

---

* Many will remember that delightful little story, so pleasantly
told in Edwardes's "Year on the
Punjab Frontier," of Reynell Taylor's
invitation to prayer on a Sunday
morning in February, 1848, and of
the question whether the half-caste
colonel, "John Holmes," who had
"always attended prayers at Peshawur" in George Lawrence's house,
was sufficiently a Christian to be
admitted to swell the two or three
into three or four.

† On the abolition of the Board,
Mr. Montgomery, who had succeeded
Mr. Mansel as third member, became
Judicial Commissioner, and Mr. Mac-
leod was appointed Financial Com-
missioner.

tercourse. To find just cause, according to European notions, for chastising these people would at any time have been easy. But their insolence did us very little harm. We could tolerate, without loss of credit or of prestige, the discourtesies of a barbarian Government on the outskirts of civilisation. An insult on the banks of the Irrawaddy was very different from an insult on the banks of the Jumna. The Princes and chiefs of India knew nothing and cared nothing about our doings far out beyond the black waters of the Bay of Bengal. But at last these discourtesies culminated in an outrage which Lord Dalhousie thought it became the British Government to resent. Whether, under more discreet management, redress might have been obtained and war averted, it is now of little moment to inquire. A sea-captain was appointed to conduct our diplomacy at Rangoon, and he conducted it successfully to a rupture. A war ensued, to which the future historian of India may devote a not very inviting chapter, but its details have nothing to do with the story of this book. English arms were triumphant, and the province of Pegu lay at our feet. Dalhousie annexed it to the British Empire, "in order that the Government of India might hold from the Burmese State both adequate compensation for past injury, and the best security against future danger." Thus did the British Empire, which had so recently been extended to the north-west, stretch itself out to the south-east; and the white man sat himself down on the banks of the Irrawaddy as he had seated himself on the banks of the Indus. There were not wanting those who predicted that the whole of Burmah would soon become British territory, and that then the "uncontrollable principle," by reference to which a great English statesman justified the

seizure of Sindh, would send the English conqueror 1840.
to grope his way through the Shan States and Siam
to Cochin-China. But these apprehensions were
groundless. The administrator began his work in
Pegu, as he had begun his work in the Punjab, and
there was no looking beyond the frontier; but, on the
other hand, a desire to avoid border disputes, or, if
they could not be avoided, to treat them as matters
of light account, inevitable and soon to be forgotten.
There was a military officer, admirably fitted for the
work, who had served long and successfully, as a
civil administrator, in Arracan ; who knew the Burmese language and the Burmese people, and had a
great name along the eastern coast. Those isolated
regions beyond the Bay of Bengal are the grave of all
catholic fame. Whilst the name of Lawrence was in
all men's mouths, Phayre was pursuing the even
tenor of his way, content with a merely local reputation. But the first, and as I write the only commis-'
sioner of Pegu, is fairly entitled to a place in the very
foremost rank of those English administrators who
have striven to make our rule a blessing to the people
of India, and have not failed in the attempt.

In India the native mind readily pervades vast
distances, and takes little account of space that the
foot can travel. But it is bewildered and confused by
the thought of the "black water." The unknown is
the illimitable. On the continent of India, therefore,
neither our war-successes nor our peace-successes in
the Burmese country stirred the heart of Indian
society. In the lines of the Sepoy or the shops of the
money-changer they were not matters of eager interest and voluble discourse. We might have sacked
the cities of Ava and Amarapoora, and caused their
sovereign lord to be trodden to death by one of his

1849.   white elephants without exciting half the interest
engendered by a petty outbreak in Central India, or
the capture of a small fort in Bundelkund.   The
Princes and chiefs of the great continent of Hindostan
knew little and cared less about a potentate, however
magnificent in his own dominions, who neither worshipped their gods nor spoke their language, and
who was cut off from their brotherhood by the intervention of the great dark sea.   We gained no
honour, and we lost no confidence, by the annexation
of this outlying province ; but it opened to our Native
Soldiery a new field of service, and unfortunately it
was beyond the seas.

CHAPTER II.

THE ADMINISTRATION OF LORD DALHOUSIE—ADOPTION—THE "RIGHT OF LAPSE"—SATTARAH—NAGPORE—JHANSI—KEROWLEE—THE CARNATIC—TANJORE—THE CASE OF THE PEISHWAH—DUNDOO PUNT, NANA SAHIB—SUMBHULPORE.

So, three years after his arrival in India, Dalhousie 1848-1856. had brought to a close two great military campaigns, and had captured two great provinces. He had then done with foreign wars; his after-career was one of peaceful invasion. Ere long there was a word which came to be more dreaded than that of Conquest. The native mind is readily convinced by the inexorable logic of the sword. There is no appeal from such arbitration. To be invaded and to be conquered is a state of things appreciable by the inhabitant of India. It is his "kismut;" his fate; God's will. One stronger than he cometh and taketh all that he hath. There are, however, manifest compensations. His religion is not invaded; his institutions are not violated. Life is short, and the weak man, patient and philosophical, is strong to endure and mighty to wait. But LAPSE is a dreadful and an appalling word; for it pursues the victim beyond the grave. Its significance in his eyes is nothing short of eternal condemnation.

"The son," says the great Hindoo lawgiver, "delivers his father from the hell called Put." There are, he tells us, different kinds of sons; there is the son begotten; the son given; the son by adoption; and other filial varieties. It is the duty of the son to perform the funeral obsequies of the father. If they be not performed, it is believed that there is no resurrection to eternal bliss. The right of adoption is, therefore, one of the most cherished doctrines of Hindooism. In a country where polygamy is the rule, it might be supposed that the necessity of adopting another man's offspring, for the sake of these ceremonial ministrations, or for the continuance of an ancestral name, would be one of rare occurrence. But all theory on the subject is belied by the fact that the Princes and chiefs of India more frequently find themselves, at the close of their lives, without the solace of male offspring than with it. The Zenana is not an institution calculated to lengthen out a direct line of Princes. The alternative of adoption is one, therefore, to which there is frequent resort; it is a source of unspeakable comfort in life and in death; and politically it is as dear to the heart of a nation as it is personally to the individual it affects.

It is with the question of Adoption only in its political aspects that I have to do in this place. There is a private and personal, as there is a public and political, side to it. No power on earth beyond a man's own will can prevent him from adopting a son, or can render that adoption illegal if it be legally performed. But to adopt a son as a successor to private property is one thing, to adopt an heir to titular dignities and territorial sovereignty is another. Without the consent of the Paramount State no adoption

ot the latter kind can be valid. Whether in this case
of a titular Prince or a possessor of territorial rights,
dependent upon the will of the Government, Hindooism is satisfied by the private adoption and the penalties of the sonless state averted, is a question for the
pundits to determine; but no titular chief thinks the
adoption complete unless he can thereby transmit his
name, his dignities, his rights and privileges to his
successor, and it can in no wise be said that the son
takes the place of his adoptive father if he does not
inherit the most cherished parts of that father's possessions.

But whether the religious element does or does not
rightly enter into the question of political adoptions,
nothing is more certain than that the right, in this
larger political sense, was ever dearly prized by the
Hindoos, and was not alienated from them by the
Lords-Paramount who had preceded us.   The imperial recognition was required, and it was commonly
paid for by a heavy "nuzzurana," or succession-duty,
but in this the Mogul rulers were tolerant.   It was
reserved for the British to substitute for the right of
adoption what was called "the right of lapse," and in
default of male heirs of the body lawfully begotten to
absorb native principalities into the great amalgam
of our British possessions.   "In 1849," wrote Lord
Dalhousie, in his elaborate farewell minute, "the
principality of Sattarah was included in the British
dominions by right of lapse, the Rajah having died
without male heir." The Princes of Sattarah were the
descendants of Sevajie, the founder and the head of
the Mahratta Empire.   Their power and their glory
had alike departed.   But they were still great in
tradition, and were looked up to with respect by the

1848.   Mahrattas of Western India. In April, 1848, the last
Rajah died;* and a question arose as to whether, no
direct male heir of the body having been left by the
deceased, a son by adoption, or a collateral member
of the family, should be permitted to succeed him, or
whether the rights and titles of the principality should
be declared to be extinct. Sir George Clerk was then
Governor of Bombay. He looked at the Treaty of
1819; saw that "the British Government agreed to
cede in perpetual sovereignty to the Rajah of Sattarah,
his heirs and successors," the territories which he had
held, and at once declared himself in favour of the
continuance of the native Raj. The members of his
Council looked upon the question as purely one of
expediency, and considered it the duty of the British
Government to decide it in the manner most advantageous to ourselves. But the Governor refused to
admit any secondary considerations, saying, "If it be
inconsistent with justice to refuse confirmation to the
act of adoption, it is useless to inquire whether it is
better for the interests of the people or of the empire
at large to govern the Sattarah territories through the
medium of a native Rajah, or by means of our own
administration." The trumpet of that statesman was
not likely to give an uncertain sound.

When this question first arose, the Governor-General was in his novitiate. But new as he was to the
consideration of such subjects, he does not appear to
have faltered or hesitated. The opinions, the practical expression of which came subsequently to be called

---

* Appa Sahib. He had suc-
ceeded his brother, who in 1839
was deposed, and, as I think, very
rightly, on account of a series of
intrigues against the British Government, equally foolish and dis-
creditable. It is worthy of remark,
that Sir Robert Grant, being satisfied
of the Rajah's guilt, proposed to
punish him in the manner least
likely to be advantageous to ourselves.

the "policy of annexation," were formed at the very
outset of his career, and rigidly maintained to its
close.   Eight months after his first assumption of the
Government of India, he placed on record a confession of faith elicited by this agitation of the Sattarah
question.   Subsequent events of far greater magnitude dwarfed that question in the public mind, and
later utterances of the great minute-writer caused
this first manifesto to be comparatively forgotten;
but a peculiar interest must ever be associated with
this earliest exposition of Dalhousie's political creed,
and therefore I give it in the words of the statesman
himself: "The Government," he wrote on the 30th
August, 1848, "is bound in duty, as well as policy,
to act on every such occasion with the purest integrity, and in the most scrupulous observance of
good faith.   Where even a shadow of doubt can be
shown, the claim should at once be abandoned.   But
where the right to territory by lapse is clear, the
Government is bound to take that which is justly
and legally its due, and to extend to that territory
the benefits of our sovereignty, present and prospective.   In like manner, while I would not seek to lay
down any inflexible rule with respect to adoption, I
hold that, on all occasions, where heirs natural shall
fail, the territory should be made to lapse, and adoption should not be permitted, excepting in those cases
in which some strong political reason may render it
expedient to depart from this general rule.   There
may be conflict of opinion as to the advantage or the
propriety of extending our already vast possessions
beyond their present limits.   No man can more sincerely deprecate than I do any extension of the
frontiers of our territory which can be avoided, or
which may not become indispensably necessary from

considerations of our own safety, and of the maintenance of the tranquillity of our provinces.   But I
cannot conceive it possible for any one to dispute the
policy of taking advantage of every just opportunity
which presents itself for consolidating the territories
that already belong to us, by taking possession of
States that may lapse in the midst of them ; for thus
getting rid of these petty intervening principalities,
which may be made a means of annoyance, but which
can never, I venture to think, be a source of strength,
for adding to the resources of the public Treasury,
and for extending the uniform application of our system of government to those whose best interests, we
sincerely believe, will be promoted thereby.   Such is
the general principle that, in our humble opinion,
ought to guide the conduct of the British Government in its disposal of independent States, where
there has been a total failure of heirs whatsoever, or
where permission is asked to continue by adoption a
succession which fails in the natural line."

The Court of Directors of the East India Company
confirmed the decision of the Governor-General, and
Sattarah was annexed.   There were men, however, in
the Direction who protested against the measure as an
act of unrighteous usurpation.   " We are called upon,"
said Mr. Tucker, ever an opponent of wrong, " to
consider and decide upon a claim of right, and I have
always felt that our best policy is that which most
closely adheres to the dictates of justice."   " We
ought not to forget," said Mr. Shepherd, who, on
great questions of this kind, was commonly to be
found side by side with his veteran friend, contending
for the rights of the native Princes of India, " that
during the rise and progress of our empire in the
East, our Governments have continued to announce

and proclaim to the people of India that not only 1842. should all their rights and privileges which existed under preceding Governments be preserved and maintained, but that their laws, habits, customs, and prejudices should be respected."* And what right more cherished, what custom more honoured, than the right and custom of adoption? But the majority of the Court of Directors supported the views of the Governor-General. They had heard the voice of the charmer. And from that time the policy of Dalhousie became the policy of Leadenhall-street, and the "Right of Lapse" was formally acknowledged.

And it was not, for reasons which I have already 1853. given, likely long to remain a dead letter. Soon Nagpore. another of the great Mahratta chiefs was said to be dying, and in a few days news came to Calcutta that he was dead. It was the height of the cold season of 1853—a few days before Christmas—when the slow booming of minute guns from the Saluting Battery of Fort William announced the death of Ragojee Bonslah, Rajah of Nagpore. At the age of forty-seven he succumbed to a complication of disorders, of which debauchery, cowardice, and obstinacy were the chief. There have been worse specimens of royalty, both in Eastern and Western Palaces, than this poor, worn-out, impotent sot; for although he was immoderately addicted to brandy and dancing-girls, he rather liked his people to be happy, and was not incapable of kindness that caused no trouble to himself. He had no son to succeed him; a posthumous son was an impossibility; and he had not adopted an heir.

It may seem strange and contradictory that if the

* Colonel Oliphant and Mr. Leslie Melville recorded minutes on the same side.

1853. right of adoption as sanctioned by religion and prescribed by ancestral usage be so dear to the people of
India, they should ever fail to adopt in default of heirs
of their body. But we know that they often do; and
the omission is readily explicable by a reference to the
ordinary weaknesses of humanity. We know that
even in this country, with all the lights of civilisation
and Christianity to keep us from going astray, thousands of reasoning creatures are restrained from
making their wills by a vague feeling of apprehension
that there is something "unlucky" in such a procedure; that death will come the sooner for such a
provision against its inevitable occurrence. What
wonder, then, that in a country which is the very
hotbed of superstition, men should be restrained by
a kindred feeling from providing against the event of
their dissolution? But in this case there is not only
the hope of life, but the hope of offspring, to cause the
postponement of the anticipatory ceremony. Men,
under the most discouraging circumstances, still cling
to the belief that by some favourable reaction of
nature they may, even when stricken in years, beget
an heir to their titles and possessions. In this sense,
too, adoption is held to be unlucky, because it is
irreligious. It is like a surrender of all hope, and a
betrayal of want of faith in the power and goodness
of the Almighty. No man expects to beget a son
after he has adopted one.

In the case, too, of this Mahratta Prince, there were
special reasons why he should have abstained from
making such a provision for the continuance of his
House. According to the law and usage of his
country, an adoption by his widow would have been
as valid as an adoption by himself. It was natural,
therefore, and assuredly it was in accordance with

the character of the man, who was gormandising and
dallying with the hand of death upon him, that he
should have left the ceremony to be performed by
others. Whether it was thus vicariously performed is
not very clearly ascertainable. But it is certain that
the British Resident reported that there had been no
adoption. The Resident was Mr. Mansel, who had
been one of the first members of the Lahore Board of
Administration—a man with a keen sense of justice,
favourable to the maintenance of native dynasties,
and therefore, in those days, held to be crotchety and
unsound. He had several times pressed the Rajah on
the subject of adoption, but had elicited no satisfactory
response. He reported unequivocally that nothing had
been done, and asked for the instructions of the
Supreme Government.

Lord Dalhousie was then absent from Calcutta.
He was making one of his cold-weather tours of inspection—seeing with his own eyes the outlying province of Pegu, which had fallen by right of conquest
into his hands. The Council, in his absence, hesitated
to act, and all the instructions, therefore, which they
could send were to the effect that the Resident should
provide for the peace of the country, and keep things
quiet until further orders. There was no doubt about
Dalhousie's decision in such a case. Had the Rajah
adopted a son, there was little likelihood of the
Governor-General's sanction of the adoption; but as
he had wilfully failed to perform the ceremony, it appeared to be as clear as noon-day that the great organ
of the Paramount State would pronounce the fatal
sentence of Lapse.

Dalhousie returned to Calcutta, and with characteristic energy addressed himself to the mastery of
the whole question. Before the first month of the

new year had worn to a close, he attached his signature to an elaborate minute, in which he exhausted
all the arguments which could be adduced in favour
of the annexation of the country. Printed at full
length, it would occupy fifty pages of this book. It
was distinguished by infinite research and unrivalled
powers of special pleading. It contended that there
had been no adoption, and that if there had been, it
would be the duty of the British Government to
refuse to recognise it. "I am well aware," he said,
"that the continuance of the Raj of Nagpore under
some Mahratta rule, as an act of grace and favour on
the part of the British Government, would be highly
acceptable to native sovereigns and nobles in India;
and there are, doubtless, many of high authority who
would advocate the policy on that special ground. I
understand the sentiment and respect it; but re-
membering the responsibility that is upon me, I cannot bring my judgment to admit that a kind and
generous sentiment should outweigh a just and
prudent policy."

Among the members of the Supreme Council at
that time was Colonel John Low. An old officer of
the Madras army, who long years before, when the
Peishwah and the Bonslah were in arms against the
British, had sate at the feet of John Malcolm, and
had graduated in diplomacy under him, he had never
forgotten the lessons which he had learnt from his
beloved chief; he had never ceased to cherish those
"kind and generous sentiments" of which the Governor-General had spoken in his minute. His whole
life had been spent at the Courts of the native Princes
of India. He had represented British interests long
and faithfully at the profligate Court of Lucknow.
He had contended with the pride, the obstinacy, and

the superstition of the effete Princes of Rajpootana.
He had played, and won, a difficult game, with the
bankrupt State of Hyderabad. He knew what were the
vices of Indian Princes and the evils of native misrule.
But he had not so learnt the lesson presented to him
by the spectacle of improvident rulers and profligate
Courts; of responsibilities ignored and opportunities
wasted; as to believe it to be either the duty or the
policy of the Paramount Government to seek "just occasions" for converting every misgoverned principality into a British province. Nor had he, knowing
as he did, better perhaps than any of his countrymen,
the real character of such misgovernment, ever cherished the conviction that the inhabitants of every
native State were yearning for the blessings of this
conversion. There were few such States left—Hindoo
or Mahomedan—but what remained from the wreck
of Indian dynasties he believed it to be equally just
and politic to preserve. And entertaining these
opinions, he spoke them out; not arrogantly or
offensively, but with what I believe may be described
as the calm resolution of despair. He knew that he
might speak with the tongue of angels, and yet that
his speech would no more affect the practical result
than a sounding brass or a tinkling cymbal. What
am I against so many? he said; nay, what am I
against one? Who will listen to the utterance of
my ideas when opposed to the "deliberately-formed
opinion of a statesman like the Marquis of Dalhousie,
in whose well-proved ability and judgment and integrity of purpose they have entire confidence?"* But
great statesmen in times past had thought that the
extension of British rule in India was,-for our own
sakes, to be arrested rather than accelerated; that the

* Minute of Colonel John Low. February 10, 1854.

1854. native States were a source to us of strength rather than of weakness, and that it would go ill with us when there were none left.*

Strong in this belief, Colonel Low recorded two minutes, protesting against the impolicy and the injustice of the proposed annexation of Nagpore. He said that already the annexation of Sattarah had in many parts of India had a bad moral effect ;† that it had shaken the confidence of the people in the justice and good faith of the British Government; that people had asked what crime Sattarah had committed that sentence of political death should thus have been pronounced against it; that throughout India acquisition by conquest was well understood, and in many cases admitted to be right; that the annexation of the Punjab, for example, had not been regarded as a wrong, because the chiefs and people had brought it on themselves, but that the extinction of a loyal native State, in default of heirs, was not appreciable in any part of India, and that the exercise of the alleged right of lapse would create a common feeling of uncertainty and distrust at every Durbar in the

---

* "If Great Britain shall retain her present powerful position among the States of Europe, it seems highly probable that, owing to the infringement of their treaties on the part of native Princes and other causes, the whole of India will, in the course of time, become one British province; but many eminent statesmen have been of opinion that we ought most carefully to avoid unnecessarily accelerating the arrival of that great change; and it is within my own knowledge that the following five great men were of that number—namely, Lord Hastings, Sir Thomas Munro, Sir John Malcolm, the Hon. Mountstuart Elphinstone, and Lord Metcalfe."—*Minute, Feb.* 10, 1854.

† "When I went to Malwa, in 1850, where I met many old acquaintances, whom I had known when a very young man, and over whom I held no authority, I found these old acquaintances speak out much more distinctly as to their opinion of the Sattarah case; so much so, that I was, on several occasions, obliged to check them. It is remarkable that every native who ever spoke to me respecting the annexation of Sattarah, asked precisely the same question: 'What crime did the late Rajah commit that his country should be seized by the Company?' Thus clearly indicating their notions, that if any crime had been committed our act would have been justifiable, and not otherwise."—*Minute of Colonel Low, Feb.* 10, 1854.

country. He dwelt upon the levelling effects of British dominion, and urged that, as in our own provinces, the upper classes were invariably trodden down, it was sound policy to maintain the native States, if only as a means of providing an outlet for the energies of men of good birth and aspiring natures, who could never rise under British rule. He contended that our system of administration might be far better than the native system, but that the people did not like it better ; they clung to their old institutions, however defective, and were averse to change, even though a change for the better. " In one respect," he said, "the natives of India are exactly like the inhabitants of all parts of the known world ; they like their own habits and customs better than those of foreigners."

Having thus in unmeasured opposition to the Dalhousie theory flung down the gauntlet of the old school at the feet of the Governor-General, Low ceased from the enunciation of general principles, and turned to the discussion of the particular case before him. He contended that the treaty between the British Government and the late Rajah did not limit the succession to heirs of his body, and that, therefore, there was a clear title to succession in the Bonslah family by means of a son adopted by either the Rajah himself or by his eldest widow, in accordance with law and usage. The conduct, he said, of the last Prince of Nagpore had not been such as to alienate this right ; he had been loyal to the Paramount State, and his country had not been misgoverned ; there had been nothing to call for military interference on our part, and little to compel grave remonstrance and rebuke. For what crime, then, was his line to be cut off and the honours of

1854.

his House extinguished for ever? To refuse the right of adoption in such a case would, he alleged, be entirely contrary to the spirit, if not to the letter, of the treaty—But how was it to be conceded when it was not claimed; when no adoption had been reported; when it was certain that the Rajah had not exercised his right, and there had been no tidings of such a movement on the part of his widow? The answer to this was, that the Government had been somewhat in a hurry to extinguish the Raj without waiting for the appearance of claimants, and that if they desired to perpetuate it, it was easy to find a fitting successor.

Of such opinions as these Low expected no support in the Council-chamber of Calcutta—no support from the authorities at home. It little mattered, indeed, what the latter might think, for the annexation of Nagpore was decreed and to be accomplished without reference to England. As the extinction of the Sattarah State had been approved by the Company, in the face of an undisputed adoption asserted at the right time, Dalhousie rightly judged that there would be no straining at a gnat in the Nagpore case, where there had been no adoption at all. Indeed, the general principles upon which he had based his proceedings towards Sattarah, in the first year of his administration, having been accepted in Leadenhall-street, there could be no stickling about so mild an illustration of them as that afforded by the treatment of Nagpore. The justification of the policy in the latter instance is to be found in the fact that there was no assertion of an adoption—no claim put forward on behalf of any individual—at the time when the British Government was called upon to determine

the course to be pursued. It is true that the provi-
sional Government might, for a time, have been
vested in the eldest widow of the deceased Prince,
adoption by whom would have been recognised by
Hindoo law and Mahratta usage; but it was not
probable that the British Government would have
thus gone out of its way to bolster up a decayed
Mahratta dynasty, when the head of that Government conscientiously believed that it was the duty of
the Paramount State to consolidate its dominions by
recognising only among these effete Princes succession
by direct heirship of the body. Cherishing the faith
which he did, Dalhousie would have gone grievously
wrong, and he would have stood convicted of a
glaring inconsistency, if he had adopted any other
course; so the kingdom of Berar was declared to
have lapsed to the British Government, and the
family of the Bonslah was extinct.

The country passed under British rule, and the
people became British subjects, without an audible
murmur of discontent except from the recesses of the
palace. There the wretched ladies of the royal household, at first dismayed and paralysed by the blow
which had fallen upon them, began, after a little
space, to bestir themselves and to clamour for their
asserted rights. Liberal pensions had been settled
upon them; but their family was without a head,
and that which might soon have faded into an idea
was rendered a galling and oppressive reality by the
spoliation of the palace, which followed closely upon
the extinction of the Raj. The live stock and dead
stock of the Bonslah were sent to the hammer. It
must have been a great day for speculative cattle-
dealers at Seetabaldee when the royal elephants,

1854. horses, and bullocks were sold off at the price of carrion :* and a sad day, indeed, in the royal household, when the venerable Bankha Baee,† with all the wisdom and moderation of fourscore well-spent years upon her, was so stung by a sense of the indignity offered to her, that she threatened to fire the palace if the furniture were removed. But the furniture was removed, and the jewels of the Bonslah family, with a few propitiatory exceptions, were sent to the Calcutta market. And I have heard it said that these seizures, these sales, created a worse impression, not only in Berar, but in the surrounding provinces, than the seizure of the kingdom itself.‡

But even in the midst of their degradation, these unfortunate ladies clung to the belief that the Bonslah family would some day be restored and rehabilitated. The Governor-General had argued that the widow, knowing that her husband was disinclined to adopt, had, for like reasons, abstained from adoption. He admitted the right according to Mahratta usage, but declared that she was unwilling to exercise it. He contended, too, that the Bankha Baee, the most influential of the royal ladies, would naturally be averse to a measure which would weaken her own authority in the palace. But his logic halted, and

* Between five and six hundred elephants, camels, horses, and bullocks were sold for 1300*l*. The Ranees sent a protest to the Commissioner, and memorialised the Governor-General, alleging, in the best English that the Palace could furnish, that "on the 4th instant (Sept.) the sale of animals, viz. bullocks, horses, camels, and elephants, commenced to sell by public auction and resolution—a pair her hackery bullocks, valued 100 rupees, sold in the above sale for 5 rupees."

† The Bankha Baee was a widow of the deceased Rajah's grandfather.
‡ I know that the question of public and private property, in such cases, is a very difficult one, and I shall not attempt to decide it here. I only speak of the intense mortification which these sales create in the family itself, and the bad impression which they produce throughout the country. Rightly or wrongly, they cast great discredit on our name; and the gain of money is not worth the loss of character.

his prophecy failed. Both the elder and the younger 　
lady were equally eager to perpetuate the regal dignities of their House. Mr. Mansel had suggested a
compromise, in the shape of an arrangement somewhat similar to that which had been made with the
Newabs of the Carnatic, by which the title might be
maintained, and a certain fixed share of the revenue
set apart for its dotation. But he had been severely
censured for his indiscretion, and had left Nagpore
in disgrace. He was, perhaps, the best friend that
the Ranees had in that conjuncture; but—such is
the value of opinion—they accused him, in the
quaint Palace-English of their scribe, of " endeavouring to gain baronetage and exaltation of rank by re-
porting to the Governor-General that the late Rajah
was destitute of heirs to succeed him, with a view to
his Lordship being pleased to order the annexation
of the territory."* But there was not a man in the
country less disposed to annex provinces and to
humour Governors than Charles Mansel, and instead
of being exalted in rank, he sacrificed his prospects
to his principles and retired from the Service.

Failing altogether to move the Governor-General,
the Ranees sent agents to London, but with no better

* Lord Dalhousie, in his Nagpore Minute, says that the Rajah did not adopt, partly because he did not like to acknowledge his inability to beget a son, and partly because he feared that the existence of an adopted son might some day be used as a pretext for deposing him. He then observes: " The dislike of the late Rajah to the adoption of a successor, was of course known to his widow; and although the custom of the Mahrattas exempts her from that necessity for having the concurrence of her husband in adoption, which general Hindoo law imperatively requires, in order to render the act of adoption valid, still the known disinclination of the Rajah to all adoption could not fail to disincline his widow to have recourse to adoption after his decease." It will be seen at once that the ordinary logical acumen of the Governor-General failed him in this instance, for the very reasons given by the writer himself for the failure of adoption by the Rajah ceased altogether to be operative, *ipso facto*, " after his decease."

1854   result. After the manner of native emissaries from Indian Courts, they spent large sums of money in feeing lawyers and printing pamphlets, without making any impression on Leadenhall-street or Cannon-row, and at last, being recalled by their employers, and having nothing wherewith to pay their debts, they flung themselves on the generosity of their opponents, and were sent home by the help of the great Corporation whom they had reviled. Meanwhile, the elder widow of the late Rajah died, and a boy, of another branch, whom the Ranees called Janojee Bonslah, and in whose person they desired to prolong the Nagpore dynasty, was formally adopted by the dying lady. Clutching at any chance, however desperate, an attempt was made to revive the question of the political adoption; but the sagacity of the Bankha Baee must have seen that it was too late, and that nothing but the private property of the deceased Princess could be thus secured to the adopted heir. The country of the Bonslahs had become as inalienably a part of the Company's possessions as the opium go-downs of Patna, or the gun-factory at Cossipore.

Thus, within a few years of each other, the names of two of the great rulers of the Mahratta Empire ceased from off the roll of Indian Princes; and the territories of the Company were largely increased. Great in historical dignity as was the Sattarah Raj, it was comparatively limited in geographical extent, whilst the Bonslah, though but a servant in rank, owned rich and productive lands, yielding in profusion, among other good gifts, the great staple of our English manufactures.* Whilst the annexation of

* Lord Dalhousie put forth the cotton-growing qualities of the Berar country as one of the many argu-ments which he adduced in favour of the annexation of the territory.

the Punjab and of Pegu extended the British Empire
at its two extreme ends, these Mahratta acquisitions
helped to consolidate it. Some unseemly patches,
breaking the great rose-hued surface, which spoke of
British supremacy in the East, were thus effaced from
the map; and the Right of Lapse was proclaimed to
the furthermost ends of our Indian dominions.

There is a circumstantial difference between these
two cases, inasmuch as that, in the one, there was an
actual and undisputed adoption by the deceased
Rajah, and in the other there was none; but as
Dalhousie had frankly stated that he would not have
recognised a Nagpore adoption had there been one, the
two resumptions were governed by the same principle.
And this was not a mere arbitrary assertion of the
power of the strong over the weak, but was based, at
all events, on a plausible substratum of something
that simulated reason and justice. It was contended
that, whenever a native Prince owed his existence
as a sovereign ruler to the British Government, that
Government had the right, on failure of direct heirs,
to resume, at his death, the territories of which it
had originally placed him in possession. The power
that rightly gives, it was argued, may also rightfully
take away. Now, in the cases both of Sattarah and
Nagpore, the Princes, whom the British Government
found in possession of those States, had forfeited their
rights: the one by hidden treachery and rebellion,
the other by open hostility. The one, after full inquiry, had been deposed; the other, many years
before, had been driven into the jungle, and had
perished in obscurity a fugitive and an outcast.* In

---

* It is to be observed, too, with
respect to Sattarah, that not only had
the last Rajah been elevated by the
British Government, but that the
Raj itself had been resuscitated by
us in the person of his predecessor.
We had found the Rajah prostrate
and a prisoner, almost, it may be

both cases, therefore, the "crime" had been committed which the natives of India are so willing to recognise as a legitimate reason for the punishment of the weaker State by the stronger.   But the offence had been condoned, and the sovereignty had been suffered to survive; another member of the reigning family being set up by the Paramount State in place of the offending Prince.   Both Pertaub Singh and Ragojee Bonslah, as individuals, owed their sovereign power to the grace and favour of the British Government.   All this is historical fact.   It may be admitted, too, that when the crimes of which I have spoken were committed by the heads of the Sattarah and Nagpore families, the British Government would have been justified in imposing conditions upon the restoration of the Raj, to the extent of limiting the succession to heirs of the body, or even in making a personal treaty with the favoured Prince conferring no absolute right of sovereignty upon his successors. But the question is whether, these restrictions not having been penally imposed, at the time of forfeiture, the right which then might have been exercised could be justly asserted on the occurrence of a subsequent vacancy created by death?   Lord Dalhousie thought that it could—that the circumstances under which the Sattarah and Nagpore Princes had received their principalities as free gifts from the British Government conferred certain rights of suzerainty on that Government, which otherwise they could not have properly asserted.   But, on the other hand, it is contended that both principalities, what-

said, at his last gasp; we had rescued him from his enemies, and set him up in a principality of his own; a fact which, assuming the validity of the argument against adoption, necessarily imparted additional force to it.   The same may be said of the Nagpore Raj. It was "resuscitated" by the British Government.

soever might have been the offences committed years
before by their rulers, had been re-established in their
integrity—that no restrictions as to their continuance
had then been imposed—that treaties had been concluded containing the usual expressions with respect
to succession—in a word, that the condonation had
been complete, and that both the Sattarah and the
Nagpore Houses really possessed all the rights and
privileges which had belonged to them before the
representative of the one compromised himself by a
silly intrigue, and the head of the other, with equal
fatuity, plunged into hostilities which could result
only in his ruin.

This justificatory plea, based upon the alleged
right of the British Government to resume, in default
of direct heirs, tenures derived from the favour of the
Lord Paramount, was again asserted about the same
time, but with some diversity of application. Comparatively insignificant in itself, the case claims especial attention on account of results to be hereafter
recorded in these pages. In the centre of India,
among the small principalities of Bundelkund, was
the state of Jhansi, held by a Mahratta chief, origi- Jhansi.
nally a vassal of the Peishwah. But on the transfer
to the British Government of that Prince's possessions in Bundelkund, the former had resolved "to
declare the territory of Jhansi to be hereditary in the
family of the late Sheo Rao Bhow, and to perpetuate
with his heirs the treaty concluded with the late
Bhow;" and, accordingly, a treaty was concluded
with the ruling chief, Ram Chand, then only a
Soubahdar, constituting "him, his heirs and successors," hereditary rulers of the territory. Loyal and
well disposed, he won the favour of the British Government, who, fifteen years after the conclusion of

1864. the treaty, conferred upon him the title of Rajah, which he only lived three years to enjoy.

For all purposes of succession he was a childless man; and so various claimants to the chiefship appeared. The British agent believed that the most valid claim was that of the late Rajah's uncle, who was at all events a direct lineal descendant of one of. the former Soubahdars. He was a leper, and might have been rejected, but, incapable as he was, the people accepted him; and, for three years, the administration of Jhansi was carried on in his name. At the end of those three years he died, also without
1838. heirs of the body, and various claimants as before came forward to dispute the succession. Having no thought of absorbing the State into our British territories, Lord Auckland appointed a commission of British officers to investigate and report upon the pretensions of the several claimants; and the result was, that Government, rightly considering that if the deceased Rajah had any title to the succession, his brother had now an equally good title, acknowledged Gungadhur Rao's right to succeed to the hereditary chiefship.

Under the administration of Ragonath the Leper the country had been grossly mismanaged, and as his successor was scarcely more competent, the British Government undertook to manage the State for him, and soon revived the revenue which had dwindled down under the native rulers. But, in 1843, after the amputation of a limb of the territory for the support of the Bundelkund Legion, the administration was restored to Gungadhur Rao, who carried on the government for ten years, and then, like his predecessors, died childless.

Then again arose the question of succession; but

the claims of the different aspirants to the Raj were
regarded with far other eyes than those which had
scrutinised them in times past. The Governor-General recorded another fatal minute, by which the
death-warrant of the State was signed. It was ruled.
that Jhansi was a dependent State, held by the favour
of the Peishwah, as Lord Paramount, and that his
powers had devolved upon the British Government.
A famous minute recorded, in 1837, by Sir Charles
Metcalfe, was cited to show the difference between
Hindoo sovereign Princes and " chiefs who hold
grants of land or public revenue by gift from a sovereign or paramount Power," and to prove that, in the
latter case, " the Power which made the grant, or
that which by conquest or otherwise has succeeded to
its rights, is entitled to limit succession," and to
" resume on failure of direct heirs of the body."* To
demonstrate the right to resume was in those days
tantamount to exercising it. So Jhansi was resumed.
In vain the widow of the late Rajah, whom the Political Agent described as " a lady bearing a high character, and much respected by every one at Jhansi,"
protested that her husband's House had ever been
faithful to the British Government—in vain she
dwelt upon services rendered in former days to that
Government, and the acknowledgments which they
had elicited from our rulers—in vain she pointed to
the terms of the treaty, which did not, to her simple
understanding, bar succession in accordance with the
laws and usages of her country—in vain she quoted

---

* But what Sir Charles Metcalfe
really said was, that the paramount
Power was "entitled to limit succession *according to the limitations of
the grant*, which in general confirms
it to heirs male of the body, and
consequently precludes adoption. *In
such cases*, therefore, the Power which
granted, or the Power standing in its
place, would have a right to resume
on failure of heirs male of the body."
This passage is very fairly quoted in
Lord Dalhousie's Minute.

1853. precedents to show that the grace and favour sought for Jhansi had been yielded to other States. The fiat was irrevocable. It had been ruled that the interests both of the Jhansi State and the British Government imperatively demanded annexation. "As it lies in the midst of other British districts," said Lord Dalhousie, "the possession of it as our own will tend to the improvement of the general internal administration of our possessions in Bundelkund. That its incorporation with the British territories will be greatly for the benefit of the people of Jhansi a reference to the results of experience will suffice to show." The results of experience have since shown to what extent the people of Jhansi appreciated the benefits of that incorporation.

Kerowlee. Whilst this question was being disposed of by Lord Dalhousie and his colleagues, another lapse was under consideration, which had occurred some time before, but regarding which no final decision had been passed. In the summer of 1852, the young chief of Kerowlee, one of the smaller Rajpoot States, had died, after adopting another boy, connected with him by ties of kindred. At that time Colonel Low represented the British Government in Rajpootana, and he at once pronounced his opinion that the adoption ought immediately to be recognised.

The Governor-General hesitated. It appeared to him that Kerowlee might, rightly and expediently, be declared to have lapsed. But his Council was divided; his Agent in Rajpootana had declared unequivocally for the adoption; and the case differed in some respects from the Sattarah question, which had already been decided with the sanction and approval of the Home Government. How great the difference really was appeared far more clearly to the

1852.

experienced eye of Sir Frederick Currie than to the vision of the Governor-General, clouded as it was by the film of a foregone conclusion.* The name of Sattarah had, by the force of accidental circumstances, become great throughout the land, both in India and in England; it was a familiar name to thousands and tens of thousands who had never heard of Kerowlee. With the Mahrattas, too, the House of Sivajee had been held in high veneration; but the Mahrattas could only boast of recent sovereignty; their high estate was one of modern usurpation. Their power had risen side by side with our own, and had been crushed down by our greater weight and greater vigour. But the Houses of Rajpootana had flourished centuries before the establishment of British rule; and the least of them had an ancestral dignity respected throughout the whole length and breadth of Hindostan, and treaty rights not less valid than any possessed by the greatest of territorial Princes. To men who had graduated, from boyhood upwards, in Indian statesmanship, there was something almost sacrilegious in the idea of laying a destroying hand even upon the least of the ancient Houses of Rajpootana—of destroying titles that had been honoured long years before the face of the white man had been seen in the country. But impressions of this kind are the growth of long intercourse with the people themselves, and we cannot be surprised that, after a year or two of Indian government, Lord Dalhousie, with all his unrivalled quickness of perception, should not have thoroughly understood the vital differences between the various

---

* Sir Frederick Currie's Minute on the Kerowlee question is an admirable state-paper—accurate in its facts, clear in its logic, and unexceptionable in its political morality.

races inhabiting the great continent of India. Had he done so, he would at once have sanctioned the proposed adoption ; as it was, he referred the question to the final decision of the Home Government.

Eager as they were at that time to support the policy of Lord Dalhousie, and entire as was the faith of many of them in his wisdom, the Directors could not look with favour upon a proposal to commence the gradual extinction of the ancient principalities of Rajpootana.
"It appears to us," they said, "that there is a marked distinction in fact between the case of Kerowlee and Sattarah, which is not sufficiently adverted to in the Minute of the Governor-General. The Sattarah State was one of recent origin, derived altogether from the creation and gift of the British Government, whilst Kerowlee is one of the oldest of the Rajpoot States, which has been under the rule of its native Princes from a period long anterior to the British power in India. It stands to us only in the relation of protected ally, and probably there is no part of India into which it is less desirable, except upon the strongest grounds, to substitute our government for that of the native rulers. In our opinion, such grounds do not exist in the present case, and we have, therefore, determined to sanction the succession of Bhurt Pal."

But before the arrival of the despatch expressing these just sentiments and weighty opinions, all chance of the succession of Bhurt Pal had passed away. Had the adoption been granted at once, it would, in all probability, have been accepted by the members of the late Rajah's family, by the principal chiefs, and by the people of the country. But it is the inevitable tendency of delay in such a case to unsettle the public mind, to raise questions which but for this suspense

would not have been born, and to excite hopes and
stimulate ambitions which otherwise would have lain
dormant. So it happened that whilst London and
Calcutta were corresponding about the rights of
Bhurt Pal, another claimant to the sovereignty of
Kerowlee was asserting his pretensions in the most
demonstrative manner. Another and a nearer kins-
man of the late Prince—older, and, therefore, of a
more pronounced personal character—stood forward
to proclaim his rights, and to maintain them by arms.
The ladies of the royal family, the chiefs, and the
people, supported his claims; and the representative
of the British Government in Rajpootana recognised
their validity. That representative was Sir Henry
Lawrence. Succeeding General Low in the Agency,
he cherished the same principles as those which had
ever been so consistently maintained by that veteran
statesman; but circumstances had arisen which moved
him to give them a different application. This new
pretender to the throne had better claims on the score
of consanguinity than Bhurt Pal, but Adoption over-
rides all claims of relationship, and, if the adoption
were valid, the latter was legally the son and heir of
the deceased. In this view, as consonant with the
customs of the country, Henry Lawrence would have
supported the succession of Bhurt Pal; but, on investigation, it appeared that all the requirements and
conditions of law and usage had not been fulfilled,
and that the people themselves doubted the validity
of the adoption. It appeared to him, therefore, that
the British Government would best discharge its duty
to Kerowlee by allowing the succession of Muddun
Pal. Even on the score of adoption his claims were
good, for he had been adopted by the eldest of the
late Rajah's widows, which, in default of adoption by

the Rajah himself, would have been good against all claimants.   But, in addition to this, it was to be said of the pretensions of this man that he was older than the other; that a minority would thus be avoided altogether; that he had some personal claims to consideration; and that the voice of the chiefs and the people had decided in his favour.   As the succession, therefore, of Bhurt Pal had not been sanctioned, and as the decision of the Home Government in his favour had not been published, there would be no wrong to him in this preference of his rival, so Henry Lawrence recommended, and the Government of Lord Dalhousie approved, the succession of Muddun Pal to the sovereignty of Kerowlee.

So Lapse, in this instance, did not triumph; and the ancient Houses of Rajpootana, which, during these two years of suspense, had awaited the issue with the deepest interest, felt some temporary relief when it was known that the wedge of annexation had not been driven into the time-honoured circle of the States.   But it is not to be supposed that because no wrong was done at last no injury was done by the delay.   Public rumour recognises no Secret Department.   It was well known at every native Court, in every native bazaar, that the British Government were discussing the policy of annexing or not annexing Kerowlee.   The mere fact that there was a question to be discussed, in such a case, was sufficient to fill the minds of the people with anxiety and alarm.   For two years Kerowlee was without any other ruler than the Political Agent of the British Government; and this was a significant fact, the impression of which was not to be removed by the subsequent decision. The Rajpoot Princes lost their confidence in the good faith of the British Government.   Kerowlee had been spared, they scarcely knew how; some were fain to attribute it to the well-known justice and liberality of Henry Lawrence. But the same moderation might not be displayed again; there were childless men amongst them; and from that time a restless, uneasy feeling took possession of them, and no man felt sure that his House would not perish with him. It was not strange, indeed, that a year or two afterwards there should have been in circulation all over the country ominous reports to the effect that the policy of Lord Dalhousie had eventually triumphed, and that the gradual absorption of all the Rajpoot States had been sanctioned by the Home Government. It was a dangerous lie; and even the habitual reticence of the Court of Directors was not proof against the grossness of the calumny; so it was authoritatively contradicted. But not before it had worked its way in India, and done much to undermine the foundations of that confidence which is one of the main pillars of our strength.

There is one other story of territorial annexation yet to be told—briefly, for it was not thought at the time to be of much political importance, and now is held but little in remembrance. Beyond the south-western frontier of Bengal was the territory of Sum-bhulpore. It had formerly been an outlying district of the Nagpore principality, but had been ceded by the Bonslah family, and had been bestowed by the British on a descendant of the old Sumbhulpore Rajahs, under terms which would have warranted the resumption of the estate on the death of the first incumbent. But twice the sovereign rights had been bestowed anew upon members of the family, and not until 1849, when Narain Singh lay at the point of death, was it determined to annex the territory to

the British dominions. There were no heirs of the
body; no near relatives of the Rajah. No adoption
had been declared. The country was said to have
been grievously misgoverned. And so there seemed
to be a general agreement that the Lapse was perfect, and that annexation might be righteously proclaimed. Dalhousie was absent from the Presidency;
but the case was clear, and the Government neither
in India nor in England hesitated for a moment.
And, perhaps, though it was not without its own
bitter fruit, there is less to be said against it, on the
score of abstract justice, than against anything of
which I have written in this division of my work.

But there were lapses of another kind, lapses
which involved no gain of territory to the British
Government, for the territory had been gained before. There were several deposed princes in the land,
representatives of ancient Houses, whose sceptres had
passed by conquest or by treaty into the white man's
hand, but who still enjoyed the possession of considerable revenues, and maintained some semblance of
their former dignity and state. It happened that,
whilst Dalhousie reigned in India, three of these
pensioned princes died. Of the story of one of them

I must write in detail. There had once been three
great Mahratta Houses: the Houses of Sattarah, of
Nagpore, and of Poonah. It has been told how
Dalhousie extinguished the two first; the third had
been for some thirty years territorially extinct,
when he was sent out to govern India. In 1818,
at the close of the second great Mahratta war,
the Peishwah, Badjee Rao, surrendered to Sir John
Malcolm. He had been betrayed into hostility, and
treacherous hostility; he had appealed to the sword,
and he had been fairly beaten; and there was nothing

left for him but to end his days as an outcast and a
fugitive, or to fling himself upon the mercy of the
British Government. He chose the latter course;
and when he gave himself to the English General,
he knew that he was in·the hands of one who sympathised with him in his fallen fortunes, and would
be a generous friend to him in adversity. Malcolm
pledged the Government to bestow upon the Peishwah, for the support of himself and family, an annual
pension of not less than eight lakhs of rupees. The
promise was said to be an over-liberal one; and
there were those who at the time condemned Malcolm for his profuseness. But he replied, that "it
had been the policy of the British Government, since
its first establishment in India, to act towards princes,
whose bad faith and treachery had compelled it to
divest them of all power and dominion, with a generosity which almost lost sight of their offences. The
effect of this course of proceeding in reconciling all
classes to its rule had been great. The liberality and
the humanity which it had displayed on such occasions had, I was satisfied, done more than its arms
towards the firm establishment of its power. It was,
in fact, a conquest over mind, and among men so
riveted in their habits and prejudices as the natives
of their country, the effect, though unseen, was great
beyond calculation." It was a solace to him to think
that these sentiments were shared by such·men as
Mountstuart Elphinstone, David Ochterlony, and
Thomas Munro.

So Badjee Rao went into honourable seclusion, and
an asylum was found for him at Bithoor, distant
some twelve miles from the great military station
of Cawnpore, in the North-Western Provinces of
India. He was not then an old man, as age is calcu-

1818-51. lated by years, but he was said to be of debauched habits and feeble constitution ; and no one believed that he would very long survive to be a burden upon the Company. But he outlived his power for a third part of a century, living resignedly, if not contentedly, in his new home, with a large body of followers and dependents, mostly of his own race, and many others of the outward insignia of state. From the assemblage, under such circumstances, of so large a body of Mahrattas, some feeling of apprehension and alarm might have arisen in the mind of the British Government, especially in troubled times ; but the fidelity of the ex-Peishwah himself was as conspicuous ·as the good conduct and the orderly behaviour of his people. Nor was it only a passive loyalty that he manifested ; for twice in critical conjunctures, when the English were sore-pressed, he came forward with offers of assistance. When the War in Afghanistan had drained our Treasury, and money was grievously wanted, he lent the Company five lakhs of rupees; and when, afterwards, our dominions were threatened with an invasion from the Punjab, and there was much talk all over the country of a hostile alliance between the Sikhs and the Mahrattas, the steadfastness of his fidelity was evidenced by an offer made to the British Government to raise and to maintain at his own cost a thousand Horse and a thousand Foot. As he had the disposition, so also had he the means to serve us. His ample pension more than sufficed for the wants even of a retired monarch ; and as years passed, people said that he had laid by a great store of wealth, and asked who was to be its inheritor ? For it was with him, as it was with other Mahratta princes, he was going down to the grave leaving no son to succeed him. So he adopted a son, from his own family stock,[*] and, some years before his death, sought the recognition of the British Government for an adoption embracing more than the right of succession to his savings (for this needed no sovereign sanction) the privilege of succeeding to the title and the pension of the Peishwah. The prayer was not granted ; but the Company did not shut out all hope that, after the death of Badjee Rao, some provision might be made for his family. The question was reserved for future consideration—that is, until the contingency of the ex-Peishwah's death should become an accomplished reality ; and as at this time the old man was feeble, paralytic, and nearly blind, it was not expected that his pension would much longer remain a burden on the Indian revenues.

But not until the 28th of January, 1851, when there was the weight of seventy-seven years upon him, did the last of the Peishwahs close his eyes upon the world for ever. He left behind him a will, executed in 1839, in which he named as his adopted son, " to inherit and be the sole master of the Guddee of the Peishwah, the dominions, wealth, family possessions, treasure, and all his real and personal property," a youth known as Doondoo Punt, Nana Sahib. When Badjee Rao died, the heir was twenty-seven years old ; described as " a quiet, unostentatious young man, not at all addicted to any extravagant habits, and invariably showing a ready disposition to attend to the advice of the British Commissioner."

1818-51.

Death of Badjee Rao

The Nana Sahib.

---

* Strictly it should be said that he adopted three sons and a grandson. His will says : " That Doondoo Punt, Nana, my eldest son, and Gungadhur Rao, my youngest and third son, and Sada-Sheo Punt Dada, son of my second son, Pundoo Rung Rao, my grandson ; these three are my sons and grandson. After me Doondoo Punt, Nana, my eldest son, Mookh Perdan, shall inherit and be the sole master of the Guddee of the Peishwah, &c."—*MS. Records.*

What he was safe to inherit was about 300,000*l.*, more than one-half of which was invested in Government securities;* but there was an immense body of dependents to be provided for, and it was thought that the British Government might appropriate a portion of the ex-Peishwah's stipend to the support of the family at Bithoor. The management of affairs was in the hands of the Soubahdar Ramchunder Punt, a faithful friend and adherent of Badjee Rao, who counselled his master with wisdom, and controlled his followers with vigour; and he now, with all due respect for the British Government, pleaded the cause of the adopted son of the Peishwah. "Nana Sahib," he said, "considering the Honourable Company in the room of the late Maharajah as his protector and supporter, is full of hopes and free of care on this subject. His dependence in every way is on the kindness and liberality of the British Government, for the increase of whose power and prosperity he has ever been, and will continue to be, desirous." The British Commissioner at Bithoor† supported the appeal in behalf of the family, but it met with no favour in high places. Mr. Thomason was then Lieutenant-Governor of the North-Western Provinces. He was a good man, an able man, a man of high reputation, but he was one of the leaders of the New School, and was no friend to the princes and nobles of the land; and he told the Commissioner to dis-. courage all hopes of further assistance in the breasts

---

* The official report of the Commissioner said, 16 lakhs of Government paper, 10 lakhs of jewels, 3 lakhs of gold coins, 80,000 rupees gold ornaments, 20,000 rupees silver plate.

† It should rather be said, "two British Commissioners." Colonel Manson was Commissioner when the Peishwah died, but he left Bithoor shortly afterwards, and Mr. Morland, then magistrate at Cawnpore, took his place, and on him devolved the principal business of the settlement of the ex-Peishwah's affairs.

of the family, and to "strive to induce the numerous retainers of the Peishwah speedily to disperse and return to the Deccan." Lord Dalhousie was Governor-General; and, in such a case, his views were little likely to differ from those of his Lieutenant. So he declared his opinion that the recommendations of the Commissioner were "uncalled for and unreasonable." "The Governor-General," it was added, "concurs in opinion with his Honour (Mr. Thomason) in thinking that, under any circumstances, the Family have no claim upon the Government; and he will by no means consent to any portion of the public revenues being conferred on them. His Lordship requests that the determination of the Government of India may be explicitly declared to the Family without delay." And it was so declared; but with some small alleviation of the harshness of the sentence, for the Jagheer, or rent-free estate, of Bithoor was to be continued to the Nana Sahib, but without the exclusive jurisdiction which had been enjoyed by the ex-Peishwah.

When Doondoo Punt learnt that there was no hope of any further assistance to the family at Bithoor from the liberality of the Government of India, he determined to appeal to the Court of Directors of the East India Company. It had been in contemplation during the lifetime of Badjee Rao to adopt such a course, and a son of the Soubahdar Ramchunder had been selected as the agent who was to prosecute the appeal. But discouraged by the Commissioner, the project had been abandoned, and was not revived until all other hope had failed after the ex-Peishwah's death. Then it was thought that a reversal of the adverse decision might be obtained by memorialising the authorities in England, and a

Memorial of the Nana.

memorial was accordingly drawn up and despatched, in the usual manner, through the Government in India. "The course pursued by the local governments," it was said, "is not only an unfeeling one towards the numerous family of the deceased prince, left almost entirely dependent upon the promises of the East India Company, but inconsistent with what is due to the representative of a long line of sovereigns. Your memorialist, therefore, deems it expedient at once to appeal to your Honourable Court, not merely on the ground of the faith of treaties, but of a bare regard to the advantages the East India Company have derived from the last sovereign of the Mahratta Empire. . . . . It would be contrary to the spirit of all treaties hitherto concluded to attach a special meaning to an article of the stipulations entered into, whilst another is interpreted and acted upon in its most liberal sense." And then the memorialist proceeded to argue, that as the Peishwah, on behalf of his heirs and successors, had ceded his territories to the Company, the Company were bound to pay the price of such cession to the Peishwah and his heirs and successors. If the compact were lasting on one side, so also should it be on the other. "Your memorialist submits that a cession of a perpetual revenue of thirty-four lakhs of rupees in consideration of an annual pension of eight lakhs establishes a *de facto* presumption that the payment of one is contingent upon the receipt of the other, and hence that, as long as those receipts continue, the payment of the pension is to follow." It was then argued that the mention, in the treaty, of the "Family" of the Peishwah indicated the hereditary character of the stipulation, on the part of the Company, as such mention would be unnecessary and unmeaning in its applica-

tion to a mere life-grant, "for a provision for the 1852.
support of the prince necessarily included the maintenance of his family ;" and after this, from special
arguments, the Nana Sahib turned to a general assertion of his rights as based on precedent and analogy.
"Your memorialist," it was said, "is at a loss to
account for the difference between the treatment, by
the Company, of the descendants of other princes
and that experienced by the family of the Peishwah,
represented by him. The ruler of Mysore evinced
the most implacable hostility towards the Company's
government; and your memorialist's father was one of
the princes whose aid was invoked by the Company
to crush a relentless enemy. When that chieftain
fell, sword in hand, the Company, far from abandoning his progeny to their fate, have afforded an asylum
and a liberal support to more than one generation of
his descendants, without distinction between the legitimate and the illegitimate. With equal or even
greater liberality the Company delivered the dethroned Emperor of Delhi from a dungeon, re-in-
vested him with the insignia of sovereignty, and
assigned to him a munificent revenue, which is continued to his descendants to the present day. Wherein
is your memorialist's case different? It is true that
the Peishwah, after years of amity with the British
Indian Government, during which he assigned to
them revenues to the amount of half a crore of
rupees, was unhappily engaged in war with them, by
which he perilled his throne. But as he was not
reduced to extremities, and even if reduced, closed
with the terms proposed to him by the British Commander, and ceded his rich domains to place himself
and his family under the fostering care of the Company, and as the Company still profit by the revenues

of his hereditary possessions; on what principle are his descendants deprived of the pension included in those terms and the vestiges of sovereignty? Wherein are the claims of his family to the favour and consideration of the Company less than those of the conquered Mysorean or the captive Mogul?" Then the Nana Sahib began to set forth his own personal claims as founded on the adoption in his favour; he quoted the best authorities on Hindoo law to prove that the son by adoption has all the rights of the son by birth; and he cited numerous instances, drawn from the recent history of Hindostan and the Deccan, to show how such adoptions had before been recognised by the British Government. "The same fact," he added, "is evinced in the daily practice of the Company's Courts all over India, in decreeing to the adopted sons of princes, of zemindars, and persons of every grade, the estates of those persons to the exclusion of other heirs of the blood. Indeed, unless the British Indian Government is prepared to abrogate the Hindoo Sacred Code, and to interdict the practice of the Hindoo religion, of both of which adoption is a fundamental feature, your memorialist cannot understand with what consistency his claim to the pension of the late Peishwah can be denied, merely on the ground of his being an adopted son."

Another plea for refusal might be, nay, had been, based upon the fact that Badjee Rao, from the savings of his pension, had accumulated and left behind him a large amount of private property, which no one could alienate from his heirs. Upon this the Nana Sahib, with not unreasonable indignation, said: "That if the withholding of the pension proceeded from the supposition that the late Peish-

wah had left a sufficient provision for his family, it 1852.
would be altogether foreign to the question, and unprecedented in the annals of the History of British
India. The pension of eight lakhs of rupees per
annum has been agreed upon on the part of the
British Government, to enable his Highness the late
Badjee Rao to support himself and family; it is im-
material to the British Government what portion of
that sum the late prince actually expended, nor has
there been any agreement entered into to the effect
that his Highness the late Badjee Rao should be
compelled to expend every fraction of an annual
allowance accorded to him by a special treaty, in
consideration of his ceding to the British Government territories yielding an annual and perpetual
revenue of thirty-four lakhs of rupees. Nobody on
earth had a right to control the expenditure of that
pension, and if his Highness the late Badjee Rao had
saved every fraction of it, he would have been perfectly justified in doing so. Your memorialist would
venture to ask, whether the British Government ever
deigned to ask in what manner the pension granted
to any of its numerous retired servants is expended?
or whether any of them saves a portion, or what
portion, of his pension? and, furthermore, in the
event of its being proved that the incumbents of such
pensions had saved a large portion thereof, it would
be considered a sufficient reason for withholding the
pension from the children in the proportions stipulated by the covenant entered into with its servant?
And yet is a native prince, the descendant of an ancient scion of Royalty, who relies upon the justice
and liberality of the British Government, deserving
of less consideration than its covenanted servants?
To disperse, however, any erroneous impression that

may exist on the part of the British Government on that score, your memorialist would respectfully beg to observe that the pension of eight lakhs of rupees, stipulated for by the treaty of 1818, was not exclusively for the support of his Highness the late Badjee Rao and his family, but also for the maintenance of a large retinue of faithful adherents, who preferred following the ex-Peishwah in his voluntary exile. Their large number, fully known to the British Government, caused no inconsiderable call upon the reduced resources of his Highness; and, furthermore, if it be taken into consideration the appearance which Native princes, though rendered powerless, are still obliged to keep up to ensure respect, it may be easily imagined that the savings from a pension of eight lakhs of rupees, granted out of an annual revenue of thirty-four lakhs, could not have been large. But notwithstanding this heavy call upon the limited resources of the late Peishwah, his Highness husbanded his resources with much care, so as to be enabled to invest a portion of his annual income in public securities, which, at the time of his death, yielded an income of about eighty thousand rupees. Is then the foresight and the economy on the part of his Highness the late Badjee Rao to be regarded as an offence deserving to be visited with the punishment of stopping the pension for the support of his

MS. Records. family guaranteed by a formal treaty ?"

But neither the rhetoric nor the reasoning of the Nana Sahib had any effect upon the Home Government. The Court of Directors of the East India Company were hard as a rock, and by no means to be moved to compassion. They had already expressed an opinion that the savings of the Peishwah were sufficient for the maintenance of his heirs and dependents;* and when the memorial came before 1853. Decision of the Company. them, they summarily rejected it, writing out to the Government to " inform the memorialist that the pension of his adoptive father was not hereditary, that he has no claim whatever to it, and that his application is wholly inadmissible." Such a reply as May 4, 1853. this must have crushed out all hope from the Bithoor Family, and shown the futility of further action; but it happened that, before this answer was received, the Nana Sahib had sent an agent to England to prosecute his claims. This agent was not the son of the old Mahratta Soubahdar, to whom the mission first contemplated was to have been entrusted, but a young and astute Mahomedan, with a good presence, a plausible address, and a knowledge of the English language. His name was Azim-oollah Khan. In the summer of 1853 he appeared in England, and in conjunction with an Englishman, named Biddle, prosecuted the claims of the Nana, but with no success. Judgment had already been recorded, and nothing that these agents could say or do was likely to cause its reversal.

 So Azim-oollah Khan, finding that little or nothing could be done in the way of business for his employer, devoted his energies to the pursuit of pleasure on his own account. Passing by reason of his fine clothes for a person of high station, he made his way into good society, and is said to have boasted of favours received from English ladies. Outwardly he was a gay, smiling, voluptuous sort of person; and

* " *May* 19, 1852.—We entirely approve of the decision of the Governor-General that the adopted son and dependents on Badjee Rao have no claim upon the British Government. The large pension which the ex-Peishwah enjoyed during thirty- three years afforded him the means of making an abundant provision for his family and dependents, and the property, which he is known to have left, is amply sufficient for their support."—*The Court of Directors to the Government of India.—MS.*

even a shrewd observer might have thought that he was intent always upon the amusement of the hour. There was one man, however, in England at that time, who, perhaps, knew that the desires of the plausible Mahomedan were not bounded by the enjoyment of the present. For it happened that the agent, who had been sent to England by the deposed Sattarah Family, in the hope of obtaining for them the restoration of their principality, was still resident in the English metropolis. This man was a Mahratta named Rungo Bapojee. Able and energetic, he had pushed his suit with a laborious, untiring conscientiousness, rarely seen in a Native envoy; but though aided by much soundness of argument and much fluency of rhetoric expended by others than hired advocates, upon the case of the Sattarah Princes, he had failed to make an impression on their judges. Though of different race and different religion, these two men were knit together by common sympathies and kindred tasks, and in that autumn of 1853, by like failures and disappointments to brood over and the same bitter animosities to cherish. What was said and what was done between them no Historian can relate. They were adepts in the art of dissimulation. So the crafty Mahratta made such a good impression even upon those whom his suit had so greatly troubled, that his debts were paid for him, and he was sent back at the public expense to Bombay with money in his pocket from the Treasury of the India House;* whilst the gay Mahomedan floated about the surface of society and made a conspicuous figure at crowded watering-places, as if he dearly loved England and the English, and could not per-

* Rungo Bapojee returned to India in December, 1853. The East India Company gave him 2500l. and a free passage.

suade himself to return to his own dreary and be- 1853.
nighted land.

So little material are they to this History that I Carnatic and
need not write in detail of the circumstances attend- Tanjore.
ing the extinction of the titular sovereignties of the
Carnatic and Tanjore, two ancient Houses, one Mahomedan, the other Hindoo, that had once flourished
in the Southern Peninsula. Lord Wellesley had
stripped them of territorial power. It remained,
therefore, only for Lord Dalhousie, when the Newab 1854.
of the Carnatic and the Rajah of Tanjore died with- 1855.
out heirs of the body, to abolish the titular dignities
of the two Families and " to resume the large stipends
they had enjoyed, as Lapses to Government." Pensions were settled upon the surviving members of
the two Families; but in each case, the head of the
House made vehement remonstrance against the extinction of its honours, and long and loudly cla-
moured for restitution. There were many, doubtless, in Southern India who still clung with feelings
of veneration to these shadowy pageants, and deplored the obliteration of the royal names that they
had long honoured; and as a part of the great system of demolition these resumptions made a bad impression in more remote places. But empty titular
dignities are dangerous possessions, and it may be,
after all, only mistaken kindness to perpetuate them
when the substance of royalty is gone.

₊ In this chapter might have been included other cases of Lapse, as those of the Pergunnah, of Odeipoor, on the South-Western Frontier, and of Jeitpore, in Bundlekhund; but, although every additional absorption of territory tended to increase, in some measure, the feeling of insecurity in men's minds, they were comparatively of little political importance; and Lord Dalhousie did not think them worth a paragraph in his Farewell Minute.

CHAPTER III.

THE ANNEXATION OF OUDE—EARLY HISTORY OF THE PROVINCE—THE TREATY
OF 1801—EFFECTS OF THE DOUBLE GOVERNMENT—CREATION OF THE
KINGSHIP—PROGRESS OF MISRULE—REPEATED WARNINGS—THE UN-
RATIFIED TREATY—COLONEL SLEEMAN'S REPORTS—LORD DALHOUSIE'S
MINUTE—VIEWS OF THE COURT OF DIRECTORS—SIR JAMES OUTRAM
RESIDENT—ANNEXATION PROCLAIMED.

1856.   THERE was still another province to be absorbed
into the British Empire under the administration of
Lord Dalhousie; not by conquest, for its rulers had
ever been our friends, and its people had recruited
our armies; not by lapse, for there had always been
a son or a brother, or some member of the royal
house, to fulfil, according to the Mahomedan law of
succession, the conditions of heirship, and there was
still a king, the son of a king, upon the throne; but
by a simple assertion of the dominant will of the
British Government.   This was the great province of
Oude, in the very heart of Hindostan, which had long
tempted us, alike by its local situation and the reputed
wealth of its natural resources.

It is a story not to be lightly told in a few sentences.
Its close connexion with some of the more important
passages of this history fully warrants some ampli-
tude of narration. Before the British settler had established himself on the peninsula of India, Oude was

a province of the Mogul Empire. When that empire was distracted and weakened by the invasion of Nadir Shah, the treachery of the servant was turned against the master, and little by little the Governor began to govern for himself. But holding only an official, though an hereditary title, he still acknowledged his vassalage; and long after the Great Mogul had shrivelled into a pensioner and a pageant, the Newab-Wuzeer of Oude was nominally his minister.

Of the earliest history of British connexion with the Court of the Wuzeer, it is not necessary to write in detail. There is nothing less creditable in the annals of the rise and progress of the British power in the East. The Newab had territory; the Newab had subjects; the Newab had neighbours; more than all, the Newab had money. But although he possessed in abundance the raw material of soldiers, he had not been able to organise an army sufficient for all the external and internal requirements of the State, and so he was fain to avail himself of the superior military skill and discipline of the white men, and to hire British battalions to do his work. At first this was done in an irregular, desultory kind of way, job-work, as in the infamous case of the Rohilla massacre; but afterwards it assumed a more formal and recognised shape, and solemn engagements were entered into with the Newab, by which we undertook, in consideration of certain money-payments, known as the Subsidy, to provide a certain number of British troops for the internal and external defence of his Excellency's dominions.

In truth it was a vicious system, one that can hardly be too severely condemned. By it we established a Double Government of the worst kind. The Political and Military government was in the hands

I

1796. of the Company; the internal administration of the Oude territories still rested with the Newab-Wuzeer. In other words, hedged in and protected by the British battalions, a bad race of Eastern Princes were suffered to do, or not to do, what they liked. Under such influences it is not strange that disorder of every kind ran riot over the whole length and breadth of the land. Never were the evils of misrule more horribly apparent; never were the vices of an indolent and rapacious Government productive of a greater sum of misery. The extravagance and profligacy of the Court were written in hideous characters on the desolated face of the country. It was left to the Nabob's Government to dispense justice: justice was not dispensed. It was left to the Nabob's Government to collect the revenue; it was wrung from the people at the point of the bayonet. The Court was sumptuous and profligate; the people poor and wretched. The expenses of the royal household were enormous. Hundreds of richly-caparisoned voracious elephants ate up the wealth of whole districts, or carried it in glittering apparel on their backs. A multitudinous throng of unserviceable attendants; bands of dancing-girls; flocks of parasites; costly feasts and ceremonies; folly and pomp and profligacy of every conceivable description, drained the coffers of the State. A vicious and extravagant Government soon beget a poor and a suffering people; a poor and a suffering people, in turn, perpetuate the curse of a bankrupt Government. The process of retaliation is sure. To support the lavish expenditure of the Court the mass of the people were persecuted and outraged. Bands of armed mercenaries were let loose upon the ryots in support of the rapacity of the Aumils, or Revenue-farmers, whose appearance was a terror to the people. Under such a system of cruelty and extortion, the country soon became a desert, and the Government then learnt by hard experience that the prosperity of the people is the only true source of wealth. The lesson was thrown away. The decrease of the revenue was not accompanied by a corresponding diminution of the profligate expenditure of the Court, or by any effort to introduce a better administrative system. Instead of this, every new year saw the unhappy country lapsing into worse disorder, with less disposition, as time advanced, on the part of the local Government to remedy the evils beneath which it was groaning. Advice, protestation, remonstrance were in vain. Lord Cornwallis advised, protested, remonstrated: Sir John Shore advised, protested, remonstrated. At last a statesman of a very different temper appeared upon the scene.

Lord Wellesley was a despot in every pulse of his heart. But he was a despot of the right kind; for he was a man of consummate vigour and ability, and he seldom made a mistake. The condition of Oude soon attracted his attention; not because its government was bad and its people were wretched, but because that country might either be a bulwark of safety to our own dominions, or a sea of danger which might overflow and destroy us. That poor old blind ex-King, Shah Zemaun, of the Suddozye family of Caubul, known to the present generation as the feeble appendage of a feeble puppet, had been, a little while before the advent of Lord Wellesley, in the heyday of his pride and power, meditating great deeds which he had not the ability to accomplish, and keeping the British power in India in a chronic state of unrest. If ever there had been any real peril, it had passed away before the new century was a year old. But it

might arise again.   Doubtless the military strength
of the Afghans was marvellously overrated in those
days; but still there was the fact of a minacious Mahomedan power beyond the frontier, not only meditating invasion, but stirring up the Mahomedan
Princes of India to combine in a religious war against
the usurping Feringhee.   Saadut Ali was then on the
musnud of Oude; he was the creature and the friend
of the English, ·but Vizier Ali, whom he had supplanted, had intrigued with Zemaun Shah, and would
not only have welcomed, but have subsidised also an
Afghan force in his own dominions.   At the bottom
of all our alarm, at that time, were some not unreasonable apprehensions of the ambitious designs of the
first Napoleon.   At all events, it was sound policy to
render Oude powerful for good and powerless for
evil.   To the accomplishment of this it was necessary
that large bodies of ill-disciplined and irregularly
paid native troops in the service of the Newab-Wuzeer
—lawless bands that had been a terror alike to him
and to his people—should be forthwith disbanded,
and that British troops should occupy their place.
Now, already the Wuzeer was paying seventy-six
lakhs of rupees, or more than three-quarters of a
million of money, for his subsidised British troops,
and though he was willing to disband his own levies,
and thereby to secure some saving to the State, it
was but small in proportion to the expense of the
more costly machinery of British military defence
now to be substituted for them.   The additional burden to be imposed upon Oude was little less than half
a million of money, and the unfortunate Wuzeer,
whose resources had been strained to the utmost to
pay the previous subsidy, declared his inability to
meet any further demands on his treasury.   This was

what Lord Wellesley expected—nay, more, it was
what he wanted. If the Wuzeer could not pay in
money, he could pay in money's worth. He had rich
lands that might be ceded in perpetuity to the Company for the punctual payment of the subsidy. So
the Governor-General prepared a treaty ceding the
required provinces, and with a formidable array of
British troops at his call, dragooned the Wuzeer into
sullen submission to the will of the English Sultan.
The new treaty was signed; and districts then yielding a million and a half of money, and now nearly
double that amount of annual revenue, passed under
the administration of the British Government.

Now, this treaty—the last ever ratified between
the two Governments—bound the Newab Wuzeer to
"establish in his reserved dominions such a system of
administration, to be carried on by his own officers,
as should be conducive to the prosperity of his subjects, and be calculated to secure the lives and properties of the inhabitants," and he undertook at the
same time "always to advise with and to act in con-
formity to the counsels of the officers of the East
India Company." But the English ruler knew well
that there was small hope of these conditions being
fulfilled. "I am satisfied," he said, "that no effectual security can be provided against the ruin of the
province of Oude until the exclusive management of
the civil and military government of that country
shall be transferred to the Company under suitable
provisions for the maintenance of his Excellency and
his family." He saw plainly before him the break-
down of the whole system, and believed that in the
course of a few years the entire administration of the
province would be transferred to the hands of our
British officers. There was one thing, however, on

which he did not calculate—the moderation of his successors. He lived nearly half a century after these words were written, and yet the treaty outlived him by many years.

If there was, at any time, hope for Oude, under purely native administration, it was during the wuzeership of Saadut Ali, for he was not a bad man, and he appears to have had rather enlightened views with respect to some important administrative questions.* But the opportunity was lost; and whilst the counsels of our British officers did nothing for the people, the bayonets of our British soldiers restrained them from doing anything for themselves. Thus matters grew from bad to worse, and from worse to worst. One Governor-General followed another; one Resident followed another; one Wuzeer followed another: but still the great tide of evil increased in volume, in darkness, and in depth.

But, although the Newab-Wuzeers of Oude were, doubtless, bad rulers and bad men, it must be admitted that they were good allies. False to their people—false to their own manhood—they were true to the British Government. They were never known to break out into open hostility, or to smoulder in hidden treachery against us; and they rendered good service, when they could, to the Power to which they owed so little. They supplied our armies, in time of war, with grain, they supplied us with carriage-cattle; better still, they supplied us with cash. There was money in the

---

* Sir Henry Lawrence says that he was "in advance of the Bengal Government of the day on revenue arrangements," and gives two striking instances of the fact. With characteristic candour and impartiality, Lawrence adds that Saadut Ali's mal-administration was "mainly attributable to English interference, to the resentment he felt for his own wrongs, and the bitterness of soul with which he must have received all advice from his oppressors, no less than to the impunity with which they enabled him to play the tyrant."—*Calcutta Review*, vol. iii. See also Lawrence's Essays, in which this paper is printed.

Treasury of Lucknow, when there was none in the Treasury of Calcutta; and the time came when the Wuzeer's cash was needed by the British ruler. Engaged in an extensive and costly war, Lord Hastings wanted more millions for the prosecution of his great enterprises. They were forthcoming at the right time; and the British Government were not unwilling in exchange to bestow both titles and territories on the Wuzeer. The times were propitious. The successful close of the Nepaul war placed at our disposal an unhealthy and impracticable tract of country at the foot of the Hills. This "terai" ceded to us by the Nepaulese was sold for a million of money to the Wuzeer, to whose domains it was contiguous, and he himself expanded and bloomed into a King under the fostering sun of British favour and affection.* The interest of the other million was paid away by our Government to a tribe of Oude pensioners, who were not sorry to exchange for a British guarantee the erratic benevolence of their native masters.

It would take long to trace the history of the progressive misrule of the Oude dominions under a succession of sovereigns all of the same class—passive permitters of evil rather than active perpetrators of iniquity, careless of, but not rejoicing in, the sufferings of their people. The rulers of Oude, whether Wuzeers or Kings, had not the energy to be tyrants.

---

* Sir John Malcolm said that the very mention of "his Majesty of Oude" made him sick. "Would I make," he said, "a golden calf, and suffer him to throw off his subordinate title, and assume equality with the degraded representative of a line of monarchs to whom his ancestors have been for ages really or nominally subject?" Sir Henry Lawrence seems to have thought that this was precisely what was intended. "The Newab Ghazee-oodeen Hyder," he wrote, "was encouraged to assume the title of King; Lord Hastings calculated on this exciting a rivalry between the Oude and Delhi Families."—*Calcutta Review*, vol. iii.; and Essays, page 119.

1817. They simply allowed things to take their course. Sunk in voluptuousness and pollution, often too horribly revolting to be described, they gave themselves up to the guidance of pandars and parasites, and cared not so long as these wretched creatures administered to their sensual appetites. Affairs of State were pushed aside as painful intrusions. Corruption stalked openly abroad. Every one had his price. Place, honour, justice—everything was to be bought. Fiddlers and barbers, pimps and mountebanks, became great functionaries. There were high revels at the capital, whilst, in the interior of the country, every kind of enormity was being exercised to wring from the helpless people the money which supplied the indulgences of the Court. Much of the land was farmed out to large contractors, who exacted every possible farthing from the cultivators; and were not seldom, upon complaint of extortion, made, unless inquiry were silenced by corruption, to disgorge into the royal treasury a large portion of their gains. Murders of the most revolting type, gang-robberies of the most outrageous character, were committed in open day. There were no Courts of Justice except at Lucknow; no Police but at the capital and on the frontier. The British troops were continually called out to coerce refractory landholders, and to stimulate revenue-collection at the point of the bayonet. The sovereign—Wuzeer or King—knew that they would do their duty; knew that, under the obligations of the treaty, his authority would be supported; and so he lay secure in his Zenana, and fiddled whilst his country was in flames.

And so years passed; and ever went there from the Residency to the Council-chamber of the Supreme Government the same unvarying story of frightful misrule. Residents expostulated, Governors-General

protested against it. The protests in due course became threats. Time after time it was announced to
the rulers of Oude that, unless some great and immediate reforms were introduced into the system of
administration, the British Government, as lords-
paramount, would have no course left to them but
to assume the direction of affairs, and to reduce the
sovereign of Oude to a pensioner and a pageant.

By no man was the principle of non-interference
supported more strenuously, both in theory and in
practice, than by Lord William Bentinck. But in
the affairs of this Oude State he considered that he
was under a righteous necessity to interfere. In April,
1831, he visited Lucknow; and there, distinctly and
emphatically told the King that "unless his territories were governed upon other principles than those
hitherto followed, and the prosperity of the people
made the principal object of his administration, the
precedents afforded by the principalities of the Carnatic and Tanjore would be applied to the kingdom
of Oude, and to the entire management of the country, and the King would be transmuted into a State
prisoner." This was no mere formal harangue, but
the deliberate enunciation of the Government of
India; and to increase the impression which it was
calculated to make on the mind of the King, the
warning was afterwards communicated to him in
writing. But, spoken or written, the words were of
no avail. He threw himself more than ever into the
arms of parasites and pandars; plunged more deeply
into debauchery than before, and openly violated all
decency by appearing drunk in the public streets of
Lucknow.* With the corruption of the Court the

* This was Nussur-ood-deen Hyder
—the second of the Oude kings, and
perhaps the worst. I speak du-
biously, however, of their comparative merits. Colonel Sleeman seems
to have thought that he might have
extracted more good out of Nussur-
ood-deen than out of any of the rest.

disorders of the country increased. The crisis seemed
now to have arrived. A communication was made
to the Court of Oude, that "instructions to assume
the government of the country, if circumstances
should render such a measure necessary, had arrived,
and that their execution was suspended merely in the
hope that the necessity of enforcing them might be
obviated."

But in what manner was the administration to be
assumed—in what manner was the improvement of
the country to be brought about by the intervention
of the British Government? There were different
courses open to us, and they were all diligently considered. We might appoint a Minister of our own
selection, and rule through him by the agency of the
Resident. We might depose the ruling sovereign,
and set up another and more hopeful specimen of
royalty in his place. We might place the country
under European administration, giving all the surplus revenues to the King. We might assume the
entire government, reducing the King to a mere
titular dignitary, and giving him a fixed share of the
annual revenues. Or we might annex the country
outright, giving him so many lakhs of rupees a year,
without reference to the revenues of the principality.
The ablest and most experienced Indian statesmen of
the day had been invited to give their opinions.
Malcolm and Metcalfe spoke freely out. The first of
the above schemes seemed to represent the mildest
form of interference ; but both the soldier and the
civilian unhesitatingly rejected it as the most odious,
and, in practice, the most ruinous of all interposition. Far better, they said, to set up a new King, or
even to assume the government for ourselves. But
those were days when native dynasties were not considered unmixed evils, and native institutions were not

pure abominations in our eyes. And it was thought that we might assume the administration of Oude, but not for ourselves. It was thought that the British Government might become the guardian and trustee of the King of Oude, administer his affairs through native agency and in accordance with native institutions, and pay every single rupee into the royal treasury.

This was the scheme of Lord William Bentinck, a man of unsurpassed honesty and justice; and it met with favourable acceptance in Leadenhall-street. The Court of Directors at that time, true to the old traditions of the Company, were slow to encourage their agents to seek pretexts for the extension of their dominions. The despatches which they sent out to India were for the most part distinguished by a praiseworthy moderation; sometimes, indeed, by a noble frankness and sincerity, which showed that the authors of them were above all disguises and pretences. They now looked the Oude business fairly in the face, but hoping still against hope that there might be some amelioration, they suffered, after the receipt of Lord William Bentinck's report, a year to pass away, and then another year, before issuing authoritative orders, and then they sent forth a despatch, which was intended to bring the whole question to a final issue. They spoke of the feelings which the deplorable situation of a country so long and so nearly connected with them had excited in their minds—of the obligations which such a state of things imposed upon them—of the necessity of finding means of effecting a great alteration. They acknowledged, as they had acknowledged before, that our connexion with the country had largely contributed to the sufferings of the people, inasmuch as it had afforded protection to tyranny, and rendered

1832.

July 16,
1834.

1834. hopeless the resistance of the oppressed.* This made it the more incumbent upon them to adopt measures for the mitigation, if not the removal, of the existing evil. They could not look on whilst the ruin of the country was consummated. It was certain that some‑ thing must be done. But what was that something to be? Then they set in array before them, some‑ what as I have done above, the different measures which might be resorted to, and, dwelling upon the course which Bentinck had recommended, placed in the hands of the Governor-General a discretionary power to carry the proposed measure into effect at such period, and in such a manner as might seem advisable, but with the utmost possible consideration for the King, whose consent to the proposed arrange‑ ment was, if possible, to be obtained. It was sug‑ gested that all the titles and honours of sovereignty should remain with his Majesty as before; that the revenues should be mainly expended in the adminis‑ tration and the improvement of the country, and that either the surplus, or a fixed stipend, should be assigned to the King. But, at the same time, the Government were instructed, in the event of their proceeding to assume the administration of the coun‑ try, distinctly to announce that, so soon as the neces‑ sary reforms should have been effected, the admi‑ nistration of the country, as in the case of Nagpore, would be restored to its native rulers.

Colonel John Low, of whose character and career I have already spoken, was then Resident at Luck‑

---

* For a long time, as we have said, our troops were employed by the King's officers to aid them in the collection of the revenue; thereby active, as the Court frankly described it, as "instruments of extortion and vengeance." This scandal no longer existed; but our battalions were still stationed in the country, ready to dragoon down any open insur‑ rection that might result from the misgovernment of Oude.

now. The despatch of the Court of Directors, authorising the temporary assumption of the Government of Oude, was communicated to him, and he pondered over its contents. The scheme appeared in his eyes to be distinguished by its moderation and humanity, and to be one of a singularly disinterested character. But he was convinced that it would be misunderstood. He said that, however pure the motives of the British Government might be, the natives of India would surely believe that we had taken the country for ourselves. So he recommended the adoption of another method of obtaining the same end. Fully impressed with the necessity of removing the reigning King, Nussur-ood-deen, he advised the Government to set up another ruler in his place; and in order that the measure might be above all suspicion, to abstain from receiving a single rupee, or a single acre of ground, as the price of his elevation. "What I recommend is this," he said, "that the next heir should be invested with the full powers of sovereignty; and that the people of Oude should continue to live under their own institutions." He had faith in the character of that next heir; he believed that a change of men would produce a change of measures; and, at all events, it was but bare justice to try the experiment.

But, before anything had been done by the Government of India, in accordance with the discretion delegated to them by the Court of Directors, the experiment which Low had suggested inaugurated itself. Not without suspicion of poison, but really, I believe, killed only by strong drink, Nussur-ood-deen Hyder died on a memorable July night. It was a crisis of no common magnitude, for there was a disputed succession; and large bodies of lawless native troops in Lucknow were ready to strike at a moment's notice.

The cool courage of Low and his assistants saved the city from a deluge of blood.   An uncle of the deceased Prince—an old man and a cripple, respectable in his feebleness—was declared King, with the consent of the British Government; and the independence of Oude had another lease of existence.

Lord Auckland was, at that time, Governor-General of India.   The new King, who could not but feel that he was a creature of the British, pledged himself to sign a new treaty.   And soon it was laid before him.   That the engagements of the old treaty had been violated, day after day, year after year, for more than a third part of a century, was a fact too patent to be questioned.   The misgovernment of the country was a chronic breach of treaty.   Whether the British or the Oude Government were more responsible for it was somewhat doubtful to every clear understanding and every unprejudiced mind.   The source of the failure was in the treaty itself, which the author of it well knew from the first was one of impossible fulfilment.   But it was still a breach of treaty, and there was another in the entertainment of vast numbers of soldiers over and above the stipulated allowance.   Those native levies had gradually swollen, according to Resident Low's calculations, to the bulk of seventy thousand men.   Here was an evil not to be longer permitted; wonder, indeed, was it that it should have been permitted so long.   This the new treaty was to remedy; no less than the continued mal-administration of the country by native agency. It provided, therefore, that in the event of any further - protracted misrule, the British Government should be entitled to appoint its own officers to the management of any part, small or great, of the province; that the old native levies should be abandoned, and a new force, commanded by British officers, organised in its place, at the cost of the Oude Government. But there was no idea of touching, in any other way, the revenues of the country. An account was to be rendered of every rupee received and expended, and the balance was to be paid punctually into the Oude Treasury.

This was the abortion, often cited in later years as the Oude Treaty of 1837. Authentic history recites that the Government of India were in throes with it, but the strangling hand of higher authority crushed all life out of the thing before it had become a fact. The treaty was wholly and absolutely disallowed by the Home Government.* They took especial exception to the establishment of the new auxiliary force, which was to cost the Oude Treasury sixteen lakhs of rupees a year; for, with all the pure logic of honesty, they said that the treaty of 1801 had made it compulsory on the British Government to provide for the defence of the country, and that a large tract of territory had been ceded with the express object of securing the payment of the troops necessary for this purpose. If, then, it were expedient to organise a fresh force under British officers, it was for the Company, not for the Oude Government, to defray the expenses of the new levy. But not only on these grounds did they object to the treaty. It is true that, a few years before, they had given the Governor-General discretionary power to deal, as he thought best, with the disorders of Oude, even to the extent of a temporary assumption of the government; but this authority had been issued at a time when Nussur-ood-deen, of whose vicious incapacity they had had

* That is to say, by the Secret Committee, who had, by Act of Parliament, special powers in this matter of Treaty-making.

many years' experience, sat upon the throne; and the Home Government were strongly of opinion that the new King, of whose character they had received a favourable account, ought to be allowed a fair trial, under the provisions of the treaty existing at the time of his accession to the throne. They there-fore directed the abrogation, not of any one article, but of the entire treaty. Wishing, however, the annulment of the treaty to appear rather as an act of grace from the Government of India than as the result of positive and unconditional instructions from Eng-land, they gave a large discretion to the Governor-General as to the mode of announcing this abrogation to the Court of Lucknow.

The receipt of these orders disturbed and perplexed the Governor-General. Arrangements for the orga-nisation of the Oude auxiliary force had already ad-vanced too far to admit of the suspension of the measure. It was a season, however, of difficulty and supposed danger, for the seeds of the Afghan war had been sown. Some, at least, of our regular troops in Oude were wanted to do our own work; so, in any view of the case, it was necessary to fill their places. The Auxiliary Force, therefore, was not to be arrested in its formation, but it was to be maintained at the Company's expense. Intimation to this effect was given to the King in a letter from the Governor-General, which, after acquainting his Majesty that the British Government had determined to relieve him of a burden which, in the existing state of the country, might have imposed heavier exactions on the people than they were well able to bear, ex-pressed a strong hope that the King would see, in the relaxation of this demand, good reason for apply-ing his surplus revenues firstly to the relief of oppressive taxation, and, secondly, to the prosecution of useful public works. But nothing was said, in this letter, about the abrogation of the entire treaty, nor was it desired that the Resident, in his conferences with the King or his minister, should say anything on that subject. The Governor-General, still hoping that the Home Government might be induced to consent to the terms of the treaty (the condition of the auxiliary force alone excluded), abstained from an acknowledgment which, he believed, would weaken the authority of his Government. But this was a mistake, and worse than a mistake. It betrayed an absence of moral courage not easily to be justified or forgiven. The Home Government never acknowledged the validity of any later treaty than that which Lord Wellesley had negotiated at the commencement of the century.

Such is the history of the treaty of 1837. It was never carried out in a single particular, and seldom heard of again until after a lapse of nearly twenty years, except in a collection of treaties into which it crept by mistake.* And, for some time, indeed,

---

* Much was attempted to be made out of this circumstance—but the mistake of an under Secretary cannot give validity to a treaty which the highest authorities refused to ratify. If Lord Auckland was unwilling to declare the nullity of the treaty because its nullification hurt the pride of his Government, the Home Government showed no such unwillingness, for, in 1838, the following return was made to Parliament, under the signature of one of the Secretaries of the Board of Control:

"There has been no treaty concluded with the present King of Oude, which has been ratified by the Court of Directors, with the approbation of the Commissioners for the affairs of India. (Signed) "R. GORDON.
"India Board, 3rd July, 1838."
It must, however, be admitted, on the other hand, that, years after this date, even in the Lucknow Residency, the treaty was held to be valid. In October, 1853, Colonel Sleeman wrote to Sir James Hogg: "The treaty of 1837 gives our Government ample authority to take the whole administration on ourselves." And again, in 1854, to Colonel Low: "Our Government would be fully authorised at any time to enforce the penalty prescribed in your treaty of 1837." This was doubly a mistake. The treaty was certainly not Low's.

K

1838-46. little was heard of Oude itself. A Native State is never so near to death, but that it may become quite hale and lusty again when the energies and activities of the British are engrossed by a foreign war. Now, it happened that, for some time to come, the British had quite a crop of foreign wars. First, the great Afghanistan war of Auckland, which made him wholly forgetful of Oude—her People and her King —her sorrows and her sensualities. Then there was the Sindh war of Ellenborough, intended to wash out by a small victory the stain of a great defeat, but fixing a still deeper stain upon the character of the nation ; and next the fierce Mahratta onslaught, which followed closely upon it. Then there was the invasion from beyond the Sutlej, and the first Sikh war, in which Hardinge was most reluctantly immersed. Altogether, some eight years of incessant war, with a prospect of further strife, kept the sword out of the scabbard and the portfolio out of the hand. Then Oude was safe in its insignificance and obscurity. Moreover, Oude was, as before, loyal and sympathising, and, although the hoardings of Saadut Ali had long since been squandered, there was still money in the Treasure-chests of Lucknow. But peace came, and with it a new birth of danger to the rulers of that misruled province. There had been no change for the better ; nay, rather there had been change for the worse, during the years of our conflicts beyond the frontier. One Prince had succeeded another only to emulate the vices of his ancestors with certain special variations of his own. And when Lord Hardinge, in the quiet interval between the two

1847. Sikh wars, turned his thoughts towards the kingdom of Oude, he found Wajid Ali Shah, then a young man in the first year of his reign, giving foul pro mise of sustaining the character of the Royal House.[*]

With the same moderation as had been shown by Lord William Bentinck, but also with the same strong sense of the paramount duty of the British Government to arrest the disorders which had so long been preying upon the vitals of the country, Lord Hardinge lifted up his voice in earnest remonstrance and solemn warning; and the young King cowered beneath the keen glance of the clear blue eyes that were turned upon him. There were no vague words in that admonition; no uncertain sound in their utterance. Wajid Ali Shah was distinctly told that the clemency of the British Government would allow him two years of grace; but that if at the end of that period of probation there were no manifest signs of improvement, the British Government could, in the interests of humanity, no longer righteously abstain from interfering peremptorily and absolutely for the introduction of a system of administration calculated to restore order and prosperity to the kingdom of Oude. The discretionary power had years before been placed in the hands of the Governor-General, and these admonitions failing, it would assuredly be exercised. A general outline of the means, by which the administration might be reformed, was laid down in a memorandum read aloud to the King; and it was added that, if his Majesty cordially entered into the plan, he might have the satisfaction,

---

[*] There was something in the number *seven* fatal to the Princes of Oude. Ghazee-ood-deen Hyder died in 1827; Nussur-ood-deen in 1837; and Umjid Ali Shah in 1847. The last named succeeded, in 1842, the old King, whom we had set up, and from whose better character there appeared at one time to be some hope of an improved administration. But, *capax imperii nisi imperasset*, he was, for all purposes of government, as incompetent as his predecessors. His besetting infirmity was avarice, and he seemed to care for nothing so long as the treasure-chest was full.

within the specified period of two years, of checking and eradicating the worst abuses, and, at the same time, of maintaining his own authority and the native institutions of his kingdom unimpaired—but that if he should adhere to his old evil ways, he must be prepared for the alternative and its consequences.

Nervous and excitable at all times, and greatly affected by these words, the King essayed to speak; but the power of utterance had gone from him. So he took a sheet of paper and wrote upon it, that he thanked the Governor-General, and would regard his counsels as though they had been addressed by a father to his son. There are no counsels so habitually disregarded; the King, therefore, kept his word. Relieved from the presence of the Governor-General his agitation subsided, and he betook himself, without a thought of the future, to his old courses. Fiddlers and dancers, singing men and eunuchs, were suffered to usurp the government and to absorb the revenues of the country. The evil influence of these vile panders and parasites was felt throughout all conditions of society and in all parts of the country. Sunk in the uttermost abysses of enfeebling debauchery, the King pushed aside the business which he felt himself incapable of transacting, and went in search of new pleasures. Stimulated to the utmost by unnatural excitements, his appetites were satiated by the debaucheries of the Zenana, and, with an understanding emasculated to the point of childishness, he turned to the more harmless delights of dancing, and drumming, and drawing, and manufacturing small rhymes. Had he devoted himself to these pursuits in private life, there would have been small harm in them, but overjoyed with his success as a musician, he went about the crowded streets of Lucknow with a big drum round his neck, striking as much noise out of it as he could, with all the extravagance of childish delight.

The two years of probation had passed away, and the British Resident reported that "the King had not, since the Governor-General's visit in October, 1847, shown any signs of being fully aware of the responsibility he incurred." "In fact," he added, "I do not think that his Majesty can ever be brought to feel the responsibilities of sovereignty strongly enough to be induced to bear that portion of the burden of its duties that must necessarily devolve upon him; he will always confide it to the worthless minions who are kept for his amusements, and enjoy exclusively his society and his confidence." So the time had arrived when the British Government might have righteously assumed the administration of Oude. The King had justly incurred the penalty, but the paramount power was in no haste to inflict it. Lord Dalhousie was Governor-General of India; but again the external conflicts of the British were the salvation of the sovereignty of Oude. The Punjab was in flames, and once more Lucknow was forgotten. The conquest of the Sikhs; the annexation of their country; the new Burmese war and its results; the lapses of which I have spoken in my last chapter; and many important affairs of internal administration of which I have yet to speak, occupied the ever-active mind of Lord Dalhousie until the last year of his reign; but it was felt by every one, who knew and pondered over the wretched state of the country, that the day of reckoning was approaching, and that the British Government could not much longer shrink from the performance of a duty imposed upon it by every consideration of humanity.

Colonel Sleeman was then Resident at Lucknow. He was a man of a liberal and humane nature, thoroughly acquainted with the character and feelings, the institutions and usages of the people of India. No man had a larger toleration for the short-comings of native Governments, because no one knew better how much our own political system had aggravated, if they had not produced, the evils of which we most complained. But he sympathised at the same time acutely with the sufferings of the people living under those native Governments; and his sympathy overcame his toleration. Having lived all his adult life in India—the greater part of it in, or on the borders of, the Native States—he was destitute of all overweening prepossessions in favour of European institutions and the "blessings of British rule." But the more he saw, on the spot, of the terrible effects of the misgovernment of Oude, the more convinced he was of the paramount duty of the British Government to step in and arrest the atrocities which were converting one of the finest provinces of India into a moral pesthouse. In 1849 and 1850 he made a tour through the interior of the country. He carried with him the prestige of a name second to none in India, as that of a friend of the poor, a protector of the weak, and a redresser of their wrongs. Conversing freely and familiarly in the native languages, and knowing well the character and the feelings of the people, he had a manner that inspired confidence, and the art of extracting from every man the information which he was best able to afford. During this tour in the interior, he noted down, from day to day, all the most striking facts which were brought to his notice, with the reflections which were suggested by them; and the whole presented a revolting picture of the worst type

of misrule—of a feebleness worse than despotism, of 1850.
an apathy more productive of human suffering than
the worst forms of tyrannous activity. In the absence
of all controlling authority, the strong carried on
everywhere a war of extermination against the weak.
Powerful families, waxing gross on outrage and rapine,
built forts, collected followers, and pillaged and murdered at discretion, without fear of justice overtaking
their crimes. Nay, indeed, the greater the criminal
the more sure he was of protection, for he could purchase immunity with his spoil. There was hardly,
indeed, an atrocity committed, from one end of the
country to the other, that was not, directly or indirectly, the result of the profligacy and corruption of
the Court.*

Such was Colonel Sleeman's report of the state of
the Oude country; such was his account of what he
had seen with his own eyes or heard with his own
ears. There was not a man in the Two Services who
was more distressed by the fury for annexation which

* "The Talookdars keep the country in a perpetual state of dis-turbance, and render life, property, and industry, everywhere insecure. Whenever they quarrel with each other, or with the local authorities of the Government, from whatever cause, they take to indiscriminate plunder and murder—over all lands not held by men of the same class—no road, town, village, or hamlet, is secure from their merciless attacks—robbery and murder become their diversion, their sport, and they think no more of taking the lives of men, women, and children, who never offended them, than those of deer and wild hogs. They not only rob and murder, but seize, confine, and torture all whom they seize, and suppose to have money or credit, till they ransom themselves with all they have, or can beg or borrow. Hardly a day has passed since I left Luck-now, in which I have not had abun-dant proof of numerous atrocities of this kind committed by landholders within the district through which I was passing, year by year, up to the present day." And again: " It is worthy of remark that these great landholders, who have recently ac-quired their possessions by the plun-der and the murder of their weaker neighbours, and who continue their system of plunder in order to ac-quire the means to maintain their gangs and add to their possessions, are those who are most favoured at Court, and most conciliated by the local rulers, because they are more able and more willing to pay for the favour of the one and set at defiance the authority of the other."—Slee-man's Diary.

was at that time breaking out in the most influential public prints and the highest official circles. He saw clearly the danger into which this grievous lust of dominion was hurrying us, and he made a great effort to arrest the evil;* but he lifted up a warning voice in vain. The letters which he addressed to the Governor-General and to the Chairman of the East India Company appear to have produced no effect. He did not see clearly, at that time, that the principles which he held in such abhorrence were cherished by Lord Dalhousie himself, and he did not know that the Court of Directors had such faith in their Governor-General that they were content to substitute his principles for their own. But, utterly distasteful to him as were the then prevailing sentiments in favour of absorption and confiscation, Sleeman never closed his eyes against the fact that interference in the affairs of Oude, even to the extent of the direct assumption of the government, would be a righteous interference. Year after year he had pressed upon the Governor-General the urgent necessity of the measure. But, perhaps, had he known in what manner his advice was destined to be followed, and how his authority would be asserted in justifica-

---

* See Sleeman's Correspondence, *passim*. *Exempli gratiá:* "In September, 1848, I took the liberty to mention to your Lordship my fears that the system of annexing and absorbing Native States—so popular with our Indian Services, and so much advocated by a certain class of writers in public journals—might some day render us too visibly dependent upon our Native Army; that they might see it, and that accidents might occur to unite them, or too great a portion of them, in some desperate act."—(*Colonel Sleeman to Lord Dalhousie*, April, 1852.) And again : " I deem such doctrines to be dangerous to our rule in India, and prejudicial to the best interests of the country. The people see that these annexations and confiscations go on, and that rewards and honorary distinctions are given for them and for the victories which lead to them, and for little else; and they are too apt to infer that they are systematic and encouraged and prescribed from home. The Native States I consider to be breakwaters, and when they are all swept away we shall be left to the mercy of our Native Army, which may not always be sufficiently under our control."—*Colonel Sleeman to Sir James Hogg*, January, 1853.

tion of an act which he could never countenance, he would rather have suffered the feeble-minded debauchee who was called King of Oude still to remain in undisturbed possession of the throne, than have uttered a word that might hasten a measure so at variance with his sense of justice, and so injurious as he thought to our best interests, as that of which the interference of Government eventually took the shape.

Sleeman's advice had been clear, consistent, unmistakable. "Assume the administration," he said, "but do not grasp the revenues of the country." Some years before the same advice had been given by Henry Lawrence,* between whom and Sleeman there was much concord of opinion and some similitude of character. The private letters of the latter, addressed to the highest Indian functionaries, and, therefore, having all the weight and authority of public documents, were as distinct upon this point as the most emphatic words could make them. "What the people want, and most earnestly pray for," he wrote to the Governor-General, "is that our Government should take upon itself the responsibility of governing them well and permanently. All classes, save the knaves, who now surround and govern the King, earnestly pray for this—the educated classes, because they would then have a chance of respectable employment, which none of them now have; the middle classes, because they find no protection or encouragement, and no hope that their children will be permitted to inherit

---

* "Let the management," he said, "be assumed under some such rules as those which were laid down by Lord William Bentinck. Let the administration of the country, as far as possible, be native. *Let not a rupee come into the Company's coffers.*" (The italics are Lawrence's.) "Let Oude be at last governed, not for one man, the King, but for him and his people."—*Calcutta Review*, vol. iii. (1845); and Lawrence's Essays, p. 132.

the property they leave, not invested in our Government Securities; and the humbler classes, because they are now abandoned to the merciless rapacity of the starving troops and other public establishments, and of the landholders driven or invited to rebellion by the present state of misrule." But he added: " I believe that it is your Lordship's wish that the whole of the revenues of Oude should be expended for the benefit of the Royal Family and People of Oude, and that the British Government should disclaim any wish to derive any pecuniary advantage from assuming to itself the administration." And again, about the same time, he had written to the Chairman of the Court of Directors, urging the expediency of assuming the administration, but adding: " If we do this, we must, in order to stand well with the rest of India, honestly and distinctly disclaim all interested motives, and appropriate the whole of the revenues for the benefit of the People and Royal Family of Oude. If we do this, all India will think us right." And again, a few months later, writing to the same high authority, he said, mournfully and prophetically, that to annex and confiscate the country, and to appropriate the revenues to ourselves, would "be most profitable in a pecuniary view, but most injurious in a political one. It would tend to accelerate the crisis which the doctrines of the absorbing school must sooner or later bring upon us."*

Such was the counsel Sleeman gave; such were the warnings he uttered. But he did not remain in India, nay, indeed he did not live, to see his advice ignored, his cautions disregarded. After long years of arduous and honourable service, compelled to retire in broken

* Private correspondence of Sir W. H. Sleeman, printed at the end of the English edition of his " Diary in Oude."

health from his post, he died on his homeward voyage, 1853.
leaving behind him a name second to none upon the
roll of the benefactors and civilisers of India, for he
had grappled with her greatest abomination, and had Thuggee.
effectually subdued it. Some solace had it been to
him when he turned his back upon the country to
know that his place would be well and worthily filled.
"Had your Lordship left the choice of a successor to
me," he wrote to the Governor-General, "I should September, 1854.
have pointed out Colonel Outram; and I feel very
much rejoiced that he has been selected for the office,
and I hope he will come as soon as possible."

An officer of the Company's army on the Bombay
establishment, James Outram had done good service
to his country, good service to the people of India,
on many different fields of adventure; and had risen,
not without much sore travail and sharp contention,
to a place in the estimation of his Government and
the affections of his comrades, from which he could
afford to look down upon the conflicts of the Past
with measureless calmness and contentment. Versed
alike in the stern severities of war and the civilising
humanities of peace, he was ready at a moment's
notice to lead an army into the field or to superintend
the government of a province. But it was in rough
soldier's work, or in that still rougher work of mingled
war and diplomacy which falls to the share of the Political officer in India, that Outram's great and good
qualities were most conspicuously displayed. For in
him, with courage of the highest order, with masculine energy and resolution, were combined the gentle-
ness of a woman and the simplicity of a child. No
man knew better how to temper power with mercy
and forbearance, and to combat intrigue and perfidy
with pure sincerity and stainless truth. This truth-

fulness was, indeed, perhaps the most prominent, as it was the most perilous, feature of his character. Whatsoever he might do, whatsoever he might say, the whole was there before you in its full proportions. He wore his heart upon his sleeve, and was incapable of concealment or disguise. A pure sense of honour, a strong sense of justice, the vehement assertions of which no self-interested discretion could hold in restraint, brought him sometimes into collision with others, and immersed him in a sea of controversy. But although, perhaps, in his reverential love of truth, he was over-eager to fight down what he might have been well content to live down, and in after life he may have felt that these wordy battles were very little worth fighting, he had still no cause to regret them, for he came unhurt from the conflict. It was after one of these great conflicts, the growth of serious official strife, which had sent him from an honourable post into still more honourable retirement, that, returning to India with strong credentials from his masters in Leadenhall-street, Lord Dalhousie selected him to succeed Sleeman as Resident at Lucknow.

The choice was a wise one. There was work to be done which required a hand at once gentle and strong. The fame of Outram was not the fame of a spoliator, but of a just man friendly to the native Princes and chiefs of India, who had lifted up his voice against wrongs done to them in his time, and who would rather have closed his public career than have been the agent of an unrighteous policy. But a measure which Low, and Sleeman, and Henry Lawrence had approved, nay, which in the interests of humanity they had strenuously recommended, was little likely to be an unrighteous one, and Outram, whilst rejoicing that his past career had thus been stamped by

his Government with the highest practical approval, 1854
accepted the offer in the full assurance that he could
fulfil its duties without a stain upon his honour or a
burden upon his conscience.*

Making all haste to join his appointment, Outram
quitted Aden, where the summons reached him, and
took ship for Calcutta, where he arrived in the first
month of the cold season. His instructions were soon November,
prepared for him; they were brief, but they suggested 1854.
the settled resolution of Government to wait no longer
for impossible improvements from within, but at once
to shape their measures for the assertion, in accordance with Treaty, of the authority of the Paramount State. But it was not a thing to be done in a
hurry. The measure itself was to be deliberately
carried out after certain preliminary formalities of
inquiry and reference. It was Outram's part to
inquire. A report upon the existing state of Oude
was called for from the new Resident, and before the
end of March it was forwarded to Calcutta. It was 1855.
an elaborate history of the misgovernment of Oude
from the commencement of the century, a dark cata-
logue of crime and suffering " caused by the culpable
apathy of the Sovereign and the Durbar." " I have
shown," said the new Resident, in conclusion, " that
the affairs of Oude still continue in the same state, if
not worse, in which Colonel Sleeman from time to time
described them to be, and that the improvement which
Lord Hardinge peremptorily demanded, seven years
ago, at the hands of the King, in pursuance of the
Treaty of 1801, has not, in any degree, been effected.
And I have no hesitation in declaring my opinion,

---

* I speak, of course, of the mere ing out the measure had not then
fact of the assumption of the ad- been decided.
ministration. The manner of carry-

1855. therefore, that the duty imposed on the British Government by that treaty, cannot any longer admit of
our 'honestly indulging the reluctance which the Government of India has felt heretofore to have recourse
to those extreme measures which alone can be of any
real efficiency in remedying the evils from which the
state of Oude has suffered so long.' "

To this report, and to much earlier information of
the same kind with which the archives of Government
were laden, the Governor-General gave earnest and
sustained attention amidst the refreshing quiet of the
Blue Mountains of Madras. The weighty document
had picked up, on its road through Calcutta, another
March 28,
1855. still more weighty, in the shape of a minute written
by General Low. Few as were the words, they exhausted all the arguments in favour of intervention,
and clothed them with the authority of a great name.
No other name could have invested them with this
authority, for no other man had seen so much of the
evils of native rule in Oude, and no man was on
principle more averse to the extinction of the native
dynasties of India. All men must have felt the case
to be very bad when John Low, who had spoken the
brave words in defence of the Princes and chiefs of
India which I have cited in the last chapter, was
driven to the forcible expression of his conviction
that it was the paramount duty of the British Government to interfere at once for the protection of
the people of Oude.*

* Low said that he was in favour of interference, "because the public and shameful oppressions committed on the people by Government officers in Oude have of late years been constant and extreme; because the King of Oude has continually, during many years, broken the Treaty by syste- matically disregarding our advice, instead of following it, or even endeavouring to follow it; because we are bound by *Treaty* (quite different in that respect from our position relatively to most of the great Native States) to prevent serious interior misrule in Oude; because it has

It was not possible to add much in the way of fact **1855.** to what Outram had compiled, or much in the way of argument to what Low had written. But Dalhousie, to whom the fine bracing air of the Neilgherries had imparted a new-born capacity for sustained labour, sat himself down to review the whole question in a gigantic minute. He signed it on the 18th June; and, indeed, it was his Waterloo—the crowning victory of annexation. It is not necessary to repeat the facts, for I have stated them, or the arguments, for I have suggested them. No reader can have followed me thus far, without a strong assurance on his mind that it would have been a grievous wrong done to humanity to have any longer abstained from interference. But what was the interference to be? Here was a question for the Governor-General to solve in the invigorating atmosphere of Ootacamund—a question, the solution of which was to yield the crowning measure of his long vice-regal career.

There may have been many ways of working out the practical details of this measure; but there was only one uncertain point which was of much substantial importance. All men agreed that the Treaty of 1801 might rightfully be declared to have ceased by reason of repeated violations, and that with the consent of the King, if attainable, or without it, if unattainable, the Government of the country might be transferred to the hands of European administrators. That the King must be reduced to a mere cypher was

been fully proved that we have not prevented it, and that we cannot prevent it by the present mode of conducting our relations with that State; and because no man of common sense can entertain the smallest expectation that the present King of Oude can ever become an efficient ruler of his country." And he added to these pungent sentences an expression of opinion that the unfulfilled threats of Lord Hardinge had increased the evil, inasmuch as that they had produced an impression in Oude that the Indian Government were restrained from interference by the orders of higher authority at home.

certain; it was certain that all possible respect ought to be shown to him in his fallen fortunes, and that he and all his family ought to be splendidly endowed; no question could well be raised upon these points. The question was, what was to be done with the surplus revenue after paying all the expenses of administration? Just and wise men, as has been shown, had protested against the absorption of a single rupee into the British Treasury. They said that it would be as politic as it would be righteous, to demonstrate to all the States and Nations of India, that we had not deposed the King of Oude for our own benefit— that we had done a righteous act on broad principles of humanity, by which we had gained nothing. But Lord Dalhousie, though he proposed not to annex the country, determined to take the revenues.

It is not very easy to arrive at a just conception of his views: "The reform of the administration," he said, "may be wrought, and the prosperity of the people may be secured, without resorting to so extreme a measure as the annexation of the territory and the abolition of the throne. I, for my part, therefore, do not recommend that the province of Oude should be declared to be British territory." But he proposed that the King of Oude, whilst retaining the sovereignty of his dominions, should "vest all power, jurisdiction, rights and claims thereto belonging, in the hands of the East India Company," and that the surplus revenues should be at the disposal of the Company. What this territorial sovereignty was to be, without territorial rights or territorial revenues, it is not easy to see. When the Newab of the Carnatic and the Rajah of Tanjore were deprived of their rights and revenues, they were held to be not territorial, but titular sovereigns. The Nizam, on the other hand, might properly be described as "territorial sovereign" of the Assigned Districts, although the administration had been taken from him, because an account of the revenue was to be rendered to him, and the surplus was to be paid into his hands. But the King of Oude, in Dalhousie's scheme, was to have had no more to do with his territories, than the titular sovereigns of the Carnatic and Tanjore; and yet he was to be told that he was "to retain the sovereignty of all the territories" of which he was then in possession.

Strictly interpreted to the letter, the scheme did not suggest the annexation of Oude. The province was not to be incorporated with the British dominions. The revenues were to be kept distinct from those of the empire; there was to be a separate balance-sheet; and thus far the province was to have a sort of integrity of its own. This is sufficiently intelligible in itself; and, if the balance being struck, the available surplus had been payable to the King of Oude, the rest of the scheme would have been intelligible also, for there would have been a quasi-sovereignty of the territories thus administered still remaining with the King. But the balance being payable into the British Treasury, it appears that Oude, in this state of financial isolation, would still have substantially been British territory, as much as if it had become a component part of the empire. Again, under the proposed system, Oude would have been beyond the circle of our ordinary legislation, in which respect it would not have differed much from other "Non-Regulation Provinces;" and if it had, even this Legislative segregation superadded to the Financial isolation of which I have spoken, would not have made it any the less British territory. The Channel Islands have a separate

L

Budget and distinct laws of their own, but still they are component parts of the British Empire, although they do not pay their surplus into the British Treasury. But in everything that really constitutes Kingship, the Bailiff of Jersey is as much the territorial sovereign of that island as Wajid Ali would have been territorial sovereign of Oude under Lord Dalhousie's programme of non-annexation.

But this transparent disguise was not to be worn; this distinction without a difference was not to be asserted, anywhere out of Lord Dalhousie's great Minute. The thing that was to be done soon came to take its proper place in the Councils of the Indian Empire as the Annexation of Oude; and it was as the annexation of Oude that the measure was considered by the Government at home. The Court of Directors consented to the annexation of Oude. The Board of Control consented to the annexation of Oude. The British Cabinet consented to the annexation of Oude. The word was not then, as it since has been, freely used in official documents, but it was in all men's minds, and many spoke it out bluntly instead of talking delicately about "assuming the Government of the Country." And, whether right or wrong, the responsibility of the measure rested as much with the Queen's Ministers as with the Merchant Company. That the Company had for long years shown great forbearance is certain. They had hoped against hope, and acted against all experience. So eager, indeed, had they been to give the native Princes of India a fair trial, that they had disallowed the proposed treaty of 1837, and had pronounced an authoritative opinion in favour of the maintenance of the then existing Native States of India. But twenty more years of misrule and anarchy had

raised in their minds a feeling of wondering self-
reproach at the thought of their own patience ; and
when they responded to the reference from Calcutta,
they said that the doubt raised by a survey of the
facts before them, was not whether it was then incumbent upon them to free themselves from the responsibility of any longer upholding such a Government, but whether they could excuse themselves for
not having, many years before, performed so imperative a duty.

The despatch of the Court of Directors was signed
in the middle of November. At midnight on the
2nd of January, the Governor-General mastered its
contents. Had he thought of himself more than of
his country he would not have been there at that
time. The energies of his mind were undimmed; but
climate, and much toil, and a heavy sorrow weighing
on his heart, had shattered a frame never constitutionally robust, and all men said that he was "breaking." Without any failure of duty, without any
imputation on his zeal, he might have left to his
successor the ungrateful task of turning into stern
realities the oft-repeated menaces of the British
rulers who had gone before him. But he was not
one to shrink from the performance of such a task
because it was a painful and unpopular one. He
believed that by no one could the duty of bringing
the Oude Government to solemn account be so fitly
discharged as by one who had watched for seven
years the accumulation of its offences, and seen the
measure of its guilt filled to the brim. He had intimated, therefore, to the Court of Directors his willingness to remain at his post to discharge this duty,
and in the despatch, which he read in the quiet of
that January night, he saw on official record the

1856.· alacrity with which his offer was accepted, and he girded himself for the closing act of his long and eventful administration.*

Next morning he summoned a Council. It was little more than a form. Dalhousie had waited for the authoritative sanction of the Home Government; but he knew that sanction was coming, and he was prepared for its arrival. The greater part of the work had, indeed, been already done. The instructions to be sent to the Resident; the treaty to be proposed to the King; the proclamation to be issued to the people had all been drafted. The whole scheme of internal government had been matured, and the agency to be employed had been carefully considered. The muster-roll of the new administration was ready, and the machinery was complete. The system was very closely to resemble that which had been tried with such good success in the Punjab, and its agents were, as in that province, to be a mixed body of civil and military officers, under a Chief Commissioner. All the weighty documents, by which the revolution was to be effected, were in the Portfolio of the Foreign Secretary; and now, at this meeting of the Council, they were formally let loose to do their work.

The task which Outram was commissioned to perform was a difficult, a delicate, and a painful one. He was to endeavour to persuade the King of Oude formally to abdicate his sovereign functions, and to make over, by a solemn treaty, the government of his territories to the East India Company. In the event of his refusal, a proclamation was to be issued, declaring the whole of Oude to be British territory.

* The Court of Directors to the Government of India, November 19, 1855. Paragraph 19.

By a man of Outram's humane and generous nature
no counsel from his Government was needed to
induce him to do the work entrusted to him in the
manner least likely to wound the feelings of the King.
But it was right that such counsel should be given.
It was given; but the decree of the Paramount State,
tempered as it might be by outward courtesy of manner, was still to be carried out, with stern and resolute action. No protests, no remonstrances, no promises, no prayers were to be suffered to arrest the
retributive measure for a day. It need not be added
that no resistance could avert it. A body of British
troops, sufficient to trample down all possible opposition, had been moved up into a position to overawe
Lucknow, and for the doomed Government of Oude
to attempt to save itself by a display of force would
have been only to court a most useless butchery.

Outram received his instructions at the end of
January. On the last day of the month he placed
himself in communication with the Oude Minister,
clearly stated the orders of the British Government,
and said that they were final and decisive. Four
days were spent in preliminary formalities and negotiations. In true Oriental fashion, the Court endeavoured to gain time, and, appealing to Outram,
through the aged Queen Mother—a woman with far
more of masculine energy and resolution than her
son—importuned him to persuade his Government to
give the King another trial, to wait for the arrival
of the new Governor-General, to dictate to Wajid Ali
any reforms to be carried out in his name. All this had
been expected; all this provided for. Outram had
but one answer; the day of trial, the day of forbearance was past. All that he could now do was to
deliver his message to the King.

On the 4th of February, Wajid Ali announced his willingness to receive the British Resident; and Outram, accompanied by his lieutenants, Hayes and Weston, proceeded to the palace. Strange and significant symptoms greeted them as they went. The guns at the palace-gates were dismounted. The palace-guards were unarmed. The guard of honour, who should have presented arms to the Resident, saluted him only with their hands. Attended by his brother and a few of his confidential Ministers, the King received the English gentlemen at the usual spot; and after the wonted ceremonies, the business commenced. Outram presented to the King a letter from the Governor-General, which contained, in terms of courteous explanation, the sentence that had been passed upon him, and urged him not to resist it. A draft of the proposed treaty was then placed in his hands. He received it with a passionate burst of grief, declared that treaties were only between equals; that there was no need for him to sign it, as the British would do with him and his possessions as they pleased; they had taken his honour and his country, and he would not ask them for the means of maintaining his life. All that he sought was permission to proceed to England, and cast himself and his sorrows at the foot of the Throne. Nothing could move him from his resolution not to sign the treaty. He uncovered his head; placed his turban in the hands of the Resident, and sorrowfully declared that title, rank, honour, everything were gone; and that now the British Government, which had made his grandfather a King, might reduce him to nothing, and consign him to obscurity.

In this exaggerated display of helplessness there was something too characteristically Oriental for any

part of it to be assigned to European prompting. But 1856.
if the scene had been got up expressly for an English
audience, it could not have been more cunningly contrived to increase the appearance of harshness and
cruelty with which the friends of the King were prepared to invest the act of dethronement. No man
was more likely than Outram to have been doubly
pained, in the midst of all his painful duties, by the
unmanly prostration of the King. To deal harshly
with one who declared himself so feeble and defenceless, was like striking a woman or a cripple. But
five millions of people were not to be given up, from
generation to generation, to suffering and sorrow,
because an effeminate Prince, when told he was no
longer to have the power of inflicting measureless
wrongs on his country, burst into tears, said that he
was a miserable wretch, and took off his turban instead of taking out his sword.

There was nothing now left for Outram but to
issue a proclamation, prepared for him in Calcutta,
declaring the province of Oude to be thenceforth, for
ever, a component part of the British Indian Empire.
It went forth to the people of Oude; and the people
of Oude, without a murmur, accepted their new
masters. There were no popular risings. Not a
blow was struck in defence of the native dynasty of
Oude. The whole population went over quietly to
their new rulers, and the country, for a time, was
outwardly more tranquil than before.

This was the last act of Lord Dalhousie's Ministry.
When he placed the Portfolio of Government in the
hands of Lord Canning, the British officers to whom
had been entrusted the work of reforming the administration of Oude, were discharging their prescribed duties with an energy which seemed to

1856. promise the happiest results. The King was still
obstinate and sullen. He persisted in refusing to
sign the treaty or to accept the proposed stipend of
£120,000 twelve lakhs; and though he had thought better of
the idea of casting himself at the foot of the British
Throne, he had made arrangements to send his nearest
kindred—his mother, his brother, and his son—to
England to perform a vicarious act of obeisance,
and to clamour for his rights.

With what result the administration, as copied
closely from the Punjabee system, was wrought out
in detail, will be shown at a subsequent stage of this
narrative. It was thought, as the work proceeded
in quietude and in seeming prosperity, that it was a
great success; and it gladdened the heart of the
Government in Leadenhall-street, to think of the
accomplishment of this peaceful revolution. But
that the measure itself made a very bad impression
on the minds of the people of India, is not to be
doubted; not because of the deposition of a King
who had abused his powers; not because of the introduction of a new system of administration for the
benefit of the people; but because the humanity of
the act was soiled by the profit which we derived
from it; and to the comprehension of the multitude
it appeared that the good of the people, which we
had vaunted whilst serving ourselves, was nothing
more than a pretext and a sham; and that we had
simply extinguished one of the few remaining Mahomedan States of India that we might add so
many thousands of square miles to our British territories, and so many millions of rupees to the revenues
of the British Empire in the East. And who, it was
asked, could be safe, if we thus treated one who had
ever been the most faithful of our allies?

CHAPTER IV.

DESTRUCTION OF THE NATIVE ARISTOCRACY — RETROSPECT OF REVENUE
ADMINISTRATION—THE SETTLEMENT OF THE NORTH-WEST PROVINCES—
THE OUSTING OF THE TALOOKHDARS—RESUMPTION OPERATIONS—THE
INAM COMMISSION—DECAY OF PRIESTLY POWER—SOCIAL REFORMS—
MORAL AND MATERIAL PROGRESS.

WHILST great principalities were thus being ab- 1806 1856.
sorbed and ancient sovereignties extinguished, a war
of extermination no less fatal in its effects, but more
noiseless in its operations, was being waged against
the nobility and gentry of the country. The original
proclamation of this war did not emanate from Lord
Dalhousie. The measures by which the native aristocracy were destroyed were not primarily his measures. It was the policy of the times to recognise
nothing between the Prince and the Peasant; a policy
which owed its birth not to one but to many; a policy,
the greatest practical exposition of which was the Settlement of the North-West Provinces. It was adopted
in pure good faith and with the most benevolent intentions. It had the sanction of many wise and good
men. It was not the policy by which such statesmen
as John Malcolm, George Clerk, and Henry Lawrence, sought to govern the people; but it was sanctified by the genius of John Lawrence, and of the
Gamaliel at whose feet he had sat, the virtuous, pure-
minded James Thomason.

To bring the direct authority of the British Government to bear upon the great masses of the people, without the intervention of any powerful section of their own countrymen—to ignore, indeed, the existence of all governing classes but the European officers, who carried out the behests of that Government—seemed to be a wise and humane system of protection. It was intended to shelter the many from the injurious action of the interests and the passions of the few. The utter worthlessness of the upper classes was assumed to be a fact; and it was honestly believed that the obliteration of the aristocracy of the land was the greatest benefit that could be conferred on the people. And thus it happened that whilst the native sovereigns of India were one by one being extinguished, the native aristocracy had become well-nigh extinct.

Doubtless, we started upon a theory sound in the abstract, intent only on promoting the greatest happiness of the greatest number; but if we had allowed ourselves to understand the genius and the institutions of the people, we should have respected the rights, natural and acquired, of all classes of the community, instead of working out any abstract theory of our own. It was in the very nature of things necessary, inevitable, that the extension of British rule, followed always by a reconstruction of the administration, and a substitution of civil and military establishments fashioned upon our own models and composed of our own people, should have deprived many of the chief people of their official rank and official emoluments, and cast them adrift upon the world, either to seek new fields of adventure in the unabsorbed Native States, or to fester into a disaffected and dangerous class sullenly biding their time. This

is an old story; an old complaint. Half a century
before the time of which I am now writing, it had
been alleged to be one of the main causes of that
national outburst in Southern India known as the
mutiny of Vellore. But this very necessity for the
extinction of the old race of high native functionaries,
often hereditary office-bearers, ought to have rendered us all the more desirous to perpetuate the
nobility whose greatness was derived from the Land.
It is true that the titles of the landed gentry whom
we found in possession were, in some cases, neither of
very ancient date nor of very unquestionable origin.
But, whatsoever the nature of their tenures, we found
them in the possession of certain rights or privileges
allowed to them by the Governments which we had
supplanted, and our first care should have been to
confirm and secure their enjoyment of them. We
might have done this without sacrificing the rights
of others. Indeed, we might have done it to the full
contentment of the inferior agricultural classes. But
many able English statesmen, especially in Upper
India, had no toleration for any one who might
properly be described as a Native Gentleman. They
had large sympathies and a comprehensive humanity,
but still they could not embrace any other idea of the
Native Gentry of India than that of an institution
to be righteously obliterated for the benefit of the
great mass of the people.

There were two processes by which this depression
of the privileged classes was effected. The one was
known by the name of a Settlement, the other was
called Resumption. It would be out of place here, if
I had the ability, to enter minutely into the difficult
question of landed tenures in India. It is an old story
now, that when that clever coxcomb, Victor Jacque-

mont, asked Holt Mackenzie to explain to him in a five minutes' conversation the various systems of Land Revenue obtaining in different parts of the country, the experienced civilian replied that he had been for twenty years endeavouring to understand the sub-ject and had not mastered it yet.   Such a rebuke ought to be remembered.   The little that I have to say on the subject shall be said with the least possible use of technical terms, and with the one object of making the general reader acquainted with the process by which the substance of the great landholders in Upper India was diminished by the action of the British Government.

Settlement
Operations.
· In the Literature of India the word "Settlement" is one of such frequent occurrence, and to the Indian resident it conveys such a distinct idea, that there is some danger of forgetting that the general reader may not be equally conversant with the exact meaning of the term.   It may therefore, perhaps, be advantageously explained that as the Indian Revenue is mainly derived from the land, it is of the first im-portance, on the acquisition of new territory, clearly to ascertain the persons from whom the Government dues are to be exacted, and the amount that is payable by each.   We may call it Rent or we may call it Revenue, it little matters.   The adjustment of the mutual relations between the Government and the agriculturists was known as the Settlement of the Revenue.   It was an affair of as much vital interest and concernment to the one as to the other, for to be charged with the payment of the Revenue was to be acknowledged as the proprietor of the land.

When we first took possession of the country ceded by the Newab-Wuzeer of Oude, or conquered from the Mahrattas, all sorts of proprietors presented themselves, and our officers, having no special theories and no overriding prejudices, were willing to consider the claims of all, whether small or great holders, whom they found in actual possession; and brief settlements or engagements were made with them, pending a more thorough investigation of their rights. There was, doubtless, at first a good deal of ignorance on our part, and a good deal of wrong-doing and usurpation on the part of those with whom we were called upon to deal. But the landed gentry of these Ceded and Conquered Provinces, though they suffered by the extension of the British Raj, were not deliberately destroyed by a theory. It was the inevitable tendency of our Regulations, especially of that great Mystery of Iniquity, the Sale Law, and of the immigration of astute native functionaries from the Lower Provinces, which inaugurated our rule, to subvert the supremacy of the old landholders. Under the system, which we introduced, men who had been proprietors of vast tracts of country as far as the eye could reach, shrivelled into tenants of mud-huts and possessors only of a few cooking-pots. The process, though certain in its results, was gradual in its operation; and the ruin which it entailed was incidental, not systematic. It was ignorantly suffered, not deliberately decreed. But, at a later period, when a new political creed had grown up among our British functionaries in India, and upon officers of this new school devolved the duty of fixing the relations of the agricultural classes with the British Government, the great besom of the Settlement swept out the remnant of the landed gentry from their baronial possessions, and a race of peasant-proprietors were recognised as the legitimate inheritors of the soil.

How this happened may be briefly stated. A Per-

1806-56.   manent Settlement on the Bengal model had been
talked of, ordered and counter-ordered; but for nearly
a third part of a century, under a series of brief
engagements with holders of different kinds, uncertainty and confusion prevailed, injurious both to the
Government and to the People.   But in the time
1833.   of Lord William Bentinck an order went forth for
the revision of this system or no-system, based upon
a detailed survey and a clearly recorded definition of
rights, and what is known in History as the Settlement of the North-West Provinces, was then formally
commenced.

That it was benevolently designed and conscientiously executed, is not to be doubted.   But it was
marred by a Theory.   In the pursuit of right, the
framers of the settlement fell into wrong.   Striving
after justice, they perpetrated injustice.   Nothing
1845.   could be sounder than the declared principle that " it
was the duty of the Government to ascertain and protect all existing rights, those of the poor and humble
villager as well as those of the rich and influential
Talookhdar."*   It was said that this principle had
been not only asserted, but acted upon.   But the fact
is, that the practice halted a long way behind the
principle.   Such were the feelings with which many of
our officers regarded the great landholders, that equal
justice between the conflicting claims and interests
of the two classes was too often ignored.   There
were scales over the eyes of commonly clear-sighted
men when they came to look at this question in the
face, and therefore the "poor and humble villager"

* See letter of Mr. John Thorn-   undeniable truth, that "in so far as
ton, Secretary to Government, North-   this is done with care and diligence
West Provinces, to Mr. H. M. El-   will the measure be successful in
liot, Secretary to Board of Revenue,   placing property on a healthy and
April 30, 1845.   It is added, with   sound footing."

had a full measure of justice, pressed down and running over, whilst the "rich and influential Talookhdar" had little or none.

There are few who have not become familiar with this word *Talookhdar*; who do not know that an influential class of men so styled in virtue of certain rights or interests in the land, were dispossessed of those rights or interests and reduced to absolute ruin. It must be understood, however, that the proprietary rights of which I speak were very different from the rights of landed property in England. The Talookhdar was little more than an hereditary revenue-contractor. His right was the right to all the just rents paid by the actual occupants, after satisfaction of the Government claims. His property was the rent *minus* the revenue of a particular estate. This Talookhdaree right, or right of collection, was distinct from the Zemindaree right, or proprietary right in the soil. The Talookhdar, who paid to Government the revenue of a large cluster of villages, had, perhaps, a proprietary right in some of these small estates; perhaps, in none. The proprietary right, in most instances, lay with the village communities. And it was the main effort of the English officers, engaged in the Settlement of the North-West Provinces, to bring these village occupants into direct relations with the Government, and to receive from them the amount of the assessment fixed upon their several estates.

Now it was a just and fitting thing that the rights of these village proprietors should be clearly defined. But it was not always just that the Government should enter into direct engagements with them and drive out the intervening Talookhdar. The actual occupants might, in a former generation, have been a consequence only of a pre-existing Talookhdaree right, as in cases where cultivators had been located on waste lands by a contractor or grantee of the State; or the Talookhdar might have acquired his position by purchase, by favour, perhaps by fraud, after the location of the actual occupants; still it was a proprietary interest, perhaps centuries old. Let us explain their position as we may, these Talookhdars constituted the landed aristocracy of the country; they had recognised manorial rights; they had, in many instances, all the dignity and power of great feudal barons, and, doubtless, often turned that power to bad account. But whether for good or for evil, in past years, we found them existing as a recognised institution; and it was at the same time a cruel wrong and a grievous error to sweep it away as though it were an incumbrance and an usurpation.

The theory of the Settlement officers was that the village Zemindars had an inalienable right in the soil, and that the Talookhdar was little better than an upstart and an impostor. All the defects in his tenure were rigidly scanned; all the vices of his character were violently exaggerated. He was written down as a fraudulent upstart and an unscrupulous oppressor. To oust a Talookhdar was held by some young Settlement officers to be as great an achievement as to shoot a tiger; and it was done, too, with just as clear a conviction of the benefit conferred upon the district in which the animal prowled and marauded. It was done honestly, conscientiously, laboriously, as a deed entitling the doer to the gratitude of mankind. There was something thorough in it that wrung an unwilling admiration even from those who least approved. It was a grand levelling system, reducing everything to first principles and a delving Adam. Who was a gentle- man and a Talookhdar, they asked, when these time-honoured Village Communities were first established on the soil? So the Settlement Officer, in pursuit of the great scheme of restitution, was fain to sweep out the Landed Gentry and to applaud the good thing he had done.*

And if one, by happy chance, was brought back by a saving hand, it was a mercy and a miracle; and the exception which proved the rule. The chances against him were many and great, for he had divers ordeals to pass through, and he seldom survived them all. It was the wont of many Settlement officers to assist the solution of knotty questions of proprietary right by a reference to personal character and conduct, so that when the claims of a great Talookhdar could not be altogether ignored, it was declared that he was a rogue or a fool—perhaps, an atrocious compound of both—and that he had forfeited, by oppressions and cruelties, or by neglects scarcely less cruel, all claim to the compassion of the State. They gave the man a bad name, and straight-way they went out to ruin him. A single illustration will suffice. One of the great landholders thus consigned to perdition was the Rajah of Mynpooree. Of an old and honoured family, distinguished for loyalty and good service to the British Government, he was the Talookhdar of a large estate comprising nearly two hundred villages, and was amongst the most influential of the landed aristocracy of that part of the country. The Settlement officer was one of

---

* In sober official language, described by Lieutenant-Governor Robertson as "the prevailing, and perhaps excessive, readiness to reduce extensive properties into minute portions, and to substitute, whenever there was an opportunity, a village community for an individual landholder."

the ablest and best of his class. Fulfilling the great
promise of his youth, he afterwards attained to the
highest post in those very Provinces, an eminence
from which he might serenely contemplate the fact
that the theory of the Dead-Level is against nature,
and cannot be enforced without a convulsion. But,
in the early days of which I am speaking, a great
Talookhdar was to him what it was to others of the
same school; and he represented that the Rajah,
himself incompetent almost to the point of imbecility,
was surrounded by agents of the worst character,
who in his name had been guilty of all kinds of
cruelty and oppression. Unfit as he was said to be
for the management of so large an estate, it would,
according to the prevailing creed, have been a
righteous act to exclude him from it; but it was
necessary, according to rule, to espy also a flaw in
his tenure; so it was found that he had a just proprietary right in only about a fourth of the two
hundred villages.* It was proposed, therefore, that
his territorial greatness should to this extent be
shorn down in the future Settlement, and that the
bulk of the property should be settled with the village communities, whose rights, whatever they might
originally have been, had lain for a century in
abeyance.

Above the Settlement officer, in the ascending
scale of our Administrative Agency, was the Commissioner; above the Commissioner, the Board of
Revenue; above the Board of Revenue, the Lieutenant-Governor. In this cluster of graduated authorities the Old and New School alternated like the
Black and White of a chess-board. The recommen-

---

* The exact number was 189, of
which it was ruled that the Rajah
could justly be recorded as proprietor only of 51. A money-compensation, in the shape of a per-
centage, was to be given him for the
loss of the rest.

dations of George Edmonstone were stoutly opposed by Robert Hamilton. The sharp, incisive logic of the Commissioner cut through the fallacious reasoning of the Settlement officer. "He was of opinion that the value of landed possessions and the importance attached to them could never be made up by a money allowance; that the imbecility of the Rajah, if affording a justification for his being relieved from the management of his estate, could be none for depriving his family of their inheritance; and that it was inconsistent to denounce as oppressive in a native ruler the same measures of sale and dispossession which were adopted by our own Government towards Revenue defaulters."* But the Board, of which the living principle was Robert Bird, dissented from the views of the Commissioner, and upheld the levelling processes of the Settlement officer. Then Lieutenant-Governor Robertson appeared upon the scene, and the decision of the Board was flung back upon them as the unjust growth of a vicious, generalising system, which would break up every large estate in the country into minute fractions, and destroy the whole aristocracy of the country. He could not see that, on the score either of invalidity of tenure or of administrative incapacity, it would be just to pare down the Rajah's estate to one-fourth of its ancestral dimensions; so he ruled that the settlement of the whole ought rightly to be made with the Talookhdar.† But the vicissitudes of the case were not even then at an

---

* Despatch of Court of Directors, August 13, 1851.

† "The Lieutenant-Governor recorded his opinion, that no proof of the Rajah's mismanagement, such as could justify his exclusion, had been adduced; that the evidence in support of the proprietary claims of the Zemindars was insufficient and inconclusive; that if the Zemindars ever possessed the rights attributed to them, they had not been in the active enjoyment of them for upwards of a century, while the Rajah's claims had been admitted for more than four generations; that, admitting the inconvenience which might sometimes result from the recognition of

1836-46.

end. The opposition of the Board caused some delay in the issue of the formal instructions of Government for the recognition of the Talookhdar, and before the settlement had been made with the Rajah, Robertson had resigned his post to another. That other was a man of the same school, with no greater passion than his predecessor for the subversion of the landed gentry; but sickness rendered his tenure of office too brief, and, before the close of the year, he was succeeded by one whose name is not to be mentioned without respect—the honoured son of an honoured father—the much-praised, much-lamented Thomason. He was as earnest and as honest as the men who had gone before him; but his strong and sincere convictions lay all in the other way. He was one of the chief teachers in the New School, and so strong was his faith in its doctrines that he regarded, with feelings akin to wondering compassion, as men whom God had given over to a strong delusion that they should believe a lie, all who still cherished the opinions which he had done so much to explode.*

Mr. George Clerk.

1844.

Mr. Thomason.

the superior malgoosar, it would not be reconcilable with good feeling or justice to deal as the Board proposed to do, with one found in actual and long-acknowledged possession. He condemned the practice of deciding cases of this nature on one invariable and generalising principle; stated that he could discover no sufficient reason for excluding the Rajah of Mynpooree from the management of any of the villages composing the Talook of Minchunnah; and finally withheld his confirmation of the settlement concluded with the village Zemindars, directing the engagements to be taken from the Talookhdar."—*Despatch of Court of Directors, August* 13, 1851.

* See, for example, his reflections on the contumacy of Mr. Boulderson, of whom Mr. Thomason says: "With much honesty of principle he is possessed of a constitution of mind which prevents him from readily adopting the principles of others, or acting upon their rules. A great part of his Indian career has been passed in opposition to the prevailing maxims of the day, and he finds himself conscientiously adverse to what has been done." With respect to these prevailing maxims, Mr. F. H. Robinson, of the Civil Service, in a pamphlet published in 1855, quotes the significant observation of an old Ressaldar of Gardener's Horse, who said to him: "No doubt the wisdom of the new gentlemen had shown them the folly and the ignorance of the gentlemen of the old time, on whom it pleased God, nevertheless, to bestow the government of India."

Supreme in the North-West Provinces, he found the
case of the Mynpooree Rajah still formally before the
Government. No final orders had been issued, so he
issued them. The besom of the Settlement swept the
great Talookhdar out of three-fourths of the estate,
and the village proprietors were left to engage with
Government for all the rest in his stead.

It is admitted now, even by men who were personally concerned in this great work of the Settlement
of Northern India, that it involved a grave political
error. It was, undoubtedly, to convert into bitter
enemies those whom sound policy would have made
the friends and supporters of the State. Men of the
Old School had seen plainly from the first that by these
measures we were sowing broadcast the seeds of future
trouble. ·Foremost among these was the veteran Director Tucker, who had been engaged in the first settlement of the Ceded and Conquered Provinces, and
who knew as well as any man what rights existed on
our original assumption of the government of those
territories. "The way to conciliate the peasantry,"
he wrote, "or to improve their condition, is not, I
think, by dissolving the connexion between them and
the superior Talookhdars, or village Zemindars. The
one we have, I fear, entirely displaced; but we cannot
destroy the memory of their past or the consciousness
of their present state. They were once prosperous,
and they and their descendants must feel that they are
no longer so. They are silent, because the natives of
India are accustomed to endure and to submit to the
will of their rulers; but if an enemy appear on our
Western frontier, or if an insurrection unhappily take
place, we shall find these Talookhdars, I apprehend,
in the adverse ranks, and their ryots and retainers
ranged under the same standard." And a quarter of

a century later, one who had received the traditions of this school unbroken from Thomas Campbell Robertson, at whose feet he had sat, wrote that he had long been pointing out that, "although the old families were being displaced fast, we could not destroy the memory of the past, or dissolve the ancient connexion between them and their people; and said distinctly that, in the event of any insurrection occurring, we should find this great and influential body, through whom we can alone hope to keep under and control the rural masses, ranged against us on the side of the enemy, with their hereditary followers and retainers rallying around them, in spite of our attempts to separate their interests." "My warnings," he added, "were unheeded, and I was treated as an alarmist, who, having hitherto served only in the political department of the State, and being totally inexperienced in Revenue matters, could give no sound opinion on the subject."[*]

Treatment of the native gentry.

Warnings of this kind were, indeed, habitually disregarded; and the system, harsh in itself, was carried out, in some cases harshly and uncompromisingly, almost indeed as though there were a pleasure in doing it. It is true that men deprived of their vested interests in great estates were recommended for money-payments direct from the Treasury; but this was no compensation for the loss of the land, with all the dignity derived from manorial rights and baronial privileges, and it was sometimes felt to be an insult. It was not even the fashion in those days to treat the Native Gentry with personal courtesy and conciliation. Some of the great masters

[*] Personal Adventures during the Indian Rebellion. By William Edwards, B.C.S., Judge of Benares, and late Magistrate and Collector of Budaon, in Rohilcund.

of the school, men of the highest probity and benevolence, are said to have failed in this with a great
failure, as lamentable as it was surprising. "In the
matter of discourtesy to the native gentry," wrote
Colonel Sleeman to John Colvin, "I can only say
that Robert Mertins Bird insulted them, whenever
he had an opportunity of doing so; and that Mr.
Thomason was too apt to imitate him in this as
in other things. Of course their example was followed by too many of their followers and admirers."[*]

And whilst all this was going on, there was another
process in active operation by which the position of
the privileged classes was still further reduced.
There is not one of the many difficulties, which the
acquisition of a new country entails upon us, more
serious than that which arises from the multiplicity
of privileges and prescriptions, territorial and official,
which, undetermined by any fixed principle, have
existed under the native Government which we have
supplanted. Even at the outset of our administrative
career it is difficult to deal with these irregular
claims, but the difficulty is multiplied tenfold by
delay. The action of our Government in all such
cases should be prompt and unvarying. Justice or
Injustice should be quick in its operation and equal
in its effects. Accustomed to revolutions of empire
and mutations of fortune, the native mind readily
comprehends the idea of confiscation as the immediate result of conquest. Mercy and forbearance at
such time are not expected, and are little understood.
The descent of the strong hand of the conqueror upon
all existing rights and privileges is looked for with a

---

[*] See Correspondence annexed to
published edition of Sleeman's Oude
Diary. I have been told by men
whose authority is entitled to respect, that the statement is to be
received with caution.

1-46.   feeling of submission to inevitable fate; and at such
a time no one wonders, scarcely any one complains,
when the acts of a former Government are ignored,
and its gifts are violently resumed.

Under former Governments, and indeed, in the
earlier days of our own, there had been large alienations of revenue in favour of persons who had rendered
good service to the State, or had otherwise acquired
the favour of the rulers of the land.   These rent-free
tenures were of many different kinds.   A volume
might be filled with an account of them.   Some were
burdened with conditions; some were not.   Some
were personal life-grants; some were hereditary and
perpetual.   Some were of old standing; some were
of recent origin.   Some had been fairly earned or
justly acquired ; others were the vile growth of fraud
and corruption.   They varied no less in the circumstances of their acquisition than in their intrinsic
character and inherent conditions.   But anyhow they
were for some time a part of our system, and had
come to be regarded as the rights of the occupants.
Every year which saw men in undisturbed possession seemed to strengthen those rights.   An inquiry,
at the outset of our career of administration, into the
validity of all such tenures would have been an intelligible proceeding.   Doubtless, indeed, it was expected.   But years passed, and the danger seemed to
have passed with them.   Nay, more, the inactivity,
seemingly the indifference of the British Government,
with respect to those whom we found in possession,
emboldened others to fabricate similar rights, and to
lay claim to immunities which they had never enjoyed under their native masters.

1   In Bengal this manufacture of rent-free tenures

was carried on to an extent that largely diminished **1836-46.**
the legitimate revenue of the country. A very considerable portion of these tenures was the growth of
the transition-period immediately before and immediately after our assumption of the Dewanee, or
Revenue - Administration, of Bengal, Behar, and
Orissa. At the time of the great Permanent Set- **1793.**
tlement the rent-free holders were called upon to
register their claims to exemption from the payment
of the Government dues, and their grounds of exemption; and as they still remained in possession, they
believed that their rights and privileges had been
confirmed to them. The Permanent Settlement,
indeed, was held to be the Magna Charta of the
privileged classes; and for more than forty years
men rejoiced in their freeholds, undisturbed by any
thoughts of invalidity of title or insecurity of
tenure.

But after this lapse of years, when Fraud itself **Resumption**
might reasonably have pleaded a statute of limita- **operations.**
tions, the English revenue-officer awoke to a sense of
the wrongs endured by his Government. So much
revenue alienated; so many worthless sinecurists
living in indolent contentment at the cost of the State,
enjoying vast privileges and immunities, to the injury
of the great mass of the People. Surely it was a
scandal and a reproach! Then well-read, clever
secretaries, with a turn for historical illustration, discovered a parallel between this grievous state of
things in Bengal and that which preceded the great
revolution in France, when the privileges of the old
nobility pressed out the very life of the nation, until
the day of reckoning and retribution came, with a
more dire tyranny of its own. Viewed in this light,

it was held to be an imperative duty to Colbertise the Lakhirajdars of the Lower Provinces.* So the resumption-officer was let loose upon the land. Titles were called for; proofs of validity were to be established, to the satisfaction of the Government functionary. But in families, which seldom last a generation without seeing their houses burnt down, and in a climate, which during some months of the year is made up of incessant rains, and during others of steamy exhalations—where the devouring damp, and the still more devouring insect, consume all kinds of perishable property, even in stout-walled houses, it would have been strange if genuine documentary evidence had been forthcoming at the right time. It was an awful thing, after so many years of undisturbed possession, to be called upon to establish proofs, when the only proof was actual incumbency. A reign of terror then commenced. And if, when thus threatened, the weak Bengalee had not sometimes betaken himself in self-defence to the ready weapons of forgery, he must have changed his nature under the influence of his fears. That what ensued may properly be described as wholesale confiscation is not to be doubted. Expert young revenue-officers settled scores of cases in a day; and families, who had held possession of inherited estates for long years, and never doubted the security of their tenure, found

* "In a memoir of the Great Colbert I read the following words, which are exactly descriptive of the nature of the pretensions of the great mass of the Lakhirajdars, and of the present measures of the Government: 'Under the pernicious system which exempted the nobility from payment of direct taxes, a great number of persons had fraudulently assumed titles and claimed rank, while another class had obtained immunity from taxation by the prostitution of Court favour, or the abuse of official privileges. These cases Colbert caused to be investigated, and those who failed in making out a legal claim to immunity were compelled to pay their share of the public burdens, to the relief of the labouring classes, on whom nearly the whole weight of taxation fell.'"—See *Letters of* GAUNTLET, *addressed to the Calcutta Papers of* 1838.

themselves suddenly deprived of their freeholds and compelled to pay or to go. That the State had been largely defrauded, at some time or other, is more than probable. Many, it is admitted, were in possession who had originally no good title to the exemption they enjoyed. But many also, whose titles were originally valid, could produce no satisfactory evidence of their validity; so the fraudulent usurper and the rightful possessor were involved in one common ruin.

The success of these operations was loudly vaunted at the time. A social revolution had been accomplished, to the manifest advantage of the State, and at no cost, it was said, of popular discontent. The Bengalee is proverbially timid, patient, and long-suffering. But there were far-seeing men who said, even at that time, that though a strong Government might do this with impunity in those lower provinces, they must beware how they attempt similar spoliation in other parts of India, especially in those from which the Native Army was recruited. If you do, it was prophetically said, you will some day find yourselves holding India only with European troops. The probability of alienating by such measures the loyalty of the military classes was earnestly discussed in the European journals of Calcutta;* and it was said, by those who defended the measure, that it was not intended to extend these resumption operations to other

* The following, written a quarter of a century ago, affords a curious glimpse of the apprehensions even then entertained by far-seeing men: " We would just hint by the way to those who have planned this very extraordinary attack upon vested rights, that the Sepoys are almost all landholders, many of them Brahmins, whose families are supported by the charitable foundations which it is now sought to confiscate and destroy. The alarm has not yet, we believe, spread to the Army, but it has not been without its causes of complaints; and we would very calmly and respectfully put it to our rulers, whether it is wise or prudent to run the risk to which this Resumption measure would sooner or later in-

1836-46.   parts' of the country. But scarcely any part of the country escaped; scarcely any race of men, holding rent-free estates of any kind, felt secure in the possession of rights and privileges which they had enjoyed under Mogul and Mahratta rule, and had believed that they could still enjoy under the Raj of the Christian ruler.

North-West Provinces.   In the North-West Provinces it was part of the duty of the Settlement officer to inquire into rent-free tenures, and to resume or to release from assessment the lands thus held. The feelings with which the task imposed upon him was regarded varied with the character and the opinions of the functionary thus employed; but whilst those who were disposed to look compassionately upon doubtful claims, or believed that it would be sound policy to leave men in undisturbed possession even of what might have been in the first instance unrighteously acquired, were few, the disciples of Bird and Thomason, who viewed all such alienations of revenue as unmixed evils, and considered that any respect shown to men who were described as " drones who do no good in the public hive" was an injury done to the tax-paying community at large, were many and powerful, and left their impression on the land. Rejoicing in the great principle of the Dead-Level, the Board commonly supported the views of the resumptionist; and but for the intervention of Mr. Robertson, the Lieutenant-

fallibly lead. The native soldier has long been in the habit of placing implicit reliance upon British faith and honour; but let the charm once be broken, let the confiscation of rent-free land spread to those provinces out of which our Army is recruited, and the consequences may be that we shall very soon have to trust for our security to British troops alone. The Government may then learn rather late that revenue is not the only thing needful, and that their financial arithmetic, instead of making twice two equal to one, as Swift says was the case in Ireland, may end by extracting from the same process of multiplication just nothing at all."—*Englishman, November* 2, 1838.

Governor, there would scarcely, at the end of the Settlement operations, have been a rent-free tenure in the land. There was sometimes a show of justice on the side of resumption, for the immunity had been granted, in the first instance, as payment for service no longer demanded, or what had been originally merely a life-grant had assumed the character of an hereditary assignment. Perhaps there was sometimes more than suspicion that in unsettled times, when there was a sort of scramble for empire, privileges of this kind had been fabricated or usurped; but in other instances strong proofs of validity were ignored, and it has been freely stated, even by men of their own order, that these earnest-minded civilians "rejected royal firmans and other authentic documents," and brought upon the great rent-roll of the Company lands which had been for many generations free from assessment. Nay, even the highest authority, in the great Settlement epoch, declared that "the Settlement officer swept up, without inquiry, every patch of unregistered land; even those exempted by a subsequent order, which did not come out until five-sixths of the tenures had been resumed." In one district, that of Furruckabad, "the obligations of a treaty and the direct orders of Government were but lightly dealt with; and in all, a total disregard was evinced for the acts even of such men as Warren Hastings and Lord Lake."* In every case what was done was done conscientiously, in the assured belief that it was for the general good of the people; but the very knowledge that was most vaunted, a knowledge of the institutions and the temper of the natives,

* Minute of Mr. Robertson, Lieutenant-Governor of the North-West Provinces, quoted in Despatch of the Court of Directors, August 13, 1851.

was that which they most lacked. They were wrecked upon the dangerous coast of Little Learning.

There were, however, it has been said, some men engaged in those great Settlement operations who were not smitten with this unappeasable earth-hunger, and who took altogether another view both of the duty and of the policy of the State. Mr. Mansel, of whose eager desire, so honourably evinced at a later period, to uphold the Native States of India I have already spoken, was the principal exponent of these exceptional opinions. "If it be of importance," he wrote, in his Report on the Settlement of the Agra District, "to conciliate the affections of the people, as well as to govern by the action of naked penal laws; if it be important that the natural tendency of every part of native society in these provinces, to sink into one wretched level of poverty and ignorance, should, as a principle, be checked as far as possible by the acts of Government; if it be important that the pride of ancestry and nobility, the valour of past times, and the national character of a country, should be cherished in recollection, as ennobling feelings to the human mind, I know of no act to which I could point with more satisfaction, as a zealous servant of Government, than the generous manner in which the restoration of the family of the Buddawar Rajah to rank and fortune was made by the Lieutenant-Governor of Agra; and I cannot refrain from allowing myself to echo, for the inhabitants of this part of the country, that feeling, in a report of necessity, largely connected with the welfare and happiness of the district of Agra." Mr. Robertson had granted the Buddawar Jagheer to the adopted son of the deceased Rajah, and it was the recognition of this adoption which so rejoiced the heart of the sympathising Settlement officer.

As the events of which I am about to write occurred, 1817-52.
for the most part, in Northern India, it is to the disturbing causes in that part of the country that the introductory section of this book is mainly devoted. But before it passes altogether away from the subject of Resumption, something should be said about the operations of that great confiscatory Tribunal known as the Inam Commission of Bombay. This was but *The Inam Commission* the supplement of a series of measures, of which it *of Bombay* would take a long time to write in detail. A great part of the territory, now constituting the Presidency of Bombay, was in 1817 conquered from the Peishwah. With conquest came the old difficulty, of which I have spoken*—the difficulty of dealing with the privileges and prescriptions, the vested interests of all kinds, territorial and official, derived from the Mahratta Government. As in Bengal and in the North-Western Provinces, these difficulties were greatly aggravated by delay. Had we instituted a searching inquiry at once, and resumed every doubtful tenure; had we cancelled even the undoubted grants of former governments, and suddenly annulled all existing privileges, such proceedings in the eyes of the people would have been the intelligible tyranny of the conqueror, and, at all events, in accordance with the custom of the country. But our very desire to deal justly and generously with these privileged classes generated delaid and unequal action. At different times, and in different parts of Western India, these old alienations of Revenue were dealt with after different fashions; and it was a source of bitter discontent that, under like circumstances, claims were settled by Government with far greater rigour in one part of the country than in another.

* *Ante,* page 167.

1852.   Years passed, various regulations were framed, for
the most part of restricted operation; and still, after
the country had been for more than a third of a
century under British rule, the great question of
alienated revenue had only been partially adjusted.
So in 1852 an act was passed, which empowered a
little body of English officers, principally of the
military profession—men, it was truly said, "not
well versed in the principles of law, and wholly un-
practised in the conduct of judicial inquiries"—to
exercise arbitrary jurisdiction over thousands of
estates, many of them held by men of high family,
proud of their lineage, proud of their ancestral privileges, who had won what they held by the sword, and
had no thought by any other means of maintaining
possession. In the Southern Mahratta country there
were large numbers of these Jagheerdars, who had
never troubled themselves about title-deeds, who
knew nothing about rules of evidence, and who had
believed that long years of possession were more
cogent than any intricacies of law. If they had ever
held written proofs of the validity of their tenures,
they had seldom been so provident as to preserve
them. But, perhaps, they had never had better proof
than the memory of a fierce contest, in the great
gurdee-ka-wukht, or time of trouble, which had pre-
luded the dissolution of the Mahratta power in
Western India, and placed the white man on the
Throne of the Peishwah.* Year after year had

* See the admirably-written memorial of Mr. G. B. Seton-Karr:
"Chiefs, who had won their estates
by the sword, had not been careful
to fence them in with a paper barrier,
which they felt the next successful
adventurer would sweep away as un-
ceremoniously as themselves. Instead of parchments, they transmitted arms and retainers, with
whose aid they had learnt to consider mere titles superfluous, as without it they were contemptible. In
other instances, men of local influence and energetic character
having grasped at the lands which
lay within their reach in the general
scramble which preceded the down-

passed, one generation had followed another in undisturbed possession, and the great seal of Time stood
them in stead of the elaborate technicalities of the
Conveyancer.   But the Inam Commission was established.   The fame of it went abroad throughout the
Southern Mahratta country.   From one village to
another passed the appalling news that the Commissioner had appeared, had called for titles that could
not be produced, and that nothing but a general confiscation of property were likely to result from the
operations of this mysterious Tribunal.   "Each day,"
it has been said, " produced its list of victims ; and
the good fortune of those who escaped but added to
the pangs of the crowd who came forth from the
shearing-house, shorn to the skin, unable to work,
ashamed to beg, condemned to penury."*   The titles
of no less than thirty-five thousand estates, great and
small, were called for by the Commission, and during
the first five years of its operations, three-fifths of 1852-57.
them were confiscated.†

Whilst the operations of the Revenue Department Operation of
were thus spreading alarm among the privileged the Civil
classes in all parts of the country, the Judicial Department was doing its duty as a serviceable ally in
the great war of extermination.   Many of the old
landed proprietors were stripped to the skin by the
decrees of our civil courts.   The sale of land in
satisfaction of these decrees was a process to which
recourse was often had among a people inordinately

---

fal of the Peishwah's Government,
had transmitted their acquisitions to
the children, fortified by no better
titles than entries in the village
account-books, which a closer examination showed to be recent or
spurious.   Roused from the dreams
of thirty years, these proprietors of

precarious title, or of no title at all,
found themselves suddenly brought
face to face with an apparatus,
which, at successive strokes, peeled
away their possessions with the harsh
precision of the planing machine."
   * Memorial of G. B. Seton-Karr.
   † Ibid.

1836-56.   addicted to litigation.   We must not regard it altogether with English eyes; for the Law had often
nothing else to take.   There was many a small landed
proprietor whose family might have been established
for centuries on a particular estate, with much pride
of birth and affection for his ancestral lands, but
possessing movable goods and chattels not worth
more than a few rupees.   He might have owned a pair
of small bullocks and a rude country cart consisting
of two wheels and a few bamboos, but beyond such
aids to husbandry as these, he had nothing but a
drinking-vessel, a few cooking-pots, and the blankets
which kept the dews off at night.   Justice in his
case might not be satisfied without a surrender of his
interests in the land, which constituted the main portion of his wealth.*   So a large number of estates
every year were put up to sale, under the decrees of
the courts, in satisfaction of debts sometimes only of
a few shillings, and bought by new men, perhaps from
different parts of the country, not improbably the
agents or representatives of astute native functionaries from the lower provinces; whilst the ancient
proprietors, still rooted to the soil, shrunk into small
farmers or under-tenants on their old ancestral domains.   Thus a revolution of landed property was ·
gradually brought about by means of English application, which, acting coincidentally with the other
agencies of which I have spoken, swelled the number

---

* I have stated here the principle
upon which the law was based.   But
I believe that in many cases no pains
were taken to ascertain in the first
instance what were the movable
goods of the debtor.   Recourse was
had to the register of landed property, even when the debt amounted
to no more than four or five rupees.
" I have seen," says an officer of the
Bengal Civil Service, in a Memorandum before me, " estates put up for
sale for four rupees (eight shillings),
which appears to me just the same as
if an English grocer, getting a decree
in a small-debt court against a squire
for half a sovereign, put up his estate
in Cheshire for the same, instead
of realising the debt by the sale of
his silk umbrella."

of the disaffected, dangerous classes, who traced their 183
downfal to the operations of British rule, and sullenly
bided their time for the recovery of what they had
lost, in some new revolutionary epoch.

This general system of depression, which, thus assuming many different forms and exercising itself in
many different ways, struck with uniform precision at
the most cherished privileges of the upper classes, had
not its origin in the fertile brain of Lord Dalhousie.
He only confirmed and extended it; confirmed it in
our older provinces, and extended it to those which
he had himself acquired. In the Punjab it sorely disquieted some few of our more chivalrous English
officers connected with the Administration,* and it
was carried into the Oude dominions, as will hereafter
be shown, with a recklessness which in time brought
down upon us a terrible retribution. Every new
acquisition of territory made the matter much worse.
Not merely because the privileged classes were in
those territories struck down, but because the extension of the British Raj gradually so contracted the
area on which men of high social position, expelled by
our system from the Company's provinces, could find
profitable and honourable employment, that it seemed
as though every outlet for native enterprise and ambition were about to be closed against them. It was
this, indeed, that made the great difference between

* Sir Herbert Edwardes, in a Memorandum quoted by Mr. Charles Raikes in his graphic "Notes of the Revolt of the North-West Provinces of India," says of Arthur Cocks, that he "imbibed Sir Henry Law-rence's feelings, and became greatly attached to the chiefs and people. He hardly stayed a year after annex-ation, and left the Punjab because he could not bear to see the fallen state of the old officials and Sirdars." Of Henry Lawrence himself, Mr. Raikes says: "He fought every losing battle for the old chiefs and Jagheerdars with entire disregard for his own interest, and at last left the Punjab, to use Colonel Edwardes's words, dented all over with defeats and disappointments, honourable scars in the eyes of the bystanders."

N 2

resumptions of rent-free estates under the Native Governments and under our own. It has been said that under the former there was no security of tenure; and it is true that the Native Princes did not consider themselves bound to maintain the grants of their predecessors, and often arbitrarily resumed them. But the door of honourable and lucrative employment was not closed against the sufferers. All the great offices of the State, civil and military, were open to the children of the soil. But it was not so in our British territories. There the dispossessed holder, no longer suffered to be an unprofitable drone, was not permitted to take a place among the working bees of the hive. And what place was there left for him, in which he could serve under other masters? We had no room for him under us, and we left no place for him away from us. And so we made dangerous enemies of a large number of influential persons, among whom were not only many nobles of royal or princely descent, many military chiefs, with large bodies of retainers, and many ancient landholders for whom a strong feudal veneration still remained among the agricultural classes, but numbers of the Brahminical, or priestly order, who had been supported by the alienated revenue which we resumed, and who turned the power which they exercised over the minds of others to fatal account in fomenting popular discontent, and instilling into the minds of the people the poison of religious fear.

The Priest-hood.

Other measures were in operation at the same time, the tendency of which was to disturb the minds and to inflame the hatred of the Priesthood. It seemed as though a great flood of innovation were about to

1848-56.

sweep away all their powers and their privileges. The pale-faced Christian knight, with the great Excalibar of Truth in his hand, was cleaving right through all the most cherished fictions and superstitions of Brahminism. A new generation was springing up, without faith, without veneration; an inquiring, doubting, reasoning race, not to be satisfied with absurd doctrines or captivated by grotesque fables. The literature of Bacon and Milton was exciting a new appetite for Truth and Beauty; and the exact sciences of the West, with their clear, demonstrable facts and inevitable deductions, were putting to shame the physical errors of Hindooism. A spirit of inquiry had been excited, and it was little likely ever to be allayed. It was plain that the inquirers were exalting the Professor above the Pundit, and that the new teacher was fast displacing the old.

Rightly to understand the stake for which the Brahmin was playing, and with the loss of which he was now threatened, the reader must keep before him the fact that Brahminism is the most monstrous system of interference and oppression that the world has ever yet seen, and that it could be maintained only by ignorance and superstition of the grossest kind. The people had been taught to believe that in all the daily concerns of life Brahminical ministrations were essential to worldly success. The Deity, it was believed, could be propitiated only by money-payments to this favoured race of holy men. "Every form and ceremony of religion," it has been said; "all the public festivals; all the accidents and concerns of life; the revolutions of the heavenly bodies; the superstitious fears of the people; births, sicknesses, marriages, misfortunes; death; a future state—have all been seized as sources of revenue to the Brahmins

1849-56.   "The farmer does not reap his harvest without paying a Brahmin to perform some ceremony; a tradesman cannot begin business without a fee to a Brahmin; a fisherman cannot build a new boat, nor begin to fish in a spot which he has farmed, without a ceremony and a fee."* "The Brahmin," says another and more recent writer, "does not only stand in a hierarchical, but also in the highest aristocratical position; and he has an authoritative voice in all pursuits of industry. All processes in other arts, as well as agriculture, are supposed to have been prescribed and imparted through the Brahmins. Every newly-commenced process of business, every new machine, or even repair of an old one, has to go through the ceremony of 'poojah,' with a feeing of the Brahmin."† And as the Brahmin was thus the controller of all the ordinary business concerns of his countrymen, so also was he the depositary of all the learning of the country, and the regulator of all the intellectual pursuits of the people. There was, indeed, no such thing among them as purely secular education. "It is a marked and peculiar feature in the character of Hindooism," says another writer, himself by birth a Hindoo, "that instead of confining itself within the proper and lawful bounds prescribed to every theological system, it interferes with and treats of every department of secular knowledge which human genius has ever invented; so that grammar, geography, physics, law, medicine, metaphysics, &c., do each form as essential a part of Hindooism as any religious topic with which it is concerned. . . . In their religious works they have treated of all the branches of secular

---

* Ward on the Hindoos.   is much interesting and valuable
† Jeffreys on the "British Army   matter.
in India," Appendix, in which there

knowledge known among them, in a regular, systematic manner; and have given them out to the world in a tone of absolute authority, from which there could be no appeal."* But the English had established a Court of Appeal of the highest order, and Brahminism was being continually cast in it. In a word, the whole hierarchy of India saw their power, their privileges, and their perquisites rapidly crumbling away from them, and they girded themselves up to arrest the devastation.

All this had been going on for years; but the progress of enlightenment had been too slow, and its manifestations too little obtrusive, greatly to alarm the sacerdotal mind. As long as the receptacles of this new wisdom were merely a few clever boys in the great towns, and the manhood of the nation was still saturated and sodden with the old superstition, Brahminism might yet flourish. But when these boys grew up in time to be heads of families, rejoicing in what they called their freedom from prejudice, laughing to scorn their ancestral faith as a bundle of old wives' fables, eating meat and drinking wine, and assuming some at least of the distinguishing articles of Christian apparel, it was clear that a very serious peril was beginning to threaten the ascendancy of the Priesthood. They saw that a reformation of this kind once commenced, would work its way in time through all the strata of society. They saw that, as new provinces were one after another brought under British rule, the new light must diffuse itself more and more, until there would scarcely be a place for Hindooism to lurk unmolested. And some at least, confounding cause and effect, began to argue that all this annexation and absorption was brought about for the

* *Calcutta Review*, vol. xi. Article: "Physical Errors of Hindooism."

1848-56.   express purpose of overthrowing the ancient faiths of the country, and establishing a new religion in their place.

Education.   Every monstrous lie exploded, every abominable practice suppressed, was a blow struck at the Priesthood; for all these monstrosities and abominations had their root in Hindooism, and could not be eradicated without sore disturbance and confusion of the soil. The murder of women on the funeral-pile, the murder of little children in the Zenana, the murder of the sick and the aged on the banks of the river, the murder of human victims, reared and fattened for the sacrifice, were all religious institutions, from which the Priesthood derived either profit, power, or both. Nay, even the wholesale strangling of unsuspecting travellers was sanctified and ceremonialised by religion. Now all these cruel rites had been suppressed, and, what was still worse in the eyes of the Brahmins, the foul superstitions which nurtured them were fast disappearing from the land. Authority might declare their wickedness, and still they might exist as part and parcel of the faith of the people. But when Reason demonstrated their absurdity, and struck conviction into the very heart of the nation, there was an end of both the folly and the crime. The Law might do much, but Education would assuredly do much more to sweep away all these time-honoured superstitions. Education, pure and simple in its secularity, was quite enough in itself to hew down this dense jungle of Hindooism; but when it was seen that the functions of the English schoolmaster and of the Christian priest were often united in the same person, and that high officers of the State were present at examinations conducted by chaplains or missionaries, a fear arose lest even secular educa-

tion might be the mask of proselytism, and so the   1848-56.
Brahmins began to alarm the minds of the elder
members of the Hindoo community, who abstained,
under priestly influence, from openly countenancing
what they had not the energy boldly to resist.*

And, every year the danger increased. Every
year were there manifestations of a continually increasing desire to emancipate the natives of India
from the gross superstitions which enchained them.
One common feeling moved alike the English Government and the English community. In other matters
of State-policy there might be essential changes, but
in this there was no change. One Governor might
replace another, but only to evince an increased hostility to the great Baal of Hindooism. And in no
man was there less regard for time-honoured abominations and venerable absurdities—in no man did
the zeal of iconoclasm work more mightily than
in Lord Dalhousie. During no former administration had the vested interests of Brahminism in moral
and material error been more ruthlessly assailed.
There was nothing systematic in all this. Almost,
indeed, might it be said that it was unconscious.
It was simply the manifestation of such love as any
clear-sighted, strong-headed man may be supposed
to have for truth above error, for intelligent progress above ignorant stagnation. From love of
this kind, from the assured conviction that it was
equally humane and politic to substitute the strength
and justice of British administration for what he
regarded as the effete tyrannies of the East, had
emanated the annexations which had distinguished

---

* The English journalists sometimes remarked in their reports of
these school-examinations upon the
absence of the native gentry—*e. g.*:
"We cannot help expressing great
surprise at the absence of natives of
influence."—*Bengal Hurkaru, March*
14, 1853.

his rule. And as he desired for the good of the people
to extend the territorial rule of Great Britain, so he
was eager also to extend her moral rule, and to make
those people subject to the powers of light rather
than of darkness. And so he strove mightily to extend among them the blessings of European civilisation, and the Priesthood stood aghast at the sight of
the new things, moral and material, by which they
were threatened.

Many and portentous were these menaces. Not
only was Government Education, in a more syste-
matised and pretentious shape than before, rapidly
extending its network over the whole male population of the country, but even the fastnesses of the
female apartments were not secure against the intrusion of the new learning and new philosophy of the
West. England had begun to take account of its
short-comings, and, among all the reproaches heaped
upon the Company, none had been so loud or so
general as the cry that, whilst they spent millions on
War, they grudged hundreds for purposes of Education. So, in obedience to this cry, instructions had
been sent out to India, directing larger, more comprehensive, more systematic measures for the instruction of the people, and authorising increased expenditure upon them. Whilst great Universities were to
be established, under the immediate charge of the
Government, the more humble missionary institutions were to be aided by grants of public money,
and no effort was to be spared that could conduce to
the spread of European knowledge. It was plain to
the comprehension of the guardians of Eastern learning, that what had been done to unlock the flood-
gates of the West, would soon appear to be as
nothing in comparison with the great tide of Euro-

pean civilisation which was about to be poured out
upon them.

Most alarming of all were the endeavours made, Female Edu-
during Lord Dalhousie's administration, to penetrate cation.
the Zenana with our new learning and our new customs.
The English at the large Presidency towns began to
systematise their efforts for the emancipation of the
female mind from the utter ignorance which had been
its birthright, and the wives and daughters of the
white men began to aid in the work, cheered and encouraged by the sympathies of their sisters at home.
For the first time, the education of Hindoo and
Mahomedan females took, during the administration
of Lord Dalhousie, a substantial recognised shape.
Before it had been merely a manifestation of missionary zeal addressed to the conversion of a few
orphans and castaways. But now, if not the immediate work of the Government in its corporate capacity,
it was the pet project and the especial charge of a Mr. Bethune.
member of the Government, and, on his death, passed
into the hands of the Governor-General himself, and
afterwards was adopted by the Company's Government. Some years before, the Priesthood, secure in
the bigotry and intolerance of the heads of families,
might have laughed these efforts to scorn. But now
young men, trained under English Professors, were
becoming fathers and masters, sensible of the great
want of enlightened female companionship, and ill-
disposed to yield obedience to the dogmas of the
Priests. So great, indeed, was this yearning after
something more attractive and more satisfying than
the inanity of the Zenana, that the courtesans of the
Calcutta Bazaars taught themselves to play on instruments, to sing songs, and to read poetry, that
thereby they might lure from the dreary environ-

ments of their vapid homes the very flower of Young
Bengal.

About the same time the wedge of another startling
innovation was being driven into the very heart of
Hindoo Society.   Among the many cruel wrongs to
which the womanhood of the nation was subjected was
the institution which forbade a bereaved wife ever to
re-marry.   The widow who did not burn was condemned to perpetual chastity.   Nay, it has been
surmised that the burning inculcated in the old religious writings of the Hindoos was no other than
that which, centuries afterwards, the great Christian
teacher forbade, saying that it is better to marry than
to burn.   Be this as it may, the re-marriage of Hindoo
widows was opposed both to the creeds and the
customs of the land.   It was an evil and a cruel thing
itself, and the prolific source of other evils.   Evil and
cruel would it have been in any country and under
any institutions, but where mere children are married,
often to men advanced in years, and are left widows,
in tender youth, when they have scarcely looked upon
their husbands, its cruelty is past counting.   To the
more enlightened Hindoos, trained in our English
colleges and schools, the evils of this prohibition were
so patent and so distressing, that they were fain to see
it abrogated by law. . One of their number wrote a
clever treatise in defence of the re-marriage of widows,
and thousands signed a petition, in which a belief
was expressed that perpetual widowhood was not en-
joined by the Hindoo scriptures.   But the orthodox
party, strong in texts, greatly outnumbered, and,
judged by the standard of Hindooism, greatly out-
argued them.   The Law and the Prophets were on
their side.   It was plain that the innovation would
inflict another deadly blow on the old Hindoo law of

inheritance. Already had dire offence been given to the orthodoxy of the land by the removal of those disabilities which forbade all who had forsaken their ancestral faith to inherit ancestral property. A law had been passed, declaring the abolition of " so much of the old law or usage as inflicted on any person forfeiture of rights or property, by reason of his or her renouncing, or having been excluded from, the communion of any religion." Against this the old Hindoos had vehemently protested, not without threats, as a violation of the pledges given by the British Government to the natives of India; pledges, they said, issued in an hour of weakness and revoked in an hour of strength.* But Lord Dalhousie had emphatically recorded his opinion " that it is the duty of the State to keep in its own hands the right of regulating succession to property," and the Act had been passed. And now there was further authoritative interference on the part of the State, for it was proposed to bestow equal rights of inheritance on the offspring of what the old-school Hindoos declared to be an illicit, God-proscribed connexion. This, however, was but a part of the evil. Here was another step towards the complete emancipation of woman; and Hindoo orthodoxy believed, or professed to believe, that if widows were encouraged to marry new husbands instead of burning with the corpses of the old,

---

* The Bengal Memorial said: " Your memorialists will not conceal that from the moment the proposed act becomes a part of the law applicable to Hindoos, that confidence which they hitherto felt in the paternal character of their British rulers will be most materially shaken. No outbreak, of course, is to be dreaded; but the active spirit of fervent loyalty to their sovereign will be changed into sullen submission to their will, and obedience to their power." The Madras Memorial was couched in much stronger language. It denounced the measure as a direct act of tyranny, and said that the British Government, " treading the path of oppression," "would well deserve what it will assuredly obtain—the hatred and detestation of the oppressed."

wives would be induced to make themselves widows by poisoning or otherwise destroying their lords. It was apprehended, too—and not altogether without reason*—that the re-marriage of Hindoo widows would soon be followed by a blow struck at Hindoo polygamy, especially in its worst but most honoured form of Kulinism; and so the Brahmins, discomfited and alarmed by these innovations, past, present, and prospective, strove mightily to resist the tide, and to turn the torrent of destruction back upon their enemies.†

The Railway and the Telegraph.

Nor was it only by the innovations of moral progress that the hierarchy of India were alarmed and offended. The inroads and encroachments of physical science were equally distasteful and disquieting. A privileged race of men, who had been held in veneration as the depositaries of all human knowledge, were suddenly shown to be as feeble and impotent as babes and sucklings. It was no mere verbal demonstration; the arrogant self-assertion of the white man, which the Hindoo Priesthood could contradict or explain away. There were no means of contradicting or explaining away the railway cars,

---

* See the following passage of a speech delivered by Mr. Barnes Peacock, in the Legislative Council, July 19, 1856: "There was a great distinction between preventing a man from doing that which his religion directed him to do, and preventing him from doing that which his religion merely allowed him to do. If a man were to say that his religion did not forbid polygamy, and therefore that he might marry as many wives as he pleased, when it was impossible for him to carry out the contract of marriage, it would be no interference with his religion for the Legislature to say that the marrying of a hundred wives, and the subse-

quent desertion of them, was an injury to society, and therefore that it should be illegal to do so. He" (Mr. Peacock) "maintained that it was the duty of the Legislature, in such a case, to prevent him from doing that which his religion merely permitted, but did not command him to do."

† The "Bill to remove all legal obstacles to the marriage of Hindoo widows," though introduced and discussed during the administration of Lord Dalhousie, was not finally passed till after his retirement. It received the assent of Lord Canning in July, 1856.

which travelled, without horses or bullocks, at the rate of thirty miles an hour, or the electric wires, which in a few minutes carried a message across the breadth of a whole province.

These were facts that there was no gainsaying. He who ran might read. The prodigious triumphs over time and space achieved by these " fire-carriages " and "lightning-posts," put to shame the wisdom of the Brahmins, and seemed to indicate a command over the supernatural agencies of the Unseen World, such as the Pundits of the East could never attain or simulate. They, who for their own ends had imparted a sacred character to new inventions, and had taught their disciples that all improvements in art and science were derived from the Deity through their especial intercession, and were to be inaugurated with religious ceremonies attended with the usual distribution of largesses to the priests, now found that the white men could make the very elements their slaves, and call to their aid miraculous powers undreamt of in the Brahminical philosophy. Of what use was it any longer to endeavour to persuade the people that the new knowledge of the West was only a bundle of shams and impostures, when any man might see the train come in at a given moment, and learn at Benares how many pounds of flour were sold for the rupee that morning in the bazaars of Delhi and Calcutta?

To the introduction into India of these mysterious agencies the Hour and the Man were alike propitious. When Lord Dalhousie went out to India, England was just recovering from the effects of that over-activity of speculation which had generated such a disturbance of the whole financial system of the country. She had ceased to project lines of Railway between towns without Traffic, and through countries without Population, and had subsided, after much suffering, into a healthy state of reasonable enterprise, carefully estimating both her wants and her resources. As President of the Board of Trade, Dalhousie had enjoyed the best opportunities of acquainting himself with the principles and with the details of the great question of the day, at the one central point to which all information converged, and he had left England with the full determination, God willing, not to leave the country of his adoption until he had initiated the construction of great trunk-roads of iron between all the great centres of Government and of Commerce, and had traversed, at railway speed, some at least of their first stages. A little while before, the idea of an Indian railway had, in the estimation of the greater number of English residents, been something speculative and chimerical, encouraged only by visionaries and enthusiasts. A few far-seeing men, foremost among whom was Macdonald Stephenson, predicted their speedy establishment, and with the general acceptance of the nation; but even after Dalhousie had put his hand to the work, and the Company had responded to his efforts, it was the more general belief that railway communication in India would be rather a concern of Government, useful in the extreme for military purposes, than a popular institution supplying a national want. It was thought that Indolence, Avarice, and Superstition would keep the natives of the country from flocking to the Railway Station. But with a keener appreciation of the inherent power of so demonstrable a benefit to make its own way, even against these moral obstructions, Dalhousie had full faith in the result. He was right. The people now learnt to estimate at its full worth the great truth that Time is Money; and having so learned, they were not to be deterred from profiting by it by any tenderness of respect for the feelings of their spiritual guides.

That the fire-carriage on the iron road was a heavy blow to the Brahminical Priesthood is not to be doubted. The lightning post, which sent invisible letters through the air and brought back answers, from incredible distances, in less time than an ordinary messenger could bring them from the next street, was a still greater marvel and a still greater disturbance. But it was less patent and obtrusive. The one is the natural complement of the other; and Dalhousie, aided by the genius of O'Shaughnessy, had soon spread a network of electric wires across the whole length and breadth of the country. It was a wise thing to do; a right thing to do; but it was alarming and offensive to the Brahminical mind. It has been said, that as soon as we had demonstrated that the earth is a sphere revolving on its axis, there was an end to the superstitions of Hindooism. And so there was—in argument, but not in fact. The Brahminical teachers insisted that the new doctrines of Western civilisation were mere specious inventions, with no groundwork of eternal truth, and as their disciples could not bring the test of their senses to such inquiries as these, they succumbed to authority rather than to reason, or perhaps lapsed into a state of bewildering doubt. But material experiments, so palpable and portentous that they might be seen at a distance of many miles, convinced whilst they astounded. The most ignorant and unreasoning of men could see that the thing was done. They knew that Brahminism had never done it. They saw plainly the fact that there were wonderful things in the world which their own Priests could not teach them—of which, indeed, with all their boasted wisdom, they had never dreamt; and from that time the Hindoo Hierarchy lost half its power, for the People lost half their faith.

Caste.   But clear as was all this, and alarming as were the prospects thus unfolded to the Pundits, there was something more than this needed to disturb the popular mind.   Hindooism might be assailed; Hindooism might be disproved; and still men might go about their daily business without a fear for the future or a regret for the past.   But there was something about which they disturbed themselves much more than about the abstract truths of their religion.   The great institution of Caste was an ever-present reality. It entered into the commonest concerns of life. It was intelligible to the meanest understanding.   Every man, woman, and child knew what a terrible thing it would be to be cast out from the community of the brotherhood, and condemned to live apart, abhorred of men and forsaken by God.   If, then, the people could be taught that the English by some insidious means purposed to defile the Hindoos, and to bring them all to a dead level of one-caste or of no-caste, a great rising of the Natives might sweep the Foreigners into the sea.   This was an obvious line of policy; but it was not a policy for all times.   It needed opportunity for its successful development. Equally patient and astute, the Brahmin was content to bide his time rather than to risk anything by an inopportune demonstration.   The English were loud in their professions of toleration, and commonly cautious in their practice. Still it was only in the nature of things that they should some day make a false step.

As the Brahmin thus lay in wait, eager for his

opportunity to strike, he thought he espied, perhaps in an unexpected quarter, a safe point of attack. It required some monstrous invention, very suitable to troubled times, but only to be circulated with success after the popular mind, by previous excitement, had been prepared to receive it, to give any colour of probability to a report that the Government had laid a plot for the defilement of the whole mass of the people. But there were certain classes with which Government had a direct connexion, and whose bodies and souls were in the immediate keeping of the State. Among these were the inmates of our gaols. As these people were necessarily dependent upon Government for their daily food, it appeared to be easy, by a well-devised system of Prison Discipline, either to destroy the caste of the convicts or to starve them to death. The old tolerant regulations allowed every man to cater and to cook for himself. A money-allowance was granted to him, and he turned it into food after his own fashion. But this system was very injurious to prison discipline. Men loitered over their cooking and their eating and made excuses to escape work. So the prisoners were divided into messes, according to their several castes; rations were issued to them, and cooks were appointed to prepare the daily meals at a stated hour of the day. If the cook were of a lower caste than the eaters, the necessary result was the contamination of the food and loss of caste by the whole mess. The new system, therefore, was one likely to be misunderstood and easily to be misinterpreted. Here, then, was one of those openings which designing men were continually on the alert to detect, and in a fitting hour it was turned to account. Not merely the inmates of the gaols, but the inhabitants of the towns in which pri-

The Messing System in Gaols.

o 2

sons were located, were readily made to believe that
it was the intention of the British Government to
destroy the caste of the prisoners, and forcibly to
convert them to Christianity.   It mattered not whether Brahmin cooks had or had not, in the first instance, been appointed.   There might be a Brahmin
cook to-day; and a low-caste man in his place to-
morrow.   So the lie had some plausibility about it;
and it went abroad that this assault upon the gaol-
birds was but the beginning of the end, and that by
a variety of different means the religions of the
country would soon be destroyed by the Government
of the Feringhees.

Reports of this kind commonly appear to be of
Hindoo origin; for they are calculated primarily
to alarm the minds of the people on the score
of the destruction of caste.   But it seldom hap-
pens that they are not followed by some auxiliary
lies expressly designed for Mahomedan reception.
The Mahomedans had some especial grievances of
their own.   The tendency of our educational measures, and the all-pervading Englishism with which
the country was threatened, was to lower the dignity
of Mahomedanism, and to deprive of their emoluments
many influential people of that intolerant faith.   The
Moulavees were scarcely less alarmed by our innovations than the Pundits.   The Arabic of the one fared
no better than the Sanskrit of the other.   The use
of the Persian language in our law courts was abolished; new tests for admission into the Public Service
cut down, if they did not wholly destroy, their
chances of official employment.   There was a general
inclination to pare away the privileges and the perquisites of the principal Mahomedan seats of learning.
All the religious endowments of the great Calcutta

Madrissa were annihilated; and the prevalence of the   184
English language, English learning, and English law,
made the Mahomedan doctors shrink into insignificance, whilst the resumption of rent-free tenures,
which, in many instances, grievously affected old
Mussulman families, roused their resentments more
than all the rest, and made them ripe for sedition.
A more active, a more enterprising, and a more intriguing race than the Hindoos, the latter knew well
the importance of associating them in any design
against the State.* So their animosities were stimulated, and their sympathies were enlisted, by a report,
sedulously disseminated, to the effect that the British
Government were about to issue an edict prohibiting
circumcision, and compelling Mahomedan women to
go abroad unveiled.

Small chance would there have been of such a lie
as this finding a score of credulous Mussulmans to
believe it, if it had not been for the little grain of
truth that there was in the story of the messing-
system in the gaols. The innovation had been originated some years before Lord Dalhousie appeared
upon the scene. At first it had been introduced with

* It must be admitted, however, that it is a moot question, in many instances, whether the first move-ment were made by the Hindoos or the Mahomedans. Good authorities sometimes incline to the latter sup-position. Take, for example, the fol-lowing, which has reference to a se-ditious movement at Patna in the cold season of 1845-46: "From inquiries I have made," wrote Mr. Dampier, Superintendent of Police in the Lower Provinces, "in every quarter, I am of opinion that the Mahomedans of these parts, amongst whom the resumption of the Maa-fee Tenures, the new educational system, and the encouragement given to the English language, have pro-duced the greatest discontent and the bitterest animosity against our government, finding that the en-forcement of the messing-system in the gaols had produced a consider-able sensation amongst the people, were determined to improve the op-portunity, especially as our troops were weak in numbers, and we were supposed to be pressed in the North-West." Of the event to which this refers, more detailed mention will be found in a subsequent chapter of this work, in connexion with the attempt then made to corrupt the regiments at Dinapore.

1845-46. a discretion signifying a full knowledge of the lurking
danger ;* but, as time advanced, one experiment followed another, and some of the old caution was
perhaps relaxed. So in many places the prisoners
broke into rebellion and violently resisted the proposed change. Eager and excited, under the influence of a common alarm, the townspeople cheered
them on, and were ready to aid them, with all their
might, in what they believed to be the defence of
their religion. At Shahabad, Sarun, Behar, and
Patna, there were serious disturbances, and at a later

1852. period, Benares, the very nursery and hotbed of
Hindooism, the cherished home of the Pundits, was
saved only by prudential concessions, from becoming
the scene of a sanguinary outbreak.

The Hindoo The experience thus gained of the extreme sensi-
and his Lotah. tiveness of the native mind, given up as it was to
gross delusions, does not appear to have borne the
fruit of increased caution and forbearance. For not
long afterwards another improvement in prison discipline again stirred up revolt in the gaols; and, for the
same reason as before, the people sided with the convicts. A Hindoo, or a Hindooised Mahomedan, is
nothing without his Lotah. A Lotah is a metal
drinking-vessel, which he religiously guards against
defilement, and which he holds as a cherished possession when he has nothing else belonging to him in
the world. But a brass vessel may be put to other
uses than that of holding water. It may brain a
magistrate,† or flatten the face of a gaoler, and truly

* See Circular Orders of Lieutenant-Governor of the North-West
Provinces, July, 1841 :—" Government are of opinion that these measures ought not to be compulsorily
enforced, if there be any good ground
to believe that they will violate or
offend the religious prejudices of the
people, or injure the future prospects
of those who may be subjected to
temporary imprisonment."

† My earliest recollection of India
is associated with the sensation
created in Calcutta, in April, 1834,

it was a formidable weapon in the hands of a desperate man. So an attempt was made in some places to deprive the prisoners of their lotahs, and to substitute earthenware vessels in their place. Here, then, in the eyes of the people, was another insidious attempt to convert prison discipline into a means of religious persecution—another attempt covertly to reduce them all to one caste. So the prisoners resisted the experiment, and in more than one place manifested their resentment with a fury which was shared by the population of the towns. At Arrah the excitement was so great that the guards were ordered to fire upon the prisoners, and at Mozufferpore, in Tirhoot, so formidable was the outburst of popular indignation, that the magistrate, in grave official language, described it as " a furious and altogether unexpected outbreak on the part of the people of the town and district in support and sympathy with the prisoners." The rioters, it was said, "included almost all the inhabitants of the town, as well as a vast number of ryots, who declared that they would not go away until the lotahs were restored;" and so great was the danger of the prisoners escaping, of their plundering the Treasury and pillaging the town, before the troops which had been sent for could be brought up, that the civil authorities deemed it expedient to pacify the insurgents by restoring the lotahs to the people in the gaols. And this was not held at the time to be a sudden outburst of rash and misguided ignorance, but the deliberate work of some of the rich native inhabitants of the town, and some of the higher native functionaries of our Civil Courts.

when Mr. Richardson, magistrate of Alipore gaol by a blow from a brass the 24 Pergunnahs, was killed in lotah.

1856.

It was clear, indeed, that the inflammability of the native mind was continually increasing; and that there were many influential persons, both Hindoo and Mahomedan, running over with bitter resentments against the English, who were eagerly awaiting a favourable opportunity to set all these combustible materials in a blaze. The gaol-business was an experiment, and, as far as it went, a successful one. But it was not by an outbreak of the convict population that the overthrow of the English was to be accomplished. There was another class of men, equally under the control of the Government, whose corruption would far better repay the labours of the Moulavees and the Pundits.

BOOK II.—THE SEPOY ARMY.

[1756—1856.]

———•———

CHAPTER I.

THE SEPOY ARMY OF THE COMPANY—ITS RISE AND PROGRESS—THE FIRST
MUTINY, IN BENGAL—DETERIORATING INFLUENCES—DEGRADATION OF
THE NATIVE OFFICER—THE REORGANISATION OF 1796—PROGRESS OF IN-
NOVATION—THE MUTINY OF VELLORE—LATER SIGNS OF DISAFFECTION—
CAUSES OF THE MUTINY.

WHILST the hearts of the Aristocracy and of the   1856.
Priesthood of the country were thus turned against
the government of the English, there was a third
great class, esteemed to be more powerful than all,
whom it was believed that our policy had propitiated.
There was security in the thought that the Soldiery
were with us. It was the creed of English statesmen
that India had been won by the Sword, and must be
retained by the Sword. And so long as we held the
sword firmly in our hands, there was but little apprehension of any internal danger. The British power
in the East was fenced in and fortified by an army
of three hundred thousand men.

A small part only of this Army was composed of
our own countrymen. Neither the manhood of England nor the revenues of India could supply the
means of defending the country only with British
troops. A large majority of our fighting-men were,
therefore, natives of India, trained, disciplined, and

equipped after the English fashion. We had first learnt from the French the readiness with which the "Moors" and the "Gentoos" could be made to adapt themselves to the habits and forms of European warfare, and, for a hundred years, we had been improving on the lesson.   Little by little, the handful of Blacks which had helped Robert Clive to win the battle of Plassey had swollen into the dimensions of a gigantic army.   It had not grown with the growth of the territory which it was intended to defend; but still, nerved and strengthened by such European regiments as the exigencies of the parent state could spare for the service of the outlying dependency, it was deemed to be of sufficient extent to support the Government which maintained it against all foreign enmity and all intestine revolt.

It was, doubtless, a strange and hazardous experiment upon the forbearance of these disciplined native fighting-men, held only by the bondage of the Salt in allegiance to a trading Company which had usurped the authority of their Princes and reduced their countrymen to subjection.   But it was an experiment which, at the date of the commencement of this history, had stood the test of more than a century of probation.   The fidelity of the Native Army of India was an established article of our faith. Tried in many severe conjunctures, it had seldom been found wanting.   The British Sepoy had faced death without a fear, and encountered every kind of suffering and privation without a murmur. Commanded by officers whom he trusted and loved, though of another colour and another creed, there was nothing, it was said, which he would not do, there was nothing which he would not endure.   In an extremity of hunger, he had spontaneously offered his scanty food to sustain the robuster energies of his English 1756-1856. comrade. He had planted the colours of his regiment on a spot which European valour and perseverance had failed to reach. He had subscribed from his slender earnings to the support of our European wars. He had cheerfully consented, when he knew that his Government was in need, to forego that regular receipt of pay, which is the very lifeblood of foreign service. History for a hundred years had sparkled with examples of his noble fidelity; and there were few who did not believe, in spite of some transitory aberrations, that he would be true to the last line of the chapter.

If there were anything, therefore, to disturb the 1856. mind of Lord Dalhousie when he laid down the reins of government on that memorable spring morning, the trouble which oppressed him was not the growth of any mistrust of the fidelity of the Sepoy. "Hardly any circumstance of his condition," he said, in his Farewell Minute, "is in need of improvement." And there were few who, reading this passage, the very slenderness of which indicated a more settled faith in the Sepoy than the most turgid sentences could have expressed, did not feel the same assurance that in that direction there was promise only of continued repose. It was true that Asiatic armies were ever prone to revolt—that we had seen Mahratta armies and Sikh armies, Arab armies and Goorkha armies, all the military races of India indeed, at some time or other rising in mutiny against their Government, and perhaps overthrowing it. But fifty years had passed away since the minds of our British rulers had been seriously disturbed by a fear of military revolt, and that half century, it was believed, had brought full conviction home to the understanding of the Sepoy

1856.   that the Company was a good and generous master,
whose colours it was a privilege to bear. Outwardly,
there was only a great calm ; and it was not thought
that beneath that smooth surface there were any
latent dangers peculiar to the times. The Sepoy was
esteemed to be "faithful to a proverb;" and his
fidelity was the right arm of our strength.

First Sepoy
Levies in
Bombay and
Madras.

Our first Sepoy levies were raised in the Southern
Peninsula, when the English and the French powers
were contending for the dominant influence in that
part of the country. They were few in number, and
at the outset commonly held in reserve to support
our European fighting-men. But, little by little, they
proved that they were worthy to be entrusted with
higher duties, and, once trusted, they went boldly to
the front. Under native commandants, for the most
part Mahomedans or high-caste Rajpoot Hindoos, but
disciplined and directed by the English captain, their
pride was flattered and their energies stimulated by
the victories they gained. How they fought in the
attack of Madura, how they fought in the defence of
Arcot, how they crossed bayonets, foot to foot, with
the best French troops at Cuddalore, historians have
delighted to tell. All the power and all the responsibility, all the honours and rewards, were not then
monopolised by the English captains. Large bodies
of troops were sometimes despatched, on hazardous
enterprises, under the independent command of a
native leader, and it was not thought an offence to a
European soldier to send him to fight under a black
commandant. That black commandant was then a
great man, in spite of his colour. He rode on horse-
back at the head of his men, and a mounted staff-

officer, a native adjutant, carried his commands to
the Soubahdars of the respective companies. And a
brave man or a skilful leader was honoured for his
bravery or his skill as much under the folds of a
turban as under a round hat.

When the great outrage of the Black Hole called The Bengal
Clive's retributory army to Bengal, the English had Army.
no Sepoy troops on the banks of the Hooghly. But
there were fourteen native battalions in Madras,
numbering in all ten thousand men, and Clive took
two of these with him, across the black water, to
Calcutta. Arrived there, and the first blow struck,
he began to raise native levies in the neighbourhood,
and a battalion of Bengal Sepoys fought at Plassey
side by side with their comrades from Madras. Eight
years after this victory, which placed the great province of Bengal at our feet, the one battalion had
swollen into nineteen, each of a thousand strong. To
each battalion three English officers were appointed
—picked men from the English regiments.* The
native element was not so strong as in the Southern
Army; but a good deal of substantive authority still
remained with the black officers.

And that the Bengal Sepoy was an excellent soldier, was freely declared by men who had seen the
best troops of the European powers. Drilled and
disciplined in all essential points after the English
model, the native soldier was not called upon to
divest himself of all the distinctive attributes of his
race. Nothing that his creed abhorred or his caste
rejected was forced upon him by his Christian
masters. He lived apart, cooked apart, ate apart,
after the fashion of his tribe. No one grudged him

---

* In 1765, the number was in- native commandant and ten Soubah-
creased to five. There were then a dars to each battalion.—*Broome.*

1757.   his necklace, his ear-rings, the caste-marks on his
forehead, or the beard which lay upon his breast.
He had no fear of being forcibly converted to the religion of the white men, for he could not see that the
white men had any religion to which they could
convert him.   There was no interference from the
Adjutant-General's office, no paper government, no
perpetual reference to order-books bristling with innovations; and so he was happy and contented,
obedient to the officers who commanded him, and
faithful to the Government he served.

His predominant sentiment, indeed, was fidelity to
his Salt, or, in other words, to the hand that fed him.
But if he thought that the hand was unrighteously
closed to withhold from him what he believed his due,
he showed himself to be most tenacious of his rights,
and he resolutely asserted them.   This temper very
soon manifested itself.   The Bengal Army was but
1764.   seven years old, when it first began to evince some
The First   symptoms of a mutinous spirit.   But in this instance
Mutiny in   the contagion came from the Europeans.   The white
Bengal.   troops had mutinied because the promise of a donation
to the Army from Meer Jaffier had halted on the way
to performance; and when the money came, the Sepoys
followed their example, because they thought that they
were denied their rightful share of the Prize.   They
had just ground of complaint in this instance, and
they were soothed by a reasonable concession.*   But
the fire had not burnt itself out; and before the close
of the year some regiments were again in rebellion.
One battalion seized and imprisoned its English officers,
and vowed that it would serve no more.   It was one
of those childish ebullitions, of which we have since

* Whilst a private of the Euro-   six.   The share of the latter was
pean Army was to receive forty ru-   afterwards fixed at twenty rupees.
pees, it was proposed to give a Sepoy

seen so many in the Bengal Army.   But it was plain
that the evil was a growing one, and to be arrested
with a strong hand.   So twenty-four Sepoys were
tried, at Chuprah, by a drum-head Court-Martial, for
mutiny and desertion, found guilty, and ordered to be
blown away from the guns.

A century has passed since the order was carried
into execution, and many strange and terrible scenes
have been witnessed by the Sepoy Army ; but none
stranger or more terrible than this.   The troops
were drawn up, European and Native, the guns were
loaded, and the prisoners led forth to suffer.   Major
Hector Munro, the chief of the Bengal Army, superintended that dreadful punishment parade, and gave
the word of command for the first four of the criminals
to be tied up to the guns.   The order was being
obeyed; the men were being bound; when four tall,
stately Grenadiers stepped forward from among the
condemned, and represented that as they had always
held the post of honour in life, it was due to them that
they should take precedence in death.   The request
was granted ; a brief reprieve was given to the men
first led to execution ; the Grenadiers were tied to
the guns, and blown to pieces at the word of command.

Then all through the Sepoy battalions on that ghastly
parade, there ran a murmur and a movement, and it
seemed that the black troops, who greatly outnumbered the white, were about to strike for the rescue of
their comrades.   There were signs and sounds not to
be misunderstood ; so the officers of the native regiments went to the front and told Munro that their
men were not to be trusted; that the Sepoys had resolved not to suffer the execution to proceed. On the
issue of that reference depended the fate of the Bengal
Army.   The English troops on that parade were few.

1764. There was scarcely a man among them not moved to tears by what he had seen ; but Munro knew that they could be trusted, and that they could defend the guns, which once turned upon the natives would have rendered victory certain. So he closed the Europeans on to the battery; the Grenadiers upon one side, the Marines on the other, loaded the pieces with grape, and sent the Sepoy officers back to their battalions. This done, he gave the word of command to the native regiments to ground arms.   In the presence of those loaded guns, and of the two lines of white troops ready to fire upon them, to have disobeyed would have been madness.   They moved to the word of command, laid down their arms, and when another word of command was given, which sent the Sepoys to a distance from their grounded muskets, and the Europeans with the guns took ground on the inter-vening space, the danger had passed away.   The native troops were now completely at Munro's mercy, and the execution went on in their presence to its dreadful close.   Twenty men were blown away from the guns at that parade.   Four were reserved for execution at another station, as a warning to other regiments, which appeared to be mutinously disposed, and six more, tried and sentenced at Bankepore, were blown away at that place.   Terrible as was this example, it was the act of a merciful and humane man, and Mercy and Humanity smiled sorrowfully, but approvingly, upon it.   It taught the Sepoy Army that no British soldier, black or white, can rebel against the State without bringing down upon himself fearful retribution, and by the sacrifice of a few guilty forfeited lives checked the progress of a disease which, if weakly suffered to run its course, might have resulted in the slaughter of thousands.

The lesson was not thrown away. The Sepoy learnt
to respect the stern authority of the Law, and felt
that the Nemesis of this new Government of the
British was certain in its operations, and not to be
escaped. And the time soon came when his constancy was tested, and found to have the ring of
the true metal. The European officers broke into
rebellion; but the natives did not falter in their *Mutiny of the*
allegiance. Conceiving themselves aggrieved by the *Bengal Officers.*
withdrawal of the extraordinary allowances which
they had enjoyed in the field, the former determined
to remonstrate against the reduction, and to clamour
for what they called their rights. In each brigade
meetings were called, consultations were held, and
secret committees were formed, under the disguise of
Freemasons' Lodges. Headstrong and obstinate, the
officers swore to recover the double batta which had
been taken from them, or to resign the service in a
body. Large sums of money were subscribed, and
the Company's civilians contributed to the fund, which
was to enable their military brethren to resist the
authority of their common masters. It was a formidable conjuncture, and one to try the courage
even of a Clive. The orders of the Company were
peremptory; and he was not a man to lower the authority of Government by yielding to a threat. But
he could not disguise from himself that there were
contingencies which might compel him to make a
temporary concession to the insubordinates; one was
an incursion of the Mahrattas,* the other the defection
of the Sepoys. Had the native soldiers sympathised
with and supported the English officers, the impetus

---

* "In case the Mahrattas should case, you have authority to make
still appear to intend an invasion, terms with the officers of your bri-
or in case you apprehend a mutiny gade."—*Lord Clive to Col. Smith, May*
among the troops, but in no other 11, 1766. [See also following note.]

P

1766.   thus given to the movement would have overborne
all power of resistance, and Government must have
succumbèd to the crisis.   In this emergency, Clive
saw clearly the importance of securing "the fidelity
and attachment of the Soubahdars, or commanding
officers of the black troops," and he wrote urgently
to his lieutenants, Smith and Fletcher, instructing
them to attain this end.   But the Sepoys had never
wavered.   True to their colours, they were ready at
the word of command to fire on the white mutineers.
Assured of this, Clive felt that the danger was over—
felt that·he could hold out against the mutiny of the
English officers, even though the European troops
should break into revolt.*

The founders of the Native Army had conceived
the idea of a force recruited from among the people
of the country, and commanded for the most part by
men of their own race, but of higher social position
—men, in a word, of the master-class, accustomed to
exact obedience from their inferiors.   But it was the
inevitable tendency of our increasing power in India
to oust the native functionary from his seat, or to lift
him from his saddle, that the white man might fix himself there, with all the remarkable tenacity of his race.
An Englishman believes that he can do all things
better than his neighbours, and, therefore, it was doubt-

---

* "The black Sepoy officers, as
well as men, have given great proofs
of fidelity and steadiness upon this
occasion, and so long as they remain
so, nothing is to be apprehended
from the European soldiery, even if
they should be mutinously inclined."
—*Clive to Smith, May* 15, 1760, *MS.
Records.*—They had just afforded a
striking proof that they were prepared, if necessary, to fire upon the
Europeans. See Broome's History of
the Bengal Army, vol. i. 589: "The
European battalion had got under
arms, and were preparing to leave
the fort and follow their officers, and
the artillery were about to do the
same, but the unexpected appearance of this firm line of Sepoys, with
their bayonets fixed and arms loaded,
threw them into some confusion, of
which Captain Smith took advantage, and warned them, that if they
did not retire peaceably into their
barracks, he would fire upon them
at once."

less with a sincere conviction of the good we were doing 1764.
that we gradually took into our own hands the reins of
office, civil and military, and left only the drudgery
and the dirty work to be done by the people of the
soil.   Whether, if we had fairly debated the question, it would have appeared to us a safer and a wiser
course to leave real military power in the hands of
men who might turn it against us, than to cast upon
the country a dangerous class of malcontents identi-
fying the rise of the British power with their own
degradation, it may now be difficult to determine.
But any other result than that before us would have
been utterly at variance with the genius of the
English nation, and, theorise as we might, was not to
be expected.   So it happened, in due course, that
the native officers, who had exercised real authority
in their battalions, who had enjoyed opportunities of
personal distinction, who had felt an honourable
pride in their position, were pushed aside by an incursion of English gentlemen, who took all the substantive power into their hands, and left scarcely
more than the shadow of rank to the men whom
they had supplanted.   An English subaltern was Increase of
appointed to every company, and the native officer English
then began to collapse into something little better Officers.
than a name.

As the degradation of the native officer was thus
accomplished, the whole character of the Sepoy army
was changed.   It ceased to be a profession in which
men of high position, accustomed to command,
might satisfy the aspirations and expend the energies of their lives.   All distinctions were effaced.
The native service of the Company came down to a
dead level of common soldiering, and rising from the
ranks by a painfully slow process to merely nominal

command. There was employment for the many; there was no longer a career for the few. Thenceforth, therefore, we dug out the materials of our army from the lower strata of society, and the gentry of the land, seeking military service, carried their ambitions beyond the red line of the British frontier, and offered their swords to the Princes of the Native States.

But in those lower strata there were elementary diversities of which in England we know nothing. The lower orders amongst us are simply the lower orders—all standing together on a common level of social equality; we recognise no distinctions among them except in respect of the callings which they follow. Thus one common soldier differs only from another common soldier in the height of his stature, or the breadth of his shoulders, or the steadiness of his drill. But in India the great institution

of Caste—at once the most exclusive and the most levelling system in the world—may clothe the filthiest, feeblest mendicant with all the dignities and powers of the proudest lord. So, in our native army, a Sepoy was not merely a Sepoy. He might be a Brahmin, or he might be a Pariah; and though they might stand beside each other shoulder to shoulder, foot to foot, on the parade-ground, there was as wide a gulf between them in the Lines, as in our own country yawns between a dustman and a duke.

In the Bengal Army the Sepoys were chiefly of high Caste. Deriving its name from the country in which it was first raised, not from the people composing it, it was recruited in the first instance from among the floating population which the Mahomedan conquest had brought from the northern provinces—from Rohilcund, from Oude, from the country be-

tween the two rivers; men of migratory habits, and
martial instincts, and sturdy frames, differing in all
respects, mind and body, from the timid, feeble deni-
zens of Bengal. The Jat, the Rajpoot, and the
priestly Brahmin, took service, with the Patan, under
the great white chief, who had humbled the pride of
Soorajah Dowlah. And as time advanced, and the
little local militia swelled into the bulk of a magnificent army, the aristocratic element was still dominant
in the Bengal Army. But the native troops of
Madras and Bombay were made up from more mixed
and less dainty materials. There were men in the
ranks of those armies of all nations and of all castes,
and the more exclusive soon ceased from their exclu-
siveness, doing things which their brethren in the
Bengal Army shrunk from doing, and solacing their
pride with the reflection that it was the "custom of
the country." Each system had its advocates. The
Bengal Sepoy, to the outward eye, was the finest
soldier; tallest, best-formed, and of the noblest presence. But he was less docile and serviceable than
the Sepoy of the Southern and the Western Armies.
In the right mood there was no better soldier in the
world, but he was not always in the right mood; and
the humours which he displayed were ever a source
of trouble to his commanders, and sometimes of danger to the State.

In an army so constituted, the transfer of all substantive authority to a handful of alien officers
might have been followed by a fatal collapse of the
whole system, but for one fortunate circumstance,
which sustained its vitality. The officers appointed
to command the Sepoy battalions were picked men;
men chosen from the European regiments, not merely
as good soldiers, skilled in their professional duties,

1784-96. but as gentlemen of sound judgment and good
temper, acquainted with the languages and the
habits of the people of the country, and prone to
respect the prejudices of the soldiery. The command
of a native battalion was one of the highest objects
of ambition. It conferred large powers and often
great wealth upon the Sepoy officer; and though
the system was one pregnant with abuses, which
we see clearly in these days, it contained that
great principle of cohesion which attached the English officer and the native soldier to each other—
cohesion, which the refinements of a later civilisation
were doomed rapidly to dissolve.

1796. It lasted out the century, but scarcely survived it.*
The English Sepoy-officer having become a great
substantive fact, not a mere excrescence upon the
general body of the English Army, it became necessary to define his position. He had many great
advantages, but he had not rank; and the Company's officer found himself continually superseded by
younger men in the King's army. Very reasonably,
if not always very temperately, he began then to
assert his rights; and the result was an entire reor-

* That the national basis, which
had originally distinguished the
foundation of the Madras Army, did
not very long survive the establishment of the reformed system of Bengal, and that the native officers soon
lost the power and the dignity in
which they had once rejoiced, may
be gathered from an early incident in
the Life of Sir John Malcolm. It
was in 1784, when an exchange of
prisoners with Tippoo had been negotiated, that a detachment of two
companies of Sepoys was sent out
from our side of the Mysore frontier
to meet the escort under Major
Dallas conveying the English prisoners from Seringapatam. "In
command of this party," says the
biographer, "went Ensign John
Malcolm. This was his first service;
and it was long remembered by
others than the youthful hero himself. When the detachment met the
prisoners' escort, a bright-faced,
healthy English boy was seen by the
latter riding up to them on a rough
pony. Dallas asked him after his
commanding officer. 'I am the commanding officer,' said young Malcolm." As Malcolm was born in
1769, he must at this time have been
a boy of fifteen; yet he commanded
a detachment of two companies of
Sepoys, and all the old native officers
attached to them.

ganisation of the Company's army, which greatly im-   179
proved the status of its old officers and opened a door
for the employment of a large number of others. By the
regulations then framed, two battalions of Sepoys were
formed into one regiment, to which the same number .
of officers were posted as to a regiment in the King's
army, and all took rank according to the date of
their commissions. It was believed that the increased
number of European officers would add to the efficiency of the Native Army. But it was admitted,
even by those who had been most active in working
out the new scheme, that it did not develop all the
good results with which it was believed to be laden.
The little authority, the little dignity, which still
clung to the position of the native officers was then
altogether effaced by this new incursion of English
gentlemen;* and the discontent, which had been
growing up in the minds of the soldiery, began then
to bear bitter fruit.

But this was not all. The new regulations, which
so greatly improved the position of the Company's
officers, and in no respect more than in that of the
pensions which they were then permitted. to enjoy,
held out great inducements to the older officers of the
Company's army to retire from active service, and to
spend the remainder of their days at home. Many of
the old commandants then prepared to leave the battalions over which they had so long exercised paternal
authority, and to give up their places to strangers. Not only was there a change of men, but a
change also of system. The English officer rose by
seniority to command. The principle of selection

---

* It was alleged to be an advantage of the new system that the increased number of English officers
would obviate the necessity of ever
sending out a detachment under
native command.

was abandoned. And men, who could scarcely call for a glass of water in the language of the country, or define the difference between a Hindoo and a Mahomedan, found themselves invested with responsibilities which ought to have devolved only on men of large local experience and approved good judgment and temper.

The Mysore and Mahratta Wars. But the evil results of the change were not immediately apparent. The last years of the eighteenth, and the first years of the nineteenth century were years of active Indian warfare. In the Mysore and in the Mahratta countries the Sepoy had constant work, under great generals whom he honoured and trusted; he had strong faith in the destiny of the Company; and his pride was flattered by a succession of brilliant victories. But it is after such wars as those of Harris, Lake, and Wellesley, when a season of stagnation succeeds a protracted period of excitement, that the discipline of an army, whether in the East or in the West, is subjected to its severest trials. All the physical and moral properties which have so long sustained it in high health and perfect efficiency then seem to collapse; and the soldier, nerveless and languid, readily succumbs to the deteriorating influences by which he is surrounded. And so it was with the Sepoy after those exhausting wars. He was in the state which, of all others, is most susceptible of deleterious impressions. And, unhappily, there was one especial source of annoyance and alarm to irritate and disquiet him in the hour of peace. Amidst the stern realities of active warfare, the European officer abjures the pedantries of the drill-sergeant and the fopperies of the regimental tailor. He has no time for small things; no heart for trifles. It is enough for him that his men are in a condition to

fight battles and to win them. But in Peace he 1805.
sometimes shrivels into an Arbiter of Drill and Dress,
and worries in time the best of soldiers into malcontents and mutineers.

And so it was that, after the fierce excitement of
the Mysore and Mahratta wars, there arose among our
English officers an ardour for military improvement;
and the Sepoy, who had endured for years, without a
murmur, all kinds of hardships and privations, under
canvas and on the line of march, felt that life was less
endurable in cantonments than it had been in the
field, and was continually disturbing himself, in his
matted hut, about the new things that were being
forced upon him. All sorts of novelties were bristling
up in his path. He was to be drilled after a new
English fashion. He was to be dressed after a
new English fashion. He was to be shaved after
a new English fashion. He was not smart enough
for the Martinets who had taken him in hand to
polish him up into an English soldier. They were
stripping him, indeed, of his distinctive Oriental character; and it was not long before he began to see in
these efforts to Anglicise him something more than
the vexatious innovations and crude experiments of
European military reform.

To these annoyances and vexations the Madras Mutiny of
Army were especially subjected. Composed as were its the Coast
Army.
battalions of men of different castes, and not in any
way governed by caste principles, they were held to be
peculiarly accessible to innovation; and, little by
little, all the old outward characteristics of the native
soldier were effaced, and new things, upon the most
approved European pattern, substituted in their place.

1805-6,   At last the Sepoy, forbidden to wear the distinguishing marks of Caste on his forehead, stripped of his
ear-rings, to which, by ties alike of vanity and superstition, he was fondly attached,* and ordered to shave
himself according to a regulation cut,† was put into
a stiff round hat, like a Pariah drummer's, with a flat
top, a leather cockade, and a standing feather. It was
no longer called a "turband;" it was a hat or cap; in
the language of the natives, a *topi;* and a *topi-wallah,*
or hat-wearer, was in their phraseology a synonym
for a Feringhee or Christian.

The Sepoy is not logical, but he is credulous and
suspicious. It was not difficult to persuade him that
there were hidden meanings and occult designs in all
this assimilation of the native soldier's dress to that of
the European fighting-man. The new hat was not
merely an emblem of Christianity, and therefore
possessed of a grave moral significance, but materially,
also, it was discovered to be an abomination. It was
made in part of leather prepared from the skin of the
unclean hog, or of the sacred cow, and was, therefore,
an offence and a desecration alike to Mahomedan and
Hindoo. The former had no distinguishing marks of
caste to be rubbed off on parade with a dirty stick, but
he venerated his beard and his ear-rings, and, under
the force of contact and example, he had developed
many strong generic resemblances to the caste-
observing Hindoo. The Mahomedan of India differs

---

* By the Mahomedan Sepoy the
ear-ring was often worn as a charm.
It was given to him at his birth, and
dedicated to some patron saint.

† See the following, Para. 10,
Sec. 11, Standing Orders of Madras
Army: "It is ordered by the Regulations that a native soldier shall not
mark his face to denote his caste, or
wear ear-rings when dressed in his
uniform; and it is further directed,
that at all parades, and on all duties,
every soldier of the battalion shall
be clean-shaved on the chin. It is
directed, also, that uniformity shall,
as far as is practicable, be preserved
in regard to the quantity and shape
of the hair on the upper lip."

greatly in his habits and his feelings from the Mahomedan of Central Asia or Arabia; he accommodates himself, in some sort, to the usages of the country, and being thus readily acclimatised, he strikes strong root in the soil. Christianity does not differ more than Mahomedanism, doctrinally or ethically, from the religion of the Hindoos; but in the one case there may be social fusion, in the other it is impossible. Even in the former instance; the fusion is imperfect, and there is in this partial assimilation of races one of the chief elements of our security in India. But the security derived from this source is also imperfect; and circumstances may at any time, by an unfortunate coincidence, appeal to the ethnical resemblances and the common instincts of different nationalities, in such a manner as to excite in both the same fears and to raise the same aspirations, and so to cause all diversities to be for a time forgotten. And such a coincidence appears now to have arisen. Different races, moved by the sense of a common danger, and roused by a common hope, forgot their differences, and combined against a common foe.

And so it happened that in the spring of 1806, the Hindoo and Mahomedan Sepoy in the Southern Peninsula of India were talking together, like caste-brothers, about their grievances, and weaving plots for their deliverance. It is partly by accident, partly by design, that such plots ripen in the spring. By accident, because relieved from cold-weather exercises, parades, field-days, and inspections, the soldier has more leisure to ruminate his wrongs, and more time to discuss them. By design, because the coming heats and rains paralyse the activities of the white man, and are great gain to the native mutineer. In April and

May the English officer sees little of his men; his visits to the Lines are few; few are his appearance on parade. He is languid and prostrate. The morning and evening ride are as much as his energies can compass. The Sepoy then, disencumbered of dress and dismissed from drill, can afford to snatch some hours from sleep to listen to any strange stories, told by wandering mendicants, with the odour of sanctified filth about them, and to discuss the most incredible fables with all the gravity of settled belief. There is always more or less of this vain talk. It amuses the Sepoy and for a while excites him with a visionary prospect of higher rank and better pay, under some new dispensation. But he is commonly content to regard this promised time as a far-off Hegira, and, as he turns himself round on his charpoy for another nap, he philosophically resolves in the mean while to eat the Company's salt in peace, and to wait God's pleasure in quietude and patience.

But there was at this time something more to excite the imagination of the Sepoy in Southern India than the ordinary vain talk of the Bazaars and the Lines. The travelling fakeers were more busy with their inventions; the rumours which they carried from place to place were more ominous; the prophecies which they recited were more significant of speedy fulfilment. There was more point in the grotesque performances of the puppet-shows — more meaning in the rude ballads which were sung and the scraps of verse which were cited. Strange writings were dropped by unseen hands, and strange placards posted on the walls. At all the large military stations in the Carnatic and in the Deccan there was an uneasy feeling as of something coming. There were manifold signs which seemed to indicate that the time to strike had arrived, and so the Sepoy began to take stock of his grievances and to set before him all the benefits of change.

The complaints of the Sepoy were many. If he were to pass his whole life in the Company's service and do what he might, he could not rise higher than the rank of Soubahdar; there had been times when distinguished native soldiers had been appointed to high and lucrative commands, and had faithfully done their duty; but those times had passed, and, instead of being exalted, native officers were habitually degraded. A Sepoy on duty always presented or carried arms to an English officer, but an English soldier suffered a native officer to pass by without a salute. Even an English Sergeant commanded native officers of the highest rank. On parade, the English officers made mistakes, used the wrong words of command, then threw the blame upon the Sepoys and reviled them. Even native officers, who had grown grey in the service, were publicly abused by European striplings. On the line of march the native officers were compelled to live in the same tents with the common Sepoys, and had not, as in the armies of native potentates, elephants or palanquins assigned to them for their conveyance, how great soever the distance which they were obliged to traverse. And if they rode horses or ponies, purchased from their savings, the English officer frowned at them as upstarts. "The Sepoys of the Nizam and the Mahratta chiefs," they said, "are better off than our Soubahdars and Jemidars." Then it was urged that the Company's officers took the Sepoys vast distances from their homes, where they died in strange places, and that their wives and children were left to beg their bread; that native Princes, when they conquered new

806   countries, gave grants of lands to distinguished
soldiers, but that the Company only gave them sweet
words; that the concubines of the English gentlemen
were better paid than the native officers, and their
grooms and grass-cutters better than the native
soldiers; that the English officers could import into
their Zenanas the most beautiful women in the
country, whilst the natives hardly dared look at the
slave-girls; and, to crown all, it was declared that
General Arthur Wellesley had ordered his wounded
Sepoys to be mercilessly shot to death.

Preposterous as were some of the fables with which
this bill of indictment was crusted over, there was
doubtless beneath it a large substratum of truth.
But the alleged grievances were, for the most part,
chronic ailments which the Sepoy had been long
enduring, and might have endured still longer, patiently and silently, had they not culminated in
the great outrage of the round hat, with its auxiliary
vexations of the shorn beard, the effaced caste-marks,
and the despoiled ear-rings. Then, it was not difficult to teach him that this aggregation of wrongs
had become intolerable, and that the time had
come for him to strike a blow in defence of his
rights. And the teacher was not far distant. The
great Mahomedan usurpation of Mysore had been
overthrown, but the representatives of the usurper
were still in the country. The family of the slain
Sultan were living in the fort of Vellore, as the
clients rather than the captives of the English, with
abundant wealth at their command, and a numerous
body of Mussulman attendants. But generous as
was the treatment they had received, and utterly at
variance with their own manner of dealing with
fallen enemies, they had not ceased to bewail the

loss of the sovereign power which had passed from
their House, or to hate the conquerors who had
unkinged them.   In the luxurious idleness of Vellore they dreamed of the recovery of their lost
empire.   There was but one way to the attainment
of that cherished object, and that way was through
the corruption of the Sepoy.   The time was propitious, and the work commenced.

It ought not to have been easy work, but so it
was.   If there had been relations of confidence between the English officer and the native soldier, the
corruption of the latter would have been a task of
sore difficulty and danger; but those relations were
not what they had been a few years before.   It was
not that the officers themselves had deteriorated, but
that a new system had been introduced, which, greatly
improving their state and prospects, and, it may be
said, permanently increasing their efficiency as a
body, still caused some temporary relaxation of the
ties which bound them to the soldiery of the country.
The new regulations of 1796, it has been said, opened
out to the elder generation of officers a door by which
they might retire on advantageous terms from the
service.   Some took their pensions at once; but a
period of active warfare supervened, and many
veteran officers waited for the restoration of peace
to take advantage of the boon that was offered.
They went; and a new race of men, young and inexperienced, took their places.   And so, for a time, the
Sepoy did not know his officer, nor the officer his
men; they met almost as strangers on parade, and
there was little or no communion between them.   It
was a transition-period of most untoward occurrence,
when so many other adverse influences were destroying the discipline of the army; and, therefore, again

I say the hour was propitious, and the work of' corruption commenced.

At the end of the first week of May, as Adjutant-General Agnew was rising from his work, in the white heat of Fort St. George, there came tidings to his office of general disaffection among the native troops at Vellore. One battalion, at least, already had broken into open mutiny. The chief of the Madras army, Sir John Cradock, had retired for the evening to his garden-house in the pleasant suburbs of Madras, so Agnew drove out to see him with the important missive in his hand. A few days afterwards, Cradock was posting to Vellore. Arrived there, he found that there had been no exaggeration in the reports which had been furnished to him, but that more judicious treatment at the outset might have allayed the excitement among the troops, and restored the confidence of the Sepoy. So said a Court of Inquiry; so said the Commander-in-Chief. A gentle sudorific, almost insensibly expelling the pent-up humours, may suffice at the beginning, though only much blood-letting can cure at the end. But ailments of this kind, in the military body, seldom reveal themselves in their full significance until the time for gentle treatment is past. When Cradock went to Vellore no mere explanations could repair the mischief that had been done. The mutinous troops were sent down to the Presidency, and others substituted for them. Military discipline was vindicated for the time by a court-martial, and two of the ringleaders were sentenced to be—flogged. But the infection still clung to Vellore. The whole native garrison was tainted and corrupted.

Nor was it a mere local epidemic. At other military stations in the Carnatic there was similar excitement.

Midnight meetings were being held in the Lines; oaths of secresy were being administered to the Sepoys; threats of the most terrible vengeance were fulminated against any one daring to betray them. The native officers took the lead, the men followed, some roused to feelings of resentment, others huddling together like sheep, under the influence of a vague fear. In the bungalows of the English captains there was but small knowledge of what was passing in the Sepoys' Lines, and if there had been more, discretion would probably have whispered that in such a case "silence is gold." For when in the high places of Government there is a general disinclination to believe in the existence of danger, it is scarcely safe for men of lowlier station to say or to do anything indicating suspicion and alarm.

At Vellore, after the first immature demonstration, there was a lull; and the quietude had just the effect that it was intended to have; it disarmed the suspicion and suspended the vigilance of the English. The most obvious precautions were neglected. Even the significant fact that the first open manifestation of disaffection had appeared under the shadow of the asylum of the Mysore Princes, had not suggested any special associations, or indicated the direction in which the watchful eye of the British Government should be turned. Nothing was done to strengthen the European garrison of Vellore.* No pains were taken to cut off the perilous intercourse which existed be-

* "That neither the Government nor the Commander-in-Chief entertained any serious apprehensions from the agitation having first occurred at Vellore, is obvious. The battalion that most opposed the innovation was, indeed, ordered to Madras, but nothing was directed indicative of any jealousy of the Princes. No precautions seem to have been taken within the Fort, and notwithstanding the discontent manifested by the native troops, the garrison was still left with only four companies of Europeans."—*Barry Close to John Malcolm. Poonah, Aug.* 12, 1806. *MS. Correspondence.*

tween the native soldiery and the occupants of the Palace. So the latter went about the Fort jeering the Sepoys, and telling them that they would soon be made Christians to a man. The different parts of their uniform were curiously examined, amidst shrugs and other expressive gestures, and significant " Wah-wahs !" and vague hints that everything about them in some way portended Christianity. They looked at the Sepoy's stock, and said, "What is this? It is leather ! Well !" Then they would look at his belt, and tell him that it made a cross on his breast, and at the little implements of his calling, the turnscrew and worm, suspended from it, and say that they also were designed to fix the Christian's cross upon his person. But it was the round hat that most of all was the object of the taunts and warnings of the people from the Palace. " It only needed this," they said, " to make you altogether a Feringhee. Take care, or we shall soon all be made Christians—Bazaar-people, Ryots, every one will be compelled to wear the hat; and then the whole country will be ruined." Within the Fort, and outside the Fort, men of all kinds were talking about the forcible conversion to Christianity which threatened them; and everywhere the round hat was spoken of as the instrument by which the Caste of the Hindoo was to be destroyed, and the faith of the Mussulman desecrated and demolished.

But all this was little known to the officers of the Vellore garrison, or, if known, was little heeded. So unwilling, indeed, were they to believe that any danger was brewing, that a Sepoy who told his English officer that the regiments were on the eve of revolt was put in irons as a madman. The native officers declared that he deserved condign punishment for blackening the faces of his corps, and they were readily believed. But the time soon came when the prophecy of evil was verified, and the prophet was exalted and rewarded. Deeply implicated as he was said to be in the plot—a traitor first to the English, and then to his own people—his name became an offence and an abomination to the Army, and the favour shown to him a source of the bitterest resentment. "The disposition of the gentlemen of the Company's service," they said, "and the nature of their government, make a thief happy, and an honest man afflicted."*

On the 10th of July the mine suddenly exploded. It was remembered afterwards that on the preceding afternoon an unusual number of people had passed into the Fort, some mounted and some on foot, seemingly on no especial business; all with an insolent, braggart air, laughing and rollicking, making mimic battle among themselves, and otherwise expressing a general expectancy of something coming. It was remembered, too, that on that evening there had been more than the common tendency of the times to speak abusively of the English. The Adjutant of a Sepoy regiment had been called, to his face, by the vilest term of reproach contained in the language of the country.† But it has been doubted whether the day and hour of the outburst were those fixed for the development of the plot. The con-

* From a paper in Hindostanee, transmitted to Adjutant-General Agnew from the Hyderabad Subsidiary Force: "In the affair at Vellore," said the Sepoys, "when the mutiny first commenced, it was on account of Mustapha Beg; and the gentlemen of the Company's Government have bestowed upon him a reward of two thousand pagodas from the public treasury, with the rank of Soubah-dar. The same Mustapha Beg, Sepoy, was the man who gave the signal for revolt to the people at Vellore, and this is the man whom the Company have distinguished by their favour."

† Unhappily it is one of the first words which the Englishman in India learns to speak, and by which many young officers, when displeased, habitually call their native servants.

1806.   spirators, it is said, were not ripe for action. Two or three days later, the first blow was to have been struck, but that a Jemadar, inflamed with strong drink, could not control the passionate haste within him, and he precipitated the collision which it was the policy of his party to defer.* Numbers thus suddenly roused to action were unprepared to play their parts; and letters which had been written to disaffected polygars and others in Mysore had not yet been despatched. It was confidently believed that in a few days ten thousand faithful adherents of the House of Hyder would rally round the standard of the Mussulman Princes. All that was required of the Sepoys was, that they should hold Vellore for a week. At the end of that time it was believed that the whole country would be in the hands of the insurgents.

His Majesty's 69th.   The European garrison of Vellore, at this time, consisted only of four companies of a Line regiment. To fall suddenly, in the dead of the night, on all who might happen to be on guard, to overpower them by numbers, and then to murder the rest in their beds, was apparently an easy task. Two hours after midnight the work commenced. The sentries were shot down. The soldiers on main guard were killed as they lay on their cots, and the white men in the

---

* In the private correspondence of the time, it is stated that the day fixed for the outbreak was the 14th. It appeared, however, in the evidence of the first Committee of Inquiry assembled at Vellore, that it was agreed that the first blow should be struck fifteen days after the Mysore standard, prepared in the Palace, was ready to be hoisted, and that thirteen days had then passed. The story of the drunken Jemadar appears in Madras Secret Letter, Sept. 30, 1806. It happened, too, that the European officer commanding the native guard fell sick, that the Soubahdar was also indisposed, and that Jemadar Cossim Khan, one of the most active of the mutineers, was eager to go the grand rounds; and it is possible that this accident helped to precipitate the crisis. On the other hand, it is to be observed that Major Armstrong, who had been absent from Vellore, and who returned on the night of the 10th, was warned by people outside the Fort not to enter, as something was about to happen.

hospital were ruthlessly butchered. There was then
a scene of unexampled confusion. Roused from their
beds by the unaccustomed sound of firing in the Fort,
the English officers went out to learn the cause of the
commotion, and many of them were shot down by the
mutineers in the first bewilderment of surprise. The
two senior officers of the garrison were among the
first who fell. On the threshold of his house, Fan-
court, who commanded the garrison, was warned, for
dear life's sake, not to come out, but answering with
the Englishman's favourite formula of " Never mind,"
he made for the Main Guard, and was shot with the
" Fall in !" on his lips. Of the survivors two or
three made their way to the barracks, and took command of such of the Europeans as had escaped the
first murderous onslaught of the Sepoys. But it was
little that the most desperate resolution could do in
this extremity to stem the continually increasing tide
of furious hostility which threatened to overwhelm
them. It was no mere military revolt. The inmates
of the Palace were fraternising with the Sepoys. From
the apartments of the Princes went forth food to re-
fresh the weary bodies of the insurgents, and vast
promises to stimulate and sustain the energies of their
minds. One of the Princes, the third son of Tippoo, Prince Moiz-
personally encouraged the leaders of the revolt. With ood-deen.
his own hands he gave them the significant bhetal-nut.
With his own lips he proclaimed the rewards to be
lavished upon the restorers of the Mahomedan dynasty.
And from his apartments a confidential servant was
seen to bring the tiger-striped standard of Mysore,
which, amidst vociferous cries of " Dheen ! Dheen !"
was hoisted above the walls of the Palace. But the
family of the Sultan were soon forgotten. There was
no combination to aid their escape. The Sepoys at

1806.

first gave themselves up to the work of massacre. The people from the Palace, following in their wake, gorged themselves with the plunder of the white men, and aided the mutineers without sharing their danger. After a time the Sepoys betook themselves also to plunder; and the common object was forgotten under the excitement of personal greed. The white women in the Fort were spared. The tender mercies of the wicked, with a refined cruelty, preserved them for a worse fate than death. The people from the Palace told the Sepoys not to kill them, as all the English would be destroyed, and the Moormen might then take them for wives.*

But whilst these terrible scenes were being enacted, and the sons of Tippoo were swelling with the proud certainty of seeing the rule of the Sultan again established in Mysore, retribution swift and

Major Coats. certain was overtaking the enterprise. An officer of the English regiment, who happened to be on duty outside the Fort, heard the firing, thoroughly apprehended the crisis, and, through the darkness of the early morning, made his way to Arcot, to carry thither the tidings of insurrection, and to summon succours to the aid of the imperilled garrison. There

The 19th was a regiment of British Dragoons at Arcot, under
Dragoons. the command of Colonel Gillespie. By seven o'clock Coats had told his story. Fifteen minutes afterwards, Gillespie, with a squadron of his regiment, was on his way to Vellore. The rest were saddling and mounting; the galloper-guns were being horsed and limbered; and a squadron of Native Cavalry was responding to the trumpet-call with as much alacrity

---

* The massacre included fourteen officers and ninety-nine soldiers killed. There were, moreover, seve- ral officers and men wounded, some of the latter mortally.

as the British Dragoons. The saving virtues of
promptitude and preparation were never more conspicuously manifested. A little vacillation, a little
blundering, a little delay, the result of nothing being
ready when wanted, and all might have been lost.
Never had the sage precept of Hyder Ali, that the
English should keep their white soldiers like hunting-
leopards in cages, and slip them suddenly and fiercely
at the enemy, been wrought into practice with more
terrible effect, than now against the followers and
supporters of his descendants.

Once under the walls of Vellore, Gillespie was
eager to make his way into the Fort, that he might
rally the remnant of the European garrison and
secure the safe admission of his men. The outer
gates were open, but the last was closed, and in possession of the enemy. There was no hope of forcing
it without the aid of the guns. But these were now
rapidly approaching. There were good officers with
the relieving force, to whom the conduct of external
operations might be safely entrusted; and Gillespie
longed to find himself with the people whom he had
come to save. So, whilst preparations were being
made for the attack, he determined to ascend alone
the walls of the Fort. In default of ladders, the men
of the 69th let down a rope, and, amidst the shouts
of the delighted Europeans, he was drawn up, unhurt, to the crest of the ramparts, and took command
of the survivors of the unhappy force. Quickly
forming at the word of command, they came down
eagerly to the charge, and, cheered by the welcome
sound of the guns, which were now clamouring for
admission, and not to be denied, they kept the mutineers at a distance till the gates were forced; and
then the cavalry streamed in, and victory was easy.

1800. The retribution was terrible, and just. Hundreds fell beneath the sabres of the Dragoons and of the native horsemen, who emulated the ardour of their European comrades. Hundreds escaped over the walls of the Fort, or threw down their arms and cried for mercy. But the excited troopers, who had seen Tippoo's tiger-standard floating over the citadel of Vellore, could not, after that hot morning-ride, believe that they had done their work until they had destroyed the "cubs." They were eager to be led into the Palace, and there to inflict condign punishment on those whom they believed to be the real instigators of the butchery of their countrymen. For a moment there was a doubt in Gillespie's mind; but an appeal from Colonel Marriott, in whose charge was the Mysore family, removed it; and he put forth a restraining hand. He would not soil his victory with any cruel reprisals. The members of Tippoo's family were now at his mercy, and the mercy which he showed them was that which the Christian soldier delights to rain down upon the fallen and the helpless. *

* For all the facts given in the text, I have the authority of a mass of official, semi-official, and private contemporary correspondence, which I have very carefully collated. In doing so, I have been compelled to reject some personal incidents which have hitherto generally formed part of the narrative of the "Massacre of Vellore," but which, however serviceable they may be for purposes of effective historical writing, are, I am sorry to say, at best apocryphal. It has been said that the officer who carried the tidings to Arcot escaped through a sally-port, and swam the ditch of the Fort so famous for the number and size of its alligators. Sober official correspondence states that Major Coats, who was bearer of the news, was outside the Fort at the time of the outbreak. It is very generally stated, too, that when Gillespie wished to enter the Fort in advance of his men, as there were no ladders and no ropes, the survivors of the 69th fastened their belts together, and thus drew him up the walls. But I have before me two letters, signed " R. Gillespie," which state that he was drawn up by a rope. Among the fictitious incidents of the mutiny may be mentioned the whole of the stories which tell of the foul murder of English women, and the braining of little children before their mothers' eyes.

But the storm had not expended itself in this fierce 1806. convulsion. Taught by so stern a lesson, the Government resolved that "all orders which might be liable to the objection of affecting the usages of the troops," should be abandoned. But the obnoxious hats might have been burnt before the eyes of the troops, and the caste-marks and ear-rings restored on parade, in the presence of the Governor, the Commander-in-Chief, and all the magnates of the land; and still a return to quietude and contentment might have been far distant. Individual causes of anger and bitterness might be removed, but still there would remain, together with the mistrust they had engendered, all the vague anxieties on the one side, and the indefinite expectations on the other, which designing men had excited in the minds of the soldiery.* Rebellion had been crushed for a time at its Head-Quarters. The British flag floated again over Vellore; but there were other strong posts, which it had been intended to seize, and efforts might yet be made to establish revolt in other parts of the Southern Peninsula.

Nor was it only in Mysore and the Carnatic that Hyderabad. the spirit of disaffection was rife. In the Deccan, also, it was manifesting itself in a manner which, for a while, created serious alarm. At Hyderabad, the capital of the Nizam's dominions, there was a high

---

* "The subversion of the British Empire in India by foreign invasion and domestic revolt, seems to have been the common theme of discourse all over the country, and opinions have generally prevailed that such a revolution was neither an enterprise of great difficulty, nor that the accomplishment of it was far distant. . . . . . A most extraordinary and unaccountable impression has been made upon the Sepoys, which has been fomented by prophecies and predictions inducing a belief that wonderful changes are about to take place, and that the Europeans are to be expelled from India."—*General Hay Macdowall. Nundydroog, Oct. 31. MS. Correspondence.*

1806. tide of excitement. It was apprehended that the
native troops of the Subsidiary Force, encouraged
and aided by some of the chief people of this Mahomedan State, if not by the Nizam himself, would
break out into revolt. They were wrought upon by
nearly the same influences as had destroyed the
loyalty of the troops in Mysore, with some peculiar
aggravations of their own. A new commanding
Colonel Mon- officer had recently been placed over them—a smart
tresor.   disciplinarian of the most approved European pattern.
They had been worried and alarmed before his ar
rival. Montresor's appearance soon made matters
worse. Knowing little or nothing of the habits and
feelings of the people of the country, he enforced
the new orders with more than common strictness,
and supplemented them with some obnoxious regulations of his own. An order had been issued just
before his arrival forbidding the Sepoy to leave his
Guard and to divest himself of his uniform during
his period of duty; and now the new English commandant prohibited the beating of taum-taums in the
bazaars. It was not seen that these prohibitions were,
in effect, orders that the Hindoo Sepoy should take no
sustenance on duty, and that there should be no marriage and no funeral processions. When the discovery was made, the new local regulations were re-
scinded; but it was not possible to rescind the mischief that was done. There was a profound conviction among the Sepoys that it was the intention of
the English to destroy their caste, to break down
their religion, and forcibly to convert them to Christianity. And all through the long straggling lines of
Hyderabad there was a continual buzz of alarm, and
the Sepoys were asking each other if they had heard

how the English General, Wemyss Sahib, at Colombo, had marched his native soldiers to Church.[*]

That the feeling of mingled fear and resentment, which had taken possession of the minds of the soldiery, was much fomented by emissaries from the city of Hyderabad, is not to be doubted. Many leading men, discontented and desperate, at all times prone to intrigue and ripe for rebellion, looked eagerly for a crisis out of which might have come some profit to themselves. It is probable that they were in communication with dependents of the House of Tippoo. It is certain that they fostered the resentments and stimulated the ambition of the native officers, and that a programme of action had been agreed upon, of which murder and massacre were the prelude.[†] But happily the Nizam and his minister, Meer Allum—the one in word, the other in spirit—were true to the English alliance. Wisely, in that conjuncture, did Sydenham confide all his troubles to them. It is a sad necessity to be compelled to communicate to a native Prince the belief of the English Government that their troops are not to be trusted. But concealment in such a case is impossible, and any attempt to disguise the truth helps

---

[*] "It is astonishing how strong and how general the impression was of a systematic design to enforce the conversion of the Sepoys to Christianity. The men here heard, and talked of the late arrival of some clergymen from England, and of the story of General Wemyss marching the Sepoys to church at Colombo."— *Captain Thomas Sydenham (Resident at Hyderabad) to Mr. Edmonstone, July 27, 1806. MS. Correspondence.*

[†] Captain Sydenham wrote that, from the best information he could obtain at Hyderabad, it appeared that "the native troops had been invited to desert their colours, to break out in open mutiny, and to murder their officers. It was intended that a commotion should have taken place in the city at the moment of the insurrection in cantonments; that Meer Allum, and all those in the interests of the English, were to be destroyed; that the Soubahdar (Nizam) was to be confined, and Feridoom Jah either made Dewan or placed on the musnud, as circumstances might suggest."—*MS. Correspondence.*

others to exaggerate and to distort it. The Nizam knew all that had been going on, perhaps before the British Resident had even a suspicion of it. Eager for his support, and willing to raise the standard of revolt in his name, the conspirators had conveyed to him a written paper signifying their wishes. He did not answer it. He did not give it to the Resident. He simply waited and did nothing. It was not in the nature of the man to do more. He knew the power of the English; but he secretly hated them, and naturally shrank from opposing or betraying a cause which appealed to him in the name of his religion. Perhaps it is hardly fair to expect from a native Prince, under such conflicting circumstances, more than this negative support.

The feeling among the native troops was so strong, the danger appeared to be so imminent, that Montresor was besought by some old Sepoy officers not to enforce the obnoxious regulations. But he replied that he had been selected for that especial command as a fitting agent for their enforcement, and how could he turn his back upon his duty? But when tidings of the massacre at Vellore reached Hyderabad, he saw at once that concession must be made to the prejudices of the Sepoy, and the orders were revoked in anticipation of instructions from the Madras Government. Still the troops were not satisfied. Having gained one victory they determined to attempt another. So they fell back upon the old grievance of the leather stock, and the men of some of the battalions, encouraged by their native officers, were seen disencumbering themselves of this article of their uniform on parade, and casting it contemptuously on the ground. A display of vigour at the right time crushed the mutiny ere it was matured. On the

14th of August, the troops at Hyderabad were ordered under arms.   The English regiment was
posted near the park of artillery, and the cavalry
were drawn up *en potence* on both flanks.   Then four
Soubahdars of Native Infantry, who were believed to
be the ringleaders in the mutinous movement, were
called to the front and marched off under a guard of
thirty Europeans and a company of Sepoys.   Under
this escort they were sent to Masulipatam.   This
movement had the best possible effect both in the
cantonment and the city.   Mutiny was awe-struck ;
sedition was paralysed ; conciliatory explanations
and addresses, which had before failed, were now
crowned with success, and early in the following
month Sydenham wrote from Hyderabad that everything was " perfectly tranquil, both in the city and
the cantonments."   " The Sepoys," it added, " appear cheerful and contented, and the Government
goes on with considerable vigour and regularity."

But ere long the anxieties of the Government
again turned towards the old quarter.   It was clear
that, in the former domains of the Sultan, the fire,
though suppressed for a time, had not been extinguished.   At Nundydroog, in the heart of the
Mysore territory, there had been symptoms of uneasiness from the commencement of the year.   The
native troops were few ; but the fortress, built upon
a high scarped rock, was one of uncommon strength,
and, well defended, might have defied attack.   In
itself, therefore, a coveted possession for the rebel
force, it was rendered doubly important by its
position.   For it was within a night's march of
the great station of Bangalore, and the mutineers
from that post would have flocked to it as a
rallying-point and a stronghold, admirably suited

1806.   for the Head-Quarters of Rebellion.* The influences, therefore, of which I have spoken—the fakeers, the conjurors, the puppet-showmen, the propagators of strange prophecies—were more than commonly operative in that direction, and had success attended the first outbreak at Vellore, the Nundydroog garrison would then have turned upon their officers, hoisted the rebel flag on the walls of the Fort, and displayed signals which might have been seen at Bangalore. But a season of suspended activity naturally followed this failure; and it was not until the month of October that they ventured to resolve on any open demonstration. Then the Mahomedan and Hindoo Sepoys feasted together, bound themselves by solemn engagements to act as brethren in a common cause, and swore that they would rise against and massacre their English officers.

October 18, 1806.   The day and the hour of the butchery were fixed. The native soldiery had quietly sent their families out of the Fort, and otherwise prepared for the struggle.† Two hours before midnight on the 18th of October the Sepoys were to have rushed upon their English officers, and not left a white man living in the place.

Capt. Baynes. But about eight o'clock on that evening an English officer galloped up to the house of the Commandant Cuppage, and told him that no time was to be lost; that the Sepoys were on the point of rising, and that

---

* Mark Wilks wrote to Barry Close, with reference to this movement at Nundydroog: "I do not know what to make of all this; men who had any great combination in view could scarcely have any design to act on so small a scale." But Barry Close, taking a more comprehensive view, replied: "The great object of the Insurgents at Vellore seems to have been to secure to themselves a strong post on which to assemble in force. Cuppage's garrison, though small, may have had it in view to seize on Nundydroog. Possessed of this strong post, the conspirators would have probably assembled upon it in force, and proceeded to act against us openly."— *MS. Correspondence.*

† Colonel Cuppage to Barry Close. —*MS. Correspondence.*

means of safety must at once be sought. Scarce had 1806.
the story been told, when an old and distinguished
native officer came breathless with the· same intelligence. There was no room for doubt; no time for
delay. An express, calling for reinforcements, was
despatched to Bangalore; and the officers, selecting
one of their houses in the Pagoda-square, which
seemed best adapted to purposes of defence, took post
together and waited the issue. The night passed
without an attack; and on the morrow afternoon
safety came in the shape of a squadron of Dragoons
from Bangalore. Colonel Davis had received the
tidings soon after daybreak, and by three o'clock his
troopers were clattering into Nundydroog.

November came, and with it came new troubles. Pallamcottah
Far down the coast, not many leagues removed from
the southernmost part of the Peninsula, lies the station
of Pallamcottah. There Major Welsh, with six European officers under him, commanded a Sepoy battalion,
in which many relatives of the mutineers cut up at
Vellore were brooding over their loss of kindred.
Towards the end of the third week of the month, it
was believed that the Mahomedan Sepoys were about
to rise and to massacre all the Europeans in the place.
The story ran that, rejecting with contempt the idea
of banding themselves with the Hindoos, they had
met at a mosque and concerted their murderous plans.
Some buildings were to be fired in the cantonment to
draw the English officers from their homes. In the
confusion, the whole were to be slain, the Fort was to
be seized, and the rebel flag hoisted on the ramparts.
Scenting the plot, a Malabar-man went to the mosque
in disguise, and carried tidings of it to the English
Commandant. The danger appeared to be imminent,
and Welsh at once took his measures to avert it

Whatever may have been the judgment and discretion of the man, his courage and determination were conspicuous; and his comrades were of the same temper. Assuming the bold, intrepid front, which has so often been known to overawe multitudes, this little handful of undaunted Englishmen seized and confined thirteen native officers, and turned five hundred Mussulman Sepoys out of the Fort. That they were able to accomplish this, even with the support of the Hindoos, was declared to be a proof that no desperate measures had really been designed. But the premature explosion of a plot of this kind always creates a panic. In a state of fear and surprise, men are not capable of reasoning. There is a vague impression that boldness presages power; that there is something behind the imposing front. A single man has ere now routed a whole garrison. I am not sure, therefore, that there was no danger, because it was so easily trodden out.

Two days afterwards Colonel Dyce, who commanded the district of Tinnivelly, threw himself into Pallamcottah; assembled the Hindoo troops; told them that he had come there to maintain the authority of the Company, or to die in the defence of the colours which he had sworn to protect. He then called upon those who were of the same mind to approach the British flag for the same purpose, but if not, to depart in peace. They went up and took the oath to a man, presented arms to the colours, gave three unbidden cheers in earnest of their unshaken loyalty, and fell in as on a muster-parade.

On the first appearance of danger, Welsh had despatched a letter by a country-boat to Ceylon, calling for European troops, and the call was responded to with an alacrity beyond all praise. But so effectual were the measures which had been already adopted, or so little of real danger had there been, that when the succour which had been sent for arrived from Trichinopoly, the alarm had passed, and the work was done.

Told as I have told this story—a simple recital of facts, as written down in contemporary correspondence —it would appear to afford an instructive example of the virtue of promptitude and vigour. But this is not the only lesson to be learnt from it. It is more instructive still to note that Major Welsh was severely condemned as an alarmist, the tendency of whose precipitate action was to destroy confidence and to create irritation. Another officer,* who, apprehending danger, had disarmed his regiment as a precaution, was denounced with still greater vehemence.† Apprehensions of this kind were described as "disgraceful and groundless panics;" and political officers chuckled to think that it was proposed at Madras to remove from their commands and to bring to Courts-Martial the officers who had considered it their duty not to wait to be attacked.‡ With these lessons before

---

* Lieutenant-Colonel Grant.

† I find this fact recorded in the correspondence of the day with three notes of exclamation : "With regard to Colonel Grant," wrote Major Wilks from Mysore, "it appears that he disarmed his troops simply as a measure of precaution!!! Whether we are in danger from our own misconduct, or from worse causes, the danger is great. . . . I conclude that Chalmers will be sent to supersede Grant, and Vesey to Pallamcottah, and my best hope is that there will be found sufficient grounds for turning Welsh and Grant out of the service, but this will not restore the confidence of the Sepoys." — *M.S. Correspondence.* Grant's conduct was at once repudiated in a general order,

and he and Welsh ordered for Court-Martial. Both were honourably acquitted.

‡ Many years after the occurrence of these events, Major, then Colonel Welsh, published two volumes of Military Reminiscences. Turning to these for some account of the affair at Pallamcottah, I was disappointed to find only the following scanty notice of it : "Towards the end of the year an event took place, which, although injurious to my own prospects and fortune, under the signal blessing of Providence terminated fortunately. Time has now spread his oblivious wings over the whole occurrence, and I will not attempt to remove the veil."

1806.

us, we cannot wonder that men, in such conjunctures, should hesitate to strike the blow which any one may declare uncalled-for, and the wisdom of which no one can prove—should pause to consider whether they are more likely to develop the evil by an assertion of strength, or to encourage its growth by the feebleness of inaction.*

Wallajaha-bad.

But it was plain that, whatsoever might be the wisest course in such a conjuncture, the Government of Lord William Bentinck was all in favour of the milder and more sedative mode of treatment. In remarkable contrast to the manner in which the symptoms of coming mutiny were grappled with at Pallamcottah stands the story of Wallajahabad. Some of the earliest signs of disaffection, on the score of the turban, had manifested themselves at that place; and Gillespie, with his dragoons, had been despatched thither at the end of July, not without a murmur of discontent at the thought of his "poor hard-worked fellows" being sent to counteract what appeared to him a doubtful danger. It was believed, however, that the uneasiness had passed away, and for some months there had been apparent tranquillity. But in November the alarm began to revive; and a

---

* The difficulties of the English officer at that time were thus described by a contemporary writer, in a passage which I have chanced upon since the above was written: "The massacre at Vellore had naturally created a great degree of mistrust between the European officers and the Sepoys throughout the Army; and the indecision of measures at Head-Quarters seemed further to strengthen this mistrust. If an officer took *no* precautionary measures on receiving information of an intended plot, he was liable to the severest censure, as well as responsible for his own and the lives of his European officers. On the contrary, if he took precautionary measures he was accused of creating unnecessary distrust; and equally censured for being premature and not allowing the mutiny to *go on* till satisfactorily proved, when it would have been too late to prevent."—*Strictures on the present Government of India, &c. In a Letter from an Officer resident on the spot. Trichinopoly,* 1807; *London,* 1808.

detailed statement of various indications of a coming
outbreak, drawn up by Major Hazlewood, was sent to
the authorities. On the morning of the 2nd of December the members of the Madras Government met
in Council. Hazlewood's statement was laid before
them and gravely discussed; but with no definite
result. The Council broke up without a decision, but
only to meet again, refreshed by the sea-breeze and
the evening ride. Then it was resolved that a discreet
officer, in the confidence of Government, should be
sent to Wallajahabad to inquire into and report on
the state of affairs; and on the same evening Colonel
Munro, the Quartermaster-General, received his instructions, and prepared to depart. The event appeared to justify this cautious line of action; but
one shudders to think what might have happened at
Wallajahabad whilst Government were deliberating
over written statements of danger, and drafting instructions for a Staff-officer in the Council-Chamber
of Madras.

Six months had now passed since the Madras Government had been made acquainted with the state
of feeling in the Native Army, and understood that a
vague apprehension of the destruction of caste and of
"forcible conversion to Christianity" had been one
of the chief causes of the prevailing disquietude.
The obnoxious regulations had been abandoned, but
this was a concession obviously extorted from fear;
and nothing had yet been done to reassure the
minds of the soldiery by a kindly paternal address
to them from the fountain-head of the local Government. But at last Bentinck and his colleagues
awoke to a sense of the plain and palpable duty
which lay before them; and at this Council of the
2nd of December a Proclamation was agreed upon,

1806.

Dec., 1806.

R 2

and on the following day issued, which, translated into the Hindostanee, the Tamul, and Telegoo dialects, was sent to every native battalion in the Army, with orders to commanding officers to make its contents known to every native officer and Sepoy under their command. After adverting to the extraordinary agitation that had for some time prevailed in the Coast Army, and the reports spread for malicious purposes, by persons of evil intention, that it was the design of the British Government to convert the troops by forcible means to Christianity, the Proclamation proceeded to declare that the constant kindness and liberality at all times shown to the Sepoy should convince him of the happiness of his situation, "greater than what the troops of any other part of the world enjoy," and induce him to return to the good conduct for which he had been distinguished in the days of Lawrence and Coote, and "other renowned heroes." If they would not, they would learn that the British Government "is not less prepared to punish the guilty than to protect and distinguish those who are deserving of its favour." But this was something more than the truth. The British Government did not show itself, in this conjuncture, to be "prepared to punish the guilty" in a manner proportionate to the measure of their offences. Lord William Bentinck and his Councillors were all for clemency. Sir John Cradock counselled the adoption of more vigorous punitory measures, and the Supreme Government were disposed to support the military chief. Something of a compromise then ensued, the result of which was a very moderate instalment of the retribution which was justly due. A few only of the most guilty of the murderers were executed; whilst others, clearly convicted of taking part in the sanguinary revolt, were merely dismissed the service. And **1806.** if it had not been for the overruling authority of the Government at Calcutta—that is, of Sir George Barlow, with Mr. Edmonstone at his elbow*—the numbers of the assassin-battalions would not have been erased from the Army List. But penal measures did not end here. The higher tribunals of the Home Government condemned the chief authorities of Madras, and, justly or unjustly, the Governor, the Commander-in-Chief, and the Adjutant-General, were summarily removed from office.

The mutiny died out with the old year; the active **1807.** danger was passed; but it left behind it a flood Alleged of bitter controversy which did not readily subside. causes of th What was the cause of the revolt? Whose fault was Revolt. it? Was it a mere military mutiny, the growth of internal irritation, or was it a political movement fomented by agitators from without? The controversialists on both sides were partly wrong and partly right—wrong in their denials, right in their assertions. It is difficult in such a case to put together in proper sequence all the links of a great chain of events terminating even in an incident of yesterday, so little do we know of what is stirring in the occult heart of native society. After a lapse of half a century it is impossible. There is often in the Simultaneous, the Coincidental, an apparent uniformity of tendency, which simulates design, but which, so far as human agency is concerned, is wholly fortuitous. We see

---

* Many years afterwards, Sir George Barlow gracefully acknowledged the valuable assistance which, in this conjuncture, Mr. Edmonstone had rendered to him, saying that his "unshaken firmness and resolution in times of internal difficulty and danger" were "signally displayed on the discovery of the conspiracy formed at Vellore." "His wise and steady counsel," added Barlow, "afforded me important aid and support in carrying into effect the measures necessary for counteracting the impressions made by that alarming event, which threatened the most serious consequences to the security of our power."—*MS. Documents.*

1807.

this in the commonest concerns of life. We see it in events affecting mightily the destinies of empires. Under a pressure of concurrent annoyances and vexations, men often cry out that there is a conspiracy against them, and the historical inquirer often sees a conspiracy when in reality there is only a coincidence. A great disaster, like the massacre at Vellore, acts like iodine upon hidden writings in rice-water. Suddenly is proclaimed to us in all its significance what has long been written down on the page of the Past, but which, for want of the revealing agent, has hitherto lain illegibly before us. Doubtless, many hidden things were disclosed to us at this time; but whether they were peculiar to the crisis or of a normal character, at any period discernible, had we taken proper steps to develop them, was matter of grave dispute. The political officers, headed by Mark Wilks, the historian of Southern India, who was then representing British interests in Mysore, laughed to scorn the discoveries of the military officers, and said that the things which they spoke of as so portentous were in reality only phenomena of every-day appearance, familiar to men acquainted with the feelings and habits of the people. He derided all that had been said about seditious conversations in the Bazaars and the Lines, the wild prophecies and mysterious hints of wandering Fakeers, and the suggestive devices of the puppet-shows.* There was nothing in all this, he contended, of an exceptional character, to be regarded as the harbingers of mutiny and massacre. And his arguments culminated in the chuckling assertion that the military authorities had discovered

* There were two subjects which the *Kootpootlee-Wallahs* extremely delighted to illustrate—the degradation of the Mogul, and the victories of the French over the English, the one intended to excite hatred, the other contempt, in the minds of the spectators.

a cabalistic document of a most treasonable character, which appeared to their excited imaginations to be a plan for partitioning the territory to be wrested from the English, but which, in reality, was nothing more portentous than the scribblement of the Dervish Bazee, or "royal game of goose."

With equal confidence on the other hand, the military authorities protested that the new regulations had nothing to do with the mutiny—that it was altogether a political movement. The new cap, they said, had been accepted and worn by the Sepoys. Three representative men, types of the principal nationalities composing the Coast Army, had signified their satisfaction with the new head-dress, and one or two regiments *en masse* had been paraded in it without a murmur. The fact, they alleged, was that the movement had emanated solely from the deposed family of Tippoo Sultan; that its object was to restore, in the first instance, the Mahomedan dynasty in Southern India, and eventually to recover the imperial throne for the Mogul. If proper precautions had been taken by Government — if Tippoo's family, eager for a taste of blood, had not been left to disport themselves at will in Vellore—if they had not been gorged with money, and attended by countless Mussulman followers eager to recover the posts and the privileges which they had lost, there would, said the military leaders, have been no massacre and no mutiny and, some said, not even a murmur of discontent. But the military critic was as wrong as the political, and for the same reason. Each was blinded by professional interests and professional prejudices. Each argued in self-defence. The truth, as it commonly does in such cases, lay midway between the two extremes. But for the intrigues of Tippoo's family

1807. there would have been no outbreak at that time, and but for the new military regulations they might have intrigued in vain. It so happened that the political and military influences were adverse to us at the same moment, and that from the conjuncture arose the event known in history as the Massacre of Vellore, but which was in reality a much more extensive military combination, prevented only by repeated local failures from swelling into the dimensions of a general revolt of the Coast Army.

Nor is it to be forgotten that there was a third party, which attributed the calamity less to political and to military causes than to the general uneasiness, which had taken possession of the native mind in consequence of the supposed activity of Christian missionaries and of certain "missionary chaplains." The dread of a general destruction of Caste and forcible conversion to Christianity was not confined to the Sepoys. The most preposterous stories were current in the Bazaars. Among other wild fables, which took firm hold of the popular mind, was one to the effect that the Company's officers had collected all the newly-manufactured salt, had divided it into two great heaps, and over one had sprinkled the blood of hogs, and over the other the blood of cows; that they had then sent it to be sold throughout the country for the pollution and the desecration of Mahomedans and Hindoos, that all might be brought to one caste and to one religion like the English. When this absurd story was circulated, some ceased altogether to eat salt, and some purchased, at high price, and carefully stored away, supplies of the necessary article, guaranteed to have been in the Bazaars, before the atrocious act of the Feringhees had been committed. Another story was that the Collector of

Trincomalee had, under the orders of Government, laid the foundation of a Christian Church in his district close to the great Pagoda of the Hindoos; that he had collected all the stone-cutters and builders in the neighbourhood; that he was taxing every household for the payment of the cost of the building; that he had forbidden all ingress to the Pagoda, and all worshipping of idols; and that to all complaints on the subject he had replied that there was nothing extraordinary in what he was doing, as Government had ordered a similar building to be erected in every town and every village in the country. In India, stories of this kind are readily believed. The grosser the lie the more eagerly it is devoured.* They are circulated by designing persons with a certainty that they will not be lost. That the excitement of religious alarm was the principal means by which the enemies of the British Government hoped to accomplish their objects is certain; but if there had not been a foregone determination to excite this alarm, nothing in the actual progress of Christianity at that time would have done it. A comparison, indeed, between the religious status of the English in India and the wild stories of forcible conversion, which were then circu-

1807.

* Not immediately illustrating this point of inquiry, but even more preposterous in itself than the rumours cited in the text, was a story which was circulated at Hyderabad. It was stated that an oracle in a neighbouring Pagoda had declared that there was considerable treasure at the bottom of a well in the European barracks, which was destined not to be discovered until a certain number of human heads had been offered up to the tutelar deity of the place; and that accordingly the European soldiers were sacrificing the necessary number of victims with all possible despatch. It happened that the dead body of a native without a head was found near the Residency, and that a drunken European artilleryman, about the same time, attacked a native sentry at his post. These facts gave new wings to the report, and such was the alarm that the natives would not leave their homes or work after dark, and it was reported both to the Nizam and his minister that a hundred bodies without heads were lying on the banks of the Moose River.—*Captain Sydenham to the Government of India. MS. Records.*

1807.

lated, seemed openly to give the lie to the malignant inventions of the enemy. There were no indications on the part of Government of any especial concern for the interests of Christianity, and among the officers of the Army there were so few external signs of religion that the Sepoys scarcely knew whether they owned any faith at all.* But in a state of panic men do not pause to reason; and if at any time the doubt had been suggested, it would have been astutely answered that the English gentlemen cared only to destroy the religions of the country, and to make the people all of one or of no caste, in order that they might make their soldiers and servants do everything they wished.

Views of the Home Government.

The authoritative judgment of a Special Commission appointed to investigate the causes of the outbreak confirmed the views of the more moderate section of the community, which recognised, not one, but many disturbing agencies; and the Home Government accepted the interpretation in a candid and impartial spirit. That " the late innovations as to the dress and appearance of the Sepoys were the leading cause of the mutiny, and the other was the residence of the family of the late Tippoo Sultan at Vellore," was, doubtless, true as far as it went. But the merchant-rulers of Leadenhall-street were disposed to sound the lower depths of the difficulty. Those were not days when the numerous urgent claims of the Present imperatively forbad the elaborate investigation of the Past. So the Directors began seriously to consider what had been the more remote predisposing causes of the almost general disaffection

* Sir John Cradock said, after the occurrence of these events, that " from the total absence of religious establishments in the interior of the country, from the habits of life prevalent among military men, it is a melancholy truth that so unfrequent are the religious observances of officers doing duty with battalions, that the Sepoys have not, until very lately, discovered the nature of the religion professed by the English."

of the Coast Army. And the "Chairs," in a masterly letter to Mr. Dundas, freighted with the solid intelligence of Charles Grant, declared their conviction that the general decline of the fidelity of the Army and of the attachment of the People to British rule, was to be traced to the fact that a new class of men, with little knowledge of India, little interest in its inhabitants, and little toleration for their prejudices, had begun to monopolise the chief seats in the Government and the chief posts in the Army; that the annexations of Lord Wellesley had beggared the old Mahomedan families, and had shaken the belief of the people in British moderation and good faith; and that the whole tendency of the existing system was to promote the intrusion of a rampant Englishism, and thus to widen the gulf between the Rulers and the Ruled.*

* The Chairman and Deputy-Chairman of the East India Company (Mr. Parry and Mr. Grant) to the President of the Board of Control (Mr. Dundas).—*May* 18, 1807. *MS. Records.*

CHAPTER II.

SUBSIDENCE OF ALARM—THE SOLDIER IN ENGLAND AND IN INDIA—THE
SEPOY AND HIS OFFICER—DETERIORATING INFLUENCES—THE DRAINAGE
OF THE STAFF—PROGRESS OF CENTRALISATION—THE REORGANISATION
OF 1824—THE BARRACKPORE MUTINY—THE HALF-BATTA ORDER—ABO-
LITION OF CORPORAL PUNISHMENT.

.807-1809.   IT was not strange that for some time after the occurrence of these events in the Coast Army, the English in Southern India should have been possessed by
a common sense of anger, and that this feeling should
have spread to some other parts of the country.   For
a while the white man saw a conspirator beneath the
folds of every turban, and a conspiracy in every
group of people talking by the wayside.   In every
laugh there was an insult, and in every shrug there
was a menace.   English officers pillowed their heads on
loaded fire-arms, and fondled the hilts of their swords
as they slept.   But gradually they lived down the sensitiveness that so distressed them.   Other thoughts and
feelings took possession of the bungalow ; other subjects were dominant in the mess-room.   And ere long
a new grievance came to supersede an old danger ;
and the officers of the Madras Army forgot the rcbel-
lion of the Sepoys as they incubated a rebellion of
their own.   How the mutiny of the officers grew out
of the mutiny of the men of the Coast Army, it
would not be difficult to show ; but the chapter of

utiny of
idras
ficers,
09.

Indian history which includes the former need not be re-written here.   The objects for which the officers contended were altogether remote from the interests and sympathies of the Sepoys ; and although the latter, in ignorance, might at first have followed their commanders, it is not probable that they would have continued to cast in their lot with the mutineers, after the true character of the movement had been explained to them, and an appeal made to their fidelity by the State.   But they were not unobservant spectators of that unseemly strife; and the impression made upon the Sepoy's mind by this spectacle of disunion must have been of a most injurious kind. There is nothing so essential to the permanence of that Opinion, on which we so much rely, as a prevailing sense that the English in India are not Many but One.

Nor was it strange that, after these unfortunate events, the fame of which went abroad throughout the whole country, there should have been for a little space less eagerness than before to enlist into the service of the Company.   But the reluctance passed away under the soothing influence of time.   In the prompt and regular issue of pay, and in the pensions, which had all the security of funded property, there were attractions, unknown to Asiatic armies, not easily to be resisted.   And there were other privileges, equally dear to the people of the country, which lured them by thousands into the ranks of the Company's Army.   As soon as his name was on the muster-roll, the Sepoy, and through him all the members of his family, passed under the special protection of the State.

It is difficult to conceive two conditions of life The English more dissimilar in their social aspects than soldiering Soldier.

1807-1809. in India and soldiering in England. In England, few men enlist into the Army as an honourable profession, or seek it as an advantageous source of subsistence. Few men enter it with any high hopes or any pleasurable emotions. The recruit has commonly broken down as a civilian. Of ruined fortune and bankrupt reputation, he is tempted, cheated, snared into the Army. Lying placards on the walls, lying words in the pot-house, the gaudy ribbons of Sergeant Kite, the drum and the fife and the strong drink, captivate and enthral him when he is not master of himself. He has quarrelled with his sweetheart or robbed his employer. He has exhausted the patience of his own people, and the outer world has turned its back upon him. And so he goes for a soldier. As soon as he has taken the shilling, he has gone right out of the family circle and out of the circle of civil life. He is a thousandth part of a regiment of the Line. Perhaps he has changed his name and stripped himself of his personal identity. Anyhow, he is as one dead. Little more is heard of him; and unless it be some doting old mother, who best loves the blackest sheep of the flock, nobody much wishes to hear. It is often, indeed, no greater source of pride to an English family to know that one of its members is serving the Queen, in the ranks of her Army, than to know that one is provided for, as a convict, at the national expense.

The Indian Soldier.

But the native soldier of India was altogether of a different kind. When he became a soldier, he did not cease to be a civilian. He severed no family ties; he abandoned no civil rights. He was not the outcast, but the stay and the pride of his house. He visited his home at stated times. He remitted to it a large part of his pay. It was a decorous boast in

many families that generation after generation had 1807-1809.
eaten the Company's salt. Often, indeed, in one
household you might see the Past, the Present, and
the Future of this coveted military service. There
was the ancient pensioner under the shade of the
banyan-tree in his native village, who had stories to
tell of Lawrence, Coote, and Medows; of battles
fought with the French; of the long war with Hyder
and the later struggles with his son. There was the
Sepoy, on furlough from active service, in the prime
of his life, who had his stories also to tell of "the
great Lord's brother," the younger Wellesley, of
Harris and Baird, perhaps of "Bikrum Sahib" and Abercrombie and Lake.
Egypt, and how "Lick Sahib," the fine old man,
when provisions were scarce in the camp, had ridden
through the lines, eating dried pulse for his dinner.
And there was the bright-eyed, supple-limbed, quick-
witted boy, who looked forward with eager expectancy to the time when he would be permitted to
take his father's place, and serve under some noted
leader. It was no fond delusion, no trick of our self-
love, to believe in such pictures as this. The Company's Sepoys had a genuine pride in their colours,
and the classes from which they were drawn rejoiced
in their connexion with the paramount State. It was
honourable service, sought by the very flower of the
people, and to be dismissed from it was a heavy
punishment and a sore disgrace.

Strong as were these ties, the people were bound
to the military service of the Company by the still
stronger ties of self-interest. For not only were the Civil privi-
Sepoys, as has been said, well cared-for as soldiers leges of the Sepoy.
—well paid and well pensioned—but, as civilians,
they had large privileges which others did not enjoy.
Many of them, belonging to the lesser yeomanry of

1807-1809. the country, were possessors of, or shareholders in, small landed estates. And thus endowed, they rejoiced greatly in a regulation which gave the Sepoy on furlough a right to be heard before other suitors in our civil courts.* In a country whose people are inordinately given to litigation, and where justice is commonly slow-paced, this was so prodigious a boon, that entrance to the service was often sought for the express purpose of securing this valuable precedence, and the soldier-member of the family thus became the representative of his whole house. In this connexion of the soldiery with hereditary rights in the soil, there was an additional guarantee for his loyalty and good conduct. He was not merely a soldier—a component unit of number two company, third file from the right; he was an important member of society, a distinct individuality in his native village no less than in his cantonment Lines. He retained his self-respect and the respect of others; and had a personal interest in the stability of the Government under which his rights were secured.

And whilst these extraneous advantages were attached to his position as a soldier of the Company, there was nothing inherent in the service itself to render it distasteful to him. His officers were aliens of another colour and another creed; but the Hindoo was accustomed to foreign supremacy, and the Mahomedan, profoundly impressed with the mutabilities of fortune, bowed himself to the stern necessities of fate. As long as the Sepoy respected the personal

The Sepoy and his Officer.

---

* This was a part only of the civil privileges enjoyed by the native soldier. A memorandum in the Appendix will show the full extent of the advantages conferred upon him by this class-legislation. Sir Jasper Nicolls, in his evidence before the Parliamentary Committee of 1832, said that the withdrawal of these privileges had been regarded as an especial grievance by the Sepoys—but I have failed to discover that they ever were withdrawn.

qualities of the English officer, and the English officer 1809-1822. felt a personal attachment for the Sepoy, the relations between them were in no degree marred by any considerations of difference of race. There was a strong sense of comradeship between them, which atoned for the absence of other ties. The accidental severance of which I have spoken was but short-lived.* In that first quarter of the present century, which saw so much hard fighting in the field, the heart of the Sepoy officer again turned towards his men, and the men looked up and clung to him with child-like confidence and affection. To command a company, and, in due course, a regiment of Sepoys, was still held to be a worthy object of professional ambition. The regiment, in those days, was the officer's home, whether in camp, or cantonment, or on the line of march. There was but little looking beyond ; little hankering to leave it. To interest himself in the daily concerns of the Sepoys, to converse with them off parade, to enter into their feelings, to contribute to their comforts, were duties, the performance of which occupied his time, amused his mind, and yielded as much happiness to himself as it imparted to others. There was, in truth, little to divert him from the business of his profession or to raise up a barrier between him and his men. Intercourse with Europe was rare and difficult. Neither the charms of English literature nor the attractions of English womanhood alienated his affections from the routine of

---

* There had certainly been, before the mutiny in Southern India, a very culpable want of kindly consideration on the part of our English officers for the native officers and men of the Sepoy army. In the letter, written by the Chairman and Deputy-Chairman of the East India Company, to Mr. Dundas, referred to above, this is alleged to have been one of the remote causes of the mutiny. It is stated that the English had ceased to offer chairs to their native officers when visited by them. A favourable reaction, however, seems afterwards to have set in.

military life, and made its details dull and dreary in his sight. He had subdued his habits, and very much his way of thinking, to the Orientalism by which he was surrounded. He was glad to welcome the native officer to his bungalow, to learn from him the news of the Lines and the gossip of the Bazaar, and to tell him, in turn, what were the chances of another campaign and to what new station the regiment was likely to be moved at the approaching annual Relief. If there were any complaints in the regiment, the grievance was stated with freedom on the one side, and listened to with interest on the other. If the men were right, there was a remedy; if they were wrong, there was an explanation. The Sepoy looked to his officer as to one who had both the power and the will to dispense ample justice to him. In every battalion, indeed, the men turned to their commandant as the depository of all their griefs, and the redresser of all their wrongs. They called him their father, and he rejoiced to describe them as his "babalogue"—his babes.

Progress of Centralisation.

But in time the power was taken from him, and with the power went also the will. A variety of deteriorating circumstances occurred—some the inevitable growth of British progress in the East, and some the results of ignorance, thoughtlessness, or miscalculation on the part of the governing body. The power of the English officer was curtailed and his influence declined. The command of a regiment had once been something more than a name. The commanding-officer could promote his men, could punish his men, could dress them and discipline them as he pleased. The different battalions were called after the commander who had first led them to victory, and they rejoiced to be so distinguished. But, little by little, this power, by the absorbing action of *1822-1835* progressive centralisation, was taken out of his hands; and he who, supreme in his own little circle, had been now a patriarch and now a despot, shrivelled into the mouthpiece of the Adjutant-General's office and the instrument of Head-quarters. The decisions of the commanding officer were appealed against, and frequently set aside. In the emphatic language of the East, he was made to eat dirt in the presence of his men. The Sepoy, then, ceased to look up to him as the centre of his hopes and fears, and the commanding officer lost much of the interest which he before took in his men, when he knew how much their happiness and comfort depended upon his individual acts, and how the discipline and good conduct of the corps were the reflexion of his personal efficiency.

And it happened that, about the same time, new *England in India.* objects of interest sprung up to render more complete the severance of the ties which had once bound the English officer to the native soldier. The second quarter of the nineteenth century in India was a period of progressive reform. We reformed our Government and we reformed ourselves. Increased facilities of intercourse with Europe gave a more European complexion to society. English news, English books, above all, English gentlewomen, made their way freely and rapidly to India. The Overland Mail bringing news scarcely more than a month old of the last new European revolution; the book-club yielding its stores of light literature as fresh as is commonly obtained from circulating libraries at home; and an avatar of fair young English maidens, with the bloom of the Western summer on their cheeks, yielded attractions beside which the gossip of the lines and the feeble garrulity of the old Soubahdar

were very dréary and fatiguing. Little by little, the
Sepoy officer shook out the loose folds of his Orientalism. Many had been wont, in the absence of other
female society, to solace themselves with the charms
of a dusky mate, and to spend much time in the recesses of the Zenana. Bad as it was, when tried in
the crucible of Christian ethics, it was not without its
military advantages. The English officer, so mated,
learnt to speak the languages of the country, and to
understand the habits and feelings of the people; and·
he cherished a kindlier feeling for the native races
than he would have done if no such alliances had
been formed. But this custom passed away with the
cause that produced it. The English wife displaced
the native mistress. A new code of morals was recognised; and the Zenana was proscribed. With the appearance of the English gentlewoman in the military
cantonment there grew up a host of new interests
and new excitements, and the regiment became a
bore.

Staff employ-
ment.
Whilst these influences were sensibly weakening
the attachment which had existed between the native
soldier and his English officer, another deteriorating
agent was at work with still more fatal effect. The
Staff was carrying off all the best officers, and un-
settling the rest. As the red line of British Empire
extended itself around new provinces, and the administrative business of the State was thus largely increased, there was a demand for more workmen than
the Civil Service could supply, and the military establishment of the Company was, therefore, indented
upon for officers to fill the numerous civil and political posts thus opened out before them. Extensive
surveys were to be conducted, great public works
were to be executed, new irregular regiments were to

be raised, and territories not made subject to the "regulations" were, for the most part, to be administered by military men. More lucrative, and held to be more honourable than common regimental duty, these appointments were eagerly coveted by the officers of the Company's army. The temptation, indeed, was great. The means of marrying, of providing for a family, of securing a retreat to Europe before enfeebled by years or broken down by disease, were presented to the officer by this detached employment. And if these natural feelings were not paramount, there was the strong incentive of ambition or the purer desire to enter upon a career of more active utility. The number of officers with a regiment was thus reduced; but numbers are not strength, and still fewer might have sufficed, if they had been a chosen few. But of those who remained some lived in a state of restless expectancy, others were sunk in sullen despair. It was not easy to find a Sepoy officer, pure and simple, with no aspirations beyond his regiment, cheerful, content, indeed, proud of his position. All that was gone. The officer ceased to rejoice in his work, and the men saw his heart was not with them.

There were some special circumstances, too, which at this time—during the administrations of Lord Amherst and Lord William Bentinck—tended to aggravate these deteriorating influences both upon the officers and the men of the Sepoy regiments. Since the subsidence of the spirit of disaffection, which had pervaded the Coast Army in 1806, there had been no obtrusive manifestations of discontent in the Sepoy's mind. He had done his duty faithfully and gallantly in the great wars, which Lord Hastings

1822.   had conducted to a triumphant issue; but when peace
came again, he again, after a while, began to take
stock of his troubles and to listen to strange reports.
One more illustration may be drawn from Madras,
before the Bengal Army claims a monopoly of the
record.   In the early spring of 1822, a paper was
dropped in the Cavalry Lines of Arcot, setting forth
that the followers of Mahomed, having been subjected to the power of the English, suffered great
hardships—that being so subjected, their prayers were
not acceptable to the Almighty, and that, therefore,
in great numbers they were dying of cholera morbus
—that the curse of God was upon them; and that,
therefore, it behoved them to make a great effort for
the sake of their religion.   There were countless
Hindoos and Mussulmans between Arcot and Delhi.
But the Europeans being few, it would be easy to slay
the whole in one day.   Let them but combine, and
the result would be certain.   There was no time, it
said, to be lost.   The English had taken all the
Jagheers and Inams of the people of the soil, and
now they were about to deprive them of employment.
A number of European regiments had been called
for, and in the course of six months all the native
battalions would be disbanded.   Let, then, the senior
Soubahdar of each regiment instruct the other Soubahdars, and let them instruct the Jemadars, and so
on, till all the Sepoys were instructed, and the same
being done at Vellore, at Chittore, at Madras, and
other places, then, on a given signal, the whole
should rise on one day.   The day fixed was Sunday,
the 17th of March.   A Naick and ten Sepoys were
to proceed at midnight to the house of each European, and kill him, without remorse, in his bed.
This done, the regiments would be placed under the

Mahomedan Grievances.

command of the native officers, and the Soubahdars
should have the pay of Colonels. It was always thus.
It is always thus. A little for the Faith, and all for
the Pocket.

From whomsoever this paper may have emanated,
the attempt to corrupt the Sepoys was a failure. It
was picked up in the Lines of the Sixth Cavalry, and
another nearly resembling it was dropped in the Lines
of the Eighth—but both were carried at once to the
commanding officer of the station. Colonel Foulis
took his measures with promptitude and vigour. He
assembled the regimental commanders, imparted to
them the contents of the paper, and desired them to
place themselves in communication with the native
officers whom they most trusted. Having done this,
he wrote to the commandants of the several stations
named in the paper. But they could see no signs of
disaffection ; and the appointed day passed by without
even an audible murmur of discontent. But not
many days afterwards, the Governor of Madras re- Sir Thomas
ceived by the post a letter in Hindostanee, purporting Munro.
to come from the principal native officers and Sepoys
of the Army, setting forth the grievances under which
they suffered as a body. The complaint was that all
the wealth and all the honour went to the white
Sirdars, especially to the civilians, whilst for the
soldier there was nothing but labour and grief. "If
we Sepoys take a country," they said, "by the sword,
these whore-son cowardly civil Sirdars enter that
country and rule over it, and in a short time fill
their coffers with money and go to Europe—but if a
Sepoy labour all his life, he is not five couries the
better." Under the Mahomedan Government, it had
been different, for when victories were gained,
Jagheers were given to the soldiers, and high offices

1822.   distributed among them. But under the Company, everything was given to the Civil Service. "A single Collector's peon has an authority and greatness in the country which cannot be expressed. But that peon does not fight like a Sepoy." Such, in effect, was the plaint of the native soldiery, as conveyed to Governor Munro. It may have been the work of an individual, as might have been also the papers picked up in the lines of Arcot; but it is certain that both documents expressed sentiments which may be supposed at all times to lie embedded in the Sepoy's mind, and which need but little to bring them, fully developed, above the surface.[*]

The relations between the English officer and the native soldier were better then than they had been sixteen years before. But these relations were sadly weakened, and a heavy blow was given to the discipline and efficiency of the Indian army, when, two years later, the military establishments of the Three Presidencies were reorganised. Then every regiment of two battalions became two separate regiments, and the officers attached to the original corps were told off alternately to its two parts—"all the odd or uneven numbers," said the General Order, "to the first, and the even numbers to the second;" by which process it happened that a large number of officers were detached from the men with whom they had been associated throughout many years of active service. The evil of this was clearly seen at the time, and a feeble compromise was attempted. "It is not intended," said the General Order, "that in carrying the present orders into effect, officers should be permanently removed from the particular battalion in which they

The Reorganisation.

May 6, 1824.

* It was to this event that Sir Thomas Munro alluded in his remarkable minute on the dangers of a Free Press in India.

may long have served and wished to remain, provided that by an interchange between officers standing the same number of removes from promotion, each could be retained in his particular battalion, and both are willing to make the exchange." In effect, this amounted to little or nothing, and a large number of officers drifted away from the battalions in which they had been reared from boyhood, and strangers glided into their place.

Bad as at any time must have been such a change as this, in its influence upon the morale of the Sepoy army, the evil was greatly enhanced by falling upon evil times. The best preservative, and the best re- storative of military spirit and discipline, is commonly a good stirring war. But the Sepoy, though not un- willing to fight, was somewhat dainty and capricious about his fighting-ground. A battle-field in Hin- dostan or the Deccan was to his taste; but he was disquieted by the thought of serving in strange regions, of which he had heard only vague fables, beyond inaccessible mountain-ranges, or still more dreaded wildernesses of water. With the high-caste, fastidious Bengal Sepoy the war with Burmah was not, therefore, a popular war. The Madras Sepoy, more cosmopolitan and less nice, took readily to the transport vessel; and a large part of the native force was drawn from the Coast Army. But some Bengal regiments were also needed to take part in the opera- tions of the war, and then the system began to fail us. To transport troops by sea from Calcutta to Rangoon would have been an easy process. But the Bengal Sepoy had enlisted only for service in coun- tries to which he could march; to take ship was not in his bond. The regiments, therefore, were marched to the frontier station of Chittagong, and there as-

1824.

The Mutiny at Barrack-pore.

sembled for the landward invasion of the Burmese country.

Without any apparent symptoms of discontent, some corps had already marched, when, in October, the incident occurred of which I am about to write, an incident which created a most powerful sensation from one end of India to the other, and tended greatly to impair the loyalty and discipline of the Bengal Sepoy. The Forty-seventh Regiment had been warned for foreign service, and was waiting at Barrackpore, a few miles from the Presidency, whilst preparations were being made for its march in the cold weather. To wait is often to repent. Inactive in cantonments during the rainy season, and in daily intercourse with the men of other regiments, who had been warned for the same service, the Forty-seventh, uninfluenced by any other external causes, would have lost any ardour which might have possessed them when first ordered to march against a barbarous enemy who had insulted their flag. But it happened that ominous tidings of disaster came to them from the theatre of war. The British troops had sustained a disaster at Ramoo, the proportions of which had been grossly exaggerated in the recital, and it was believed that the Burmese, having cut up our battalions, or driven them into the sea, were sweeping on to the invasion of Bengal. The native newspapers bristled with alarming announcements of how the Commander-in-Chief had been killed in action and the Governor-General had poisoned himself in despair; and there was a belief throughout all the lower provinces of India that the rule of the Company was coming to an end. The fidelity of the Sepoy army requires the stimulus of continued success. Nothing tries it so fatally as disaster. When, therefore, news came that the war had opened with a great failure, humiliating to the British power, and all kinds of strange stories relating to the difficulties of the country to be traversed, the deadliness of the climate to be endured, and the prowess of the enemy to be encountered, forced their way into circulation in the Bazaars and in the Lines, the willingness which the Sepoys had once shown to take part in the operations beyond the frontier began to subside, and they were eager to find a pretext for refusing to march on such hazardous service. And, unhappily, one was soon found. There was a scarcity of available carriage-cattle for the movement of the troops. Neither bullocks nor drivers were to be hired, and fabulous prices were demanded from purchasers for wretched starvelings not equal to a day's journey. For the use of the regiments which had already marched, Bengal had been well-nigh swept out, and the reports which had since arrived rendered it difficult to persuade men voluntarily to accompany as camp-followers an expedition fraught with such peculiar perils. All the efforts of the Commissariat failed to obtain the required supply of cattle; and so the Sepoys were told to supply themselves. In this conjuncture, it would seem that a new lie was circulated through the Lines of Barrackpore. It was said that as the Bengal regiments could not, for want of cattle, be marched to Chittagong, they would be put on board ship and carried to Rangoon, across the Bay of Bengal. Murmurs of discontent then developed into oaths of resistance. The regiments warned for service in Burmah met in nightly conclave, and vowed not to cross the sea.

Still foremost in this movement, the Forty-seventh Regiment was commanded by Colonel Cartwright.

1824. Rightly measuring the difficulty, and moved with compassion for the Sepoy, who really had just ground of complaint, he offered to provide cattle from his private funds; and all the refuse animals, either too old or too young for service, were got together, and the Government offered to advance money for their purchase. But the terrible ban of "Too Late" was written across these conciliatory measures. The regiment was already tainted with the ineradicable virus of mutiny, which soon broke out on parade. The Sepoys declared that they would not proceed to Burmah by sea, and that they would not march unless they were guaranteed the increased allowances known in the jargon of the East as "double batta." This was on the 30th of October. On the 1st of November, another parade was summoned. The behaviour of the Sepoys was worse than before—violent, outrageous, not to be forgiven; and they remained masters of the situation throughout both the day and night. Then the Commander-in-Chief appeared on the scene. A hard, strict disciplinarian, with no knowledge of the native army, and a bitter prejudice against it, Sir Edward Paget was a man of the very metal to tread down insurrection with an iron heel, regardless both of causes and of consequences. He carried with him to Barrackpore two European regiments, a battery of European artillery, and a troop of the Governor-General's Body-guard. Next morning the native regiments found themselves in the presence of the English troops; but still they did not know the peril that awaited them, and, with a child-like obstinacy, they were not to be moved from their purpose of resistance. Some attempt was made at explanation—some attempt at conciliation. But it was feeble and ineffectual; perhaps not understood.

They were told, then, that they must consent to
march, or to ground their arms. Still not seeing
the danger, for they were not told that the Artillery
guns were loaded with grape, and the gunners ready
to fire,* they refused to obey the word; and so the
signal for slaughter was given. The guns opened
upon them. The mutineers were soon in panic flight.
Throwing away their arms and accoutrements, they
made for the river. Some were shot down; some
were drowned. There was no attempt at battle.
None'had been contemplated. The muskets with
which the ground was strewn were found to be un.
loaded.

Then the formalities of the military law were called
in to aid the stern decisions of the grape-shot. Some
of the leading mutineers were convicted, and hanged;
and the regiment was struck out of the Army List.
But this display of vigour, though it checked mutiny
for the time, tended only to sow broadcast the seeds
of future insubordinations. It created a bad moral
effect throughout the whole of the Bengal army.
From Bazaar to Bazaar the news of the massacre ran
with a speed almost telegraphic. The regiments,
which had already marched to the frontier, were discussing the evil tidings with mingled dismay and disgust before the intelligence, sent by special express,
had reached the ears of the British chiefs. "They
are your own men whom you have been destroying,"
said an old native officer; and he could not trust
himself to say more.† The Bengal regiments, with
the expeditionary force, had soon a grievance of
their own, and the remembrance of this dark tragedy

---

* It is doubtful, indeed, whether they knew that the guns were in the rear of the European regiments.

† "Political Incidents of the first Burmese War." By T. C. Robertson to whom was entrusted the political conduct of the war.

increased the bitterness with which they discussed it. The high-caste men were writhing under an order which, on the occupation of Arracan, condemned the whole body of the soldiery to work, as labourers, in the construction of their barracks and lines. The English soldier fell to with a will; the Madras Sepoy cheerfully followed his example. But the Bengal soldier asked if Brahmins and Rajpoots were to be treated like Coolies, and, for a while, there was an apprehension that it might become necessary to make another terrible example after the Barrackpore pattern. But this was fortunately averted. General Morrison called a parade, and addressed the recusants. The speech, sensible and to the point, was translated by Captain Phillips; and so admirable was his free rendering of it, so perfect the manner in which he clothed it with familiar language, making every word carry a meaning, every sentence strike some chord of sympathy in the Sepoy's breast, that when he had done, the high-caste Hindostanees looked at each other, understood what they read in their comrades' faces, and forthwith stripped to their work.

Thus was an incipient mutiny checked by a few telling words. And the sad event which had gone before might have been averted also if there had been as much tact and address as " promptitude and decision." A few sentences of well-chosen, well-delivered Hindostanee, on that fatal November morning, might have brought the Sepoys back to reason and to loyalty. But they had the benefit of neither wise counsel from within nor kindly exhortation from without. Deprived, by the reconstruction of the Army, of the officers whom they had long known and trusted, they were more than ever in need of external aid to bring them back to a right state of feeling.

They wanted a General of Division, such as Malcolm or Ochterlony, to reawaken their soldierly instincts— their pride in their colours, their loyalty to their Salt. But, instead of such judicious treatment as would have shown them their own folly, as in a glass, the martinets of the Horse Guards, stern in their unsympathising ignorance, their ruthless prejudices, had, in our own territories, at the very seat of government, in the presence of no pressing danger, no other lessons to teach, no other remedies to apply, than those which were to be administered at the bayonet's point and the cannon's mouth.

With the return of peace came new disquietudes. A reign of Retrenchment commenced. Alarmed by the expenses of their military establishments, the Company sent out imperative orders for their reduction—orders more than once issued before, more than once disobeyed. Blows of this kind commonly fall upon the weakest—upon those least able to endure them. So it happened that the condition of the regimental officer having, by a variety of antecedent circumstances, been shorn of well-nigh all its advantages, was rendered still more grievous and intolerable by the curtailment of his pecuniary allowances. An order, known in military history as the Half-Batta Order, was passed, by which all officers stationed within a certain distance from the Presidency were deprived of a large per-centage of their pay.* The order excited the utmost dismay throughout the Army; but the discontent which it engendered vented itself in words. Twice before the officers of the Company's army had resented similar encroachments, and

---

* Or, in strict professional language, his allowances. The gross salary of an Indian officer was known as his "pay and allowances." The former, which was small, was enhanced by several substantial accessories, as tentage, house-rent, and batta, or field allowance.

1825-35. had been prepared to strike in defence of their asserted rights. But this last blow did not rouse them to rebellion. Never before had justice and reason been so clearly upon their side; but, keenly as they felt their wrongs, they did not threaten the Government they served, but loyally protested against the treatment to which they had been subjected. The humours of which their memorials could not wholly relieve them, a Press, virtually free, carried off like a great conduit. The excitement expended itself in newspaper paragraphs, and gradually subsided. But it left behind it an after-growth of unanticipated evils. The little zeal that was left in the regimental officer was thus crushed out of him, and the Sepoy, who had watched the decline, little by little, of the power once vested in the English captain, now saw him injured and humiliated by his Government, without any power of resistance; saw that he was no longer under the special protection of the State, and so lost all respect for an instrument so feeble and so despised.

Abolition of Corporal Punishment.
And as though it were a laudable achievement thus to divest the native soldier of all fear of his European officer, another order went forth during the same interval of peace, abolishing the punishment of the lash throughout the Sepoy army in India. So little was he a drunkard and a ruffian, that it was a rare spectacle to see a black soldier writhing under the drummer's cat. But when the penalty, though still retained in the European army, became illegal and impossible among them, the native soldiery felt that another blow was struck at military authority—another tie of restraint unloosed. It was looked upon less as a boon than as a concession—less as the growth of our humanity than of our fear. So the Sepoy did not love us better, but held us a little more in contempt.

There were great diversities of sentiment upon this point, and some, whose opinions were entitled to respect, believed in the wisdom of the measure. But the weight of authority was against it,[*] and, some ten years afterwards, Hardinge revived what Bentinck had abolished. But even before the act of abolition, by a variety of concurrent causes, the character and the conduct of the Sepoy Army were so impaired, that an officer who had served long with them, and knew them well, declared, in his evidence before a Committee of Parliament, that "in all the higher qualifications of soldiers, in devotedness to the service, readiness for any duty they may be called upon to perform, cheerfulness under privations, confidence and attachment to their officers, unhesitating and uncalculating bravery in · the field, without regard either to the number or the character of the enemy, the native soldier is allowed by all the best-informed officers of the service, by those who have most experience, and are best acquainted with their character, to have infinitely deteriorated."[†]

---

[*] Numerous illustrations might be cited, but none more significant than the following anecdote, told by Mr. Charles Raikes: " I recollect a conversation which I had in 1839 with an old pensioned Soubahdar. I inquired of him how the measure would work. He replied, that the abolition of the punishment would induce some classes to enter the Army who had not done so before. ' But, Sahib,' said the old man, ' *Fouj-beh-durr hogya.*' (The Army has ceased to fear.)" Another native officer said: " The English, to manage us rightly, should hold the whip in one hand and the *mehtoys* (sweetmeats) in the other. You have dropped the whip, and now hold out sweets to us in both hands."

[†] Evidence of Captain Macan in 1832.

CHAPTER III.

The War in Afghanistan. 1838.

PEACE is never long-lived in India, and the Army was soon again in the bustle and excitement of active service. There was a long war; and, if it had been a glorious one, it might have had a salutary effect upon the disposition of the Sepoy. But when all his soldierly qualities were thus, as it were, at the last gasp, the War in Afghanistan came to teach him a new lesson, and the worst, at that time, which he could have been taught. He learnt then, for the first time, that a British army is not invincible in the field; that the great "Ikhbal," or Fortune, of the Company, which had carried us gloriously through so many great enterprises, might sometimes disastrously fail us; he saw the proud colours of the British nation defiled in the bloody snows of Afghanistan, and he believed that our reign was hastening to a close. The charm of a century of conquest was then broken. In all parts of Upper India it was the talk of the Bazaars that the tide of victory had turned against the Feringhees, and that they would soon be driven into

the sea.   Then the Sikh arose and the Mahratta be-
stirred himself, rejoicing in our humiliation, and
eagerly watching the next move.   Then it was that
those amongst us, who knew best what was seething
in the heart of Indian society, were "ashamed to
look a native in the face."   The crisis was a perilous
one, and the most experienced Indian statesmen regarded it with dismay, not knowing what a day
might produce.   They had no faith in our allies, no
faith in our soldiery. An Army of Retribution, under
a wise and trusted leader, went forth to restore the
tarnished lustre of the British name; but ominous
whispers soon came from his camp that that Army
was tainted—that the Sepoy regiments, no longer
assured and fortified by the sight of that ascendant
Star of Fortune which once had shone with so bright
and steady a light, shrunk from entering the passes
which had been the grave of so many of their comrades.   It was too true.   The Sikhs were tampering
with their fidelity.   Brahmin emissaries were endeavouring to swear them on the Holy Water not to
advance at the word of the English commander.
Nightly meetings of delegates from the different regiments were being held; and, perhaps, we do not
even now know how great was the danger.   But the
sound discretion and excellent tact of Pollock, aided
by the energies of Henry Lawrence and Richmond
Shakespear, brought the Sepoys to a better temper,
and, when the word was given, they entered the
dreaded passes, and, confiding in their leader, carried victory with them up to the walls of the Afghan
capital.

The Sepoy did his duty well under Pollock. He
had done his duty well under Nott, who spoke with
admiration of his "beautiful regiments," and man-

1843. fully resented any imputation cast upon them. **And**
when, after the British Army had been disentangled
from the defiles of Afghanistan, war was made against
the Ameers of Scinde, the Sepoy went gallantly to
the encounter with the fierce Belloochee fighting-
man, and Napier covered him with praise. Then
there was another war, and the native regiments of
the Company went bravely up the slopes of Maharajpore, and turned not aside from the well-planted,
well-manned batteries of the turbulent Mahrattas.
But peace came, and with peace its dangers. Scinde
had become a British province, and the Sepoy, who
had helped to conquer, had no wish to garrison the
country.

Results of the Conquest of Scinde.   The direct and immediate result of well-nigh every
annexation of Territory, by which our Indian empire
has been extended, may be clearly discerned in the
shattered discipline of the Sepoy Army. To extend
our empire without increasing our means of defence
was not theoretically unreasonable; for it might
have been supposed that as the number of our enemies
was reduced by conquest and subjection, the necessity
for the maintenance of a great standing army was
diminished rather than increased. These annexations,
it was said, consolidated our own territories by eradicating some native principality in the midst of them,
or else substituted one frontier, and perhaps a securer
one, for another. But the security of our empire lay
in the fidelity of our soldiery. To diminish the number of our enemies, and to extend the area of the
country to be occupied by our troops, was at the same
time to diminish the importance of the Sepoy, and to
render his service more irksome to him; for it sent
him to strange places far away from his home, to do
the work of military Police. It frittered away in small

detached bodies the limited European force at the disposal of the Indian Government, or massed large ones on a distant frontier. This extension of territory, indeed, whilst it made us more dependent upon our native troops, made that dependence more hazardous. The conversion of Scinde into a British province, by which our long line of annexations was commenced, had burnt this truth into our history before Lord Dalhousie appeared upon the scene. For indeed it was a sore trial to the Sepoy to be posted in a dreary outlying graveyard of this kind, far away from his home and his people—far beyond the limits of the empire in which he had enlisted to serve. And when it was proposed to take from him the additional allowances, which had been issued to the troops, on active service in an enemy's country, on the plea that they had subsided into the occupation of British cantonments, he resented this severe logic, and rose against the retrenchment. He did not see why, standing upon the same ground, he should not receive the same pay, because the red line of the British boundary had been extended by a flourish of the pen, and the population of the country had by the same magic process been converted into British subjects; and still less easily could he reconcile himself to the decision when he thought that the Sepoy himself had contributed to bring about the result that was so injurious to him; that he had helped to win a province for his employers, and, in return for this good service, had been deprived of part of his pay. In the old time, when the Company's troops conquered a country, they had profited in many ways by the achievement, but now they were condemned to suffer as though gallantry were a crime.

In more than a camel-load of documents the story

lies recorded; but it must be briefly narrated here. In the month of February, 1844, Governor-General Ellenborough, being then absent from his Council in the Upper Provinces, received the disheartening intelligence that the Thirty-fourth Sepoy Regiment of Bengal, which had been warned for service in Scinde, had been halted at Ferozepore. It had refused to enter our newly-acquired province, unless its services were purchased by the grant of the additional allowances given to the soldiery beyond the Indus in time of war. The distressing character of the intelligence was aggravated by many circumstances of time and place. In a moment, Ellenborough's quick perceptions had grappled the whole portentous truth. Our troops were mutinying for pay, on the Punjab frontier, almost in the presence of the disorderly masses of Sikh troops, who, gorged with the donatives they had forced from a weak Government, were then dominating the empire. Other regiments were coming up, on the same service, who might be expected to follow the rebellious lead of the Thirty-fourth; and so Ellenborough and Napier might have found themselves with the province they had just conquered on their hands, and no means of securing its military occupation, without destroying the authority of Government by humiliating concessions.

In this conjuncture, the first thing that Ellenborough did was the best that could have been done. He delegated to the Commander-in-Chief the full powers of the Governor-General in Council for the suppression of mutiny in the Army. But, how were those powers to be exercised? Doubt and perplexity, and something nearly approaching consternation, pervaded Army Head-Quarters. The Seventh Bengal Cavalry, on the line of march to the frontier, had

broken into open mutiny, and in spite of all the efforts of their officers, who had guaranteed to pay them
from their own funds the allowances they demanded,
the troopers had refused to obey the trumpet-call to
march, and were halted, therefore, sullen and obstinate, in the neighbourhood of Ferozepore. Some
companies of Native Artillery had already refused
to march, and there were rumours of other regiments being on the eve of declaring their refusal.
The most obvious course, under such circumstances,
was to march the recusant regiments back to one or
more of the large stations, as Loodhianah and Meerut,
where European troops were posted, and there to
disband them. But sinister whispers were abroad that
the sympathies of the Europeans, in this instance, were
with the native soldiery. One regiment of the Line,
it was reported, had openly declared that it would not
act against the Sepoys, who were demanding no more
than their rights. There were Sikh emissaries from
beyond the Sutlej doing their best to debauch the
Sepoys by offering both their sympathy and their
assistance. Dick, the General of Division, declared
his belief that an order to the mutineers to march
back for disbandment would not be obeyed; and a
violent collision at such a time would have set the
whole frontier in a blaze. The project of disbandment
was, therefore, suspended; and all the more readily, as
even at Head-Quarters there was a belief that, although the recusant troops might have had no reasonable ground of complaint, the actual state of the case
with respect to the Scinde pay and allowances had not
been properly explained to them.[*]

* The extraordinary allowances—
the withdrawal of which had created
all this ill feeling—were originally
granted when the troops crossed the
Indus in 1838, on their march to
Candahar and Caubul. They were
withdrawn from the troops in Scinde
early in 1840, when there seemed to

1844.

Uncondemned, the mutinous regiments were ordered back to the stations from which they had marched, to await the result of a reference to the Governor-General; and other corps, warned for the Scinde service, came up to the frontier. Dick's first and wisest impulse had been to halt the regiments marching to Ferozepore, in order that they might not run the risk of contamination by the tainted corps, or the corrupting influence of the Sikhs. But, by some strange fatality, this judicious measure had been revoked; the regiments marched to the frontier; and Dick's difficulties increased.

The Sixty-ninth and the Fourth.

The Sixty-ninth refused to embark, unless the old Indus allowances were guaranteed to them. By the exertions of the officers, one-half of the regiment was afterwards brought round to a sense of their duty; they loaded their carriage cattle, marched to the banks of the river, and declared their willingness to embark on the boats. They ought to have been embarked at once with the colours of their regiment. Their comrades would then have followed them; and other regiments, moved by the good example, might also have asserted their fidelity. But the golden opportunity was lost; and all example was in the way of evil. The Fourth Regiment, trusted overmuch by its commanders, followed the Sixty-ninth into mutiny at Ferozepore, and such was the conduct of the Sepoys, that Philip Goldney, a man of equal courage and capacity, suddenly called to the scene of tumult, drew upon one of the foremost of the mutineers, and a younger officer, moved to passion

be no longer any extraordinary duties to be performed by them. When the insurrection broke out in Afghanistan, and retributory operations were commenced, the allowances were restored; but they were again reduced from the 1st of July, 1843, after the close of the war in Afghanistan and the conquest of Scinde.

by their violence, struck out with a bayonet, and
wounded two soldiers in the face. Those were days
when mutiny did not mean massacre, and the Sepoy
did not turn upon his officer. But neither regiment
would march. On many hard-fought fields Sir Robert
Dick had proved himself to be a good soldier, but
he was not equal to such a crisis as this: so Ellenborough at once ordered him to be cushioned in some
safer place.

In the mean while, aid to the embarrassed Government was coming from an unexpected quarter. The
Sixty-fourth Regiment of Sepoys had formed part of
that unfortunate detachment known in history as
Wilde's Brigade, which had been sent, before Pollock's
arrival at Peshawur, to carry the Khybur Pass, without guns and without provisions. It had afterwards
served with credit during the second Afghan campaign, since the close of which it had been cantoned
at the frontier station of Loodhianah. The Sepoys
had manifested a strong reluctance to serve in Scinde,
and had addressed to the Adjutant - General more
than one *urzee*, or petition, couched in language of
complaint almost akin to mutiny. From Loodhianah
the regiment had been ordered down to Benares.
On the 15th of February it reached Umballah, then
become the Head-Quarters of the Sirhind division of
the Army, which General Fast, an old officer of the
Company's service, commanded. Well able to converse in the language of the country, and knowing,
from long intercourse with them, the character and
feelings of the native soldiery, Fast believed that
something might still be done to bring the regiment
back to its allegiance. So he halted the Sixty-fourth
at Umballah, and summoned the native officers to his
presence. Questioned as to the disposition of the

1844. regiment, they one and all declared that the men had never refused to march to Scinde; that they were still willing to march; that only on the evening before the native officers had severally ascertained the fact from their respective companies; that the matter of the allowances would not influence the Sepoys; and that the mutinous *urzees* had emanated only from a few bad characters in the regiment; perhaps, it was added, from a Sepoy who had been already dismissed. From these and other representations, it appeared to the General that the Sixty-fourth really desired to wipe out the stain, which the *urzees* had fixed upon their character, and, believing in this, he recommended that they should be permitted to march to Scinde. Under certain stringent conditions, the Commander-in-Chief adopted the recommendation; and so Moseley, with his Sepoys, again turned his face towards the Indus.

The disposition of the regiment now seemed to be so good; it was marching with such apparent cheerfulness towards the dreaded regions, and setting so good an example to others, that the Commander-in-Chief was minded to stimulate its alacrity, and to reward its returning fidelity, by a voluntary tender of special pay and pension, and relaxations of the terms of service.* The language of these instructions was somewhat vague, and Moseley, eager to convey glad

---

* "In addition to the full or marching batta always allowed to regiments serving in Scinde, still higher advantages in regard to pay, together with the benefits of the regulated family pension to the heirs of those who may die from disease contracted on service." The commanding officer was also instructed "to make known to the corps that it shall be brought back to a station in the provinces in one year in the event of the ensuing season proving unhealthy, and under no circumstances be kept in Scinde beyond two years, while the indulgence of furlough to visit their homes will, in the latter case, be extended to the men in the proportion enjoyed by corps located at stations within the British frontier." — [*The Adjutant-General to Colonel Moseley, March* 15, 1844.] Scinde, however, had become a British "province," and was "within the British frontier."

tidings to his men, turned the vagueness to account
by exaggerating the boon that was offered to them.
And so the error of Head-Quarters was made doubly
erroneous, and the Governor-General was driven wild
by the blunder of the Commander-in-Chief.

Whatsoever Head-Quarters might have intended to
grant, was contingent upon the good conduct of the
regiment. But before the letter had been received by
Moseley, on the line of march, mutiny had again
broken out in the ranks of the Sixty-fourth. At
Moodkhee, now so famous in the annals of Indian
warfare, the regiment, not liking the route that had
been taken, assumed a threatening front, and attempted to seize the colours.* The petulance of the
hour was suppressed, and next day the regiment resumed its march. But transitory as was the outbreak, it was mutiny in one of its worst forms.
On the second day, the Colonel received, at Tibbee,
the letter from Head-Quarters, on the subject of
the additional allowances. The outbreak at Moodkhee had converted it into an historical document, to
be quietly put aside for purposes of future record. It
was, indeed, a dead letter. The fatal words "too
late" were already written across the page. But
Moseley laid eager hands upon it, as a living reality,
for present uses. The Sixty-fourth was plainly in an
excitable state. It had mutinied once on the march,
and, without the application of some very powerful
sedative, it might mutiny again. The outbreak at
Moodkhee had not been reported to Head-Quarters.
It might pass into oblivion as an ugly dream of the
past; and the future might be rendered peaceful and
prosperous by the letter of the Adjutant-General. So

* It was advisable to march the
troops proceeding to Scinde along a
route which would not bring them
into contact with other regiments,
either coming from that province or
stationed on the frontier; and it was
especially desirable to mask Ferozepore.

1844.   Moseley, having caused it to be translated into Hindostanee, summoned a parade, and ordered it to be read aloud to his men.

Tremendous as was this error—for it tendered to the mutinous the reward intended only for the faithful—its proportions were dwarfed by the after-conduct of the infatuated Colonel. He put a gloss of his own on the Head-Quarters' letter, and told the regiment that they would receive the old Indus allowances given to Pollock's Army.* Upon which they set up a shout of exultation. And then the Sixty-fourth pursued its journey to Scinde.

The horrible mistake which had thus been committed soon began to bear bitter fruit. The inevitable pay-day came; and Moseley, like a man who has silenced the clamorous demands of the Present by drawing a forged bill upon the Future, now saw his gigantic folly staring him in the face. The crisis came at Shikarpore. The Indus war-allowances were not forthcoming, and the Sixty-fourth refused in a body to receive their legitimate pay.

George Hunter.   There was then, under Governor Napier, commanding the troops in Scinde, an old Sepoy officer, familiarly and affectionately known throughout the Army as George Hunter. Of a fine presence, of a kindly nature, and of a lively temperament, he led all men captive by the sunny influences of his warm heart and his flowing spirits; whilst his manly courage and resolution commanded a wider admiration and respect. Of his conspicuous gallantry in action he carried about with him the honourable insignia in an arm maimed and mutilated by the crashing downward blow of a Ját swordsman, as he was forcing one of

---

* This was known among the Sepoys as "Pollock's Batta." It made up the soldier's pay to twelve rupees a month.

the gates of Bhurtpore. In the whole wide circle of 1844.
the Army, there was scarcely one man whom the Sepoy
more loved and honoured; scarcely one whose appearance on the scene at this moment could have had
a more auspicious aspect. But there are moods in
which we turn most angrily against those whom we
most love; and General Hunter in this emergency
was as powerless as Colonel Moseley.

George Hunter was not a man to coquet with Mutiny of the
mutiny. He saw at a glance the magnitude of the Sixty-fourth.
occasion, and he was resolute not to encourage its
further growth by any inopportune delay. The short
twilight of the Indian summer was already nearly
spent when news reached him that the regiment had
refused to receive its pay. Instantly calling a parade,
he declared his intention of himself paying the troops.
Darkness had now fallen upon the scene; but lamps
were lit, and the General commenced his work. The
light company, as the one that had evinced the most
turbulent spirit, was called up first; the Sepoys took
their pay to a man, and were dismissed to their Lines.
Of the company next called, four men had refused to
receive their pay, when Moseley went up to the
General, and told him that the whole regiment would
take their money quietly, if disbursed to them by
their own officers. Hunter had once refused this, but
now he consented, and again the effort to flatter the
corps into discipline was miserably unsuccessful. No
sooner was this reluctant consent wrung from the
General, than the parade was broken up with a
tumultuous roar. Filling the air with shouts, sometimes shaped into words of derision and abuse, the
Sepoys flocked to their Lines. In vain Hunter ordered
them to fall in; in vain he implored them to remember that they were soldiers. They turned upon

him with the declaration that they had been lured to
Scinde by a lie; and when he still endeavoured to
restore order and discipline to the scattered rabble
into which the regiment had suddenly crumbled, they
threw stones and bricks at the fine old soldier and the
other officers who had gone to his aid.

Nothing more could be done on that night; so
Hunter went to his quarters, and waited anxiously for
the dawn. A morning parade had been previously
ordered, and when the General went to the ground,
he saw, to his exceeding joy, that the Sixty-fourth
were already drawn up—"as fine-looking and steady
a body of men," he said, "as he could wish to see."
No signs of disorder greeted him; and as he inspected
company after company, calling upon all who had
complaints to make to come forward, the regiment
preserved its staid and orderly demeanour, and it
seemed as if a great shame held them all in inactivity
and silence.* Returning then to the head of the
column, drawn up left in front, Hunter proceeded to
resume the work which had been broken off so
uproariously on the preceding evening. Ten men of
one company refused their pay, but none others followed their example. All now seemed to be proceeding to a favourable issue; and Hunter believed
that the favourable disposition which had begun to
show itself might be confirmed by a suitable address.
So he prepared himself to harangue them.

The ways of the Sepoy are as unaccountable as the
ways of a child. It is impossible to fix the limits of
his anger, or rightly to discern the point at which his
good temper has really returned. Unstable and inconsistent, his conduct baffles all powers of human

* Only one man came forward, and his complaint was that he had been
passed over in promotion.

comprehension. So it happened that just on the
seeming verge of success the ground crumbled away
under Hunter's feet. As each company had been
called up to receive its pay, the men had piled their
arms to the word of command. But when the word
was given to un-pile, there was an immediate shudder
of hesitation, which seemed to be caught by one
company from another, until it pervaded the whole
regiment. Each man seemed to read what was in
his neighbour's heart, and without any previous con-
cert, therefore, they clung to each other in their disobedience. Three Grenadier Sepoys took their
muskets, and were promoted on the spot; but not
another man followed their example. The regiment
had again become a rabble. Nothing now could
reduce them to order.

Until the blazing June sun was rising high in the
heavens, Hunter and the regimental officers remained
on the parade-ground, vainly endeavouring to persuade the Sepoys to return to their duty. They had
only one answer to give—their Colonel and their
Adjutant had promised them what they had not
received. If the General would guarantee them the
old Indus war-allowances, they would serve as good
soldiers; if not, they wished to be discharged, and
return to their homes. All through the day, and all
through the night, without divesting themselves of
their uniform, without going to their Lines to cook
or to eat, the mutineers remained on the ground,
sauntering about in the neighbourhood of their piled
arms, and discussing their wrongs.

Day broke, and found them still on the ground.
But hunger and fatigue had begun to exhaust the
energies of their resistance, and when Hunter appeared again on the scene, accompanied only by his

aide-de-camp, and beat to arms, the men fell in, took their muskets, and evinced some signs of contrition. Then the General spoke to them, saying that he would receive at his quarters a man from each company, and hear what he had to say on the part of his comrades. Satisfied with this promise, and being no longer irritated by the presence of the officers who had deceived them, the Sixty-fourth allowed the parade to be quietly dismissed, and went to their Lines. At the appointed hour, the delegates from the several regiments waited on the General, and each man told the same story of the deception that had been practised upon the regiment. They had been promised "General Pollock's Batta," and the twelve rupees which they had expected had dwindled down into eight.

With this evidence before him, the General removed Colonel Moseley from the command of the station and from the command of the regiment,* and ordered the Sixty-fourth to march to Sukkur, on their way back to our older provinces. It was an anxious time; a hazardous march. So Hunter went with them. But the hot stage of the fever had passed, and the paroxysm seemed to have left them feeble and sore-spent. Unresistingly they went to Sukkur, and encamped in the presence of European troops; and George Hunter, thanking God that the peril was over, and that not a drop of blood had been shed, then took upon himself the responsibility of pardoning the regiment as a body, and bringing to punishment only the worst of the individual offenders.† Such moderation could hardly be misunderstood at a time

---

* Colonel Moseley was afterwards tried by court-martial, and cashiered.

† Thirty-nine prisoners were sent to trial, of whom one only was acquitted. Six were ordered for capital punishment, and the sentence of death passed upon the others was commuted to imprisonment and hard labour for various terms.

when there was present power to enforce the decrees of a sterner justice. So he addressed the regiment on parade, told them that he pardoned all but the leading mutineers, who would be tried by Court-martial; and he trusted that the mercy thus shown to them would not be thrown away, that they would repent of their misconduct and return to their allegiance. And perhaps the provocation which they had received was ample warrant for the leniency of their treatment.*

But the embarrassments of the Government did not end here. Whatsoever might be the punishment of the offence, it could not afford a remedy for the evil. The mutinous regiments might be disbanded, and their ringleaders might be hanged by the neck, or blown to atoms from the guns; but still there would be no answer to the question of how was Scinde to be garrisoned with British troops? It had been the design of the Government to employ only Bengal regiments on that service, seeking aid in other quarters from Madras. But the Bengal Army had broken down under the experiment; and there was small hope, after what had passed, of its ever being induced, except by humiliating concessions, to look that hated province in the face. There were, however, two other Presidencies, and two other Armies, not so nice as Bengal; and the defence of Scinde might be entrusted to Bombay or Madras regiments. If such had been the design in the first instance, it might, under judicious management, have been suc-

* There is something very touching in the humility which pervades the letters written at this time by George Hunter to Lord Ellenborough and Sir Charles Napier. He asks to be pardoned for all short-comings, in consideration of the difficulty of the circumstances. "I never could write," he says at the end of one letter, "and old age does not improve a man in any way, except, I trust, in seeing his own failings and praying for mercy."

1843.   cessfully carried into effect.   But after such an ex
ample as had been set by the Bengal regiments, there
was small consolation to be drawn from the prospect
of loyal service to be rendered by their comrades.
Already, indeed, were there signs that the disposition
to strike for higher pay which had manifested itself
among the Bengal troops was not confined to the
Sepoys of that "pampered and petted" Army.   The
Bombay regiments were untainted ;* but a mutinous
spirit had again displayed itself among the native
soldiery of the Coast Army.†

Mutiny of the
Sixth Madras
Cavalry.

The first symptom of this was in a Cavalry regiment at Jubbulpore.   Among the results of an
extension of empire without a corresponding augmentation of our military force, are frequent violations of old Presidential limits in the location of our
troops, which, however unobjectionable they may
appear at the Adjutant-General's office, are seldom
carried out without some disturbance of our military
system.   It might seem to be of small consequence
whether the station at which a regiment was posted
were within the limits of one Presidency or another ;
but if a Madras regiment were called upon to serve
in the Bengal Presidency, or a Bombay regiment in
Madras, or any other departure from ordinary rule
were decreed, the Government was fortunate if it
were not seriously perplexed and embarrassed by the
results.   Now, the Madras Army, though, as has been

---

* The Bombay Army was said at
that time to have more duty on its
hands than it could perform without
a severe strain, and the Bombay Government were clamouring for an
augmentation.

† There had been several recent
instances of extreme insubordination,
amounting, indeed, to mutiny, in the
Madras Army.   The 52nd Native

Infantry had mutinied at Asseeghur
and Mallegaum ; there had been a
mutiny of the Madras troops at Se-
cunderabad ; and the 2nd and 41st
Regiments had shown a bad spirit,
when ordered to embark for China.
The 3rd and 4th Native Cavalry
regiments had also mutinied ; the
former in 1838, the latter in 1842.

said, more cosmopolitan and less nice than that of
Bengal, and not deterred by caste prejudices from
proceeding to strange places, suffered even more than
the Bengal troops from being ordered to distant
stations, because the family of the Madras soldier followed his regiment, whilst the belongings of his
Bengal comrade remained in their native village.
The removal of the family from one station to another was a sore trouble and a heavy expense to the
Madras Sepoy; and whatever increased the distance
to be traversed was, therefore, a grievance to him.

To the Cavalry it was especially a grievance, for
the troopers were principally well-born Mahomedans,
and the rigid seclusion in which their women were
kept greatly increased the cost of their conveyance
from one station to another. The Sixth Cavalry had
been more than commonly harassed in this respect,
when, towards the close of 1843, just as they were
expecting to get their route for the favourite cavalry
station of Arcot, they received orders to march from
Kamptee to Jubbulpore, in the valley of the Nerbudda, which, in consequence of the demand for
Bengal troops on the Indus, it had been necessary to
occupy with regiments from Madras. The sharp disappointment, however, was in some measure miti-
gated by the assurance that the service on which
they were required was but temporary, and that they
would soon return within the proper limits of their
own Presidency. They went, therefore, leaving their
families behind them; but when they reached Jubbulpore, they found that they were to be permanently
located there upon lower allowances than they had
expected, that they must send for their families from
Kamptee, and that their next march would be nine
hundred miles southward to Arcot.

U 2

1843.

Only by savings from their pay at the higher rates could the troopers hope to defray these extraordinary expenses. On the lower rates of pay it was impossible; for the greater part of their earnings was remitted for the support of their absent families, and what remained was barely enough to keep together body and soul. When, therefore, they found that they were to receive these lower rates at Jubbulpore, they broke into open manifestations of discontent, and bound themselves by oaths to stand by each other whilst they resisted the unjust decree. The first few days of December were, therefore, days of sore vexation and disturbance to the officers of the Sixth, and most of all to the Commandant, Major Litchfield, to whose want of personal sympathy with their sufferings the Sepoys, reasonably or unreasonably, attributed a great part of their affliction. The conduct of the men was violent and outrageous. They were with difficulty induced to saddle and mount for exercise; and when the trumpet sounded for the canter, they loosened rein, urged their horses forward at a dangerous pace, and raising the religious war-cry of " Deen! deen!" broke into tumultuous disorder. Brought back to something like discipline, the regiment was dismissed; but throughout the day the greatest excitement prevailed among them, and a large body of troopers marched in a defiant manner through the Lines to the tent of a favourite officer, declaring that they would obey his orders, and serve under him, and beseeching him to place himself at their head. On the following day the excitement had increased. The troop-officers went among their men, endeavouring to pacify them. But they could report nothing more satisfactory than that the troopers were in a frantic state, and that if Litchfield

Major Litch-
field.

Capt. Byng.

ventured on parade next morning the result would be fatal to him.

Undeterred by this, the Major would have held the parade, but the Brigadier commanding the station, to whom, in due course, all the circumstances were reported, caused it to be countermanded, and an Inspection Parade, under his own command, ordered in its stead. To this the regiment sullenly responded; and when the Brigadier addressed them, saying that he was willing to hear their complaints, many of the men stepped forward and presented him with petitions, which were given over to the troop-officers, to be forwarded to him through the regular official channels. But, although it was plain that there was a bitter feeling of resentment against Litchfield, no act of violence was committed at that parade. And it happened that before its dismissal a letter reached the Brigadier announcing that the higher allowances were to be given to the men; and so the active danger was passed. But the disturbance which had been engendered did not soon pass away; the Sepoys remained sullen and discontented, and for some days it appeared to the Brigadier not improbable that he would be compelled to call the Infantry and the Artillery to his assistance. But the Madras Army was spared this calamity of bloodshed; and after a little while the regiment returned to the quiet and orderly performance of its duty.

As the old year closed upon the scene of mutiny in the Madras Cavalry, so, very soon, the new year opened upon a kindred incident in the Madras Infantry. When it was found that the Bengal troops were reluctant to serve, under the proposed terms, in the Scinde province, and serious embarrassment was, thereby, likely to be occasioned to the Supreme Government, the

1843-44. Madras authorities, believing that the crisis was one in which it behoved every one to do his best, promptly and vigorously, for the salvation of the State, determined, on a requisition from the Government of Bombay, to send two infantry regiments to Scinde.* The Sepoys were to embark on board transport vessels at Madras, to touch at Bombay, and thence to proceed to Kurrachee. One of these regiments, the Forty-seventh, was in orders for Moulmein, on the eastern coast of the Bay of Bengal—a station at which, being beyond Presidential limits, extra allowances, known as field-batta and rations, were paid to the troops. Ignorant, it would appear, of the Bengal regulations, the Madras Government, represented by the Marquis of Tweedale, who held the double office of Governor and Commander-in-Chief, guaranteed to the regiments ordered to Scinde the allowances received at Moulmein; and under these conditions the Forty-seventh embarked for Bombay.

Mutiny of the Madras Forty-seventh.

Meanwhile, the Supreme Government had been advised of the unauthorised measures of the Madras authorities. Chafing under such usurpation of the powers and prerogatives of the Governor-General, Ellenborough sent orders for the detention of the Madras regiment at Bombay, and it was disembarked on its arrival.† There the Madras Sepoys learnt that the advantages of foreign service, promised to them at Madras, and on the faith of which they had set their faces towards Scinde, were disallowed. The greater part of their pay up to the end of March had already

* Sir Charles Napier had made an urgent call on Bombay, which, Bombay not being able to comply with it, passed on to Madras.

† Intelligence of the change of destination was communicated to the officers during the voyage. It should be stated that one detachment of the regiment mutinied on board the *John Line* transport vessel; but the discontent then manifested arose from circumstances unconnected with the after-causes of disaffection.

been disbursed to them, for the benefit of the families whom they left behind, and now they found, in the middle of February, that the scanty residue, on which they had relied for their own support, was by these retrenchments taken from them, and that, far away from their homes, starvation stared them in the face. It was not strange that they should have regarded this as a cruel breach of faith; and that they should have resented it. They had been promised rations, and they asked for them, and when they found they were not likely to be supplied, they manifested their discontent, after the wonted fashion, by breaking out on parade. When the word of command was given for them to march to their Lines, by fours from the left, they stood fast. The word was repeated, but still they stood fast; and when the Adjutant rode up to the leading section and asked the men if they had not heard the word of command, they answered sullenly that they had heard it; and when a Native officer asked them why they did not move, they told him that they wanted food, and that they would not stir without it.

When the order to advance was again given, the regiment moved off; but only to renew on the following morning the exhibition of disobedience and discontent. Paraded before the General commanding the garrison, the regiment soon evinced signs of being in the same mood. After inspection, when the order was given to march by companies to their respective Lines, the Grenadiers stepped off, but presently wavered and halted; and when their captain, having ordered their arms, went off to report their conduct to the commanding officer, they insisted on following him in a body, declaring that if they then lost their chance of representing their hard case to the General, they might never find it again. Another company was even more violent in its demands. When the word of command was given to advance at the quick march, a man from the ranks cried out, "Right about face," and the whole company stood fast, as did other parts of the column. Taken in the act of flagrant mutiny, the Sepoy was disarmed, and sent to the guard, whither the greater part of the company followed, declaring that they also would go to the guard, that they wanted rice, and must have it.

After a while order was restored. The General addressed the European and Native officers, and told them to assure the men, that any complaints advanced in a soldierly manner would be inquired into and any grievances redressed, but that such conduct as had been displayed on parade could not be overlooked. The regiment was then moved off to its Lines, some of the ringleaders being carried off as prisoners; and an advance of money, at first reluctantly received, stifled the further progress of mutiny. Here, then, the story may end. The Madras Army was not destined to supply the want accruing from the defective loyalty of Bengal. It broke down at a critical time; but only under such a weight of mismanagement as might have crushed out·the fidelity of the best mercenaries. in the world.

In these, as in instances above cited, by conflicts of authority and variations of system, the Sepoy was not unreasonably alarmed for the integrity of his pay; and although we may condemn the manner in which he manifested his discontent, we must not think too harshly of the tenacity with which he asserted his rights. If an English soldier strikes for more pay, it is in most cases only another name for more drink. He seeks it, too often, as a means of personal indulgence.

There is nothing to render less greedy his greed. But the avarice of the Sepoy was purified by domestic affection, by a tender regard for the interests of others, and that strong feeling of family honour which in India renders Poor Laws an useless institution. He had so many dependents with whom to divide his slender earnings, that any unexpected diminution of his pay excited alarm lest those who were nearest and dearest to him should in his absence be reduced to want. The honour of his family was threatened; he chafed under the thought; and if he took unsoldierly means of asserting his rights, we must remember the provocation, and not forget those peculiarities of national sentiment which lighten the dark colours in which all such resistance of authority presents itself to European eyes.

Eventually Bombay troops were sent to garrison Scinde, and the province became a part of the Bombay Presidency. But it is hard to say how much these first abortive attempts to provide for its defence shook the discipline of the Sepoy Army. For the evil was one to which it was difficult to apply a remedy; and the authorities were greatly perplexed and at variance one with another. The disbandment of a mutinous regiment is, in such a case, the most obvious, as it is the easiest measure, to which Government can resort; but it may often be unjust in itself and dangerous in its results. It falls alike on the innocent and on the guilty. It fills the country with the materials of which rebellions are made, or sends hundreds of our best fighting-men, with all the lessons we have taught them, into the enemy's ranks. To be effective, it should follow closely on the commission of the crime which it is intended to punish; but it can rarely be accomplished with this essential promptitude, for it is

1844.

Penal Measures.

.844. only under certain favouring circumstances that an order to reduce to penury and disgrace a thousand trained soldiers can be carried out with safety to the State. To delay the execution of the punishment is outwardly to condone the offence. It was not strange, therefore, that when the Thirty-fourth Infantry and the Seventh Cavalry of Bengal mutinied on the frontier, almost in the presence of the Sikh Army, there should have been obstinate questionings at Head-Quarters as to the expediency of disbandment on the spot, or at some safer place remote from the scene of their crimes. It was the opinion of Lord Ellenborough, at the time, that a regiment of Europeans and a troop of European artillery should have been summoned with all haste from Loodhianah to Ferozepore, and that, in presence of this force, the mutinous corps should have been at once disbanded. But a reference, it has been said, was made to Government, and the mutinous regiments were marched down, unsentenced, to Loodhianah and Meerut, there to await the decision of supreme authority. The orders given left some discretion with the Commander-in-Chief. The Seventh Cavalry had not mutinied in a body. The Native officers and nearly two hundred troopers were true to their Salt. Discipline might, therefore, be vindicated by ordinary processes of law without involving the innocent and the guilty alike in one common ruin. But the Thirty-fourth, Native officers and Sepoys, were all tainted ; so, with every mark of infamy, in the presence of all the troops, European and Native, at Meerut, the regiment was broken up, the British uniform was stripped from the backs of the mutineers, and the number of the regiment was erased from the Army List.*

* Two or three years afterwards of a new regiment, in no degree the gap was filled up by the raising better than the old.

Propinquity to an overawing European force removes the chief difficulties which oppose themselves to the sudden dissolution of a Native regiment. But under no other circumstances is it to be counselled. The question of disbandment, therefore, perplexed the Madras authorities even more than those of Bengal. To march a regiment, with arms in its hands, some hundreds of miles across the country, to receive its services, and perhaps to witness its repentance during a period of many weeks, all that time concealing the fate that is in store for it, and then having caged it in a safe place, pinioned it, as it were, beyond all hope of resistance, to visit it with all the terrors of a long-hidden, long-delayed retribution, is altogether abhorrent to the generous nature of an English officer. To have disbanded, for example, the Sixth Madras Cavalry at Jubbulpore would have been cruel and dangerous. To have marched it to Arcot in ignorance of its fate, would have been cruel and dastardly. To have broken it up at Kamptee would have been to incur, only in a less degree, the evil of both courses. And nothing else appeared possible; for it was not to be supposed that all those indignant Mahomedans, men with whom revenge is a virtue, would have quietly gone down, mounted on good horses, and with sharpened sabres at their sides, in full knowledge of their destiny, to the disgraceful punishment awaiting them. With these considerations before them, it was not strange that the Madras authorities hesitated to carry out the comprehensive penalty of disbandment, and that, as a choice of difficulties, it should have suffered many guilty men to escape.

In this instance, Lord Ellenborough was eager for disbandment. He said that the conduct of the regiment had been equally bad in itself and pernicious in

1844.   its results, for that the disturbed state of Bundelkund
rendered it little short of mutiny before the enemy,
and it had disconcerted all the arrangements of his
Government for the general defence of the country.
But it was not his, either on principle or in practice,
to deal harshly with the errors and delusions of the
Native Army, and there were few men living who
had a more kindly appreciation of the good qualities
of the Sepoy, or who could more readily sympathise
with him.   If he did not know precisely how to deal
with a mutiny of that Army; if he could not, with
accurate calculation of the results, so apportion the
just measures of leniency and severity as in no case to
encourage by the one or to exasperate by the other,
he only failed where no one had yet succeeded, and
need not have blushed to find himself mortal.   He
often said that a general mutiny of the Native Army
was the only real danger with which our empire in
India was threatened; and he believed that the surest
means of maintaining the fidelity of the Sepoy was by
continually feeding his passion for military glory.   In
this he was right.   But the passion for military glory
cannot always be fed without injustice, and the evils
of conquest may be greater than its gains.   He had
much faith, too, in the good effect of stirring addresses, appealing to the imaginations of the soldiery,
and in the application of donatives promptly following good service.   And, although in working out his
theory he was sometimes impelled to practical expressions of it, which caused people to smile, as in
the famous Somnauth Proclamation, and in the dis-
weetmeats. tribution of the "favourite *mehtoys*" to the Sepoys
after the battle of Maharajpore, there was, doubtless,
sound philosophy at the bottom of it.   But such light
as this only served to show more clearly the many

and great difficulties with which the whole question 1844. of the Sepoy Army was beset, and to convince reflecting minds that, though human folly might accelerate the break-down of the whole system, human wisdom could not so fence it around with safeguards as to give it permanent vitality and strength.

That the treatment to which the mutinies arising out of the annexation of Scinde were subjected by the Government of the day was nothing more than a series of expedients is a fact, but one which may be recorded without censure. The disbandment of one regiment, the punishment of a few ringleaders in others, the forgiveness of the rest; the dismissal of an officer or two for culpable mismanagement, and a liberal issue of donatives to all who during the preceding year had either done well, or suffered much, in the service of the State, were so many palliatives, born of the moment, which did not touch the seat of the disease, or contribute to the future healthy action of the system. But there were circumstances, both intrinsic and extrinsic, which seemed to forbid, on grounds alike of justice and of policy, the application of more vigorous remedies. The fact, indeed, that the misconduct of the soldiery had, in a great measure, been the direct growth of the injuries which they had sustained at the hands of the Government, would have made severity a crime. But it was no less certain that leniency was a blunder. If an Army once finds that it can dictate to Government the amount of its pay, there is an end to the controlling power of the latter. What the State ought to have learnt from this lesson was the paramount obligation which rested upon it of clearly explaining to its troops all regulations affecting their pay and allowances, and especially such as entailed upon them any loss of privileges

1844.   antecedently enjoyed. Under any circumstances a reduction of pay is a delicate and hazardous operation. Even the loyalty of European officers is not always proof against such a trial. But the absence of explanation aggravates it, in the Sepoy's eyes, into a breach of faith; he believes that he is only asserting his rights when he strikes for the restoration of that of which he has been, in his own eyes unjustly, deprived; and the Government then, perplexed in the extreme, has only a choice of evils before it, and either on the side of leniency or severity is too likely to go lamentably wrong.

CHAPTER IV.

THE WAR ON THE SUTLEJ—THE PATNA CONSPIRACY—ATTEMPT TO COR-
RUPT THE SEPOYS AT DINAPORE—THE OCCUPATION OF THE PUNJAB—
ANNEXATION AND ITS EFFECTS—REDUCTION OF THE SEPOY'S PAY—THE
MUTINIES AT RAWUL PINDEE AND GOVINDGHUR—LORD DALHOUSIE AND
SIR CHARLES NAPIER.

IT was fortunate, perhaps, for the rulers of that day 1845.
that Peace was but of short duration, and that the
" passion for military glory" had again something to
feed upon.   The Sikh Army, having risen against its
own leaders, was vapouring on the banks of the Sutlej,
and threatening to cross the British frontier.   No
war could have been more welcome to the Sepoy than
a war with the Sikhs.   For they were an insolent and
minacious race, and it was known that they had
talked of overrunning Hindostan, and pouring on to
the sack of Delhi and the pillage of Calcutta.   They
took the first step, and the war commenced.

Whilst the Governor-General and the Commander- The Patna
in-Chief were at the head of the Army on the frontier, Conspiracy.
and all eyes were turned towards the scene of that
sanguinary conflict on the Sutlej, lower down, on the
banks of the Ganges, four hundred miles from Calcutta, an incident was occurring, which, in quiet
times, might have made itself heard all over the
country, but which, lost in the din of battle in that

1845-46. momentous winter, gave only a local sound. Discovery was made of an organised attempt to corrupt the soldiery in the Lower Provinces. On Christmas-eve the magistrate of Patna received a letter from Major Rowcroft, informing him that the Moonshee of his regiment—the First Native Infantry—was in treasonable correspondence with a rich and influential landholder in the neighbourhood, who had been tampering with the allegiance of the Native officers and Sepoys in the contiguous station of Dinapore.

Of the truth of the story there was no doubt. To what dimensions the conspiracy really extended, and from what central point it radiated, is not known, and now never will be known. It was a season of considerable popular excitement, aggravated in the neighbourhood of Patna by local causes, and eager efforts had been made to prepare the people for revolt. Reports had been for some time current to the effect that the British Government purposed to destroy the caste of the Hindoos, and to abolish Mahomedanism by forbidding the initial ceremony through which admission is obtained to the number of the Faithful. And to this was added another lie, scarcely less alarming, that the Purdah was also to be prohibited, and that Mahomedan females of all ranks were to be compelled to go about unveiled. Stories of this kind, it has been observed, however monstrous in themselves, are readily believed, if there be but only a very little truth to give them currency. The truth may be from within or it may be from without. It may be direct proof or indirect confirmation. It little matters so long as there is something which men may see and judge for themselves. There had been many exciting causes at this time, to rouse the resentments and to·stimulate the activities of the Moulavees and the Pundits, such as the new law of inheritance and the new educational measures; and now the introduction of the messing-system into the gaols was a patent fact which all might understand. It was an incident, moreover, of untoward occurrence, that about this time, when designing men were eagerly looking out for some false move on the part of the Government, the Magistrate of Patna, at the request of the Principal of the College, alarmed the inhabitants of the city by instituting inquiries enabling him to form something of a census of the population, showing their different castes, professions, and employments—a movement which was at once declared to be a part of the great scheme of the Government for the forcible conversion of the people.

But it was necessary that the soldiery should be gained over by some alarming fiction of especial application to the Sepoy himself. Already had indirect agency been set at work for his corruption. He found the lie in full leaf in his native village. When he went on furlough, his relatives told him that if he did not make a stand for his religion he would soon have to fight against his brethren and kinsmen.[*] When he returned to his regiment he found that every one was talking on the same subject, and that it was currently believed that the introduction of the messing-system into the gaols was to be followed by its introduction into the Army, and that the Sepoy was not much longer to be allowed to have uncontrolled dominion over his own cooking-pot.

[*] Some of the men of the First Regiment told Major Rowcroft that the villagers had said, "Our village furnishes 500 men to your Army; but if you will not listen to us, we will send 2000 juwans (young men) to oppose you."

x

į-46.   If, then, there had been nothing more than this,
the time would have been propitious, and plotters
might reasonably have thought that the opportunity
was ripe.   But in that winter of 1845-46 a seditious
enterprise of this kind in the Lower Provinces was
favoured by the circumstances of the great war with
the Sikhs, which was drawing all the resources of the
Government to the North-Western frontier.   There
was a vague belief that lakhs of Punjabee fighting-
men would soon be streaming over the country, and
that the English would be driven into the sea. Many,
then, with eager cupidity, bethought themselves of
gutting the opium godowns of Patna, where a million
and a half of Government property lay stored; and
all the dangerous classes of the city were ripe and
ready for pillage and for slaughter.   A rising of the
Sepoys at such a time, or their acquiescence in a
rising of the people, might have been fatal to the
continued supremacy of Government in that part of
the country.   The plotters scarcely hoped to accomplish more than the latter of these two means of
overthrowing the English.   At all events, it was safer
to begin with the milder experiment on the fidelity
of the Sepoy.   So delegates went about in the Lines
saying that the great King of Delhi had sent a confidential agent to give a month's pay to every Native
officer and soldier in the regiments in order that if
any outbreak should occur in their part of the country they should not lift a hand in support of the
Government.   All the landholders, and the cultivators, and the townspeople were ready, it was said,
to rise; and if the soldiery would only remain inactive, the British power might be destroyed before it
could perpetrate the outrages by which it sought to
overturn the religions of the country.

A Jemadar of the First Regiment heard this story, gravely listened to all that was urged by the emissary of sedition, and said that he would consider of the matter.* Then he repeated all that had happened to his commanding officer, and measures were soon taken to test the reality of the plot. There was at all events one substantial proof that the story was no fiction. There was money counted out for the work of corruption, and tied up in bags ready for immediate delivery. It was agreed that the Jemadar and another officer in Rowcroft's confidence should take the money, and matters were soon conveniently arranged so as to bring about the disclosure. A detachment of the regiment was about to proceed to Gya; with this went the two faithful Jemadars. On the way they met or were overtaken by two well-dressed Mahomedans in an ecka, or native wheeled-carriage, who gave them the money, saying that others had taken it, and that larger supplies were forthcoming for the same purpose. Nothing could stamp the reality of the design more surely than this. Men are in earnest when they part with their money.

Another Native officer of the First traitorously took the corrupting coin, and a Moonshee of the regiment was found to be deeply implicated in the plot. But Rowcroft's opportune discovery of the attempt to debauch his men, and the measures which he wisely adopted, rendered the further efforts of the conspirators utterly futile and hopeless. The military offenders were soon in confinement; the civil magistrate was tracking down the instigators of sedition; and if no great success then attended the attempt

* The Jemadar was a Brahmin, by name Mootee-Missur. He had been pay-havildar to Rowcroft, when the latter was adjutant of the regiment, and was greatly attached to him.

to bring the necks of the most guilty to the gallows, it was sufficient for the public peace that the plot was discovered. What the amount of real danger then was it is difficult to determine. Two other Native regiments at Dinapore were tampered with in like manner, but the discovery of the plot in Rowcroft's corps rendered other efforts abortive. Many great names were used by the agents of sedition, but upon what authority can only be conjectured. It was stated that a royal mandate had come from the King of Delhi; that the Rajah of Nepaul was ready to send a great army sweeping down to the plains; and again it was said that the Sikhs were the prime movers of the plot.* All this can be only obscurely shadowed on the page of history. But it is certain that a scroll was found, described by a witness as being many cubits long, on which the names of some hundred of respectable inhabitants of Patna, Hindoos and Mahomedans, were attached to a solemn declaration binding them to die in defence of their religion, and that it was honestly believed by large numbers of the educated no less than the ignorant people of that part of the country, that the one cherished object of the British Government was to reduce all the people of India to the no-caste state of the Feringhees. Of the reality of this belief there was no doubt; so a Proclamation was put forth by the Governor of Bengal, declaring that as the British Government never had interfered, so the people

---

* The principal actor in the Patna conspiracy was one Khojah Hassan Ali Khan. It seems that at the Sonepore Fair, a short time before, he had appeared in great state, and received a considerable number of influential people in his tent, with the object of instilling into them a fear of religious conversion, and encouraging their determination to resist. He escaped for want of evidence. There was also a wandering bookseller, who, on the plea of selling Persian volumes to the Moonshees of regiments, readily gained access to them without exciting suspicion.

might be assured that it never would interfere in any way with the religions of the country.

The Jemadar and the Moonshee of the First Regiment, who had been seduced into traitorous courses, were tried by court-martial, and sentenced to death, with the usual reluctance manifested by a tribunal composed only of Native officers.* But it was not necessary to strike terror into the minds of an army hovering on the brink of general mutiny; so the sentence was not carried out. Whatever danger there may have been had passed away.† The victories of Hardinge and Gough had a grand moral effect from one end of the country to the other, for it had been believed that the British were sore pressed, and that their power would be shaken to the centre by this collision with the Sikhs. Victory made all things right again, and for a while we heard nothing more of mutiny or sedition. With intervals of comparative repose, distinguished by an occupation of the Sikh country, very flattering to the Sepoy's pride, and very profitable to his purse, the operations which resulted in the fall of the Sikh empire then lasted for more than three years. The story has been told in the first chapter of this work. The Punjab, like Scinde, was turned by a stroke of the pen into a British province, and the same difficulties bristled up in the path of

---

* Not long after the discovery of this plot, Major Rowcroft was seized with severe illness, not without suspicion of poison, and obliged to proceed to England. Jemadar Mootee-Missur told him that on his return to India, he would, doubtless, be able to lay before the Major further facts illustrative of the extent of the conspiracy. But when Rowcroft rejoined the regiment both Mootee-Missur and the other faithful Jemadar were dead.

† It is stated in an interesting pamphlet, published by Mr. Stocqueler, in 1857, that it was said at Dinapore, after the discovery of this conspiracy, that although the English had then escaped, there would be, in 1857, when they had ruled a hundred years, such a *tomasha* as the country had never seen. I can find no trace of this in any contemporary documents, nor have my inquiries from officers who were then at Dinapore enabled me to confirm the truth of the story.

1845-46.   the Annexer. The Sepoy, called to serve in the Punjab, had no longer the privileges of foreign service; and, in spite of the lesson taught by the Scinde annexation, he could not understand why the conquest of the country should be inaugurated by the reduction of his pay.

Mutiny in the Punjab. 1849-50.   And so the regiments in the Punjab at that time, and those which were moved across the Sutlej from our older provinces, determined to refuse the reduced rates, and to stand out boldly for the higher allowances. All the regiments, suffering or soon to suffer from the incidence of the reduction, took counsel with each other, and promised mutual support. Delegates from the several corps went about from station to station, and letters were exchanged between those at a distance. The first manifestation of open discontent was at Rawul Pindee. There, one morning in July, Sir Colin Campbell, a soldier of the highest promise, already budding into fame—the "war-bred Sir Colin," as Napier then called him—received the significant

July, 1849.   intelligence that the Twenty-second Regiment had refused to receive their pay. Outwardly, the Sepoys were calm and respectful; but their calmness indicated a sense of strength, and Campbell felt that all the other Native regiments in the Punjab would probably follow their example. Such a combination at any time and in any place would have been dangerous and alarming; but the peril was greatly aggravated by the peculiar circumstances of the times. For it had grown up in a newly-conquered country, swarming with the disbanded fighting-men of the old Sikh Army, and it was believed that our discontented Sepoys, if they had once broken into rebellion, would have soon found their ranks swollen by recruits from the Kalsa soldiery, eager to profit by the crisis, and

again to strike for the recovery of their lost dominion.
We had just seen the downfal of an empire precipitated by the lawlessness of an army, driven onward
by the impulses of its greed; and now it seemed as
though our own soldiery, having caught the contagion, were clamouring for donatives, and that it required very careful steering to save us from being
wrecked upon the same rock.

Sir Charles Napier had, at that time, just appeared
upon the stage. He had hastened from Calcutta to
Simlah to meet the Governor-General, who was refreshing himself with the cool mountain air; and
there the news reached him, not that one, but that
two regiments at Rawul Pindee had refused to take
their pay, and that there was every prospect of four
more regiments at Wuzeerabad, and two at the inter-
mediate station of Jhelum, following their example.
Then Dalhousie and Napier took counsel together,
with some of their staff-officers, and it was debated
whether it would not be wise to strike a vigorous blow
at the incipient mutiny by disbanding the regiments
which had already refused to accept their pay. To
this course, proposed by Colonel Benson, an old officer
of the Company's service, held in deserved regard by
many successive Governors-General, Napier resolutely
objected, and Dalhousie concurred with the Chief.
Hoping for the best, but still prepared for the worst,
the old soldier instructed Campbell to point out to the
recusant regiments the folly and wickedness of their
course; but he wrote privately to him that in the
event of their obduracy, he and other commanding
officers must bring the power of the European regiments in the Punjab to bear upon the coercion of the
mutinous Sepoys. But before these letters arrived,
Campbell had tided over the difficulty. "The com-

1849.   bination amongst the men of the Thirteenth and
Twenty-second Regiments," he wrote to Napier, on
the 26th of July, " gave way to fear on the 18th, the
day before your prescription for bringing them to
their senses was despatched from Simlah." The fact
is that, at that time, they were not ready; they were
not strong enough for the resistance of authority;
and they were not prepared to be the protomartyrs in
such a cause.   There was a European regiment at
Rawul Pindee; there were European regiments at
other stations not far removed; and so it was held to
be a wiser course to wait until the new regiments
should arrive from the older provinces and unite with
them in the dangerous work of military rebellion.

That these regiments were prepared to resist was
soon too apparent.   From Simlah, Napier proceeded
on a tour of inspection to the principal military
stations in the Northern Provinces of India; and at
Delhi he found unmistakable signs of a confederation
of many regiments determined not to serve in the
Punjab except on the higher pay.   One regiment
there, warned for service beyond the Sutlej, declared
its intention not to march; but it was conciliated by
a liberal grant of furloughs, which had before been
withheld; and it went on to its destination.   Napier
believed that the spirit of disaffection was wide-spread.
He had heard ominous reports of twenty-four regiments prepared to strike, and when he entered the
Punjab, he was not surprised to find that mutiny was
there only in a state of suspended activity, and that
at any moment it might burst out, all the more
furiously for this temporary suppression.

At Wuzeerabad it soon openly manifested itself. In
command of that station was one of the best soldiers
of the Company's service.   At an early age John

Hearsey had earned a name in History, as one of the heroes of Seetabuldee, and thirty years of subsequent service had thoroughly ripened his experience, so that at this time he had perhaps as large a knowledge of the Sepoy, of his temper, of his habits, of his language, as any officer in the Native Army. With this large knowledge dwelt also in him a large sympathy. It commonly happened in those days that the man who best knew the Sepoy best loved him; and Hearsey, who had seen how good a soldier he could be, before the enemy, respected his good qualities, and looked leniently on his bad. He believed that, with good management, a Sepoy regiment might be kept, under almost any circumstances, in the right temper, and he had great faith in the magic efficacy of a good speech. When, therefore, one of the regiments at Wuzeerabad openly refused its pay, Hearsey drew up the men on parade, and addressed them in language so touching, so forcible, and so much to the point, that many hung down their heads, ashamed of what they had done, and some even shed tears of penitence. The pay was then offered to them again. The first four men who refused were tried at once, and sentenced to imprisonment with hard labour. The whole brigade was then turned out to see the sentence carried into effect. There were four Native regiments at Wuzeerabad; but there was also a Regiment of the Line and detachments of European Artillery, Horse and Foot. In the presence of this force, the convicted Sepoys were manacled as felons and sent off to work on the roads. After this, there were no more refusals; the men took their pay and did their work.

But discipline had not yet been fully vindicated. Three ringleaders, who had been known to go from company to company, instigating and fomenting re-

1844. bellion, were tried by court-martial, and sentenced to fourteen years' imprisonment. But Napier, who regarded in a far stronger light both the enormity of the offence and the magnitude of the danger, ordered a revision of the sentence, and death was recorded against the culprits; and against two others who were tried for the same offence by the same Court.* Then justice was satisfied, and mercy might stretch forth its hand. The sentence was commuted to transportation for life. "In eternal exile," said Napier, in his general order to the troops, "they will expiate their crimes. For ever separated from their country and their relations, in a strange land beyond the seas, they will linger out their miserable lives. It is a change, but I do not consider it an amelioration of their punishment. They will remain living examples of the miserable fate which awaits traitors to their colours."

January 25, 1850.

But the spirit of disaffection was not suppressed, though locally for a time it was subdued. It was declared that the Post-office runners laboured under the weight of the Sepoys' letters, which were then passing from cantonment to cantonment; but a large number of these letters were seized and examined, and they were found to contain nothing on the subject of the allowances.† Napier, however, anticipated a crisis, and was prepared for it. Taking post at Peshawur, the extremest corner of our new Punjab territory, where was a strong European force, he believed that he would ere long be compelled to sweep down with the English regiments, picking up reinforcements as he went from station to station, and to

---

* Sir Charles Napier, in his Indian Misgovernment, says that four were tried at first, and one afterwards; but the fact is as stated in the text.

† Sir Henry Lawrence, in *Calcutta Review*, vol. xxii. The statement is made on the authority of Major W. Mayne, President of the Govindghur Court of Enquiry.

crush a general rising of the Sepoy troops. And soon it appeared to him that the crisis had come. The Sixty-sixth Regiment broke into mutiny at Govindghur. Bursting out, on parade, with vehement shouts of disapprobation, they attempted to seize the gates of the Fort, so as to cut off all communication with the loyal troops outside the walls. There was no European regiment at Govindghur, but the First Native Cavalry, under Bradford, were faithful among the faithless, and, aided by the cool courage of Macdonald, of the Sixty-sixth, they made good their entrance through the gate.* The Fort was saved. The European officers were saved. And the guilty regiment was doomed to a moral death. The Sixty-sixth was struck out of the Army List. The men were disbanded in a body, and their colours given to a corps of Goorkhas, from the hill-tracts of Nepaul, who were known to be good soldiers, with no Brahminical daintiness about them, and a general fidelity to their Salt.

"When the Sixty-sixth was disbanded," says Sir Charles Napier, "the mutiny ceased entirely. Why? The Brahmins saw that the Goorkhas, another race, could be brought into the ranks of the Company's Army—a race dreaded, as more warlike than their own. Their religious combination was by that one stroke rendered abortive." But, far other causes than this helped to subdue the spirit of disaffection which was then ripening in the Punjab. The Sepoys had struck for higher allowances than those which had been granted to them by the strict letter of the Regulations; but Napier thought, that however unsoldierly, however culpable their conduct might be,

---

* An opportune blow from Macdonald's sword appears to have caused the gate to be opened. See statement published by Sir H. Lawrence in *Calcutta Review*, vol. xxii.

1850.

some grounds of dissatisfaction existed. The change, which the Sepoys resented, was declared by the Chief to be "impolitic and unjust;" and, pending a reference to Government, orders were issued for the payment of compensation to the troops, on a higher scale than that sanctioned by the latest regulations.*

Dalhousie and Napier.

Then arose that memorable conflict between Napier and Dalhousie, which ended in the resignation by the former of an office which many had predicted that he could not long continue to hold. Both were men of imperious temper, and a collision between them was, from the first, clearly foreseen. When the Military Chief took upon himself to readjust the allowances of the troops in the Punjab, the Civil Go-

* The bare statement in the text will suffice for the general reader, but not, perhaps, for the professional one. It may be stated, therefore, that it had been for many years the rule of the Indian Government, whenever the prices of the common articles of consumption used by the Native soldiery exceeded a certain fixed price, to grant them compensation proportionate to the additional cost of supplies. This bounty seems first to have been bestowed in the year 1821 on the Native troops serving in the Western Provinces, and was limited to the single article of ottah, or flour. Whenever ottah was selling at less than fifteen seers (or thirty pounds) the rupee, a proportionate compensation was granted. But, subsequently, in 1844, the application of this order was extended by Lord Ellenborough, and compensation also was granted to the Native troops serving in Scinde, when certain minor articles of consumption were selling at a high price. In the following year a new order relative to this same subject of compensation-money was issued by Lord Hardinge, who had by this time succeeded to the government. Instead of granting a separate money-compensation for each particular high-priced article of consumption, all the several articles were massed, and some being cheaper than elsewhere, a general average was struck. It was then officially announced that thenceforth compensation would be granted to the Sepoys "whenever the price of provisions, forming the Native soldier's diet, should exceed 3 rupees and 8 annas, the aggregate of the rates for the several articles laid down in the General Orders of the 26th of February, 1844." Whenever, in other words, the Sepoy was unable to obtain his daily rations at a cost of 3 rupees 8 annas a month (which cost was calculated in accordance with the aggregate fixed rates of the prices of provisions, beyond which compensation, under the old regulations, was granted for each article), the excess was to be defrayed by the Government. The regulation of 1845 was not so favourable to the troops as that of 1844, and Sir Charles Napier, believing that the application of the former rule to the troops in the Punjab was a mistake, directed the regulation of 1844 again to be brought into force.

vernor was at sea beyond the reach of an official reference. He returned to find what had been done, and he resented such an encroachment upon the prerogative of the Government. Napier had justified the exercise of an authority not constitutionally belonging to his office, by the assertion that the danger was pressing, and that action, in such an emergency, did not admit delay. Dalhousie denied the premises; he insisted that there had been no danger. " I cannot sufficiently express," he wrote, in an elaborate Minute on Napier's proceedings, "the astonishment with which I read, on the 26th of May, the intimation then made to the Government by the Commander-in-Chief, that in the month of January last a mutinous spirit pervaded the army in the Punjab, and that insubordination had risen so high and spread so wide, as to impress his Excellency with the belief that the Government of the country was placed at that time in a position of 'great peril.' I have carefully weighed the statements which his Excellency has advanced. I have examined anew the records that bear on the state of public affairs at that period, and I have well reflected upon all that has passed. While I do not seek to question in any way the sincerity of the convictions by which Sir Charles Napier has been led to declare that the army was in mutiny and the empire in danger, I, on my part, am bound to say that my examination and reflection have not lessened in any degree the incredulity with which I first read the statements to which I have referred." "There is no justification," continued his Lordship, " for the cry that India was in danger. Free from all threat of hostilities from without, and secure, through the submission of its new subjects, from insurrection within, the safety of India has never for one moment been imperilled by the partial insubordination in the ranks of its army. I have confronted the assertions of the Commander-in-Chief on this head with undisputed facts, and with the authority of recorded documents, and my convictions strengthened by the information which the Government commands, I desire to record my entire dissent from the statement that the army has been in mutiny, and the empire in danger."

This was, doubtless, the popular view of the matter; and it was readily accepted at the time. What amount of danger really existed was never known, and now never will be known. Whatever it may have been, it was tided over; and the quietude that followed this temporary explosion seemed to warrant the confidence which the Governor-General had expressed. But Napier held to his opinion with as much tenacity as Dalhousie. Nothing could shake the belief of the old soldier that the exceptional course he had adopted was justified by the exceptional circumstances of the times. Still he knew the duty of obedience; he knew that in a conflict between two authorities the lower must yield to the higher, and that he had no right to complain if the latter asserted the power vested in him by the Law. "And I do not complain," he emphatically added. But, strong in his conviction of right, and master of himself, though not of the situation, he felt that he could retire with dignity from a position which he could not hold with profit to the State. And he did retire. On the 22nd of May, he addressed a letter to the Horse-Guards, requesting that the Duke of Wellington would obtain her gracious Majesty's permission for him to resign the chief command of the Indian Army. "And the more so," he added, "as being now nearly seventy

years of age—during the last ten years of which I
have gone through considerable fatigue of body and
mind, especially during the last year—my health
requires that relief from climate and business which
public service in India does not admit."

But there is no blame, in such a case, to be recorded against the Governor-General. When an old
and distinguished soldier—a warrior of high repute,
and a man of consummate ability—deliberately de-
clares that he regards the system under which he has
been called upon to command an army as a system at
once faulty and dangerous; that he conceives the
power of the civil magistrate to be so absolute that
the arm of the chief soldier is paralysed; and that, so
enervated and emasculated by restrictions imposed
upon him by law, he cannot wield the sword with
honour to himself or advantage to the State, and that,
therefore, he desires to lay it down, he utters words
which, whether he be right or wrong in his estimate
of what ought to be the just balance between the civil
and the military power, are honest, manly, dignified
words, and ought everywhere to be received with
respect. Few men had a better right than Sir Charles
Napier to criticise an Act of Parliament. He had a
right to think that the law was a bad law; and he had
a right to say that it was bad. But the law, whether
good or bad, was not made by Lord ·Dalhousie, but
by the British Parliament. It was Dalhousie's business to administer that law, and to maintain the authority vested in him by the Imperial Legislature. Of
this Napier had no right to complain; and he declared
that he did not complain. But the contest was on
every account an unseemly and an unfortunate one.
It was another and a culminating instance of that
excessive centralisation which weakened the authority

and degraded the character of the military arm, and taught the soldiery that the greatest chief whom England could send them was as much a subaltern of the civil governor as the youngest ensign on the Army List.

And it taught even more than this. It taught thinking men, not for the first time, that even the chief members of the Government were at war among themselves, and the lesson shook their faith in the stability of a power thus disunited, thus incoherent. " I am now sixty years of age," wrote an intelligent native official to Sir George Clerk. " I have heard three sayings repeated by wise men, and I myself have also found out, from my own experience, that the sovereignty of the British Government will not be overthrown save by the occurrence of three objectionable circumstances." And the first of these circumstances he thus stated : " Formerly the high, dignified Sahibs had no enmity among themselves, or at least the people of India never came to know that they had enmity. Now enmity exists among them, and it is as well seen as the sun at noonday that they calumniate and bear malice against each other."* Such conflicts of authority are keenly watched and volubly discussed ; and a significance is attached to them out of all proportion to the importance with which amongst.us like contentions are invested. The natives of India know that we are few ; but they feel that union makes us many. Seen to be at discord among ourselves, we shrivel into our true proportions, and it is believed that our power is beginning to crumble and decay.

During the administration of Lord Ellenborough there had been disunion among the higher authorities, arising out of nearly similar causes. The unauthorised

* MS. Correspondence, translated from the Persian.

promises given by the Commander-in-Chief to the Native troops proceeding to Scinde had stirred the resentment of the Governor-General, and his grave displeasure was excited by the zealous indiscretions of the Madras Government. But he had studiously veiled from the public eye the differences that had arisen. There was nothing to which he was more keenly alive than to the necessity, especially in troubled times, of maintaining a show of union and co-operation in the high places of Government. It was his hard fate at last to be compelled, by the fiat of a higher power, to exhibit to the people of India, in his own person, the very spectacle which he had striven to conceal from them, and to declare, trumpet-tongued, that the English were vehemently contending among themselves. But so long as he exercised the supreme control he was careful not to reveal the local dissensions of the Government, lest he should weaken the authority it was so essential to uphold; and little even is now known of the strife that raged at the time, when the great difficulty of garrisoning Scinde was filling the minds of the rulers of the land. But the strife between Dalhousie and Napier was proclaimed, almost as it were by beat of drum, in all the Lines and Bazaars of the country; and all men knew that the English, who used so to cling to one another, that it seemed that they thought with one strong brain and struck with one strong arm, were now wasting their vigour by warring among themselves, and in their disunion ceasing to be formidable.

This was apparent to all men's eyes; but the Sepoy had his own particular lesson to learn, and did not neglect it. How it happened that the bitter experience which the English Government had gained, on the annexation of Scinde, made no impression upon

Y

1850.   the minds of those whose duty it was to provide
against the recurrence of similar disasters, it is impossible to explain. All we know is, that five years after
a misunderstanding between the Government and the
Army with respect to the rates of pay and allowance
to be disbursed to the Sepoy, in a newly-acquired
country, had driven into mutiny a large number of
Native regiments, and greatly perplexed the rulers of
the day, a similar conjuncture arose, and there was
a similar misunderstanding, with similar results.* The
Sepoy had not learnt to reconcile himself to the British
theory of Annexation, and so he resented it in the
Punjab as he had before resented it in Scinde. In the
latter country the excitement was far greater, and the
danger more serious, than in the former; but in both
there was an outburst on the one side, and a concession
on the other. That was given to the mutinous soldier,
not without loss of character by Government, which
might before have been given to the loyal one with
befitting dignity and grace. When the emergency
arises, it is hard to say whether there be greater evil
in concession or in resistance. Napier thought the

---

* This uncertainty with respect
to the pay and allowances of different branches and different ranks
of the Indian Army was emphatically
commented upon by Sir Henry Lawrence in an article bearing his name
in the *Calcutta Review:* "Of all
the wants of the Army, perhaps the
greatest want is a simple pay-code,
unmistakably showing the pay of
every rank, in each branch, under all
circumstances. At present there
are not three officers in the Bengal
Army who could, with certainty, tell
what they and the people under
them are entitled to in every position
in which they are liable to be placed.
The Audit-office seldom affords help.
It is considered an enemy ready to
take advantage of difficulties, not
an umpire between man and man.
During the last thirty years, I have
seen much hardship on officers in
matters of accounts, and of the several instances of discontent that I
have witnessed in the Native Army,
all were more or less connected with
pay, and in almost every instance
the men only asked for what they
were by existing rules entitled to.
Half a sheet of paper ought to show
every soldier his rate of pay, by sea,
by land, on leave, on the staff, in
hospital, on duty, &c. There ought
to be no doubt on the matter. At
present there is great doubt, though
there are volumes of Pay and Audit
Regulations."

one thing, Dalhousie thought the other; and each 1850. had strong argument on his side. But both must have bitterly regretted that the contingency was ever suffered to arise, that no one in authority, warned by the lessons of the Past, had learnt to look at the consequences of Annexation with a Sepoy's eyes, and anticipated, by small concessions, the not irrational expectations which, at a later stage developing into demands, had all the force and significance of mutiny. Had this been done; had the Sepoy been told that in consideration of increased distance from home, and other circumstances rendering service in Scinde and the Punjab more irksome to him than in our older provinces, certain especial advantages would be conferred upon him—advantages which might have been bestowed at small cost to the State—he would have received the boon with gratitude, and applauded the justice of his masters; but after he had struck for it, he saw not their justice, but their fear, in the concession, and he hugged the feeling of power, which lessons such as these could not fail to engender.

CHAPTER V.

CHARACTER OF THE BENGAL SEPOY—CONFLICTING OPINIONS—CASTE—THE SENIORITY SYSTEM—THE OFFICERING OF THE ARMY—REGULAR AND IRREGULAR REGIMENTS—WANT OF EUROPEANS—THE CRIMEAN WAR— INDIAN PUBLIC OPINION—SUMMARY OF DETERIORATING INFLUENCES.

1851-56.   AFTER this, there was again a season of quiet. The remaining years of Lord Dalhousie's administration passed away without any further military outbreaks to disturb his rooted conviction of the fidelity of the Sepoy. There were not wanting those who declared that there was an ineradicable taint in the constitution of the Bengal Army, that it was rotten to the very core. But the angry controversies which arose —the solemn warnings on the one side, and the indignant denials on the other—proved nothing more than that among men, entitled to speak with authority on the subject, there were vast diversities of opinion. Much of this was attributed to class prejudices and professional jealousies. One voice, very loud and very earnest, pealing from the West, sustained for years a continual remonstrance against the laxities of the Bengal System. But Bengal resented the outrage. A genuine man, above all pettiness, John Jacob, was declared to be the exponent only of small Presidential envyings and heart-burnings. The voice of Truth was proclaimed to be the voice of

Bombay. And when officers of the Bengal Army wrote, as some did most wisely, of the evil symptoms which were manifesting themselves, and of the dangers which appeared to be looming in the distance, they were denounced as defilers of their own nest, and as feeble-minded alarmists, to whose utterances no heed should be given. There was a general unwillingness to believe in the decay of discipline throughout one of the finest armies of the world; and in the absence of any outward signs of mischief, we willingly consented not to look beneath the surface for the virus of undeveloped disease.

There is nothing that is strange, and little that is blamable in this. The Bengal Sepoy had evinced signs of a froward, petulant nature, and he had, on several occasions, broken out after a fashion which, viewed by European military eyes, is criminality of the deepest dye. But these aberrations were merely a few dark spots upon a century of good service. It was not right that rare exceptions of this kind should cancel in our minds all the noble acts of fidelity which were chronicled in the history of our empire. Nor was it to be forgotten that, in most instances, the criminality of the Sepoy had been the direct growth of some mismanagement on the part either of the officers whom he followed or the Government which he served. To have looked with suspicion on the Sepoy, because from time to time some component parts of our Army had done that, which the Armies of every Native State had done, with their whole accumulated strength, would have been equally unwise and unjust. For although it might be said that the examples, which those Native States afforded, ought to have taught us to beware of the destroying power of a lawless soldiery, the English were justified in be-

1851-56. lieving that there were special reasons why their own
mercenaries should not tread in the footsteps of the
Mahratta and Sikh Armies.   They did not believe in
the love of the Sepoy; but they believed in his fidelity
to his Pay.

Character of   Whilst it was natural, and indeed commendable,
the Sepoy.   that the remembrance of all the good service which
the Native soldiery had done for their English masters,
should have sustained our confidence in them as a
body, there was nothing in the individual character
of the Sepoy to subvert it.   Even his outbreaks of
rebellion had recently partaken more of the naughti-
ness of the child than of the stern resolution of manhood.   He had evinced a disposition, indeed, rather
to injure himself than to injure others; and it was
not easy for those who knew him to believe that he
was capable of any violent and sanguinary excesses.
His character was made up of inconsistencies, but the
weaker and less dangerous qualities appeared to have
the preponderance; and though we knew that they
made him a very difficult person to manage, we did
not think that they made him a dangerous one.   From
the time when, in the very infancy of the Sepoy Army,
a Madras soldier cut down Mr. Haliburton, and was
immediately put to death by his own comrades, to the
day when Colin Mackenzie was well-nigh butchered at
Bolarum by troopers of his own brigade, there had
been ever and anon some murderous incidents to dis-
figure the Military History of our Indian Empire.* But
outrages of this kind are common to all armies; and
there was no reason to regard them in any other light
than that of exceptional aberrations.   It was not to

---

* See Williams's Bengal Army   section on the Sepoy Army in Suther-
and Mackenzie's Narrative of the   land's Sketches of the Native States
Mutiny at Bolarum; compare also   of India.

1851-56.

be said that the Sepoy was a ruffian because he had done some ruffianly deeds.

He was, indeed, altogether a paradox. He was made up of inconsistencies and contradictions. In his character, qualities, so adverse as to be apparently irreconcilable with each other, met together and embraced. He was simple and yet designing; credulous and easily deceived by others, and yet obstinately tenacious of his own in-bred convictions; now docile as a child, and now hard and immovable in the stubbornness of his manhood. Abstemious and yet self-indulgent, calm and yet impetuous, gentle and yet cruel, he was indolent even to languor in his daily life, and yet capable of being roused to acts of the most desperate energy. Sometimes sportive, and sometimes sullen, he was easily elevated and easily depressed; but he was for the most part of a cheerful nature, and if you came suddenly upon him in the Lines you were more likely to see him with a broad grin upon his face than with any expression of moroseness or discontent. But light-hearted as was his general temperament, he would sometimes brood over imaginary wrongs, and when a delusion once entered his soul it clung to it with the subtle malevolence of an ineradicable poison.

And this, as we now understand the matter, was the most dangerous feature of his character. For his gentler, more genial qualities sparkled upon the surface and were readily appreciated, whilst all the harsher and more forbidding traits lay dark and disguised, and were not discernible in our ordinary intercourse with him. There was outwardly, indeed, very much to rivet the confidence of the European officer, and very little to disturb it. It is true that if we reasoned about it, it did not seem to be altogether reasonable to expect from the Sepoy any strong affection for the alien officer who had usurped all the high places of the Army, and who kept him down in the dead level of the dust. But Englishmen never reason about their position in the midst of a community of strangers; they take their popularity for granted, and look for homage as a thing of course. And that homage was yielded to the British officer, not for his own sake, for the Sepoy hated his colour and his creed, his unclean ways, and his domineering manners; but because he was an embodiment of Success. It was one of the many inconsistencies of which I have spoken, that though boastful and vain-glorious beyond all example, the Native soldier of India inwardly acknowledged that he 'owed to the English officer the aliment which fed his passion for glory and sustained his military pride. This, indeed, was the link that bound class to class, and resisted the dissolving power of many adverse influences. It was this that moved the Sepoy to light up the tomb of his old commanding officer; it was this that moved the veteran to salute the picture of the General under whom he had fought. But there was a show also of other and gentler feelings, and there were instances of strong personal attachment, of unsurpassed fidelity and devotion, manifested in acts of charity and love. You might see the Sepoy of many fights, watchful and tender as a woman, beside the sick-bed of the English officer, or playing with the pale-faced chil-dren beneath the verandah of his captain's bungalow. There was not an English gentlewoman in the country who did not feel measureless security in the thought that a guard of Sepoys watched her house, or who would not have travelled, under such an escort, across the whole length and breadth of the

land. What was lurking beneath the fair surface we
knew not. We saw only the softer side of the
Sepoy's nature; and there was nothing to make us
believe that there was danger in the confidence which
we reposed in those outward signs of attachment to
our rule.

But whilst cherishing this not unreasonable confidence in the general good character of the Sepoy,
the British Government might still have suffered
some doubts and misgivings to arise when they looked
into the details of the System. They might, it has
been urged, have believed in the soundness of the
whole, but admitted the defectiveness of parts, and
addressed themselves earnestly and deliberately to
the details of the great work of Army Reform. Instead of boasting that the condition of the Native
soldier left nothing to be desired, Lord Dalhousie, it
is said, ought to have looked beneath the surface, to
have probed all the vices of the existing system, and
to have striven with all his might to eradicate them.
Information was not wanting. " Officers of experience" were at all times ready to tell him what it
behoved him to do. But in the multitude of counsellors there was inextricable confusion. As with the
whole, so with the parts. The forty years' experience
of one greybeard belied the forty years' experience
of another. And when the responsible ruler had
been almost persuaded to see a blot and to promise
to erase it, another adviser came, straightway declared it to be a beauty, and besought him to leave it
as it was. Thus distracted by the conflicting judgments of the best military critics, Dalhousie did, as
others had done before him; he admitted that if he
had then for the first time to construct a Native
Army it would in some respects differ from that

1851-56.   which he saw before him, the growth not of systems
and theories but of circumstances; but that as it had
grown up, so on the whole it was better to leave it,
as Change is sometimes dangerous, and almost always
misunderstood.

That, indeed, there was no more difficult question
to understand than that of the Sepoy Army, was a
fact which must have been continually forced upon
the mind of the Governor-General, by the discordant
opinions which were pronounced on points vitally
affecting its fidelity and efficiency.   Even on the
great question of Caste, men differed.   Some said it
was desirable that our Native regiments should be
composed mainly of high-caste men; because in such
men were combined many of the best qualities, moral
and physical, which contribute to the formation of
an accomplished soldier.   The high-caste man had a
bolder spirit, a purer professional pride, a finer frame,
and a more military bearing, than his countryman of
lower social rank.   Other authorities contended that
the Native soldiery should be enlisted indiscriminately,
that no account should be taken of Caste distinctions,
and that the smaller the proportion of Brahmins and
Rajpoots in the service the better for the discipline
of the Army.*   Comparisons were drawn between the
Bengal and the Bombay Armies.   There was a strong
and not unnatural prejudice in favour of the Bengal
Sepoy; for he was a fine, noble-looking fellow, and in
comparison with his comrades from the Southern and
Western Presidencies, was said to be quite a gentleman; but there were those who alleged that he was
more a gentleman than a soldier; and it was urged
that the normal state of the Bengal Army was Mutiny,
because in an Army so constituted Caste was ever

Caste.

* For the statistics of Caste in the Sepoy Army, see Appendix.

stronger than Discipline; and the social institutions of the Sepoy domineered over the necessities of the State.

It was contended, for this reason, that the Bengal Army required a larger infusion of low-caste men. But it was alleged, on the other hand, that this very mixture of castes tended to destroy the discipline of which it was proposed to make it the preservative; for that military rank was held to be nothing in comparison with Brahminical Elevation, and that the Sepoy was often the "master of the officer."* To this it was replied that the presumption of Caste was favoured and fostered by the weakness and indulgence of the officers of the Bengal Army; that, in the armies of Madras and Bombay, Caste had found its level; that it had neither been antagonistic to good service, nor injurious to internal discipline; that high-caste men in those armies did cheerfully what they refused to do in Bengal, and that low-caste native officers met with all the respect from their social superiors due to their superior military rank. It was asserted, indeed, that Brahminism was arrogant and exacting in Bengal, because it saw that it could play upon the fears of the English officers. To this it was replied, that disregard Caste as we might, we could never induce the natives to disregard it. And then again the rejoinder was, that in the other Presidencies we had taught them to disregard it, why, then, might not the same lesson be taught in Bengal? The answer to this was, that men will often do in other countries what they cannot be persuaded to do

* "I cannot conceive the possibility of maintaining discipline in a corps where a low-caste non-commissioned officer will, when he meets off duty a Brahmin Sepoy, crouch down to him with his forehead on the ground. I have seen this done. The Sepoy thus treated is the master of the officer."—*Evidence of Major-General Birch.*

1851-56. in their own; that high-caste Hindostanees enlisting into the Bombay or Madras Armies were, to a great extent, cut off from the brotherhood, that they were greatly outnumbered in their several regiments, that it was convenient to conform to the custom of the country, and that what he did in a foreign country among strangers was little known at home. In a word, when he took service in the Bombay Army, he did what was done in Bombay; just as among ourselves, men who, fearful of losing caste, would on no account be seen to enter a London hell, think nothing of spending whole days in the gambling-rooms of Homburg or Baden-Baden.

Nationalities. Of a kindred nature was the question hotly discussed, whether it were wiser to compose each regiment of men of the same race, or to mix up different races in the same corps. On the one hand, it was alleged that the fusion of different nationalities had a tendency to keep internal combinations in check; but that if men of one tribe were formed into separate regiments; if we had Patan regiments and Goorkha regiments, Sikh regiments and Mahratta regiments, facilities for mutinous combinations would be greatly increased. On the other hand, it was contended that the fusion of different tribes and castes in the several regiments encouraged external combinations by imparting common interests to the whole Army; that if safety were to be sought in the antagonism of nationalities, it was more likely to be attained by keeping them apart than by fusing them into a heterogeneous mass; that it was easier to keep one regiment from following the example of another composed of different materials, raised and stationed in a different part of the country, than to keep one half of a regiment from following the example of the other; easier to make men fight against those whom they had never seen, than against those with whom they had long lived, if not in brotherhood of caste, at least in brotherhood of service.

Again, men discussed, with reference to this question of combination, the relative advantages and disadvantages of localisation and distribution. Whilst some contended that the different Sepoy regiments should serve respectively only in certain parts of the country, except under any peculiar exigencies of war —in other words, that they should be assimilated as much as possible to a sort of local militia—others were in favour of the existing system, under which there were periodical reliefs, and regiments marched from one station to another, often many hundreds of miles apart. On the one hand it was argued that there was much danger in the local influence which would be acquired by men long resident in the same place, and that intrigues and plots, rendered perilous by the fusion of the civil and military classes, might result from this localisation; and, on the other, it was urged that it was far more dangerous to suffer the Sepoy regiments to become extensively acquainted with each other, for the men to form friendships, and therefore to have correspondents in other corps, and thus to afford them the means, in times of excitement, of forming extensive combinations, and spreading, as it were, a network of conspiracy over the whole face of the country. Thus, again, men of wisdom and experience neutralised one another's judgments, and from amongst so many conflicting opinions it was impossible to evolve the truth.

It was a question also much debated whether the fidelity and efficiency of the Sepoy were best maintained by keeping him apart from his family, or by

Local and General Service.

Families.

1851-56. suffering the wives, the children, and the dependents of the soldier to attach themselves to his regiment, and to follow his fortunes. The former was the system in the Bengal Army; the latter, in the Army of Madras, and partially in that of Bombay. Each system had its advocates; each its special advantages. The Bengal Sepoy visited his family at stated times, and remitted to them a large part of his pay. If he failed to do this he was a marked man in his regiment; and, it was said, that the knowledge that if he failed in his duty as a soldier, a report of his misconduct would surely reach his native village, and that his face would be blackened before his kindred, kept him in the strict path of his duty. The presence of the Family led to much inconvenience and embarrassment, and the necessity of moving it from one station to another, when the regiments were relieved, strained the scanty resources of the Sepoy, and developed grievances out of which mutiny might arise.* It was said, indeed, that there was " hardly a Native regiment in the Bengal Army in which the twenty drummers, who were Christians, and had their families with them, did not cause more trouble to their officers than the whole eight hundred Sepoys."† On the other hand, it was urged that the presence of the Family afforded the best guarantee for the fidelity and good conduct of the Sepoy. His children were hostages in our hands; the honour of his women was in our keeping. These were held to be safeguards against mutiny and massacre. It was urged, too, that the system tended more to keep them, as a race, apart from the general mass of their countrymen; that the ties which bound them to the country were

---

* See the case of the Sixth Madras Cavalry, *ante*, page 291.   † Sleeman on the Spirit of Discipline in the Native Army.

thus weakened, and their interests more indissolubly 1851-56.
associated with the State.   They were less representative men than their brethren of the Bengal Army,
and more a part of the machinery of Government.
And so each system had its advocates, and each was
left to work itself out and develop its own results.

Great, also, was the difference of opinion with respect Promotion.
to Promotion.   Some said that the Bengal Army was
destroyed by the Seniority system, which gave to every
Sepoy in the service an equal chance of rising to the
rank of a Commissioned Officer.*   Others maintained
that this was the very sheet-anchor which enabled it
to resist all adverse influences.   Strong arguments
were adduced, and great names were quoted upon
both sides.   It was said that under such a system
there was no incentive to exertion; that the men
were independent of their officers, that they had no
motive to earn the good opinion of their superiors, that
it was enough for them to drowse through a certain
number of years of service, to slide quietly into a
commission, and then to end their military lives in a
state of senile somnolence and apathy.   The Native
officers of the Bengal Army were, therefore, for the
most part, respectable, worn-out, feeble-minded old
men, with no influence in their regiments, and no desire beyond that of saving-themselves as much trouble
as possible, and keeping things as quiet as they could.
On the other hand, it was alleged that the seniority
system was the very prop and support of the Sepoy
service; that all men were happy and contented, and
had some aliment of hope, so long as they felt that
nothing but their own misconduct could deprive them
of the right of succession to the highest grades of the

* To every regiment of Native   dar-major, ten Soubahdars, and ten
infantry were attached one Soubah-   Jemadars.

1851-56.   Native Army.   It was said that to pass over a man at the head of the list, and to give promotion to others of shorter service, would be to flood the regiments with desperate malcontents, or else with sullen, broken-spirited idlers.   Whilst Henry Lawrence and John Jacob were descanting on the evil of filling the commissioned ranks of the Sepoy Army with "poor old wretches, feeble in body and imbecile in mind,"[*] Charles Napier was peremptorily commanding that " the fullest attention and consideration should invariably be given to the claim of seniority in every grade" of the Native Army, and William Sleeman was asserting, not less emphatically, in his published writings, that "though we might have in every regiment a few smarter Native officers, by disregarding the rule of promotion than by adhering to it, we should, in the diminution of good feeling towards the European officers and the Government, lose a thousand times more than we gained."[†]   What wonder, then, that Governor-General after Governor-General was perplexed and bewildered, and left things, when he passed away from the scene, as he found them on his first arrival.

---

[*] *Views and Opinions of General John Jacob*, p. 120; compare also Sir Henry Lawrence's *Essays, Military and Political*, p. 24 *et seq.*

[†] Sleeman relates, that " an old Soubahdar, who had been at the taking of the Isle of France, mentioned that when he was the senior Jemadar of his regiment, and a vacancy had occurred to bring him in as Soubahdar, he was sent for by his commanding officer, and told that by orders from Head-Quarters he was to be passed over, on account of his advanced age and supposed infirmity. ' I felt,' said the old man, ' as if I had been struck by lightning, *and fell down dead.* The Colonel was a good man, and had seen much service. He had me taken into the open air, and when I recovered he told me that he would write to the Commander-in-Chief and represent my case. He did so immediately, and I was promoted, and I have since done my duty as Soubahdar for ten years.' "   But, it may be asked, *how?*   It must be borne in mind, too, that Sleeman speaks here of the effect of supersession under a Seniority system. Under a system of selection such results would not be apparent, because there would not be the same disgrace in being passed over.

Then, again, there were wide diversities of opinion
with respect to the European officering of regiments.
There were those who contended for the Irregular and
those who were loud in their praises of the Regular
system; some who thought it better to attach to each
regiment a few select officers, as in the old times,
giving them some power and authority over their
men; and others who believed it to be wiser to officer
the regiments after the later English system, like regiments of the Line, with a large available surplus for
purposes of the General Staff, and to leave all the
centralised power and authority in the hands of the
Adjutant-General of the Army.* There was a continual cry, not always, it must be admitted, of the
most unselfish character, for " more officers;" and
yet it was plain that the Irregular regiments, to
which only three or four picked officers were attached, were in a perfect state of discipline in peace,
and capable of performing admirable service in war.
It was said that in action the Sepoys, losing their
officers, killed or carried wounded to the rear, lost
heart, and were soon panic-struck; and that if officers
were so few, this contingency must often happen. To
this, however, it was replied, that if the Native
officers were of the right class, they would keep their
men together, and still do good service; but if they
were worn-out imbeciles, or over-corpulent and scant
of breath, of course disorder and ruin must follow
the fall of the English officers. Then, hearing this,
the disputant on the other side would triumphantly
ask how many years' purchase our empire in India
were worth, if our Native officers were as efficient as

* A regiment of Native Infantry   5 ensigns. A few months after-
in March, 1856, was officered by 1 wards another captain and another
colonel, 1 lieutenant-colonel, 1 ma- lieutenant were added to each regi-
jor, 6 captains, 10 lieutenants, and ment.

z

1851-56.   ourselves.   It was often argued, indeed, that our instructions might some day return to plague the inventor; that to make men qualified to lead our battalions to battle against our enemies is to qualify them to command troops to fight against ourselves. But there were others, and chief among them Henry Lawrence, who, taking a larger and more liberal view of the question, contended that it was sound policy to give to every man, European and Native, a motive for exertion; who declared that it was one of the crying wants of our system that it afforded no outlet for the energies of Native soldiers of superior courage and ability, and urged that we could not expect to have an efficient Native Army so long as we rigidly maintained in it the theory of the Dead Level, and purposely excluded every possible inducement to superior exertion.

Nor less curious were the fundamental diversities of opinion which manifested themselves, when thinking men began to consider whether the English in India carried into their daily lives too much or too little of their nationality.   It was asserted on the one side that the English officer was too stiff-necked and exclusive, that he dwelt apart too much, and subdued himself too little to surrounding influences; and on the other side, that he fell too rapidly into Oriental habits, and soon ceased to be, what it should have been his ambition to remain to the last, a model of an English Gentleman.   It was urged by some that increased facilities of intercourse with Europe rendered men more dissatisfied with the ordinary environments of Eastern life and professional duty, whilst others declared that one of the most serious defects in the Indian Military System was the difficulty with which the English officer obtained furlough to Europe.* The stringency of the Furlough Regulations had, however, been greatly relaxed during the administration of Lord Dalhousie, and the establishment of regular steam-communication between the two countries had made the new rules practical realities. But whatsoever increased intercourse with Europe may have done to promote the application of Western science to our Indian Military System, it did not improve the regimental officer. It was contended that he commonly returned to his duty with increased distaste for cantonment life; and that he obeyed the mandate, "Let it be the fashion to be English," by suffering a still greater estrangement to grow up between him and the Native soldier.

Indeed, there was scarcely a single point, in the whole wide range of topics connected with the great subject of the efficiency of the Native Indian Army, which did not raise a doubt and suggest a controversy. And there was so much of demonstrable truth in the assertions, and so much cogency in the arguments adduced, on both sides, that in the eyes of the looker-on it was commonly a drawn battle between the two contending parties; and so, as it was the easier and perhaps the safer course to leave things as they were, the changes which Army Reformers so earnestly advocated were practically rejected, and we clung to evils which had grown up in the system rather than we would incur the risk of instituting others of our own.

But perplexing as were these practical details, there Intermixture was nothing so difficult of solution as the great doubt Troops. which arose as to the amount of confidence in the Sepoy Army which it was expedient outwardly to manifest. It was said, upon the one hand, that any

* *Views and Opinions of Brigadier-General John Jacob.*

diminution of our confidence would be fatal to our rule, and, on the other, that our confidence was leading us onward to destruction. Some said that the Native Army should be narrowly watched, and held in control by sufficient bodies of European soldiery; others contended that we could commit no more fatal mistake than that of betraying the least suspicion of the Sepoy, and suggesting even a remote possibility of one part of our Army ever being thrown into antagonism to the other. This controversy was half a century old. When, after the Massacre of Vellore, the Madras Government urged upon the Supreme Authority in Bengal the expediency of sending some reinforcements of European troops to the Coast, the latter refused to respond to the call, on the ground that such a movement would betray a general want of confidence in the Native Army, and might drive regiments still loyal into rebellion under an impulse of fear. There was force in this argument, which will be readily appreciated by all who understand the character of the Sepoy Army; and its cogency was not diminished by the fact put forth by the Madras Government that the European troops under their command were fewer by two thousand men than they had been before the recent large extension of territory. But a great lesson was to be learnt from the embarrassment which then arose; a lesson which ought to have been taken to the hearts of our rulers from one generation to another. It was then clearly revealed, not merely that " prevention is better than cure," but that prevention may be possible when cure is not; that we may hold danger in check by quietly anticipating it, but that, when it has arisen, the measures, to which we might have resorted before the fact, cannot be pursued, after it, without increasing the evil. If anything should teach us the wisdom of never suffering our European force, even in the most tranquil times, to decline below what we may call " the athletic standard," it is the fact that, when the times cease to be tranquil, we cannot suddenly raise it to that standard without exciting alarm and creating danger.

But this lesson was not learnt. Or, if Indian statesmen ever took it to their hearts, it was remorselessly repudiated in the Councils of the English nation. Other considerations than those of the actual requirements of our Indian Empire were suffered to determine the amount of European strength to be maintained on the Company's establishment. Stated in round numbers, it may be said that the normal state of things, for some years, had been that of an Army of three hundred thousand men, of which forty thousand were European troops.* Of these, roughly calculated, about one-third were the local European troops of the Company, raised exclusively for Indian service; the rest were the men of royal regiments, Horse and Foot, periodically relieved according to the will of the Imperial Government, but paid out of the Revenues of India. In the five years preceding the departure of Lord Dalhousie from India, the strength of the Company's European troops had been somewhat increased, but the force which England lent to India was considerably reduced. In 1852, there were twenty-nine Royal regiments in the three Presidencies of India, mustering twenty-eight thousand men; in 1856, there were twenty-four Royal regiments, mustering twenty-three thousand men. During those five years there had been a vast extension of empire; but the aggregate European strength was lower in

* For the details of the Native Army of India, see Tables in Appendix.

1851-56.

1856 than in 1852 by nearly three thousand men. Between those two dates England had been engaged in a great war, and she wanted her troops for European service.

The Crimean War.

We deceive ourselves, when we think that European politics make no impression on the Indian Public. The impression may be very vague and indistinct; but ignorance is a magnifier of high power, and there are never wanting a few designing men, with clearer knowledge of the real state of things, to work upon the haziness of popular conceptions, and to turn a little grain of truth to account in generating a harvest of lies. That a number of very preposterous stories were industriously circulated, and greedily swallowed, during the Crimean war, and that these stories all pointed to the downfal of the British power, is not to be doubted. It was freely declared that Russia had conquered and annexed England, and that Queen Victoria had fled and taken refuge with the Governor-General of India. The fact that the war was with Russia gave increased significance to these rumours; for there had long been a chronic belief that the Russlogue would some day or other contend with us for the mastery of India; that, coming down in immense hordes from the North, and carrying with them the intervening Mahomedan States, they would sweep us, broken and humbled, into the sea. And it required no great acuteness to perceive that if a popular insurrection in India were ever to be successful, it was when the military resources of the empire were absorbed by a great European war. It is at such times as these, therefore, when there is always some disturbance of the public mind, that especial care should be taken to keep the European strength in India up to the right athletic standard. But, in these very times, the dependency is called upon to aid the empire, and her European regiments are reluctantly given up at the critical moment when she most desires to retain them. "The idea broached in Parliament," said a Native gentleman, "of drawing troops from India for the Crimean War, took intelligent natives of India by surprise." They saw plainly the folly of thus revealing our weakness to the subject races; for we could not more loudly proclaim the inadequacy of our resources than by denuding ourselves in one quarter of the world in order that we might clothe ourselves more sufficiently in another.

Nor was it this alone that, during the last years of Lord Dalhousie's administration, "took intelligent natives of India by surprise." They saw us increasing our territory, in all directions, without increasing our European force. There were those who argued that territorial increase did not necessarily demand increased means of defence, as it might be a change, not an extension of frontier; indeed, that the consolidation of our empire, by diminishing the numbers of our enemies, ought rather to be regarded as a reason for the diminution of our military strength. And this, in respect to our external enemies, it has already been observed, was not untrue.* But our dangers were from within, not from without; and it was forgotten that false friends might be more dangerous than open enemies. The English in India were, indeed, continually in a state of siege, and the conquest of their external enemies increased the perils of their position, for it deprived them of those safety-valves which had often before arrested a ruinous explosion. We were far too sanguine in our estimates of the results of conquest or annexation. We saw everything as we wished

* *Ante*, p. 276.

1851-56. to see it. We saw contentment in submission, loyalty
in quiescence; and took our estimate of national sentiment from the feelings of a few interested individuals
who were making money by the change. But "intelligent natives" seeing clearly our delusion, knowing
that we believed a lie, wondered greatly at our want
of wisdom in suffering vast tracts of territory, perhaps only recently brought under British rule, to lie
naked and defenceless, without even a detachment of
English fighting men to guard the lives of the new
masters of the country. And little as we gave them
credit for sagacity in such matters, they touched the
very kernel of our danger with a needle's point, and
predicted that our confidence would destroy us.

It was fortunate that, when we conquered the
Punjab, it was impossible to forget that Afghanistan,
still festering with animosities and resentments born
of the recent invasion, lay contiguous to the frontier
of our new province. It was fortunate, too, that
Henry Lawrence, being a man of a quick imagination, could feel as a Sikh chief or a Sikh soldier would
feel under the new yoke of the Feringhee, and could
therefore believe that we were not welcomed as deliverers from one end of the country to the other.
But it was not fortunate that the obvious necessity
of garrisoning this frontier Province with a strong
European force should have been practically regarded
as a reason for denuding all the rest of India of English troops. Acting in accordance with the old traditions, that the only danger with which our position
in India is threatened, is danger coming from the
North-West, we massed a large body of Europeans
in the Punjab, and scattered, at wide intervals, the
few remaining regiments at our disposal over other
parts of our extended dominions. Thus we visibly

became more and more dependent on our Native **1851-56.**
Army; and it needed only the declaration of weakness made, when England called on India for regiments to take part in the Crimean war, to assure "intelligent natives" that the boasted resources of England were wholly insufficient to meet the demands made upon them from different quarters, and that we could only confront danger in one part of the world by exposing ourselves to it in another.[*]

And this impression was strengthened by the fact Effects of the that when Oude was annexed to our British terri- Annexation of tories, although the province was thereby filled with Oude. the disbanded soldiery of the destroyed Native Government, and with a dangerous race of discontented nobles, whom the revolution had stripped of their privileges and despoiled of their wealth, the English appeared not to possess the means of garrisoning with European troops the country which they had thus seized. As Oude was not a frontier province, there was no necessity to mass troops there, as in the Punjab, for purposes of external defence; and the English, emboldened by success, were stronger than ever in their national egotism, and believed that, as they could not be regarded in Oude in any other light than that of deliverers, there was small need to make provision against the possibility of internal disturbance. They left the province, therefore, after annexation had been proclaimed, with only a small handful of European fighting men; and "intelligent natives" were again surprised to see that the English gentlemen were carrying out their new scheme of administration, to the ruin of almost every pre-existing interest

---

[*] It has been alleged, too, that the subscriptions raised towards the support of the Patriotic Fund, during the Crimean War, impressed intelligent natives with the belief that we were as short of money as we were of men.

1851-56. in the country, with as much confidence as if every
district of Oude were bristling with British bayonets.
They saw, too, that the English had absorbed one of
the last remaining Mahomedan States of India; and
they felt that not only would this prodigious appro-
priation be regarded from one end of India to the
other as the precursor of new seizures, and that it
would thus greatly disturb the public mind, but that
the very class of men on whom we appeared to rely
for the continued security of our position were, of all
others, most likely to resent this act of aggression.

For the annexation of Oude had some results injurious to the Sepoy. A very large portion of the
Bengal Army was drawn from that province. In
every village were the families of men who wore the
uniform and bore the arms of the English. Being for
the most part high-caste Hindoos, they might not
have regarded the peaceful revolution by which a
Mahomedan monarchy was destroyed with any strong
feelings of national resentment; and it is certain that
this extension of territory was not provocative of the
feelings of aversion and alarm with which they regarded those other seizures which had sent them to
rot in the charnel-house of Scinde, or to perish in
exile on the frontiers of Afghanistan. Their griefs
were of another kind. The old state of things had
suited them better. They had little sympathy, perhaps, with Wajid Ali, and service in Oude brought
them nearer to their homes. But so long as it was a
foreign province, they derived certain special privileges and advantages from their position as the
servants of the Company, and increased importance
in the eyes of the people of the province. They had,
indeed, been a favoured race, and as such the Sepoy
families had held up their heads above those of their

countrymen who had no such bonds of privilege.and protection to unite them to the Paramount State. "The Sepoy," wrote the man who had studied the character and probed the feelings of the Native more deeply and philosophically perhaps than any of his. contemporaries—"the Sepoy is not the man of consequence he was. He dislikes annexations; among other reasons, because each new province added to the Empire widens his sphere of service, and at the same time decreases our foreign enemies and thereby the Sepoy's importance. . . . . . The other day, an Oude Sepoy of the Bombay Cavalry at Neemuch, being asked if he liked annexation, replied, ' No ; I used to be a great man when I went home. The best in my village rose as I approached. Now the lowest puff their pipes in my face.' "[*]   Under the all-prevailing lawlessness and misrule, which had so long overridden the province, the English Sepoy, whatever might be the wrongs of others, was always sure of a full measure of justice on appeal to the British Resident. If he himself were not, some member of his family was, a small yeoman, with certain rights in the land—rights which commonly among his countrymen were as much a source of trouble as a source of pride—and in all the disputes and contentions in which these interests involved him, he had the protection and assistance of the Resident, and right or wrong carried his point. In the abstract it was, doubtless, an evil state of things, for the Sepoys'

---

[*] Sir Henry Lawrence to Lord Canning, MS. Correspondence. I may give here in a note the words omitted in the text, as bearing, though not immediately, upon the Oude question, and upon the general subject of annexation: "Ten years ago, a Sepoy in the Punjab asked an officer what we would do without them. Another said, ' Now you have got the Punjab, you will reduce the Army.' A third remarked, when he heard that Scinde was to be joined to the Bengal Presidency, ' Perhaps there will be an order to join London to Bengal.'"

1851-56. privileges were often used as instruments of oppression, and were sometimes counterfeited with the help of an old regimental jacket and pair of boots, by men who had never gone right-face to the word of command. But for this very reason they were dearly valued; and when the Sepoys were thus brought down by annexation to the dead level of British subjects, when the Residency ceased to be, and all men were equally under the protection of the Commissioner, the Sepoy families, like all the other privileged classes in Oude, learnt what the revolution had cost them, and, wide apart as their several grievances lay from each other, they joined hands with other sufferers over a common grief.

Summary of deteriorating influences. Looking, then, at the condition of the Native Army of India, and especially at the state of the Bengal regiments, as it was in the spring of 1856, we see that a series of adverse circumstances, culminating in the annexation of Oude, some influencing him from without and some from within, had weakened the attachment of the Sepoy to his colours. We see that, whilst the bonds of internal discipline were being relaxed, external events, directly or indirectly affecting his position, were exciting within him animosities and discontents. We see that as he grew less faithful and obedient, he grew also more presuming; that whilst he was less under the control of his officers and the dominion of the State, he was more sensible of the extent to which we were dependent upon his fidelity, and therefore more capricious and exacting. He had been neglected on the one hand, and pampered on the other. As a soldier, he had in many ways deteriorated, but he was not to be regarded only as a soldier. He was a representative man, the embodiment of feelings and opinions shared by large classes of his countrymen, and circumstances might one day render him their exponent. He had many opportunities of becoming acquainted with passing events and public opinion. He mixed in cantonments, or on the line of march, with men of different classes and different countries; he corresponded with friends at a distance; he heard all the gossip of the Bazaars, and he read, or heard others read, the strange mixture of truth and falsehood contained in the Native newspapers. He knew what were the measures of the British Government, sometimes even what were its intentions, and he interpreted their meanings, as men are wont to do, who, credulous and suspicious, see insidious designs and covert dangers in the most beneficent acts. He had not the faculty to conceive that the English were continually originating great changes for the good of the people; our theories of government were beyond his understanding, and as he had ceased to take counsel with his English officer, he was given over to strange delusions, and believed the most dangerous lies.

But in taking account of the effect produced upon the Sepoy's mind by the political and social measures of the British Government, we must not think only of the direct action of these measures—of the soldier's own reading of distant events, which might have had no bearing upon his daily happiness, and which, therefore, in his selfishness he might have been content to disregard. For he often read these things with other men's eyes, and discerned them with other men's understandings. If the political and social revolutions, of which I have written, did not affect him, they affected others, wiser in their generation, more astute,

1851-56. more designing, who put upon everything that we did the gloss best calculated to debauch the Sepoy's mind, and to prepare him, at a given signal, for an outburst of sudden madness. Childish, as he was, in his faith, there was nothing easier than to make him believe all kinds and conditions of fictions, not only wild and grotesque in themselves, but in violent con- tradiction of each other. He was as ready to believe that the extension of our territory would throw him out of employment, as that it would inflict upon him double work. He did not choose between these two extremes; he accepted both, and took the one or the other, as the humour pleased him. There were never wanting men to feed his imagination with the kind of aliment which pleased it best, and reason never came to his aid to purge him of the results of this gross feeding.

Many were the strange glosses which were given to the acts of the British Government; various were the ingenious fictions woven with the purpose of un- settling the minds and uprooting the fidelity of the Sepoy. But diverse as they were in many respects, there was a certain unity about them, for they all tended to persuade him that our measures were di- rected to one common end, the destruction of Caste, and the general introduction of Christianity into the land. If we annexed a province, it was to facilitate our proselytising operations, and to increase the num- ber of our converts. Our resumption operations were instituted for the purpose of destroying all the religious endowments of the country. Our legislative enactments were all tending to the same result, the subversion of Hindooism and Mahomedanism. Our educational measures were so many direct assaults upon the religions of the country. Our penal system, according to their showing, disguised a monstrous attempt to annihilate caste, by compelling men of all denominations to feed together in the gaols. In the Lines of every regiment there were men eager to tell lies of this kind to the Sepoy, mingled with assurances that the time was coming when the Feringhees would be destroyed to a man; when a new empire would be established, and a new military system inaugurated, under which the high rank and the higher pay monopolised by the English would be transferred to the people of the country. We know so little of what is stirring in the depths of Indian society; we dwell so much apart from the people; we see so little of them, except in full dress and on their best behaviour, that perilous intrigues and desperate plots might be woven, under the very shadow of our bungalows, without our perceiving any symptoms of danger. But still less can we discern that quiet under-current of hostility which is continually flowing on without any immediate or definite object, and which, if we could discern it, would baffle all our efforts to trace it to its source. But it does not the less exist because we are ignorant of the form which it assumes, or the fount from which it springs. The men, whose business it was to corrupt the minds of our Sepoys, were, perhaps, the agents of some of the old princely houses, which we had destroyed,* or members of old baronial families which we had brought to poverty and disgrace. They were, perhaps, the emissaries of Brahminical Societies, whose precepts we were turning into folly, and whose power we were setting at naught. They were, perhaps, mere visionaries and enthusiasts, moved only by their

---

* It was asserted at the time of the "Mutiny of Vellore," that not only were agents of the House of Tippoo busy in all the Lines of Southern India, but that there was scarcely a regiment into which they had not enlisted.

1851-56. own disordered imaginations to proclaim the coming of some new prophet or some fresh avatar of the Deity, and the consequent downfal of Christian supremacy in the East. But whatsoever the nature of their mission, and whatsoever the guise they assumed, whether they appeared in the Lines as passing travellers, as journeying hawkers, as religious mendicants, or as wandering puppet-showmen, the seed of sedition which they scattered struck root in a soil well prepared to receive it, and waited only for the ripening sun of circumstance to develop a harvest of revolt.

BOOK III.—THE OUTBREAK OF THE MUTINY.

[1856—1857.]

CHAPTER I.

DEPARTURE OF LORD DALHOUSIE—HIS CHARACTER—THE QUESTION OF SUCCESSION—ARRIVAL OF LORD CANNING—HIS EARLY CAREER—COMMENCEMENT OF HIS ADMINISTRATION—HIS FELLOW - COUNCILLORS—GENERAL LOW—MR. DORIN—MR. GRANT—MR. BARNES PEACOCK—THE COMMANDER-IN-CHIEF.

WHEN, on the last day of February, 1856, "the   1856. Most Noble" the Marquis of Dalhousie placed the Portfolio of the Indian Empire in the hands of his successor, all men said that a great statesman and a great ruler was about to depart from the land.   The praises that were bestowed upon him had been well earned.   He had given his life to the public service; and many feared, as they sorrowfully bade him farewell, that he had given it up for the public good.

He stood before men at that time as the very embodiment of Success.   Whatsoever he had attempted to do he had done with his whole heart, and he had perfected it without a failure or a flaw.   The policy which during those eventful eight years had been so consistently maintained was emphatically his policy. The success, therefore, was fairly his.   No man had ever stamped his individuality more clearly upon the public measures of his times.   There are periods when the Government fades into an impersonality; when

2 A

men cease to associate its measures with the idea of one dominant will. But during the reign then ended we heard little of "the Government;" in every one's mouth was the name of the individual Man.

Character of Lord Dalhousie.

And in this remarkable individual manhood there was the very essence and concentration of the great national manhood; there was an intense Englishism in him such as has seldom been equalled. It was the Englishism, too, of the nineteenth century; and of that particular epoch of the nineteenth century when well-nigh every one had the word "progress" on his lips, and stagnation was both disaster and disgrace. A man of strong convictions and extraordinary activity of mind, he laid fast hold of the one abstract truth that English government, English laws, English learning, English customs, and English manners, are better than the government, the laws, the learning, the customs, and the manners of India; and with all the earnestness of his nature and all the strength of his understanding he wrought out this great theory in practice. He never doubted that it was good alike for England and for India that the map of the country which he had been sent to govern should present one surface of Red. He was so sure of this, he believed it so honestly, so conscientiously, that, courageous and self-reliant as he was, he would have carried out this policy to the end, if all the chief officers and agents of his government had been arrayed against him. But he commenced his career at a time when the ablest of our public functionaries in India, with a few notable exceptions, had forsaken the traditions of the old school—the school of Malcolm, of Elphinstone, and of Metcalfe—and stood eager and open-armed to embrace and press closely to them the very doctrines of which they perceived in

Dalhousie so vigorous an exponent. He did not found the school; neither were his opinions moulded in accordance with its tenets. He appeared among them and placed himself at their head, just at the very time when such a coming was needed to give consistency to their faith, and uniformity to their works. The coincidence had all the force of a dispensation. No prophet ever had more devoted followers. No king was ever more loyally served. For the strong faith of his disciples made them strive mightily to accomplish his will; and he had in a rare degree the faculty of developing in his agents the very powers which were most essential to the fitting accomplishment of his work. He did not create those powers, for he found in his chief agents the instincts and energies most essential to his purpose; but he fostered, he strengthened and directed them, so that what might have run to weed and waste withou this cherishing care, yielded under his culture, in ripe profusion, a harvest of desired results.

As his workmen were admirably suited to his work, so also was the field, to which he was called, the one best adapted to the exercise of his peculiar powers. In no other part of our empire could his rare administrative capacity have found such scope for development. For he was of an imperious and despotic nature, not submitting to control, and resenting opposition; and in no situation could he have exercised a larger measure of power in the face of so few constitutional checks. His capacities required free exercise, and it may be doubted whether they would have been fully developed by anything short of this absolute supremacy. But sustained and invigorated by a sense of enormous power, he worked with all the energies of a giant. And he was successful beyond all example, so far as success is the full accomplishment of one's own desires and intentions. But one fatal defect in his character tainted the stream of his policy at the source, and converted into brilliant errors some of the most renowned of his achievements. No man who is not endowed with a comprehensive imagination can govern India with success. Dalhousie had no imagination. Lacking the imaginative faculty, men, after long years of experience, may come to understand the national character; and a man of lively imagination, without such experience, may readily apprehend it after the intercourse of a few weeks. But in neither way did Dalhousie ever come to understand the genius of the people among whom his lot was cast. He had but one idea of them —an idea of a people habituated to the despotism of a dominant race. He could not understand the tenacity of affection with which they clung to their old traditions. He could not sympathise with the veneration which they felt for their ancient dynasties. He could not appreciate their fidelity to the time-honoured institutions and the immemorial usages of the land. He had not the faculty to conceive that men might like their own old ways of government, with all their imperfections and corruptions about them, better than our more refined systems. Arguing all points with the preciseness of a Scotch logician, he made no allowance for inveterate habits and ingrained prejudices, and the scales of ignorance before men's eyes which will not suffer them rightly to discern between the good and the bad. He could not form a true dramatic conception of the feelings with which the representative of a long line of kings may be supposed to regard the sudden extinction of his royal house by the decree of a stranger and an infidel, or the bitterness of spirit in which a greybeard chief, whose family from generation to generation had enjoyed ancestral powers and privileges, might contemplate his lot when suddenly reduced to poverty and humiliation by an incursion of aliens of another colour and another creed. He could not see with other men's eyes; or think with other men's brains; or feel with other men's hearts. With the characteristic unimaginativeness of his race he could not for a moment divest himself of his individuality, or conceive the growth of ancestral pride and national honour in other breasts than those of the Campbells and the Ramsays.

And this egotism was cherished and sustained by the prevailing sentiments of the new school of Indian politicians, who, as I have said, laughed to scorn the doctrines of the men who had built up the great structure of our Indian Empire, and by the utterances of a Press, which, with rare ability, expounded the views of this school, and insisted upon the duty of universal usurpation. Such, indeed, was the prevailing tone of the majority, in all ranks from the highest to the lowest, that any one who meekly ventured to ask, "How would you like it yourself?" was reproached in language little short of that which might be fitly applied to a renegade or a traitor. To suggest that in an Asiatic race there might be a spirit of independence and a love of country, the manifestations of which were honourable in themselves, however inconvenient to us, was commonly to evoke as the very mildest result the imputation of being "Anti-British," whilst sometimes the "true British feeling" asserted itself in a less refined choice of epithets, and those who ventured to sympathise in any way with the people of the East were at once de-

1856. nounced as "white niggers." Yet among these very
men, so intolerant of anything approaching the
assertion of a spirit of liberty by an Asiatic people,
there were some who could well appreciate and sympathise with the aspirations of European bondsmen,
and could regard with admiration the struggles of
the Italian, the Switzer, or the Pole to liberate himself, by a sanguinary contest, from the yoke of the
usurper.   But the sight of the dark skin sealed up
their sympathies.   They contended not merely that
the love of country, that the spirit of liberty, as
cherished by European races, is in India wholly unknown, but that Asiatic nations, and especially the
nations of India, have no right to judge what is best
for themselves ; no right to revolt against the beneficence of a more civilised race of white men, who
would think and act for them, and deprive them, for
their own good, of all their most cherished rights and
their most valued possessions.

So it happened that Lord Dalhousie's was a strong
Government; strong in everything but its confor-
mity to the genius of the people.   It was a Government admirably conducted in accordance with
the most approved principles of European civilisation,
by men whose progressive tendencies carried them
hundreds of years in advance of the sluggish Asiatics,
whom they vainly endeavoured to bind to the chariot-
wheels of their refined systems.   There was everything to give it complete success but the stubbornness
of the national mind.   It failed, perhaps, only because
the people preferred darkness to light, folly to
wisdom.   Of course the English gentlemen were
right and the Asiatics lamentably wrong.   But the
grand scriptural warning against putting new wine
into old bottles was disregarded.   The wine was good

wine, strong wine; wine to gladden the heart of
man.   But poured into those old bottles it was sure,
sooner or later, to create a general explosion.   They
forgot that there were two things necessary to successful government: one, that the measures should be
good in themselves; and the other, that they should be
suited to the condition of the recipients.   Intent upon
the one, they forgot the other, and erred upon the
side of a progress too rapid and an Englishism too
refined.

But at the bottom of this great error were benign
intentions.   Dalhousie and his lieutenants had a
strong and steadfast faith in the wisdom and benevolence of their measures, and strove alike for the
glory of the English nation and the welfare of the
Indian people.   There was something grand and even
good in the very errors of such a man.   For there
was no taint of baseness in them; no sign of anything sordid or self-seeking.   He had given himself
up to the public service, resolute to do a great work,
and he rejoiced with a noble pride in the thought
that he left behind him a mightier empire than he
had found, that he had brought new countries and
strange nations under the sway of the British sceptre,
and sown the seeds of a great civilisation.   To do
this, he had made unstinting sacrifice of leisure, ease,
comfort, health, and the dear love of wedded life,
and he carried home with him, in a shattered frame
and a torn heart, in the wreck of a manhood at its
very prime, mortal wounds nobly received in a great
and heroic encounter.

Great always is the interest which attaches to the
question of succession; greatest of all when such a
ruler as Dalhousie retires from the scene.   Who was
to take the place of this great and successful states-

1856.

man? Who was to carry out to its final issue the grand policy which he had so brilliantly inaugurated? This was the question in all men's mouths as the old year passed away and the new year dawned upon India; in some sort a remarkable year, for was it not the centenary of the great disaster of the Black Hole which had brought Clive's avenging army to Bengal? Ever at such times is there much talk of the expected advent of some member of the English Cabinet, some successful Colonial Governor, or some great Lord little experienced in statesmanship, of high lineage and dilapidated fortune. And so now there was the wonted high tide of speculation and conjecture, wild guesses and moonshine rumours of all kinds, from dim possibilities to gigantic nonsenses, until at last there came authentic tidings to India that the choice had fallen on Her Majesty's Post-master-General, one of the younger members of Lord Palmerston's Cabinet.

Antecedents of Lord Canning.

Scarcely within bounds of possibility was it, that, in the midst of so great an epidemic of faith in Lord Dalhousie, England could send forth a statesman to succeed him, whom her Anglo-Indian sons would not receive with ominous head-shakings, denoting grave doubts and anxious misgivings. Another great man, it was said, was needed to understand, to appreciate, to maintain the policy of the hero whom they so glorified. But they knew little or nothing of Viscount Canning, except that he was the bearer of a great

1822.

name. Thirty-four years before, all England had been talking about the acceptance of the Governor-Generalship by this man's father. There were a

few, then, who, looking at the matter solely from
an Indian point of view, exulted in the thought that
one who had done such good service at the Board of
Control, and whose abilities were known to be of the
very highest order, was about to devote some of the
best years of his life to the government of our great
Eastern empire.   There was another and a baser
few, who, festering with jealousies, and animosities,
and dishonourable fears, joyed most of all that they
should see his face no more for years, or perhaps for
ever.   But the bulk of the English people deplored
his approaching departure from among them, because
they felt that the country had need of his services, '
and could ill bear the loss of such a man.   And it
was a relief to them when the sad close of Lord
Castlereagh's career brought George Canning back
from the visit, which was to have been his farewell,
to Liverpool, to take his place again in the great
Council of the nation.

Great, also, was the relief to George Canning
himself—great for many reasons; the greatest, perhaps, of all, that he was very happy in his family.
In the first year of the century he had married a
lady, endowed with a considerable share of the
world's wealth, but with more of that better wealth
which the world cannot give; the daughter and co-
heiress of an old general officer named Scott.   No
man could have been happier in his domestic life;
and domestic happiness is domestic virtue.   Blind to
the attractions of that Society in which he was so
pre-eminently formed to shine, he found measureless
delight in the companionship of his wife and children.
And as an Indian life is more or less a life of separa-
tion, it was now a joy to him to think that the brief

1856.

vision of Government House, Calcutta, had been replaced by the returning realities of the English fireside.[*]

Gloucester Lodge, 1822.

At this time the great statesman had a son in his tenth year, at school with Mr. Carmalt, of Putney, on the banks of the Thames. He was the third son born to George Canning;[†] born during what was perhaps the happiest period of his father's life, his residence at Gloucester Lodge. This was the boy's birthplace. Lying between Brompton and Kensington, it was at that time almost in the country. There was not, perhaps, a pleasanter place near Town. It had a strange, memorable history, too, and it was among the notabilities of suburban London. In the days of Ranelagh, it had been, under the name of the Florida Gardens, a lesser rival to that fashionable haunt; and from this state, after an interval of desertion and decay, it had developed into a royal residence.[‡] The Duchess of Gloucester bought the

1807.

Gardens, built there a handsome Italian villa, lived and died there, and, passing away, bequeathed her interest in the estate to the Princess Sophia, who sold it to Mr. Canning. And there, in this pleasant umbrageous retreat, on the 14th of December, 1812, was born the third son of George Canning, who, in due course, was christened Charles John.

The Putney School.

In 1822, as I have said, when George Canning

---

[*] "The unsullied purity of Mr. Canning's domestic life," says his last and pleasantest biographer, "and his love of domestic pleasures (for after his marriage he seldom extended his intercourse with general society beyond those occasions which his station rendered unavoidable), were rewarded by as much virtue and devotion as ever graced the home of an English statesman."— *Bell's Life of Canning.*

[†] At this time Charles was the second surviving son. The eldest, George Charles, born in April, 1801, died in March, 1820. The second brother was in the navy.

[‡] See Bell's Life of Canning, chapter x., which contains an animated sketch of the early history of Gloucester Lodge, and of the social and domestic environments of the great statesman's residence there.

woke from his brief dream of Indian vice-regal power to take the seals of the Foreign Office, this boy Charles was under the scholastic care of Mr. Carmalt, of Putney. In those days his establishment enjoyed a great reputation. It was one of the largest and best private schools in the neighbourhood of London, perhaps in the whole kingdom, and as the sons of our highest noblemen mingled there with those of our middle-class gentry, not a bad half-way house to the microcosm of Eton or Harrow. The impression which Charles Canning made upon the minds of his school-fellows was, on the whole, a favourable one. He was not a boy of brilliant parts, or of any large popularity; but he was remembered long afterwards as one who, in a quiet, unostentatious way, made it manifest to ordinary observers that there was, in schoolboy language, " something in him." One, whose letter is now before me, and who was with him for nearly two years in the same room at the Putney school, remembered, after a lapse of more than a third part of a century, the admiration with which he then regarded young Canning's "youthful indications of talent, and amiable and attractive manners."

Two years after George Canning's surrender of the Governor-Generalship, his son Charles left Mr. Carmalt's and went to Eton. Eton was very proud of the father's great reputation, and eager to embrace the son; for, verily, George Canning had been an Etonian of Etonians, and had done as much, as a scholar and a wit, to make Eton flourish, as any man of his age. It was, perhaps, therefore, in a spirit of pure gratitude and veneration, and with no "hope of future favours," that worthy Provost Goodall, than whom perhaps no man ever had a keener appreciation both

.856.   of scholarship and of wit, on intimation made to him that George Canning wished his son to be entered as an oppidan, sent Mr. Chapman, one of the masters of the school,[*] who had been selected as the boy's tutor, to examine him at Gloucester Lodge. These examinations, which determine the place in the school which the boy is to take, are commonly held in the tutor's house at Eton, not beneath the parental roof. But the Minister's son was examined in his father's library and in his father's presence at Gloucester Lodge; a double trial, it may be thought, of the young student's nerve, and not provocative of a successful display of scholarship. But it was successful.[†] Charles Canning was declared to be fit for the fourth form, and on the 4th of September, 1824, he commenced his career. It is on record that he was "sent up for good" for his proficiency in Latin verse. It is on record, also, if the recording minister at Eton does not kindly blot out such traces of boyish error, that he was also sent up for bad; in more correct Etonian phraseology, "in the bill," marked for the flogging block. And it is traditional that the avenging hand of Head-master Keate was sometimes stayed by a tender reluctance to apply the birch to the person of Secretary Canning's son. On the whole, perhaps, it is historically true that, at Eton, he had no very marked reputation of any kind. He was good-looking, and a gentleman, which goes for something; but I do not know that he was a great rower,

---

* Afterwards Bishop of Colombo; now retired.

† I am indebted for this incident to Sir Robert Phillimore, Queen's Advocate. The memorandum from which it is taken adds: "The well-known description of the storm in the first Æneid, 'Interea magno misceri murmure pontum,' &c., was the passage chosen for the trial of his proficiency, and the Bishop now remembers the anxiety with which the father watched the essay of his son, and the smile of approval which greeted his reading of the rather difficult transition, 'Quos ego — sed motos,' &c., and the final 'Not so bad,' which followed at the close of the whole translation."

a great cricketer, or a great swimmer, or was in any sense an athlete of the first water and the admiration of his companions; and, scholastically, it is remembered of him that he had "a reputation rather for intelligence, accuracy, and painstaking, than for refined scholarship, or any remarkable powers of composition."

But on passing away from Eton, the stature of his mind was soon greatly enlarged. At the close of 1827, having risen to the Upper division of the fifth form, he received the parting gifts of his schoolfellows; and soon afterwards became the private pupil of the Rev. John Shore, a nephew of Sir John Shore, Governor-General of India, and known to a later generation as Lord Teignmouth. This worthy Christian gentleman and ripe scholar lived, but without Church preferment, at Potton, a quiet little market-town in Bedfordshire, receiving pupils there of the better sort. Among the inmates of his house was the grandson of the first Lord Harris, with whom Charles Canning entered into bonds of friendship, riveted at Oxford, strengthened in public life at home, and again by strange coincidence in India, and broken only by death. Here, doubtless, he made great progress in scholarship. Perhaps the death of his father, and the after-honours which were conferred on the family, and, more than all, the subsequent calamitous end of his elder brother,* awakened within him a sense of the responsibilities of his position, and roused him to new exertions. Though born the third in succession of George Canning's sons, he was now the eldest, the only one. He and his sister alone survived. He was now the heir to a peerage, sufficiently, though not splendidly, en-

---

* William Pitt Canning, then a Captain in the Royal Navy, was drowned while bathing at Madeira, in September, 1828.

1850.   dowed, and there was a public career before him.
He applied himself to his books.[*]

Oxford.   His next step was to the University.   In December, 1828, he was entered on the roll as a Student of
Christ Church, Oxford, as his father had been entered just forty years before.   Among the foremost of his fellow-students were Mr. Gladstone, Mr.
Bruce, and Mr. Robert Phillimore,[†] all of whom
lived to take parts, more or less prominent, in public
affairs.   Among other members of the same distinguished house, at that time, was the young Lord
Lincoln, heir to the Dukedom of Newcastle, and the
representative of the great Scotch House of Ramsay,
ennobled by the Earldom of Dalhousie.   But the
most intimate of all his associates was the present
Lord De Tabley, with whom he lived in the closest
bonds of friendship to the latest day of his life.   By
him, and a few other chosen companions, he was
dearly loved and much respected; but neither achiev-
ing nor seeking extensive popularity among his cotemporaries, he was regarded by the outer University
world as a man of a reserved and distant manner,
and of a somewhat cold and unimpulsive temperament.   The few in the inner circle knew that he was
not cold; knew that he had a true loving heart, very
loyal and constant in its affections; knew that in the
society of his familiar friends he had a pleasant, a
genial, and sometimes a playful manner, that he had
a fine scholarly taste, a fund of quiet humour, a keen
appreciation of character, and that he was all in all a
delightful companion.   They had great hope, too, of
his future career, though he did not seem to be ambi-

* It need scarcely be indicated
that the widow of George Canning,
on his death, was created a Viscountess, with remainder to his eldest
son.

† The present (1864) Chancellor
of the Exchequer; the late Lord
Elgin, Governor-General of India;
and the present Queen's Advocate.

tious; nay, rather, it appeared to those who closely observed him, that he was haunted and held back by the thought of his father's renown, and a diffidence of his own capacity to maintain the glories of the name. But, although he did not care to take part in the proceedings of debating societies, and, apparently, took small interest in the politics of the great world, he was anxious that at least his University career should do no dishonour to his lineage, and that if he could not be a great statesman, he might not stain the scholarly reputation enjoyed by two generations of Cannings before him. He strove, therefore, and with good results, to perfect himself in the classic languages; and even more assiduous were his endeavours to obtain a mastery over his own language. At an early age he acquired a thoroughly good English style; not resonant or pretentious; not splintery or smart; but pure, fluent, transparent, with the meaning ever visible beneath it, as pebbles beneath the clearest stream.

His efforts bore good fruit. In 1831, he wrote a Latin Prize Poem, on the " Captivity of Caractacus;" and recited it in the great hall of Christ Church, standing beneath his father's picture.* And in the

1856.

---

* I am indebted for this to Sir Robert Phillimore. I give the incident in his own words: "In the year 1831, he won the Christ Church prize for Latin verse. The subject was 'Caractacus Captivus Romam ingreditur.' The verses were, as usual, recited in the hall. It was a remarkable scene. In that magnificent banqueting-room are hung the portraits of students who have reflected honour upon the House which reared them by the distinctions which they have won in after life. Underneath the portrait of George Canning, the recollection of whose brilliant career and untimely end was still fresh in the memory of men, stood the son, in the prime of youth, recalling by his eminently handsome countenance the noble features of the portrait, while repeating the classical prize poem, which would have gladdened his father's heart. Generally speaking, the resident members of Christ Church alone compose the audience when the prize poem is recited. But on this occasion there was a stranger present—the old faithful friend of Mr. Canning, his staunch political adherent through life—Mr. Sturges Bourne. He had travelled from London for the purpose of witnessing the first considerable achievement of the younger Canning."— MS. Memorandum.

Easter term of 1833 he took his degree, with high honours: a first class in Classics, and a second in Mathematics. He was then in his twenty-first year; and Parliament would soon be open to him. But he was in no hurry to enter upon the realities of public life. He was diffident of his oratorical powers; he was constitutionally shy; and it did not appear to him that the House of Commons was a theatre in which he was ever likely to make a successful appearance. Moreover, he had other work in hand at that time; other yearnings to keep down any young ambitions that might be mounting within him. Love and courtship filled up a sweet interlude in his life, as they do in the lives of most men whose story is worth telling; and, in due course, they bore the rich fruit of happy wedlock. On the 5th of September, 1835, the Honourable Charles John Canning espoused the Honourable Charlotte Stuart, eldest daughter of Lord Stuart De Rothesay; a lady of a serene and gentle beauty, and many rare gifts of mind.

But, after a year of wedded life, he was prevailed upon to enter Parliament; and in August, 1836, he was returned for Warwick. In that month, however, Parliament was prorogued; and on its reassembling at the commencement of the following year he was content to be a silent member. His opportunities, indeed, were very few, for his whole career in the House of Commons extended over a period of little more than six weeks. During the month of February and the early part of March he attended in his place with praiseworthy regularity.* But, on the 15th of the latter month, his mother, Viscountess Canning, died; and, on the 24th of April, he took his seat in the House of Lords.

* His name is to be found in all the principal division lists. He voted sometimes against Lord Melbourne's Government, but more frequently with it.

For nearly twenty years he sate in that House, taking no very prominent part in the debates, but doing his duty in a quiet, unostentatious way, and gradually making for himself a reputation as a conscientious, painstaking young statesman, who might some day do good service to his country and honour to his great name. His political opinions, which were shared by most of his distinguished cotemporaries at Christ Church, were characterised by that chastened liberalism which had found its chief exponent in Sir Robert Peel; and when, in 1841, that great Parliamentary leader was invited to form a Ministry, Lord Canning, Lord Lincoln, and Mr. Gladstone were offered, and accepted, official seats. The seals of the Foreign Office had been placed in the hands of Lord Aberdeen. He had a high opinion of, and a personal regard for, Lord Canning, and there was no one whom the veteran statesman wished so much to associate with himself in office as George Canning's son. About the same time another distinguished member of the House of Lords was also moved by a strong desire to have the benefit of the young statesman's official co-operation and personal companionship. This was Lord Ellenborough, who, on the formation of the Peel Ministry, had been appointed President of the Board of Control, but who had subsequently been selected to succeed Lord Auckland as Governor-General of India. He offered to take Canning with him in the capacity of Private Secretary.

Creditable as this offer was to the discernment of Lord Ellenborough, and made in perfect sincerity, it was one little likely to be accepted by a man of high social position, good political prospects, and a sufficient supply of the world's wealth. Lord Canning

2 B

elected to remain in England, and entered official life as Under-Secretary of State for Foreign Affairs. He liked his work ; he did it well; and he had the entire confidence of his chief. But he did not take an active part in the debates and discussions of the House of Lords. The presence, in the same Chamber, of the Chief of his Department relieved him from the responsibility of ministerial explanations and replies, and his constitutional reserve forbade all unnecessary displays. It was not, indeed, until the Session of 1846 found him in the office of Chief Commissioner of Woods and Forests, that he took any prominent part in the business of the House. If the position which he then held afforded no opportunity for the development of his powers either as an orator or a debater, it kept him continually in Parliamentary harness, and the training was of service to him. It lasted, however, but a little time. At the end of June, 1846, Sir Robert Peel and his colleagues resigned; and a Whig Cabinet was formed under the leadership of Lord John Russell.

Lord Canning was then "in opposition;" but, in heart, he was a Liberal, and willing to support liberal measures, without reference to the distinctions of party. When, therefore, in May, 1848, Lord Lansdowne moved the second reading of the Jewish Disabilities Bill, Lord Canning was the first to speak in support of it. He answered Lord Ellenborough, who had moved the amendment, and he voted against all his old colleagues then in the Upper House, with the exception of Lord Hardinge. But in 1850 he supported, in a speech displaying an entire mastery of the subject, the resolution of Lord Derby condemnatory of the Foreign Policy of Lord Palmerston ; and he spoke against the Ecclesiastical Titles Bill, introduced by Lord John Russell. So little, indeed, was he considered to be pledged to any party, that when the Russell Cabinet resigned in the spring of 1851, and Lord Derby was invited to form an administration, the great Conservative leader saw no reason why he should not invite Canning to become a member of it. The offer then made was a tempting one, for it was the offer of a seat in the Cabinet second in importance only to that of the First Minister. To the son of George Canning it was especially tempting, for it was the offer of the seals of the Foreign Office. In that office the father had built up his reputation, and the son had already laid the foundation of an honourable career of statesmanship. It was the department which, above all others, Lord Canning best knew and most desired. He had served a long apprenticeship in it, and if his humility suggested any doubts of his capacity to direct its affairs, they must have been removed by the manner in which he was invited to take their direction.

The offer now made to him was made through his old official chief, Lord Aberdeen, who pressed him to accept it. But there were many grave considerations which caused him to hesitate. He had sat for some years on the same ministerial bench with Lord Derby, but the latter had separated himself from his party, and the cause of the disruption was the liberal commercial policy of Sir Robert Peel, in favour of which Canning had freely declared his opinions. He had condemned the foreign policy of the Whig party; but, on the other hand, there were matters of home government, in which his liberality was far in advance of the opinions of Lord Derby and his colleagues; and, on the whole, he felt that he could not honestly and consistently support the Administration which he was invited to enter. He judged rightly, and in such a case he judged wisely. Lord Derby failed to construct a Ministry, and the Whigs resumed office for another year. This was the turning-point of Lord Canning's career; and it is impossible to say how different might have been the story which I am now about to write, if these overtures had been accepted.

In the following year, Lord Derby again endeavoured, and with better success, to form a Ministry, but its career was of brief duration. In November, its place was filled by an Administration under the premiership of Lord Aberdeen, composed of the leading members of the Governments both of Sir Robert Peel and Lord John Russell. In this Coalition Ministry Lord Canning held the office of Postmaster-General. Though held by many a distinguished man, the post was not one to satisfy the desires of an ambitious one. But he was not disappointed or discouraged. He knew the difficulties which lay in the path of his leader,[*] and he addressed himself cheerfully and assiduously to his work, with a steadfast resolution to elevate the importance of the appointment he held, by doing in it the largest possible amount of public good. In this office he had first an opportunity of displaying that high conscientious courage which bears up and steers right on, in spite of the penalties and mortifications of temporary unpopularity. What was wrong he endeavoured to set right; and knowing how much depended on the personal exertions of individual men, he strove, even

[*] In a "coalition ministry" there is necessarily an exceptional number of claimants for the higher offices with seats in the Cabinet. In the arrangements then made the seals of the Foreign Office fell, in the first instance, to Lord John Russell.

at the expense of certain very clamorous vested interests, to obtain the utmost possible amount of com-
petency for the performance of all the higher departmental duties. During his administration of the
Post-office many important reforms were instituted,
and much progress made in good work already commenced. So effectually, indeed, had he mastered all
the complicated details of the department, that when
the Coalition Ministry was dissolved and a new Government formed under Lord Palmerston, the public
interests required that there should be no change at
the Post-office; so Lord Canning was reappointed to
his old office, but with further acknowledgment of
his good services in the shape of a seat in the Cabinet.
But it was not ordered that he should hold the office
much longer. There was more stirring work in store
for him. His old friend and cotemporary, Lord Dalhousie, was coming home from India, and it was
necessary that a new Governor-General should be
appointed in his place. Practically the selection, in
such cases, was made by the Imperial Government,
but constitutionally the appointment emanated from
the East India Company. The President of the
Board of Control and the Chairman of the Court
of Directors commonly took counsel together, when
the Cabinet had chosen their man; and then the
nomination was formally submitted to the Court.
There is always, in such cases, much internal doubt
and conflict among those with whom the selection
rests, and much speculation and discussion in the
outer world. It was believed in this instance, that
some member of the Ministry would be appointed;
but people said in England, as they said in India,
that it would be no easy thing to find a fit successor
for Lord Dalhousie; and when at last it transpired

that the choice had fallen on Lord Canning, men shook their heads and asked each other whether there was anything great about him but his name. In Parliament the propriety of the appointment was questioned by some noisy speakers, and there was a general feeling in society that the appointment was rather a mistake. But those who knew Lord Canning—those especially who had worked with him— knew that it was no mistake. They knew that there was the stuff in him of which great administrators are made.

On the first day of August a Court of Directors was held at the India House, and Lord Canning was introduced to take the accustomed oath. On the evening of that day the Company gave, in honour of their new servant, one of those magnificent entertainments at which it was their wont to bid God-speed to those who were going forth to do their work. Those banquets were great facts and great opportunities. It was discovered soon afterwards that the expenditure upon them was a profligate waste of the public money. But the Government of a great empire, spending nothing upon the splendid foppery of a Court, was justified in thinking that, without offence, it might thus do honour to its more distinguished servants, and that, not the turtle and the venison, but the hospitality and the courtesy of the Directors, thus publicly bestowed upon the men who had done their work well in civil or military life, would find ample recompense in increased loyalty and devotion, and more energetic service. Many a gallant soldier and many a wise administrator carried back with him to India the big card of the East India Company inviting him to dinner at the London Tavern, and religiously preserved it as one of the most cherished records of an honourable career. There were many, too, who hoarded among their dearest recollections the memory of the evening when they saw, perhaps for the first and the last time, England's greatest statesmen and warriors, and heard them gravely discourse on the marvel and the miracle of our Indian Empire. Nor was it a small thing that a man selected to govern a magnificent dependency beyond the seas, should thus, in the presence of his old and his new masters, and many of his coadjutors in the great work before him, publicly accept his commission, and declare to the people in the West and in the East the principles which were to regulate his conduct and to shape his career. The words uttered on these occasions rose far above the ordinary convivial level of after-dinner speeches. There was a gravity and solemnity in them, appreciated not merely by those who heard them spoken, but by thousands also, to whom the Press conveyed them, in the country which they most concerned; and on the minds of the more intelligent Natives the fact of this grand ceremonial of departure made a deep impression, and elevated in their imaginations the dignity of the coming ruler.

Seldom or never had this ceremonial assumed a more imposing character than that which celebrated the appointment of Lord Canning to the Governor-Generalship of India. In the great Banqueting Hall of the London Tavern were assembled on that 1st of August many members of the Cabinet, including among them some of Canning's dearest friends; others besides of his old companions and fellow-students; and all the most distinguished of the servants of the Company at that time in the country. Mr. Elliot Macnaghten, Chairman of the East India Company, presided, and after dinner proposed the accustomed toasts. It was natural and right that, when doing honour to the newly-appointed Governor-General, the speaker should pay a fitting tribute to the distinguished statesman who was then bringing his work to a close; it was natural and graceful that tribute should be paid also to the worth of the elder Canning, who had done India good service at home, and had been selected to hold the great office abroad which his son was proceeding to fill; but there was something to a comparatively untried man perilous in such associations, and the younger Canning, with instinctive modesty, shrunk from the invidious suggestion. Perhaps there were some present who drew comparisons, unfavourable to the son, between the early careers of the two Cannings, which had entitled them to this great distinction; but when the younger stood up to speak, every one was struck—the many judging by busts and pictures, and the few recalling the living likeness of George Canning—by his great resemblance to his father. The singularly handsome face, the intellectual countenance, and, above all, the noble " Canning brow," like a block of white marble, bespoke no common capacity for empire, and gave emphatic force to the words he uttered. He said, after the usual expression of thanks for the kind words spoken, and the kind reception accorded to them, that the kindness which he had received had not created any delusion in his mind, for whether he contemplated the magnitude of the task that awaited him, or the great achievements of the distinguished men who had preceded him, he was painfully sensible that the labourer was unequal to the great work that had been entrusted to his hands. He was not ashamed to confess that there were times when he was tempted to shrink from the responsibility that awaited him. But this feeling, he added, was not inconsistent with his determination to devote all the energies of his mind, every hour, nay, every minute of his time, every thought and every inspiration, to the discharge of the duties which he had that day accepted from the hands of the Company. There were, however, other considerations, which had greatly reassured and encouraged him: "You have," he said, turning to the Chairman, "assured me, this day, of what you rightly describe as the generous confidence and co-operation of the Court of Directors. I thank you for that assurance, and I rely on it implicitly, for I know that the body of which you are the head are, wherever they bestow their confidence, no niggards in supporting those who honestly and faithfully serve them." And then, not perhaps without a knowledge of what, more than a quarter of a century before, his father had said on a similar occasion,* he added, "I feel that I can also rely on the cordial support and sympathy of my noble friend at the head of the Government, and of all those colleagues with whom I have had the proud satisfaction of serving as a Minister of the Crown, but, above all, I delight in the co-operation—for on that I must daily and hourly rely—of those two admirable bodies, the Civil Service and the Army of India. I hardly know whether there is any feature of our Government, any portion of our institutions, upon which Englishmen may look with more honest exultation than those two noble

---

* The occasion alluded to was the farewell banquet given by the East India Company to Sir John Malcolm, on his appointment to the government of Bombay. Then it was that George Canning said: "There cannot be found in the history of Europe the existence of any monarchy which, within a given time, has produced so many men of the first talents, in civil and military life, as India has first trained for herself, and then given to their native country."

branches of our Public Service. The men of those branches have done much for the advancement of India, and have sent forth from their ranks men who were efficient in war and peace, in numbers of which any monarchy in Europe might be proud, and who have rescued their countrymen from charges formerly, and not unjustly, levelled against them of dealing sometimes too harshly with those whom they were bound to succour and protect. Sir, it is the possession of such men which enables you to exhibit a spectacle unequalled in the world's history—that of a hundred and fifty millions of people submitting in peace and contentment, in a country teeming with wealth, to the government of strangers and aliens."

Then, after a few more words on the high character of the Services, and a brief declaration of the fact that he assumed office "without a single promise or pledge to any expectant," he proceeded with increased gravity and solemnity of utterance, almost, indeed, as one under the spell of prophecy: "I know not what course events may take. I hope and pray that we may not reach the extremity of war. I wish for a peaceful time of office, but I cannot forget that in our Indian Empire that greatest of all blessings depends upon a greater variety of chances and a more precarious tenure than in any other quarter of the globe. We must not forget that in the sky of India, serene as it is, a small cloud may arise, at first no bigger than a man's hand, but which, growing larger and larger, may at last threaten to burst, and overwhelm us with ruin. What has happened once may happen again. The disturbing causes have diminished certainly, but they are not dispelled. We have still discontented and heterogeneous peoples united under our sway; we have still neighbours before whom we

cannot altogether lay aside our watchfulness; and we
have a frontier configuration that renders it possible
that in any quarter, at any moment, causes of collision may arise. Besides, so intricate are our relatio:.s
with some subsidiary states, that I doubt whether in
an empire so vast and so situated it is in the power
of the wisest Government, the most peaceful and the
most forbearing, to command peace. But if we cannot command, we can at least deserve it, by taking
care that honour, good faith, and fair dealing are on
our side; and then if, in spite of us, it should become
necessary to strike a blow, we can strike with a clear
conscience. With blows so dealt the struggle must
be short and the issue not doubtful. But I gladly
dismiss from my mind apprehensions that may not
be realised, and joyfully recognise a large arena of
peaceful usefulness, in which I hope for your kind
assistance and co-operation."

Equally surprised were the few then present, who
were familiar with Lord Canning's parliamentary
utterances, and the many, who had never heard him
speak, but had been told that he was "no orator;"
for the speech which they now heard from his lips
was all that such a speech ought to have been. It was
impressive rather than impassioned; slowly spoken,
with a deliberate gravity, every sentence making
itself felt, and every word making itself heard in the
farthest corners of that great Banqueting Hall.
There were few present in whose estimation the
speaker had not risen before he resumed his seat;
few present who did not, years afterwards, remember
with strong emotion that picture of the little cloud
rising in an unexpected quarter, and in time obscur-
ing the firmament and overshadowing the land.
Some, perhaps, thought also of another speech, then

1-56. delivered by a more practised speaker; for the First
Minister of the Crown, on that August evening, let
fall some memorable words.   It was only in common
course that he should speak of the qualifications of
his colleague for the high office to which he had been
appointed; only in common. course that he should
express his gratitude to the Company who so materially lightened the cares of the Sovereign and her
Ministers.   But when Lord Palmerston dwelt on
" the significant fact that, whereas of old all civilisation came from India, through Egypt, now we, who
were then barbarians, were carrying back civilisation
and enlightenment to the parent source," and added,
" perhaps it might be our lot to confer on the countless millions of India a higher and a holier gift than
any real human knowledge; but that must be left
to the hands of time and the gradual improvement
of the people," he supplemented Lord Canning's prophecy, though he knew it not, and pointed to the
quarter from which the little cloud was to arise.

But although Lord Canning had been sworn in at
the India House, and had stood before the magnates
of the land as Governor-General elect, he was still a
member of the Cabinet and her Majesty's Postmaster-
General.   Parliament was prorogued on the 14th of
August, and in accordance with that wise official
usage, which recognises the necessity of holidays no
less for statesmen than for schoolboys, the Queen's
Ministers dispersed themselves over the country, and
Lord Canning went to Scotland.   It had been settled
that he should receive from the hands of Lord Dalhousie the reins of Indian Government on the 1st of
February, 1856, and his arrangements, involving a
short sojourn in Egypt, and visits to Ceylon, Bombay,
and Madras, had been made with a view to his arrival

at Calcutta on that day. But at Dalhousie's own request, his resignation was subsequently deferred to the 1st of March. When this request was first made to him, Canning thought that the intention of the change was simply to allow the old Governor-General more time not only to consummate the annexation of Oude, but to confront the first difficulties of the revolution; and it appeared to him, thinking this, that the postponement might be interpreted alike to his own and to his predecessor's disadvantage. It might have been said that the new Governor-General shrank from encountering the dangers of the position, or that the measure was so distasteful to him, on the score of its injustice, that he could not bring himself to put his hand to the work. Both assumptions would have been utterly erroneous. The question of the Annexation of Oude had been a Cabinet question, and as a member of the Cabinet, Lord Canning had given his assent to the policy, which, after much discussion in Leadenhall and in Downing-street, found final expression in the Court's despatch of the 19th of November. The policy itself had been already determined, although the precise terms of the instructions to be sent to the Government of India were still under consideration, when Dalhousie's proposal reached him; and he was willing to accept all the responsibilities of the measure. The proposed delay, therefore, did not at first sight please him; but when, from a later letter, he learnt that Dalhousie required a few more weeks of office, not for special, but for general purposes; that he needed time to gather up the ends of a large number of administrative details, the case was altered, and he assented, with the concurrence of the Court of Directors, to the change.*

* "As long," he wrote to the Chairman, "as it turned upon Oude

i-56.   A few days afterwards, Lord Canning turned his
face again towards the South, to superintend the final
arrangements for his departure, and to take leave of
his friends. Thus the month of October and the
greater part of November were passed; but not without some study of Indian questions, some useful training for the great work upon which he was about to
enter. On the 21st of November he went by command to Windsor, accompanied by Lady Canning,
who was among her Majesty's cherished friends, and
on the 23rd returned to London, after taking final
leave of the Queen. Another day or two, and he had
commenced his overland journey to the East. From
the French capital he wrote, on the last day of November: "I intended to leave Paris this afternoon,
but I received notice in the morning that the Emperor
wished to see me to-morrow, so that it will be Tuesday
morning (December 4th) before we embark at Mar-
seilles. We still hope to reach Alexandria on the
10th." He arrived there, however, not before the
12th, and after a day's halt pushed on to Cairo,
where he was received and entertained magnificently
by orders of the Pacha, who was at that time absent
from his capital.

The party consisted of Lord and Lady Canning,
his nephew Lord Hubert de Burgh,* Captain Bou-

---

alone, I felt that there was some
difficulty in making the change proposed by Lord Dalhousie, and some
risk of its intention being misrepre-
sented to the disadvantage of both
of us. But it is now clear that for
other reasons, apart from Oude, and
for the general winding up of the
work on his hands, it will be a great
help to him to have a month more
time. These are his very words to
me; and I cannot hesitate, so far as
I am concerned, to do that which

will be agreeable and convenient to
him, and probably advantageous to
the public interests. I hope, therefore, that you will feel no difficulty
in complying with Lord Dalhousie's
wish, by putting off my succession
until the day he names."—*Lord
Canning to Mr. Macnaghten, September 20, 1855.—MS. Correspondence.*

* Afterwards Lord Hubert Canning.

verie, A.D.C., and Dr. Leckie. There was abundant time for an exploration of the wonders of Egypt, and, as the fine climate of the country invited a protracted sojourn there, it was arranged that some weeks should be spent in pleasant and profitable excursions, and that they should embark at Suez about the middle of the month of January. "The Pacha was in Upper Egypt until to-day," wrote Lord Canning to Mr. Macnaghten, on the 17th of December, "when he returned to this neighbourhood. I am to see him to-morrow, and on the following day we set out on our expedition up the Nile. Thanks to a steamer, which the Pacha lends us, we shall be able to accomplish all we wish, and to embark on the *Feroze* immediately upon its arrival at Suez, which, according to a letter from Lord Dalhousie, that met me at Alexandria, will not be until close upon the 12th of January. . . . The magnificence, not to say extravagance, of our reception here far exceeds anything that I had expected. I shall need to be very profuse of my thanks to the Pacha to-morrow."

It would be pleasant to follow Lord Canning and his family on their river-voyage, the grateful experiences of which he has himself recorded, but these personal incidents have no connexion with the stern story before me, and the temptation, therefore, to enlarge upon them must be resisted. The programme of his movements given in the above letter to the Chairman of the Company, was realised with but little departure from the original design. The Governor-General elect halted at Aden, where, under the guidance of Brigadier Coghlan*—an officer of the Company's Artillery, one of those excellent

---

* Afterwards Sir William Coghlan, K.C.B.

public servants who, partly in a military, partly in a diplomatic capacity, represent great interests and undertake great responsibilities in the East—Lord Canning made his first acquaintance with the Sepoy Army of India. From Aden he steamed to Bombay, where he arrived on the 28th of January, 1856, and first planted his foot on Indian soil. "I found," he wrote to Mr. Macnaghten on the 2nd of February, "that Lord Dalhousie had given orders that I should be received with the full honours of Governor-General in possession; and of course I did nothing to check or escape from the demonstrations with which we were met, though I did not desire or expect them. I have been unceasingly busy for two-thirds of every twenty-four hours since our arrival; and by the 5th or 6th, I hope to have seen nearly all that calls for ocular inspection in the city and its neighbourhood. We shall then embark for Madras; for I have given up all thoughts of stopping at Ceylon, unless to coal, and hope to arrive there on the 14th or 15th. I cannot sufficiently congratulate myself on having come round by this Presidency. It has shown me much that I should not easily have learnt otherwise." It was a disappointment to him that he had not time to visit Ceylon, for his old Eton tutor, Chapman, had developed into Bishop of Colombo, and there would have been a grand old Etonian pleasure, on both sides, in talking over old times. But there was consolation in the thought that his friend Lord Harris, his fellow-pupil in the Bedfordshire market-town, was Governor of Madras. In that presidency he spent a few pleasant days, sojourning at Guindy, and then on the 25th of February set out to face the realities of Indian Government, and steamed up the Bay of Bengal.

On the last day of February, Lord Canning dis- February 29, embarked at Calcutta; and, proceeding to Govern- 1856. ment House, at once took his oaths of office and his seat in Council. It is the custom in such cases. No time is left for any question to arise as to who is Governor-General of India. So brief did the whole operation appear to him, that he wrote home that he had been sworn in and installed " within five minutes after touching land." As his dignities and responsi- bilities commenced at once, so did his work. At the end of his first week of office, he wrote that such had been the pressure of public business, that he had found time only for " one look out of doors " since he arrived. During that first week Lord Dalhousie tarried in Calcutta, and the past and future of the Government of India were discussed with interest, the depths of which were stirred by varying circum- stances, between those earnest-minded men ; the one all readiness to teach, the other all eagerness to learn. Dull and prosaic as its details often appear to Eng- lishmen at a distance, it is difficult to describe the living interest with which statesmen in India of all classes, from the highest to the lowest, perpetually regard their work.

No man ever undertook the office of Governor- First days of General of India under the impression that it would Government. be a sinecure. But it is scarcely less true that no man, whatever opinion he may have formed in Eng- land, ever entered upon its duties without discover- ing that he had greatly underrated the extent of its labours. The current of work is so strong and so continuous ; so many waters meet together to swell the stream ; that at first even a strong man trying to breast it may feel that he is in danger of being over- whelmed. Time lessens the difficulty ; but at the

2 c

outset, the multiplicity of unfamiliar details distracts and bewilders even the sharpest wit and the clearest brain; and the first result is apt to be a chaos. Box after box is placed upon the Governor-General's table; and each box is crammed with papers rugged with the names of strange men and stranger places, and references to unknown events and incomprehensible states of society. By some means or other, he must master the antecedents of every case that comes before him for decision; and there are often very intricate cases purposely left for his decision, that he may not be embarrassed by the judgments of his predecessor. Week after week goes by and little impression is made upon this pile of work. "Another fortnight is gone," wrote Lord Canning towards the end of March, "and I am beginning to gather up by slow degrees the threads of business, as it passes before me; but it is severe work to have to give so much time to the bygones of almost every question that comes up; and some weeks more must pass before I shall feel myself abreast of current events." There was a strong conscientiousness within the new Governor-General which would not suffer him to pass anything lightly over, and he endeavoured to understand all that came before him even at the risk of some inconvenient delays.

So he did not rush at his work; but quietly confronted it, and was in no haste to impress people with a sense of the profundity of his wisdom and the greatness of his self-reliance. He knew that he had much to learn, and he adopted the best means of learning it; for he invited all the chief agents of his Government, scattered over the country, especially those who were representing British interests at the Native Courts, to correspond confidentially with him on matters relating to their respective charges; an invitation which gave to every man thus addressed full liberty to declare his sentiments and to expound his views. And thus he escaped the danger on the one hand of surrendering his own judgment, by succumbing to the influence of some two or three public functionaries immediately attached to the Executive Government, and, on the other, of the over-confident. exercise of a dominant self-will rejecting all external aids, and refusing to walk by other men's experiences. He knew that there was no royal road to a knowledge of India; and he was well content that the first year of his administration should be unostentatiously devoted to the great duty of learning his work.

There were able men, too, at his elbow to assist him to a correct knowledge of facts, and to the formation of sound opinions. The Supreme Council consisted at that time of General John Low, Mr. Dorin, Mr. John Peter Grant, and Mr. Barnes Peacock. Of the first I can say little in this place that has not been already said. The only charge laid against him by the assailants of the Government was, that he was well stricken in years. But, although one who had fought beside Malcolm at Mehidpore, and then not in his first youth, must have lost some of the physical energy that animated him in his prime, his intellect was unimpaired. Ceasing to be a man of action, he had subsided gracefully into the condition of a councillor, the Nestor of the Political Service, a veteran without a stain. No man had so large an acquaintance with the Native Courts of India; no man knew the temper of the people better than John Low. He could see with their eyes, and speak with their tongues, and read with their understandings. And, therefore, he looked with some dismay at the wide-spread Englishism of the Dalhousie school, and sorrowfully regarded the gradual dying out of the principles in which he had been nurtured and trained, and to which, heedless of their unpopularity, he clung with honest resolution to the last. Dalhousie had too often disregarded his counsel; but he had always respected the man. And now Canning equally admired the personal character of his colleague, but was not equally minded to laugh his principles to scorn.

Mr. Dorin.

Of the two Bengal civilians who sat in that Council, it may be said that the one owed his position there apparently to chance, the other to his unquestionable abilities. Mr. Dorin was not a man of great parts; he was not a man of high character. If he had any official reputation, it was in the capacity of a financier; and finance was at that time the weakest point of our Government. He had limited acquaintance with the country, and but small knowledge of the people. He had no earnestness; no enthusiasm; no energy. He had a genius for making himself comfortable, and he had no superfluous activities of head or heart to mar his success in that particular direction. He had supported the policy of Lord Dalhousie, and had recorded in his time a number of minutes expressing in two emphatic words, which saved trouble and gained favour, his concurrence with the most noble the Governor-General; and now if the new ruler was not likely to find in him a very serviceable colleague, there was no greater chance of his being found a troublesome one.

John Peter Grant.

In John Grant the Governor-General might have found both. He was many years younger than his brother civilian, but he had done infinitely more work. In him, with an indolent sleepy manner was strangely combined extraordinary activity of mind. **1856.** He was one of the ablest public servants in the country. With some hereditary claim to distinction, he had been marked out from the very commencement of his career, no less by a favourable concurrence of external circumstances than by his own inherent qualifications, for the highest official success. No young civilian in his novitiate ever carried upon him so clearly and unmistakably the stamp of the embryo Councillor, as John Grant. In some respects this was a misfortune to him. His course was too easy. He had found his way; he had not been compelled to make it. He had not been jostled by the crowd; he had seen little or none of the rough work of Indian administration or Indian diplomacy. It had been his lot, as it had been his choice, to spend the greater part of his official life in close connexion with the Head-Quarters of the Government; and, therefore, his opportunities of independent action had been few; his personal acquaintance with the country and the people was not extensive; and his work had been chiefly upon paper. But as a member of a powerful bureaucracy his value was conspicuous. Quick in the mastery of facts, clear and precise in their analytical arrangement, and gifted with more than common powers of expression, he was admirably fitted to discharge the duties of the Secretariat. He was a dead hand at a report; and if Government were perplexed by any difficult questions, involving a tangled mass of disordered financial accounts, or a great conflict of authority mystifying the truth, he was the man of all others to unravel the intricate or to elucidate the obscure. Comparatively young in years, but ripe in bureaucratic experience, he entered the Supreme Council towards the close of Lord Dalhousie's administration. But he had sat long enough at the Board to establish his independence. He expressed his opinions freely and fearlessly; and his minutes, when minute-writing was in vogue, were commonly the best State papers recorded by the Government of the day. Closely reasoned, forcibly expressed, with here and there touches of quiet humour or subdued sarcasm, they cut through any sophistries put forth by his colleagues, with sharp incisive logic, and clearly stated the points at issue without disguises and evasions. On the whole, he was a man of large and liberal views, the natural manifestations of which were, perhaps, somewhat straitened by an acquired official reserve; and no one questioned the honesty of his intentions or the integrity of his life.

Barnes Peacock.

Mr. Barnes Peacock was the fourth, and, as is commonly called, the "Law Member" of Council. An English lawyer, appointed to aid the great work of Indian legislation, he was a member of the Executive rather by sufferance than by right. In a limited sense, he was supposed to represent the popular element in the Council. There was no very violent conflict of class-interests in those days. But so far as such division existed at all, he was regarded as the exponent of the views of the non-official Englishman and of the Europeanised Natives of the large towns, whose interests are bound up with our own. For the institution of the Company he was believed to have no respect, and for the exclusive system of Government by the Company's servants no toleration. He had a clear head, an acute understanding, but by no means a large mind. Assiduous in the work of law-making, he was the very soul of the Legislative Council; and had he confined his efforts to the work of moulding into draft-acts the ideas of other men, he would have been an invaluable public servant. But he sometimes went beyond this; and, when he did so, he commonly went wrong. For knowing little of the people of India, and having only thoroughly English notions of philanthropic reforms and legislative beneficences, he would have taught the people better manners with a rapidity for which they were not prepared, if he had unrestrainedly followed out his own ideas of social improvement. Indeed, he had already threatened to limit the polygamies of the Natives of India, and, doubtless, had a draft-act for the purpose on the legislative anvil, when circumstances arrested his career of reform. But, although it was in the legislative department that his especial strength lay, he did not confine himself to it. He grappled manfully with all the varied details of the general administration. There were times when his legal penetration was of service in the disentanglement of knotty questions of executive government, and he sometimes recorded minutes distinguished by no common powers of special pleading. But, on the whole, this laborious addiction to business was an encumbrance and an embarrassment to the Ministry; and Lord Canning had soon reason to complain of the conscientious excesses of his colleague. A general disinclination to take anything for granted impeded the progress of business; and the Governor-General, not without a feeling of admiration for a defect that had its root in honesty of purpose, endeavoured, and with good success, to wean the law member from his habit of mastering details which he was not expected to understand, and keeping back business which it was desirable to dispose of, whilst he was working up the past history of a Native State, or calculating grain-

1856. bags in a commissariat account. There must have
been some inward promptings of self-knowledge in
Canning's own mind to assure him that this laborious conscientiousness was a part of his own nature;
but he felt, at the same time, that his larger scope of
responsibility demanded from him a larger scope of
action, and that what was right in the Governor-
General was not therefore right in his departmental
colleague.

Such were the fellow-labourers with whom Lord
Canning was now about to prosecute the work of
Government. On the whole, the Council was not
badly constituted for ordinary purposes of administration in quiet times. It contained, indeed, many
of the essential elements of a good Board. What it
most wanted was military knowledge; for General
Low, though an old soldier of the Madras Army, had
seen more of the Court than of the Camp; and it
was rather in the diplomacies of the Native States
than in the conduct of warlike operations, or in the
details of military administration, that he had earned,
by hard service, the right to be accepted as an authority.* It was a constitutional fiction that, in an
Indian Council, the necessary amount of military
knowledge was supplied in the person of the Commander-in-Chief, who had a seat in it. The seat,
though legally occupied, was for the most part practically empty, for duty might not, and inclination
did not, keep the military chief at the Head-Quarters
of the Civil Government. But it happened that,
when Lord Canning arrived in India, he found
General Anson in Calcutta. And it was a pleasure
to him to see in the Indian capital a face that had
been familiar to him in the English.

* Shortly after Lord Canning's
arrival, General Low went to Eng
land, but returned at the commencement of the cold weather (1856-57).

The appointment of the Honourable George Anson to the chief command of the Indian Army took by surprise the English communities in the three Presidencies, who had seen his name only in the Racing Calendar, or in other records of the Turf. But there was one thing at least to be said in his favour: he was not an old man. It was not in the nature of things, after a long European peace, that good service should be found in the officers of the Queen's Army unaccompanied by the weight of years. But the scandal of imbecility had risen to such a height, the military world had grown so sick of infirmity in high places—of the blind, the lame, the deaf, the obesely plethoric—that they were prepared to welcome almost any one who could sit a horse, who could see from one end to the other of a regiment in line, and hear the report of a nine-pounder at a distance of a hundred yards. There was nothing to be said against George Anson on this score. He could hear and see; he could ride and walk. He was of a light spare figure, well framed for active exercise; and his aspect was that of a man who could "stand the climate." But with all men who first brave that climate in the maturity of life, there is a risk and an uncertainty; and appearances belied Anson's capabilities of resistance. During the hot weather and rainy season of 1856, the heats and damps of Bengal tried him severely; and Lord Canning more than once wrote home that his military colleague was reduced to a skeleton, and had lost all his bodily strength and all his buoyancy of spirit. But, at the same time, he spoke of the Chief as one who had many excellent points, both as an officer and as a man. The precise limits of authority vested in the chief civil and military functionaries are so ill defined, that, when the powers of both are combined in one individual, it is

1856.

General
Anson.

1856. a mercy if he does not quarrel with himself. When they are divided, as is commonly the case, a conflict of authority is inevitable. And so at this time, the Governor-General and the Commander-in-Chief soon came into official collision; but it never grew into personal strife between Lord Canning and General Anson. The public prints hinted that there was a rupture between them; and the same story travelled homewards and penetrated Cannon-row. But the Civilian wrote, that though there had been some special points of difference between them, the temper of the Soldier was so charming, and he was so thoroughly a gentleman, that it was quite impossible to quarrel with him. The inevitable antagonism of official interests could not weaken the ties of personal regard; and when Anson, in the month of September, left Calcutta on a tour of military inspection in the Upper Provinces, he carried with him no kindlier wishes than those which attended him warm from the heart of the Governor-General.[*]

* What Lord Canning wrote about General Anson is so honourable to both, that it is quite a pleasure to quote it. "We get on admirably together," wrote the Governor-General in June. "His temper is charming, and I know no one whom I should not be sorry to see substituted for him." And again, in October: "I am not surprised at the report you mention that Anson and I do not get on well together, because such a rumour was current in Calcutta two or three months ago, and even found its way into the newspapers. I believe it originated in a difference between us on two points; one (of much interest to the Indian Army), the power of the Commander-in-Chief to withhold applications for furlough, transmitted through him to the Governor-General in Council; the other, an authority to exercise something very like a veto upon the Governor-General's selections of officers for civil and political service. Upon both of which I found it necessary to disallow his pretensions. But neither these disagreements, nor the reports to which they gave rise, have for a moment caused any misunderstanding or reserve between us. It would be very difficult to quarrel with any one so imperturbably good tempered, and so thoroughly a gentleman."—MS. Correspondence.

CHAPTER II.

LORD CANNING'S FIRST YEAR—THE OUDE COMMISSION—WAJID ALI AND
THE EMBASSY TO ENGLAND—THE PERSIAN WAR—THE QUESTION OF
COMMAND—JAMES OUTRAM—CENTRAL-ASIAN POLICY—DOST MAHOMED—
JOHN LAWRENCE AND HERBERT EDWARDES AT PESHAWUR—HENRY
LAWRENCE IN LUCKNOW.

WITH these colleagues in the Council Chamber, and
with a staff of able, well-trained secretaries, of whom
I shall speak hereafter, in the several Departments,
the new Governor-General found the burden of his
work, though it pressed heavily upon him, in no way
galling or dispiriting.   There are always small vexations and embarrassments; incidental details, that will
not run smoothly in the administrative groove, but
grind and grate and have a stubborn obstructiveness
about them.   But the great sum-total of the business
before him wore an aspect cheerful and encouraging.   There was tranquillity in India.   Outwardly,
it seemed that Lord Dalhousie had left only a
heritage of Peace.   Even in Oude, just emerging
from a revolution, there were external signs of general
quietude; of contentment, or at least of submission;
and of the satisfactory progress of the administration.   But a new administrator was wanted.   Outram
had done his work.   He had been selected to fill the
office of Resident, and no man could have more be-

1856.

The Adminis-
tration of
Oude.

comingly represented British interests at a corrupt and profligate Court. In that capacity it had fallen to his lot to accomplish ministerially the revolution which had been decreed by the British Government. But it was work that sickened him ; for although he believed that it was the duty of the Paramount State to rescue Oude from the anarchy by which it had so long been rent, he was one whose political predilections were in favour of the maintenance of the Native States, and he knew that much wrong had been done to the Princes and Chiefs of India under the plea of promoting the interests of the people. When the Proclamation converted Oude into a British province, the Resident became Chief Commissioner, and the superintendence of the administration was the work that then devolved upon him. But it was work that Outram was not now destined to perform. His health had broken down ; the hot season was coming on apace ; and a voyage to England had been urgently pressed upon him by his medical advisers. So he sought permission to lay down the Portfolio for a while, and asked the Governor-General to appoint an officer to act for him in his absence.

Question of succession.

It would have been comparatively easy to find a successor suited to the work, if the appointment to be disposed of had been a permanent one. But Lord Canning had to find a man able to conduct the administration at its most difficult stage, and yet willing to forsake other important work for the brief tenure of another's office. Outram said that there was one man in whom both the ability and the will were to be found. That man was Henry Ricketts, a Bengal civilian of high repute, whose appointment was pressed upon Lord Canning as the best that could be made. But Ricketts was wanted for other work.

The authorities at home were clamouring for a reduction of expenditure; and as retrenchment, public or private, commonly begins in the wrong place, a revision of official salaries was to be one of the first efforts of our economy. So Mr. Ricketts had been specially appointed to furnish a Report on the best means of extracting from the officers of Government the same amount of good public service for a less amount of public money. Lord Canning shook his head doubtfully at the experiment; but Cannon-row was urgent, and nothing was to be suffered to interrupt the labours of the man who was to suggest the means of increasing the financial prosperity of the Company by sapping out the energies of those upon whom that prosperity mainly depended.

Whilst Outram and the Governor-General were corresponding about this arrangement, another plan for the temporary administration of Oude was suggesting itself; but it never became more than a suggestion. Ever since the dissolution of the Lahore Board, Sir Henry Lawrence had held office as chief of the Political Agency in Rajpootana. It was a post of honour and responsibility; but there was not in the work to be done enough to satisfy so ardent and so active a mind, and he had longed, during that great struggle before Sebastopol, which he had watched with eager interest from the beginning, to show, when all the departments were breaking down, what a rough-and-ready Indian Political might do to help an army floundering miserably in a strange land. But this field of adventure was closed against him. Peace was proclaimed: and Henry Lawrence, who had studied well the history and the institutions of Oude, and who had advocated the assumption of the government, but not the annexation of the pro-

vince or the absorption of its revenues, thought that
he might do some good by superintending the administration during the first year of our tenure.
There were many interests to be dealt with in that
conjuncture, which require! a strong but a gentle
hand to accommodate them to the great revolution
that had been accomplished, and he felt some apprehension lest civilian-government, harsh and precise,
should forthwith begin to systematise, in utter disregard of the institutions and the usages of the
country, and should strike at once for a flourishing
balance-sheet. It was too little the fashion to sympathise with the fallen fortunes of men ruined by
the dominant influence of the White Race. In the
chivalrous benevolence of the out-going Commissioner, Henry Lawrence had full confidence. The
great-hearted compassion which Outram had shown
for the Ameers of Scinde, proclaimed the mercy and
the justice of the man. But a civilian of the new
school from the Regulation Provinces might bring
with him a colder heart and a sharper practice, and
might overbear all ancient rights and privileges in
pursuit of the favourite theory of the Dead Level.
Anxious to avert this, which he believed would be a
calamity alike to the people of Oude and to his own
government, Henry Lawrence offered to serve, during
the transition-period, in Outram's place; and the first
misfortune that befel the ministry of Lord Canning
was that the letter, conveying the proposal, arrived a
little too late. A Commissioner had already been appointed.

The New
Commis-
sioner.
The choice had fallen on Mr. Coverley Jackson, a
civilian from the North-West Provinces, an expert
revenue-officer, held in high esteem as a man of
ability, but more than suspected of some infirmity of

temper. Aware of this notorious failing, but not deeming it sufficient to disqualify one otherwise so well fitted for the post, Lord Canning accompanied his offer of the appointment with a few words of caution, frank but kindly, and Jackson in the same spirit received the admonition, assuring the Governor-General that it would be his earnest endeavour to conciliate the good feelings of all who might be officially connected with him, so far as might be consistent with the claims of the public service and the maintenance of the authority entrusted to him. But he did not accomplish this; and there is slight evidence that he resolutely attempted it. It was an untoward occurrence that the man next in authority, and the one with whom the circumstances of the province brought him most frequently into official communication, was as little able to control his temper as Jackson himself. Mr. Martin Gubbins, of the Bengal Civil Service, was the Financial Commissioner. Upon him devolved the immediate superintendence of the revenue administration of our new territory, whilst Mr. Ommaney, of the same service, superintended the department of Justice. A man of rare intelligence and sagacity, eager and energetic, Martin Gubbins would have been a first-rate public servant, if his utility had not been marred by a contentious spirit. His angularities of temper were continually bringing him into collision with others, and his pertinacious self-assertion would not suffer him, when once entangled in a controversy, ever to detach himself from it. Of all men in the service he Jackson and was the one least likely to work harmoniously with Gubbins. the Chief Commissioner. So it happened that, in a very short time, they were in a state of violent antagonism. Whether, in the first instance, Jackson

1856. overstrained his authority, and unwisely and unkindly expressed his displeasure in language calculated to excite irritation and resentment, or whether Gubbins was the first to display an insubordinate spirit, and to provoke the censure of his chief by the attempted usurpation of his powers, it is of little importance now to inquire. The sharp contention that grew up between them was soon made known to the Governor-General, who deplored and endeavoured to arrest it. How wisely and calmly he conveyed to the Commissioner an expression, less of his displeasure than of his regret, his correspondence pleasantly illustrated. * But no kindly counsel from Government House could smoothe down the asperities of Jackson's temper. As time advanced, the feud between him and Gubbins grew more bitter and more irreconcilable. In India, a paper war once commenced lasts out many a military campaign. There is something so exciting, so absorbing in it, that even the best public servants sometimes forget the public interests whilst they are wasting their time and expending their energies in personal conflicts and criminations. Had Coverley Jackson taken half as much pains to see that the pledges of the British Government were fulfilled, and the annexation of Oude rendered as little ruinous

---

* Take, for example, the following: "Judging by my own experience, I should say that in dealing with public servants who have incurred blame, everything is to be gained by telling them their faults in unmistakable language, plainly and nakedly; but that one's purpose (their amendment) is rather defeated than otherwise by the use of terms that sting them, or amplify their offences to them unnecessarily—even though all be done within the strict limits of truth and fact. I believe that if a man has at bottom a sense of his duty, and is possessed of the feelings and temper of a gentleman, the more simply his error is put before him, and the more plain and quiet the reproof, the better chance there is of his correcting himself readily and willingly, and that if we wish to get work done hereafter out of some one whom it is necessary to rebuke, we ought to give him as little excuse as possible (he will too often find it where it is not given) for feeling irritated against ourselves." —Lord Canning to Mr. Coverley Jackson, July 7, 1856.—MS. Correspondence.

as possible to all the chief people of the province, 1856.
as he did to convict his subordinates of official mis-
demeanours, it would have been better both for his
own character and for the character of the nation.
But whilst Jackson and Gubbins were in keen contention with each other, covering reams of paper with
their charges and counter-charges and their vehement
self-assertions, the generous nature of the Governor-
General was grieved by complaints and remonstrances
from the King, who declared, or suffered it to be
declared for him, that the English officers in Lucknow were inflicting grievous wrongs and indignities
upon him and upon his Family, seizing or destroying
his property, and humiliating the members and dependents of his House.

It has been shown that Wajid Ali, when he saw Movements
that all hope of saving his dominions from the great of the ex-
white hand that had been laid upon them had utterly King.
gone from him, had talked about travelling to England and laying his sorrows at the foot of the Throne.
But, in truth, travelling to England, or to any other
place, was a thing rather to be whined about than
to be done, by one so destitute of all activities,
physical and mental, and it was almost certain that
he would hitch somewhere; not improbably at the
first stage. And so he did. Halting not far from
Lucknow, the King awaited the on-coming of his
minister, Ali Nuckee Khan, a man not wanting in
activities of any kind, who had been detained at
the capital to aid in the " transfer of the Government," out of which he had been ousted. But after
a while King and Minister, and other regal appen-
dages, male and female, moved on towards Calcutta
—the first stages by land; then afterwards taking the
river-steamer, at a time of year when there is ever a

scant supply of water for such travelling, they were
constrained to go ".round by the Sunderbunds," and
make a long and by no means a pleasant voyage to
the English capital; of which necessity Lord Canning shrewdly observed that it would give his Majesty
such a foretaste of life on board as would inevitably
drive out of him any lingering thought of the passage
across the black water to England.

And so it was. The King arrived at Calcutta when
the month of May had burnt itself half out, and was
soon domiciled in a house on the river-side, which had
erst been the suburban villa of an English Chief-
Justice. It was enough for him to see the steamers
smoking past him sea-wards; and to keep steadily
before him the conviction that for a man of his tastes
and habits, to take no account of his girth, Garden-
Reach was a more recommendable place than the Bay
of Bengal, the Red Sea, or the Mediterranean. But
still the pilgrimage to the foot of the Throne was to
be undertaken, not by but for the last of the Oude
Kings. Without any sacrifice of his personal ease,
or any abandonment of the delights of the Zenana, he
might enter a vicarious appearance at St. James's by
sending the chief members of his family—the nearest
of his kindred, in each stage and relation, before,
beside, and after him—his mother, his brother, and
his son, with agents and ministers, black and white,
to plead against the seizure of his dominions.

The Oude
Mission.
There was one of the royal party with some substance of masculine vigour still left as God had given
it; and that one was not the Heir-Apparent, or the
so-called General, or a born manhood of any kind,
but the Queen-Mother, who set the example of going
across the dreary waste of black water and level sand
straight to the feet of the Queen of England. And

they went, not scantily attended either, those three, like thieves in the night, embarking secretly in the darkness, and taking Government House by surprise with the report of the accomplished fact of their departure. Not that Government House would have opposed any obstacle to their going in broad daylight, with drums beating and flags flying; but that the steam-company, with an eye to business, thought it better to make a secret of it; such fellow-travellers, according to European notions, not increasing the comforts of the voyage. As to the Governor-General, all he could say was, "Let them go;" pitying the East India Company, thus compelled to receive such troublesome visitors, but claiming for them kindly and courteous treatment at the hands of the magnates of Leadenhall. And so those representatives of the exploded kingship of Oude went westward, with vague but extensive ideas of a recovery past looking for on this side of eternity, buoyed up and encouraged by men who well knew the hopelessness of the endeavour. The "case" was miserably mismanaged. There was much internal strife, and scarcely an attempt to strike out against the common foe. The so-called "Mission" went to pieces and rotted piecemeal. Not merely waste of treasure was there, but waste of life. The Queen-Mother and the Prince-General died, and were buried in the great cemetery of Père la Chaise. The Heir-Apparent, money-bound and helpless, threw himself upon the mercy of the enemy, borrowed from them half a lakh of rupees, and was carried homewards, somewhat dazed and bewildered as to the upshot or no upshot of the whole affair, but with a prevailing sense of escape and relief that it was all over. And the rest of the luckless embassy went at last, leaving behind

1856.   them some scum of official trouble and mishap, and
some legal perplexities not readily soluble by any
" perfection of human reason" known in our English
courts.

Grievances of   Meanwhile, in the name of the King himself,
the ex-King.   ministerial activities had not been wanting in India
to make substantial grievance, not so much of the
thing done (for that was left to the " Mission") as
of the manner of doing it, which had not been all
right.   In the Humanities, wherein is included the
great art of letting down easily, good to be learnt
alike by Men and by Governments, we had not
taken first-class honours.   Not without some red-
denings of shame is it to be recorded that the
wrongs inflicted upon the Princes of India in the
shape of territorial dispossessions and titular extinctions had been sometimes supplemented by lesser
wrongs, more grievous to bear upon the one side and
less to be justified on the other.   For there is some
dignity in great wrong, doing or suffering; and a
persuasion, in one case, not without sincerity at the
bottom, that wrong is right.   But look at the matter
in what light we may, it can be nothing but miserable
wrong to make these dispossessions and extinctions,
which may be for the national good, the forerunners
of personal distresses and humiliations to individuals
thus dispossessed and extinguished.   Yet men and,
redder shame still, feeble Zenana-bred women had
brought this charge against the strong Government of
the British, before the kingdom of Oude was marked
for extinction; and now again the same complaint of
supplemental cruelties and indignities, more galling
than the one great wrong itself, went up from Wajid
Ali, or was uttered in his name.   It was charged
against us that our officers had turned the stately
palaces of Lucknow into stalls and kennels, that

1856.

delicate women, the daughters or the companions of Kings, had been sent adrift, homeless and helpless, that treasure-houses had been violently broken open and despoiled, that the private property of the royal family had been sent to the hammer, and that other vile things had been done very humiliating to the King's people, but far more disgraceful to our own.

Not only so disgraceful, but so injurious to us, so great a blunder, indeed, would such conduct have been, that all who had any hope of the restoration of the Oude monarchy must have devoutly wished the story to be true. There were those who had such hope. How could it be hopeless, when it was remembered that the Sepoy Army of the Company was full of men whose homes were in Oude; when it was believed that the great flood of English rule was sweeping away all existing interests, and destroying all the influential classes alike in the great towns and in the rural districts? The ministers and courtiers of the King of Oude were at large in Calcutta and the neighbourhood, and might journey whithersoever they pleased. Vast fields of intrigue were open before them. The times were propitious. It was plain that there was a feeling of inquietude in the native mind, and that fear had engendered discontent. It was certain that the British Government were weak, for the country was stripped of European troops. The good day might yet come. Meanwhile, it might be something to spread abroad, truly or falsely, a story to the effect that the English, adding insult to injury, had cruelly humiliated all the members of the Oude family left behind in Lucknow.

In these stories of official cruelty Canning had small faith. But the honour of his Government demanded that they should be inquired into and contradicted, and he urged the Chief Commissioner at once to investigate and report upon the charges put forth by the creatures of the King. But Jackson, full of his own wrongs, failed to see the importance of the task assigned to him, and his answers were unsatisfactory and apparently evasive. Privately as well as publicly he was urged by the Governor-General to address himself seriously to the work of effacing from the nation the dishonour with which the dependents of the old Court of Lucknow had endeavoured to besmear the British name. But the result was not what Lord Canning had sought, not what he had expected. So at last, bitterly grieved and disappointed by the manner in which his representative had dealt with a subject, at once of so delicate and so important a nature, the Governor-General thus becomingly poured forth his indignation : " I will not conceal from you," he wrote to Mr. Jackson, " my disappointment at the manner in which from first to last you have treated this matter. Instead of enabling the Government to answer distinctly and categorically every complaint which the King has preferred, you have passed over unnoticed some upon which you must have known that the Government were without materials for reply. Upon placing your answers, now that all have been received, side by side with the King's letters, I find myself quite unable to say whether any buildings such as he describes have been pulled down, and if so, why?—although one building, the Jelwa Khana, had been especially mentioned to the King, as in course of demolition—whether dogs or horses have been quartered in the Chutter Munzil, and especially whether a stoppage of the allowances to the King's descendants has been threatened, a statement to this effect being pointedly made in the King's letter of the 14th of September You tell me that you have delayed your answers in order that they may be more complete. I can hardly think, therefore, that these matters have escaped you, and yet I do not know how otherwise to account for their being passed by. Be this as it may, the result of your course of proceeding is that the Governor-General is placed in an unbecoming, not to say humiliating position towards the King of Oude. The King brings complaints, which, whether true or false, are plain enough against the officers of Government, and the Governor-General, after assuring the King that as soon as reference shall have been made to the Chief Commissioner, satisfactory explanation shall be given, and relying, as he has a right to do, that that officer will obey his instructions and do his duty, finds himself altogether mistaken, and defeated upon points which, however unworthy of notice they may appear to the Chief Commissioner at Lucknow, cannot be slurred over by the Government in Calcutta. It matters nothing that these charges are instigated by disreputable hangers-on of the King, or that they are wholly or partly untrue, or even impossible. There they are in black and white, and they must be answered. It is surprising to me that you should have failed to appreciate the necessity."

And it was surprising; but Coverley Jackson, at that time, could scarcely appreciate any necessity save that of riding roughshod over Gubbins and Ommaney, and keeping them down to the right subordinate level. How far these charges of cruel indifference to the feelings of the Oude family were true, to what extent the dependents of the late King were wronged and humiliated, and the nobles of the land despoiled and depressed; how, indeed, the revolution affected all existing interests, are subjects reserved for future inquiry. It would have been well if the Chief Commis-

sioner had done as much to mollify these poor people
as to exasperate his own colleagues.   But the temper
of the man was to the last degree arbitrary and exacting, and Lord Canning, though with admirable
patience and moderation he strove to control the excesses of his agent, could not hold them in check.
Pointing to the great exemplar of John Lawrence, the
Oude administration having been constructed on the
Punjabee model, he showed that the reins of government might be held with a firm and vigorous hand by
one not grasping at all departmental authority.   But
these kindly teachings were in vain.   The old strife
continued.   Striking with one hand at Gubbins, and
with the other at Ommaney, the Chief Commissioner
was continually in an attitude of offence; and the administration was likely to be wrecked altogether upon
the lee-shore of these internal contentions.   So, at
last, the Governor-General was forced upon the conviction that he had selected the wrong man to preside
in Oude, and that the sooner he could be removed
from it the better for the province.

The readiest means of effecting this, without any
public scandal or any recorded reproach injurious to
Jackson's career, was by the restoration of James
Outram to the post which the civilian had been holding for him. Very unfit, doubtless, was the "officiating
Chief Commissioner" for that post; but he had done
good service to the State, he had some commendable
points of character, and even at the bottom of his
proved incapacity for this particular office there might
be nothing worse than a distempered zeal.   So Lord
Canning, in the exercise of what is called a "sound
discretion," as well as in obedience to the dictates of a
kind heart, sought to accomplish the end in view by
a return to the *status ante* in the natural order of
things, rather than by any violent supersession of his

unfortunate nominee. It was doubly a source, therefore, of satisfaction to him to learn that Outram,
whose shattered health at the time of his departure in
the spring had excited sad forebodings in the mind of
the Governor-General, now in the autumn declared
himself convalescent and about to return to his work.
But the work, the very thought of which had breathed
into the veins of the soldier-statesman new health, and
revived all his prostrate activities, was not administrative business in Oude. It was altogether work of
another kind and in another place, far enough away
from the scene of all his former endeavours; work
the account of which must be prefaced by some
historical explanations.

Scarcely had Lord Canning taken his place in The rupture
Government House, when the question of a war with with Persia.
Persia began to assume portentous dimensions. Truly,
it was not his concern. Ever since the days when,
nearly half a century before, there had been a strange
mad scramble for diplomatic supremacy in Persia between the delegates of the Governor-General and of
the Court of St. James's, the position of the Government of India towards our Persian Mission and our
Persian policy had been very indistinctly defined. The
financial responsibility of the Company had been at
all times assumed, and the executive assistance of the
Indian Government had been called for, when our relations with that perfidious Court had been beset with
difficulties beyond the reach of diplomatic address.
But the political control had been vested in the Imperial Government, as represented by the Foreign
Office;* and the officers of the Mission had been

---

* Except during a brief interval; delegated partially the management
that is, between the years 1826 and of affairs to the Governor-General,
1835, when the King's Government only to resume it wholly again.

1856.

nominated by the Crown. Affairs were still in this state when Lord Canning assumed the Government of India, and found that Great Britain was rapidly drifting into a war with Persia, which it would be his duty to direct, and the resources for which must be supplied from the country under his charge.

Herat.

The difficulties, which now seemed to render war inevitable, were chronic difficulties, which were fast precipitating an acute attack of disease. They were an after-growth of the great convulsion of 1838, which had culminated in the war in Afghanistan. We had tried to forget that hated country; but there was a Nemesis that forbade oblivion. It was an article of our political faith that Herat must be an independent principality, and we clung to it as if the very salvation of our Indian Empire depended on the maintenance of this doctrine. But there was nothing in the whole range of Eastern politics so certain to engender continual tribulation, and at last to compel us to apostatise in despair. The independence of Herat was a shadowy idea; it never could be a substantial reality. With an Army of Occupation in Afghanistan, and with British officers freely disbursing British gold at the "gate of India," we had for a while maintained the outward independence of the principality under Shah Kamran of the Suddozye House of Caubul; but even then the minister, Yar Mahomed, was continually declaring that his heart was with Iran, and threatening to throw himself into the arms of the Persian King. When the British Army had evacuated Afghanistan, the bold, unscrupulous minister, having soon relieved himself of the nominal sovereignty of the Suddozye, began to rule the country on his own account. And he ruled it well: that is, he ruled it with vigour; and for some ten years, by astute diplomacy, the soul of which was a system of small concessions to Persia, which soothed her pride and averted great demands, he governed the principality in peace, and maintained its nominal integrity.   But his son, Syud Mahomed, who succeeded him, had none of the essentials of a great ruler.   Plentifully endowed with his father's wickedness, he lacked all his father's vigour.   Treacherous and unscrupulous, but feeble in the extreme, he was ready, on the first appearance of danger, to become a creature of the Persian Court.   Persia eagerly seized the opportunity; and again England appeared upon the scene.

In the course of 1852, a Persian Army marched upon Herat. Not, indeed, in open defiance; not with any avowed object of conquest; but nominally, as a powerful ally, to perform an office of friendship.   On the death of Yar Mahomed the affairs of the principality had fallen into confusion, and the Persian Army went forth with the benevolent design of restoring them to order and prosperity.   But the mask was soon thrown aside.   The real object of the expedition proclaimed itself. Herat was declared to be an appendage of the Persian monarchy.   This was not to be borne. To maintain the independence of Herat, England a few years before had been prepared to send her legions to the gates of the city.   And now Persia was destroying it by a trick.   So, fortified by instructions from Downing-street, the British minister resisted the outrage.   On pain of an entire forfeiture of the friendship of Great Britain, the Persian Government were called upon to withdraw their army, and to enter into a solemn covenant binding them to recognise and respect the independence of Herat.   There were then the usual displays of trickery and evasiveness; but overawed at last by the resolute bearing of

1853.   the British minister, the required pledge was given, and Persia bound herself to acknowledge the independence which she was so eager to crush. But she was sorely disturbed and irritated by our interference with her schemes of ambition; and thenceforth the British Mission became an object of dislike and suspicion at Tcheran; and a rupture between the two Courts was only a question of time.

The war in the Crimea delayed—it did not avert— the inevitable crisis. The genius of Persia had then free scope for exercise, and turned to the best account its opportunities of double-dealing. Waiting the sentence of the great Judge of Battles, she coquetted both with Russia and with the Allies, and was ready to sell her good offices to the stronger party, or in a time of uncertainty to the higher bidder. But when the war ceased, her importance was gone; she had not been able to turn her position to account during the day of strife, and when peace dawned again upon Europe, she tried in vain to be admitted to the great international Council, which made the work of reconciliation complete. Disappointed and offended, perhaps, not thinking much of our boasted victory, for Russia had been successful in Asiatic Turkey, and Persia knew less about Sebastopol than about Kars, she could see no profit in the English alliance. The minister who then directed her affairs had no feeling of affection for the British representative at her Court. A strong personal prejudice, therefore, came in to aggravate the national antipathy; and before the end of 1855, the Mission had been so grievously insulted that Mr. Murray hauled down the British Flag, and set his face towards the Turkish frontier.

1855.   Into the details of this affair it is unnecessary to enter. Another event occurred about the same time.

A rebellion broke out in Herat. Syud Mahomed was killed. In his place was installed a member of the old Suddozye House, a nephew of Shah Kamran, Yusoof Khan by name, who had no peculiar qualifications for empire, but who could not be worse than the man whom he had supplanted. A revolution of this kind is so much in the common course of Afghan history, that we need not seek to account for it by any other than internal causes. But it was said that it had been fomented by Persian intrigue; and it is certain that the Government of the Shah were eager to profit by the crisis. The times were propitious. There was in Central Asia at that time one great man, whose movements were regarded at the Persian Court with alarm not altogether feigned, though sometimes exaggerated for a purpose. Ever since the British had set the seal on their confession of gigantic failure in Afghanistan by restoring Dost Mahomed to empire, the energies and activities of the old Ameer had expended themselves on the consolidation of his former dominions; and now he was hot to extend them to the westward. It was not merely an impulse of ambition. In part, at least, it was an instinct of self-preservation. The pretensions of Persia were not limited, and her encroachments were not likely to be confined, to the principality of Herat. Already she had established a dominant influence in Candahar, and did not scruple to talk about her rights of dominion. It was impossible for Dost Mahomed to regard this with unconcern. That Persia had views of extended influence, if not of actual conquest, in Afghanistan was certain. She had proposed to the Ameer himself to reduce the whole country to the condition of a protected State. The time had now come for him to put forth a mighty hand and a stretched-out arm for the maintenance of the independence of Afghanistan. Kohun-dil-Khan, his half-brother, the Chief of Candahar, died in the autumn of 1855. Dost Mahomed had never trusted him; and his son was not to be trusted. So the Ameer, who had no love for half-measures, annexed Candahar to the kingdom of Caubul; and the Persian Government believed, or pretended to believe, that he included Herat itself in his scheme of conquest.

He had at that time no such design. But it was a favourite trick of Persia to justify her own acts of aggression by a reference to some alleged danger and the necessity of self-preservation. So, seeing in the internal state of Herat an encouraging opportunity, and in the movements of Dost Mahomed a plausible pretext for evading their obligations, the Government of the Shah tore the convention of 1853 into shreds, and again marched an army upon Herat. But it met with no welcome there. Alarmed by the movements of the Caubul Ameer, and threatened with a counter-revolution at home, the nominal ruler of Herat had turned towards the Persians for assistance, but when he found that the chief people of the place were opposed to such an alliance, and that a strong national Sooneeism prevailed among them, he hoisted British colours and invited Dost Mahomed to come to his aid. The characteristic bad faith of the Suddozye Princes was conspicuous in this wretched man. His own people could not trust him. The Persians were investing the place, and it was feared that Yusoof Khan would betray the city into their hands. It was easy, therefore, to raise a party against him. So Eesa Khan, the Deputy or Lieutenant-Governor of the place, caused him to be seized, and sent him a prisoner into the enemy's camp, with a letter declaring that he was of ·

no use in Herat, and that the Persians might do with
him as they liked.

To this point events had progressed when Lord
Canning was called upon to address himself seriously
to the consideration of the troubled politics of Central
Asia. To the new Governor-General these complications were a source of no common anxiety, for he could
see clearly that England was drifting into war, and
that, however little he might have to do with it in its
origin and conception, its execution would be entrusted to him. There was a bitter flavour about the
whole affair that was distasteful in the extreme to the
Governor-General. "My hope of an accommodation,"
he wrote to the President in August, "has almost
died out, and I contemplate the prospect of the in-
glorious and costly operations which lie before us
with more disgust than I can express."* He had
gone out, as others had gone before him, with an
avowed and a sincere desire for peace; but warned
by their cruel disappointments, he had laid fast hold
in India of the resolution which he had formed in England, and he was not by any adverse or any alluring
circumstances to be driven or enticed into unnecessary
war. "Do not," he said, "be afraid of my being
unduly hasty to punish Persia. Unless the Shah
should steam up the Hooghly, with Murray swinging
at his yard-arm, I hope that we shall be able to keep
the peace until your instructions arrive."† And he
was anxious to avoid, not only aggressive measures
from the side of India, but any diplomatic entangle-
ments that might at some future time be a cause of
perplexity to his Government. The politics of Central
Asia he regarded with extreme aversion. Remember-

* Lord Canning to Mr. Vernon   † The same to the same, April 22,
Smith, August 8, 1856.—*MS.*   1856.—*MS.*

ing the fearful lessons of the Past, he determined not, of his own free will, to send a single man into Afghanistan; and he resisted the promptings of Ministers at home, when it was suggested to him somewhat prematurely that seasonable donatives might convert Dost Mahomed into an effective ally, willing and ready to apply a blister from the side of Candahar.

And when, at a later period, instructions came from England to supply the Ameer with arms and money and authority was given to the Governor-General to send a British Mission to Herat, he shrunk from acting upon the latter suggestion. "I do not purpose," he wrote, "to use the permission to send British officers to Herat. We know much too little of things there to justify this step, which would for certain be full of risk. The place is hard pressed by famine as well as by the enemy. Our officers could take with them no relief nor any promise of it, for we are not going to march to Herat ourselves, and we cannot afford to promise on the faith of the Ameer's performances."

But unwilling as was Lord Canning to adopt the measures, to which reference was made in these letters, he could not maintain this policy of non-interference in Afghanistan after the Home Government had determined upon the declaration of war against Persia. The year had scarcely dawned, when such an upshot began to be discussed as something of no very remote reality, and before Parliament had broken up and her Majesty's Ministers had dispersed for the autumn, the equipment of an expedition to the Persian Gulf had been decreed. The orders from Home were that all preparations should be made for the despatch of a military and naval expedition from

Bombay to the Persian Gulf; but that pending the progress of some further diplomacies in Europe, which might end in concessions, no actual start should be made. It was not until the end of September that her Majesty's Government, through the legal channel of the Secret Committee of the Court of Directors of the East India Company, sent out final instructions for the sailing of the expedition and the commencement of the war.* On the evening of the last day of October, these instructions reached the Governor-General in Calcutta, and on the following morning—day of evil omen, for eighteen years before it had delivered itself of the sad Afghan manifesto—a proclamation of war was issued. On the same day it was sent to Lord Elphinstone at Bombay, and the General in command was charged with instructions respecting the conduct of the expedition, and ordered straightway to begin.

The question of the command of the expedition had been one, which Lord Canning by no means found it easy to solve. Many names had been suggested to him, and among them that of General Windham—"Windham of the Redan"—who had performed feats of gallantry in the Crimea, and was ready for hard service in any part of the world.

margin notes: 1856.   November 1st.   The question of command.

---

* The orders were, under date July 22, 1856, that measures were to be "immediately taken at Bombay for the preparation of an expedition sufficiently powerful to occupy the island of Karrack in the Persian Gulf, and the district of Bushire on the mainland; but the expedition is not to sail until further orders shall have been received from this country." On the 26th of September the Secret Committee forwarded to Lord Canning copies of Lord Clarendon's instructions to the British Consuls in Persia to withdraw from that country, and of a letter addressed by his Lordship to the Commissioners for the Affairs of India, "requiring that the expedition, which will have been prepared, under instructions of the 22nd of July, shall, as soon as it can be completed, proceed to its destination in the Persian Gulf."

But Lord Canning, whilst thoroughly appreciating Windham's gallant services in the field, and knowing well that his appointment would be "popular in England," saw that there were strong reasons against it. "In a mixed force of Queen's and Company's troops," he said, "it is of great importance that there should be a willing and earnest co-operation of all subordinate officers with the Commander, and it is more difficult to obtain this for a stranger than for one who is known. The Commander should have some acquaintance with the Indian Army, if he has to lead a large force of it into an unknown and difficult country. He should know something of its constitution, temper, and details—of what it can and what it can not do. This would not be the case with Windham, fresh landed from England." And it is not to be doubted that he was right. If the force had been on a larger scale, the Commander-in-Chief himself might perhaps have been placed at its head; but Lord Canning, with the highest possible opinion of General Anson's fine temper, of the assiduity with which he had addressed himself to the business of his high office, and the ability with which he had mastered its details, had still some misgivings with respect to his prejudices, and doubted whether he had not formed certain conclusions unjust to the Company's Army.

On the whole, it was better, in any circumstances, that an Indian officer should command; and Lord Canning was resolute that such should be the arrangement. But he had been somewhat perplexed at first as to the choice to be made, and he had consulted Sir John Lawrence, as the man of all others who, not being by profession a soldier, had the finest soldierly instincts and the keenest appreciation of the essential qualities demanded for the command of such

an expedition. What the great Punjabee administrator said in reply was an utterance of good sense
and good feeling, the fulness of which, however, was
not then as discernible as it now is, viewed by the
light of intervening history. About the answer to be
given there was no doubt; but clearly there was some
difficulty. For the man whom of all men in India he
held to be best fitted for the work in hand was his
own brother, Sir Henry Lawrence; and if he could Henry
go, accompanied by Colonel Sydney Cotton, all would Lawrence.
be well. "Cotton," wrote John Lawrence to the
Governor-General, "is one of the best officers I have
seen in India. He is a thorough soldier, loves his
profession, and has considerable administrative talent.
Of all the officers I have noted, with one exception,
Sydney Cotton is the best." But his experiences,
great as they were, had not lain in the line of diplomatic action, and, if it were necessary, as Lawrence
believed, to unite the political and the military authority in the same person, Cotton, good soldier as he
was, might clearly lack some of the essential qualifications for the double office. So John Lawrence proceeded to say: "The man whom I would name for
the command of such an expedition is my brother
Henry. I can assure your lordship that I am not in
the slightest degree biased in his favour. He has
seen a good deal of service, having been in the first
Burmese war, in the second Afghan war, and in both
the Sutlej campaigns. He is not an officer of much
practical knowledge, except in his own branch (the
Artillery), and he is not fond of details. But, on the
other hand, he has great natural ability, immense
force of character, is very popular in his service, has
large political acumen, and much administrative
ability. I do not think that there is a military man

in India who is his equal in these points.   He is also in possession of his full vigour, both of mind and body, and there is not a good soldier of the Bengal Army, in the Punjab or perhaps in Upper India, but would volunteer to serve under him.   With him as the Commander, and Sydney Cotton as the Second-in-Command, the arrangement would be complete. Cotton is master of all technical details of every arm of the service, and devotes his entire energies and thoughts to the welfare of his soldiers."

All this might have been misunderstood; and a little man, in such a case, would perhaps have hesitated to recommend his brother; but John Lawrence knew that the advice was good, and that he was incapable of offering it, if it had not been.   "If I know myself," he wrote, "I would revolt against such conduct."   But though strong in the conviction that of all men living Henry Lawrence was the best suited to the work in hand, he was loud in his praise of other good officers, and had various plans to recommend, any one of which might have a successful issue.   If Sydney Cotton were sent in command, it would be well to associate with him such an officer as Herbert Edwardes, in the character of political adviser.   "But, in such matters," said John Lawrence, "unity in council and action is of the highest importance, and a commander who unites the military and political functions is most desirable.   If your lordship does not take my brother, and Outram is available, I would be inclined to recommend him.   I never met this officer; but he has a high reputation."   And John Jacob, as having much military ability and considerable political experience, was a man not to be overlooked in the account of available capacity for such an enterprise.

But not only in Calcutta and in the Punjab was this question of the command of the expedition being considered. It was well pondered at Bombay and in England, taking a shape eventually to overrule all other decisions. The expedition was to sail from Bombay, and all the arrangements for its organisation and equipment were proceeding there. Lord Elphin- stone was Governor of that Presidency. Twenty years before he had been Governor of Madras. At that time he was young, and not so serious and sedate as some people thought the head of a Government ought to be. " We want a Governor," it was said, somewhat bitterly, "and they send us a Guardsman; we want a statesman, and they send us a dancer." But he had ripened into what these people wanted, and now with a higher sense of the responsibilities of office, with a keener pleasure in his work, and a statesmanlike assiduity, for which the companions of his youth had not given him credit, he was, a second time, administering the affairs of an Indian Presidency, and busying himself with our external relations. The troops to be despatched, in the first instance, to the Persian Gulf were mainly Bombay troops, and it seemed fitting that the choice of a Commander should be made from the Bombay Army. If under stress of circumstance the war should assume more important dimensions, and the military force be proportionably extended, another selection might be made. But meanwhile, Elphinstone was requested to name some officer attached to his own Presidency, in whom the troops of all arms would have common confidence. So he named General Stalker, not without a pang of regret that he could not select Colonel Hancock—Hancock, the Adjutant-General of the Bombay Army—whom ill health was driving to England. Stalker was the senior of the available officers, so there were no heart-burnings from supersession; he had seen much service, he was experienced in command, and it was believed that the appointment would be both a popular and a safe one. "I hear favourable accounts of his good sense and temper," said Lord Canning; "and that is what is wanted for the service before him, which will require more of patient and enduring than of brilliant qualities."

So General Stalker was appointed to the command of the expedition to the Persian Gulf. But whilst these and other arrangements were being made in India, in the belief that ere long they would be merged into others of a more comprehensive character, the question of the chief command was being solved in England in a manner hardly anticipated by the Governor-General. In the month of May he had taken leave of Sir James Outram, with painful misgivings raised in his mind by the sight of the General's shattered frame and feeble bearing. He had suspected that the mischief was far greater than Outram himself acknowledged or believed, and thought that years must elapse before he would be fit again for active service. And so thought all his friends in England. He appeared among them as the wreck only of the strong man who had left them a short time before; and they grieved to see the too visible signs of weakness and suffering which every look and gesture afforded. The summer faded into autumn; but there was little change for the better apparent in his outer aspect, when suddenly they were startled by the announcement that he was about forthwith to proceed to the Persian Gulf and take command of the expedition.

Nobody knew, nobody knows, how it happened

that suddenly in this conjuncture, James Outram
shook off the incumbrances of disease, rose up from
the prostration of the sick-room, and stood erect,
active, robust before the world with the harness of
war on his back. It was the autumnal season, when
men scatter and disperse themselves in strange places,
and elude in a vagrant life the rumours of the distant
world; so there were many friends who, having left
him at the summer's close a feeble invalid, were struck
with a strange surprise when, returned or returning
homewards, they were met by the news that Outram
had gone or was going to Persia to take command of
the invading force. The wonder soon gave place to
delight; for they knew that though he was moved by
strong ambitions, there was ever within him a sense
of duty still stronger, and that on no account would
he jeopardise the interests of the State by taking upon
himself responsibilities which he had not full assurance
in his inmost self of his ample competence to discharge. And so it was. The sound of the distant
strife had rekindled all his smouldering energies.
There was work to be done, and he felt that he could
do it. On the pleasant Brighton esplanade, sauntering alone meditative, or perhaps in the stimulating
companionship of a stalwart friend and high functionary, the Chairman of the Court of Directors of the Colonel
East India Company, Master of Masters, new hopes Sykes.
were wafted upon him with the sea-breezes, and his
step grew firmer, his carriage more erect, as with
strong assurance of support from Leadenhall-street,
he resolved to tender his services to her Majesty's
Government for employment in Persia with a joint
military and diplomatic command.

This was at the beginning of the last week of
October. On the 26th he wrote to Lord Canning

that he purposed returning to India by the mail of the 20th of December, " having perfectly recovered from the illness which drove him home." And he added, "In the supposition that I may be more usefully employed with the army about to proceed to Persia than necessary to your lordship in Oude, where everything is progressing so satisfactorily, I have offered my services to the President (of the Board of Control), should it be deemed advisable to entrust to me diplomatic powers in conjunction with the military command, and I believe that, should your lordship be disposed so to employ me, the home authorities would not object. In that case your lordship's commands would meet me at Aden, whence I would at once proceed to Bombay."*

This letter reached Calcutta on the 2nd December. By the outgoing mail of the 8th, Lord Canning wrote to Outram at Aden, rejoicing in his complete recovery, " on every account, public and private," but questioning the policy of the Persian appointment. The expedition, he said, was not likely to increase in magnitude; it was not probable that there would be any operations beyond the seaboard during the winter, or that any diplomatic action would be taken to call for the employment of a high political functionary; if, indeed, overtures were to be made, they would most probably be addressed through some friendly power to London; there would be little scope, therefore, for his services with the Persian expedition, and it would be better, therefore, that he should return to his old appointment. "Oude is completely tranquil," wrote Lord Canning, " and generally prospering. Nevertheless,

* So full was Outram at this time of the thought of his departure in December, and so eager for the advent of the happy day of release, that he dated this letter "December" instead of October.

I shall be very glad to see you resume your command there." The fact was that the Administration was by this time plunged into such a hopeless condition of internecine strife, that the Governor-General could in no way see any outlet of escape from the perplexities besetting him except by the removal of Chief-Commissioner Jackson; and now here was the opportunity, for which he had been waiting, to accomplish this end in an easy natural manner, without any official scandal, or the infliction of any personal pain.

But it was not to be so accomplished. Before the end of November the question of Outram's command of the Persian expedition had been fully discussed in the English Cabinet. Downing-street had laid fast hold of the idea, and pronounced its full satisfaction with it. Her Majesty the Queen had stamped the commission with the seal of her approbation, and the public voice, with one accord, had proclaimed that a good thing had been done, and that the right man would soon be in the right place. That it was thus virtually settled, past recal, went out, under the President's hand by the mail of the 26th of November, and greeted Lord Canning with the new year. In official language, however, of Court of Directors, or Secret Committee thereof, it took the shape not of an announcement of a thing done, but of a recommendation that it should be done; for it was substantially an interference with the prerogative of the Governor-General, and was to be softened down so as in no wise to give offence. But Lord Canning was not a man, in such a case, to raise a question of privilege, or, assured that it was, actually or presumedly, for the official good, to shoot out any porcupine-quills from his wounded official dignity. He took the interference in good part; thanked the Chairman for the delicacy with which it had been communicated, and promised to give Outram his best support. He had doubted, he said, whether Outram's health and strength would be sufficient to bear the burdens that would be imposed upon him. "But the Queen's Government," he continued, "and the Secret Committee have seen him in recovered health, and if they are satisfied that he is in a condition to undertake the labour and trial of such a command, without risk to the interest confided to him, I have no objection to make, nor any wish to shake myself clear of responsibility." And then, with a reference to a memorandum on the future conduct of the campaign which Outram had drawn up in England, the Governor-General added, "It is a pleasure to me to declare that I have been greatly struck by all that has proceeded from General Outram in regard to future operations in Persia. I think his plans excellent, prudent for the present, and capable of easy expansion hereafter, and the means which he proposes for carrying them out for the most part well suited. For everything that I have yet heard of his proposals he shall have my cordial support."

1857. Whilst the first division of the expeditionary force
Central-Asian under Stalker was commencing operations with good
Policy. success in the Persian Gulf, the new year found Outram at Bombay superintending the despatch of the second. But it was not only by these movements from the sea-board that an impression was now to be made on the fears of the Court of Teheran. Diplomácy was to do its work in the country which lay between India and Persia. Reluctant as he had been, in the earlier part of the year, to commit himself to any decided course of Central-Asian policy, Lord Canning now began to discern more clearly

the benefits that might arise from a friendly alliance with the Ameer of Caubul. There was no longer any chance of a pacific solution of our difficulties. War had been proclaimed. Herat had fallen. Dost Mahomed had put forth plentiful indications of a strong desire for an English alliance; and the English Government at home appeared to be not unwilling to meet his wishes. That some action must now be taken in that direction was certain. Already had arms and money been sent into Afghanistan; but with no specific undertaking on the one side or the other, and it appeared desirable to put the matter now upon a more secure and a more dignified footing than that of temporary shifts and expedients. But there were great diversities of opinion as to the shape which should be taken by British action in the Afghan countries. Lord Canning had always had at least one clear conception about the matter; that it was better to do little than to do much, and wise not to do that little a day sooner than was needed. The terrible lessons which had been burnt into us fifteen years before had lost none of their significance. The warning voice was still sounding in our ears; the saving hand was still beckoning us away from those gloomy passes. It could never again enter into our imaginations to conceive the idea of turning back the tide of Russo-Persian invasion by making war against the national will and the substantive Government of the Afghans. But the monitions of the Past did not stop there. They cautioned us against ever sending a single British regiment across the Afghan frontier. Neither the Princes nor the People of Afghanistan were to be trusted, if the memories of their wrongs were to be reawakened within them by the presence of that which had done them such grievous harm.

So, although among the schemes which were discussed, and in some military quarters advocated, was
the project of an auxiliary British force, acting in
close alliance with the Afghans, it was never for a
moment seriously entertained in the Council Chamber.   But to assail Persia in some measure from that
side, whilst we were operating upon the sea-board;
to recover Herat, and, at the same time, to occupy
some of the littoral provinces of the Persian Empire;
was doubtless to put enormous pressure upon the
Shah, to hold him, as it were, in a vice, helpless and
agonised, and to extort from him all that we might
want.   This, peradventure, might be done, by con-
tinuing to send British bayonets into Afghanistan,
but without, as of old, British valour to wield them;
so many thousands of stands of arms, not so many
thousands of soldiers; and British money, lakhs
upon lakhs, but no British hands to dispense it.   In
a word, if we could manage successfully to subsidise
Dost Mahomed, and hold him, by the bonds of self-
interest, to a friendly covenant, whereby, whilst aiding us he would aid himself, we might bring the war
much more rapidly to a conclusion than if no such
alliance were formed.

Dost
Mahomed.
   But there were strong doubts of the good faith of
Dost Mahomed.   The wily old Ameer, it was said,
was waiting upon the shore of circumstance, willing
to sail in the same boat with us, if tide and stream
should be in our favour and a fair wind setting in
for success.   For some time, there had been going on
between the Governor-General of India and the
Ruler of Caubul certain passages of diplomatic
coquetry, which had resulted rather in a promise
of a close alliance, a kind of indefinite betrothal,
than in the actual accomplishment of the fact.   We

had condoned the offence committed by the Ameer at the close of the last war in the Punjab, when he had sent some of his best troops, in the uniforms of our own slaughtered soldiers, to aid the Sikhs in their efforts to expel us; and whilst Dalhousie was still the ruler of India, an engagement of general amity had been negotiated by John Lawrence on the one side, and Hyder Khan on the other, between the English and the Afghans. It was probably intended, with a forecast of the coming rupture with Persia, that this should in time be expanded into a more definite treaty with Dost Mahomed; and more than two years before the occasion actually arose, the subsidising of the Ameer loomed in the distance.* It was an old idea. Mr. Henry Ellis had entertained it; Sir John M'Neill had entertained it;[†] and if Lord Auckland's Secretaries had' allowed him to entertain it, it is probable that the events of which I am about to write would never have afforded me a subject of History. In an hour of miserable infatuation, we had played the perilous game of King-making, and had forced an unpopular pageant upon

1849.

March 30, 1855.

---

* It was talked of, indeed, before the compact of 1855, but did not form a part of it. In 1854 (June 19), Sir Henry Lawrence wrote to the author: "I fancy that we shall have some sort of Treaty with Dost Mahomed, unless Lord Dalhousie overreach himself by too great anxiety and by agreeing to pay him a subsidy. If Persia attack Afghanistan, the help we should give the latter should be by attacking Persia from the Gulf. We should not send a rupee or a man into Afghanistan. We should express readiness to forgive and forget, to cry quits in Afghan matters, and pledge ourselves to live as good neighbours in future; but there ought to be no interference beyond the passes, and no backing of one party or another."

† One passage in Sir John M'Neill's early correspondence I cannot help quoting. There is rare prescience in it: "Dost Mahomed Khan, with a little aid from us, could be put in possession of both Candahar and Herat. I anxiously hope that aid will not be withheld. A loan of money would probably enable him to do this, and would give us a great hold upon him. . . . Until Dost Mahomed or some other Afghan shall have got both Candahar and Herat into his hands, our position here must continue to be a false one."

a reluctant people. Now, after bitter experience, we were reverting to the first conception of our diplomatists; but mild as comparatively the interference was, it was held by some great authorities to be wiser to leave Afghanistan and the Afghans altogether alone. In spite of the present benefit to be derived from applying in that quarter a blister to the side of Persia, it might be better to suffer the old Ameer to make the most of the crisis after his own fashion. He would not fight our battles for us without substantial help; but he might fight his own, and there could be no time, for the extension of his dominion to Herat, so opportune as that which saw Persia entangled in a war with England. But Dost Mahomed had too clear a knowledge of the English, and Afghan cupidity was too strong within him, to suffer this gratuitous co-operation. He knew that, if he waited, we should purchase his aid; so he magnified the difficulties of the march to Herat, talked of the deficiency of his resources, and otherwise pretended that he lacked strength for a successful enterprise without continuous pecuniary aid from the English. Whether, having received such assistance from us, he would render effectual service in return for it, seemed to some of our Indian statesmen extremely doubtful, for there was the lowest possible estimate in their minds of Afghan truth and Afghan honour. There was the fear that the old Ameer would set an extravagant price on his services, and that by disappointing his expectations, if not scouting his pretensions, we might inopportunely excite his animosities against us. Some, indeed, thought that he looked eagerly to the conjuncture as one that might help him to realise his old day-dream, the recovery of Peshawur. There was, in truth, no lack of sagacity in these anticipations; but, perhaps, at the bottom of them there lay too deep a distrust of the personal character of the Ameer. He had, in all candour it must be admitted, too much reason to doubt the good faith of the English. He could fathom the depths of our selfishness as well as we could fathom the depths of his guile. In truth, there were causes of mutual suspicion; and little good was likely to come from the distant fencing of diplomatic correspondence. So at last it was resolved to test the sincerity of the Ameer by inviting him to a conference on the frontier.

At that time, Herbert Edwardes, he of whose Herbert glorious youthful impulses I have spoken in the first Edwardes. chapter of this work, was Commissioner of Peshawur. He had grown, by good-service brevet, rather than by the slow process of regimental promotion, from Lieutenant to Lieutenant-Colonel. His career had been a prosperous one, and its prosperity was well deserved. The great reputation which he had gained as an ambitious subaltern, brought down upon him at one time a shower of small jealousies and detractions. He had been feasted and flattered in England, and there were some who, doubtless, with a certain self-consciousness of what would be likely to flow from such adulations, said that his head was turned, and that he had been overrated. But one, the noble helpmate of a truly noble man, wrote to me at this Honoria time, as one, however, not doubting, for I had like Lawrence. faith, that Herbert Edwardes was one of Nature's true nobility, and that surely I should live to know it. It was right. Under the Lawrences, Henry and John, both of whom he dearly loved, he grew to be one of the main-pillars of the Punjabee Administration; and now' he was in charge of that part of the

old dominions of Runjit Singh which lay beyond
the Indus; the Proconsulate of Peshawur. Planted
thus upon the frontier of Afghanistan, it was one of
his special duties to watch the progress of events in
that country, and duly to report upon them to the
higher authorities. Of direct diplomatic action there
had been little or none; but no one knew what a
day might produce, and it was ever therefore among
the responsibilities of the Peshawur Commissioner to
be well versed in the politics of Caubul, and prepared, in any conjuncture, to counsel the course to be
taken by the British Government.

For some time there had been much to observe
and much to report, and now a conjuncture had
arisen, which seemed to require from us that we
should act. Persia was doing all that could be done
to enlist the sympathies of Central Asia on her side,
even in the far off regions of Bokhara and Kokund,
by sending abroad, as a proof of the dangers of English friendship, copies of the pro-Christian Firman
of the Sultan, which had been issued at the close of
the Russian war. It was fortunate, therefore, that at
this time the political animosities of the Afghans
were strongly excited against the Persians, for, perhaps, under such pressure, the chronic sectarian jealousies which kept the two nations apart might for a
while have been merged in a common religious
hatred of the Feringhees. A very little done, or left
undone on our part, to offend the old Ameer, might
have lost to us for ever the only serviceable Mahomedan alliance that could have availed us in such a
crisis. To no man was the value of this alliance so
apparent as to Herbert Edwardes; no man pressed
its importance so earnestly upon the Governor-General. He believed that Dost Mahomed would respond

with pleasure to an invitation to meet on the
frontier of the two States a representative of the
British Government, and to discuss the terms of a
friendly alliance; and he recommended that this invitation should be sent to him. Reluctant as Lord
Canning had been in the earlier part of the year to
commit himself to any decided course of Afghan
policy, he now before the close of it, in the altered
circumstances that had arisen, yielded to this suggestion, and afterwards, with that frankness which sat
so becomingly upon him, gracefully acknowledged
its wisdom, and thanked the suggester.

So Dost Mahomed was invited to a conference at
Peshawur. He was, if willing to meet the representatives of the British Government, to discuss personally with them the terms of the alliance. Either
Sir John Lawrence, accompanied by Colonel Edwardes, or Colonel Edwardes alone, as might be determined between them, was to meet the old Ameer
on the frontier, to feel his pulse, and to prescribe
accordingly. It would have been a great opportunity for the younger man; but Edwardes, to whom
the decision was left by Lawrence, for ever giving
the lie to all that had been charged against him on
the score of vanity and self-assertion, strongly urged
that the Mission should be headed by his beloved
Chief. Lawrence much doubting, however, whether
the Ameer would come, and little expecting a successful issue if he should come, lauded the magna-
nimity of his more sanguine friend, and prepared
himself with all the earnestness of his nature to prove
the groundlessness of his own anticipations of failure.

They were groundless. The Ameer accepted the
invitation, marched down with two of his sons, some
of his chosen counsellors, and a body of picked troops,

2 F

January 1,
1857.
to the frontier; and on the first day of the new year received in the Khybur Pass the first visit of the British Commissioners. It was with no common interest that Lawrence, Edwardes, Sydney Cotton, and the other English officers who accompanied them, looked into the face of the old Ameer, whose white beard and venerable aspect had, fifteen years before, been so familiar to the eyes of the dwellers in Calcutta, and who in his fallen fortunes, half-prisoner and half-guest, had been a not unworthy object of our sympathies. When, nearly half a century before, the representatives of the British Government had been received almost on the same spot by Shah Soojah, they had found the Caubul ruler arrayed in gorgeous apparel, his whole person a blaze of jewellery, with the Koh-i-noor outshining it all; but the English gentlemen now saw before them only a hale old man, very simply attired in a garment of the coarse camel-hair of the country. They found him full of energy, full of sagacity; courteous and friendly in his outer manner; glad to welcome them to his camp. It was only a visit of ceremony; repaid, two days later, by the Ameer, who was received in the grand English style near Peshawur. Our troops formed a street more than a mile long, and after the Durbar marched past the Ameer and his host in review order. More than seven thousand British fighting men were assembled there, and among them were three complete European regiments, whose steady discipline, and solidity, and fine soldierly bearing, made a strong impression on the minds of the Afghan visitors, from the aged Ameer himself to the youngest trooper of his escort.

The formal interviews thus accomplished, the serious business of the conference commenced on the

5th of January. The Ameer had pitched his Camp at Jumrood, and there Lawrence and Edwardes visited him, accompanied by Major Lumsden of the Guides. Dost Mahomed, his sons standing behind him, and a few chosen Sirdars on his left, opened the discussions with a long exposition of the recent struggles in Herat, and of the policy which he had himself pursued. He had entertained no schemes of conquest embracing that principality. The movements which the Persians had thus pretended to interpret were directed only towards Candahar. But he frankly avowed his eager longing to recover Herat; and, please God and the English, he would take it from the Persians. Swearing by Allah and the Prophet that, from that time, he would be our friend, let all the world be against him, he declared, as his enthusiasm kindled, that let the English but make a diversion in the Persian Gulf and supply him with money and with arms, he would mine the walls of Herat, blow up the towers, and take the place at the point of the sword; or raise such a flame in the surrounding country as fairly to burn the Persians out of it. The Toorcomans and the Usbegs would rise at his bidding, and join against a common foe.

From that distant-frontier post, on the very outskirts of our empire, the telegraphic wires ran right up to the vice-regal capital, and the Governor-General and the Chief Commissioner were corresponding by the "lightning post" between Calcutta and Peshawur. So it happened that whilst John Lawrence and Dost Mahomed were in conference, a horseman galloped up with a message from the former, despatched on the preceding day. In it Lord Canning told Lawrence that a reinforcement of five thousand men would be sent as quickly as possible to the Persian

1857 Gulf; and that amongst the conditions of Peace with Persia would be a stipulation that she should withdraw her troops from Herat, and renounce for ever her pretensions to interfere with Afghanistan. The significant words, "You may make use of this," were included in the message. But the time had not then come for the best use to be made of it; so John Lawrence, reserving the rest for more opportune disclosure, announced only that the reinforcements were about to be despatched to the Gulf. It was his design, at that first meeting, to elicit the views and intentions of the Ameer rather than to disclose those of his own Government.* So, making no promises of any kind, he indicated the difficulties that seemed to lie in the way of the Afghan ruler, and asked for a recital of the means and resources, by which they were to be overcome, already at his disposal, and the extent of the aid which he would require from the English. But this was too momentous a question to be answered, without much thought and calculation; so the Ameer, seeking time for deliberation, said that he would unfold his views fully at the next meeting; and so the conference broke up for the day.

January 7, 1857.   On the 7th, Dost Mahomed, attended by a few chosen counsellors, visited the British Camp, and the conferences were renewed in the Chief Commissioner's tent. Pursuing the old process of drawing-out, John Lawrence, at the outset, reminded the Ameer of his

---

* This course, though doubtless the one that would have suggested itself to John Lawrence's unaided judgment, was expressly dictated by Lord Canning, who had written on the 2nd of December to the Chief Commissioner, saying, "It is not certain that our object will continue the same as the Ameer's; neither is it certain to what extent the Ameer can contribute towards it, even whilst it continues the same. For these reasons, it is necessary first that we should know what he can do; and next, that we should come to a clear understanding as to the conditions upon which he shall receive aid in doing it. The meeting ought to clear up the first point at once."—*MS. Correspondence.*

promise to state fully his views and intentions; but it required some resolution and perseverance to keep the old Afghan to this point, and it was not without difficulty that the promised revelation was extorted from him. At last he explained that, owing to the state of the season, he could not commence his march on Herat until after the expiration of a period of two months; grass and young grain would then be springing up, and with the aid of some not very elaborate commissariat arrangements, he would be able to find provisions for his troops; that he proposed to march one column from Balkh and another from Candahar. The muster-roll of his troops showed some thirty-five thousand men and sixty guns. These, he said, should be raised to fifty thousand men with a hundred guns; four-fifths of the men and nearly the whole of the guns should, he said, be moved upon Herat. "But," he added, "if you say take more troops, I will take more; if you say less will suffice, I will take less. I have given you my own opinion, but you Sahibs know Persia best." But when pressed for a statement of the amount of aid he would require, he said, that on the morrow morning his son, Azim Jah, would wait upon the English gentlemen with all the required information in a digested form, in order that they might judge for themselves.

So the conference broke up; and on the following day the Ameer's sons, accompanied by a few of his ministers, waited upon John Lawrence, and laid before him a detailed statement of the finances of Afghanistan, and of the military resources of the empire; together with an estimate of the aid that would be required from the English to enable the Afghans to drive the Persians out of Herat, and to hold their own against all comers. The aid that was thus sought amounted in money to sixty-four lakhs of rupees a year, whilst the war lasted, and in munitions to more than fifty guns, eight thousand stands of small arms, and ammunition at discretion. It was more than the English Government were likely to be willing to give, but not more than appeared really to be wanted. The largeness of the demand, however, suggested the idea of a less extensive enterprise; and so Lawrence asked what would be required to enable the Afghans, abandoning all aggressive movements, to hold their own, without danger of encroachments from the westward. The question was not a welcome one. The Afghans were hot for an advance on Herat. If they were to sit down within their own dominions, the Persians would assuredly occupy Furrah. It was for the English, of course, to decide upon the course to be pursued, but it was more in accordance with the genius and temper of the Afghans to take vigorous action in advance. Still, however, John Lawrence pressed for a statement of the requirements of the Afghans if a strictly defensive policy were maintained. The Sirdars could give no answer without consulting the Ameer, so the conference broke up; and next day they returned with the statement that, in addition to what had already been supplied, four thousand muskets would be required, and money to pay eight thousand regular troops; one-half to be employed in the Candahar country, and the other half in Balkh. But still they were eager for the larger enterprise; and one of them whispered to Edwardes that the enmity between the Afghans and the Persians was not merely an affair of this world, for that Sheeahs and Soonees must always hate each other in the world to come. There was nothing more now to be said. The Afghans, on their part, had made known their wishes; and all the English gentlemen could say in reply was, that they would at once communicate with their Government.

So the telegraphic wires were again set in motion, and the substance of what had passed at the two last meetings was communicated to the Governor-General at Calcutta. Then there was doubt in the Council Chamber. Would it be better to await detailed reports from Peshawur by post, or at once to send telegraphic instructions to Sir John Lawrence? The former course was determined upon, and a message to that effect despatched to Peshawur. Lawrence had sent in detailed reports of the meetings, and had added to the last an expression of his own views as to what should be done. He recommended that assistance on the larger scale, for the siege of Herat, should not be given to Dost Mahomed, but that we should give him the four thousand muskets that he required, and an annual subsidy of twelve lakhs of rupees, so long as England and Persia might be at war with each other. But it did not seem to him to be wise to await the slow process of correspondence by letter. The Ameer was eager to depart; and some time must be necessarily occupied in the negotiation of a formal agreement. So Lawrence telegraphed the substance of his recommendation to Calcutta, urged that nothing would be gained by awaiting his more detailed reports, and asked permission to communicate to the Ameer the proposal which he thought it best to make. To this a message was promptly returned, saying: "You may tell the Ameer that the terms are agreed to. Four thousand stand of arms and twelve lakhs a year, whilst England is at war with Persia. You will proceed to arrange the articles of agreement and report them by telegraph."

This message was despatched on the 13th of January. On the following morning Lawrence and Edwardes proceeded to Dost Mahomed's camp, and unfolded to him the views and intentions of the British Government. With less appearance of disappointment than had been expected, the Ameer assented to the abandonment of the expedition to Herat, and accepted the modified proposal of the English. But the despatch of. a party of British officers to Caubul, which was to form part of the agreement, appeared to be distasteful to him. When active offensive warfare against Persia had been contemplated, he cherished the thought of their presence with his troops; but now the state of affairs was altered. The point, however, was one not to be yielded. If the British were to give the subsidy, they were entitled to see it rightly appropriated. Then the Ameer lowered his tone, and said that he was ready to do what was expedient; and finally he agreed to all that was proposed. But next day, when his son Azim Khan, accompanied by other chiefs, visited, according to agreement, the English Commissioners, to settle the precise terms of agreement, the question of the Mission to Caubul was reopened. It was urged that the appearance of British officers at the Afghan capital might compromise the Ameer either with his own people or with his English friends. There would be danger in their path at Caubul; but at Candahar, threatened by the Persians, their presence would be better understood, and they might abide in perfect security. Nearly fifteen years had passed since our retributive Army had set its mark upon the Afghan capital; but still the hatred which our usurpation had engendered was fresh in the minds of the people, and. Dost Mahomed knew that

there were those in Caubul whom he could not trust
within reach of an English throat. It was a sad
thought; and Lawrence could not but ask how the
alliance between the two nations could ever strike
deep root when in one country such suspicions and
animosities were never suffered to sleep. What the
English wanted was not a temporary alliance dictated by an emergency of self-interest, but an enduring friendship based upon mutual confidence and
respect. But Dost Mahomed knew the Afghans well,
and little wisdom would there have been in disregarding a warning which every Englishman's heart
must have told him was an utterance of the voice of
truth. So it was resolved that, although we should
claim, and duly record, our right to send British
officers to Caubul, as to other parts of Afghanistan,
yet that practically the Mission should, in the first
instance, proceed only to Candahar. It was better
than that our officers should be smuggled into the
capital, surrounded by the Ameer's troops, virtually
prisoners under the name of protected guests. There
was, at all events, some definite meaning in their
proceeding to the more western city, for it was a
better point from which to observe the movements of
the Persians. But what route were they to take?
It was the Ameer's wish that the Mission should proceed by way of the Bolan Pass; but this, although
the route by which Shah Soojah and the Army of
the Indus had marched into Afghanistan, was said to
be entering the country by a back door. It was,
therefore, finally determined that the Mission should
proceed by way of the Paiwar Pass,* an unexplored

* "It was deemed advisable that
the Mission should journey to Candahar by the route of the Paiwar
Pass, a road that had never before
been traversed by Europeans, and
was consequently unknown ground,
and full of interest to the British in
a military point of view, as being one

road, to Candahar; and that Major Henry Lumsden, of the Guide corps, an officer of great courage and capacity, versed in the politics of Afghanistan, who had been marked from the first for the conduct of this enterprise, should be placed at its head. His brother, Lieutenant Peter Lumsden, was to accompany him, and Mr. Henry Bellew was selected to take medical charge of the Mission; a post of more importance than it appears to be in an official gazette, for in such diplomacies as these the Medicine-chest and the Lancet are often more serviceable than the Portfolio and the Pen.

On the 26th of January, the Articles of Agreement, having by the aid of the telegraph been approved by the Government at Calcutta, were ready for seal and signature; and a meeting for the conclusion of the compact was held in Dost Mahomed's tent. In attendance on the Ameer were his son Azim Khan and several of his chief counsellors, whilst Lawrence, Edwardes, and Lumsden appeared on behalf of the English. Written in Persian and in English, the articles of agreement were read aloud in Durbar. By these the Ameer engaged to maintain a force of eighteen thousand men; to allow British officers to be stationed at Caubul, Candahar, or Balkh, or wherever Afghan troops might be posted; to receive a Wakeel at Caubul, and to send one to Calcutta; and to communicate to the Government of India any overtures that he might receive from Persia and from the Allies of Persia during the war. On their part, the English undertook, during the continuance of hostilities, to pay to the Ameer a monthly subsidy of a lakh of rupees, to send him

of the approaches by which an invading force from the West might enter and attack their Indian Empire."—*Bellew's Journal of a Political Mission to Afghanistan in* 1857.

four thousand stands of arms, and, as if the wrong 1857. done had been all against us, to forget and forgive the past. It was explained that the British officers would in the first instance proceed to Candahar; and with this assurance the Ameer was satisfied. So the Articles of Agreement were signed and sealed. Then came some discussion and some interchange of compliments. A message from the Governor-General had been received by telegraph, desiring Sir John Lawrence to express to Dost Mahomed "the satisfaction which he had derived from his frank dealing, and from the clear understanding on which affairs had been placed," together with the best wishes for his health and long life, and a word of regret that he had not himself been able to meet the Ameer. The message was now delivered and received with manifest gratification. It would have delighted him, he said, to meet Lord Canning, but he could not expect his Lordship to take so long a journey to see him. He had known two Governor-Generals, Lord Auckland and Lord Ellenborough, who had been kind to him in old times; he remembered also with gratitude the kindness of two other English gentlemen, Mr. Wilberforce Bird and Mr. Thoby Prinsep,* who had paid him much attention in Calcutta. "And now," he said, in conclusion, "I have made an alliance with the British Government, and come what may, I will keep it till death." And the promise thus given was never broken. He was true to the English alliance to the last.

On the following day a Durbar was held in the January 27, Camp of the British Commissioner, and the chief 1857. officers of the Ameer's suite attended to take their leave of the English gentlemen. Dost Mahomed had

* Then members of the Supreme Council of India.

excused himself on the plea of age and infirmity. The visit to Peshawur, with its attendant anxieties and excitements, had visibly affected the Ameer's health. The hale old man, who, three or four weeks before, had spent hours in the saddle, and seemed to be full of health and energy, had lost much of his bodily vigour and his elasticity of spirit. A sharp attack of gout had prostrated him; and he seemed to be growing impatient under his protracted detention in Camp. So the conclusion of the Terms of Agreement was a manifest relief to him; and it was with no common satisfaction that, on the day following the Farewell Durbar, he set his face towards Jellalabad, carrying with him, in bills on Caubul, a lakh of rupees and some costly presents from the British Government.*

Nor was the gratification experienced at this time confined to the Ameer's camp. Lawrence and Edwardes were well pleased to think that all had gone off so smoothly; that the friendship of the Afghans had been secured at no very extravagant cost; and that, on the whole, although Dost Mahomed had not obtained all that he had asked, he had taken his departure tolerably well satisfied with the favourable issue of the meeting. Lord Canning, too, was more than well satisfied with the manner in which the negotiations had been conducted, and with the apparent result. He was one not stinting in free outspoken expressions of praise and gratitude to those who did good service to his Government; and, both

---

* The only present made by the Afghan ruler to his allies consisted of a batch of wretched horses, all of which, John Lawrence wrote, were spavined or worn out. The whole were sold for not more than 100*l.* Perhaps Dost Mahomed, remember- ing the "pins and needles" brought by Burnes, which had caused so much disappointment some twenty years before at Caubul, did not expect, on this occasion, to be the recipient of anything more valuable.

in public and private letters, he cordially thanked the Commissioners, even before their work was done, for the admirable judgment and good tact which they had displayed at the conferences; giving an especial word of thanks to Edwardes as the original suggester of the meeting,* and, it might have been added, the originator of the new policy which had more recently been observed towards the Afghans. To Major Lumsden he wrote, at the same time, a letter of kindly encouragement and good advice, cordially approving the selection, " not only from his trust in Sir John Lawrence's judgment on such matters, but from everything that the Governor-General had been able to hear of Lumsden from those who knew him." He knew the power of such words; as a statesman he felt assured that they would bear good fruit; but as a man he uttered them from the kindness of his heart.

So Dost Mahomed set his face towards Caubul, and Sir John Lawrence, after a month of administrative journeying about the province, returned to Lahore. It need be no subject of surprise if the latter, as he went about his work, thinking of all that had been done at Peshawur, sometimes asked himself, What good? and wished that the monthly lakh of rupees to be expended on the Afghan Army were available

---

* " I must ask you," wrote Lord Canning to Colonel Edwardes on the 19th of January, " to accept my best thanks for the part you have taken in the recent negotiations, and for their satisfactory issue. I feel the more bound to do this, because the first suggestion of a meeting came from you; and so far as I can judge from the reports as yet received, and from the tone of the discussion shown in them, I believe that the suggestion has proved a very wise and useful one. It would be a good thing if all diplomatic conferences were conducted so satisfactorily, and set forth as lucidly as these have been." All this was well deserved; for the policy was emphatically Edwardes's policy; he had been the first to recommend, in Lord Dalhousie's time, that we should try the effect of trusting the Afghans, and his recommendations had resulted in the general compact of 1855.

for the improvement of the province under his charge; for he had never liked the project from the beginning. He had no faith in Dost Mahomed. He had detected him in at least one palpable falsehood, and the detection had excited in the Ameer no sense of shame, but rather a feeling of admiration at the clever incredulity of the Feringhees. The expulsion of the Persians from Herat, or even the raising of the Turcoman tribes, was, in Lawrence's opinion, so far beyond the power of the Ameer, that he believed, on the other hand, that the Persians would have little difficulty in seizing Candahar. This belief in the weakness of Dost Mahomed was based upon a somewhat exaggerated estimate of the disunion among the chief people of the country. But even if the Ameer had the power, Lawrence could not believe that he had the will to serve the British; and he doubted, therefore, whether the subsidy would produce any tangible results. As to the question of the future of Herat, it had never even approached a solution. Dost Mahomed had been assured that the evacuation of the place by the Persians would be an essential condition of peace; but he had not been able to offer, without manifest doubt and hesitation, any suggestion as to the best means of providing for its future government. In truth, there was a lack of available capacity in the direction in which it was most natural that we should look for a new ruler. When the Ameer was asked if there was any member of Yar Mahomed's family to whom the government could be entrusted, he replied that there was a brother of Syud Mahomed, but that, if possible, he was a greater reprobate and a greater fool than that unlucky chief. Syud Mahomed, however, had left a

son, a boy of some ten years, in whose name a competent Wuzeer might administer the affairs of the
principality ; but a competent Wuzeer was not to be
found more readily than a competent Prince. The
future of Herat was, therefore, left to the development of the Chapter of Accidents. In the mean
while, Lord Canning, though he had slowly come to
this point, believed that the subsidising of the Ameer
was not a bad stroke of policy. It bound the Afghan
ruler by strong ties of self-interest to remain faithful
to the British Government. Even neutrality was
great gain at a time when Persia was doing her best
to raise a fervour of religious hatred against the
English throughout all the countries of Central Asia.
The very knowledge, indeed, of the fact that Dost
Mahomed had gone down to Peshawur to negotiate a
closer alliance with the British, must have had a
moral effect at Teheran by no means conducive to an
increased confidence in the Shah's powers of resistance. Altogether, it was not an inefficacious, whilst
comparatively it was an inexpensive, mode of pressing
upon Persia from the side of Afghanistan. But whilst
he went thus far, Lord Canning was resolute to go
no farther. He had made up his mind that the independence of Herat could be written only on sand ;
that the waves of circumstance from one direction or
another must utterly efface it after a while ; and that
it would be wiser to abandon an effort that was so
fraught with tribulation, and so sure to result in
failure. Certain he was that nothing would ever induce him to send a single regiment into Afghanistan
to maintain the integrity of a petty state, which
Nature seemed to have intended to be a part of
Persia or a part of Afghanistan, and which, as in a

national and religious sense it assuredly belonged to the latter, was certain, if left to itself, eventually to fall into the right hands.*

Whilst thus, in this first month of the new year, Lord Canning was eagerly watching the progress of his foreign policy, he was grappling with the great difficulty which beset his internal administration. The question of the Persian command had been settled; but it unsettled, by its solution, that other question of the Oude Commissionership. It was clearer than ever that Jackson must be removed; but it was no longer possible that his tenure of office should come to a natural end and peacefully die out. It was necessary to lay violent hands upon it, and bring it to an ignominious close. The necessity was painful to Lord Canning; but the interests of the State demanded it, and the Governor-General, in such a case, properly overrode the man. Therefore, as Outram could not quietly resume his old seat, another officer was to be found to take the place of Commissioner Jackson. Ample admissions were there of zeal and ability, of assiduous devotion to public business, of much good work well done in the province; but the tone and temper of the man, his contentious spirit, his insolent treatment of his colleagues, were past bear-

* Dost Mahomed and his counsellors, during the conferences at Peshawur, frequently asserted that Persia had, on this as on a former occasion, been instigated and aided by Russia to occupy Herat. I can discern no evidence of this. Prince Gortschakoff assured Lord Granville at Moscow that the Russian minister at Teheran had urged the Persian Government to evacuate Herat, and so to place themselves in a better position to demand from others a like observance of treaty obligations. It may be noted here, that the Ameer told Lawrence at Peshawur that he would show him the letter which the unfortunate Russian diplomatist, Viktcvitch, had carried with him to Caubul from the Government of the Czar. But he did not produce it after all.

ing; and communication to that effect, with notice of appointment of a successor, was made to him in due course.

The choice was an admirable one. It has been said that in the spring of 1856, Sir Henry Lawrence had offered his services to the Governor-General, to officiate as Chief Commissioner of Oude, in Outram's absence, and that the first disaster that befel Lord Canning was that the offer was received too late.[*] When Henry Lawrence found that it was so, he saw at once the weak point of the arrangement, and an idea struck him that if whilst the civil administration of the province was placed in Jackson's hands, he himself were vested with political and military authority in Oude, all objects might be advantageously secured. It was but a passing thought, a fleeting suggestion; but it found expression in a letter addressed to the Governor-General, who said, "Two Consuls and Two Tribunes have worked well enough in old times, as we all know; but Two Commissioners at Lucknow would have been at a dead lock within a month I could not have delayed for a day the sending of a Third." A truth not to be disputed. So Henry Lawrence had fallen back upon his duties among those intractable Rajpoots; grieving over their degeneracy, striving mightily, but with no great success, to evolve something of good out of their transition-state, and at last admitting that the peace and security we had given them had not yet much improved the race. All through the year he had gone on, in his old earnest, unstinting way, doing what he could, through divers channels of beneficence, alike for the Ancient Houses and the national Chivalries, whereof History and Tradition had given such grand accounts.

[*] *Ante*, page 398.

But often had he turned aside from the thought of the Princes and the people by whom he was surrounded to consider the general condition of our empire in the East, and most of all our Military System, wherein he discerned some rottenness, which needed to be arrested lest the entire edifice should some day become nothing but a prostrate ruin.

But as the new year approached, certain promptings of failing health inwardly admonished him that it would be well to turn his face towards England for a while; and he had just communicated his wishes upon this score to the Governor-General, when there sprung up a great need for his services on a new and more hopeful field of action. So the answer that went back contained the expression of a hope that he would reconsider his determination to go home and accept the Chief Commissionership of Oude. "There is no person in whose hands I would so gladly and confidently place the charge," wrote Lord Canning, "and my only scruple in offering it to you is, that I am proposing that which will interfere with the immediate recruiting of your health. But I will not for this refrain from executing my intention to do so, which was formed many days before I received your letter." And truly a most wise intention; formed without any doubts and misgivings upon his part, for he knew the real character of the man; but not without some counsel against it, given in perfect honesty and good faith by one honest and faithful to the core, but under a false impression, an error afterwards frankly admitted. Had the counsellors been many, and all of the same singleness and sincerity, and the same ripe experience, they could not have turned Lord Canning from his good purpose, or shaken his conviction that he was right.

The invitation reached Henry Lawrence at Nee- much. It came to him, weak and dispirited as he was, with all the renovating influence of a breath of his native air. It was to him what the distant sound of the Persian war had been to James Outram. It made the blood course less languidly through his veins. With such work as lay before him in Oude, he could not be an invalid. The head-shakings of the medical profession were nothing, if the practitioners learned in physical symptoms took no account of the action of the mind. It was the spirit, not the flesh, that required rousing. Two great clouds, coming from opposite directions, had overshadowed his life, blighting both his honourable ambitions and his domestic affections; a heavy disappointment followed by a cruel loss. The black-edged paper on which he wrote still spoke of the latter; a certain sadness of tone in all his allusions to his public life told how fresh were the wounds of the former. " Annoyances try me much more than work," he now wrote to Lord Canning. " Work does not oppress me." He could work at his desk, he said, for twelve or fifteen hours at a time. He had just made a tour of Guzrat, riding thirty or forty miles a day, sometimes being in the saddle from morning to night, or from night to morn- ing. " But," he added, " ever since I was so cavalierly elbowed out of the Punjab, I have fretted even to the injury of my health. Your lordship's handsome letter has quite relieved my mind on that point; so I re- peat that if, on this explanation, you think fit to send me to Oude, I am quite ready, and can be there within twenty days of receiving your telegraphic reply."

The substance of this letter was telegraphed to Calcutta, and it brought back a telegraphic answer.

The convictions on both sides were so strong in favour of the arrangement that it was not likely to break down under any conditions or reservations on either part; and so it was settled that Henry Lawrence should be Chief Commissioner of Oude. " I am in great hopes," wrote Lord Canning, " that the task being so thoroughly congenial to you, it will sit more lightly upon you than, measured by its labour alone, might be expected; and as to my support, you shall have it heartily. The field before you is a noble one, full of interest and of opportunities for good; and I look forward with the greatest confidence to the results of your exertions in it." So Henry Lawrence prepared himself to proceed to Lucknow, and was soon on his way thither by easy stages; for it was not desired that he should assume office before the middle of the following month. Halting at Bhurtpore, where he took counsel with the Political agent and the Engineer officer, and did much to give a right direction to their energies, he proceeded thence to Agra, which was then the seat of the Lieutenant-Governorship of the North-Western Provinces. It was vividly remembered afterwards by

Mr. E. A. Reade.

one old friend with whom he held sweet communion at that time, that though his thoughts were pregnant with many grave matters begotten of the great Condition-of-India Question, and though he conversed of many things and many men, there was nòthing that seemed to press more heavily on his mind than an anxious, uncertain feeling with respect to the state of the Sepoy Army. There were few civilians in the service who knew the Native soldier so well as this friend; and as they talked over certain manifest signs and symptoms, and narrated what they had seen and heard, each saw plainly that there was a painful sense of coming danger in the other's mind. For twelve years Henry Lawrence had been publicly discoursing of the defects of our Indian military system, and emphatically indicating the dangers which might some day overtake the State in the most terrible of all shapes, an outburst of the Native Soldiery;* and he now playfully told his friend, but with more of sadness than of pleasantry in his speech, that the time was not far distant when the Sepoys would hold him and the Lieutenant-Governor and other "big Brahmins," as hostages in the Fort of Agra, until all their demands were granted.

Still thinking much of this, and mindful that in the province to which he was proceeding he would stand on vantage-ground for the clear discernment of the real causes of the malady, Henry Lawrence passed on to Lucknow. And before day had broken on the 20th of March, he had been received, at the Residency, by the man whom he had come to supplant. There must have been pain and embarrassment on both sides in such a meeting. But before he had broken his fast, the new Commissioner sat down and wrote a letter to Lord Canning, saying that he had had two hours' friendly conversation with Mr. Jackson, who had received him altogether "like a gentleman." He had found a long and encouraging letter from the Governor-General awaiting him on his arrival; and now he emphatically replied, "With your lordship's cordial support I

---

* See Lawrence's Essays, reprinted from the *Calcutta Review*: "How unmindful we have been that what occurred in the city of Caubul may some day occur at Delhi, Meerut, or Bareilly" (page 51). Again: "What the European officers *have* repeatedly done (*i.e.* mutinied) may surely be expected from Natives. We shall be unwise to wait for such occasion. *Come it will, unless anticipated.* A Clive may not be then at hand." The emphatic italics are Lawrence's. Other passages to the same effect might be cited.

have no fear of success." His spirit rose as he thought of the work before him. What that work was, what he found done and what he found undone in the province, when he assumed charge of his new office, will be told in a subsequent page of this story.

₊ No better opportunity than this may be afforded for a note on the opinions of Sir Henry Lawrence with respect to the maintenance of the Native States of India. Having said elsewhere that he was on principle opposed to the "Annexation Policy," I recently elicited the following reply from a distinguished writer in the *Edinburgh Review:* "A writer so well informed as Mr. Kaye need not have thus held on to the skirts of a popular delusion. The course which Sir Henry Lawrence favoured in respect to Oude, by whatever name it may be called, is plain enough. It is a course which, if submitted to the 'Law Officers of the Crown,' as a question of international law, would, probably, receive from these authorities some name harsher than 'annexation.' " To this I think it right to reply, that as any opinion which I may have formed of the sentiments, on this or any other subject, of Sir Henry Lawrence, has been derived either from oral communication with him or from his letters to myself, I ought not to be charged with "hanging on to the skirts of a popular delusion." That those sentiments were what I have represented them to be, I have numerous proofs in his own handwriting. A single extract, however, from his correspondence will suffice for all purposes. Writing to me from Mount Aboo on the 16th of July, 1856, with reference to the office under the Home Government of India which had recently been conferred on me, he said : "The appointment must be one of the pleasantest, unless, indeed, you feel as I do, that Government is going too fast, and that we are losing our good name among the Native States. I confess that I do not like the present system, and that I would gladly give up salary to change to a purely civil or military berth. When I read the tirades of the *Friend of India,* I half think myself (with many better men, including Elphinstone, Munro, and Clerk) a fool. The doctrine now is that it is wicked not to knock down and plunder every Native prince. My views are exactly what they were when I wrote the articles for you on the Mahrattas and on Oude. My paper on Oude would serve as a guide to present doings in all points save the disposal of the surplus revenue, which assuredly ought to be spent *in Oude.* Nor, indeed, do I think that we should materially lose, or fail to gain thereby. Is it nothing that we should make a garden of the nursery of our Sepoys, and open out the resources of a province bordering for a thousand miles on our old ones ? . . . . . But I repeat, that my taste for politics is gone. There is no confidence left in the country; and one does not feel that the people about Government House care one straw about one's exertions on behalf of the Native States." Surely, the trumpet here gives no " uncertain sound."

CHAPTER III.

LORD CANNING AND THE NATIVE ARMY—THE CALL FOR "MORE OFFICERS"
—DREAD OF THE BLACK WATER—THE GENERAL SERVICE ENLISTMENT
ACT—ANXIETIES AND ALARMS—LORD CANNING AND THE MISSIONARY
CAUSE—PROSELYTISING OFFICERS—POLITICAL INQUIETUDES—THE PRO-
PHECY OF FIFTY-SEVEN.

THE anxieties which Henry Lawrence carried with The little
him to Lucknow had then, for some weeks, been dis- cloud. January,
quieting the mind of the Governor-General. The old 1857.
year had died out, apparently leaving to its successor
no greater troubles than those which were inseparable
from the Persian war; but before the new year was
many days old, there arose upon the horizon that
little cloud no bigger than a man's hand, of which
Lord Canning, at the great Farewell Banquet of the
Company, had prophetically spoken. It might be
little; it might be much. It might be blown away
by a breath of wind; or it might expand into terrific
dimensions, covering the whole heaven as with a pall.
Anyhow, it had an angry threatening aspect; and
the looker-on, being no alarmist, might well wish it
away.

Memorable, and, doubtless, well remembered is it Retrospect
that, when Lord Dalhousie bade farewell to the cares 1856.

of Indian Government, he placed upon record an opinion that the condition of the Native soldiery left nothing to be desired. There was no reason why Lord Canning, at the outset of his career, should not take this assertion on trust; no reason why he should not hold to it for a while. He went out to India, prepossessed in favour of "the faithful Sepoy." He had, doubtless, read the noble picture which, nearly forty years before, his father had drawn of the fidelity of the Native soldiery of the Company, unshaken by threats, unallured by temptations.* There were no flutterings of disquiet apparent on the surface to raise anxious doubts and misgivings. But he had not long taken up the reins of Government, when the subject of the Native Army began to occupy his thoughts and to afford matter for much grave correspondence. The vast extension of territory which had made famous the career of Lord Dalhousie had not been followed by any corresponding extension of the Agency by which all this new country was to be administered. As so much more civil duty was to be

---

* As President of the Board of Control, George Canning had moved, in the House of Commons, the vote of thanks to Lord Hastings's Army for its service in the Second Mahratta war, and in the course of his speech had paid this fine tribute to the Native Army: "In doing justice," he said, "to the bravery of the Native troops, I must not overlook another virtue, their fidelity. Many of the Bombay Army had been recruited in the territories of the Peishwah; their property, their friends, their relatives, all that was valuable and dear to them, were still in that prince's power. Previously to the commencement of hostilities, the Peishwah had spared no pains to seduce and corrupt these troops; he abstained from no threats to force them from their allegiance, but his utmost arts were vain. The Native officers and soldiers came to the British Commanders with the proofs of these temptations in their hands, and renewed the pledges of their attachment. One man, a non-commissioned officer, brought to his captain the sum of 5000 rupees, which had been presented to him by the Peishwah in person, as an earnest of reward for desertion. The vengeance denounced by the Peishwah was not an unmeaning menace; it did, in many instances, fall heavily on the relatives of those who resisted his threats and his entreaties; but the effect was rather to exasperate than to repress their ardour in the service to which they had sworn to adhere."

done, it seemed, in strict logical sequence, that there
was an increased demand for civil servants, and that
this demand should have been supplied. But government by the Civil Service of the Company was
costly ; and to have called for increased agency of
this kind would perhaps have supplied Leadenhall-
street with an argument against the profitableness of
annexation. Moreover, there was much rough work
to be done in our newly-acquired provinces, for
which, on the whole, perhaps, military administrators
were better suited than civilians. So the military
officer, as has before been said, was taken from his
regimental duties to share in the civil administration
of the country. Great had been, for this purpose,
the drain upon the Native regiments, before the
annexation of Oude. That event brought the ascendant evil to a climax; and Lord Canning wrote
home that it had become necessary to add two
officers to each Native Infantry regiment and four
to the Europeans. "A request," he wrote, in the
early part of April, "for an addition to the number
of officers in each Infantry regiment—European and
Native—goes home by this mail. Four for each
European and two for each Native regiment are
asked. The application comes singly and in a bald
shape; because the necessity of an immediate increase is urgent, and because I have had no time to
go into the complicated questions of .our military
wants generally."

There was, indeed, nothing more difficult to under- "More
stand aright than these military questions; difficult officers."
to experienced statesmen: altogether embarrassing
and bewildering to a Governor in his novitiate.
Even this matter of "more officers," so smooth as it
appeared to be on the surface, when you came to

gauge it, was found to contain a deposit of doubt and conflict. It was held by some, who had studied well all the deteriorating influences of which so much has been said in these pages, that the cry for " more officers" was one to be responded to with caution; that, indeed, the Native Army had already too many officers; and that now to increase their number would be to increase one of the evils that had long been impairing its efficiency. That Lord Canning, fresh from England, should have taken the more popular view of this want of officers, was natural; and, indeed, it may be said that it was a plain common-sense view, not wanting in a certain kind of logic. It had become a proverb that the English officer was the Backbone of the Native regiment; and, assuredly, the administrative demands of our new provinces had left these Native regiments, according to the recognised reading, sadly enfeebled and incapacitated. All that he now sought to do was to restore them somewhat more nearly to their normal condition. The remedy seemed to lie on the surface, and straightway he exerted himself to supply it. But, the theory of the Backbone accepted, it was still possible that the vertebral column might be weakened by having too many joints; and therefore it was said by a few thoughtful and experienced men, emphatically by Sir George Clerk,* that there was more danger. in giving our Native regiments too many English officers than in giving them too few; and for this reason, that being many they formed a society apart and kept aloof from their men, and became altogether in their ways of life too European. Doubts such as these, and from such a quarter, brought clearly to Lord Canning's mind the fact that

* Then Secretary to the Board of Control.

the Native Army question was a very difficult one; that it was almost impossible, indeed, whilst avoiding one rock, to escape from steering upon another. But the call for more officers had been made; and, perhaps, with no want of wisdom. For, although there was profound truth in what was said about the evil of too much Englishism in the Native Army, the Regular Regiments of the Company had been formed upon the European model, and the principle of command by many officers was a vital part of the system. The Irregular system might have been better than the Regular, but a Regular Regiment denuded of its officers fulfilled the condition of neither. So the Home Government recognised the want of more officers, and responded to the appeal.

Another, and still more important question, soon came up for solution. The specific evils, which resulted from the extension of our dominions, varied in accordance with the direction in which we had extended them. · The acquisition of new territory on the south-eastern coast had caused but little political excitement in India; but the very circumstance to which we owed our exemption from evils of one kind was the immediate source of another class of evils. It has been said that the intervention of the black waters of the Bay of Bengal cut off the sovereigns of Burmah from the brotherhood of the Princes of the great continent of India, and made it a matter of small concern whether we gained battles or lost them in that part of the world.[*] But that very black water made it difficult for us to garrison the country which we had won. The new province of Pegu had been brought administratively under the Supreme Government of India, and in the first

Evils of extended dominion.

Military defence of Peg

[*] *Ante,* pp. 67-68.

1856. arrangements made for its military defence, the regiments planted there had been drawn from the Bengal Army. But the great bulk of that Army eschewed Foreign service.[*] It was not part of the conditions, under which they had enlisted, that they should cross the seas. The Sepoy, on taking service, swore that he would never forsake or abandon his colours, and that he would march whithersoever he was directed, whether within or beyond the territories of the Company. Out of the seventy-four regiments composing the Native Infantry of the Bengal Army, six only were recruited for general service. When more Native troops had been required to take part in operations beyond the séas, it had been customary to call for volunteers from the limited-service regiments. There had been often a free response to this invitation, and the volunteer corps had done their duty well upon Foreign service. In the old times, indeed, before the new organisation, they had in this respect shown signal devotion; they had gone willingly to remote places beyond the seas and cheerfully endured all the miseries and privations of long and boisterous voyages. In one year, seven thousand Bengal Sepoys had volunteered for service against the French in the Mauritius and in Java; and had served for many years in those islands with unvarying fidelity and good conduct.[†] But, even in those days, they had

Volunteer corps.

1811.

---

[*] "The natives of India have, generally speaking, a rooted dislike to the sea; and when we consider the great privations and hardships to which Hindoos of high caste are subject on a long voyage, during which some of them, from prejudices of caste, subsist solely on parched grain, we feel less surprised at the occasional mutinies, which have been caused by orders for their embarkation, than at the zeal and attachment they have often shown upon such trying occasions."—*Sir John Malcolm in the Quarterly Review*, vol. xviii. p. 399.

[†] The battalions thus formed were the basis of the six general-service regiments, in the later organisation, of which mention is made in the text.

·been at times capricious; and their caprices, as time advanced and their devotion to their officers diminished, had grown more frequent and more embarrassing.* The mutiny and massacre at Barrackpore had risen out of the demands of the first Burmese war, and the second war in those transmarine regions had raised up a new crop of difficulties of the old type.

A few sentences will tell all that need be told of this last story: The Native troops employed in the conquest of Pegu were either Madras troops or the general-service regiments of the Bengal Army. But reinforcements were needed, and so a call was to be made for volunteers. The Thirty-eighth Native Regiment was then at the Presidency. It had served long and fought gallantly in Afghanistan, and it was believed that it would follow its officers to any part of the world. But when the day of trial came, the result was a bitter disappointment. The Sepoys were asked whether they would embark for Rangoon to take part in the war, or for Arracan, there to relieve a general-service regiment, which in that case would be sent on to Burmah. Their reply was, that they were willing to march anywhere, but that they would not volunteer to cross the seas. Perfectly respectful in their language, they were firm in their refusal. Doubt and suspicion had taken possession of their minds. How it happened I do not know, but a belief was afterwards engendered among them, that the English Government had a foul design to entrap them, and that if they commenced the march to the banks of the Irrawaddy, they would at a con-

---

* Sir John Malcolm, writing in 1817-18, says, that all the mutinies in the Bengal Army up to that time had arisen from the blunders of their commanding officers, or from orders given to go beyond the seas. See article, above quoted, in *Quarterly Review*.

1856. venient point be taken to the sea-board and forcibly compelled to embark. Lord Dalhousie, taking, therefore, the prudent rather than the vigorous view of the situation, and availing himself of the advanced state of the season as a plea for the adoption of the feebler of the two courses before him, yielded to these first symptoms of danger, and decreed that the Thirty-eighth should be sent neither to Rangoon nor to Arracan, but to the nearer and more inland station of Dacca. And so nothing more was heard for a time of the disaffection of the Bengal Army.

The Court of Directors of the East India Company, when this business was reported to them, saw clearly that it had become difficult to carry on the concerns of their vastly extended empire with one-half of their Army, and that the more important half, bound to render them only a restricted obedience; so they wrote out to the Governor-General that they hoped soon to be put in possession of the "senti-

October 20, 1852. ments of his Government on the expediency of adopting such a change in the terms of future enlistments as might eventually relieve them from similar embarrassments." But no action was taken during the remaining years of Lord Dalhousie's administration, and Lord Canning found, on his accession, that still but a twelfth part of the Bengal Army was available for service beyond the seas. What then

Reliefs for Pegu. was to be done, when reliefs were required for Pegu? Even if the old professional ardour of the Sepoy had been restored, the occasion was scarcely one on which the Government could have called for volunteers. The formation of volunteer regiments had been confined to periods of actual warfare; and now that we required them merely to garrison our acquisitions in time of peace, the difficulty that confronted

Lord Canning was one not readily to be overcome. He found at this time that of the six general-service regiments three were then in Pegu. They had embarked on a specific understanding that they should not be called upon to serve there for more than three years, and, in the rainy season of 1856, two of the three regiments were in their third year of transmarine service. In the early part of the following year, therefore, a relief would be necessary; but not one of the other three regiments could be despatched; for they had all returned only a year or two before from service in the same part of the country. It was clear, therefore, that the Bengal Army could not provide the means of despatching the required reliefs by water transport to Pegu.

So a question arose as to whether the relieving regiments might not, according to their bond, be marched to the Burmese coast. It was a circuitous and toilsome journey, but it had been done, under pressure of like difficulty, thirty years before, and might yet be done again. But although the improvement of the communications between the Hooghly and the Irrawaddy was then being urged forward by the Government, there was still a break on the line from Chittagong to Akyab, of which our Engineers could not give a sufficiently encouraging account to satisfy the Governor-General that the relieving regiments could be sent by land in the ensuing cold season. "A part of the road," said Lord Canning, "could not be made passable for wheels by that time without the addition of eight thousand labourers to those already employed. If the use of wheeled carriages were abandoned, there would still remain encamping ground to be cleared on many parts of it; the jungle, which is already choking the tract, to be removed; preparation to be made for halting the men on the march; wells to be dug, or water to be stored, where none has yet been found; and stations and storehouses provided. Simple operations enough in themselves, but which in this case would have to be begun and completed, on two hundred miles of road, between the beginning of December, before which no work on that coast can be attempted, and February, when the troops must begin to pass over the ground, the supply of labour, as well as its quality, being very little trustworthy." "Obstacles of this kind," continued the Governor-General, "have been overcome again and again by the Sepoys of Bengal in their marches, whenever it has been necessary to do so; but I am of opinion that it will be better in the present instance to seek some other solution of the difficulty. And I believe that the one most available is a recourse to the Madras Army."

Demands on the Madras Army.

And why not? The Madras, or, as it was once called, the Coast Army, was enlisted for general service. Posted in the Southern Peninsula, and to a great extent along the sea-board, it was as readily available for service on the other side of the Bay as the Army in Lower Bengal. If the duty were unpalatable, it could not, when diffused over fifty regiments, press very heavily upon any individual soldier. Besides, service of this kind had some compensations of its own, and was not altogether to be regarded as a grievance.* So it was thought that the

---

* It must not be supposed, however, that the Madras Army had always cheerfully accepted this necessity for going upon foreign service. On several occasions they had broken into mutiny on the eve of embarkation. Once, towards the close of the last century, they had risen upon their European officers, when about to embark at Vizagapatam, and shot all but one or two, who had contrived to escape on board the ship which was waiting to receive the regiment. In a former chapter I have given some later instances, and others might have been cited. But there are some noble examples on record of another kind,

garrison of Pegu might, for a time at least, be drawn from the Madras Army. But ready as the solution appeared to be, it was found that here also there was some hard, gritty, insoluble matter at the bottom of the scheme. The Madras Government, though not unwilling to send troops to Pegu, as a temporary arrangement, protested against being called upon to supply a permanent garrison to that part of our dominions. Such an arrangement would bring round to every regiment a tour of service beyond the sea once in every nine years, instead of once in twelve years; it would render service in the Madras Army unpopular; make recruiting difficult among the better class of Natives whom it was desired to enlist; and, inasmuch as every regiment lost much of its morale on Foreign service, and took two or three years to recover what was lost, the efficiency of the Madras Army would be permanently deteriorated.

So Lord Canning turned his thoughts in another

and one adduced by Sir John Malcolm, in the article above quoted, deserves to be recorded here, if only as an illustration of the influence for good of a trusted commanding officer. Speaking of the services of the Twenty-second Madras Regiment, he says: "This fine corps was commanded by Lieutenant-Colonel James Oram, an officer not more distinguished for his personal zeal and gallantry than for a thorough knowledge of the men under his command, whose temper he had completely preserved, at the same time that he had imparted to them the highest perfection in their dress and discipline. When he proposed to his corps on parade to volunteer for Manilla, they only requested to know whether Colonel Oram would go with them? The answer was, 'He would.' 'Will he stay with us?' was the second question. The reply was in the affirmative; the whole corps exclaimed, 'To Europe! —to Europe!' And the alacrity and spirit with which they subsequently embarked, showed that they would as readily have gone to the shores of the Atlantic as to an island of the Eastern Ocean. Not a man of the corps deserted, from the period they volunteered for service until they embarked; and such was the contagion of their enthusiasm, that several Sepoys who were missing from one of the battalions in garrison at Madras, were found, when the expedition returned, to have deserted to join the Twenty-second under Colonel Oram. We state this anecdote," adds Sir John Malcolm, "with a full impression of the importance of the lesson it conveys. It is through their affections alone that such a class of men can well be commanded."

dircction. Madras troops might be sent for the nonce to Pegu, but the permanent defence of that outlying province across the Bay must, it appeared to him, be provided for by drawing, in some way, upon the Bengal Army. There was then lying, un-responded to, among the Records of the Military Department, that despatch of the Court of Directors in which the Government of India had been urged to devise the means of relieving themselves from all such embarrassments by a change in the terms of future enlistments. After much inward thought and much consultation with others, he determined, there-fore, to institute such a radical change in the con-stitution of the Bengal Army as four years before had been indicated by the Home Government. The reform which he contemplated was to have only a prospective effect. It was to touch no existing in-terests; but to be applied prospectively to all who might enlist into the military service of the State. Thenceforth every recruit was to engage himself for general service. There might be an alteration in the form of the oath, or it might simply be left to the European officer to explain to every recruit that he had been enlisted for general service. Such had been the custom with respect to the six general-service regiments of the Bengal Army, and it had been found to answer every requirement. An ex-planatory order might be issued by the Governor-General in Council, and then the military autho-rities might follow up, in their own way, the blow struck at the niceties of the old system. The Go-vernor-General argued, with irresistible force, that every Government should be master of its own Army. He was, however, at that time, fresh from England; and he might be forgiven for not knowing how the Government could best make itself the 1856. master of such an Army as that with which he was then dealing.   But he would have had no legitimate claim to forgiveness if he had failed to take counsel with those among his constitutional advisers who had spent all their adult lives in India, and who were presumedly familiar with the feelings and opinions of the people. He did take counsel with them; and they urged him to pursue this course.   He who, of all the Councillors, best knew the Native character, General Low. was then in England; but the ablest man amongst them argued that there was no place like Calcutta Mr. J. P. for shipping off a large military force, and that the Grant. Bay of Bengal had become an Indian Lake.   It does not seem that there was any one at Lord Canning's elbow to tell him that, whatsoever might be the facilities of transport, the Bay of Bengal would still be the black water, the salt water, in the thoughts of the people from whom our recruits were to be drawn; still regarded with mysterious awe, and recoiled from with unconquerable aversion.

So, on the 25th of July, 1856, a general order was issued by the Government of India, declaring that, thenceforth, they would not accept the service of any Native recruit who would not, "at the time of his enlistment, distinctly undertake to serve beyond the sea, whether within the territories of the Company or beyond them."   In what light Lord Canning regarded this important change, with what arguments he supported the measures, may be gathered from his correspondence.   "You will see," he wrote to the President of the India Board, "that August 9, a General Order has been published putting an end 1856. to the long-established, but most impolitic, embarrassing, and senseless practice of enlisting the Native

2 H 2

1856. Army of Bengal for limited service only; the sole exceptions being six regiments of Native Infantry, which are recruited on the condition of serving any-where, and the Artillery. It is marvellous that this should have continued so long, and that the Government of India should have tolerated, again and again, having to beg for volunteers, when other Governments, including those of Madras and Bombay, would have ordered their soldiers on their duty. It is the more surprising, because no one can allege any reason for conceding this unreasonable immunity to the Bengal Sepoy. The difficulties of Caste furnish none whatever, for the Bombay Army is recruited in great part from the same classes and districts as that of Bengal; and even in the latter the best Brahmin in the ranks does not scruple to set aside his prejudices, whenever it suits him to do so. There seems to have been a dim apprehension that there might be risk in meddling with the fundamental conditions upon which the bargain between the Army and the Government has hitherto rested, and there are some few alarmists on the present occasion, but I have seen no reason to fear that the order will cause any bad feeling in the Bengal Army. As it touches no existing rights, it could only do so by exciting apprehensions that something more remains behind; and, probably, this may prove to be the case, for whenever I can propose a reduction in the numbers of the Bengal Regiments, I shall endeavour to do so upon terms that will give a preference of remaining in the ranks to such men as may be willing to accept general service. But this is no part of, and is not necessarily connected with the present change; moreover, as yet

November 8, 1856. it is only in my own breast." And again, a few months later, he wrote, with still greater confidence:

"There is no fear of feelings of Caste being excited by the new enlistment regulations in the Bengal Army. No one will come under it otherwise than voluntarily; and the fact that a vast number of the recruits who join the Bombay regiments come from the same country, and are of the same caste, and in every respect of the same condition with the bulk of the Army in Bengal, proves that they do not, on first entering the service, hold very closely to Caste privileges. You are aware that the Bombay Army is enlisted for general service without exception. The only apprehension I have ever had (and that has vanished) is, that the Sepoys already enlisted on the old terms might suspect that it was a first step towards breaking faith with them, and that on the first necessity they might be compelled to cross the sea. But there has been no sign of any such false alarm on their part."

No signs truly apparent at Government House; but many and great in the Native villages, and much talk in the Lines and Bazaars. It was hardly right even to say that there was no interference with existing interests. For the interest of the Sepoy in the Bengal Army was an hereditary interest. If the British Government did not at once assume the right to send him across the sea, it seemed certain that his sons would be sent. There was an end, indeed, of the exclusive privileges which the Bengal Sepoy had so long enjoyed; the service never could be hereafter what it had been of old; and all the old pride, therefore, with which the veteran had thought of his boys succeeding him was now suddenly extinguished. Besides, the effect, he said, would be, that high-caste men would shrink from entering the service, and that, therefore, the vacant places of his brethren would be filled by men with whom he could have no feeling of comradeship. And this was no imaginary fear. No sooner had the order made its way through the Provinces, than it became patent to all engaged in the work of enlistment that the same high-caste men as had before been readily recruited were no longer pressing forward to enter the British service.[*] As it was believed that we had too many Brahmins and Rajpoots in the Bengal Army, this in itself might have been no great evil. But it was of all things the least likely that such an order should pass into general circulation without being ignorantly misunderstood by some, and designedly misinterpreted by others.

Enlistment of Sikhs. So it was soon said that the English gentlemen were trying to rid themselves of their old high-caste Sepoys, and that soon the profession which had been followed, with honourable pride, by generation after generation of old soldier-families would not be open to them. And this belief was greatly strengthened by a rumour which went forth about the same time, to the effect that Government had determined on enlisting thirty thousand more Sikhs. The conquest of the Punjab had placed at our disposal the services of a warlike race, always eager to wear the uniform of a successful ruler, for in their eyes success was plunder. Less dainty in the choice of their battle-

---

[*] Take, in proof of this, the following extract from a letter written by Sir Henry Lawrence to Lord Canning, on the 1st of May, 1857: "The General Service Enlistment Oath is most distasteful, keeps many out of the service, and frightens the old Sepoys, who imagine that the oaths of the young recruits affect the whole regiment. One of the best captains of the 13th Native Infantry, in this place, said to me last week that he had clearly ascertained this fact: Mr. E. A. Reade, of the Sudder Board, who was for years collector of Goruckpore, had the General Service Order given to him as a reason last year, when on his tour, by Rajpoots, for not entering the service. The salt water, he told me, was the universal answer." —*MS. Correspondence.*

fields, and not less brave or robust in battle, they were the very kind of mercenaries that we wanted to give new bone and sinew to the body of our Native Army. Whether there were or were not, at this time, a tendency to over-work this new and promising recruiting-ground, it is certain that the old race of Sepoys believed that we were designedly working it to their injury and their overthrow. They gave ready credence, therefore, to exaggerated reports of Sikh enlistments, and, coupling them with the New General Service Order, leapt to the conclusion that the English had done with the old Bengal Army, and were about to substitute for it another that would go anywhere and do anything, like coolies and pariahs.

Moreover, there were not wanting those who were eager to persuade the Sepoys of the Bengal Army that this new Act was another insidious attempt to destroy the Caste of the people, and to make men of all creeds do the bidding of the English, by merging all into the one faith of the Feringhee. It was another link in the great chain of evidence which had been artfully employed to convict the British Government of the charge of aiming at the compulsory conversion of the people. The season was most propitious. The coming of Lord Canning had, by some strange process of association which I find it impossible to trace, been identified with certain alleged instructions from England, emanating from the Queen herself in Council, for the Christianisation, by fair means or by foul, of the great mass of the people; and now one of the first acts of his Government was to issue an order making it compulsory on the Sepoy to take to the transport vessel, to cross the black water, and to serve in strange parts of the world, far away, perhaps, from all the emblems and observances of his religion, among a people sacrilegious and unclean.

. The native mind was, at this time, in a most sensitive state, and easily wrought upon by suspicious appearances. What these appearances were, has, in some measure, been shown in former chapters of this narrative. Even the Railway and the Electric Telegraph had been accounted as blows struck at the religions of the country. Nor was this purely a creation of the Native mind, an unaided conception of the Priests or the People; for the missionaries themselves had pleaded the recent material progress of the English as an argument in favour of the adoption by the inhabitants of India of one universal religion. "The time appears to have come," they said in an Address which was extensively circulated in Bengal during the closing years of Lord Dalhousie's administration, "when earnest consideration should be given to the question, whether or not all men should embrace the same system of religion. Railways, Steam-vessels, and the Electric Telegraph are rapidly uniting all the nations of the earth. The more they are brought together, the more certain does the conclusion become that all have the same wants, the same anxieties, and the same sorrows;" and so on, with manifest endeavour to prove that European civilisation was the forerunner of an inevitable absorption of all other faiths into the one faith of the White Ruler. This had gone forth, an egregious Christian manifesto, not wanting in fundamental truth, or in certain abstract proprieties of argument and diction, to "Educated Natives," especially to respectable Mahomedans in Government employment, some of the leading Native functionaries of Bengal. What might truly be the purport of it, and whence it came, was not very clear at first; but ere long it came to be accepted as a direct emanation from Government, intended to invite the people to apostatise from the religions of their fathers. And such was the excitement that Commissioner Tayler, of the great Patna division, wherein some disquietudes had before arisen, mainly of the Mahomedan type, reported to Lieutenant-Governor Halliday that intelligent natives, especially the better class of Moslems, were " impressed with a full belief that Government were immediately about to attempt the forcible conversion of its subjects." It was added, that "a correspondence on this head had for some time been going on between native gentlemen in various parts of the Lower Provinces;" and Lieutenant-Governor Halliday saw so clearly that this was no impalpable mare's-nest, no idle scum of an alarmist brain, that he forthwith issued a sedative Proclamation; which sedative proclamation was speedily answered anonymously, but beyond doubt by an "intelligent native," or conclave of "intelligent natives," clearly showing by the inevitable logic of facts that if this notion of a war against the religions of India had laid hold of the national mind, the Government had by their own measures given encouragement to the dangerous belief.

Very obstinate, indeed, and hard to be removed, was this belief; so hard, that the very efforts made to efface it might only fix more ineffaceably the damaging impression on the native mind. For if the wondering multitude did not think, there were a crafty few ready to teach them, that if Government designed, by foul means, to destroy the caste of the people and the religions of the country, they would not hesitate to make the issuing of a lying proclamation a part of the process. The conviction that it was the deliberate design of the British Government, by force or fraud, to attain this great object, was growing stronger and stronger every month, when Lord Canning arrived in India, and at once became, all unwittingly, a special object of suspicion and alarm. The lies which attended, perhaps preceded, his advent, caused all his movements to be narrowly watched; and it began soon to be bruited abroad that he had subscribed largely to missionary societies, and that Lady Canning, who was known to be in the especial confidence of the Queen, was intent on making great personal exertions for the conversion of the women of the country.

Lord Canning and the Religious Societies.

But there was no truth in all this. The Governor-General had done no more than other Governors-General had done before him. He had sent a donation to the Bible Society, a society for the translation of the Scriptures into the Oriental languages, and the circulation of these new versions among the people. But the translation of the Scriptures had been carried on more than half a century before, in the College of Fort William, under the especial patronage of Lord Wellesley; and Lord Wellesley's successor, during whose reign the Calcutta Bible Society was established, headed the list with a large subscription. Lord Hastings, Lord William Bentinck, and Sir Charles Metcalfe, had all contributed to the funds of the society. But Lord Canning had also given a donation to the Baptist College at Serampore. What then? It had been established in 1818, under the auspices of Lord Hastings, whose name had been published as the "First Patron" of the Institution, and it had received the support of subsequent Governors-General without question or comment. Besides these donations, he had made a contribution to the support of the excellent school of the Free Church Mission, under the management of Dr. Duff, as Lord Dalhousie had done before him. "I admit," he said, "that the Head of the Government in India ought to abstain from acts which may have the appearance of an exercise of power, authority, solicitation, or persuasion towards inducing natives to change their religion. But if it is contended that a school like this, thoroughly catholic and liberal, open to students of every creed, doing violence to none, and so conducted as to disarm hostility and jealousy (the number of the Hindoo and Mussulman scholars shows this), is not to have countenance and support from the Governor-General because it is managed by missionaries, I join issue on that point. I am not prepared to act upon that doctrine."

And what had Lady Canning done? She had taken a true womanly interest in the education of native female children. She had visited the female schools of Calcutta in a quiet, unobtrusive way; but once only in each case, save with a notable exception in favour of the Bethune Institution, which had been taken by Lord Dalhousie under the special care of the Government.* In this Lady Canning had taken some observable interest. But as the Managing Committee of the school was composed of high-caste Hindoo gentlemen, there was assuredly no apparent necessity for restraining her womanly instincts and shrinking into apathy and indolence, as one regardless of the happiness and the dignity of her sex. Whatsoever may have been the zeal for the conversion of the Heathen that pervaded Government House, there were no indiscreet manifestations of it. There are times, how-

* *Ante*, page 187.

ever, when no discretion can wholly arrest the growth of dangerous lies. A very little thing, in a season of excitement, will invest a colourable falsehood with the brightest hues of truth, and carry conviction to the dazzled understanding of an ignorant people. The sight of Lady Canning's carriage at the gates of the Bethune school may have added, therefore, Heaven only knows, some fresh tints to the picture of a caste-destroying Government, which active-minded emissaries of evil were so eager to hang up in the public places of the land.

Progress of social reform. It was not much; perhaps, indeed, it was simply nothing. But just at that time there was a movement, urged on by John Grant and Barnes Peacock, in the purest spirit of benevolence, for the rescue of the women of India from the degradation in which they were sunk. It happened—truly, it happened, for it was wholly an accident—that one of the first measures, outwardly, of Lord Canning's Government was the formal passing of the bill " to remove all legal obstacles to the marriage of Hindoo widows," which had been introduced, discussed, and virtually carried, during the administration of his predecessor.* And this done, there was much said and written about the restraints that were to be imposed on Hindoo polygamy; and every day the appearance of a Draft Act, formidable in the extreme to Brahminism, was looked for, with doubt and aversion, by the old orthodox Hindoos. For they saw that in this, as in the matter of Re-Marriage, some of their more free-thinking countrymen, mostly of the younger generation, moved by the teachings of the English, or by some hope of gain, were beseeching Government to relieve the nation from what they called the reproach of Ku-

* *Ante*, page 190.

linism. And, at such a time, Orthodoxy, staggering under blows given, and shrinking from blows to come, looked aghast even at such small manifestations as the visits of the wife of the Governor-General to the Bethune female school. It was clear that the English, with their overpowering love of rule, were about now to regulate in India, after their own fashion, the relations of the two sexes to each other.*

Lord Canning found this movement afoot; he in no wise instituted it. He found that Lord Dalhousie, after an experience of many years, believed these social reforms to be practicable and safe; he found that the ablest member of his Council, who had spent all his adult life in India, was with all his heart and soul eager for their promotion, and with all the activity of his intellect promoting them. As to this movement against Hindoo polygamy, which was intended to prune down the evil, not wholly to eradicate it, there was something, to his European understanding, grotesque in the notion of a Christian Legislature recognising certain forms of polygamy, and addressing itself only to the abuses of the system, as though to Christian eyes it were not altogether an abuse. But he could see plainly enough that only by admitting such a compromise could the good thing be done at all; and seeing also the necessity of proceeding warily with such a delicate operation, he was not disposed, in the first instance, to do more than to feel the pulse of the people. It would be wise to delay

* Sir Henry Lawrence clearly discerned the danger of this, and in an article in the *Calcutta Review*, written in 1856, pointed it out: "Of late years," he wrote, "the wheels of Government have been moving very fast. Many native prejudices have been shocked. Natives are now threatened with the abolition of polygamy. It would not be difficult to twist this into an attack on Hindooism. At any rate, the faster the vessel glides, the more need of caution, of watching the weather, the rocks, and the shoals."

actual legislation until public opinion should have been more unmistakably evoked.[*]

In the personal action of Lord Canning during this year of his novitiate, in the promotion either of the religious conversion or the social reformation of the people, I can see no traces of intemperate zeal. But it is not to be questioned that just at this time there was a combination of many untoward circumstances to strengthen the belief, which had been growing for some years, that the English Government were bent upon bringing, by fair means or by foul, all the nations of India under the single yoke of the White Man's faith. Nor is it less certain that at such a time the order for the enlistment of Native troops for general service appeared to their unaided comprehensions, and was designedly declared by others, to be a part of the scheme. There were those, indeed, who

[*] Lord Canning's opinions are so clearly expressed in the following passage, that it is right that his words should be given: "It will, no doubt, be a little staggering to find ourselves drawing up a law by which, although a horrible abuse of polygamy will be checked, a very liberal amount of it will be sanctioned, and which must recognise as justifying it reasons which we believe to be no justification whatever. It may be said that we shall only be enforcing Hindoo law, and that we are constantly doing this in many ways which abstractedly we should not approve. But I do not know that we have any examples of laws of our own making and wording, by which anything so contrary to our convictions of right and wrong as the taking of a second wife, for the reasons allowed by Menu (or at least for eight of them out of ten), is declared lawful. This, however, is a matter of appearance and feeling rather than of substance. Practically, a monstrous horror would be put an end to, and we might keep ourselves straight even in appearance by making it very clear in the preamble that the act is passed at the desire of the Hindoos to rescue their own law and custom from a great abuse, and that in no respect is it proposed to substitute English law for the laws of that people. . . . . Upon the whole, I come, without hesitation, to the conclusion that the movement ought to be encouraged to our utmost, and that the existence and strength of it ought to be made generally known. The presentation of the petitions to the Legislative Council, and their publication, will effect this. How soon the introduction of a bill should follow, or how much time should be given to seeing whether serious opposition is evoked, I should like to talk over with you some day, as also the scope of the bill."—*Lord Canning to Mr. J. P. Grant, June 20, 1856. MS. Correspondence.*

saw, or professed to see, in this matter, the very root of our cherished desire for the conversion of the people. It was said that we wished to bring them all to our own faith in order that we might find them willing to do our bidding in all parts of the world, that they might shrink from no kind of work by sea or by land, and even fight our battles in Europe; for it was plain that England had sad lack of fighting men, or she would not have drawn upon India for them during the Crimean war. In the art of what is called "putting two and two together," there were many 'intelligent natives by no means deficient, and deeper and deeper the great suspicion struck root in the popular mind.

There was another ugly symptom, too, at this time, which greatly, in some particular quarters, strengthened this impression of coming danger among the Sepoys of the Bengal Army. There were among the European officers of that army many earnest-minded, zealous Christians; men whose hearts were wrung by the sight of the vast mass of heathendom around them, and who especially deplored the darkness which brooded over their companions in arms, their children in the service of the State, the Sepoys who looked up to and obeyed them. Some, in their conscientious prudence, grieved in silence, and rendered unto Cæsar the homage of a wise forbearance. Others, conscientiously imprudent, believed that it was their duty to render unto God the just tribute of an apostolic activity. It was the creed of these last that all men were alike to them, as having souls to be saved, and that no external circumstances affected their own inalienable right to do their great Master's work. If under the pressure of these convictions they had changed the red coat for the black, and the sword for the shepherd's crook, they would have fairly earned the admiration of all good men. But holding fast to the wages of the State, they went about with the order-book in one hand and the Bible in the other; and thus they did a great and grievous wrong to the Government they professed to serve. To what extent this missionary zeal pervaded our English officers, it is not easy, with much precision, to declare. But there were some of whose missionary zeal there is now no remnant of a doubt—some who confessed, nay, openly gloried in their proselytising endeavours. One officer, who in 1857 was commandant of a regiment of Infantry, said vauntingly in that year: "I beg to state that during the last twenty years and upwards, I have been in the habit of speaking to natives of all classes, Sepoys and others, making no distinction, since there is no respect of persons with God, on the subject of our religion, in the highways, cities, bazaars, and villages—not in the Lines and regimental Bazaars. I have done this from a conviction that every converted Christian is expected, or rather commanded, by the Scriptures to make known the glad tidings of salvation to his lost fellow-creatures, Our Saviour having offered himself up as a sacrifice for the sins of the whole world, by which alone salvation can be secured. He has directed that this salvation should be freely offered to all without exception." Again, in another letter, he wrote: "As to the question whether I have endeavoured to convert Sepoys and others to Christianity, I would humbly reply that this has been my object, and I conceive is the aim and end of every Christian who speaks the word of God to another—merely that the Lord would make him the happy instrument of converting his neighbour to God, or, in other words, of rescuing him from eternal destruction." "On matters connected with religion," he added, " I feel myself called upon to act in two capacities—'to render unto Cæsar (or the Government) the things that are Cæsar's, and to render unto God the things that are God's.' Temporal matters and spiritual matters are thus kept clearly under their respective heads. When speaking, therefore, to a native on the subject of religion, I am then acting in the capacity of a Christian soldier under the authority of my heavenly superior; whereas in temporal matters I act as a general officer, under the authority and order of my earthly superior."* Reading this, one does not know whether more to admire the Christian courage of the writer or to marvel at the strange moral blindness which would not suffer him to see that he could not serve both God and Mammon; that ignoring the known wishes and instructions of his temporal master, he could not do his duty to his spiritual Lord; and that if in such a case the two services were antagonistic to each other, it was his part, as a Christian, to divest himself of his purchased allegiance to the less worthy Government, and to serve the Other and the Higher without hindrance and without reproach. He was not bound to continue to follow such a calling, but whilst following it he was bound to do his duty in that state of life to which it had pleased God to call him.

Whilst all these disturbing influences were at work, and on many accounts most actively in the neighbourhood of Calcutta, there came from afar, across the North-Western frontier, a current of political agitation, which was met by other streams of

* Lieutenant-Colonel Wheler to Government, April 15, 1857.—*Printed Papers.*

2 I

native origin, turgid also with troublous rumours. The Persian Government, in best of times given to treachery and trickery, even under the fairest outside show of friendship, were not likely in such a conjuncture as had arisen at the end of 1856, to let slip any available means of damaging an enemy. Holding fast to the maxim that " All is fair in war," they endeavoured, not unwisely after their kind, to ' raise manifold excitements on our Northern frontier, and somehow to "create a diversion." There might be some inflammable materials strewn about, to which a firebrand skilfully applied, or even a spark dropped seemingly haphazard, might produce the desired result of combustion. Truly it was worth a trial. In spite of Sectarian differences something perhaps might be done by an appeal to the common faith of the followers of the Prophet. The King of Delhi, though not much as a substantial fact, was a great and potential name; there was some vitality in the traditions which were attached to it and the associations by which it was surrounded. The Mogul himself was a Soonee, and the people of Delhi and its surroundings were mostly Soonees, and there was doubtless a difficulty in this, but not one that might not be surmounted. So Persia sent forth her emissaries noiselessly to the gates of the Imperial City, perhaps with no very clear conception of what was to be done, but with a general commission to do mischief to the English. Mahomedans of all sects might be invited to lay aside their doctrinal differences for a while and to unite against a common enemy. There might be great promises of the restoration of a magnificent Mahomedan Empire; and, as the least result of the scattering of such seed, the minds of the people might be unsettled, and something might come of it in good time. A Proclamation was therefore prepared, and in due course it found its way to the walls of Delhi, and even displayed itself on the Jumma Musjid, or Great Mosque. There were stories, too, in circulation to the effect that the war on the shores of the Persian Gulf was going cruelly against us. It was bruited abroad, also, that though the English thought that they had secured the friendship of Dost Mahomed, the Ameer was really the friend and vassal of Persia, and that the amity he had outwardly evinced towards them was only a pretext for beguiling them to surrender Peshawur to the Afghans.

It was believed in Upper India that this was to be done; and it was reported also about the same time that the English intended to compensate themselves for this concession by annexing the whole of Rajpootana. This last story was not one of merely native acceptance. It had been set forth prominently in some of the Anglo-Indian newspapers, and unhappily there had been nothing in our past treatment of the Native States of India to cause it to be disbelieved. In the North-Western regions of India disturbing rumours commonly assume a political colour, whilst lower down in Bengal and Behar, their complexion is more frequently of a religious cast. The rumour of the coming absorption of these ancient Hindoo principalities into the great new Empire of the British was well contrived, not only to excite the anxieties and resentments of the Rajpoot races, but to generate further political mistrust throughout all the remaining states of the country. It was so mischievous a report that, when it reached England and obtained further currency in our journals, even the Court of Directors of the East India

1856. Company, the most reticent of all political bodies, broke, as I have before said, through their habitual reserve, and authoritatively contradicted it.

Seldom is it that the English themselves discern the effects of these disquieting rumours upon the minds of the people. In ordinary official language, at this time, all was quiet in Upper India. But ever and anon some friendly Mahomedan or Hindoo spoke of certain significant symptoms of the unrest which was not visible to the English eye ;* and vague reports of some coming danger which no one could define, reached our functionaries in the North-West; and some at last began to awaken slowly to the conviction that there were evil influences at work to unsettle the national mind. The new year dawned, and there was something suggestive in the number of the year. In 1757 the English had established their dominion in India by the conquest of

---

* The old Afghan chief, Jan Fishan Khan, who had followed our fortunes and received a pension from the British Government, told Mr. Greathed, Commissioner at Cawnpore, in February, 1857, that these rumours had produced a very bad effect. A private note from that officer to Mr. Colvin, the Lieutenant-Governor, is worthy of citation in this place: "Jan Fishan Khan paid me a visit a few days ago with the special object of communicating his apprehensions on the present state of political affairs in India. He brought several members of his family, evidently to be witnesses of the interview, and prefaced his address with a recitation of the fruitless warnings he had given Sir Wm. MacNaghten of the course affairs were taking in Cabul. His fears for our safety rested on his belief that we intended to give up Peshawur to Dost Mahomed, and to annex Rajpootana. He said our maxim should be, 'Prevention better than cure,' and that, with enemies at the gate, we should take care to keep the inmates of the house our friends. He appeared quite relieved to receive my assurance that there was no probability of either of the apprehended events coming to pass. It would hardly have been worth while to mention this incident, but that we so rarely receive any indication of the political gossip of the day among the native community; and we may feel quite sure that Jan Fishan was actuated by fears for our welfare, and not by hopes of our overthrow, when he gave credence to the reports. I am afraid the frequent reports of annexation in Rajpootana have agitated the public mind and bred distrust among the Rajpoots. It is a pity so many years have elapsed since a Governor-General had an opportunity of personally assuring them of their political safety."

1856.

Bengal. For a hundred years they had now, by the progressive action of continued encroachments, been spreading their paramount rule over the whole country; and there were prophecies, said to be of ancient date, which foretold the downfal of the English power at the end of this century of supremacy. Ever in times of popular excitement are strange prophecies afloat in the social atmosphere. Whether they are revivals of old predictions, or new inventions designed to meet the requirements of the moment, it is often difficult even to conjecture.* But whether old or new, whether uttered in good faith or fraudulently manufactured, they seldom failed to make an impression on the credulous minds of the people. Coming upon them not as the growth of human intelligence, but as the mysterious revelations of an unseen power, they excited hopes and aspirations, perhaps more vital and cogent from their very vagueness. The religious element mingled largely with the political, and the aliment which nourished the fanaticism of believers fed also their ambition and their cupidity. In the particular prophecy of which men at this time were talking there was at least something tangible, for it was a fact that the first century of British rule was fast coming to an end. This in itself was sufficient to administer largely to the superstition and credulity of the people, and it was certain, too, that the prediction based upon it was not now heard for the first time. Lightly heeded, when long years were to intervene before its

* It is certain, however, that the most preposterous claims to antiquity are sometimes advanced on their behalf. For example, it was gravely stated in a leading Calcutta journal, that a prophecy had been discovered, a thousand years old, pointing to the downfal of the English at this time; in other words, that our destruction had been predicted many hundred years before we had ever been seen in the country, or ever heard of by the people.

1856.   possible realisation, now that the date of the prediction had arrived, it took solemn and significant
shape in the memories of men, and the very excitement that it engendered helped in time to bring
about its fulfilment.*

* Whether the prophecy was of Hindoo or Mahomedan origin is still a moot question. The following, from a memorandum furnished to me by Mr. E. A. Reade, throws some light on the subject and will be read with no little interest :—" I do not think I ever met one man in a hundred that did not give the Mahomedans credit for this prediction. I fully believe that the notion of change after a century of tenure was general, and I can testify with others to have heard of the prediction at least a quarter of a century previously. But call it a prediction or superstition, the credit of it must, I think, be given to the Hindoos. If we take the Hejra calendar, 1757 A.D. corresponds with 1171 Hejra; 1857 A.D. with 1274 Hejra. Whereas by the luni-solar year of the Sumbut, 1757 A.D. is 1814 Sumbut, and 1857 A.D. 1914 Sumbut. I remember on my remarking to a chowvey Brahmin, whose loyalty was conspicuous throughout the period (he was afterwards killed in action with the rebels), soon after the battle of Oct. 11, 1857, that the Sumbut 1915 was passing away without the fulfilment of the centenary prophecy, that he replied with some anxiety, there was yet a remainder of the year, i. e. till March 20, 1858; and before that time, in 1832, the Subadar, a Tewaree, of a cavalry regiment, in his farewell to a brother of mine leaving the service in that year, coolly telling him that in another twenty-five years the Company's Raj would be at an end, and the Hindoo Raj restored. It certainly does not much matter, but I think it is the safe view to accept the tradition as of Hindoo rather than Mahomedan origin."

CHAPTER IV.

THE NEW RIFLED MUSKET—THE STORY OF THE GREASED CARTRIDGES—
DUM-DUM AND BARRACKPORE—EXCITEMENT IN THE NATIVE REGIMENTS
—EVENTS AT BERHAMPORE—MUTINY OF THE NINETEENTH REGIMENT
—CONDUCT OF COLONEL MITCHELL.

THE new year dawned upon India with a fair Jan., 1857.
promise of continued tranquillity. But it was only a
few weeks old when the storm began to arise. It is The storm
in the cold weather that the British officer sees most rising.
of the Sepoy, and best understands his temper. Company drills, and regimental parades, and brigade
exercises, are continually bringing him face to face
with his men, and he roams about Cantonments as he
cannot roam in the midst of the summer heats and
autumnal deluges. But this winter of 1856-57 had
nearly passed away, and he had seen no indications
of anything to disturb his settled faith in the fidelity
of the native soldier. There was outward serenity
everywhere, and apparent cheerfulness and content,
when suddenly a cloud arose in an unexpected quarter; and a tremendous danger, dimly seen at first,
began to expand into gigantic proportions.

For years the enemies of the English, all who had
been alarmed by our encroachments, all who had
suffered by our usurpations, all who had been shorn

by our intervention of privileges and perquisites which they had once enjoyed, and who saw before them a still deeper degradation and a more absolute ruin, had been seeking just such an opportunity as now rose up suddenly before them. They had looked for it in one direction; they had looked for it in another; and more than once they thought that they had found it. They thought that they had found something, of which advantage might be taken to persuade the Native soldiery that their Christian masters purposed to defile their caste and to destroy their religion. But the false steps, which we had hitherto taken, had not been false enough to serve the purposes of those who had sought to destroy the British Government by means of a general revolt of the Native Army. For half a century there had been nothing of a sufficiently palpable and comprehensive character to alarm the whole Sepoy Army, Mahomedan and Hindoo. But now, suddenly, a story of most terrific import found its way into circulation. It was stated that Government had manufactured cartridges, greased with animal fat, for the use of the Native Army; and the statement was not a lie.

Brown Bess. The old infantry musket, the venerable Brown Bess of the British soldier, had been condemned as a relic of barbarism, and it was wisely determined, in the Indian as in the English Army, to supersede it by the issue of an improved description of fire-arm, with grooved bores, after the fashion of a rifle. As a ball from these new rifled muskets reached the enemy at a much greater distance than the ammunition of the old weapon, the Sepoy rejoiced in the advantage which would thus be conferred upon him in battle, and lauded the Government for what he regarded as

a sign both of the wisdom of his rulers and of their
solicitude for his welfare. And when it was learnt
that depôts had been established at three great military stations for the instruction of the Sepoy in the
use of the new weapon, there was great talk in the
Lines about the wonderful European musket that
was to keep all comers at a distance. But, unhappily,
these rifled barrels could not be loaded without the
lubrication of the cartridge. And the voice of joy
and praise was suddenly changed into a wild cry of
grief and despair when it was bruited abroad that the
cartridge, the end of which was to be bitten off by
the Sepoy, was greased with the fat of the detested
swine of the Mahomedan, or the venerated cow of the
Hindoo.

How the truth first transpired has been often told. Story of the
Eight miles from Calcutta lies the military station of greased
Dum-Dum. For many years it had been the head- cartridges.
quarters of the Bengal Artillery. There all the many
distinguished officers of that distinguished corps had
learnt the rudiments of their profession, and many
had spent there the happiest years of their lives. But
it was suddenly discovered that it was not suited to
the purpose for which it was designed. The head-
quarters of the Artillery were removed to Meerut.
The red coat displaced the blue. The barracks and the
mess-house, and the officers' bungalows, were given
up to other occupants; and buildings, which from
their very birth had held nothing but the appliances
of ordnance, were degraded into manufactories and
storehouses of small-arm ammunition. Thus, by a
mutation of fortune, when the Enfield Rifle began to
supersede Brown Bess, Dum-Dum became one of
three Cantonments at which the Government established Schools of Musketry for instruction in the use

1857. of the improved rifled weapon. Now, it happened that, one day in January, a low-caste Lascar, or magazine-man, meeting a high-caste Sepoy in the Cantonment, asked him for a drink of water from his lotah. The Brahmin at once replied with an objection on the score of caste, and was tauntingly told that caste was nothing, that high-caste and low-caste would soon be all the same, as cartridges smeared with beef-fat and hog's-lard were being made for the Sepoys at the depôts, and would soon be in general use throughout the army.[*]

The Brahmin carried this story to his comrades, and it was soon known to every Sepoy at the depôt. A shudder ran through the Lines. Each man to whom the story was told caught the great fear from his neighbour, and trembled at the thought of the pollution that lay before him. The contamination was to be brought to his very lips; it was not merely to be touched, it was to be eaten and absorbed into his very being. It was so terrible a thing, that, if the most malignant enemies of the British Government had sat in conclave for years, and brought an excess of devilish ingenuity to bear upon the invention of a scheme framed with the design of alarming the Sepoy mind from one end of India to the other, they could not have devised a lie better suited to the purpose. But now the English themselves had placed in the hands of their enemies, not a fiction, but a fact of tremendous significance, to be turned against them as a deadly instrument of destruction. It was the very thing that had been so long sought, and up to this time sought in vain. It required no explanation. It

---

[*] No greased cartridges had been issued at Dum-Dum. The Sepoys in the musketry school there were only in the rudiments of their rifle-education, and had not come yet to need the application of the grease.

needed no ingenious gloss to make the full force of the thing itself patent to the multitude. It was not a suggestion, an inference, a probability; but a demonstrative fact, so complete in its naked truth, that no exaggeration could have helped it. Like the case of the leathern head-dresses, which had convulsed Southern India half a century before, it appealed to the strongest feelings both of the Mahomedan and the Hindoo; but though similar in kind, it was incomparably more offensive in degree; more insulting, more appalling, more disgusting.

We know so little of Native Indian society beyond its merest externals, the colour of the people's skins, the form of their garments, the outer aspects of their houses, that History, whilst it states broad results, can often only surmise causes. But there are some surmises which have little less than the force of gospel. We feel what we cannot see, and have faith in what we cannot prove. It is a fact, that there is a certain description of news, which travels in India, from one station to another, with a rapidity almost electric. Before the days of the "lightning post," there was sometimes intelligence in the Bazaars of the Native dealers and the Lines of the Native soldiers, especially if the news imported something disastrous to the British, days before it reached, in any official shape, the high functionaries of Government.* We cannot trace the progress of these evil-tidings. The Natives of India have an expressive saying, that "it is in the air." It often happened that an uneasy feel-

* The news of the first outbreak and massacre at Caubul, in 1841, and also of the subsequent destruction of the British Army in the Pass, reached Calcutta through the Bazaars of Meerut and Kurnal some days before they found their way to Government House from any official quarter; and the mutiny at Barrackpore was known by the Sepoys of the British force proceeding to Burmah before it reached the military and political chiefs by special express. See ante, p. 269.

ing—an impression that something had happened, though they "could not discern the shape thereof"— pervaded men's minds, in obscure anticipation of the news that was travelling towards them in all its tangible proportions. All along the line of road, from town to town, from village to village, were thousands to whom the feet of those who brought the glad tidings were beautiful and welcome. The British magistrate, returning from his evening ride, was perhaps met on the road near the Bazaar by a venerable Native on an `ambling pony—a Native respectable of aspect, with white beard and whiter garments, who salaamed to the English gentleman as he passed, and went on his way freighted with intelligence refreshing to the souls of those to whom it was to be communicated, to be used with judgment and sent on with despatch. This was but one of many costumes worn by the messenger of evil. In whatsoever shape he passed, there was nothing outwardly to distinguish him. Next morning there was a sensation in the Bazaar, and a vague excitement in the Sepoys' Lines. But when rumours of disaster reached the houses of the chief English officers, they were commonly discredited. Their own letters were silent on the subject. It was not likely to be true, they said, as they had heard nothing about it. But it was true; and the news had travelled another hundred miles whilst the white gentlemen, with bland scepticism, were shaking their heads over the lies of the Bazaar.

It is difficult, in most cases, to surmise the agency to whose interested efforts is to be attributed this rapid circulation of evil tidings. But when the fact of the greased cartridges became known, there were two great motive powers, close at hand, to give an immediate impulse to the promulgation of the story.

The political and the religious animosities, excited by
the recent measures of the English, were lying in
wait for an opportunity to vent themselves in action.
It happened at this time, that the enmities which we
had most recently provoked had their head-quarters
in Calcutta. It happened, also, that these enmities
had their root partly in Hindooism, partly in Mahomedanism. There was the great Brahminical Institution, the Doorma Soobha of Calcutta, whose
special function it was to preserve Hindooism pure
and simple in all its ancestral integrity, and, therefore, to resist the invasions and encroachments of the
English, by which it was continually threatened.
There were bygone injuries to revenge, and there
were coming dangers to repel. On the other side,
there was the deposed king-ship of Oude, with all its
perilous surroundings. Sunk in slothfulness and self-
indulgence, with little real care for anything beyond
the enjoyment of the moment, Wajid Ali himself may
have neither done nor suggested anything, in this
crisis, to turn to hostile account the fact of the greased
cartridges. But there were those about him with
keener eyes, and stronger wills, and more resolute activities, who were not likely to suffer such an opportunity to escape. It needed no such special agencies
to propagate a story, which would have travelled, in
ordinary course of accidental tale-bearing, to the different stations in the neighbourhood of the capital.
But it was expedient in the eyes of our enemies that
it should at once be invested with all its terrors, and
the desired effect wrought upon the Sepoy's mind, before any one could be induced, by timely official explanation, to believe that the outrage was an accident,
an oversight, a mistake. So, from the beginning, the
story went forth that the English, in prosecution of a

long-cherished design, and under instructions from the Queen in Council, had greased the Sepoys' cartridges with the fat of pigs and cows, for the express purpose of defiling both Mahomedans and Hindoos.

On the banks of the Hooghly River, sixteen miles from Calcutta by land, is the great military station of Barrackpore. It was the head-quarters of the Presidency division of the Army. There was assembled the largest body of Native troops cantoned in that part of India. There, on the green slopes of the river, stood, in a well-wooded park, the country-seat of the Governor-General. Both in its social and its military aspects it was the foremost Cantonment of Bengal. As the sun declined on the opposite bank, burnishing the stream with gold, and throwing into dark relief the heavy masses of the native boats, the park roads were alive with the equipages of the English residents. There visitors from Calcutta, escaping for a while from the white glare and the dust-laden atmosphere of the metropolis, consorted with the families of the military officers; and the neighbouring villas of Titaghur sent forth their retired inmates to join the throng of "eaters of the evening air." There the young bride, for it was a rare place for honey-moons, emerging from her seclusion, often looked out upon the world for the first time in her new state. There many a young ensign, scarcely less hopeful and less exultant, wore for the first time the bridal garments of his profession, and backed the capering Arab that had consumed a large part of his worldly wealth. It was a pleasant, a gay, a hospitable station; and there was not in all India a Cantonment so largely known and frequented by the English. There was scarcely an officer of the Bengal Army to whom the name of Barrackpore did not suggest some familiar associations, whilst to numbers of the non-military classes, whose occupations tied them to the capital, it was, for long years, perhaps throughout the whole of their money-getting career, the extreme point to which their travels extended.

At Barrackpore, in the early part of 1857, were stationed four Native Infantry regiments. There were the Second Grenadiers* and the Forty-third, two of the "beautiful regiments" which had helped General Nott to hold Candahar against all comers, and had afterwards gained new laurels in desperate conflict with the Mahrattas and Sikhs. There was the Thirty-fourth, an ill-omened number, for a few years before it had been struck out of the Army List for mutiny,† and a new regiment had been raised to fill the dis-honourable gap. There also was the Seventieth, which had rendered good service in the second Sikh war. Three of these regiments had been recently stationed in the Punjab, or on its frontier, and the Thirty-fourth had just come down from Lucknow. This last regiment was commanded by Colonel S. G. Wheler, who had but recently been posted to it from another corps; the Forty-third was under Colonel J. D. Kennedy, whose tenure of command had also been brief; whilst the Seventieth and the wing of the Second were commanded by officers who had graduated in those regiments, and were there-fore well known to the men. The station was com-manded by Brigadier Charles Grant; and the General of Division was that brave soldier and distinguished officer, John Hearsey, of whose services I have al-ready spoken in a previous chapter of this work.‡

---

* A wing of this regiment was at Ran egunge. *Ante*, p. 298.

‡ See Book II.—Account of the Mutiny in the Punjab.

1857.
On the 28th of January, Hearsey reported officially to the Adjutant-General's office that an ill-feeling was "said to subsist in the minds of the Sepoys of the regiments at Barrackpore." " A report," he said, " has been spread by some designing persons, most likely. Brahmins, or agents of the religious Hindoo party in Calcutta (I believe it is called the 'Dharma Sobha'), that the Sepoys are to be forced to embrace the Christian faith." "Perhaps," he added, " those Hindoos who are opposed to the marriage of widows in Calcutta* are using underhand means to thwart Government in abolishing the restraints lately removed by law for the marriage of widows, and conceive if they can make a party of the ignorant classes in the ranks of the army believe their religion or religious prejudices are eventually to be abolished by force, and by force they are all to be made Christians, and thus, by shaking their faith in Government, lose the confidence of their officers by inducing Sepoys to commit offences (such as incendiarism), so difficult to put a stop to or prove, they will gain their object." The story of the greased cartridges was by this time in every mouth. There was not a Sepoy in the Lines of Barrackpore who was not familiar with it. There were few who did not believe that it was a deliberate plot, on the part of the English, designed to break down the caste of the Native soldier. And many were persuaded that there was an ultimate design to bring all men, along a common road of pollution, to the unclean faith of the beef-devouring, swine-eating Feringhee, who had conquered their country and now yearned to extirpate the creeds of their countrymen.

There was a time, perhaps, when the Sepoy would

---

* The General, doubtless, meant to say, "those Hindoos in Calcutta who are opposed to the marriage of widows."

have carried the story to his commanding officer, and sought an explanation of it. Such confidences had ceased to be a part of the relations between them. But it was not the less manifest that the Native soldiery at Barrackpore were boiling over with bitter discontent. They had accepted not only the fact as it came to them from Dum-Dum, but the accompanying lies which had been launched from Calcutta; and they soon began, after the fashion of their kind, to make a public display of their wrath. It is their wont in such cases to symbolise the inner fires that are consuming them by acts of material incendiarism. No sooner is the Sepoy troubled in his mind, and bent on resistance, than he begins covertly in the night to set fire to some of the public buildings of the place. Whether this is an ebullition of childish anger—an outburst of irrepressible feeling in men not yet ripe for more reasonable action; or whether it be intended as a signal, whether the fires are beacon-fires lit up to warn others to be stirring, they are seldom or never wanting in such conjunctures as this. A few days after the story of the greased cartridges first transpired at Dum-Dum, the telegraph station at Barrackpore was burnt down. Then, night after night, followed other fires. Burning arrows were shot into the thatched roofs of officers' bungalows. It was a trick learnt from the Sonthals, among whom the Second Grenadiers had served; and the fact that similar fires, brought about by the same means, were breaking out at Raneegunge, more than a hundred miles away, stamped their complicity in the crime, for one wing of the regiment was stationed there. These incendiary fires were soon followed by nocturnal meetings. Men met each other with muffled faces, and discussed, in excited language, the intole-

2 K

rable outrage which the British Government had deliberately committed upon them. It is probable that they were not all Sepoys who attended these nightly musters. It is probable that they were not all Sepoys who signed the letters that went forth from the post-offices of Calcutta and Barrackpore, calling upon the soldiery at all the principal stations of the Bengal Army to resist the sacrilegious encroachments of the English. All that is clearly known is, that the meetings were held, that the letters were sent; and Cantonment after Cantonment fermented with the story of the greased cartridges.

The mutiny at Berhampore.

A hundred miles from Barrackpore, to the northward, on the banks of the river, lies the military station of Berhampore. It was one well suited, by its position, for the development of the desired results. For only a few miles beyond it lay the city of Moorshedabad, the home of the Newab Nazim of Bengal, the representative of the line of Soubahdars, who, under the Imperial Government, had once ruled that great province. It was known that the Newab, who, though stripped of his ancestral power, lived in a palace with great wealth and titular dignity and the surroundings of a Court, was rankling under a sense of indignities put upon him by the British Government, and that there were thousands in the city who would have risen at the signal of one who, weak himself, was yet strong in the prestige of a great name. At Berhampore, there were no European troops; there were none anywhere near to it. A regiment of Native Infantry, the Nineteenth, was stationed there, with a corps of Irregular Cavalry, and a battery of post guns manned by native gunners. It was not difficult to see that if these troops were to rise against their English officers, and the people of Moorshedabad

1857.

were to fraternise with them, in the name of the
Newab, all Bengal would soon be in a blaze. No
thoughts of this kind disturbed the minds of our
people, but the truth was very patent to the understandings of their enemies.

It happened, too, unfortunately at this time, that
the routine-action of the British Government favoured
the growth of the evil; for when the excitement was
great at Barrackpore, detachments went forth on
duty from the most disaffected regiments of all to
spread by personal intercourse the great contagion of
alarm. Firstly, a guard from the Thirty-fourth went
upwards in charge of stud-horses; and then, a week
later, another detachment from this regiment marched
in the same direction with a party of European con-
valescents. At Berhampore they were to be relieved
by men from the regiment there, and then to return
to their own head-quarters; so that they had an
opportunity of communicating all that was going on
at Barrackpore to their comrades of the Nineteenth,
of learning their sentiments and designs, and carrying back to their own station, far more clearly and
unmistakably than could any correspondence by
letter, tidings of the state of feeling among the troops
at Berhampore, and the extent to which they were
prepared to resist the outrage of the greased cartridges.

When the men of the Thirty-fourth reached Berhampore, their comrades of the Nineteenth received
them open-armed and open-mouthed. They were old
associates, for, not long before, they had been stationed
together at Lucknow; and now the Nineteenth asked
eagerly what strange story was this that they had
heard from Barrackpore about the greasing of the
cartridges. It was not then a new story in the Lines

1857 of Berhampore, but was already two weeks old.[*] It had been carried as quickly as the post or special messenger could carry it from the one station to the other, and it was soon afterwards in every man's mouth. But it had wrought no immediate effect upon the outer bearing of the Sepoys of the Nineteenth. The story was carried to the commanding officer, who gave an assuring reply, saying that, if there were any doubts in their minds, the men might see for themselves the grease applied to their cartridges; and so for a while the excitement was allayed. But when the men of the Thirty-fourth went up from Barrackpore and spoke of the feeling there—spoke of the general belief among the Sepoys at the Presidency that the Government deliberately designed to defile them, and of the intended resistance to this foul and fraudulent outrage—the Nineteenth listened to them as to men speaking with high authority, for they came from the very seat of Government, and were not likely to err. So they took in the story as it was told to them with a comprehensive faith, and were soon in that state of excitement and alarm which is so often the prelude of dangerous revolt.

On the day after the arrival of the detachment from Barrackpore, a parade of the Nineteenth was **Feb. 27.** ordered for the following morning. It was an ordinary parade, "accidental," meaning nothing. But it was a parade "with blank ammunition," and a meaning was found. There were in the morning no ap-

---

[*] The first detachment of the Thirty-fourth reached Berhampore on the 18th of February, the second on the 25th. Colonel Mitchell, writing on February 16, says, that about a fortnight before a Brahmin Pay-Havildar had asked him, "What is this story that everybody is talking about, that Government intend to make the Native Army use cow's fat and pig's fat with the ammunition for their new rifles?" It must have reached Berhampore, therefore, either by the post or by Cossid (messenger) at the very beginning of the month of February.

parent signs of disaffection, but, before the evening had passed away, Adjutant M'Andrew carried to the quarters of Colonel Mitchell a disquieting report, to the effect that there was great excitement in the Lines; that when their percussion-caps had been served out to them for the morning's parade, the men had refused to take them, and that they had given as the ground of their refusal the strong suspicion they entertained that the cartridges had been defiled. It was the custom not to distribute the cartridges among the men before the morning of parade; but the general supply for the regiment had been served out from the magazine, and, before being stored away for the night, had been seen by some of the Sepoys of the corps. Now, it happened that the paper of which the cartridges were made was, to the outward eye, of two different kinds, and, as the men had heard that fresh supplies of ammunition had been received from Calcutta in the course of the month, they leapt at once to the conviction that new cartridges of the dreaded kind had been purposely mixed up with the old, and the panic that had been growing upon them culminated in this belief.*

Upon receipt of this intelligence, Mitchell at once started for the Lines, and summoned his native officers to meet him in the front of the Quarter-Guard. In such a conjuncture, a calm but resolute demeanour, a few words of kindly explanation and of solemn warning, as from one not speaking for himself but for a benignant and a powerful Government, might have done much to convince those Native officers, and through them the Sepoys of the regi-

* The fact, however, was, that there were no cartridges among the stores recently received from Cal-cutta, which consisted mainly of powder in barrels.

ment, that they had laid hold of a dangerous delusion. But Mitchell spoke as one under the excitement of anger, and he threatened rather than he warned. He said that the cartridges had been made up, a year before, by the regiment that had preceded them in cantonments, that there was no reason for their alarm, and that if, after this explanation, they should refuse to take their ammunition, the regiment would be sent to Burmah or to China, where the men would die,* and that the severest punishment would overtake every man known to have actively resisted the orders of his Government. So the Native officers went their way, with no new confidence derived from the words that had fallen from their Colonel, but, on the other hand, strengthened in all their old convictions of imminent danger to their caste and their religion. He would not have spoken so angrily, they argued, if mischief had not been intended. They looked upon the irritation he displayed as a proof that his sinister designs had been inopportunely discovered.†

Such was the logic of their fears. Colonel Mitchell went to his home; but as he drove thither through the darkness of the night, with the Adjutant beside him, he felt that there was danger in the air, and that

---

* After reading all the evidence that I can find throwing light upon this scene at the Quarter-Guard, I am forced upon the conviction that Colonel Mitchell did use some such words as these. Lord Canning was, however, under an erroneous impression when he wrote in his minute of May 13, "The inconsiderate threat, that if the men did not receive their cartridges he would take them to Burmah or to China, where they would die, which is not denied by Lieutenant-Colonel Mitchell,"

&c. &c.; for Mitchell had denied it on the 18th of March, saying, " I certainly did not make use of the expression above quoted."—*Lieutenant-Colonel Mitchell to Assistant-Adjutant-General. Published Papers.*

† "He gave this order so angrily, that we were convinced that the cartridges were greased, otherwise he would not have spoken so."— *Petition of the Native Officers of the Nineteenth Regiment. Published Papers.*

something must be done to meet it. But what could be done? There were no white troops at Berhampore, and the Nineteenth Régiment composed the bulk of the black soldiery. But there were a regiment of Irregular Cavalry and a detachment of Native Artillery, with guns, posted at the station, and, as these dwelt apart from the Infantry, they might not be tainted by the same disease. Weaker in numbers, as compared with the Infantry, they had a countervailing strength in their guns and horses. A few rounds of grape, and a charge of Cavalry with drawn sabres, might destroy a regiment of Foot beyond all further hope of resistance. Mitchell might not have thought that things would come to this pass ; it was his object to overawe, and, by overawing, to prevent the crisis. But, whatsoever his thoughts at that time, he issued his orders that the Cavalry and Artillery should be prepared to attend the morning parade.

In India, men retire early to their rest, for they seldom outsleep the dawn. It was little past the hour of ten, therefore, when Mitchell, just having betaken himself to his couch, heavy with thought of the morrow's work, was startled by the sound of a strange commotion from the direction of the Lines. There was a beating of drums, and there were shoutings from many voices, and a confused uproar, the meaning of which it was impossible to misinterpret. Plainly the Regiment had risen. Ever since the Colonel's interview with the Native officers the excitement had increased. It had transpired that the Cavalry and Artillery had been ordered out. Suspicions of foul play then grew into assured convictions, and the Regiment felt, to a man, that the greased cartridges were to be forced upon them at the muzzle of our guns. A great panic had taken hold of them, and it required but little to rouse them, in an impulse of self-preservation, to resist the premeditated outrage. How the signal was first given is not clear; it seldom is clear in such cases. A very little would have done it. There was a common feeling of some great danger, approaching through the darkness of the night. Some raised a cry of "Fire!"; some, again, said that the Cavalry were galloping down upon them; others thought that they heard in the distance the clatter of the Artillery gun-wheels. Then some one sounded the alarm, and there was a general rush to the bells-of-arms. Men seized their muskets, took forcible possession of the dreaded ammunition stored for the morning parade, and loaded their pieces in a bewilderment of uncertainty and fear.

Mitchell knew that the Regiment had risen, but he did not know that it was Terror, rather than Revolt, that stirred them; and so hastily dressing himself, he hurried off to bring down upon his men the very danger the premature fear of which had generated all this excitement in the Lines. Before any report of the tumult had reached him from European or from Native officers, he had made his way to the quarters of the Cavalry Commandant, and ordered him at once to have his troops in the saddle. Then like orders were given for the Artillery guns, with all serviceable ammunition, to be brought down to the Infantry Lines. There was a considerable space to be traversed, and the extreme darkness of the night rendered the service difficult. But, after a while, the Nineteenth heard the din of the approaching danger, and this time with the fleshly ear; saw the light of gleaming torches which was guiding it on to their destruction. But they stood there, not ripe for

action, irresolute, panic-struck, as men waiting their
doom. There were many loaded muskets in their
hands, but not one was fired.

It was past midnight when Mitchell, having gathered
his European officers from their beds, came down
with the guns to the parade-ground, where Alexander
and his troopers had already arrived. The Infantry,
in undress, but armed and belted, were drawn up in
line, vaguely expectant of something to come, but in
no mood to provoke instant collision. A very little,
at such a time, would have precipitated it, for the excitement of fear, in such circumstances, is more to be
dreaded than the bitterest resentments, and even if
the European officers had then moved forward in a
body, the movement would have been exaggerated by
the darkness into a hostile advance, and the Nineteenth, under an impulse of self-preservation, would
have fired upon them. What Mitchell did, therefore,
in the unfortunate conjuncture that had arisen, was
the best thing that could be done. He loaded the
guns, closed the Cavalry upon them, and sent the
Adjutant forward with instructions to have the call
sounded for an assembly of the Native officers. The
summons was obeyed. Again the Native officers
stood before their Colonel, and again there fell from
his lips words that sounded in their ears as words of
anger. What those words were, it is now impossible
to record with any certainty of their truth. The
Native officers believed that he said he would blow
every mutineer from a gun, although he should die
for it himself. They besought him not to be angry
and violent, and urged that the men were ignorant
and suspicious; that they were impelled only by their
fears; that believing the Cavalry and Artillery had
been brought down to destroy them, they were wild

857.   with excitement and incapable of reasoning, but that if the Colonel would send back the troopers and the guns, the men of the Regiment would soon lay down their arms and return to their duty.

Then a great difficulty arose, which, in the darkness and confusion of that February night, might have perplexed a calmer brain than Mitchell's. That the Nineteenth were rather panic-struck than mutinous, was certain. It was plain, too, that a mistake had been committed in bringing down the Cavalry and guns to overawe the Regiment. It would have been wiser, in the first instance, to have used them only for protective purposes, holding them in readiness the while to act on the offensive in case of necessity. But, as they had been brought down to the Infantry Lines, it was difficult to withdraw them, until the Nineteenth had given in their submission. The men, however, required, as a condition of their submission, that which Mitchell naturally desired should be regarded only as a consequence of it. Clinging fast to the belief that violence was intended, they would not have obeyed the order to lay down their arms; and Mitchell could not be certain that the Native troopers and gunners would fall upon their comrades at the word of command. There was a dilemma, indeed, from which it was difficult, if not impossible, to escape with safety and with honour. As men are wont to do in such extremities, he caught at a compromise. He would withdraw the guns and the Cavalry, he said, but he would hold a general parade in the morning; he commanded the station, and could order out all branches of the service. But the Native officers besought him not to do this, for the Sepoys, in such a case, would believe only that the violence intended to be done upon them was deferred for a few hours.

So he consented at last to what they asked; the Cavalry and the guns were withdrawn, and the general parade for the morning was countermanded. Whether the Sepoys of the Nineteenth had shown signs of penitence before this concession was made, and had or had not begun to lay down their arms, is a point of history enveloped in doubt. But it would seem that the Native officers told Colonel Mitchell that the men were lodging their arms, and that he trusted to their honour. The real signal for their submission was the retrocession of the torches. When the Sepoys saw the lights disappearing from the parade-ground, they knew that they were safe.

On the following morning the Regiment fell in, for parade, without a symptom of insubordination. The excitement of the hour had expended itself; and they looked back upon their conduct with regret, and looked forward to its consequences with alarm. Though moved by nothing worse than idle fear, they had rebelled against their officers and the State. Assured of their contrition, and believing in their fidelity, the former might perhaps have forgiven them; but it was not probable that the State would forgive. A Court of Inquiry was assembled, and during many days the evidence of European and Native officers was taken respecting the circumstances and causes of the outbreak; but the men, though clearly demonstrating their apprehensions by sleeping round the bells-of-arms, continued to discharge their duties without any new ebullitions; and there was no appearance of any hostile combinations, by which the mutiny of a regiment might have been converted into the rebellion of a province. Under the guidance of Colonel George Macgregor, the Newab Nazim of Bengal threw the weight of his influence into the

1857.   scales on the side of order and peace; and whatsoever might have been stirring in the hearts of the Mussulman population of Moorshedabad, in the absence of any signal from their chief, they remained outwardly quiescent

CHAPTER V.

CAUSES OF DELAYED ACTION—THE GOVERNMENT AND THE DEPARTMENTS—
INVESTIGATION OF THE CARTRIDGE QUESTION—PROGRESS OF DISAFFEC-
TION AT BARRACKPORE—THE STORY OF MUNGUL PANDY—MUTINY OF THE
THIRTY-FOURTH—DISBANDMENT OF THE NINETEENTH.

In all countries, and under all forms of government, the dangers which threaten the State, starting
in the darkness, make headway towards success
before they are clearly discerned by the rulers of the
land. Often so much of time and space is gained,
that the slow and complex action of authority cannot overtake the mischief and intercept its further
progress. The peculiarities of our Anglo-Indian
Empire converted a probability into a certainty.
Differences of race, differences of language, differences of religion, differences of customs, all indeed
that could make a great antagonism of sympathies
and of interests, severed the rulers and the ruled as ·
with a veil of ignorance and obscurity. We could
not see or hear with our own senses what was going
on, and there was seldom any one to tell us. When
by some accident the truth at last transpired, generally in some of the lower strata of the official soil,
much time was lost before it could make its way

upwards to the outer surface of that authority whence action, which could no longer be preventive, emanated in some shape 'of attempted suppression. The great safeguard of sedition was to be found in the slow processes of departmental correspondence necessitated by a system of excessive centralisation. When prompt and effectual action was demanded, Routine called for pens and paper. A letter was written where a blow ought to have been struck, and the letter went, not to one who could act, but was passed on to another stage of helplessness, and then on to another, through all gradations, from the subaltern's bungalow to the Government House.

The direction of the military affairs of our Indian Empire was supposed to be confided to the Commander-in-Chief. But there was a general power of control in the Governor-General that made the trust little more than nominal. So little were the limits of authority prescribed by law, or even by usage, that, it has already been observed, there was often a conflict between the Civil and the Military Chiefs, which in time ripened into a public scandal, or subsided into a courteous compromise, according to the particular temper of the litigants. Sensible of his power, the Governor-General was naturally anxious to leave all purely military matters in the hands of the Commander-in-Chief; but in India it was hard to say what were "purely military" matters, when once the question emerged out of the circle of administrative detail. As harmonious action was constitutionally promoted by the bestowal upon the Commander-in-Chief of a seat in Council, there would have been little practical inconvenience in the division of authority if the Civil and the Military Chiefs had always been in the same place. But it often happened that the Governor-General, with his official machinery of the Military Secretary's office, was at one end of the country, and the Commander-in-Chief, with the Adjutant-General of the Army, at the other. And so it happened in the early part of 1857. Lord Canning was at Calcutta. General Anson was officially in the Upper Provinces; personally he was somewhere in Lower Bengal.* The Adjutant-General was at Meerut. The Adjutant-General's office was in Calcutta. The Inspector-General of Ordnance was in Fort William. All these authorities had something to do with the business of the greased cartridges, and it was a necessity that out of a system which combined a dispersed agency with a centralised authority, there should have arisen some injurious delay.

But the delay, thus doubly inevitable, arose rather in this instance from the multiplicity of official agencies, than from the distance at which they were removed from each other. On the 22nd of January, Lieutenant Wright, who commanded the detachment of the Seventieth Sepoys at Dum-Dum, reported to the commanding officer of the musketry depôt the story of the greased cartridges, and the excitement it had produced. Major Bontein, on the following day, reported it to the commanding officer at Dum-Dum, who forthwith passed it on to the General commanding the Presidency division at Barrackpore. On the same day, General Hearsey forwarded the correspondence to the Deputy-Adjutant-General, who remained in charge of the office at Calcutta in the absence of his chief. But though thus acting in accordance with military regulations, he took the precaution to

---

* Just at this time General Anson was coming down to Calcutta to superintend the embarkation of his wife for England. He must have been actually in Calcutta when the Sepoys were in the first throes of their discontent; but it does not appear that the subject of the greased cartridges then attracted his attention.

857.   add that he forwarded the correspondence "for immediate submission to the Government of India,
through its Military Secretary," and suggested that
the Sepoys at the Rifle depôt should be permitted to
grease their own cartridges. General Hearsey's letter
must have reached the Adjutant-General's office on
the 24th of January; perhaps not till after office
hours. The following day was the Sabbath. The
letter of "immediate transmission" was dated, therefore, on the 26th.* On the following day, the Government of India, through its Military Secretary,
addressed a letter to the Adjutant-General's office
sanctioning Hearsey's suggestion. On the 28th, the
General received the official sanction, and at once
directed the concession to be made known to all the
regiments in Barrackpore. But it was too late. On
the previous day, a significant question had been put
by a Native officer on parade, as to whether any
orders had been received. The reply was necessarily
in the negative. Had it not been for the intervention of the Adjutant-General's office, General Hearsey might have received his reply four days before.
Whilst we were corresponding, our enemies were acting; and so the lie went ahead of us apace.

Onward and onward it went, making its way
throughout Upper India with significant embellish-
ments, aided by the enemies of the British Government, whilst that Government looked at the matter in
its naked reality, divested of all the outer crust of lies
which it had thus acquired. Confident of their own
good intentions, the English chiefs saw only an accident, an oversight, to be easily rectified and explained.
There did not seem to be anything dangerously irre-

---

* It is right that this should be
borne in mind. In all cases of alleged official delays the almanack of
the year should be consulted, that
account may be taken of a *dies non*.

parable in it. But it was, doubtless, right that they should probe the matter to its very depths, and do all that could be done to allay the inquietude in the Sepoy's mind. It was hardly to be expected that the Governor-General, who at that time had been less than a year in India, should see at once all the difficulties of the position. But he had men of large experience at his elbow; and it was wise to confide in them. In such an emergency as had then arisen, the Military Secretary to the Government of India was the functionary whose especial duty it was to inform and advise the Governor-General. That office was represented by Colonel Richard Birch, an officer of the Company's Army, who had served for many years at the head of the Judge Advocate's department, and was greatly esteemed as an able, clear-headed man of business, of unstained reputation in private life. Lord Dalhousie, no mean judge of character, had selected him for this important office, and Lord Canning soon recognised the wisdom of the choice. The Military Secretary had no independent authority, but in such a conjuncture as this much might be done to aid and accelerate the movements of Government; and had he then sate down idly and waited the result, or had he suffered any time to be lost whilst feebly meditating action, a heavy weight of blame would have descended upon him, past all hope of removal. But when he heard that the detachments at Dum-Dum were in a state of excitement, his first thought was to ascertain the truth or the falsehood of the alleged cause of alarm; so he went at once to the Chief of the Ordnance Department to learn what had been done.

At that time, the post of Inspector-General of Ordnance was held by Colonel Augustus Abbott, an Ar-

2 L

tillery officer of high repute, who had earned a name in history as one of the " Illustrious Garrison of Jellalabad." His first impression was, that some greased cartridges had been issued to the Depôt at Dum-Dum; and it was admitted that no inquiries had been made into the natural history of the lubricating material. But he was relieved from all anxiety on this score by a visit from Major Bontein, the Instructor, who asked Abbott to show him a greased cartridge. The fact was, that though large numbers had been manufactured, none had ever been issued to the Native troops at Dum-Dum or any other station in the Presidency Division.* The discovery, it was thought, had been made in time to prevent the dangerous consequences which might have resulted from the oversight. It would be easy to cease altogether from the use of the obnoxious fat; easy to tell the Sepoys that they might grease the cartridges after their own fashion. The uneasiness, it was believed, would soon pass away, under the influence of soothing explanations. It was plain, however, that what had happened at Dum-Dum might happen at the other military stations, where schools of musketry had been established and the new rifles were being brought into use. The regiments there would assuredly soon hear the alarm-note pealing upwards from Bengal. But though some time had been lost, the "lightning post" might still overtake the letters or messages of the Sepoys before they could reach Umballah and Sealkote.

So Birch, having thus clearly ascertained the real fact of the greased cartridges, went at once to the Governor-General, and asked his permission to take

---

* It should be stated that much of the laboratory work of the Arsenal of Fort William was actually carried on at Dum-Dum; but that the ammunition manufactured there was always sent to the Arsenal and issued thence to the troops.

immediate steps to re-assure the minds of the Sepoys
at all the Musketry Depôts. The permission was
granted, and orders were forthwith sent to Dum-
Dum; whilst the Electric Telegraph was set at work
to instruct the Adjutant-General of the Army, at
Meerut, to issue all cartridges free from grease, and
to allow the Sepoys to apply with their own hands
whatever suitable mixture they might prefer. For,
at Meerut, a large manufacture of greased cartridges
was going on, without any fear of the results.* At
the same time he telegraphed to the commanding
officers of the Rifle Depôts at Umballah and Sealkote,
not to use any of the greased cartridges that might
have been issued for service with the new rifles. It
was recommended, at the same time, by Birch and
Abbott, that a General Order should be published by
the Commander-in-Chief, setting forth that no greased
cartridges would be issued to the Sepoy troops, but
that every man would be permitted to lubricate his
own ammunition with any materials suitable to the
purpose. But plain as all this seemed to be, and
apparently unobjectionable, an objection was found
at Meerut to the course proposed in Calcutta; and
the Adjutant-General, when he received his message,
telegraphed back to the Military Secretary that Native troops had been using greased cartridges "for
some years," and the grease had been composed of
mutton-fat. "Will not," it was asked, "your instructions make the Sepoys suspicious about what
hitherto they have not hesitated to handle?" Further orders were requested; and, on the 29th of
January, a message went from Calcutta to the Head-

---

* Materials for 100,000 cartridges, Calcutta Arsenal to Meerut in Oc-
with implements of manufacture and tober, 1856. These were for the use
pattern cartridges, were sent from the of the Sixtieth Rifles.

Quarters of the Army, stating that the existing practice of greasing cartridges might be continued, if the materials were of mutton-fat and wax.[*]

Prompt measures having thus been taken to prevent the issue of greased cartridges prepared in Calcutta or Meerut to any Native troops—and with such success that from first to last no such cartridges ever were issued to them[†]—the authorities, perhaps a little perplexed by this sudden explosion in a season of all-prevailing quiet, began to inquire how it had all happened. Not without some difficulty, for there were apparent contradictions in the statements that reached them, the whole history of the greased cartridges was at last disentangled. It was this. In 1853, the authorities in England sent out to India some boxes of greased cartridges. The lubricating material was of different kinds ; but tallow entered largely into the composition of it all. It was sent out, not for service, but for experiment, in order that the effect of the climate upon the cartridges thus greased might be ascertained. But it did not wholly escape our high military functionaries in India, that these greased cartridges, if care were not taken to exclude all obnoxious materials from their composition, could not be served out to Native troops without risk of serious danger. Colonel Henry Tucker was, at that time, Adjutant-General of the Bengal Army, and he

---

[*] See the telegrams published in the papers laid before Parliament. I merely state the fact that such messages were sent. But I have found it impossible to reconcile the assertion of the Adjutant-General, that cartridges smeared with mutton-fat had been in use, with the actual facts of the case, as given in the following pages on the very highest authority. I am assured that the only grease used with the ammunition of the old two-grooved rifles was a mixture of wax and oil applied to the "patch."

[†] This was officially declared by Government, and in perfect good faith. I believe, however, that some greased cartridges were served out to a Goorkha regiment, at their own request.

obtained the permission of the Commander-in-Chief 1857.
to sound a note of warning on the subject. There
was in those days even a greater complication of
military authority than when Lord Canning presided
over the Government. There was an institution
called the Military Board, composed of certain ex-
officio members, one special salaried member, and a
Secretary who did the greater part of the work.
The trite adage that " Boards are Screens" was verified in this instance, if in no other, for responsibility
was effectually obscured. It fell within the range of
the Board's multifarious functions to direct the experiments which were to be made with the greased
cartridges ; so Colonel Tucker, in due official course,
addressed a letter to the Secretary to the Military
Board on the subject of these experiments, adding,
" I am at the same time to communicate the Com- December
mander-in-Chief's opinion, that, unless it be known 1853.
that the grease employed in these cartridges is not of
a nature to offend or interfere with the prejudices of
caste, it will be expedient not to issue them for test
to Native corps, but to European soldiers only to be
carried in pouch." But it does not seem that this
warning had any effect upon the Military Board.*
The ammunition to be tested was served out to Native Guards at Fort William, Cawnpore, and Ran-

---

* Colonel Tucker afterwards said in a public journal, " I do not presume to say with whom specifically the blame of this most culpable neglect may rest. Only investigation can settle that point ; but I conceive that either the Military Secretary or the officer presiding in chief over the Ordnance Department in Calcutta, is, one or both, the party implicated." Investigation proves that both officers were blameless. The routine in those days was for the Commander-in-Chief to address the Military Board, and for the Military Board to address the Governor-General. In this case, however, the correspondence never went further than the Military Board ; and it was not until after the mutiny had broken out, and Colonel (then Major-General) Tucker had publicly referred to his neglected warnings, that the Military Secretary had any knowledge of the correspondence of 1853.

857. goon, who carried it in their pouches, and handed it from man to man every time that the guard was relieved. After being thus tested for many months, the cartridges were reported upon by Committees of European officers drawn from Native Infantry Regiments, and eventually sent back to England with these reports. No objection was ever made by the Sepoys to the handling of the cartridges, and none were ever started by their regimental officers or by the Committees.

The Sixtieth (Queen's) Rifles were at this time serving in India, but the weapon which they used was that known as the two-grooved rifle; and the ammunition consisted of a cartridge of powder only, and, separate from this cartridge, a ball covered with a "patch" of fine cloth, which was smeared with a mixture of wax and oil. When rifle-companies were raised in some of the Native regiments, this two-grooved rifle was served out to them with the ammunition above described, and no kind of objection was ever raised to its use.* The grease was known to be harmless, and the paper of the cartridge was never suspected. But, in 1856, these two-grooved rifles were condemned, and new Enfield rifles issued to the Sixtieth, and also to some of the Company's European Infantry. The ammunition then, in the first instance, supplied to them, consisted of the residue of the greased cartridges sent from England for experiment; and whilst these were being used up, others of the same description, in accordance with orders from England, were being made up by the Ordnance Departments at Calcutta, at Dum-Dum, and at Meerut. The mixture of wax and oil, though it answered the purpose of lubrication at the

* See orders of 1847, given at p. 655 *Addendum.*

time of use, was not applicable to bundled cartridges,
because its greasing properties soon disappeared. So
the cartridges manufactured for the Enfield rifles
were to be smeared with a mixture of stearine and
tallow. The Ordnance Department then indented for
tallow, without any specification of the nature of the
animal fat composing it;* and, although no hog's-
lard was supplied, there is no question that some beef-
fat was used in the composition of the tallow. This
was, doubtless, an oversight, for it would have been
easy to enter into a contract for the supply of sheep
and goats' fat, to which there would not have been
the same objections; but it would seem that the
Ordnance authorities had before them the fact that
they were making ammunition, primarily for the use
of the Sixtieth Rifles, in accordance with instructions that had been received from England.

It was true, then, that cartridges smeared with
obnoxious grease had been in course of manufacture
both at Fort William and at the Head-Quarters of
Artillery at Meerut. It was true that, in October,
1856, large numbers of balled cartridges had been
sent up the country by steamer for the use of the

* It was a part of a contract for "Petty Stores," to be supplied to the Arsenal of Fort William for two years, from the 15th of August, 1856, entered into by Gungadhur Banerjea and Co. The article is described in the contract as "Grease, Tallow;" and it was to be supplied at the rate of two annas (or three-pence) a pound. From the Records of the Inspector-General's office, it appears that after the contract, dated 16th of August, 1856, was concluded, Grease and Tallow were indented for separately at various times. In an indent on the Contractor, dated September, 1856, the following entries appear:

Grease . . . { For ammunition purposes.
Tallow of { For greasing compo-
  the purest { sition for Minié
  kind. . . . { rifle ammunition.

In subsequent indents the article is sometimes called "Grease," and sometimes "Tallow"—"Required for Arsenal purposes." A circular was issued to the Department, dated January 29th, 1857, directing that, when applying tallow to articles which Native soldiers are required to handle, only the tallow of sheep or goats is to be employed, that of swine or cows being most carefully excluded.

1857.   Musketry Depôts at Umballah and Sealkote.* But it was not true that any had been issued to the Sepoy regiments; for the time had not yet come for the detachments at the Musketry Depôts to use any kind of ammunition. These detachments had received the Enfield rifle; but they were merely learning its use; learning the construction and the properties of the new weapon; learning to take it to pieces and to put it together again; learning the mode of taking sight and aim at different distances—processes which occupied many weeks, and delayed the season of target practice. Meanwhile, the old two-grooved rifles were in full service with the rifle-companies; and cartridges, as above described, with detached balls greased with oil and wax, were in constant use for practice-drill.† To these cartridges the Commander-in-Chief referred, when he telegraphed to Calcutta that greased cartridges had been long in use without exciting any alarm. It was thought at Head-Quarters that if attention were once called to the matter of the greased cartridges, every Sepoy who had used the old "patches" would be filled with alarm.

But whether this surmise were right or whether it were wrong, it is certain that the minds of the Sepoys, first in one station, then in another, were already becoming overwhelmed by the great fear. The lie had gone a-head of the truth. It is doubtful whether any orders or proclamations could have ar-

---

* The numbers were 22,500 for the Umballah Depôt, and 14,000 for the Sealkote Depôt, sent on the 23rd of October to Delhi, *viâ* Allahabad, by steamer.

† It may be advantageous to caution the non-professional reader against confounding the rifle-companies here spoken of with the detachments at the Rifle Depôts. The former were with their regiments, using the old two-grooved muskets; the latter were detached from their regiments, learning the use of the Enfield rifle in the schools of musketry at Dum-Dum, Umballah, and Sealkote.

rested the feeling of alarm, which was rushing, with
the force of an electric current, from cantonment to
cantonment, and turning the hearts of the soldiery
against us. It was plain that a very dangerous delusion had taken possession of them, and it was right
that everything reasonable should have been done
to expel it. But the Sepoys, at a very early stage,
were past all reasoning. It was not grease, animal
grease, alone that disturbed them. Grease of an obnoxious kind, for long years, had been applied by
Native hands to the wheels of gun-carriages and
waggons, and not even a murmur of discontent had
been heard. At Calcutta and at Meerut the greased
cartridges had been made up by Natives, and, at the
latter place, even Brahmin boys had been employed
in their manufacture. So it was thought that the
objection might be confined to the biting-off of the
end of the cartridge. It was true that the grease
was applied to the part farthest from that which
touched the lips of the soldier; but in a hot climate
grease is rapidly absorbed, and there was a not unreasonable apprehension that it would insidiously
spread itself from one end to the other of the cartridge. So, on the recommendation of Major Bontein, a change was introduced into the system of
Rifle drill, by which the process of pinching off by
the hand was substituted for biting off by the teeth.
This was right, as far as it went; but it could not
go far. The Sepoy was not satisfied. He argued
that he had been accustomed always to bite off the
end of the cartridge, and that the force of this strong
habit would often bring it unwittingly to his lips,
especially in the excitement of active service. There
are times, doubtless, when both the Hindoo and the
Mahomedan have an elastic conscience. But there are

seasons also when both are obdurate and unyielding. It might have been easy to persuade the Sepoys that the British Government desired to place the matter entirely in their own hands, and to leave them to grease their cartridges and to use them after their own fashion; but too many vague doubts and suspicions had been raised in past times, and too much was being poisonously instilled into them in the present, to suffer even a remnant of confidence to cling to them in this conjuncture. To beat them back at one point was only to make them take up their ground more tenaciously at another.

"We have at Barrackpore," wrote General Hearsey in February, "been dwelling upon a mine ready for explosion. I have been watching the feeling of the Sepoys here for some time. Their minds have been misled by some designing scoundrels, who have managed to make them believe that their religious prejudices, their caste, is to be interfered with by Government—that they are to be 'forced to become Christians.'" But day after day passed, and though it was manifest that there was an uneasy feeling in all the regiments, and especially in the Second and Thirty-fourth, there were no overt acts of insubordination. Their commanding officers had explained to them that Government had no such designs as were imputed to them; but even when the Sepoys were assured that no greased cartridges would ever be issued to them, and that they might themselves lubricate their ammunition with wax and oil, so deeply rooted were the misgivings that had taken possession of their minds, that they began to suspect that animal grease had been used in the composition of the cartridge-paper, and that the English were only abandoning one trick to fall back upon another. There was a glazed surface on the paper, which gave it a greasy aspect, and favoured the growth of the suspicion; and when it was burnt, it flared "with a fizzing noise, and smelt as if there was grease in it." So the suspicion soon grew into a certainty, and the fears of the Sepoy waxed stronger and stronger every day.

This was especially apparent in the Second Grenadiers; so a Court of Inquiry was held to investigate the matter. The paper was examined in Court, and the Sepoys were called upon to state their objections. This they did, with an obstinate adherence to their belief that grease had been used in its composition. When asked how this suspicion could be removed from their minds; they answered that they could not remove it—that there were no means of removing it, except by substituting another kind of paper. So Government resolved to submit the obnoxious paper to a chemical test, and the Chemical Examiner reported, after due investigation, that it had not been greased or treated with any greasy or oily matter during or since its manufacture; that by operating on a large quantity of paper he had been able to extract as much oil as could be discovered by the use of a higher power of the microscope, but that the grease was no more than might be contracted from the hands of the workmen who had packed it.* But there was little satisfaction even in this, for so obstinate was the conviction that the English designed to pollute the Sepoys, that a belief was gaining ground among them that the paper was little more than "bladder." The stiffness and transparency of it favoured this suspicion, and they could not rid themselves of the impression that it was an animal substance which

* Dr. M'Namara to the Inspector-General of Ordnance, Feb. 11, 1857. *Published napers.*

they were called upon to use. This was a far greater difficulty than the other, for it affected not merely the Rifle Depôts, but the whole Native Army; and there was no possibility of grappling with it except by ceasing altogether from musketry drill. If the fear had been only a fear of the fat of cows and swine, it might have been removed by the substitution of one grease for another; or if the external application of any kind of animal grease were objected to, oil and wax might be employed in its place; or if the touching of the unclean thing with the lips were the grievance, the end of the greased cartridge might be pinched off by the hand, and that objection removed. But to this fear of the paper used in all the cartridges issued to the Army, greased or dry, there was practically no antidote that would not have been both an admission and a concession, very dangerous for Government to make. It remained only that the English officer should persuade the Sepoy that he was wrong.

There could hardly, in such a crisis, have been a better man in command of the Division than General Hearsey; for he was one who steered wisely a middle course between the troubled waters of alarm and the dead calms of a placid sense of security. He had a large-hearted sympathy with the Sepoys in their affliction. He understood them thoroughly. He saw that they were labouring under a great fear; and he was not one, in such a case, to think that the "black fellows" had no right to suspect the designs of their white masters. He saw clearly what a tremendous significance, in the eyes both of Mahomedans and Hindoos, there was in this incident of the greased cartridges, and he could not wonder at the mingled feeling of terror and resentment that it had excited.

1857.

It was a case that in his opinion required kindly treatment and delicate handling; and he thought that much might be done by considerate explanations to restore confidence to their minds. So, on the afternoon of Monday, the 9th of February, he paraded the Brigade, and in a loud, manly voice, using good vernacular Hindostanee, addressed the assembled regiments. Earnestly and emphatically he explained to them that they had laid hold of a foolish and a dangerous delusion; that neither the Government which they served, nor the officers who commanded them, had ever thought for a moment of interfering with their religious usages or depriving them of their caste; and that it was but an idle absurdity to believe that they could by any means be forced to be Christians. He told them "that the English were Christians of the book—Protestants; that they admitted no proselytes but those who, being adults, could read and fully understand the precepts laid down therein; that if they came and threw themselves down at our feet, imploring to be made Book Christians, it could not be done; they could not be baptised until they had been examined in the truths of the book, and proved themselves fully conversant with them, and then they must, of their own good will and accord, desire to become Christians before they could be made so." He then asked them if they understood him; they nodded their assent, and it appeared both to the English and to the Native officers that the Sepoys were well pleased with what they had heard, and that a heaviness had passed away from their minds.*

But the good effect of this address was but tran- March, 185

* General Hearsey to the Secretary to Government, Feb. 11, 1857. —*Published papers.*

sitory; for when the troops at Barrackpore heard what had been done by their comrades of the Nineteenth, there was great excitement among them, great anxiety to know the result. It was plain that the game had commenced in earnest, and that they might soon be called upon to take a part in it. But it would be well first to see what move would be made by the Government; what punishment would be inflicted upon the mutinous regiment at Berhampore. Days passed, and days grew into weeks, but still the Government appeared to be inactive. The Nineteenth were quietly performing their duties, as if nothing had happened. In the excited imaginations of the Sepoys there was something ominous in this quietude. They dimly apprehended the truth, and the obscurity of their conceptions caused them marvellously to exaggerate it. They believed that an overwhelming European force, with Cavalry and Artillery, would come suddenly upon them and destroy them.[*]

Their fears were exaggerated; but they were not wholly baseless. When the tidings of the mutiny at Berhampore reached Calcutta, the Governor-General saw at once that a great danger had been providentially escaped; but with the sense of present relief came also a solemn sense of the magnitude of the crisis. The little cloud was growing larger—growing darker. Here was an act of overt mutiny, and from the very cause of all the perilous excitement at Barrackpore. The time had now come for the Govern-

---

[*] Take in illustration the following from the Barrackpore correspondence of the day: "The Drill Naick of my regiment came to me two days ago (March 8), and said the report in the Lines was, that there were five thousand Europeans assembled by the Government at Howrah—that they had arrived in two ships, and were to come up here during the Hoolee (festival)—that the men had not slept the previous night in consequence of this report."—*Major Matthews to Brigadier Grant.—MS. Correspondence.*

ment to do something to assert its authority, and to   1857.
strike terror into the minds of the soldiery. But
what was to be done? It was easy to decree the disbandment of the Nineteenth, but it was not easy to
accomplish it. There was but one European regiment H. M.'s 53rd.
along the whole line of country from Calcutta to
Dinapore, and one other at the latter place, with a H. M.'s. 10th
large extent of country to protect.   Only in the pre- Foot.
sence of an overawing European force could a thousand armed Sepoys be suddenly consigned to penury
and disgrace, and neither of these regiments could be
moved to Berhampore without dangerously laying
bare other parts of the lower provinces. For a while,
therefore, the stern resolution of Government was
shrouded from the guilty regiment. But the punishment was slowly overtaking them; though they knew
it not. A week after the commission of their offence,
Colonel Mitchell had received his orders to bring
down the Nineteenth to Barrackpore to be disbanded,
and the spacious passenger-vessel *Bentinck* was steam-
ing across the Bay of Bengal, charged with a commission to bring back with all possible haste the Eighty-
fourth British regiment from Rangoon. The English officers at Barrackpore, even Hearsey himself,
knew nothing of this, and laughed at the credulity
of the Sepoys, who believed, on the faith of their
own news from Calcutta, that this step had been
taken by the Government. But it soon became apparent that the Native soldiery were better informed
than the Division Staff, for on the 20th of March
there was great rejoicing among the English residents in Calcutta and the neighbourhood at the
thought that the *Bentinck* had returned, and that succours had arrived.

In the mean while a state of sullen quietude ob- March, 1857.

March, 1857. tained at Barrackpore. Still clinging to the belief that the Government, detected in their first design to apply the grease of cows and pigs to the new rifle cartridges, had purposely employed those materials in the manufacture of the cartridge-paper, the Sepoys went about their work under a prevailing sense of an impending danger and the aggravation of a great wrong.* It is probable that their fears were stronger than their discontents. They believed that their lives, and what was dearer to them even than their lives, were in peril, and they saw no means of escape except by obtaining the mastery over those who threatened to bring down such terrible calamities upon them. To what extent this idea of overpowering the Government had taken possession of the minds of the soldiery, and how far it was ever shaped into a definite scheme of action by those who were moved against us by religious or political animosities, can only be dimly conjectured. There was a belief in Calcutta that a general rising of the Native troops had been fixed for a particular night in March. It happened that, at this time, the Maharajah Scindiah, the greatest of the remaining Mahratta Princes, was on a visit to the English capital. No one then charged, no one has since charged him, or his sagacious minister, Dinkur Rao, with any complicity in a plot hostile to the English. They were gratified by the kind and hospitable reception which had been extended to them by the Governor-General and all the chief people of the Presidency, and were pleased with everything they saw. But it happened that

---

* So great was their uneasiness, and so strong were their suspicions, that it was believed that Colonel Wheler, who at that time went daily into Calcutta to attend a gene- ral court-martial, of which he was president, was in close consultation with the Governor-General respecting the forcible or fraudulent conversion of the Sepoys.

the Mahratta Prince invited all the principal English March, 1857. gentlemen and ladies in Calcutta to a grand entertainment on the 10th of March. The fête was to have been given at the Botanical Gardens on the opposite bank of the Hooghly river. It is said, that when the English were thus occupied with the pleasure of the moment, and the vigilance of the chief officers of Government was temporarily diverted, the Sepoys, stimulated by the agents of the King of Oude, were to have risen as one man, to have seized the Fort and all the chief buildings of Calcutta, and proclaimed war against the Feringhee. That the idea of such a rising found entrance into the active brains of some enemies of the British can hardly be doubted ; but there is no proof that it ever took practical shape as an organised conspiracy, which would have had the result I have indicated if nothing had occurred to frustrate the plot. But a circumstance did occur, which some still regard as a special interposition of Providence for the deliverance of our people. Most unexpectedly, in the dry season of the year, there was a heavy storm of rain —one of those mighty tropical down-pourings which render all out-of-doors recreation wholly an impossibility. So the great entertainment, which the Maharajah of Gwalior was then to have given to the English society of Calcutta, was postponed to a more auspicious moment, and the evening of the 10th of March passed over as quietly as its predecessors.

Of this combination of the Native troops at the Presidency there were, indeed, no visible signs. Outwardly it appeared that only the Second Grenadiers were implicated in treasonable schemes. "The Forty-

2 M

March, 1857. third," wrote Lord Canning to the Commander-in-Chief, "have refused to join in a dinner or feast to which the Second invited them; and some of the Seventieth have given up a Jemadar of the Second, who came into their Lines and tried to persuade the men not to bite the cartridges when the time for using them should come, and to deter them from finishing their huts, saying that there would soon be a great stir at Barrackpore, and that their huts would be burnt down."* Another sign of this apparent isolation of the Second Grenadiers was afforded by an incident that occurred in Calcutta. The Native Guards for the Fort and for the public buildings in the city were furnished by the regiments at Barrackpore. On the evening of the 10th of March a detachment of the Second was in the Fort, and a Soubahdar's guard from the Thirty-fourth was posted over the Calcutta Mint. In the course of the evening, two Sepoys from the Second presented themselves at the guard-house and sought out the Soubahdar. He was reading an order book by the light of a lamp when the men appeared before him. One of them then represented that they had come from the Fort; that the Calcutta Militia were to join the Fort-Guards at midnight; that the Governor-General was going up to Barrackpore with all the Artillery from Dum-Dum; and that if the Soubahdar would march his guard into the Fort and join their comrades there, they might rise successfully against the Government.†

---

* March 15, 1857.—*MS. Correspondence.* The Second and Forty-third had served together at Candahar, and were old friends. The proposed dinner was to be given during the Hooley festival, and the officers commanding the two regi- ments had agreed that there was no harm in their men dining together. The refusal of the Forty-third was not intelligible to them.

† Lord Canning to General Anson, March 12, 1857.—*MS. Correspondence.*

This last was rather implied than expressed; but the meaning of the men was sufficiently clear; so the Soubahdar ordered them to be arrested. Next morning he sent them prisoners into Fort William; and, a few days afterwards, they were tried by a Native Court-martial, found guilty, and sentenced to imprisonment for fourteen years.

This was a significant incident, but it was one, also, which might be turned to some account; so Hearsey determined not to lose the opportunity. His former speech to the Barrackpore troops had not accomplished all that was desired; but it had at least been partially successful, and he believed that something might now be done by another address to the Brigade. So he suggested to the Governor-General the expediency of such a course. On the 14th of March they talked the matter over at Government House, and Lord Canning assented to the proposal. But before the day had worn out, some misgivings assailed him, as to whether the General might not be carried away, by the strength of his feelings and the fluency of his speech, to say a little too much; so after Hearsey had returned to Barrackpore, Lord Canning sent a letter after him, recapitulating the results of the morning conversation, "in order to prevent all mistakes." This letter reached Hearsey soon after sunrise on the following morning (it was Sunday), and he at once replied to it, promising to take the greatest care not to exceed his instructions. On the next day the Native officers, who had been warned as members of the Court-martial ordered to assemble for the trial of the Sepoys of the Second, were to leave Barrackpore for Calcutta; and the General thought it advisable not to address the Brigade until after their dech, 1857. parture.* So the order went forth for a general parade of the troops at Barrackpore on the morning of Tuesday, the 17th of March.

There was no little tact requisite, in such a conjuncture, for the exact apportionment of the several parts. of the speech that was to be delivered. The main object of it was to warn the troops against designing persons, who were endeavouring to seduce them from their allegiance ; but it was desirable, also, to endeavour to pacify and reassure them, for it was plain that they were overridden by a great terror, born of the belief that the Government had sent for European troops of all arms with the intent of exterminating the Brigade. In order thus to remove the dangerous delusion which had taken possession of them, it was necessary to speak of the designs of the Government towards the mutinous Nineteenth—to show that retribution was sure to overtake all whose guilt had been proved, but that there was no thought of harming those who had committed no overt acts of rebellion. But it was not easy in such a case to avoid saying either too much or too little. " I am afraid," wrote Lord Canning to the General, " that, however brief your observations on that regiment (and they should, I think, be very brief), you will find it a nice matter to steer between exciting undue alarm and raising hopes which may be disappointed. But I feel sure that you will master the difficulty, and I leave the task in your hands with perfect confidence of the re-

* " I cannot address the Brigade until Tuesday morning, as the Native commissioned officers, who are to be members of the General Court-martial to be convened at Calcutta for the trial of the Sepoys of the Second Grenadiers must go from hence before I do so. If they heard my address to the men on parade, it might bias them in their judgment."—*General Hearsey to Lord Canning, March 15, 1857.—MS. Correspondence.*

sult."[*]   He was thinking mainly of the effect to be March, 1857.
produced upon the minds of the Sepoys of the Nineteenth. He did not wish that the decision of Government should be announced before the time of carrying
it into effect; but Hearsey saw plainly that it was
better for the general pacification of the Brigade that
the haze through which the intentions of Government
appeared to the soldiery in such exaggerated dimensions should be dispersed.   "For if the men of this
Brigade," he wrote to Lord Canning, "know beforehand what is to take place, their minds will be made
easy, and they will be disabused of the false rumours
now spread about that it is the intention of the Government to attack and destroy them by European
troops and Artillery."[†]

It was truly a great thing, at that time, to remove
from the minds of the Barrackpore regiments the
great terror that held possession of them; but the
Nineteenth had not then commenced its march from
Berhampore, and it is always a hazardous operation
to move a regiment, with sentence of disbandment
proclaimed against it, to the place of execution. These
considerations pressed heavily on .Hearsey's mind,
when, on the morning of the 17th of March, he rode
out to the parade-ground, and saw the Brigade drawn
up before him.   There was much, however, when he
prepared to address them, of which there could be no
doubt.   Most of all was it necessary to warn them of
the evil-minded and designing men who were leading
them astray; so he began by telling them to beware
of such men, who were endeavouring to take the

---

* Lord Canning to General Hearsey, March 14, 1857.—*MS. Corre-*
spondence.

† General Hearsey to Lord Canning, March 15, 1857.—*MS. Corre-*
spondence.

bread from the mouths of good Sepoys by making them the instruments of their schemes of sedition; then he spoke of the discontent still prevailing among them with respect to the cartridge-paper, in which they had never ceased to believe that animal fat had been used. Then he began to explain to them, and wisely, too, as he would explain to children, that the glazed appearance of the paper was produced by the starch employed in its composition, and that the very best paper used by the Princes of the land had the same smooth surface and shiny appearance. In proof of this, he produced, from a bag of golden tissue, a letter he had received, whilst serving in the Punjab, from the Maharajah Gholab Sing of Cashmere, and, giving it to the Native officers, told them to open it and to show it to their men, that they might see that it was even more glossy than the paper which they suspected. Having done this, he asked them if they thought that a Dogra Brahmin or Rajpoot, ever zealous in the protection of kine, would use paper made as they suspected, and, after further illustrations of the absurdity of their suspicions, told them, that if they did not then believe him, they should go to Serhampore and see the paper made for themselves. Then approaching the more dangerous subject of the Nineteenth, who had been led into open mutiny by a belief in the falsehood of the defiled paper, he said that the investigation of their conduct had been laid before him as General of the Division, and that he had forwarded it to Government, who were exceedingly angry, and would, in his opinion, order him to disband the regiment. That if he received orders to that effect, all the troops within two marches of the place—Infantry, Cavalry, and Artillery, European and Native—would be assembled

at Barrackpore to witness the disbandment, and that March, 1857.
" the ceremony of striking the name and number of
the regiment from the list of the Army would be
carried out in exactly the same manner as the old
Thirty-fourth Regiment were disbanded at Meerut."
" I inform you of this beforehand," added the General, " because your enemies are trying to make
you believe that European troops with Cavalry and
Artillery will be sent here suddenly to attack you ;
these, and such lies, are fabricated and rumoured
amongst you to cause trouble.   But no European or
other troops will come to Barrackpore without my
orders, and I will give you all timely intelligence of
their coming."   Then he told them that nothing had
been proved against them, and that therefore they
had nothing to fear ; that all their complaints would
be listened to by their officers; that their caste and
religious prejudices were safe under his protection,
and that any one who attempted to interfere with
them would meet with the severest punishment.

Having thus concluded, Hearsey deployed the
Brigade, opened out the ranks to double distance,
and rode through them, stopping to notice the men
who wore medals on their breasts, and asking them,
with kindly interest, for what special services they
had been rewarded.   The regiments were then dismissed, and went quietly to their Lines, pondering all
that they heard from their General.   What they had ·
heard was, perhaps, a little more than the Governor-
General had intended them to hear ; and Lord Canning, though he much admired and much trusted
the fine old officer, had not been wholly free from
alarm lest Hearsey should be carried away by his
feelings, and give vent to more than he had authority
for declaring.   But, he added, "it will be nothing

very mischievous even if he should do so." And he was right. Hearsey had intimated that Government would disband the Nineteenth, and in this he exceeded his instructions. But it is not certain that the Governor-General lamented the excess. He regarded the disbandment of the Nineteenth as a necessary, but "an odious business;" and, perhaps, in his inmost heart he was not sorry that he had thus escaped the painful, and to a generous mind the humiliating alternative of concealing from the regiment the doom in store for it, until he was strong enough to execute the sentence.* Indeed, he wrote to the Commander-in-Chief, saying, "The Nineteenth are marching down steadily, and will reach Barrackpore on the morning of the 31st. They do not know for certain that disbandment is to be their punishment, and, upon the whole, I think it was better not to tell them. But I admit that there were two sides to that question." The safer course on one side, and the manlier course on the other; and between these two the ruler and the man might well have oscillated. That there was danger in the knowledge, is not to be doubted. Hearsey had sought, by the partial revelations that he had made, to soothe the troubled spirit of the Barrackpore Brigade; but it soon became doubtful whether the knowledge they had gained would not excite within them more dangerous feelings than those which he had endeavoured to allay. "The regiments at Barrackpore, however, know it," wrote Lord Canning, "or, at least, fully expect it, and to-day it is confidently said in the Bazaars that the Second Grenadiers and the Thirty-fourth intend to protect the Nineteenth, and to join them in resist-

* Compare Book II., page 297 *et seq.*; Considerations on the subject of disbandment.

ing. This is leading to alarms and suggestions on all sides. Colonel Abbott, of Ishapore, advises the putting a gag upon the Native Press for a time. Major Bontein recommends bringing the Nineteenth to Calcutta instead of Barrackpore, and dealing with them under the guns of the Fort, where they will have no sympathisers within reach. Even Atkinson suggests that Dum-Dum would be better than Barrackpore. I am not in any way moved from my first intention, and nothing but the opinion of General Hearsey, who has to execute the orders, that a change of plan or place should be made, would dispose me to do so. I do not think that he will give any such opinion, and I hope that he will not."

No such opinion was given; but it was plain to Hearsey, as the month of March wore to a close, that the hopes which he had once entertained of the speedy subsidence of the alarm which had taken possession of the Sepoys were doomed to be disappointed. For when the troops at Barrackpore knew that the Nineteenth were to be disbanded, and that an English regiment had been brought across the black water to execute the punishment, they believed, more firmly than they had believed at the beginning of the month, that other white regiments were coming, and that the Government would force them to use the obnoxious cartridges, or treat them like their comrades that were marching down from Berhampore to be disgraced. So the great terror that was driving them into rebellion grew stronger and stronger, and as from mouth to mouth passed the significant words, "Gora-logue aya"—"the Europeans have come"—their excited imaginations beheld vessel after vessel pouring forth its legions of English fighting-men, under a foregone design to

March, 1857. force them all to apostatise at the point of the bayonet.

Mitchell had started with his doomed corps on the 20th of March, and was expected to reach Barrackpore at the end of the month. The behaviour of the men of the Nineteenth, ever since the outburst that had irretrievably committed them, had been orderly and respectful, and they were marching steadily down to the Presidency, obedient to their English officers. On the 30th, they were at Barasut, eight miles from Barrackpore, awaiting the orders of Government, when news reached Mitchell to the effect that the troops at the latter station were in a fever of excitement, and that on the day before an officer had been cut down on parade.

T e story
of Mungul
Pa dy. The story was too true. On the 29th of March—it was a Sunday afternoon—there was more than common excitement in the Lines of the Thirty-fourth, for it was said that the Europeans had arrived. Fifty men of the Fifty-third had come by water from Calcutta, and were disembarking at the river-side. The apprehensions of the Sepoys exaggerated this arrival, and it was believed that the cantonment would soon be swarming with English soldiers. On one man especially this impression had fixed itself so strongly, that, inflamed as he was by *bang*, which is to the Sepoy what strong drink is to the European soldier, he was no longer master of himself. He was a young man, named Mungul Pandy, a man of good character, but of an excitable disposition, and seemingly with some religious enthusiasm wrought upon by the story of the greased cartridges. He had heard of the arrival of the detachment of Europeans, and he believed that the dreaded hour had come; that the caste of the Sepoys was about to be destroyed. So,

putting on his accoutrements and seizing his musket, March, 1857 he went out from his hut, and, calling upon his comrades to follow him, if they did not wish to bite the cartridges and become infidels, he took post in front of the Quarter-Guard, and ordered a bugler to sound the assembly. The order was not obeyed; but, with an insolent and threatening manner, Mungul Pandy continued to stride up and down, and when the European sergeant-major went out, fired his piece at him, and missed.

All this time the Native officer and men of the Thirty-fourth on duty at the Quarter-Guard saw what was going on, but did not move to arrest the drugged fanatic who was so plainly bent upon mischief. But hastening to the Adjutant's house, a Native corporal reported what had occurred, and Lieutenant Baugh, without a moment of unnecessary delay, buckled on his sword, loaded his pistols, mounted his horse, and galloped down to the Quarter-Guard. He had just tightened rein, when Mungul Pandy, hidden by the station gun in front of the Guard, took aim and fired at the Adjutant; but, missing him, wounded his charger, and brought both horse and rider to the ground. Baugh then, disentangling himself, took one of his pistols from the holsters and fired at the Sepoy. The shot did not take effect, so he drew his sword and closed with the man, who also had drawn his tulwar, and then there was a sharp hand-to-hand conflict, in which the odds were against the Sepoy, for the sergeant-major came up and took part in the affray. But Mungul Pandy was a desperate man, and the strokes of his tulwar fell heavily upon his assailants; and he might, perhaps, have despatched them both, if a Mahomedan Sepoy, of the Grenadier Company, named

March, 1857. Sheikh Pultoo, had not seized the mutineer and averted his blows.

All this passed at the distance of a few yards only from the Quarter-Guard of the Thirty-fourth, where a Jemadar and twenty men were on duty. The sound of the firing had brought many others from the Lines, and Sepoys in uniform and out of uniform crowded around in a state of tumultuous excitement. But with the exception of this Sheikh Pultoo, no man moved to assist his officer; no man moved to arrest the criminal. Nor was their guilt only the guilt of inaction. Some of the Sepoys of the Guard struck the wounded officers on the ground with the butt-ends of their muskets, and one fired his piece at them; and when Sheikh Pultoo called upon them to arrest the mutineer, they abused him, and said that if he did not release Mungul Pandy, they would shoot him. But he held the desperate fanatic until Baugh and the sergeant-major had escaped, and doubtless to his fidelity they owed their lives.

Meanwhile, tidings of the tumult had reached the quarters of General Hearsey. An orderly rushed into the portico of his house and told him that the Brigade had risen. His two sons, officers of the Sepoy Army, were with him; and now the three, having ordered their horses to be saddled and brought round, put on their uniform and accoutrements and prepared at once to proceed to the scene of action. It seemed so probable that all the regiments had turned out in a frenzy of alarm, that, whilst the horses were being saddled, Hearsey wrote hasty notes, to be despatched in case of need to the officers commanding the Europeans at Chinsurah and Dum-Dum, calling upon them to march down at once to his assistance. He had just sealed them, when first the Adjutant of the

Forty-third, smeared with the blood of the wounded March, 1857. officers, and then the Commandant of the Regiment, came up to report, in detail, what had happened. The story then told him was a strange one; for it seemed not that the Brigade, but that a single Sepoy had risen, and was setting the State at defiance. It is hard to say whether the surprise or the indignation of the gallant veteran were greater, when he asked whether there was no one to shoot or to secure the madman. But it was plain that no time was to be lost. So, mounting their horses, Hearsey and his sons galloped down to the parade-ground, and saw for themselves what was passing.

There was a great crowd of Sepoys, mostly unarmed and undressed, and there were several European officers, some mounted and some on foot; much confusion and some consternation, but apparently no action. Mungul Pandy, still master of the situation, was pacing up and down, in front of the Quarter-Guard, calling upon his comrades in vehement tones, and with excited action, to follow his example, as the Europeans were coming down upon them, and to die bravely for their religion. But the crowd of Sepoys, though none remembered at that moment that they were servants of the State, none came forward to support discipline and authority, were not ripe for open mutiny; and when Mungul Pandy reviled them as cowards, who had first excited and then deserted him, they hung irresolutely back, clustering together like sheep, and wondering what would happen next. The arrival of the General solved the question. As soon as he saw Mungul Pandy in front of the Quarter-Guard, he rode towards it, accompanied by his sons and by his Division-Staff, Major Ross, and when an officer cried out to him to take care, as the mutineer's musket was loaded, answered, "Damn his musket," and rode on to do his duty.

Little inclination was there on the part of the Jemadar and the men of the Guard to obey the General's orders; but the manner of Hearsey at that moment was the manner of a man not to be denied; and supported by his sons, each of the gallant Three with his hand upon his revolver, there was instant death in disobedience. So the Jemadar and the Guard, thus overawed, followed Hearsey and his sons to the place where Mungul Pandy was striding about menacingly with his musket in his hand. As they approached the mutineer, John Hearsey cried out, "Father, he is taking aim at you." "If I fall, John," said the General, "rush upon him and put him to death." But Mungul Pandy did not fire upon Hearsey; he turned his weapon upon himself. He saw that the game was up; and so, placing the butt of his musket on the ground, and the muzzle of the piece to his breast, he discharged it by the pressure of his foot, and fell burnt and wounded to the ground.

As he lay there convulsed and shivering, with his blood-stained sword beneath him, the officers thought that he was dying. But medical assistance came promptly, the wound was examined and found to be only superficial, so the wounded man was carried to the Hospital; and then Hearsey rode among the Sepoys, telling them, as he had often told them before, that their alarms were groundless, that the Government had no thought of interfering with their religion, and that he saw with regret how lamentably they had failed in their duty, in not arresting or shooting down a man who had thus shown himself to be a rebel and a murderer. They answered that he was a madman, intoxicated to frenzy by bang.

" And if so," said Hearsey, "why not have shot him
down as you would have shot a mad elephant or a
mad dog, if he resisted you." Some answered that he
had a loaded musket. "What!" replied the General,
"are you afraid of a loaded musket?" They were
silent; and he dismissed them with scorn. It was
plain that they had ceased to be soldiers.

Hearsey returned to his quarters that Sabbath
evening, heavy with thought of the work before him.
He had received his orders to execute the sentence
that had been passed on the Nineteenth Regiment.
That sentence had now been publicly proclaimed in a
general order to the whole Army. On Tuesday morning, in the presence of all the troops, European and
Native, at the Presidency, the Berhampore mutineers
were to be turned adrift on the world, destitute and
degraded; and it was not to be doubted that they
would carry with them the sympathies of their
comrades in all parts of the country. That there was
prospective danger in this was certain, for every disbanded Sepoy might have become an emissary of
evil; but there was a great and present danger, far
too formidable in itself to suffer thoughts of the future
to prevail; for it was probable that the Nineteenth
would resist their sentence, and that all the Native
troops at the Presidency would aid them in their resistance. Some thought that the Barrackpore Brigade
would anticipate the event, and that on Monday there
would be a general rising of the Sepoys, and that the
officers and their families would be butchered by the
mutineers. The first blood had been shed. Mungul
Pandy was only the fugleman. So many of the
English ladies in Barrackpore left the cantonment
and sought safety for a while in Calcutta. But there
was no place at that time more secure than that

which they had quitted; and they found that the inmates of the asylum they had sought were as much alarmed as themselves.

It has been said that, halted at Barasut on the 30th of March, the Nineteenth learnt what had happened on the preceding evening. The Thirty-fourth had sent out their emissaries to meet their old friends and comrades of Lucknow, to prompt them to resistance, and to promise to cast in their own lot with their brethren and to die for their religion. And this, too, it is said, with murderous suggestions of a general massacre of the white officers. But the Nineteenth shook their heads at the tempters. They had expressed their sorrow for what had happened, and they had implored that they might be suffered to prove their loyalty by going on service to any part of the world. They had never at heart been mutinous, and they would not now rise against the Government whose salt they had eaten and whose uniform they had worn. But the bonds of a great sympathy restrained them from denouncing their comrades, so they suffered in silence the tempters to return to their own Lines.

As the morning dawned upon them, obedient to orders, they commenced the last march that they were ever to make as soldiers. Heavy-hearted, penitent, and with the remains of a great fear still clinging to them, they went to their doom. A mile from Barrackpore, Hearsey met them with his final orders, and placing himself in front of the column, rode back with them to the parade-ground which was to be the scene of their disbandment. There all the available troops in the Presidency division, European and Native, were drawn up to receive them. Steadily they marched on to the ground which had been marked out for them, and found themselves face to face with March, 1857. the guns. If there had been any thought of resistance, it would have passed away at the first sight of that imposing array of white troops and the two field-batteries which confronted them. But they had never thought of anything but submission. Obedient, there-fore, to the word of command, up to the last moment of their military existence, they listened in silence to the General's brief preliminary address, in silence to the General Order of Government announcing the sentence of disbandment; without a murmur, opened their ranks, piled their arms at the word of command as though they had been on a common parade, and then hung their belts upon their bayonets. The colours of the regiment were then brought to the front, and laid upon a rest composed of a little pile of crossed muskets. It was an anxious moment, for though the Nineteenth were penitent and submissive, the temper of some of the other regiments, and espe-cially of the Thirty-fourth, was not to be trusted; and for a while it was believed that the men, who two days before had thrown off the mask, were prepared to fire upon their officers. The rumour ran that many of the Sepoys of that guilty regiment were on parade with loaded muskets, and Hearsey was advised to prove them by ordering the regiment to spring ramrods. But he wisely rejected the advice, saying that all was going well, and that he would not mar the effect of the peaceable disbandment of the regi-ment by a movement that might excite a collision. He was right. The work that he had in hand was quietly completed. The men of the Nineteenth were marched to a distance from their arms, and the pay that was due to them brought out for disbursement. They had now ceased to be soldiers; but there was no

7. further degradation in store for them. Hearsey addressed them in tones of kindness, saying that though the Government had decreed their summary dismissal, their uniforms would not be stripped from their backs, and that as a reward for their penitence and good conduct on the march from Berhampore, they would be provided at the public cost with carriage to convey them to their homes. This kindness made a deep impression upon them. Many of them lifted up their voices, bewailing their fate and loudly declaring that they would revenge themselves upon the Thirty-fourth, who had tempted them to their undoing. One man, apparently spokesman for his comrades, said, "Give us back our arms for ten minutes before we go; and leave us alone with the Thirty-fourth to settle our account with them."*

Whilst the men of what had once been the Nineteenth were being paid, Hearsey addressed the other Native regiments on parade, very much as he had addressed them before; but urging upon them the consideration of the fact that the Nineteenth, in which there were four hundred Brahmins and a hundred and fifty Rajpoots, had been sent to their homes, and were at liberty to visit what shrines they pleased, and to worship where their fathers had worshipped before them, as a proof that the report which had been

* Lord Canning's reasons for sparing them the deeper degradation are thus given in a letter to General Anson: "I sent you a copy of the General Order yesterday. I have determined to omit the words which require that the men shall be deprived 'of the uniform which they have dishonoured.' Heavy as has been their crime—none heavier—it is not a mean or abject one: such as refusing to march to a post of danger; and the substance of their punishment is severe enough without being made to gall and rankle. It was for this reason that I did not originally prescribe that the number of the regiment should be removed from the Army List, or that the men should be turned out of cantonment ignominiously, as was done in the case of the Thirty-fourth thirteen years ago. The abstaining from stripping their uniforms from them will be a further relaxation in the same spirit."—*MS. Correspondence.*

circulated of the intention of Government to interfere March, 1857.
with their religion was nothing but a base falsehood.
The men listened attentively to what was said; and
when the time came for their dismissal, they went
quietly to their lines. It was nearly nine o'clock
before the men of the old Nineteenth had been paid
up; and, under an European escort, were marched
out of Barrackpore. As they moved off, they cheered
the fine old soldier, whose duty it had been to disband them, and wished him a long and a happy life;
and he went to his house with a heart stirred to its
very depths with a compassionate sorrow, feeling
doubtless that it was the saddest morning's work he
had ever done, but thanking God that it had been
done so peacefully and with such perfect success.

CHAPTER VI.

THE MONTH OF APRIL—PROGRESS OF ALARM—THE PANIC AT UMBALLAH—
GENERAL ANSON'S ADDRESS — EVENTS AT MEERUT — THE BONE-DUST
FLOUR—THE STORY OF THE CHUPATTIES—INTRIGUES OF THE NANA SAHIB
—AFFAIRS AT LUCKNOW.

Barrackpore.
April, 1857.

NOT less thankful was Lord Canning, when tidings were brought to him at Calcutta that all had passed off quietly at Barrackpore. He had sent one of his Aides-de-camp, Captain Baring, to witness the disbandment of the Nineteenth, and to bring back to him, with all possible despatch, intelligence of the events of the morning. And now that good news had come, he telegraphed it at once to the Commander-in-Chief, and made it known throughout the city, to the intense relief of many frightened residents, who had anticipated a general rising of the Native troops, and the massacre of all the European inhabitants. For the moment, at least, the danger had passed; and a little breathing-time was permitted to Government. Now that the disbandment of the Nineteenth had been effected, and the men were going quietly to their homes, there was leisure to think of the far greater crime of the Thirty-fourth. The case of Mungul Pandy, who had cut down his officer, was one to raise no questionings. Nor, indeed, could there be much doubt about the Jemadar of the

Guard, who had suffered such an outrage to be com- mitted before his eyes. The former was tried by Court-martial on the 6th of April, and sentenced to be hanged; and, on the 10th and 11th, the latter was tried, and sentenced to the same ignominious death. On the 8th, Mungul Pandy paid the penalty of his crime on the gallows, in the presence of all the troops, at Barrackpore. But although without loss of time the Jemadar was condemned to be hanged, the execution lagged behind the sentence in a manner that must have greatly marred the effect of the example. A legal difficulty arose, which, for a while, held retribution in restraint,* and the men of the Brigade began to think that Government lacked the resolution to inflict condign punishment on the offender.

Nor was this the only apparent symptom of irresolution. The Thirty-fourth had been more guilty than the Nineteenth; but punishment had not overtaken it. The men still went about with their arms in their hands; and there was scarcely a European in Barrackpore who believed that he was safe from their violence. As officers returned ‧ at night from their regimental messes, they thought that their own Sepoys would fall upon them in the darkness, and social intercourse after nightfall between the ladies

---

* "The execution of a Native officer of his rank," wrote Lord Canning to the President of the Board of Control, "convicted by his brother officers, will have a most wholesome effect. Such a thing is quite unprecedented. There has been a delay between the sentence and the execution which has vexed me, as it may give an appearance of hesitation to the proceedings of Government, which would be mischievous, and which never has existed for a moment, The delay was caused by the Commander-in-Chief not having given authority to General Hearsey, in his warrant, to carry out sentences against any but non-commissioned officers, and by an opinion utterly erroneous of the Judge Advocate, who is with the Commander-in-Chief, that the authority could not be given. Hence nearly a week was lost, and with it something of the sharpness of the example."—*MS. Correspondence of Lord Canning.*

April, 1857. of the station was suspended.* All this was known and deplored; but it was felt, upon the other hand, that if there were evil in delay, there was evil also in any appearance of haste.† Mindful that the disaffection in the Sepoy regiments had its root in fear, and believing that any undue severity would increase their irritation, the Governor-General caused all the circumstances of the excitement of the Thirty-fourth to be sifted to the bottom, and hoped thereby to elicit information which might guide him to a right understanding of the matter. The regiment once disbanded, there would be no hope of further revelations. So all through the month of April their doom was unpronounced. Courts of Inquiry were being held for the purpose of ascertaining the general temper of the regiment. It appeared that for some time there had been a want of loyalty and good feeling in the Thirty-fourth; that Native officers and Sepoys had been disrespectful in their manner towards their English officers; and altogether there had been such a lack of discipline, that the officers, when questioned, said that if the regiment had been or-

---

* It does not appear that any outrages were actually committed; but one night a Sepoy appeared suddenly in a threatening attitude before a young officer, as he was on his way home, upon which, being a stalwart and brave fellow, the English subaltern knocked him down.

† A little later the Governor-General wrote: "The mutinous spirit is not quelled here, and I feel no confidence of being able to eradicate it very speedily, although the outbreaks may be repressed easily. The spirit of disaffection, or rather of mistrust, for it is more that, has spread further than I thought six weeks ago, but widely rather than deeply, and it requires very wary walking. A hasty measure of retribution, betraying animosity, or an unjust act of severity, would confirm, instead of allaying, the temper which is abroad. It is not possible to say with confidence what the causes are; but with the common herd there is a sincere fear for their caste, and a conviction that this has been in danger from the cartridges and other causes. This feeling is played upon by others from outside, and, to some extent, with political objects. But, upon the whole, political animosity does not go for much in the present movement, and certainly does not actuate the Sepoys in the mass."—*Lord Canning to Lord Elphinstone, May 6, 1857.—MS. Correspondence.*

dered on service they would have had little faith in April, 1857. the fidelity of the great bulk of the soldiery. And at last an opinion was recorded to the effect that "the Sikhs and Mussulmans of the Thirty-fourth Regiment of Native Infantry were trustworthy soldiers of the State, but that the Hindoos generally of that corps were not to be trusted." So the Government took into deliberate consideration the disbandment of the regiment, with the exception of those officers and soldiers who had been absent from Barrackpore at the time of the outrage of the 29th of March, or who had at any time made practical demonstration of their loyalty and fidelity to the State.*

But before judgment was pronounced and sentence executed, there had been much in other parts of the country to disturb the mind of the Governor-General. He was a man of a hopeful nature, and a courageous heart that never suffered him to exaggerate the dangers of the Future, or to look gloomily at the situation of the Present; but it was plain that the little cloud which had arisen at the end of January, was now, in the early part of April, rapidly spreading itself over the entire firmament. Already the sound of the thunder had been heard from distant stations beneath the shadow of the Himalayahs,

---

* Three companies of the Thirty-fourth had been on detachment duty at Chittagong. No suspicion of disloyalty had attached to them, and when they heard of what had passed at Barrackpore, they sent in a memorial, saying that they had heard with extreme regret of the disgraceful conduct of Mungul Pandy and the Guard; that they well knew that the Government would not interfere with their religion; and that they would remain "faithful for ever." If they were sincere, their sincerity must be regarded as an additional proof of the external agency that was, I believe, at the beginning of 1857, employed to corrupt the Sepoys at the Presidency. It is a circumstance also to be noticed, that the very Soubahdar of the Mint-Guard, who had arrested the Sepoys of the Second Grenadiers, was accused, in the course of the inquiry into the conduct and temper of the Thirty-fourth, of being a prime mover of sedition.

April, 1857. and it was little likely that, throughout the intervening country, there was a single cantonment by which
the alarm had not been caught—a single Native regiment in which the new rifle and the greased cartridges were not subjects of excited discussion.

Retrospect of   The Head-quarters of the Army were at that time
events at   at Umballah, at the foot of the great hills, a thou-
Umballah.
March, 1857. sand miles from Calcutta. There General Anson,
having returned from his hasty visit to Calcutta, was
meditating a speedy retreat to Simlah, when the unquiet spirit in the Native regiments forced itself
upon his attention. This station was one of the
Depôts of Instruction, at which the use of the new
rifle was taught to representative men from the different regiments in that part of the country. These
men were picked soldiers, of more than common
aptitude and intelligence, under some of the best
Native officers in the service. The explanations of
their instructors seemed to have disarmed their suspicions, and they attended their instruction parades
without any sign of dissatisfaction. They had not
advanced so far in their drill as to require to use the
cartridges; and, indeed, the new ammunition had
not yet been received from Meerut. But the Commander-in-Chief believed that the men were satisfied, until a circumstance occurred which loudly proclaimed, and ought to have struck home to him the
conviction, that the great fear which had taken possession of men's minds was too deeply seated to be
eradicated by any single measure of the Government,
and too widely spread to be removed by any local
orders. What·solace was there in the assurance that
no cartridges lubricated with the obnoxious grease
had been, or ever would be, issued to them, if the
cartridge-paper used by them were unclean? and

even if their own minds were cleansed of all foul suspicions, what did this avail, so long as their comrades in the several regiments to which they belonged believed them to be defiled, and were, therefore, casting them out from the brotherhood?

The Thirty-sixth Regiment formed the escort of the Commander-in-Chief. There was a detachment from it in the Rifle Depôt; and it happened that one day, at the end of the third week of March, two non-commissioned officers from this detachment visited the regimental camp, and were publicly taunted by a Soubahdar with having become Christians. They carried back this story to the Depôt, and one of them, when he told it to Lieutenant Martineau, the Instructor, cried like a child in his presence, said that he was an outcast, and that the men of his regiment had refused to eat with him. A man of more than common quickness of intelligence and depth of thought, Martineau saw at once the terrible significance of this, and he pushed his inquiries further among the men of the Depôt. The result left no doubt upon his mind, that in every detachment there was the same strong feeling of terror, lest having used the new greased cartridges, or having been suspected of using them, they should become outcasts from their regiments, and shunned by their brethren on returning to their own villages. This was no mere fancy. Already had the detachments found their intercourse with their regiments suspended. They had written letters to their distant comrades and received no answers; and now they asked, not without a great show of reason, "If a Soubahdar in the Commander-in-Chief's camp, and on duty as his personal escort, can taunt us with loss of caste, what kind of reception shall we meet on our return to our own corps? No reward that Government can offer us is any equivalent for being regarded as outcasts by our own comrades." Plainly, then, it was Martineau's duty to communicate all that he knew to the Commander-in-Chief, and being his duty, he was not a man to shrink from doing it. So he wrote at once to the Assistant-Adjutant-General, Septimus Becher, and told his story—privately in the first instance, but afterwards, at Becher's suggestion, in an official letter. But already had the Commander-in-Chief learnt also from other sources the feeling of consternation that was pervading the minds of the men of the Depôt. On the 19th of March the Soubahdar had insulted the men of the detachment; on the 20th, Martineau wrote his first letter to Anson's Staff; on the morning of the 23rd the Commander-in-Chief was to inspect the Rifle Depôt; and on the previous evening a report reached him that the men of the detachments wished to speak to him, through their delegates, on parade. He determined, therefore, to take the initiative, and to address them. So, after the Inspection parade, he formed the detachments into a hollow square, and calling the Native officers to the front, within a short distance of his Staff, began his oration to the troops. He had not the advantage, which Hearsey enjoyed, of being able to address them fluently in their own language. But, if his discourse was therefore less impressive, it was not less clear; for calling Martineau to his aid, Anson paused at the end of each brief sentence, heard it translated into Hindostanee, and asked if the men understood its import. It was thus that he spoke to them:

Address of the
Commander-
in-Chief. "The Commander-in-Chief is desirous of taking this opportunity of addressing a few words to the

Native officers assembled at this Depôt, which has
been formed for the instruction of the Army in the
use of the new Rifle. The Native officers have been
selected for this duty on account of their superior intelligence upon all matters connected with the service
to which they belong. The Commander-in-Chief
feels satisfied, therefore, that they will exercise that
intelligence, and employ the influence which their
positions warrant him in supposing they possess, for
the good of the men who are placed under their
authority, and for the advantage of the Army generally. In no way can this be more beneficially
proved than in disabusing their minds of any mistaken notion which they may have been led to entertain respecting the intentions and orders of the Government whom they have engaged to serve. The
introduction of a better arm has rendered it necessary to adopt a different system of loading it, and an
improved description of cartridge. The Commander-
in-Chief finds that, on account of the appearance of
the paper used for the cartridges, and of the material
with which they are made up according to the pat-
terns sent from England, objections have been raised
to their use by Sepoys of various Religions and
Castes, and that endeavours have been made to induce them to believe that it is the express object of
the Government to subvert their Religion and to subject them to the loss of Caste on which they set so
high a value.

"A moment's calm reflection must convince every
one how utterly groundless and how impossible it is
that there can be the slightest shadow of truth in
such a suspicion. In what manner or degree could
the Government gain by such a proceeding? Can
any one explain what could be the object of it? The

Commander-in-Chief is sure that all will allow that
nothing has ever occurred to justify a suspicion that
the Government ever wished to coerce the Natives of
India in matters of Religion, or to interfere unnecessarily with their Customs, or even with the ceremonies which belong to their different Castes.

"The Commander-in-Chief regrets to hear that
there have been instances in the Army of the dis-
belief of the Sepoys in the assurances of their officers
that they would not be required to use cartridges
which were made of materials to which they could
reasonably object, and that they have acted in a
manner which must destroy all confidence in them
as soldiers, whose first duty is obedience to the Government whom they serve, and to their superiors.
The Government will know how to deal with such
instances of insubordination, and the Commander-
in-Chief does not hesitate to say that they should be
visited with the severest punishment.

"But the object of the Commander-in-Chief is not
to threaten, and he hopes that it is unnecessary even
to point out to those whose breasts are decorated
with proofs of gallantry and good service, what is
their duty. He wishes simply to assure them, on
the honour of a soldier like themselves, that it has
never been, and never will be, the policy of the
Government of this great country to coerce either
those serving in the Army or the Natives of India in
their religious feelings, or to interfere with the customs of their Castes. He trusts to the Native officers
who are present here to make this known to their
respective regiments, and to exert themselves in
allaying the fears of those who may have been mo-
mentarily seduced from their duty by evil-disposed
persons. He is satisfied that they will do everything

in their power to prevent the shame which must fall
upon all who are faithless to the colours under which
they have sworn allegiance to the Government, and
that they will prove themselves deserving of the high
character which they have always hitherto maintained in this Army."

The Native officers in front, who alone, perhaps,
were enabled by their position to hear the address
of the Chief, listened attentively and with a respectful demeanour to what was said; and when the
parade was over, they expressed to Martineau,
through the medium of three of their body acting as
spokesmen, their high sense of the honour that had
been done to them by the condescension of His Excellency in addressing them on parade. But they
urged upon him that, although they did not themselves attribute to the Government any of the evil
designs referred to in that address, it was true that
for one man who disbelieved the story, there were
ten thousand who believed it; that it was univer-
sally credited, not only in their regiments, but everywhere in their native villages; and that, therefore,
although the men of the detachments were ready to
a man to use the cartridge when ordered, they desired to represent, for the paternal consideration of
the Commander-in-Chief, the social consequences to
themselves of military obedience. They would become outcasts for ever, shunned by their comrades,
and discarded by their families, and would thus
suffer for their obedience the most terrible punishment that could be inflicted upon them upon this
side of the grave.* Martineau promised to repre-

* Lieutenant Martineau to Cap-   of intelligence and fidelity thus be-
tain Septimus Becher. The writer   comes to them the most fatal curse:
adds: "Their being selected as men   they will obey the orders of their

sent all this to the Commander-in-Chief; **and he** did so in an official letter, through the legitimate channel of the Adjutant-General's office. The matter was weighing heavily upon Anson's mind. He saw clearly what the difficulty was. "I have no doubt," he wrote on that day to the Governor-General, "that individually they (the men of the detachments) are content, and that their own minds will be set at rest; but it is the manner in which they will be received by their comrades, when they regain their regiments, that weighs upon my mind." But what was to be done? To remove from their minds all fear of the greased cartridges was only to drive them upon an equal fear of the greased paper, which it was still more difficult to remove.* He had thought at one time of breaking up the Depôt, and sending back the detachments to their regiments, on the ground of the advanced state of the season; but this would only,

military superiors, and socially perish through their instinct of obedience. That their views are not exaggerated, some knowledge of the native character, and of the temper of the Native mind (non-military as well as military) at this present moment, tend to convince me. The Asiatic mind is periodically prone to fits of religious panic; in this state, reasoning that would satisfy us is utterly thrown away upon them; their imaginations run riot on preconceived views, and often the more absurd they are, the more tenaciously do they cling to them. We are now passing through one of these paroxysms, which we might safely disregard were not unfortunately the military element mixed up in it. What the exciting causes are that at this present moment are operating on the Native mind, to an universal extent throughout these provinces, I cannot discover; no Native can or will offer any explanation, but I am disposed to regard the greased cartridges, alleged to be smeared with cows' and pigs' fat, more as the medium as the original cause of this widespread feeling of distrust that is spreading dissatisfaction to our rule, and tending to alienate the fidelity of the Native Army."

* "I am not so much surprised," wrote General Anson to Lord Canning on the 23rd of March, "at their objections to the cartridges, having seen them. I had no idea they contained, or rather are smeared with, such a quantity of grease, which looks exactly like fat. After ramming down the ball, the muzzle of the musket is covered with it. This, however, will, I imagine, not be the case with those prepared according to the late instructions. But there are now misgivings about the *paper*, and I think it so desirable that they should be assured that no animal grease is used in its manufacture, that a special report shall be made

he argued on reflection, be a cowardly staving-off of the question, so he determined merely to direct that the drill instruction should not proceed to the point of firing until a special report should have been received from Meerut on the subject of the suspected paper.

To Lord Canning, it appeared that any postponement of the target practice of the drill detachments would be a mistake. It would be a concession to unreasonable fears, which would look like an admission that there was reason in them; so, having first telegraphed to Umballah the substance of his letter, he wrote to General Anson, saying : " I gather that you are not decidedly in favour of this course, and certainly I am much opposed to it myself. The men, it seems, have no objection of their own to use the cartridges, but dread the taunts of their comrades after they have rejoined. These taunts will be founded, not on their having handled unclean grease, for against that the whole Army has been protected for many weeks past by the late orders, but upon suspicions respecting the paper. Now, although in the matter of grease the Government was in some degree in the wrong (not having taken all the precaution that might have been taken to exclude objectionable ingredients), in

to me on that head from Meerut, and until I receive an answer, and am satisfied that no objectionable material is used, no firing at the depôts by the Sepoys will take place. It would be easy to dismiss the detachments to their regiments without any practice, on the ground that the hot weather is so advanced, and that very little progress could be made, but I do not think that would be advisable. The question having been raised, must be settled. It would only be deferred till another year, and I trust that the measures taken by the Government when the objection was first made, and the example of the punishment of the Nineteenth Native Infantry, and of the other delinquents of the Seventieth, now being tried by a general court-martial, will have the effect we desire." [It is probable that General Anson here referred to the trial of the men of the Second Grenadiers.] —*MS. Correspondence.*

the matter of paper it is entirely in the right. There is nothing offensive to the Caste of the Sepoys in the paper; they have no pretence for saying so. The contrary has been proved; and if we give way upon this point I do not see where we can take our stand. It may be, as you hope, that the detachments at Umballah, being well-conditioned men, would not consider a compliance with their request as a giving way on the part of the Government, or as a victory on their own part. But I fear it would be so with their comrades in the regiments. When the detachments return to their Head-quarters, they would give an account of the concession they had obtained, which would inevitably, and not unreasonably, lead to the suspicion that the Government is doubtful of the right of its own case. It could hardly be otherwise; and if so, we should have increased our difficulties for hereafter—for I have no faith in this question dying away of itself during the idleness of the hot season, unless it is grappled with at once. I would, therefore, make the men proceed to use the cartridges at practice. It will be no violence to their own consciences, for they are satisfied that the paper is harmless; and it will, in my opinion, much more effectually pave the way towards bringing their several regiments to reason, whether the objections thereto felt are sincere or not, than any postponement. Moreover, I do not think that we can quite consistently take any other course after what has passed with the Nineteenth Regiment; for, though the climax of their crime was taking up arms, the refusal of the cartridges has been declared to be the beginning of the offence. Neither do I like the thought of countenancing consultations and references between the men of a regiment upon matters in which they have nothing to do but to obey; and I fear that postponement would look like an acquiescence in such references." So it was determined that there should be no cowardly postponement of the evil day, and the detachments in the Musketry Schools were ordered to proceed, under the new regulations, to the end of their course of instruction.*

Whilst this letter was making its way to the foot of the Hills, General Anson, whose health had been severely tried, and who had long been looking anxiously towards the cool, fresh slopes of the Himalayahs, betook himself hopefully to Simlah. That paradise of invalids, he wrote to the Governor-General, was "looking beautiful, and the climate now quite perfect." "I heartily wish," he added, "that you were here to benefit by it." But it was not a time for the enjoyment of Himalayan delights. At both ends of that long line of a thousand miles between the great Presidency town and the foot of the Hills there was that which, as the month advanced, must have sorely disquieted the minds of the civil and military chiefs. There was the great difficulty of the Thirty-fourth to disturb both the Governor-General and the Commander-in-Chief; and as time advanced, there came from other parts of the country tidings which, if they did not help them to fathom causes, brought more plainly before them the probable consequences of this great panic in the

---

* The orders issued from the Adjutant-General's office, in consequence of this decision, were, that the detachments should proceed to target practice, that they should choose and apply their own grease, and that they should pinch or tear off the end of the cartridge with their fingers. In the event of the men hesitating to use the cartridges, their officers were to reason with them, calmly in the first instance, and if the Depôt, after such an appeal to them, were to refuse to use the cartridges, more stringent measures were to be resorted to for the enforcement of discipline.—*See Letter from Adjutant-General to General Hearsey, in the Appendix.*

April, 1857.
Umballah,
Sepoy Army. Those significant fires, which had pre-
luded the outbreak at Barrackpore, were breaking
out at other stations. At Umballah especially, in
the middle of the month of April, they had become
frequent and alarming. The detachments in the
Musketry Schools were now proceeding steadily with
their target practice. They dipped their own cartridges
into a mixture of beeswax and ghee, and seemed to
be fully convinced and assured that no foul play was
intended against them. But they did not escape the
taunts of their comrades; and the nightly fires indicated the general excitement among the Native
soldiery. The European barracks, the commissariat
store-houses, the hospital, and the huts in the Lines,
night after night, burst out into mysterious conflagration. It was the belief at Head-Quarters that
these fires, made easy by the dry thatched roofs of
the buildings, were the work partly of the Sepoys
of the regiments stationed there, and partly of those
attached to the Musketry Depôt. The former still
looked askance at the latter, believing that they
had been bought over by promises of promotion to
use the obnoxious cartridges, and, as a mark of
their indignation, set fire to the huts of the apos-
tates in their absence at drill. Upon this the men
of the Musketry School retaliated, by firing the
Lines of the regimental Sepoys.* But the Courts of
Inquiry which were held to investigate the circumstances of these incendiary fires failed to elicit any
positive information; for no one was willing to give

---

* "The night before last a fire-
ball was found ignited in the hut of
a Sepoy of the Fifth Native Infantry.
The hut was empty, as the man is
attached to the School of Musketry,
and lives with them. On the following night the Lines of the Sixtieth
Native Infantry were fired, and five
huts, with all the men's property,
destroyed. This was clearly an act
of retaliation, for incendiaries do not
destroy themselves."—*General Barnard to Lord Canning. April 24,
1857.—MS. Correspondence.*

evidence, and nothing was done to put pressure upon April, 1857.
Umballah. witnesses to reveal the knowledge which they possessed.

At this time Sir Henry Barnard, an officer of Sir Henry
Barnard. good repute, who had served with distinction in the Crimea, commanded the Sirhind Division of the Army, in which Umballah was one of the chief stations. He was a man of high courage and activity, eager for service, and though he had not been many months in the country, he had begun to complain of the dreadful listlessness of Indian life, and the absence of that constant work and responsibility which, he said, had become a necessity to him. "Cannot you find some tough job to put me to? I will serve you faithfully." Thus he wrote to Lord Canning in the last week of April, seeing nothing before him at that time but a retreat to Simlah "when the burning mania is over." Little thought he then of the tough job in store for him—a job too tough for his steel, good as was the temper of it. The Commander-in-Chief wrote from Simlah that Barnard was learning his work. "It will take him some time," said Anson, "to understand the Native character and system." And no reproach to him either;[*] for nothing was more beyond the ordinary comprehension of men, trained in schools of European warfare, than Sepoy character in its normal state, except its aberrations and eccentricities. Anson had been two years in India; but he confessed that what was passing at Umballah sorely puzzled him. "Strange," he wrote to Lord Canning, "that the incendiaries should never be detected. Every one is on the alert

[*] That Sir Henry Barnard thought much and wrote very sensibly of the Sepoy Army, the defects of our Indian military system, and the causes of the prevailing disaffection, I have ample evidence in letters before me.

there; but still no clue to trace the offenders." And, again, at the end of the month, "We have not been able to detect any of the incendiaries at Umballah. This appears to me extraordinary; but it shows how close the combination is among the miscreants who have recourse to this mode of revenging what they conceive to be their wrongs, and how great the dread of retaliation to any one who would dare to become an informer." It showed, too, how little power we had of penetrating beneath the surface, and how great was the mistrust of the English throughout all classes of the Native soldiery. Let what might be the hatred and dissension among themselves, a common feeling still stronger closed their hearts and sealed their lips against their English officers.

Day after day this fact became more and more apparent. To the most observant of our people it seemed at first that, although the ministers and dependents of the deposed Mahomedan ruler of Oude might have been insidiously employed in the corruption of our Native soldiery, the alarm, and therefore the discontent among the Sepoys, was for the most part an emanation of Hindooism. The inquiries into the state of the Thirty-fourth Regiment at Barrackpore had resulted in a belief that the Mahomedan and Sikh soldiers were true to their salt; and so strong was the impression that only the Hindoos of the disbanded Nineteenth were really disaffected, that, after the dispersion of the regiment, it was believed that the whole history of the mutiny, which had ruined them, might be gathered from the Mussulman Sepoys. But, although a sagacious civil officer was put upon their track, and every effort was made to elicit the desired information, the attempt was altogether a failure. Whether these first impressions were right or wrong, whether the mutiny was, in its origin and inception, a Hindoo or a Ma- homedan movement, will hereafter be a subject of inquiry. But, before the end of the month of April, it must have been apparent to Lord Canning that nothing was to be hoped from that antagonism of the Asiatic races, which had ever been regarded as the main element of our strength and safety. Mahomedans and Hindoos were plainly united against us.

From an unexpected quarter there soon came proof of this union. As the new Enfield rifle had been the outward and visible cause of the great fear that had arisen in the minds of the soldiery, it was natural that the anxieties of the Government should, in the first instance, have been confined to the Native Infantry. In the Infantry Regiments a very large majority of the men were Hindoos; whilst in the Cavalry the Mahomedan element was proportionately much stronger.* But now there came from Meerut strange news to the effect that a Cavalry regiment had revolted.

To this station many unquiet thoughts had been directed; for it was one of the largest and most important in the whole range of our Indian territories. There, troops of all arms, both European and Native, were assembled. There, the Head-Quarters of the Bengal Artillery were established. There, the Ordnance Commissariat were diligently employed, in the Expense Magazine, on the manufacture of greased cartridges. There, the English Riflemen of the Sixtieth, not without some feelings of disgust, were using the unsavory things. More than once there had

---

* As a rule, the Mahomedans were better horsemen and more adroit swordsmen than the Hindoos, and therefore they made more serviceable troopers. It is stated, however, that in the Third Regiment of Regular Cavalry, which led off the dance of death at Meerut, there were an unusual number of Brahmins.

April, 1857.
Meerut.
been reports that the Sepoys had risen at Meerut, and that the Europeans had been let loose against them. With vague but eager expectancy the Native regiments at all the large stations in Upper India were looking in that direction, as for a signal which they knew would soon be discerned. Men asked each other what was the news from Meerut, and looked into the Native newspapers for the suggestive heading; for it was the cradle of all sorts of strange and disturbing stories. In this month of April its crowded Lines and busy Bazaars were stirred by indefinite apprehensions of something coming. Every day the excitement increased, for every day some new story, intended to confirm the popular belief in the base designs of the English, found its way into circulation. The emissary of evil, who, in some shape or other, was stalking across the country, was at Meerut in the guise of a wandering Fakeer, or religious mendicant, riding on an elephant, with many followers. That he was greatly disturbing the minds of men was certain; so the Police authorities ordered him to depart. He moved; but it was believed that he went no farther than the Lines of one of the Native regiments.*

In no place was the story of the greased cartridges discussed with greater eagerness than at Meerut; in

---

* Compare following passage in the Meerut Narrative of Mr. Williams, Commissioner First Division: "All the rumours by which the minds of the Native soldiers were prepared for revolt, were industriously disseminated at Meerut, especially those regarding the use of polluting grease in the preparation of the new cartridges, and the mixture of ground bones in flour, by which, it was said, Government desired to destroy the religion of the people. One of the many emissaries who were moving about the country appeared at Meerut in April, ostensibly as a fakeer, riding on an elephant with followers, and having with him horses and native carriages. The frequent visits of the men of the Native regiments to him attracted attention, and he was ordered, through the police, to leave the place; he apparently complied, but, it is said, he stayed some time in the Lines of the 20th Native Infantry —*Unpublished Records.*

no place was there a more disturbing belief that this
was a part of a great scheme for the defilement of
the people. It was of little use to declare to them
that not a single soldier would ever be required to
use a cartridge greased by any one but himself, for
the greasing of the cartridges was in their estimation
only one of many fraudulent devices, and every one
believed that the dry cartridges contained the obnoxious fat. So, in the beginning of the fourth week
of April, the excitement, which for many weeks had
been growing stronger and stronger, broke out into
an act of open mutiny. The troopers of the Third
Cavalry were the first to resist the orders of their
officers. They had no new weapons; no new ammunition. The only change introduced into their practice was that which substituted the pinching or tear-
ing off, for the biting off, the end of the cartridges
which they used with their carbines. This change
in the drill was to be explained to them on a parade
of the skirmishers of the regiment, which was to be
held on the morning of the 24th of April. On the
preceding evening a report ran through cantonments that the troopers would refuse to touch the
cartridges. The parade was held, and of ninety
men, to whom the ammunition was to have been
served out, only five obeyed the orders of their
officers. In vain Colonel Carmichael Smyth explained to them that the change had been introduced
from a kindly regard for their own scruples. They
were dogged and obdurate, and would not touch the
cartridges. So the parade was dismissed, and the
eighty-five troopers of the Third were ordered for
Court-martial.

All this made it manifest to Lord Canning that
the worst suspicions were deeply rooted in the Sepoy
Army; and though he at all times maintained a

The story
the groun
bones.

April, 1857. calm and cheerful demeanour, he thought much and anxiously of the signs and symptoms of the troubled spirit that was abroad. There were many indications that these suspicions were not confined to the military classes, but were disquieting also the general community. Not only in Meerut, but also in many other parts of the country, there was a belief that the English designed to defile both Hindoos and Mahomedans, by polluting with unclean matter the daily food of the people. It has been shown that a suspicion of a similar character was abroad at the time of the Mutiny at Vellore.* Now the disturbing rumour, cunningly circulated, took many portentous shapes. It was said that the officers of the British. Government, under command from the Company and the Queen, had mixed ground bones with the flour and the salt sold in the Bazaars; that they had adulterated all the ghee† with animal fat; that bones had been burnt with the common sugar of the country; and that not only bone-dust flour, but the flesh of cows and pigs, had been thrown into the wells to pollute the drinking water of the people. Of this great imaginary scheme of contamination the matter of the greased cartridges was but a part, especially addressed to one class of the community. All classes, it was believed, were to be defiled at the same time; and the story ran that the "burra sahibs," or great English lords, had commanded all the princes, nobles, landholders, merchants, and cultivators of the land, to feed together upon English bread.

Of these preposterous fables, the one which made the strongest impression on the public mind was the

* *Ante*, page 248. It was then said that the English had mixed the blood of cows and pigs with all the newly manufactured salt.

† This is the ordinary grease used for cooking purposes throughout India.

story of the bone-dust flour.   That it was current in April, 1857.
March at Barrackpore is certain.*   In the early part
of April, a circumstance occurred which proved that
the panic had then spread to the Upper Provinces.
It happened that flour having risen to an exceptionally
high price at Cawnpore, certain dealers at Meerut
chartered a number of Government boats to carry a
large supply down the canal to the former place.
When the first instalment arrived, and was offered for
sale at a price considerably below that which had
previously ruled in the Bazaars, it found a ready
market; but before the remainder reached Cawnpore, a story had been circulated to the effect that the
grain had been ground in the canal mills, under European supervision, and that the dust of cows' bones
had been mixed up with it, with the intention of
destroying the caste of all who should eat it.   Such
a story as this, circulated in the Lines and the Military Bazaars of Cawnpore, at once stopped the sale
of the Meerut flour.   Not a Sepoy would touch it,
not a person of any kind would purchase it, cheap
as was the price at which it was obtainable in comparison with all the other supplies in the market.
Rapidly spread the alarm from one station to another, and as tidings came of the arrival of imaginary
boat-loads or camel-loads of flour and bone-dust, men
threw away the bread that they were eating, and be-

---

* It was brought to the notice of
General Hearsey by a native anonymous letter, picked up at the gate of
Major Matthews, who commanded
the Forty-third. The Major sent it to
Hearsey's staff, describing it as "sad
trash;" and Hearsey, in forwarding it
to the Military Secretary, expressed
regret that the contemptible pro-
duction had not been burnt as soon
as it was found. But History re-
joices in the preservation of such
contemptible productions. I have
given it entire in the Appendix.
There are many such in my possession, but this is the earliest in date,
and gives the most comprehensive
account of the rumours circulated
by our enemies.

lieved themselves already defiled.* Whether, as some said, this was a trick of the Cawnpore grain merchants to keep up the price of flour, or whether the story had been set afloat under the same influences as those which had given so false a colouring to the accident of the greased cartridges, and had associated with all the other wild fictions of which I have spoken, cannot with certainty be declared. But, whatsoever the origin of the fable, it sunk deeply into men's minds, and fixed there more ineradicably than ever their belief in the stern resolution of the Government to destroy the caste of the people by fraudulently bringing, in one way or other, the unclean thing to their lips.

The story of
the chu-
patties.

It fixed, too, more firmly than before in the mind of Lord Canning, the belief that a great fear was spreading itself among the people, and that there was more danger in such a feeling than in a great hatred. Thinking of this, he thought also of another strange story that had come to him from the North-West, and which even the most experienced men about him were incompetent to explain. From village to village, brought by one messenger and sent onward by another, passed a mysterious token in the shape of one of those flat cakes made from flour and water, and forming the common bread of the people, which, in their language, are called Chupatties. All that was known about it was, that a messenger appeared, gave the cake to the head man of one village, and requested him to despatch it onward to the next; and

---

* Colonel Baird Smith to Mr. Colvin—Mr. Martin Gubbins to the same. "Once alarmed," wrote the latter, "they drink in the greatest follies. Bone-dust attah alarm has taken hold of men's minds at several of our stations, and Sepoys, private servants, Zemindars attending Court, have flung away their roti (bread) on hearing that five camel-loads of bone-dust attah had reached the station."—*MS. Correspondence.*

that, in this way, it travelled from place to place; no one refusing, no one doubting, few even questioning, in blind obedience to a necessity felt rather than understood. After a while, this practice became known to the functionaries of the English Government, who thought much of it, or thought little of it, according to their individual dispositions, and interpreted it, in divers ways, according to the light that was in them.* The greater number looked upon it as a signal of warning and preparation, designed to tell the people that something great and portentous was about to happen, and to prompt them to be ready for the crisis. One great authority wrote to the Governor-General that he had been told that the chupatty was the symbol of men's food, and that its circulation was intended to alarm and to influence men's minds by indicating to them that their means of subsistence would be taken from them, and to tell them, therefore, to hold together. Others, laughing to scorn this notion of the fiery cross, saw in it only a common superstition of the country. It was said that it was no unwonted thing for a Hindoo, in whose family sickness had broken out, to institute this transmission of chupatties, in the belief that it would carry off the disease; or for a community, when the cholera or other pestilence was raging, to betake themselves to a similar practice. Then, again, it was believed by others that the cakes had been sent abroad by enemies of the British Government, for the purpose of attaching to their circulation another dangerous fiction, to the effect

---

* Mr. Ford, Collector of Goorgaon, first brought it to the notice of the Lieutenant-Governor of the North-Western Provinces, Mr. Colvin, who issued circular orders on the subject to all the local officers in charge of districts.

April, 1857. that there was bone-dust in them, and that the English had resorted to this supplementary method of defiling the people. Some, too, surmised that, by a device sometimes used for other purposes,* seditious letters were in this manner forwarded from village to village, read by the village chief, again crusted over with flour, and sent on in the shape of a chupatty, to be broken by the next recipient. But whatsoever the real history of the movement, it had doubtless the effect of producing and keeping alive much popular excitement in the districts through which the cakes were transmitted; and it may be said that its action was too widely diffused, and that it lasted for too long a time, to admit of a very ready adoption of the theory that it was of an accidental character, the growth only of domestic, or even of municipal, anxieties.† Some saw in it much meaning; some saw none. Time has thrown no new

---

* In this manner communication was sometimes held with the inmates of our gaols. See the "Revelations of an Orderly," by Pannchkowree Khan: "Suppose a prisoner is confined under the bayonet of Sepoys, he must be permitted to eat bread. The preparer of food is bribed, and a short note is put into a chupatty, or a sentence is written on a plate, and when the bread is taken up the prisoner reads what is written."

† The circulation of the chupatties commenced at the beginning of the year. "The year 1857," writes Captain Keatinge, "opened in Nimar by a general distribution of small cakes, which were passed on from village to village. The same, I am aware, has occurred all over Northern India, and has been spoken of as having been a signal for the disturbances which took place later in the year. At the time they appeared in Nimar, they were everywhere brought from the direction of Indore. That city was at the time afflicted with a severe visitation of cholera, and numbers of inhabitants died daily. It was at that time understood by the people in Nimar, and is still believed, that the cakes of wheat were despatched from Indore after the performance over them of incantations that would ensure the pestilence accompanying them. The cakes did not come straight from North to South, for they were received at Bujengghur, more than half way between Indore and Gwalior, on the 9th of February, but had been distributed at Mundlaiser on the 19th of January. This habit of passing on holy and unholy things is not unknown at Nimar. When smallpox breaks out in a village, a goat is procured, a cocoa-nut tied to its neck, and it is taken by the chowkeedar to the first village on the road to Mundatta; it is not allowed to enter the town, but is

light upon it. Opinions still widely differ. And all April, 1857.
that History can record with any certainty is, that
the bearers of these strange missives went from place
to place, and that ever as they went new excitements were engendered, and vague expectations were
raised.

That in all this there was something more than Political
mere military disaffection was manifest to Lord intrigues.
Canning; but neither he nor his confidential advisers could clearly discern what it was. He had a
general conception that evil-minded men, with strong
resentments to be gratified by the ruin of the British
Government, were sending forth their emissaries; but,
with the exception of the ministers of the dethroned
King of Oude, whom he had suspected from the first, *

taken by a villager to the next
hamlet, and so passed on without
rest to its destination." This last
is the scripturally recorded scape-
goat. With respect to the chupatties,
consult also the report of Major
Erskine, Commissioner of the Saugor
and Nerbudda territories: "So far
back as January, 1857," he writes,
"small wheaten cakes (chupatties)
were passed in a most mysterious
manner from village to village in
most of the districts, and, although
all took it as a signal that something was coming, nobody in the
division, I believe, knew what it
portended, or whence it came, and
it appeared to have been little
thought about except that in the
money-market of Saugor it is said
to have had some slight effect in
bill transactions. I reported the
matter to Government at the time,
but even now it is a matter of doubt
if the signal was understood by any
one, or if it referred to the coming
rebellion, though such is now the
general opinion." I have thrown
together in the Appendix some further facts and fancies illustrative of
this interesting subject of inquiry.

* In my mind there is no doubt
of the activity, at this time, of the
Oude people at Garden Reach. The
Sepoys at Barrackpore were induced
to believe that, if they broke away
from the English harness, they would
obtain more lucrative service under
the restored kingship of Oude. I
have before me some letters, original and translated, of a Jemadar of
the Thirty-fourth Regiment, which
contain numerous allusions to the
Future of the King's service. Take
the following: "The Second Grenadiers said, in the beginning of April,
'We will go to our homes sooner
than bite the blank ammunition.'
The regiments were unanimous in
joining the King of Oude." "The
Soubahdars of the Quarter-Guard
said, 'We have sided with the King
of Oude, but nothing has come of
it.'" "Ramshaee Lalla said, 'It
would have been well for us.'" This
also has its significance: "Soubahdar Muddeh Khan, Sirdar Khan, and
Ramshaee Lalla said, 'The Feringhee Beteechoots' (a vile term of op-
probrium) 'are unequalled in their
want of faith. The King of Lucknow put down his arms, and the

he could not individualise his suspicions. How was he to know, how was any Englishman, shut up all day long in his house, and having no more living intercourse with the people than if they were clay figures, to know what was passing beneath the surface of Native society? If anything were learnt at that time to throw light upon the sources of the great events that were to happen, it was by merest accident, and the full force of the revelation was rarely discernible at the time. It was remembered afterwards that, in the early part of this year, one man, a Mahratta by race, a Brahmin by caste, of whom something has already been recorded in this narrative, was displaying, in his movements, an unwonted activity, which created surprise, but scarcely aroused suspicion. This man was Dundoo Punt, commonly known as the Nana Sahib, of Bhitoor—the adopted son of the Peishwah, Badjee Rao. He was not given to distant journeyings; indeed, he was seldom seen beyond the limits of his own estate. But in the early months of 1857, having visited Calpee, he made a journey to Delhi, and, a little later in the year, paid a visit to Lucknow. It was in the middle of April that he started on this last journey. On the 17th of that month, Mr. Morland, then one of the Agra Judges, who shortly after the Peishwah's death had been Commissioner at Bhitoor, and who had endeavoured to rescue from resumption a part of his pension, paid a visit to the Nana at that

Government have given him no allowance. We advised the King to put down his arms. The treachery of the Government is unrivalled.' " Colonel Wheler said that the writer of these letters appeared to be "affected in the head." It will be remembered that the Native officer who reported the coming massacre of Vellore was also said to be mad.

General Hearsey, sending on the correspondence to Government, said that there was " much method in his supposed madness;" and added, that " much important information on the whole cause and subject of this *supposed* Cartridge Mutiny might be elicited from him."—*MS. Correspondence.*

place. The wily Mussulman Agent, Azim-oollah Khan, who had pleaded his cause in England, was with Dundoo Punt when the English gentleman was announced, and they talked freely together, as friends talk, no suspicion on the one side, and no appearance of anything unwonted on the other. All was outwardly smooth and smiling. The Mahratta was as profuse as ever in his expressions of respect and esteem; and when Morland took his departure, the brother of Dundoo Punt told him that the Nana purposed to return the visit of the Sahib next day at Cawnpore. The next day happened to be Sunday, and Morland was anxious, therefore, to decline the visit; but the Nana Sahib went to Cawnpore, and again sent Baba Bhut to the English gentleman to propose an interview. What he wished to say to the man who had been kind to him will now never be known, for Morland declined the meeting, on the plea that it was the Sabbath, and expressed regret that the Nana Sahib should have made the journey to no purpose. To this the Brahmin replied, that his brother was on his way to Lucknow to visit one of the Newabs. There was something in all this strange and surprising. An English nobleman, in the course of three or four months, might visit all the chief cities of Europe without any one taking heed of the occurrence. But the nobility of India are little given to travelling; and the Nana Sahib had rarely gone beyond the limits of Bhitoor.*

* A different statement has, I know, been made and commonly accepted. It is the belief that the Nana Sahib was frequently to be seen at Cawnpore, riding or driving on the Mall, and mixing freely with the European residents of the place. But the truth is, he eschewed Cawnpore, for the reason which induced his adoptive father, Badjee Rao, to eschew it, namely, that a salute was not given to him on entering the cantonment. The person generally known in Cawnpore as the "Nana" was not Dundoo Punt, but Nana Nerain Rao, the eldest son of the ex-Peishwah's chief adviser and manager, the Sou-

April, 1857. That, within so short a time, he should make these three journeys, was a fact to excite speculation ; but he was held to be a quiet, inoffensive person, good natured, perhaps somewhat dull, and manifestly not of that kind of humanity of which conspirators are made, so no political significance was attached to the fact. What likelihood was there, at that time, that such a man as Dundoo Punt, heavy and seemingly impassive, who had for some years quietly accepted his position, and during that time done many acts of kindness and hospitality to the English gentlemen, should suddenly become a plotter against the State? Had any one then said that it behoved the Government to mark the movements of that man, he would have been laughed to scorn as an alarmist. We never know in India how many are the waiters and the watchers ; we never know at what moment our enemies, sluggish in their hatreds as in all else, may exact the payment of old scores which we have thought were long ago forgotten.

So Dundoo Punt, Nana Sahib, passed on, about some business known to himself, utterly unknown to European functionaries, to Calpee, on the banks of the Jumna, to the great imperial city of Delhi, and to Lucknow, the capital of Oude. In the last of these places, when the Nana arrived, Henry Lawrence was diligently, with his whole good heart, striving to make right all that had gone wrong during the time of his predecessor. But again the handwriting on the wall traced those fatal words, "Too late." If he had but gone to Lucknow when he had first offered to go, how different would all have been! It was on the 18th of April that the Nana Sahib started on his journey to Lucknow. On

bahdar Ramchunder Punt, who, after his master's death, resided at Cawnpore, and was on terms of social familiarity with many of the principal European residents.

that day Henry Lawrence wrote a long letter to the Governor-General, telling him that he had discerned signs of dangerous coalitions between the regular Sepoy regiments, the Irregulars taken into our service from the old Oude Army, and the men of the Police battalions; symptoms also of intrigues on foot among some of the chief people of the city. There were many elements of trouble; and now they were beginning to develop themselves in a manner significant of a general outburst of popular discontent. "This city," wrote Henry Lawrence on that 18th of April, "is said to contain some six or seven hundred thousand souls, and does certainly contain many thousands (twenty thousand, I was told yesterday) of disbanded soldiers, and of hungry, nay starving, dependents of the late Government. This very morning a clod was thrown at Mr. Ommaney (the Judicial Commissioner), and another struck Major Anderson (Chief Engineer) whilst in a buggy with myself. . . . . The improvements in the city here go on very fast—too fast and too roughly. Much discontent has been caused by demolition of buildings, and still more by threats of further similar measures; also regarding the seizure of religious and other edifices, and plots of ground, as Huzool or Government property. I have visited many of these places and pacified parties, and prohibited any seizure or demolition without competent authority. The Revenue measures, though not as sweeping as represented by the writer whose letter your Lordship sent me, have been unsatisfactory. The Talookhdars have, I fear, been hardly dealt with; at least, in the Fyzabad division some have lost half their villages, some have lost all." Such stated here, in the hurried outline of a letter from the spot, to be dwelt upon more

2 P

in detail hereafter, was the condition of affairs which, in the third week of April, the Nana Sahib found in Lucknow. He could have scarcely wished for any better materials from which to erect an edifice of rebellion.

By this Dundoo Punt, Nana Sahib—by all who were festering with resentments against the English and malignantly biding their time, the annexation of Oude had been welcomed as a material aid to the success of their machinations. It was no sudden thought, born of the accident of the greased cartridges, that took the disappointed Brahmin and his Mahomedan friend to Lucknow in the spring of this year of trouble. For months, for years indeed, ever since the failure of the mission to England had been apparent, they had been quietly spreading their network of intrigue all over the country. From one native Court to another native Court, from one extremity to another of the great continent of India, the agents of the Nana Sahib had passed with overtures and invitations, discreetly, perhaps mysteriously, worded, to Princes and Chiefs of different races and religions, but most hopefully of all to the Mahrattas. At the three great Mahratta families, the families of the Rajah of Sattarah, of the Peishwah, of the Boonsla, Lord Dalhousie had struck deadly blows. In the Southern Mahratta country, indeed, it seemed that Princes and Nobles were alike ripe for rebellion. It was a significant fact that the agents of the great Sattarah and Poona families had been doing their master's work in England about the same time, that both had returned to India rank rebels, and that the first year of Lord Canning's administration found Rungo-Bapojee as active for evil in the South as Azim-oollah was in the North; both able and unscrupulous men, and hating the English with a deadlier A hatred for the very kindness that had been shown to L them. But it was not until the crown had been set upon the annexations of Lord Dalhousie by the seizure of Oude, that the Nana Sahib and his accomplices saw much prospect of success. That event was the turning-point of their career of intrigue. What had before been difficult was now made easy by this last act of English usurpation. Not only were the ministers of the King of Oude tampering with the troops at the Presidency, and sowing dangerous lies broad-cast over the length and breadth of the land, but such was the impression made by the last of our annexations, that men asked each other who was safe, and what use was there in fidelity, when so faithful a friend and ally as the King of Oude was stripped of his dominions by the Government whom he had aided in its need. It is said that Princes and Chiefs, who had held back, then came forward, and that the Nana Sahib began to receive answers to his appeals.* But whatsoever may have been its effect in

---

* By those who systematically reject Native evidence, all this may be regarded as nothing but unsubstantial surmise. But there is nothing in my mind more clearly substantiated than the complicity of the Nana Sahib in wide-spread intrigues before the outbreak of the mutiny. The concurrent testimony of witnesses examined in parts of the country widely distant from each other takes this story altogether out of the regions of the conjectural. I speak only of the broad fact itself. With regard to the statement in the text, that the machinations of the Nana Sahib were much assisted by the annexation of Oude, I give the following, *quantum valeat*, from the evidence of a Native emissary detained and examined in Mysore, in January,

1858. After giving a list of numerous princes and chiefs whom the Nana had addressed, this man said : " The Nana wrote at intervals, two or three months previous to the annexation of Oude. But at first he got no answers. Nobody had any hope. After the annexation he wrote still more, and then the Sonkars of Lucknow joined in his views. Maun Singh, who is the Chief of the Poorbeah, or Poordusee, joined. Then the Sepoys began to make *tajwis* (plans) among themselves, and the Lucknow Soukars supported them. Until Oude was annexed, Nana Sahib did not get answers from any one; but when that occurred, many began to take courage and to answer him. The plot among the Sepoys first took place—the discontent about the

remote places, it cannot be questioned that in the condition of Oude itself after annexation there was that which must have gladdened the heart of every plotter against the State. Such men as Dundoo Punt and Azim-oollah Khan could not pass through the streets of Lucknow without clearly seeing what was coming. What they saw and what they heard, indeed, pleased them so greatly, that they assumed a bold and swaggering demeanour, which attracted the attention of the English functionaries to whom they were introduced. For they made no secret of their visit; but went about openly in the public streets, with numerous attendants, and even sought the presence of the Commissioner. The Nana said that he had come only to see the sights of Lucknow; so Henry Lawrence received him kindly, and ordered every attention to be shown to him by the authorities of the city. But his sojourn in Lucknow was brief, and his departure sudden. He went without taking leave of the English functionaries, saying that business required his presence at Cawnpore.

greased cartridges. Then answers began to pour in. Golab Singh, of Jummoo, was the first to send an answer. He said that he was ready with men, money, and arms, and he sent money to Nana Sahib, through one of the Lucknow Soukars." The former part of this statement may be readily accepted; the latter must be received with caution. Further extracts from this man's evidence will be found in the Appendix.

CHAPTER VII.

THE MONTH OF MAY—GENERAL SURVEY OF AFFAIRS—STATE OF FEELING AT THE RIFLE DEPÔTS—THE RISING STORM IN OUDE—THE REVOLT AT MEERUT—THE SEIZURE OF DELHI—MEASURES OF LORD CANNING—THE CALL FOR SUCCOURS.

THE month of May, with its fiery heat and glare, and its arid dust-charged winds, found Lord Canning in Calcutta watching eagerly, but hopefully, the progress of events, and the signs and symptoms of the excitement engendered in men's minds by the great lie which had been so insidiously propagated among them. From the multitude of conflicting statements and opinions which reached him from different quarters, it was difficult to extract the truth; but taking a comprehensive view of all that was manifest to him, from the plains of Bengal to the hills of the Himalayah, he could not discern in those first days of May that the clouds were gathering around him denser and blacker than before. If there were any change, indeed, it was rather a change for the brighter and the better. At Barrackpore there had been no more overt acts of mutiny. The Native regiments were doing their duty, sullenly perhaps, but still quietly. At Dum-Dum the detachments in the Rifle depôt, under the new system of drill, were proceeding to ball practice without any visible signs of discontent. It was hoped, indeed, that the troops in

May, 1857.

May, 1857. the immediate neighbourhood of Calcutta were yielding to the explanations and assurances which had been given to them, and slowly returning to reason. At the Rifle depôts also in the Upper Country the drill was quietly proceeding. At Sealkote, the detachments from the Native regiments in the Punjab, Regular and Irregular, were firing the new pieces without a murmur. Sir John Lawrence went to that station, at the beginning of the month, "to see the new School of Musketry, as well as to judge with respect to the feeling among the Sepoys;" and he wrote to Lord Canning that all were "highly pleased with the new musket, and quite ready to adopt it. They already perceive how great an advantage it will give them in mountain warfare." The officers assured him that no bad feeling had been shown, and he himself "could perceive no hesitation or reluctance on the part of any of the Sepoys."[*] From Umballah, General Barnard wrote on the first day of the month, that he had reported to Head-Quarters that so far from any insubordinate feeling existing at that place, he had reason to be satisfied with the patience, zeal, and activity that the men had shown on the severe night-picket work necessitated by the incendiary fires. "I have no reason," he added, "to accuse the Sepoy of causing these fires—no overt act has been elicited, and no instance of insubordination has occurred. The musket practice has been resumed with apparent good will and zeal. I have frequently attended it myself, and I will answer for it that no ill feeling exists in these detachments."[†]

Thus it was that, in the first days of May, there

---

[*] Sir John Lawrence to Lord Canning, May 4, 1857.—*MS. Correspondence.*

[†] Sir H. Barnard to Lord Canning, May 1, 1857.—*MS. Correspondence.*

was apparent to the eyes of the Governor-General May, 1857. something like a lull; and it seemed that at the Rifle depôts, which were the great central points of danger, the difficulty had been tided over. From Meerut, too, no fresh tidings of disturbance came. The men of the Third Cavalry were being tried by Court-martial; and it did not appear that any of their comrades were about to follow their insubordinate example. There were circumstances that rendered it probable that the motives which had driven these men into mutiny were altogether of an exceptional character. So Lord Canning, in the early part of this month of May, was able to direct his thoughts to all parts of the country, and to fix them on many topics of Indian government and administration, as calmly and as philosophically as in the quietest of times. He was corresponding with Lord Elphin-stone on the subject of the Treaty with Persia and the Expenses of the War; with Lieutenant-Governor Colvin on Education Grants and Female Schools, and the Delhi Succession—little thinking how that last question would soon settle itself; with Major David-son, the Resident at Hyderabad, about the recogni-tion of a successor to the Nizam (his Highness being nigh unto death from a surfeit of prawns); with Sir Richmond Shakespear, Resident at Baroda, on the Finances of the Guicowar; and with Colonel Durand, the Governor-General's Agent at Indore, about the large amount of Native deposits in the Residency Treasury. Indeed, the current business of Govern-ment was but little interrupted. There was no fear in Government House.

But, although at this time the Governor-General was cheerful and hopeful, and believed that the clouds of trouble would soon, by God's providence, be dispersed, he had some especial causes of anxiety. The dawn of the month of May found the Thirty-fourth Regiment at Barrackpore still awaiting its sentence. The Jemadar of the Quarter-Guard, Issuree Pandy, had been hanged on the 22nd of April, in the presence of all the troops, at Barrackpore. He had confessed his guilt on the scaffold, and with his last breath had exhorted his comrades to be warned by his example.* It was believed that this public execution of a commissioned officer would have a salutary effect upon the whole Native Army. But the punishment of one man, though that punishment were death, could not wipe out the offence of the regiment, or vindicate the authority of the Government. The great defect of Lord Canning, as a ruler in troubled times, was an excess of conscientiousness. The processes by which he arrived at a resolution were slow, because at every stage some scruple of honesty arose to impede and obstruct his conclusions. On the score both of justice and of policy he doubted whether the prompt disbandment of the Thirty-fourth would be right. It was certain that some companies were true to their colours, and he did not clearly see that all the rest were faithless. He had caused a searching inquiry to be made into the condition of the regiment, and he had hoped, up to the end of the third week of April, that all the require-

---

* There were many erroneous versions at the time of Issuree Pandy's speech from the scaffold. The words which he uttered, literally translated, were these: "Listen, Behaudur Sepoys. In such a manner do not let any one act! I have behaved in such a rascally way to the Government, that I am about to receive my just punishment. Therefore, let no Behaudur Sepoy behave in this wretched manner, or he may receive the same punishment." This is given on the authority of Colonel Mitchell of the Nineteenth, who brought the prisoner from the Quarter-Guard of the Fifty-third to the foot of the gallows, and whose own impressions were confirmed by the three orderlies who accompanied him.

ments of the case might be satisfied by the dismissal May, 1857
of some of the more patent offenders. But the weight
of military authority was strongly in favour of disbandment. General Hearsey, at Barrackpore, was
fully convinced that no measure short of this would
produce the desired effect; and General Anson wrote
earnestly from Simlah urging the expediency of such
a course. The whole question was fully and anxiously
discussed in Council; and at last, on the 30th of
April, Lord Canning recorded a minute declaratory
of his opinion that no penalty less general than disbandment "would meet the exigencies of the case,
or be effectual as an example." But even then there
were doubts with respect to the men who were to be
exempted from punishment, and not until the 4th of
May was the discussion exhausted and the order
given for the disbandment of the regiment.*

Two days afterwards, in the presence of all the Disbandment
troops at Barrackpore, of the detachments from Dum- of the Thirty-
Dum, and of the Eighty-fourth (Queen's) from Chin- fourth.
surah, the seven companies of the Thirty-fourth, who
had witnessed the great outrage of the 29th of March,
were drawn up, before the sun had risen, to receive
their sentence. There was to be no mitigation of
their punishment, as in the case of the Nineteenth;
so when they laid down their arms, the uniforms
which they had disgraced were stripped from their
backs, and they were marched out of cantonments
under an escort of Europeans. And thus a second
time the number of the guilty Thirty-fourth was
erased from the Army List; and five hundred more

---

* It is especially to be noted that a question arose as to whether the Jemadar of the Mint-Guard, who had apprehended the men of the Second Grenadiers (*ante*, page 530), should be exempted, as a faithful servant, or, on account of later reve- lations, condemned as a traitor. The decision was ultimately in his favour.

desperate men, principally Brahmins and Rajpoots, were cast adrift upon the world to work out their own schemes of vengeance.

In the quarter to which a large number of them made their way as the Nineteenth had made their way before them—in Oude, the signs of approaching trouble increased. To no place, from one end of India to another, did the mind of the Governor-General, in this conjuncture, turn, with more painful interest, than to this newly-annexed province, the nursery of the Bengal Army. Henry Lawrence's letters to the Governor-General were wholly silent on the subject of the Nana's visit to Lucknow. But they spoke of much that pressed heavily on his mind. Recognising so many causes of popular discontent in Oude, and knowing well how large a portion of the Native Army was drawn from that province, he could not, at such a time, regard without much anxiety the demeanour of the Sepoys around him. There was one regiment at Lucknow, whose conduct, although it had been betrayed into no overt act of insubordination, was of a suspicious, almost of a threatening, character, and it seemed desirable that it should be removed from the province. There was no doubt that some of the chief people of the city were tampering with its allegiance; and much danger might therefore be averted if it could be removed to another station beyond the limits of the province. The suggestion was made, and Canning responded to it, giving full authority to Henry Lawrence to move the tainted regiment to Meerut. "Let the Commander-in-Chief know," wrote the Governor-General, "if you find it necessary to send it away; but do not wait for any further authority. . . . . If you have regiments that are really untrustworthy, there must be no deli-

cacy in the matter." But before the letter sanction- May, 1857. Oude.
ing his proposal had arrived, Henry Lawrence had
thought long and deeply about the results of such a
measure; and on the 1st of May he wrote to Lord
Canning, saying: "Unquestionably we should feel
better without the Forty-eighth, but I do not feel
confident that the feeling in the other regiments is
materially better; and there is little doubt that the
Forty-eighth would not be improved by a move,
which is an important point of consideration in the
present general condition of the Army." He was
right; the removal of a single regiment could not
benefit Oude, but it might do injury elsewhere by
tainting other parts of the Army.

That other components of the Oude force were Mutiny in the Oude Irregulars
equally disaffected was presently apparent. On the
2nd of May, Captain Carnegie, who was Magistrate
of the city of Lucknow, and who had the superintendence of the Police—a man, described by his immediate superior as "prudent and active, though so
quiet in manner, and implicitly to be relied upon"
—reported to Henry Lawrence that there had been
a strong demonstration against the cartridges in the
Seventh Regiment of Oude Irregulars. At first he
was fain to believe that the story might be exaggerated; but there was soon undeniable evidence that
it was only too true. The regiment, which had been
in the King's service, was posted at a distance of
some seven miles from Lucknow. A fortnight before,
the recruits of the regiment had commenced practice
with ball-cartridge, and had done their duty without
any manifestations of discontent. But by the end of
the month it was clear that the great fear, which was
travelling about the country, had taken possession of
their minds, and that they were on the very verge of
revolt. Whether they had been wrought upon by

emissaries from the city, or whether any of the disbanded men of the Nineteenth had, by this time, found their way to Lucknow, is matter only of conjecture;[*] but as the month of May dawned upon them, they were ripe for rebellion—not only themselves prepared to resist, but eager to incite others to resistance. They had written a letter to the men of the Forty-eighth, urging them to rise for their religion; and no soothing explanations from their officers could induce them to shake off the mistrust which had fastened upon them. On the second day of the month the Brigadier rode out with his Staff to the Lines of the Seventh, and found them "as obstinate as possible with regard to the cartridges."[†] Returning at nightfall to Lucknow, he wrote at once to Lawrence, telling him the state of the regiment, and adding, "I think myself that this affair has been a long time brewing." The next morning[‡] brought with it no consolation. The Seventh were in a worse state than before. They had been sullen and obstinate on the preceding day. Now in a state

May 3.

---

[*] It has been stated that both the Nineteenth and Thirty-fourth were stationed at Lucknow at the time of annexation; and it was believed that they were there first infected with rebellion. Henry Lawrence wrote that he had ascertained that in the Nineteenth there must have been nearly seven hundred Oude men. By this time, they had mostly found their way back to their native province.

[†] The official report said that the regiment "refused to bite the cartridges when ordered by its own officers, and again by the Brigadier." How it happened that, after the change introduced into the drill, the Sepoys at Lucknow were ordered to bite the cartridge at all, it is impossible to say. This did not escape

Lord Canning, who, in a minute written on the 10th of May, said: "It appears that the revised instructions for the platoon exercise, by which the biting of the cartridge is dispensed with, had not come into operation at Lucknow. Explanation of this should be asked." But the time for explanation was past. It was ascertained, however, that the new drill instructions were sent to the Oude Irregular force in the middle of April.

[‡] So difficult is the attainment of perfect accuracy in an historical narrative, that even Mr. Gubbins, whose work on the Mutinies of Oude is the best and safest authority extant, says that these events, which he witnessed himself, happened on Sunday, the 10th of May.

of feverish excitement, violent, desperate, they as- May, 1857.
Oude.
sumed a menacing attitude, and talked openly of
murdering their officers. It was obvious that a crisis
was approaching, and that no time was to be lost;
so Henry Lawrence, when he heard that the regiment was in this defiant and dangerous state, determined at once to disarm, and, if resisted, to destroy
it. On that evening he moved up an overwhelming
force of all arms to the parade-ground of the Seventh.
The day was far spent when he commenced the
march. "It was a ticklish matter," he wrote to Mr.
Colvin, "taking the Forty-eighth down on Sunday
night; but I thought that they were safer in our
company than behind in cantonments. We had to
pass for two miles through the city; indeed, Her
Majesty's Thirty-second had four miles of it. I therefore hesitated as to moving after; but the moon was
in its third quarter; and the first blow is everything.
So off we started; and concentrated from four
points, accomplishing the seven miles in about three
hours."*

The moon had risen, bright in an unclouded sky,
on that Sabbath evening, when Henry Lawrence,
accompanied by his Staff, appeared with the Brigade
before the Lines of the Seventh. The regiment was
drawn up on parade, in a state of vague uncertainty
and bewilderment, not knowing what would come of
this strange nocturnal assembly. But when they
saw the Europeans, the Cavalry and the guns, taking
ground in their front and on their flanks, the Native
regiments being so placed as to destroy all hope of
their aiding their comrades, the mutineers knew that
their game was up, and that there would be death in

* Sir Henry Lawrence to Mr. Colvin, Lucknow, May 6, 1857.—
MS. Correspondence.

further resistance. What might then have happened if the course of events had not been determined by an accident, cannot be distinctly declared. The mutinous regiment had obeyed the word of command, and some of the men had expressed contrition ; but it happened that, by some mistake, an artilleryman lighted a port-fire. The guns were pointed towards the mutineers, and though Lawrence and his Staff were posted between them and the Artillery, and would probably have been swept away by the first round, the Sepoys of the guilty regiment believed that the battery was about to open upon them. A panic then seized the Seventh. First one man, then another, broke away from his comrades and fled, throwing down his arms as he went in the overwhelming consternation of the moment; and presently great gaps appeared in the Line, and only a remnant of the regiment was left to obey the orders of the English officer. To these men, whilst the Cavalry went in pursuit of the fugitives, Henry Lawrence rode up ; and as they broke into exclamations of " Jye Coompanee Behaudur Ko !"—" Victory to the great Lord Company !"—ordered them to lay down their arms, and to strip off their accoutrements. They obeyed without hesitation ; and, an hour after midnight, the Brigade had returned to Lucknow, carrying with it all the arms of the Seventh, and escorting, under guards of the same force, the men who had so lately borne them. In the critical state of the other Native regiments, it was not thought wise to divide the Europeans.

Next day Henry Lawrence wrote to the Governor-General, saying, "The *coup* is stated to have had great effect in the city. But people go so far as to tell me that the Forty-eighth last night abused the

Seventh for running away, and said, that if they had stood, the Forty-eighth would not have fired. I don't believe one quarter of these reports." But, although there is always, in seasons of great popular excitement, a vast amount of exaggeration afloat, and Henry Lawrence, therefore, received with caution the stories that were brought to him, he was not one to disregard the signs of the times, and to close his eyes to the dangers that were surrounding him. As time advanced, these signs increased in significance. Some fifty of the ringleaders of the Seventh Irregulars had been seized and confined, and a Court of Inquiry had been assembled to investigate the causes of the outbreak in that regiment. But little or nothing had been elicited. As at Umballah, and other places, the mouths of the Sepoys were sealed. They might contend among themselves, but in their reticence, when the English sought to probe their discontents, they acted as one man. Words were not forthcoming, but there was one form of expression, well known to the Native soldiery in times of trouble, to which they betook themselves, as they had before betaken themselves elsewhere, and thus gave utterance to the strong feelings within them. On the 7th of May, the Lines of the Forty-eighth were burnt down. The fire commenced in the hut of the Soubahdar who had given up the seditious letter addressed by the Seventh Irregulars to the men of his regiment. There could be no doubt that it was the work of an incendiary. On the following day, Lawrence visited the scene of the conflagration, and found the men outwardly civil and respectful in their demeanour, but heavy and downcast at the thought of their loss of property. It was not easy to read the state of feeling which then existed in the Oude Army, so vague and varied was it;

but if any man could have rightly discerned it, Henry Lawrence was that man.   For he had free intercourse with those who were most likely to be its exponents, and had the gift, so rare among our countrymen, of inspiring confidence in the breasts of the people.   After much communing with others and with himself, he came to the conclusion that the strongest feeling that held possession of the Sepoy's mind was a great fear, that this fear had long been growing upon him, and that it had only culminated in his belief in the story of the greased cartridges.*

Of one of these conversations a record has been left in Lawrence's handwriting.   It is so significant of the great fear that was then dominating the Army, that I give the passage as it stands.   "I had a conversation," he wrote to Lord Canning, on the 9th of May, "with a Jemadar of the Oude Artillery for more than an hour, and was startled by the dogged persistence of the man, a Brahmin of about forty years of age, of excellent character, in the belief that for ten years past Government has been engaged in measures for the forcible, or rather fraudulent conversion of all the Natives.   His argument was, that as such was the case, and that as we had made our way through India, won Bhurtpore, Lahore, &c., by fraud, so might it be possible that we mixed bone-dust with the grain sold to the Hindoos.   When I told him of our power in Europe, how the Russian war had quadrupled our Army in a year, and in another it could, if necessary, have been interminably increased,

---

* One of the earliest indications of this alarm appeared at Lucknow, when an Assistant-Surgeon in the Hospital of the Forty-eighth inadvertently put a phial of medicine to his lips to test it.   This was seen by the Sepoys, and was believed to be a deliberate scheme to pollute them.   Soon afterwards the house of the doctor was burnt to the ground by the Sepoys of his regiment.

and that in the same way, in six months, any required number of Europeans could be brought to India, and that, therefore, we are not at the mercy of the Sepoys, he replied that he knew that we had plenty of men and money, but that Europeans are expensive, and that, therefore, we wished to take Hindoos to sea to conquer the world for us. On my remarking that the Sepoy, though a good soldier on shore is a bad one at sea, by reason of his poor food, 'That is just it,' was the rejoinder. 'You want us all to eat what you like that we may be stronger, and go everywhere.' He often repeated, 'I tell you what everybody says.' But when I replied, 'Fools and traitors may say so, but honest and sensible men cannot think so,' he would not say that he himself did or did not believe, but said, 'I tell you they are like sheep; the leading one tumbles down, and all the rest roll over him.' Such a man is very dangerous. He has his full faculties, is a Brahmin, has served us twenty years, knows our strength and our weakness, and hates us thoroughly. It may be that he is only more honest than his neighbours, but he is not the less dangerous. On one only point did he give us credit. I told him that in the year 1846, I had rescued a hundred and fifty Native children, left by our army in Caubul, and that instead of making them Christians, I had restored them to their relations and friends. 'Yes,' he replied, 'I remember well. I was at Lahore.' On the other hand, he told me of our making Christians of children purchased during famines. I have spoken to many others, of all ranks, during the last fortnight; most give us credit for good intentions; but here is a soldier of our own, selected for promotion over the heads of others, holding opinions that must make him at heart a

2 Q

May, 1857. traitor." On the same day he wrote, in a similar strain, to Mr. Colvin, concluding with a significant hint to look well after the safety of the Forts in Upper India.*

If these letters from the Chief Commissioner of Oude had been read when written, they might have suggested grave thoughts of impending danger; but when they reached their destinations, they came only as commentaries upon the past, faint and feeble as seen by the glaring light of terrible realities. The Governor-General and his colleagues in the Supreme Council were discussing the conduct of the mutinous Oude regiment, and the measure of punishment which should be meted out to it. On the 10th of May Lord Canning and Mr. Dorin recorded minutes on the subject. The Governor-General declared for disbandment. Roused to a vigorous expression of opinion by this last manifestation of a growing evil, the senior member of Council wrote—and wrote well—" The sooner this epidemic of mutiny is put a stop to the better. Mild measures won't do it. A severe example is wanted. . . . . . I am convinced that timely severity will be leniency in the long run." On the same day, General Low recorded a minute, in which he expressed an opinion that " probably the main body of the regiment, in refusing to bite the cartridge, did so refuse, not from any feeling of disloyalty or disaffection towards the Government or their officers, but from an unfeigned and sincere dread that the act of biting them would involve a serious injury to their caste." On the 11th, Mr.

* In the letter to Mr. Colvin, Sir Henry Lawrence says that the Jemadar " went over all our anti-Hindoo acts of the last ten years, including Gaol-Messing, the General-Service Oath, &c., and did not conceal not only that he and all others saw no absurdity in the *grown-bone atta* belief, but that he considered we were quite up to such a dodge.' —*MS. Correspondence.*

Grant and Mr. Peacock placed on record their opinions, that it might be better to wait for fuller information before issuing the final orders of Government. On the 12th. the office-boxes were again
passing from house to house; but with the papers
then circulated, there went one, small in size, scanty
in words, but, although perhaps scarcely appreciated
at the time, of tremendous significance. "It is to
be hoped," wrote Mr. Dorin, "that the news from
Meerut (in the telegraphic message from Agra in this
box) is not true." But it was true; yet, with all its
terrors, only a small part of the truth.

The little paper, then, on that 12th of May, travelling from house to house in the office-box, was
a telegraphic message from Lieutenant-Governor
Colvin, announcing to Lord Canning that the great
military station of Meerut was in a blaze, that the
Cavalry had risen in a body, and that every European they had met had been slain by the insurgents.
There was something terribly significant in the very
form of this message. The Government at Agra had
received no official tidings of the events that had occurred at Meerut. But a lady at the former place,
who had been about to pay a visit to her friends at
Meerut, had received a message from her niece, who
was sister of the postmaster there, warning her not
to attempt the journey, as the Cavalry had risen.*

---

* The following were the words of the message: "*May* 11, 1857.— Last night, at nine o'clock, a telegraph message was received here by a lady from her niece, sister of the postmaster at Meerut, to the following effect: 'The Cavalry have risen, setting fire to their own houses and several officers' houses, besides having killed and wounded all European officers and soldiers they could find near the Lines. If aunt intends starting to-morrow evening, please detain her from doing so, as the van has been prevented from leaving the station.' No later message has been received, and the communication by telegram has been interrupted; how, not known. Any intelligence which may reach will be sent on immediately."—*Published Correspondence. Parliamentary Papers.*

May, 1857. This was the last message despatched. Before the authorities could send intelligence of what had happened, the telegraph-wires were cut by the insurgents.

The week of telegrams.

The news, therefore, which now reached Agra, and was thence communicated to Calcutta, was of a vague, fragmentary character. Scattered facts welled up from uncertain sources, and were passed on from one station to another, suggestive rather than expressive, always indicating something more terrible in the background than the truth actually revealed. Not till some time afterwards was the whole truth apparent to the Governor-General, and therefore not now do I fill up the outlines of the story. The week that followed the 12th of May was a week of telegrams. The electric wires were continually flashing pregnant messages from North to South, and from South to North. That the Sepoys at Meerut had risen, was certain from the first. Then news came that they held some part of the road between Meerut and Delhi. Then, little by little, it transpired that the Meerut mutineers had made their way in a body to the Imperial City, and that the Delhi regiments had fraternised with them. A message from Agra, despatched on the 14th, stated, on the authority of a letter from the King of Delhi, that the town and fort and his own person were in possession of the insurgents; and it was added that Fraser, the Commissioner, and many other English gentlemen and ladies, had been murdered. Then, at last, it became apparent that the King himself had cast in his lot with the insurgents, that the rebel standard had been hoisted in the palace of the Mogul, that Englishmen and Englishwomen had been ruthlessly massacred in the streets of the city, and that the mutiny of a few

regiments, by thus concentring at Delhi, was beginning to simulate a national rebellion.

Never since, a century before, the foundation of our
great Indian Empire had been laid by the conquest of
Bengal, had such tidings as these been brought to
the council-chamber of the English ruler. The little
cloud no bigger than a man's hand, which had risen
in the first month of the new year, and had been
growing in its density and darkness until it had overshadowed the heavens, was now discharging its tem-
pestuous terrors upon us. There was little before
the eyes of Lord Canning but the one naked fact of
the junction of the Meerut and Delhi troops, and the
proclamation of the restored empire of the Mogul.
With a feeling of wondering anxiety he awaited,
all through that terrible week in May, the details
which seemed as though they would never come, and
the explanations of all that seemed so inexplicable to
him. Most of all, he marvelled what our people had
been doing, or not doing in this conjuncture, that
such a post as Delhi, scarcely equalled in military,
wholly unequalled in political importance, should thus
in an hour have been wrested from their grasp. It
seemed incredible that with a regiment of British
Cavalry at Meerut, and the largest body of Artillery
in the country gathered there at its head-quarters,
such a catastrophe as this should have occurred. Was
there no one, he asked, to do with the Carabineers
and the Horse Artillery what Gillespie, half a century
before had done, with his Dragoons and galloper-
guns? But if such were the result in places where
our English officers had Cavalry and Artillery to aid
them, how would it fare with them at stations where
no such help was to be had? There was no hope
now that the conflagration would not spread from

cantonment to cantonment; no hope now that the whole country would not soon be in a blaze.

So Canning arose, and with his still, calm face, confronted the dire calamity. A braver heart than his never beat in a human breast. Happy was it for the nation that in him, to whom its honour was confided in that conjuncture, there was a resolute manhood of the finest, most enduring temper. Many thoughts pressed upon him, but dominant over all was a strong sense of the paramount duty of maintaining before all men a serene aspect and a confident demeanour. There was great work to be done, nothing less than the salvation of an empire; and with a solemn sense of his responsibility, he girded himself up for the conflict, knowing in how great a measure the deliverance of his countrymen depended, under God's good providence, upon their faith in his constancy and courage. He saw clearly that there was a tremendous danger, and he knew that the resources immediately at his command were wholly insufficient to enable him to cope with it; but even those who were nearest to his person never saw him quail for a moment, as he calculated the means and appliances of defence that could at once be brought into action, and those which might be summoned from a distance.

It was no time for lamentation; else he might have lamented that India, by a series of adverse circumstances, had been so stripped of European troops that now the whole country, with the exception of the frontier province of the Punjab, was lying naked and defenceless, without means of raising any barriers of resistance against the flood of rebellion that was pouring over Hindostan. He had lifted up his voice against the system, which placed it in the power

of England, by giving to India either too much
or too little of its manhood, to sacrifice the interests
of the dependency.* He had resisted, only a little
time before, an attempt to carry off some of the few
English regiments at his disposal, to take a part in
certain military operations against the Government
of China, with which India had no concern. It had
cost him much to send so many regiments to Persia;
but that was a call to which he had been bound to
respond, and happily now the emergency was past.
All that he had said by way of warning had been
more than verified by the event; but it was a time
for looking forward, not for looking back, so he
began to reckon up his available succours, and forthwith to summon them to the capital.

In the midst of all his tribulation there were some
sources of unspeakable comfort. Whilst the clouds
were thickening above him, before the great outburst, he had learnt with joy and gratitude that the
war with Persia had been brought to a close. Outram
had done his work rapidly and well. I cannot now
pause to speak of his successes. What he did on the
shores of the Persian Gulf must be narrated in another place. It is enough to say that Persia, alarmed
by our demonstrations on the coast, and anticipating
an advance into the interior of the country, thought
that negotiation was better than war, acceded to our
demands, and concluded, at Paris, a treaty with the
British Government. The expedition which had gone

May, 1857.

---

* "The interests of India," he
wrote on April 22nd, "do not always
make themselves heard in England,
when other important matters are
uppermost; and I am opposed to
putting into the hands of the Government at home an increased
power to diminish our main strength
here for the purpose of meeting
exigencies elsewhere. Such a diminution was made in 1854 by withholding two regiments which have
not yet been given, although six
regiments have been sent out of
India to Persia."—MS. Correspondence of Lord Canning.

forth from Bombay, was, therefore, returning to that
Presidency; and a word from the Governor-General would summon it, as fast as steam could bring
it, to his aid. This was his first thought, when
the seizure of Delhi confirmed all his worst apprehensions of the perilous want of European troops.
Then, from these Persian succours, he turned with joy
and gratitude not less profound, to the thought that
English troops were speeding to China; that the
arrogance and insolence of the Chinese Government
having provoked our chastisement, an expedition had
been fitted out under the conduct of a civil and a
military chief, and was then, perhaps, at the very
point of its journey at which it might most readily
be wrested from its original purpose, and diverted
into another and more necessitous channel. Rightly
taking the measure of the two exigencies, and never
doubting for a moment what the great interests of
the nation demanded in that conjuncture, he presently determined to call these troops to his aid. The
chastisement of China could wait; the salvation of
India could not;* and so he resolved, even at the
risk of frustrating the cherished designs of the Go- ,
vernment in England, to call upon Elgin and Ashburnham to suspend their operations, and to send
him the present help that he so much needed. It

* I did not think, when I wrote
these words, that I had done more
than express the natural feeling in
Lord Canning's breast at that time;
but I have since found that he gave
utterance almost to the very words:
"I have sent an officer," he wrote to
the Commander-in-Chief, "to Galle
by the mail to meet Ashburnham,
and I hope Elgin, with an earnest request for the first use of the regiments bound to China, if they can be
stopped at Singapore. Yeh may
wait; but Bengal, with its stretch
of seven hundred and fifty miles
from Barrackpore to Agra, guarded
by nothing but the 10th Queen's,
cannot wait, if the flame should
spread. And who shall say that it
will not? No precaution against
such a contingency can be too
great."—*MS. Correspondence of Lord
Canning.*

was a great responsibility, but he took it without a
moment's hesitation on himself; and he thanked
God, from the very depths of his heart, that by a
providential dispensation this succour, in the very
crisis of his necessities, had been placed within his
reach.

There were thus, in the peculiar circumstances of
the moment, some sources of consolation, some good
promise of relief over and above that which was to
be sought in the normal condition of the empire
under his charge. But it would take time to gather
up the strength of these Persian and Chinese expe-
ditions, and there were some available European
troops more nearly at hand. It was another happy
accident that at this time the Eighty-fourth Regiment,
which had been summoned from Pegu in March, was
still in the neighbourhood of Calcutta. The long-
delayed disbandment of the guilty companies of the
Thirty-fourth had not been carried into effect before
the 6th of May; and the regiment had been detained until after the execution of the sentence. It
seemed then that there was no further necessity for
its presence in Bengal, but the arrangements for its
return to Pegu were still incomplete, when the disastrous tidings from Upper India came to dissipate all
thought of its departure. From the quarter whence
it had come another English regiment might be
drawn. The Thirty-fifth was stationed partly at
Rangoon, partly at Moulmein; and a steamer was despatched to gather up the detachments and to bring
them with all speed to Calcutta. At the same time,
the telegraph carried to Madras a requisition to hold
the Forty-third Foot and the Madras Fusiliers ready
for immediate embarkation; and a trusted officer
was sent on board the mail-steamer to Ceylon, with

May, 1857. an urgent request to the Governor to send him all the European troops he could spare.

Whilst thus every effort was strained to bring European troops from the southern and eastern coasts, the Governor-General was intent also on the organisation of measures for the concentration of the strength already at his disposal upon the points most exposed to danger. With this object, every available river-steamer was taken up for the conveyance of troops to the Upper Provinces, and the quicker but more limited means of locomotion afforded by wheeled carriages was resorted to for the conveyance of small detachments into the interior. But it was not, in the crisis of this first peril, from the South, but from the North, that the stream of conquest was to be poured down upon the great centre of rebellion. It was not to be doubted that General Anson, whom the news of the rising at Meerut and the seizure of Delhi must have reached at Simlah as soon as it reached Lord Canning at Calcutta, was doing all that could be done to despatch troops to the seat of the revolt. The telegraph, therefore, expressed only the confidence of Government that the Commander-in-Chief was bringing down to the plains the European regiments on the hills. But the main reliance of the Governor-General in this extremity was upon the military resources of the Punjab. Though all the rest of the empire was denuded of European troops, there was no lack of this material strength in the great frontier province conquered from the Sikhs. Moreover, it was believed that the Sikhs themselves would be eager to follow their English commanders to the siege and pillage of the renowned city of the Moguls. So, whilst a message went to Kurrachee, in Scinde, directing the Commissioner to send an English regiment to the Punjab to replace any that it

might be found necessary to despatch from that pro- May, 1857.
vince to the Lower Provinces, another went to Mr.
Colvin, at Agra, saying, " Send word as quickly as
possible to Sir John Lawrence that he is to send
down such of the Punjab regiments and European
regiments as he can safely spare. Every exertion
must be made to regain Delhi. Every hour is of
importance. General Hewitt has been ordered to
press this on the Commander-in-Chief. If you find
it necessary, you may apply, in the Governor-General's name, to the Rajah of Pateeala and the Rajah
of Jheend for troops." And he added, with that
union of kindliness and sagacity which made him at
all times liberal of his encouragement to his Lieutenants, " I thank you sincerely for what you have so
admirably done, and for your stout heart."[*] The
praise, too, was well deserved. Colvin, at that time,
had done all that could be done to help others at a
distance, and to maintain the confidence of those
around him, and he had strenuously exerted himself
to forward to the Governor-General, by telegraph
and by letter, all the tidings that had made their way
to Agra.[†] " I have fairly taken upon myself," he
wrote to Lord Canning on the 15th of May, " the
position of Commander-in-Chief here. The arrangements are now on the point of completion, and
our position may be regarded as safe. There has
been a thorough co-operation and the most excellent

---

[*] In a letter to Mr. Vernon Smith
of about the same date, Lord Canning says : " South of Delhi, Colvin
at Agra is engaged in keeping the
roads quiet, collecting troops from
Gwalior (Scindiah has come forward
loyally), and encouraging his own
native garrison to fidelity. He is
confident of keeping them straight,
and he deserves to succeed. His
courage and judgment are beyond

praise."—*MS. Correspondence of Lord
Canning.*
[†] The importance of this service,
at a time when communication both
by Post and Telegraph was so greatly
interrupted, can hardly be over-esti-
mated. The Commander-in-Chief's
letters of the 14th and 16th of May
did not reach Calcutta before the
7th of June.

spirit amongst us. Scindiah and Bhurtpore will be heartily with us against the new dynasty of the House of Timour. I shall rouse the Rajpoot States to arrest the flight of the mutineers westward, when they are driven out of Delhi. The horrible murders, you will see, have been chiefly by Mahomedan troopers of the Third Cavalry. There must be a fit and fearful expiation for such atrocities."

But for this fit and fearful expiation Lord Canning knew too well that the time had not yet come. The struggle now was for bare life. For this he had done all that could be done, with the scanty means at his own disposal. "The two points to which I am straining," he wrote to the Indian Minister at home, "are the hastening of the expulsion of the rebels from Delhi, and the collection of Europeans here to be pushed up the country." But not a day was to be lost in summoning that ulterior aid, by which not only was the safety of the empire to be secured, but the honour of the nation vindicated by the infliction of just retribution upon our enemies. The succours from Bombay he was sure to obtain; and there was something exhilarating in the thought, at a time when India had need of all her heroes, that Outram would come with them. How different would it have been if those regiments had been still
Arrest of the China expedition. engaged in the Persian Gulf! But he could not calculate with the same amount of certainty upon the succours from the Eastern seas; he could not be certain that Lord Elgin would respond to his appeal. All that he could do was to throw the whole earnestness of his nature into that appeal, and to take upon himself the full responsibility of the diversion. So he wrote officially, as the Governor-General of India, to Lord Elgin, and he wrote privately to him as an

old companion and friend. In the public letter, after
setting forth in emphatic language the dangers by
which our empire in India was surrounded, he continued : " I place the matter briefly before your Lordship ; but I hope clearly enough to enable you to
come to a ready decision. I will add, that I am
anxious to bear the whole responsibility of all the
consequences of turning aside the troops from China
to India. But I beg your Lordship to believe that,
in saying this, I am not influenced by any thought
that whatever may be the course for which your
Lordship's wise judgment shall decide, you will need
any help from me in vindicating it to her Majesty's
Government."

More earnest and emphatic still was his private
letter ; not a word of it should be omitted : " My
dear Elgin,—I wish I could give you a more cheerful
and acceptable greeting than you will find in the
letter by which this is accompanied. As it is, you
will not bless me for it, but the case which I have
before me here is clear and strong. Our hold of
Bengal and the Upper Provinces depends upon the
turn of a word—a look. An indiscreet act or irritating phrase from a foolish commanding officer at
the head of a mutinous or disaffected company,
may, whilst the present condition of things at Delhi
lasts, lead to a general rising of the Native troops in
the Lower Provinces, where we have no European
strength, and where an army in rebellion would have
everything its own way for weeks and months to
come. We have seen within the last few days what
that way would be. I cannot shut my eyes to the
danger, or to the urgent necessity under which I lie,
to collect every European that can carry arms and
aid to the Government of India in the event of such

a crisis. I do not want aid to put down the Meerut and Delhi rebels; that will be done easily, as soon as the European troops can converge upon Delhi, but not sooner. Meanwhile, every hour of delay—unavoidable delay—is an encouragement to the disaffected troops in other parts; and if any one of the unwatched regiments on this side of Agra should take heart and give the word, there is not a fort, or cantonment, or station in the plains of the Ganges that would not be in their hands in a fortnight. It would be exactly the same in Oude. No help that you could give me would make us safe against this, because it cannot arrive in time. The critical moments are now, and for the next ten or twelve days to come. If we pass through them without a spread of the outbreak, I believe all will go well. If we do not, the consequences will be so frightful, that any neglect to obtain any possible accession of strength whereby to shorten the duration of the reign of terror which will ensue, would be a crime. If you send me troops, they shall not be kept one hour longer than is absolutely needed. If you come with them yourself, you shall be most heartily welcome."

With this letter went another to General Ashburnham, who commanded the troops of the China expedition; and the steamer, which carried the bearer of these important missives to Galle, bore also letters from the Governor-General to the Chairman of the Court of Directors and the President of the Board of Control, calling upon them immediately to send out reinforcements from England. "Now let me beg your attention and support," he wrote to Mr. Mangles, "to a proposal which goes to you by the mail for the immediate raising of three European regiments for Bengal. No sane man will doubt that much of increase to our European force is wanted, and that the want should be supplied with as little delay as possible is obvious from the present exposure of our weak points. I do not ask for an augmentation to the established number of Queen's troops, because for permanent purposes I much prefer an addition to the Company's Army; and for the exigencies of the moment no reinforcement, except that of the China regiments, would avail. But I do beg that you will move the Government to make up the complement of Queen's troops, irrespectively of those which now or hereafter may come to us from China. Do not let the supply of the missing regiments depend upon the turn of affairs in China, but let the gap be filled up at once."* In the same strain he wrote to Mr. Vernon Smith, looking rather to any aid that might be sent him from England, as a means of preventing the recurrence of like disasters in the future, than of combating those which had already arisen.

Whilst the first efforts of the Governor-General were thus directed towards the pressing duty of extinguishing, by sheer animal strength, the fires that had been kindled in Upper India, he was endeavouring also to prevent by moral means the flames from spreading to parts of the country not yet in a blaze. It was plain that a great fear, born of a terrible misapprehension, was driving the soldiery to madness. Might not something, then, be done—might not some authoritative declaration be put forth by Government, solemn and irresistible in its denials of the imputed treachery, to pacify men's minds, and to cast out from them the foul suspicions which were turning loyal soldiers into rebels and murderers? It

Moral force appeals.

* Lord Canning to Mr. Mangles, May 19, 1857.—*MS. Correspondence.*

May, 1857. was true that they had been told this before by the Governor-General, by the Commander-in-Chief, by Generals of Division, and Regimental Commandants; but these appeals had been of local character and limited influence, and it was thought that something might yet be done by a general Proclamation addressed to the whole Army, and distributed throughout the country. It was not doubted, that whatsoever might have been the external agencies employed to keep alive this perilous excitement, there was at the bottom of it, in the breasts of the Sepoys, a deeply-rooted fear for the sanctity of their religion and the purity of their caste. If they could once be persuaded to believe that the British Government had never meditated any injury or offence to the religious or social prejudices of the people, there might be a return to quietude and to reason. It was wise, at least, to make one more trial. So a Proclamation was issued, setting forth that the Governor-General knew that endeavours had been made to persuade Hindoos and Mussulmans, both soldiers and civil subjects, that their religion was openly as well as secretly threatened by acts of the Government, who were believed to be seeking by various ways to entrap them into loss of caste for purposes of their own; but that they had never yet deceived their subjects, and they now, therefore, called upon all men to refuse their belief to the seditious lies of designing traitors, who were leading good men to their ruin. Translated into the vernacular, this Proclamation was sent to the military authorities to be distributed among the soldiery in all parts of the country, whilst the words of it were telegraphed to the Lieutenant-Governor at Agra, with emphatic instructions to " disseminate it in every town, village, bazaar, and serai." " It is

for the people as well as for the troops." It was yet May, 1857.
hoped that it might bear the good fruit of a return
to order and tranquillity.[*]

At the same time, it appeared to the Governor-
General to be in the highest degree important to arm
the military authorities with new powers both for the
prompt reward of good and loyal soldiers, and the
prompt punishment of mutineers. The first might
be done by a simple order of the Government. The
latter required the interposition of the Legislature.
So an act was passed to facilitate the trial and punish- May 16.
ment of offences against the articles of war for the
Native Army, by which commanding officers of Divisions, Brigades, and Stations, were authorised to assemble general and other Courts-martial, and to proceed to carry sentence into effect without reference
to Head-Quarters. In such an emergency as had
then arisen, Centralisation could not stand its ground.
So whilst increased power was thus given to commanding officers to overawe rebellion, increased
power to encourage loyalty and good conduct was
delegated to them and to certain high civil and political functionaries. They were empowered to promote Native soldiers and non-commissioned officers
on the scene of their good deeds, and to confer upon

* It has been often said that this
Proclamation, which will be found
in the Appendix, ought to have been
issued at an earlier period. Colonel
Birch advised the Governor-General,
when the excited state of the Native
soldiery first became apparent, to
issue a proclamation of this kind,
and Lord Canning afterwards frankly
expressed his regret that he had not
taken the advice of his military secretary. On turning back to page
243, the reader will perceive that a
similar delay in issuing a sedative
proclamation occurred in 1806, after
the mutiny in the Madras Army. It
is, however, very doubtful whether
such manifestoes have any effect
upon the Native mind, when once
any popular belief of the intentions
of Government has taken fast hold
of it. I have already observed, that
those who entertain a conviction
that the Government have formed a
deliberate design to trick the people
out of their religion, are not likely to
find any difficulty in believing that
the issue of a lying proclamation is
a part of the plot.

2 R

May, 1857. them the " Order of Merit,"* " in order that the re-ward for eminent gallantry, loyalty, and good con-duct might be prompt, and might be conferred on the soldier in the sight of his comrades." But no General Order, May 19. proclamations and general orders—nothing that the Legislature could decree or the Executive Govern-ment publish—no words that men could utter, in that extremity, could avail to arrest the fury of the storm that was bursting over their head. It was too late for words, for none would hear. It was left to the English only to strike.

Thus Canning did all that could be done, and waited for the issue—waited, fearfully and hopefully, for tidings of new disasters in one direction, and of coming succours from another. As he thus waited and watched, and pondered new details of the great rising, which every day added something to the clearness and completeness of the story, there were times when he felt in his inmost heart that there were no better resources than a few brave hearts and a few strong heads upon whose courage and coolness he could rely. It must be said, sorrowfully, and I would fain not say it, but History admits of no such reservations, that Lord Canning felt bitterly that, with some few honourable exceptions, the Eng-lish officers at the Presidency were not giving him the moral support which, in such a crisis, would have been so grateful and refreshing to him, and for which truly he had a right to look. It is impossible to describe his mortification. Where he had hoped to see strength he saw only weakness. Men whom he thought to see sustaining and encouraging others by

* Authority in this latter respect was confined to the Lieutenant-Governor of Bengal and the North-Western Provinces, and to the Chief Commissioners in Oude and the Punjab.

their own resolute bearing and their cheerfulness of May, 1857. speech, went about from place to place infecting their friends with their own despondency, and chilling the hearts which they should have warmed by their example. Such a spectacle as this was even more painful than the tidings of disaster and death which came huddling in from all parts of the country. No one knew better, and no one more freely acknowledged that the men of whom he complained were " brave enough with swords by their sides." They would have faced death for their country's good with the courage of heroes and the constancy of martyrs; but strong as they would have been in deeds, they were weak in words, and they went about as prophets of evil, giving free utterance to all their gloomiest anticipations, and thus spreading through all the strata of English society at the capital the alarm which a more confident demeanour in the upper places might have arrested. And so strong was Lord Canning's sense of the evil that had arisen, and that might arise from this want of reserve, that he wrote specially to the authorities in England to receive with caution the stories that were likely to be sent home in the private letters which the mail was about to carry from Calcutta.

But the shame with which he beheld the failure of Harris and some of his countrymen at Calcutta, made him turn Elphinstone. with the greater pride and the greater confidence towards those who were nobly seconding his efforts from a distance. The Governors of Madras and of Bombay, Harris and Elphinstone, had responded to his appeals, and without any selfish thoughts of their own wants, any heed of dangerous contingencies at home, were sending him the succours he so much needed; and he was profoundly grateful for their

May, 1857. aid. The promptitude with which they responded to the call for help was something almost marvellous. The electric telegraph might fail us in some parts, but in others it did its work well. On the 18th of May, Canning knew that the Madras Fusiliers were already embarking, and had thanked Harris by telegraph for his " great expedition." On the 22nd he learnt that the first instalment of the troops from Persia had reached Bombay, and that a steamer had already started for Calcutta with a wing of the Sixty-fourth Queen's. The fire-ship was doing its work as well as the lightning-post.

The Law-rences.

But although there was to the Governor-General great consolation in the thought that he would lack no material or moral support that Harris and Elphin-stone could give him, it was, in a conjuncture so im-minent, to the individual characters of men actually confronting the dangers which threatened the empire, that he looked with the most eager anxiety. And there were no points to which he turned his eyes with a keener interest than to those two great provinces, the history of the annexation of which I have written in the early part of this book, the great provinces of the Punjab and of Oude. It was from Oude that so large a part of the Bengal Army had been drawn; it was in Oude, the last of our acquisitions, that the animosities and resentments born of the great revo-lution we had accomplished were festering most freshly; it was in Oude that we had to contend with the reviving energies of a dynasty scarcely yet extinct, and an aristocracy in the first throes of its humiliation. All this Lord Canning distinctly saw. It was in the Punjab that all external dangers were to be encountered; it was from the Punjab that Delhi was to be recovered. There was consolation in the thought that only a few months before the good May, 1857 offices of Dost Mahomed had been purchased in the manner most likely to secure his neutrality. But death might, any day, remove the old Ameer from the scene; there would, in such a case, be internal convulsions, out of which would probably arise an invasion of our frontier by one contending faction or another: and, therefore, much as troops were needed below, a still greater danger might be incurred by weakening the force on the frontier. In other parts of the country there might be merely a military mutiny; but in Oude and the Punjab the Government was threatened with the horrors of a popular rebellion, and the embarrassments of a foreign war.

But if there were much trouble and anxiety in these thoughts, they had their attendant consolations. Let what might happen in Oude and the Punjab, the Lawrences were there. The Governor-General had abundant faith in them both; faith in their courage, their constancy, their capacity for command; but, most of all, he trusted them because they coveted responsibility. It is only from an innate sense of strength that this desire proceeds; only in obedience to the unerring voice of Nature that strong men press forward to grasp what weak men shrink from possessing. Knowing this, when, on the 16th of May, Henry Lawrence telegraphed to the Governor-General, "Give me plenary military power in Oude; I will not use it unnecessarily," not a moment was lost in flashing back the encouraging answer, "You have full military powers. The Governor-General will support you in everything that you think necessary."

With John Lawrence it was less easy to commu-

nicate. A short time before the outbreak of the
mutiny, the Chief Commissioner of the Punjab,
whose health had been sorely tried by incessant work,
had proposed to the Governor-General to occupy a
part of the approaching hot weather in a tour
through Cashmere, but Lord Canning, on political
grounds, had discouraged the proposal; for Gholab
Singh lay dying, and it was believed that such a visit
to the dominions of the Maharajah would be associated in men's minds with some ulterior project of
their annexation. John Lawrence, therefore, had
happily not gone to Cashmere. When the news of
the outbreak at Meerut reached the Punjab he was,
on his way to the Murree Hills, at Rawul-Pindee;
and thence, having first telegraphed to them both, he
wrote, on the 13th of May, to the Governor-General
and the Commander-in-Chief. Nine days afterwards
Lord Canning received the missive which had been
addressed to him, together with a copy of the Commissioner's earnest appeal to Anson to be up and doing.
In the former, Lawrence urged upon the Governor-
General the expediency of raising for immediate service a large body of Sikh Irregulars. "Our European
force in India," he wrote, "is so small, that it may
gradually be worn down and destroyed. It is of the
highest importance, therefore, that we should increase
our Irregular troops. . . . In the event of an emergency, I should like to have power to raise as far as
one thousand Horse; I will not do this unless absolutely necessary." Five days before this letter had
reached Calcutta, Lord Canning had telegraphed his
consent to the proposal, adding, "You will be supported in every measure that you think necessary for
safety." He was unstinting in his expressions of
confidence to those who deserved it.

Those were days when the best men stood upon the least ceremony, and if they had a suggestion to offer to Government, offered it with the full assurance that they were doing their duty, and would not be charged with presumption. So General Hearsey, when he learnt the news that had come from Meerut and Delhi, had written to the Military Secretary to urge the Government to call for troops from Madras and Bombay and the Persian Gulf, and to arrest the China expedition. So Henry Lawrence had telegraphed to the Governor-General to get every available European " from China, Ceylon, and elsewhere, also all the Goorkhas from the Hills." So Patrick Grant, the Commander-in-Chief at Madras, had telegraphed to him to send a swift steamer at once to intercept the China expedition;* and John Lawrence had sent a message setting forth these and

---

* There has been some discussion, I believe, respecting the quarter whence the suggestion to intercept the China troops first emanated. I can see no reason to think that Lord Canning required any prompting. But if the question is to be solved by reference to a priority of recorded date, it is, firstly, to General Hearsey, and secondly to Sir Henry Lawrence, that the merit is to be assigned. On the 15th of May, General Hearsey wrote to Colonel Birch, saying: "Send steamers to meet and bring the European troops now on their way to China (Hong-Kong) to Calcutta. Do not delay doing this." On the 16th of May, Henry Lawrence telegraphed to Lord Canning: "Get every European you can from China, Ceylon, and elsewhere." On the 17th, Sir Patrick Grant sent his message, more detailed and emphatic: "I most earnestly recommend the despatch to Singapore of the swiftest steamer obtainable, with an earnest request to Lord Elgin to forward on to you the whole of the troops intended for China. Whether China is coerced now, or months hence, is of no moment. The moral effect of such a force being brought to the spot would be incalculable, and be regarded as something miraculous and supernatural." At what precise moment Lord Canning first determined to arrest the China expedition, is not apparent on the face of the records; but on the 18th he telegraphed to Agra: "I hope to catch the regiments on their way to China." During the week immediately following the outbreak at Meerut, Lord Canning scarcely resorted to the post-office at all. The only letter that I can find is one to General Anson, dated the 15th, in which he does not mention the intended arrest of the China troops; but at that time he had received no detailed account of events at Meerut and Delhi, and scarcely knew the extent of the evil with which he had to contend.

May, 1857 other means of meeting the crisis. For all these suggestions Lord Canning was grateful; but it was with much satisfaction, perhaps with some pride, that when the detailed plans of the Chief Commissioner of the Punjab were laid before him, he sent back a message, through the Lieutenant-Governor of Agra, saying, " Every precaution which your message suggests has been taken long ago."

Then, every effort made, and every precaution taken to save alike the Christian people and the great empire committed to his care, there was an interval of reflection ; and, with a feeling of solemn wonder, Canning dwelt upon the causes of all this tremendous excitement, and asked himself whether it could be only a military mutiny that he was combating. It did not seem as though the origin of such a commotion were to be found only in the unaided instincts of the soldiery. It might be that the activities then discernible were purely military activities, but it did not follow that external influences had not been at work to produce the state of mind that was developing such terrible results. There were even then some dawning apprehensions that, with the best possible intentions, grave mistakes might have been committed in past years, and that the tree of benignant error was now bearing bitter fruit. He thought over all that had been done by his great predecessor; the countries that had been annexed to the British Empire, the powerful interests that had suffered so grievously by our domination, the manifold encroachments, material and moral, of English muscle and English mind. Not at first did he perceive all that was afterwards made clear to him, for at the time of which I am now writing there were many breaks in the great chain of postal and telegraphic communication, and it was not easy to form a right conception of the actual situation of affairs in the Upper Provinces. But he soon ceased to speak of the mutiny, and called it a "rebellion"—a "revolt." Early in the year, he had felt disposed to attach some importance to the idea of political causes, but, as he wrote on more than one occasion, "not much."[*] Now his uncertainty upon this point began to disappear, and he wrote to the Indian Minister at home that he had not a doubt that the rebellion had been fomented "by Brahmins on religious pretences, and by others for political motives."[†] He saw, indeed, that for some years preceding the outbreak the English in India, moved by the strong faith that was in them, had striven, with a somewhat intemperate zeal, to assimilate all things to their own modes of thought, and that the Old Man had risen against the New, and resented his ceaseless innovations. To this pass had the self-assertions of the national character brought us. The Indian Empire was in flames. But, with a proud and noble confidence, Canning felt that this great national character which had raised the conflagration would, by God's blessing, ere long trample it out. Even those whose despondency had so pained him would, he knew, when called upon to act, belie the weakness of their words by the bravery of their deeds. Looking into the future, he saw the fire spreading; he saw the heathen raging furiously against him, and a great army, trained in our own

---

[*] See note, *ante*, page 550.

[†] Writing also to the Chairman of the Court of Directors (Mr. Ross Mangles), Lord Canning said: "I have learnt unmistakably that the apprehension of some attempt upon Caste is growing stronger, or at least is more sedulously spread. Mr. Colvin has found the same; and a proclamation, which goes to you herewith, has been issued with a view of arresting the evil. But political animosity goes for something among the causes, though it is not, in my opinion, a chief one."— May 19, 1857.— *MS. Correspondence.*

May, 1857. schools of warfare, turning against us the lessons we had taught them, stimulated by the Priesthood, encouraged, perhaps aided, by the nobles of the land, and with all the resources of the country at their command; but seeing this, he saw also something beyond, grand in the distance; he saw the manhood of England going out to meet it.

APPENDIX.

[THE following is the memorandum to which reference is made at page 256 :]

" By the regulations in force for the administration of Civil Justice, the Courts were prohibited from corresponding by letter with parties in suits before them, or from receiving pleadings or other applications in such cases except from the parties or their authorised representatives. All causes were required to be heard in the order in which they stood on the file of the Court, and the laws which required the use of stamped paper in judicial proceedings were very strict, and for a length of time of universal application.

" In all these respects a great change was made in the year 1816 in favour of the Bengal Sepoy.

" The regulation passed in that year made no change in respect of claims originating in loans granted by a Native officer or Sepoy, or in pecuniary transactions of a commercial nature ; but in all other respects the position of the Native soldier, as a party to a suit in a Court of Civil Justice, was materially improved.

" If a Native soldier was desirous of instituting a suit in any Court, he had only to inform his commanding officer of his intention, and to execute a deed authorising any member of his family to appear and act for him. This document was to be sent by post by the commanding officer to the Judge of the Court having jurisdiction in the matter, who was then required to take the necessary steps for giving information to the party appointed to act for the applicant, and to afford every facility for carrying on the cause. In like manner, if the Sepoy was the defendant in a case, the usual notice was to be served upon him through his commanding officer, and similar facilities were to be afforded to him in defending as in prosecuting a case. If the Sepoy himself obtained furlough for the purpose of instituting or defending a suit, he carried with him a letter from his commanding officer to the Judge, who was then required to hear the case without reference to its order on the file, and to pass judgment in it with as little delay as possible.

"No stamps were to be required, and if judgment went against the Sepoy, and any land or rent property belonging to him was attached in execution of the judgment, the Court was required to postpone the sale of it for such period as might appear reasonable for the purpose of affording the Native soldier an opportunity of discharging the amount adjudged against him.

"In like manner, if any estate belonging to a Native soldier became liable to sale for the recovery of an arrear of revenue, information of the same was to be given to him through his commanding officer, and every indulgence was to be shown to him before the last step of selling the estate was taken.

"By the same regulation, the sub-treasurer at the Presidency, the collectors of land revenue, and the several paymasters in the Presidency of Fort William, including the paymasters serving beyond the territories of the East India Company, were authorised to grant bills payable at sight without deduction of any kind, and at the usual rate of exchange, on any other treasury, for any sums which might be paid into their respective treasuries on account of Native officers or soldiers, who might be desirous of remitting money from one part of the country to another."—*MS. Memorandum.*

CASTE AND RACE IN THE SEPOY ARMY.

[The following statements, referred to at page 330, are taken from the Appendix to the Report of the Royal Commission on the organisation of the Indian Army. It will be observed that the Bengal reports relate only to the remnant of the Sepoy Army after the mutiny :]

EXTRACTS from the Official Return showing the Number, Caste, and Country of the Native Officers and Soldiers of each Regiment, Regular and Irregular, of each Presidency, confined to Regiments borne on tho Returns of each Army respectively; so far as can be stated from the Records in this House.—East India House, Sept. 1858.

BENGAL.

NATIVE INFANTRY, 7 Regiments, viz.: 21st, 31st, 47th, 65th, 66th, 70th, and 73rd.

NATIVE OFFICERS.		NON-COMMISSIONED, RANK AND FILE.	
Caste.		*Caste.*	
Mahomedans	25	Mahomedans	1,170
Brahmins	52	Brahmins	1,873
Rajpoots	39	Rajpoots	2,637
Hindus of inferior description	23	Hindus of Inferior description	2,057
		Sikhs and Punjaubees	54
	139		**7,796**

IRREGULAR AND LOCAL INFANTRY, 12 Regiments, viz.: Regiment of Khelat-i-Ghilzie, Regiment of Ferozepore, Regiment of Loodianah, Simoor Battalion, Kemaon Battalion, Nusseree Battalion, Hill Rangers, Assam Light Infantry Battalion, Mhairwarrah Battalion, Sylhet Light Infantry Battalion, Arracan Battalion, and Shekhawattee Battalion.

NATIVE OFFICERS.		NON-COMMISSIONED, RANK AND FILE.	
Caste.		*Caste.*	
Mahomedans	38	Mahomedans	1,185
Brahmins	23	Brahmins	849
Rajpoots	59	Rajpoots	2,711
Hindus of inferior description	43	Hindus of inferior description	2,247
Sikhs	17	Sikhs	1,309
Hill men	16	Hill men	1,112
Mughs	6	Mughs	705
Burmese	1	Burmese	6
Munniporees	1	Munniporees	167
		Jhats	48
	204		**10,339**

MADRAS.
NATIVE CAVALRY, 7 Regiments.

NATIVE OFFICERS.		NON-COMMISSIONED RANK AND FILE.	
Caste.		*Caste.*	
Mahomedans	68	Christians	32
Mahrattas	6	Mahomedans	1,956
Rajpoots	3	Rajpoots	90
Indo-Britons	0	Mahrattas	300
		Other castes	2
		Indo-Britons	159
	77		2,539

Country.		*Country.*	
		Hindoostan	22
Central Carnatic, Madras, Vellore, &c.	64	Northern Circars	67
Southern Carnatic, Trichinopoly	7	Central Carnatic, Madras, Vellore, &c.	1,841
Mysore	3	Southern Carnatic, Trichinopoly	205
Tanjore, Madura, and Tinnevelly	1	Baramahal	48
Ceded districts	2	Ceded districts	54
		Mysore	212
		Tanjore, Madura, and Tinnevelly	90
	77		2,539

NATIVE INFANTRY, 52 Regiments.

NATIVE OFFICERS.		NON-COMMISSIONED, RANK AND FILE.	
Caste.		*Caste.*	
Christians	4	Christians	1,853
Mahomedans	584	Mahomedans	15,273
Brahmins and Rajpoots	83	Brahmins and Rajpoots	1,922
Mahrattas	12	Mahrattas	385
Telingas (Gentoo)	242	Telingas (Gentoo)	15,371
Tamil	97	Tamil	4,275
Other castes	8	Other castes	1,616
Indo-Britons	0	Indo-Britons	1,011
	1,030		41,705

Country.		*Country.*	
Hindoostan	51	Hindoostan	1,938
Northern Circars	317	Northern Circars	16,938
Central Carnatic, Madras, Vellore, &c.	239	Central Carnatic, Madras, Vellore, &c.	8,841
Southern Carnatic, Trichinopoly	177	Southern Carnatic, Trichinopoly	4,760
Carried forward	784	Carried forward	32,477

Country.		*Country.*	
Brought forward...	784	Brought forward...	32,477
Baramahal	29	Baramahal	1,022
Ceded districts	32	Ceded districts	1,705
Mysore	59	Mysore	2,698
Tanjore, Madura, and Tin-		Tanjore, Madura, and Tin-	
nevelly	119	nevelly	3,617
Deccan and Mahratta	7	Canara, Moulmein, Jaul-	
		nah, and Belgaum	28
		Deccan and Mahratta......	99
		Portugal	1
		Other parts.................	58
	1,030		**41,705**

BOMBAY.

NATIVE CAVALRY, 3 Regiments.

NATIVE OFFICERS.		NON-COMMISSIONED, RANK AND FILE.	
Caste.		*Caste.*	
Christians	1	Christians	66
Mahomedans	12	Mahomedans	459
Brahmins and Rajpoots	9	Brahmins and Rajpoots	252
Mahrattas	1	Mahrattas	118
Telingas (Gentoo)	0	Telingas (Gentoo)............	0
Tamil	0	Tamil	0
Other castes.....................	12	Other castes	508
Indo-Britons	1	Indo-Britons	22
	36		**1,425**

Country.		*Country.*	
Hindoostan	29	Hindoostan	1,073
Northern Circars..............	1	Northern Circars	21
Central Carnatic, Madras,		Central Carnatic, Madras,	
Vellore, &c.....................	2	Vellore, &c.	30
Southern Carnatic, Trichi-		Southern Carnatic, Trichi-	
nopoly	0	nopoly	0
Deccau............................	2	Deccan	125
Concan............................	1	Concan	114
Mysore............................	0	Mysore	0
Tanjore, Madura, and Tinne-		Tanjore, Madura, and Tin-	
velly............................	0	nevelly	0
Bombay ....:	1	Guzerat........................	14
		Persia	1
		Lisbon	4
		Africa	2
		Bombay........................	4
		Punjab and Scinde	21
		Cabool and Affghanistan ...	15
		Europe	1
	36		**1,425**

NATIVE INFANTRY, 29 Regiments.

NATIVE OFFICERS.		NON-COMMISSIONED, RANK AND FILE.	
Caste.		*Caste.*	
Christians	5	Christians	270
Mahomedans	111	Mahomedans	2,048
Brahmins and Rajpoots	188	Brahmins and Rajpoots	6,421
Mahrattas	116	Mahrattas	7,980
Telingas (Gentoo)	6	Telingas (Gentoo)	107
Tamil	1	Tamil	55
Jews	3	Jews	12
Other castes	130	Other castes	7,728
Indo-Britons	0	Indo-Britons	22
Purwarrees	3	Purwarrees	170
		Mochees	29
		Sikhs	28
	563		**24,870**
Country.		*Country.*	
Hindoostan	268	Hindoostan	11,089
Northern Circars	7	Northern Circars	135
Central Carnatic, Madras, Vellore, &c.	37	Central Carnatic, Madras, Vellore, &c.	412
Southern Carnatic, Trichinopoly	13	Southern Carnatic, Trichinopoly	203
Deccan	57	Deccan	1,820
Concan	173	Concan	10,873
Mysore	4	Mysore	36
Tanjore, Madura, and Tinnevelly	0	Tanjore, Madura, and Tinnevelly	33
Guzerat	4	Mysore and Punjab	28
		Guzerat	80
		Scinde, Punjab, and Rajpootana	155
		Europe	1
	563		**24,870**

GENERAL RETURN showing the Races and Castes of which the Native Army was composed on April 1, 1858.

CORPS	European Commissioned Officers	European Non-Commissioned Officers	Native Commissioned & Non-Commissioned Officers, and Rank and File	NUMBERS of each RACE and CASTE.																			Total
				Christians	Mussulmans	Brahmins	Rajpoots	Hindoos of inferior descriptions	Seikhs	Punjabees	Hindoostanees	Cis-Sutledge	Trans-Sutledge	Hill Stations of Nepaul	Huzara Tribes	Afghans	Goorkhas	Hill Men	Mhairs	Kuhairak	Bheels	Mortyeeahs, Grasseeahs, and other predatory tribes	
Artillery	6	4	2,241	...	552	77	88	445	...	...	...	...	...	...	...	...	...	...	...	...	...	...	1,162
Light Cavalry	96	3	1,259	25	624	344	231	35	...	...	...	...	...	...	...	...	...	...	...	...	...	...	1,259
Infantry, Regular	248	47	21,928	486	3,590	6,205	6,404	4,326	135	192	...	...	...	...	...	...	590	...	...	...	...	...	21,928
Infantry, Irregular	240	29	42,715	20	1,853	1,532	2,911	3,821	3,504	15,286	1,919	2,270	2,867	358	93	105	271	3,677	566	915	803	223	41,828
Cavalry, Irregular	94	...	10,703	41	3,831	350	549	181	833	2,401	38	167	467	19	...	32	29	2	...	...	...	...	10,194
Artillery, Irregular	10	6	998	...	...	...	...	...	...	495	196	15	5	...	...	...	...	...	...	...	...	...	553
Sebundy Sappers & Miners	1	2	209	...	2	18	179	10	...	...	...	...	...	...	...	...	...	...	...	...	...	...	209
Total	625	91	80,053	572	10,452	8,526	10,362	8,818	4,472	18,374	2,153	2,452	3,339	377	93	137	890	3,679	566	915	803	223	77,133

N.B.—Aggregate of Corps the Races of which are not shown in this Return.............. 2,920

Grand Total......... 80,053

Adjutant-General's Office, Head-Quarters,
Allahabad, August 13, 1858.

(Signed)   W. MAYHEW, Lieut.-Col.,
Adjutant-General of the Army.

2 s

COMPOSITION OF THE INDIAN ARMY.—[Page 341.]

RETURN showing the Numbers of the Troops, Regular and Irregular, which were serving in the three Presidencies immediately before the Mutiny.

| | Royal Troops. | | East India Company's Troops. | | | | | | | | | | | | | Total. |
	Cavalry, 4 Regts.	Infantry, 23 Regts.	Engineers and Sappers.	Artillery. Horse, 5 Brigades.	Artillery. European Foot, 18 Battalions.	Artillery. Native Foot, 6 Battalions.	Native Cavalry. Regular, 21 Regiments.	Native Cavalry. Irregular, 33 Regiments.	Infantry. European, 9 Regiments.	Infantry. Native Regular, 135 Regiments.	Infantry. Native Irregular, 45 Regiments.	Veterans.	Medical Establishment.	Warrant Officers.	
Officers	115	693	251	119	281	138	284	106	335	2,769	162	163	814	...	6,170
European non-commissioned officers, rank and file ...	2571	20,884	110	2029	4390	37	60	...	8103	959	59	...	...	...	38,502
European veterans ...	...	...	...	...	...	...	...	...	...	...	...	466	...	...	465
Native commissioned, non-commissioned, rank and file...	...	...	3043	659	3517	...	9532	20,941	...	149,839	35,915	3613	...	...	226,352
Gun lascars	...	...	...	449	1658	343	...	...	...	...	...	...	...	...	2,450
Ordnance drivers ...	...	...	...	...	1489	848	...	...	...	...	...	...	...	...	2,337
Apothecaries and stewards	...	...	...	...	...	...	...	...	...	...	...	...	434	...	434
Native doctors	...	...	...	...	...	...	...	...	...	...	...	...	651	...	651
Warrant officers (Ordnance, &c.)..	...	...	...	...	...	...	...	...	...	...	...	...	...	385	385
Totals............	2686	21,577	3404	3256	7768	4883	9876	21,047	8438	152,860	35,496	4242	1899	385	277,746
	24,263		3404	15,907			30,923		196,794			4242	1899	385	277,746

Total Europeans—Officers 6,170
      "   Men 30,359
      "   Natives 239,994
                       277,746

Indian Army Commission.

R. B. WOOD,
Colonel and Secretary.

[In Chapter I., Book III., some extracts are given from an interesting memorandum furnished by Sir Robert Phillimore, which is now given in its integrity.]

MEMORIALS OF THE EARLY LIFE OF EARL CANNING. BY SIR ROBERT PHILLIMORE, QUEEN'S ADVOCATE.

" WHEN young Canning was eleven years old, his father took the usual steps for procuring his admission to Eton, the scene on which his own brilliant talents had given the first promise of that future excellence which they afterwards so fully realised. Mr. (afterwards Bishop) Chapman went, at the request of the Provost, Dr. Goodall, in 1824, to Gloucester Lodge, and in the presence of the great statesman examined his boy, in order that there might be no doubt as to his fitness to be placed in the upper school. The well-known description of the storm in the First Æneid, 'Interea magno misceri murmure pontum,' &c., was the passage chosen for the trial of his proficiency ; and the Bishop now remembers the anxiety with which the father watched the essay of his son, and the smile of approval which greeted his rendering of the rather difficult transition, 'Quos ego sed motos,' &c., and the final 'not so bad,' which followed at the close of the whole translation

"Young Canning was entered on the 4th September, 1824, at the house of Mr. Chapman. According to the records of the school, he was 'plus vice simplici,' sent up 'for good,' the only distinction at that time attainable at Eton. His reputation, however, at school was rather for intelligence, accuracy, and painstaking than for refined scholarship, or any remarkable powers of composition. The interval between Eton and Oxford was passed with a private tutor, the Reverend Thomas Shore, a nephew of Lord Teignmouth, who resided at Potton, Bedfordshire, but who discharged no public functions as a clergyman at that place. It is probable that he derived great benefit from the tuition of Mr. Shore. While under the care of this gentleman he formed an intimate friendship with the eldest son of the late Lord Harris (afterwards a contemporary at Christ Church), which continued without intermission to the last hour of his life. By a singular turn of fortune, Earl Canning became Governor-General of India while his friend Lord Harris was Governor of Madras. Upon the death of Mr. Canning in 1827, Mrs. Canning was created a Viscountess, with remainder to her son. It was, nevertheless, wisely determined not to send young Canning to Oxford as the son of a nobleman, but to obtain for him a studentship of Christ Church, and thereby to place him in exactly the same position at the University which his father had formerly occupied. It appears that he was nominated by Dr. Pett, the old friend and tutor of his father, and one of the canons of Christ Church, as a student on the roll which was made up December 24, 1827; but he was actually made a student by the Dean in filling up a roll dated December 20, 1828, 'in return for Dr. Pett's nomination' having been given up (a practice not unfrequent at that time) to the Dean 'in the last roll.'

"Mr. Gladstone, Lord Elgin (then Mr. Bruce), Mr. Henry Denison (a distinguished scholar), and Sir Robert Phillimore, were, among others, brother students with him; and in the number of his contemporaries at Christ Church, who afterwards became his colleagues in public life, were Lord Dalhousie and the Duke of Newcastle. He lived chiefly with a few intimate friends, among whom was Lord De Tabley, one of his executors. To them his naturally happy and cheerful temperament, his keen perception of character, his fund of quiet humour, his accomplishments as a scholar, and, above all, his loyal and affectionate heart, made him a delightful companion. He was not generally popular, and to those without his own immediate circle his manners were shy and reserved. He took at that time no particular interest in politics, and whether from a feeling that his father's great name imposed upon him an arduous responsibility, or from extreme sensitiveness to failure, did not then appear desirous to embark upon that stormy ocean of public life on which he afterwards so gallantly sailed and so nobly died.

"Those who heard his speech at the banquet given to him by the India House previous to his departure as Governor-General, know that he could, when strongly urged, put forth oratorical powers of a high order: but at Oxford, as in after-life, he showed no natural aptitude or inclination for speaking in public. His fastidious accuracy of language, his sensitive and proud nature, and a certain physical difficulty, as well, perhaps, as the ever-present recollection of his father's unrivalled success as a parliamentary chieftain, combined to dissuade him from often attempting this particular path to distinction. But at Christ Church he acquired, or matured that command of pure English, and that excellent style which in every letter or even note which he wrote excited just admiration.

"In the year 1831 he won the Christ Church prize for Latin verse. The subject was 'Caractacus captivus Romam ingreditur.' The verses were as usual recited in the hall. It was a remarkable scene. In that magnificent banqueting-room are hung the portraits of students who have reflected honour upon the House which reared them, by the distinctions which they have won in after-life.

"Underneath the portrait of George Canning, the recollection of whose brilliant career and untimely end was still fresh in the memory of men, stood the son in the prime of youth, recalling, by his eminently handsome countenance, the noble features of the portrait, while repeating the classical prize poem which would have gladdened his father's heart. Generally speaking, the resident members of Christ Church alone compose the audience when the prize is recited, but on this occasion there was one stranger present—the old, faithful friend of Mr. Canning, his staunch political adherent through life, Mr. Sturges Bourne. He had travelled from London for the express purpose of witnessing the first considerable achievement of the younger Canning.

"He closed his career at the University with distinguished success, obtaining, in Easter Term, 1833, a first-class in classical and a second-class in mathematical honours. He took the degree of B.A. in the same year, but never proceeded to the degree of M.A."—*MS. Memorandum.*

FINAL ORDERS TO THE MUSKETRY SCHOOLS.

[The following is the letter referred to at page 561—note:]

The Adjutant-General of the Army to Major-General Hearsey.

"Adjutant-General's Office, Simlah, April 13, 1857.

"SIR,—Referring to the telegraph message from this office dated the 23rd ultimo (and your acknowledgments of the 25th idem), communicating the Commander-in-Chief's orders to postpone the target practice of the Native soldiers at the Rifle Depôt at Dum-Dum, pending further instructions from this Department, I am now desired to request you will be good enough to inform the officer commanding at Dum-Dum, and through him the Depôt authorities concerned, that the course of instruction is to be completed by the Native details, and that their target practice is to be commenced as soon as practicable after the Government General Order disbanding the Nineteenth Regiment of Native Infantry has been read to the troops at the station, including the detachments of Native regiments at the Depôt.

"2. The grease for the cartridge is to be any unobjectionable mixture which may be suited for the purpose, to be provided by selected parties comprising all castes concerned, and is to be applied by the men themselves.

"3. The paper of which the cartridges are constructed having been proved by chemical test, and otherwise, to be perfectly free from grease, and in all respects unobjectionable; and all possible grounds for objection in regard to the biting of the cartridge, and the nature of the grease to be used, having been removed, it is not anticipated that the men will hesitate to perform the target practice; but, in the event of any such unexpected result, the Commander-in-Chief desires that their officers may be instructed to reason calmly with them, pointing out the utter groundlessness for any objection to the use of the cartridges now that biting the end has been dispensed with, and the provision and application of the necessary greasing material has been left to themselves; and, further, to assure them that any one who shall molest or taunt them on return to their corps, shall be visited with severe punishment.

"4. The officer commanding the Depôt will be held responsible that the above directions respecting the greasing mixture, and those recently issued in regard to the new mode of loading, are strictly observed.

"5. If, notwithstanding all these precautions and considerate measures, any disinclination to use the cartridges shall be manifested, the parties demurring are to be warned calmly and patiently, but firmly, that a persistence in such unjustifiable conduct will be viewed as disobedience of orders and insubordination, and treated accordingly, and in the event of any individuals after such warning obstinately refusing to fire, the officer commanding at Dum-Dum will at once place such parties in arrest or confinement, according to the rank of the offenders, and cause them to be tried by Court-Martial.

"6. If, however, the entire Depôt shall combinedly refuse to fire, which is very improbable, the Commander-in-Chief, under such circumstances, empowers you to place all the Native officers in arrest pending his Excellency's further orders, which you will immediately apply for; to deprive the non-commissioned officers and Sepoys of their arms and accoutrements, and to pay them up and summarily discharge them on the spot, excepting, of course, any ringleaders in these latter grades or parties whose refusal may be accompanied by insolence or insubordination, who are to be placed under arrest or confinement, in view of their being arraigned before a District or General Court-Martial, as the case may require.

"7. This communication is to be considered purely confidential, and his Excellency relies implicitly on your carrying out the instructions it contains with the utmost caution and discretion.

"I have the honour to be, Sir,
"Your most obedient servant,
"C. CHESTER, Col.
"Adjt.-Gen. of the Army."

—*MS. Records.*

THE CHUPATTIES.

[It is stated at page 571 that Mr. Ford, Magistrate and Collector of Goorgaon, was the first to call the attention of the Government of the North-Western Provinces to this subject. His letter, addressed, in official course, to the Commissioner of Delhi, is appended :]

"Goorgaon Magistracy, February 19, 1857.

"SIR,—I have the honour to inform you that a signal has passed through numbers' of the villages of this district, the purport of which has not yet transpired.

"The Chowkeydars of the villages bordering on those belonging to Mutra have received small baked cakes of atta, with orders to distribute them generally through this district.

"A Chowkeydar, upon receiving one of these cakes, has had five or six more prepared, and thus they have passed from village to village; so quickly has the order been executed, that village after village has been served with this notice.

"This day, cakes of this description have arrived and been distributed in the villages about Goorgaon, and an idea has been industriously circulated that Government has given the order.　　　　　　　"W. FORD, Magistrate.

"To Simon Fraser, Esq.,
　"Commissioner, Delhi."

––––––

[In the course of the trial of the King of Delhi great pains were taken to extract from the witnesses, both European and Native, some explanation of the "Chupatty mystery;" but nothing satisfactory was elicited. The following opinions, however, were recorded :]

From the Evidence of Jat Mall, News-writer to the Lieutenant-Governor.

"Q. Did you ever hear of the circulation of chupatties about the country some months before the outbreak; and if so, what was supposed to be the meaning of this?

A. Yes, I did hear of the circumstance. Some people said that it was a propitiatory observance to avert some impending calamity; others, that they were circulated by the Government to signify that the population throughout the country would be compelled to use the same food as the Christians, and thus be deprived of their religion; while others, again, said that the chupatties were circulated to make it known that Government was determined to force Christianity on the country by interfering with their food, and intimation of it was thus given that they might be prepared to resist the attempt.

Q. Is sending such articles about the country a custom among the Hindoos or Mussulmans; and would the meaning be at once understood without any accompanying explanation?

A. No, it is not by any means a custom; I am fifty years old, and never heard of such a thing before.

Q. Did you ever hear that any message was sent with the chupatties?

A. No; I never heard of any.

Q. Were these chupatties chiefly circulated by Mahomedans or Hindoos?

A. They were circulated indiscriminately, without reference to either religion, among the peasantry of the country."

From the Evidence of Sir Theophilus Metcalfe.

" *Q.* Can you give the Court any information about the chupatties which were circulated from village to village some months before the outbreak; and has it been ascertained how they originated, or what was the purport of their being circulated?

A. There is nothing but conjecture regarding them, but the first suggestion made by the Natives in reference to them was, that they were thus sent about in connexion with some sickness that prevailed; but this was clearly an error, as I took the trouble of ascertaining that these chupatties were never sent into any Native States, but were confined always to Government villages; they were spread through only five villages of the Delhi territory, when they were immediately stopped by authority, and they never proceeded farther up-country.

I sent for the men who had brought them from the district of Bolundshuhr, and their apology for circulating them was that they believed it to be done by order of the English Government, that they had received them elsewhere, and had but forwarded them on. I believe that the meaning of the chupatties was not understood in the Delhi district; but originally they were to be taken to all those who partook of one kind of food, connecting a body of men together in contradistinction to those who lived differently and had different customs. I think these chupatties originated at Lucknow, and were, no doubt, meant to sound a note of alarm and preparation, giving warning to the people to stand by one another on any danger menacing them."

From the Evidence of Chuni, News-writer.

" Q. Do you recollect the circumstance of chupatties being circulated from village to village ?

A. Yes, I remember hearing of it before the outbreak.

Q. Was the subject discussed in the Native newspapers; and if so, what was considered the meaning of it ?

A. Yes, it was alluded to, and it was supposed to portend some coming disturbance, and was, moreover, understood as implying an invitation to the whole population of the country to unite for some secret object afterwards to be disclosed.

Q. Do you know whence these chupatties originated, or to what quarter general opinion among the Natives attributed them ?

A. I have no knowledge as to where they were first started, but it was generally supposed that they came from Kurnaul and Paneeput."

From the Evidence of Captain Martineau.

" Q. Had you any conversation with these men (i. e. with the men assembled at Umballah for musketry instruction) relative to some chupatties that were circulated to different villages in these districts before the outbreak ?

A. Yes, I had frequent conversations with various Sepoys on this subject. I asked them what they understood in reference to them, and by whom they supposed that they were circulated; they described them to me as being in size and shape like ship biscuits, and believed them to have been distributed by order of Government through the medium of their servants for the purpose of intimating to the people of Hindoostan that they should all be compelled to eat the same food, and that was considered as a token that they should likewise be compelled to embrace one faith, or, as they termed it, ' One food and one faith.'

Q. As far as you could understand, was this idea generally prevalent among all the Sepoys of the various detachments at the Depôt ?

A. It was prevalent, as far as I could judge, among all the Sepoys of every regiment that furnished a detachment to the Depôt at Umballah.

Q. Was there any report of the Government having mixed ground bones with flour for the purpose of having it distributed to the Sepoys, and so destroying their caste ?

A. Yes, I heard of this in the month of March. It was told me that all the flour retailed from the Government Depôts for the supply of troops on the march was so adulterated.

Q. Do you think the Sepoys generally firmly believed this ?

A. I have seen correspondence from various men, which the Sepoys of the Depôt voluntarily placed in my hands, the writers of which, themselves Sepoys, evidently believed that such was the case. .

Q. Did the Sepoys ever speak to you about any other cause of complaint, or points on which they sought information ?

A. Their complaint, or rather fear, was this : they apprehended that Government was going forcibly to deprive them of their caste.

Q. Did any of them ever speak about Government interference regarding the re-marriage of Hindoo widows ?

A. Yes, they alluded to that as an invasion of their social rights."

From the Statement of Hakim Ahsan Ullah, Confidential Physician to the King of Delhi.

"Nobody can tell what was the object of the distribution of the chupatties. It is not known who first projected the plan. All the people in the palace wondered what it could mean. I had no conversation with the King on the subject; but others talked in his presence about it, wondering what could be the object.

"I consider that the chupatty affair probably originated with the Native troops, and the distribution first commenced in Oude. I also wondered what it was, but considered that it implied something.

"I consider that the distribution of the chupatties first began in Oude.

"It was the opinion of some that the Native troops had designed these chupatties as emblematical of some particular object. Others believed that there was some charm attached to them, inasmuch as they were distributed unknown all over the country, and without it being known who first originated the idea, and whence they were first sent out. People also believed that these chupatties were the invention of some adept in the secret arts, in order to preserve unpolluted the religion of the country, which, it was reported, the Government had proposed to themselves to subvert in two years."

———

[The following extracts from published works bear upon the subject of inquiry. In the first, the preceding statement that the circulation of the chupatties commenced in Oude, is corroborated:]

"Some time in February, 1857, a curious occurrence took place. It began on the confines of Oude. A Chowkeydar ran up to another village with two chupatties. He ordered his fellow-official to make ten more, and give two to each of the five nearest village Chowkeydars with the same instructions. In a few hours the whole country was in a stir, from Chowkeydars flying about with these cakes. The signal spread in all directions with wonderful celerity. The magistrates tried to stop it, but, in spite of all they could do, it passed along to the borders of the Punjab. There is reason to believe that this was originated by some intriguers of the old Court of Lucknow. Its import has not been satisfactorily explained, and was probably not understood by many who helped it along. But the same thing occurred in Behar and about Jhansi in connexion with the discontent caused by the new income-tax. It has been stated by a Native authority, published by Mr. Russell of the *Times* (see *Friend of India*, March 10, 1859), that the first circulation of the chupatties was made at the suggestion of a learned and holy pundit, who told Rajah Madhoo Singh that the people would rise in rebellion if it were done, and that the person in whose name the cakes were sent would rule all India. This, however, is very doubtful."—*Siege of Delhi, by an Officer who served there.*

———

"That remarkable and still unexplained passage through Oude, and elsewhere, of the chupatty symbol, occurred early in 1857, and, from the first movement of its advent into Oude, spread with such amazing rapidity, that it was calculated ten days more than sufficed for every village Chowkeydar in Oude to have received the little bread-cake, and made and passed on similar little bread-cakes to every village Chowkeydar within the ordinary radius of his travels. The Natives generally may have viewed this sign-manual flying through their villages—so common a method amongst men in the early stages of civilisation to warn all for either peace or war—as a forerunner of some universal popular outbreak, but by whom or with what class the standard of rebellion would be raised certainly was not generally known."—*Narrative of the Mutinies in Oude, compiled from Authentic Records, by Captain G. Hutchinson, Military Secretary to the Chief Commissioner, Oude.*

———

"In the North-West Provinces it was discovered that chupatties were being circulated throughout the country in a somewhat mysterious manner.[*] The fact was duly reported from various quarters; inquiries were ordered to be set on foot, but nothing further could be traced as to their origin or object, and they were suffered to travel on from village to village with little let or hindrance. Some fifty years before a similar appearance in Central India had perplexed the authorities,[†] but no solution of the mystery had been gained, and as nothing had then resulted from it, the hope was grasped at that in the present instance also, if not meaningless, it might prove equally harmless: it might be some superstitious spell against disease, for cholera had ravaged several districts during the previous autumn, or against some impending calamity, for the whole country teemed with forebodings of coming trouble. At all events, the idea was scouted of its having any political meaning; and far-seeing old Indians, who dared to look gravely on the 'chupatty mystery,' were denounced as croakers."—*The Punjab and Delhi in 1857, by the Rev. T. Cave-Browne, Chaplain of the Punjab Moveable Column.*

" The leaders and promoters of this great rebellion, whoever they may have been, knew well the inflammable condition, from these causes, of the rural society in the North-Western Provinces, and they therefore sent among them the chupatties, as a kind of fiery cross, to call them to action. The cakes

[*] One district officer, who saw a chupatty-laden messenger arrive in a village, and observed him breaking his cake into pieces and distributing them among the men of the village, asked what it meant; he was told that there was an old custom in Hindoostan, that when their *malik*, or chief, required any service from his people, he adopted this mode to prepare them for receiving his orders, and every one who partook of the chupatties was held pledged to obey the order whenever it might come, and whatever it might be. " What was the nature of the order in the present case?" he asked. The answer, accompanied by a suspicious smile, was, " We don't know yet."

[†] Mr. Browne, in his very interesting and trustworthy work, quotes, as his authority for this, " Kaye's Life of Metcalfe;" but I have no recollection of the statement, and I have caused a diligent search to be made through the work, but with no success. I remember, however, to have read in the papers of Sir John Malcolm a statement to the effect that, at a time of political excitement, I believe just before the mutiny of the Coast Army in 1806, there had been a mysterious circulation of sugar. There was also, in 1818, a very perplexing distribution of cocoa-nuts in Central India; but it subsequently appeared to have been the result of a mere accident.—J. W. K.

passed with the most amazing rapidity over the length and breadth of the land. Where they came from originally, it is impossible to say, but I believe Barrackpore was the starting-point, where large masses of mutinous Sepoys were congregated. The chupatties entered my district from the adjoining one of Shajehanpoor, a village watchman of that place giving to the watchman of the nearest Budaon village two of the cakes, with an injunction to make six fresh ones, retain two for his own, and give the others to the watchman of the next village, who would follow the same course, and continue the manufacture and distribution. I truly believe that the rural population of all classes, among whom these cakes spread, were as ignorant as I was myself of their real object; but it was clear they were a secret sign to be on the alert, and the minds of the people were through them kept watchful and excited. As soon as the disturbances broke out at Meerut and Delhi, the cakes explained themselves, and the people at once perceived what was expected of them."—*Personal Adventures during the Indian Rebellion in Rohilcund, Futtehghur, and Oude, by William Edwards, Esq., B.C.S., Judge of Benares, and late Magistrate and Collector of Budaon, in Rohilcund.*

[Compare also the statement at page 647.]

THE BONE-DUST STORY.

[The following translations from Native letters and papers show how general was the belief among the Sepoys in all parts of the country that the Government had mixed ground bones with the flour, and purposed to compel or to delude them to eat it:]

Translation of an Anonymous Petition sent, in March, 1857, to Major Matthews, commanding the 43rd Regiment at Barrackpore.

"The representation of the whole station is this, that we will not give up our religion. We serve for honour and religion; if we lose our religion, the Hindoo and Mahomedan religions will be destroyed. If we live, what shall we do? You are the masters of the country. The Lord Sahib has given orders, which he has received from the Company, to all commanding officers to destroy the religion of the country. We know this, as all things are being bought up by Government. The officers in the Salt Department mix up bones with the salt. The officer in charge of the ghee mixes up fat with it; this is well known. These are two matters. The third is this: that the Sahib in charge of the sugar burns up bones and mixes them in the syrup the sugar is made of; this is well known—all know it. The fourth is this: that in the country the Burra Sahibs have ordered the Rajahs, Thakurs, Zemindars, Mahajans, and Ryots, all to eat together, and English bread has been sent to them; this is well known. And this is another affair, that throughout the country the wives of respectable men, in fact, all classes of Hindoos, on becoming widows, are to be married again; this is known. Therefore we consider ourselves as killed. You all obey the orders of the Company, which we all know. But a king, or any other one who acts unjustly, does not remain.

" With reference to the Sepoys, they are your servants; but, to destroy their caste, a council assembled and decided to give them muskets and cartridges made up with greased paper to bite; this is also evident. We wish to represent this to the General, that we do not approve of the new musket and cartridge; the Sepoys cannot use them. You are the masters of the country; if you will give us all our discharge we will go away. The Native officers, Soubahdars, Jemadars, are all good in the whole Brigade, except two, whose faces are like pigs: the Soubahdar Major of the 70th Regiment, who is a Christian, and Thakur Misser, Jemadar of the 43rd Regiment Light Infantry.

" Whoever gets this letter must read it to the Major as it is written. If he is a Hindoo and does not, his crime will be equal to the slaughter of a lakh of cows; and if a Mussulman, as though he had eaten pig; and if a European, must read it to the Native officers, and if he does not, his going to church will be of no use, and be a crime. Thakur Misser has lost his religion. Chattrees are not to respect him. Brahmins are not to salute or bless him. If they do, their crime will be equal to the slaughter of a lakh of cows. He is the son of a Chumar. The Brahmin who hears this is not to feed him; if he does, his crime will be equal to the murdering of a lakh of Brahmins or cows.

"May this letter be given to Major Matthews. Any one who gets it is to give it, if he does not, and is a Hindoo, his crime will be as the slaughter of a lakh of cows; and if a Mussulman, as if he had eaten pig; and if he is an officer he must give it."

Translation of a Letter from Inayut-Oolah Goolaothee, of Boolundshuhr, to his Brother Fyzool Hussan, Extra Assistant, Rawul Pindee.

". . . . . . The reason of my letters not reaching you is this: that on the 12th of Ramyan, in Meerut 'Khas,' such a fight occurred between the Native and European troops on a point of religion as cannot be described. The foundation of the quarrel was this: that thousands of maunds of atta was taken into every ressalah and regiment; and with this atta was mixed the ground bones of the cow and pig; and the cartridges were also made with the fat of the cow and pig. The shopkeepers in the city were ordered to purchase "atta" from Government and sell it in all the villages. It was ordered by beat of drum that atta be not ground in any village, and that in every district all the mills should be confiscated to Government. It was also ordered that ten maunds of atta be thrown into every well, kuchcha or pukka, in every village and town. The troops at every station with one accord said, that if the troops at Meerut should receive the atta and cartridges, they would receive them without objection. A few European officers assembled at Meerut, and having collected the officers of the pultun and ressalah, ordered them to take the atta from the Government and to bite the cartridges with the mouth. A few Sirdars objected to do so; but two, one a Hindoo and the other a Mussulman, bit the cartridge with the mouth. A reward of one hundred rupees was immediately paid to both. The rest said that

2 T

they would consult each other during the night, and intimate the result the next morning. There were about eighty-four men. They were instantly sent to jail in irons. One among them, a Syud, who was fasting, struck his head on the ground and died. About two hours before sunset the troops girded up their loins and killed all the European soldiers and officers that were present. Only the Commissioner and the District Officer escaped. The rest of the principal Europeans were killed—women nor even children, all that were Europeans, escaped. Afterwards they went to the jail. There was a sentry at the gate, whom they asked to open it. The sentry refused, upon which a Sowar, who was a Syud, advanced, and, with the name of God in his mouth, forced open the gate with a kick. They then collected blacksmiths from the city, and, taking them to the jail, unfettered several thousand prisoners. Both the jails were broken through. Then they went to and sacked the treasury. This state of things continued for two days. The people of the city of Meerut also joined them, as also the Syuds of Ubdoollapoor, a village near Meerut. The whole of the cantonment was fired; not a single bungalow escaped. The 'Dewanee Duftur' was also burnt. On the third day they went away to Delhi; small bodies of them also scattered themselves in different districts. Three days afterwards the troops at Umballah burnt that cantonment and went away to Delhi. The Native troops at Roorkee also fired that station, and went over to Meerut. The residue of the European troops, being joined by others, demanded their arms from the Native soldiery, but they refused. The European troops surrounded them with guns. In a single volley forty of the Natives were killed, but the latter in their turn sent sixty-five Gorahs to hell by a single volley of their muskets. The Native troops then took their way to Delhi. A few went to the village of Ubdoollapoor, the Syuds of which place gave them refuge and consolation. But secretly they sent a man and informed the Commissioner, who proceeded with ten guns to Ubdoollapoor, and cut off the road to Meerut and Delhi. Then the scoundrels (Syuds of Ubdoollapoor) informed the refugees that they had given them shelter, but that Government troops had arrived.

The poor fellows then fled, but in their flight about fifteen or twenty were killed and several wounded; but they also killed about forty men, and then went to Delhi. In short, from all sides the Native troops assembled at Delhi and desired the King to ascend the throne. His Majesty refused; but the Sepoys said: 'Do you ascend the throne, else we shall cut off your head and bury your body underneath the throne, and place one from among ourselves on the throne.' They then placed Shahzadah Jewan Bukht on the throne. They then fired the Tuhseel stations at Ghazeeabad, Mooradnuggur, Mooradabad, and Cawnpore, &c., and Thanas of the Badsha were located there. One month's pay has been distributed to the troops by the King. The King also wrote to the English, telling them that their troops, having been dissatisfied with them, had come over to the King and to take them away. The English replied, that the King himself should send them back. A Moulavee from Meerut and another from some other place have gone over to Delhi with about six thousand men to make religious war. The Royal mandates were issued to the different Rajahs to wait upon the King. It is said that the Rajah of Bullubgurh has waited upon his Majesty with his troops; and it is also said that the King has raised new troops, and has fixed the pay of the Foot soldier at twelve rupees, and that of the Sowar at thirty rupees, per mensem. I have sent a man to Delhi to ascertain the course of events there; when he comes back the real state of things will be known. Traffic has ceased in several districts. The Jats and Goojurs have commenced plundering, and news arrives daily of the plundering of villages here and there. A revolution has occurred in the whole country. . . . . ."

" News from Meerut"—Translated from the " Soobah Sadik," published at Madras.

"The same newspaper* tells us that in the Patan Bélé Camp, at Meerut, the same cartridges arrived, on account of which the Barrackpore officers had earned a reputation, on

* The *Jami-Jamshid* of Meerut.

the 18th or 19th of the current month; and the flour-boxes, which had been publicly stated to contain hogs' bones mixed up in them, also came. The order was that the men of the regiment should purchase the flour. On this account no one ate food, and refused to take the flour or the cartridges. Though it is not right to suspect the Sirkars—as they have nothing to do with religion—yet in this business there is no doubt that, in the wisdom of Government, they have suddenly withdrawn from kindly feeling towards the hearts of their subjects. It is very lamentable. The sky kisses the earth from grief."

THE NANA SAHIB AND AZIM-OOLLAH KHAN

[The visit of the Nana Sahib to Lucknow, in April, 1857, referred to at page 576, is thus described by Mr. Martin Gubbins in his history of the Mutinies in Oude:]

"I must here mention a visit which was made to Lucknow, in April, by the Nana of Bithoor, whose subsequent treachery and atrocities have given him a pre-eminence in infamy. He came over on pretence of seeing the sights at Lucknow, accompanied by his younger brother and a numerous retinue, bringing letters of introduction from a former Judge of Cawnpore to Captain Hayes and to myself. He visited me, and his manner was arrogant and presuming. To make a show of dignity and importance, he brought six or seven followers with him into the room, for whom chairs were demanded. One of these men was his notorious agent, Azim-oollah. His younger brother was more pleasing in appearance and demeanour. The Nana was introduced by me to Sir Henry Lawrence, who received him kindly, and ordered the authorities of the city to show him every attention. I subsequently met him parading through Lucknow with a retinue more than usually large. He had promised before leaving Lucknow to make his final call on the Wednesday. On the Monday, we received a message from him that urgent business required his attendance at Cawnpore, and he left Lucknow accordingly. At the time his conduct excited little attention; but it was otherwise when affairs had assumed the aspect which they did at Cawnpore by the 20th of May. His demeanour at Lucknow and sudden departure to Cawnpore appeared exceedingly suspicious, and I brought it to the notice of Sir Henry Lawrence. The Chief Commissioner concurred in my suspicions, and by his authority I addressed Sir Hugh Wheeler, cautioning him against the Nana, and stating Sir Henry's belief that he was not to be depended on. The warning was unhappily disregarded, and, on the 22nd of May, a message was received stating that 'two guns and three hundred men, cavalry and infantry, furnished by the Maharajah of Bithoor, came in this morning.'"

[At pages 579-80 (note) there is an extract from the evidence of a Native emissary, taken by the Hon. H. B. Devereux, Judicial Commissioner of Mysore. This man, Seetaram Bawa by name, was very distinct and emphatic in his declaration that the Nana Sahib had been, for some time before the outbreak, stirring up this revolt against the English. The following further passages from this man's evidence, whether or not accepted as truth, will be read with interest:]

"Then Bajee Rao died at Bithoor. He left a widow and an adopted son named Nana Sahib, who was always a worthless and not very clever fellow, and never would have been anything but for the tuition of his Gooroo, Dassa Bawa (said to have come from a place called Kalee Dhar, beyond Kangra, this side of Jummoo). Three years ago, or perhaps a month less, Nana Sahib gave the Gooroo, Dassa Bawa, a sunnud, granting a five-lakh jaghir and five nachatras,* because Dassa Bawa had told him that he would become as powerful as the Peishwah had once been; and the sunnud was to take effect when he came into power. Dassa Bawa then made a Hunooman horoscope of eight angles. Nana then, after seven days of prayer, went to sleep on the horoscope, and Hunooman having revealed to him that he would be victorious, he felt that the truth of the prediction had been confirmed, and at once presented Dassa Bawa with twenty-

* Kettle-drums—marks of dignity.

five thousand rupees' worth of jewels. Dassa Bawa then went to Nepaul, &c. Dassa Bawa is the person who has helped and advised the Nana throughout. The Nana gives him much money. . . ."

" Q. How and when were the Sepoys induced to join in the revolt ?

A. Not before the annexation of Oude, but before the affair of the greased cartridges, which was a mere pretext. After that, Maun Singh sent four or five Poorbeahs to every regiment in the service of the Company, and by their means all communications took place. Even down at the French Rocks there were men. They were able to enlist in the cause the Poorbeahs, Hindostanees, and many Mussulmans, but in no instance did they attempt to gain over the Tamil or Telegoo Sepoys, or other Hindoos of this side of India, for they knew it would be useless. They eat differently, and do not inter-marry. The Hindoos of the South have no sympathy with those of the North, whereas the Mahomedans are united in feeling throughout India. If a Hindoo is glad, nobody but his own nearest people will sympathise ; but if a Mussulman is glad, all Mussulmans rejoice.

Q. Explain what the plan of attack really was.

A. A night was to have been fixed on which, without risk-ing anything, the whole of the European officers were to have been killed, and the treasuries plundered. The magazines were to have been taken possession of when possible, or else blown up. But it was never intended to injure women or children. *Nearly all* were of one mind in the different regi-ments. It is not the Brahmins and great men that have de-stroyed helpless children, women with child, and poor women. [He spoke this with great excitement.] It was the intention to destroy your men, but it was villagers and savages who de-stroyed your women and children, such as Maun Singh and his Poorbeahs. Nana Sahib, though always a worthless fellow, and nothing without Dassa Bawa, could never have ordered the massacre of the women and children. Had they no mothers or sisters! Had they no heart for them! I heard of what happened with sorrow. We object to your raj. All men have peace and freedom under it—such freedom as we never enjoyed before—but we sorrow for our caste. I am speaking of Brahmins. Brahmins love good food and ease. The Company does not give it (muft) gratis, and we wish for a return of that which will enable us to obtain it, or rather place matters in such a position that we can obtain it. We feel the pressure of your rule in this respect. Nana Sahib wrote both to Gholab Singh and to Russia, and he got an answer from Russia. In that answer he was told that no assistance could be given him unless he could take and could hold Delhi; but that, if he could succeed in that, then assistance would be given him to drive us from Calcutta. The letter was sent to Jummoo, and forwarded on from thence by the hands of the people who bring almonds and fruit. The country beyond Jummoo is said to be pure Mussulman, but I do not know anything about it. First, Gholab Singh joined, and as soon as the union of the Mussulmans and Hindoos was settled, several letters were sent to Russia.

Q. Can you explain anything about the chupatty cakes which were passed over India before the insurrection?

A. The cakes in question were a jadoo or charm, which originated with Dassa Bawa, who told Nana Sahib ·that he would make a jadoo, and, as far as these magic cakes should be carried, so far should the people be on his 'side. He then took the reed of the lotus, or rumul, called mukhana, and made an idol of it. He then reduced the idol to very small pills, and, having made an immense number of cakes, he put a pillet in each, and, as far as the cakes were carried, so far would the people determine to throw off the Company's raj. None came as far as this country.

Q. What made Nana Sahib originate this conspiracy?

A. The Company Sirkar placed all the treasure of his father under attachment, and he wanted to gain possession of it. The people about him urged him—the opportunity offered, and he took advantage of it.

·*Q.* How do you know all this?

A. Every person, particularly every Brahmin, is well acquainted with all this, and the fact of these letters having

been written. Why, every Baboo in Calcutta knew of it."—
MS. Records.

[Many readers will smile at the statement that the Nana
Sahib was in correspondence with Russia, and received an
answer to his overtures. But, it is by no means improbable
that Azim-oollah Khan entered into communication with some
Russian officers, responsible or irresponsible, and it is certain that at the time of the Crimean war nothing could have
better served the interests of Russia than a revolt in India.
That Azim-oollah visited the Crimea, we know upon the
best possible authority—that of Mr. Russell, who has given,
in his "Diary in India," the following interesting account of
his meeting with the Nana's agent in the trenches before
Sebastopol:]

" Whilst I am writing about it, I may as well relate an incident in connexion with one of the Nana's chief advisers,
which I mentioned to the Governor-General, who appeared
much struck with it. After the repulse of the allies in their
assault on Sebastopol, 18th June, an event closely followed
by the death of Lord Raglan and a cessation of any operations, except such as were connected with a renewed assault
upon the place, I went down for a few days to Constantinople,
and, whilst stopping at Misseri's Hotel, saw, on several occasions, a handsome slim young man, of dark-olive complexion,
dressed in an Oriental costume which was new to me, and
covered with rings and finery. He spoke French and English, dined at the *table d'hôte*, and, as far as I could make out,
was an Indian Prince, who was on his way back from the prosecution of an unsuccessful claim against the East India Company in London. He had made the acquaintance of Mr.
Doyne, who was going out to the Crimea as the superintendent of Sir Joseph Paxton's Army Works Corps, and by
that gentleman he was introduced to me one fine summer's
evening, as we were smoking on the roof of the hotel. I did
not remember his name, but I recollect that he expressed
great anxiety about a passage to the Crimea, ' as,' said he,
' I want to see this famous city, and those great Roostums—
the Russians—who have beaten French and English together,'

Indeed, he added that he was going to Calcutta, when the news of the defeat of June 18th reached him at Malta, and he was so excited by it that he resolved to go to Constantinople, and endeavour thence to get a passage to Balaklava. In the course of conversation he boasted a good deal of his success in London society, and used the names of people of rank very freely, which, combined with the tone of his remarks, induced me to regard him with suspicion, mingled, I confess, with dislike. He not only mentioned his *bonnes fortunes*, but expressed a very decided opinion that unless women were restrained, as they were in the East, ' like moths in candlelight, they will fly and get burned.' I never saw or heard anything more of him till some weeks afterwards, when a gentleman rode up to my hut at Cathcart's Hill, and sent me in a note from Mr. Doyne, asking me to assist his friend Azim-oollah Khan in visiting the trenches, and on going out I recognised the Indian Prince. I had his horse put up, and walked to the General's hut to get a pass for him. The sun was within an hour of setting, and the Russian batteries had just opened, as was their custom, to welcome our reliefs and working-parties, so that shot came bounding up towards the hill where our friend was standing, and a shell burst in the air at apparently near proximity to his post. Some delay took place ere I could get the pass, and when I went with it I found Azim-oollah had retreated inside the cemetery, and was looking with marked interest at the fire of the Russian guns. I told him what he was to do, and regretted my inability to accompany him, as I was going out to dinner at a mess in the Light Division. 'Oh,' said he, ' this is a beautiful place to see from; I can see everything, and, as it is late, I will ask you to come some other day, and will watch here till it is time to go home.' He said, laughingly, ' I think you will never take that strong place;' and in reply to me, when I asked him to come to dine with me at my friend's, where I was sure he would be welcome, he said, with a kind of sneer, 'Thank you, but recollect I am a good Mahomedan !' 'But,' said I, 'you dined at Misseri's ?' 'Oh, yes : I was joking. I am not such a fool as to believe in these foolish things. I am of no religion.' When I came home that night I found he was asleep in my camp-bed, and my servant told me he had enjoyed my stores very freely. In the morning he was up and off, ere I was awake. On my table I found a piece of paper—'Azim-oollah Khan presents his compliments to Russell, Esquire, and begs to thank him most truly for his kind attentions, for which I am most obliged.'

"This fellow, as we all know, was the Nana's secretary, and chief adviser in the massacres at Cawnpore. Now, is it not curious enough that he should have felt such an interest to see, with his own eyes, how matters were going on in the Crimea? It would not be strange in a European to evince such curiosity; but in an Asiatic, of the non-military caste, it certainly is. He saw the British army in a state of some depression, and he formed, as I have since heard, a very unfavourable opinion of its *morale* and *physique*, in comparison with that of the French. Let us remember, that soon after his arrival in India he accompanied Nana Sahib to Lucknow, where they remained some time, and are thought by those who recollect their tone and demeanour, to have exhibited considerable insolence and *hauteur* towards the Europeans they met. Afterwards the worthy couple, on the pretence of a pilgrimage to the hills—a Hindoo and Mussulman joined in a holy excursion!—visited the military stations all along the main trunk-road, and went as far as Umballah. It has been suggested that their object in going to Simlah was to tamper with the Goorkha regiment stationed in the hills; but that, finding on their arrival at Umballah a portion of the regiment were in cantonments, they were unable to effect their purpose with these men, and desisted from their proposed journey on the plea of the cold weather. That the Nana's demeanour towards us should have undergone a change at this time is not at all wonderful; for he had learned the irrevocable determination of the authorities to refuse what he—and, let me add, the majority of the millions of Hindoos who knew the circumstances—considered to be his just rights as adopted heir of the ex-Peishwah of the Mahrattas. When the great villany was planned is not now ascertainable; but it must be remarked, as a piece of evidence in some degree adverse to the supposition that Nana Sahib had successfully tampered with the troops at Cawnpore, that the latter did not evince any design of making him their leader, nor did they hold any communication with him on their revolt, and that they were all marching off for Delhi when he and his creatures went to their camp, and by his representations, promises, and actual disbursements, induced them to go back and assault Wheeler in his feeble entrenchments."

[The statement in the above, that the Nana Sahib visited Umballah in the spring of 1857, is new. Azim-oollah Khan was certainly there; for Captain Martineau, who had previously made acquaintance with him on board a steamer, on his return to India, met him at that station in the early part of the year, but was not aware that he accompanied the Nana.]

NATIVE VERSION OF THE BEGINNING OF THE MUTINY.

[The subjoined letter, the original of which fell into the hands of the Punjabee officials, is, on many accounts, curious and interesting. It is important, too, as showing how general was the belief that the whole army was to "take time" from the Meerut Brigade. The statement in this letter may be advantageously compared with what is said on the same subject in the letter at page 641 :]

From Nund Singh, Umritsur, to Sirdar Nehal Singh, Rawul Pindee.

"June 10, 1857.

AFTER COMPLIMENTS,—" You wrote to me to ascertain the true circumstances connected with the cartridges. I have made inquiries from different sources. The fact is this:

"Near Calcutta, five coss distant from it, there is a place called Achanuk.* There is a Government cantonment at that place. At that place a Hindostanee was drawing water out of a well. A 'Chumar' came in and asked the Hindostanee

* Barrackpore.

to give him water to drink. The Hindostanee told him that he had better go to some other place to drink water.

"'How,' said the Hindostanee, 'can I give you water to drink? You are a "Chumar."'*

"Upon this words were exchanged between them. The Chumar said:

"'You do not give me water to drink, and affect to be so religious; and the fat of the cow and pig which I prepare with my own hands you will bite off with your teeth.'

"These and similar words having been exchanged between them, they came to blows. The other people, who had heard the talk about the 'fat,' rescued the 'Chumar,' and made inquiries from him in a conciliatory manner.

"Then two men went along with him to that place,† which was a little removed from the cantonment. There they saw with their own eyes about fifty or sixty Chumars working and putting on the fat of both the animals on the cartridges. They returned from thence homewards, and described all to the Soubahdars and other officers.

"It was agreed between them that they should remain silent at the time, but refuse to receive the cartridges when they should be given to them.

"'It would then be proper to remonstrate. Let them (the Government) be doing whatever they like in private. What business have we to murmur?'

"For this reason, for some time nothing broke out. About two or one and a half months afterwards the regiment was ordered to receive these cartridges, (and it was explained to them) that, in the first place, the greased cartridges easily went down into the musket; and, secondly, they prevented the musket from being affected by the damp. But as the men already knew (all about them), they refused to receive them. The European officers at that place (Barrackpore) were very hot-tempered; therefore, in consequence of this refusal a quarrel soon sprung up. Immediately the European troops were brought out, and surrounded the regiment. The latter were ordered to give up their arms. They replied:

* The lowest class among the Hindoos, who work in leather.　† The place where cartridges were said to be made.

Give us our pay and take away the arms.' The regiments were then made to put down their arms, and they having received their pay each went away to their home. All the Sepoys in this country, at Kurnaul, Meerut, &c., were some way or other related (to those of the disbanded regiments). (The men of the latter) wrote to the former, telling them what had occurred, and stated 'that we have on this account quitted the service, and have seen all with our own eyes. We have written this to you for your information. If you should receive these cartridges, intermarriage, and eating and drinking in common, shall cease between yourselves and us.'

"When, at Dinapore, the cartridges were distributed by the English, they were refused; the men stated that 'Meerut is the principal cantonment. Distribute the cartridges there first of all, and we will take them afterwards.'

"The distribution of the cartridges having been ordered at Meerut, and the men having been already acquainted with the circumstances connected with them, refused to receive them. But a company which was sent for to receive the cartridges, not having obeyed the order, were placed in confinement by the European officers. Intelligence of this having reached the rest of the troops, all attacked the jail, and set at liberty the men of the company, and also the other prisoners. The disturbance then grew high.

"At the very first, when the regiment at Achanuk (Barrackpore) was disbanded, a requisition was made to England for twenty more European regiments. But these did not sail in steamers, but are coming in other ships which sail with the force of the wind.

"The truth appears to be, that the report of the fat being used is not altogether untrue; much is commonly made of a little thing, but it cannot be that anything can be produced from nothing. Is ever a tree produced without the seed? It cannot be. And now that orders have been read to all the regiments to the effect that these cartridges will not be served out, and shall either be cut up or flooded, consider that the very circumstance of such an order having been read, annihilates the belief that there was nothing wrong in these cartridges.

"You are wise yourself; the real foundation of this disturbance is what I have described. But all things are known to God only, who is omniscient."—*MS. Records.*

THE MAY PROCLAMATION.

[The following is the proclamation referred to at page 608 :]

"Fort William, Home Department, May 16, 1857.

"*Proclamation.*

"The Governor-General of India in Council has warned the Army of Bengal, that the tales by which the men of certain Regiments have been led to suspect that offence to their Religion or injury to their Caste is meditated by the Government of India, are malicious falsehoods.

"The Governor-General in Council has learnt that this suspicion continues to be propagated by designing and evil-minded men, not only in the Army, but amongst other classes of the people.

"He knows that endeavours are made to persuade Hindoos and Mussulmans, Soldiers and Civil Subjects, that their religion is threatened secretly, as well as openly, by the acts of the Government, and that the Government is seeking in various ways to entrap them into a loss of Caste for purposes of its own.

"Some have been already deceived and led astray by these tales.

"Once more, then, the Governor-General in Council warns all classes against the deceptions that are practised on them.

"The Government of India has invariably treated the religious feelings of all its subjects with careful respect. The Governor-General in Council has declared that it will never cease to do so. He now repeats that declaration, and he emphatically proclaims that the Government of India entertains no design to interfere with their Religion or Caste, and that nothing has been, or will be done by the Government to affect the free exercise of the observances of Religion or Caste by every class of the people.

"The Government of India has never deceived its subjects, therefore the Governor-General in Council now calls upon them to refuse their belief to seditious lies.

"This notice is addressed to those who hitherto, by habitual loyalty and orderly conduct, have shown their attachment to the Government, and a well-founded faith in its protection and justice.

"The Governor-General in Council enjoins all such persons to pause before they listen to false guides and traitors who would lead them into danger and disgrace.

"By Order of the Governor-General of India in Council,

"CECIL BEADON,

"Secretary to the Government of India."

ADDENDUM.

AMMUNITION FOR TWO-GROOVED RIFLES.

AFTER the statement at pages 516-18, respecting the composition of the greasing materials used with the old two-grooved rifles, was in type, I succeeded in tracing the original orders on the subject, drawn up by the Military Board in 1847. The following is the material part of the Board's Memorandum, approved by the Commander-in-Chief and the Governor-General:

"1st. The ammunition of two-grooved rifles is to be prepared as blank cartridge of three drachms of musketry powder, in blue paper, made up in bundles of ten.

"2nd. The balls to be put up, five in a string, in small cloth bags, with a greased patch of fine cloth—a portion carried in a ball-bag attached to the girdle on the right side, and the remainder in pouch.

"3rd. Patches to be made of calico or long cloth, and issued ready greased from magazines; a portion of greasing composition will also be issued with the patches for the purpose of renewal when required, and instructions for its preparation forwarded to magazine officers by the Military Board."

[The following were the instructions issued in accordance with this Memorandum :]

" The mode of preparing the grease and applying it to the cloth to be as follows:—To three pints of country linseed oil, add one-fourth of a pound of beeswax, which mix by melting the wax in a ladle, pouring the oil in and allowing it to remain on the fire until the composition is thoroughly melted. The cloth is then to be dipped in it until every part is saturated, and held by one corner until the mixture ceases to run, after which it is to be laid out as smooth as possible on a clean spot to cool. The above quantity of composition will answer for three yards of long cloth, from which 1200 patches can be made."

[These instructions were approved by the Governor-General (Lord Hardinge), in a letter from the Military Secretary to the Adjutant-General, dated April 6, 1847. I can trace no subsequent order cancelling the above; and as I am assured by the officer who held the post of Inspector-General of Ordnance during the administration of Lord Dalhousie and Lord Canning that this composition continued in use up to 1857, I cannot doubt that the impression at head-quarters that the "patches" were greased with mutton fat was altogether a mistake.]

END OF VOL. I.

LONDON:
Printed by C. Whiting, Beaufort House, Duke St., Lincoln's Inn Fields.

www.ingramcontent.com/pod-product-compliance
Lightning Source LLC
LaVergne TN
LVHW012209040326
832903LV00003B/202